The Geography of Transport Systems

This expanded and revised fourth edition of *The Geography of Transport Systems* provides a comprehensive and accessible introduction to the field with a broad overview of its concepts, methods and areas of application. Aimed mainly at an undergraduate audience, it provides an overview of the spatial aspects of transportation and focuses on how the mobility of passengers and freight is linked with geography.

The book is divided into ten chapters, each covering a specific conceptual dimension, including networks, modes, terminals, freight transportation, urban transportation and environmental impacts, and updated with the latest information available. The fourth edition offers new material on the issues of transport and the economy, city logistics, supply chains, security, energy, the environment, as well as a revised content structure. With over 160 updated photographs, figures and maps, *The Geography of Transport Systems* presents transportation systems at different scales ranging from global to local and focuses on different contexts such as North America, Europe and East Asia.

This volume is an essential resource for undergraduates studying transport geography, as well as those interested in economic and urban geography, transport planning and engineering. A companion website, which contains additional material, has been developed for the book and can be found here: http://people.hofstra.edu/geotrans/

Jean-Paul Rodrigue is Professor in the Department of Global Studies and Geography at Hofstra University, New York.

Claude Comtois is Professor of Geography at the University of Montreal, Canada, and is affiliated with the Research Centre on Enterprise Networks, Logistics and Transportation at the same institution.

Brian Slack is Distinguished Professor Emeritus at Concordia University, Montreal, Canada.

The Geography of Transport Systems

4th edition

Jean-Paul Rodrigue
with Claude Comtois and Brian Slack

Routledge
Taylor & Francis Group

LONDON AND NEW YORK

Fourth edition published 2017
by Routledge
2 Park Square, Milton Park, Abingdon, Oxon, OX14 4RN

and by Routledge
711 Third Avenue, New York, NY 10017

Routledge is an imprint of the Taylor & Francis Group, an informa business

First edition published by Routledge 2006
Third edition published by Routledge 2013

British Library Cataloguing in Publication Data
A catalogue record for this book is available from the British Library

Library of Congress Cataloging in Publication Data
Names: Rodrigue, Jean-Paul, 1967- author. | Comtois, Claude, 1954- author. |
Slack, Brian, 1939- author.
Title: The geography of transport systems / Jean-Paul Rodrigue, Claude Comtois
and Brian Slack. Description: Edition 4. | New York : Routledge, 2017. | Revised
edition of The geography of transport systems, 2013. | Includes bibliographical
references and index.
Identifiers: LCCN 2016022173| ISBN 9781138669567 (hardback : alk. paper) |
ISBN 9781138669574 (pbk. : alk. paper) | ISBN 9781315618159 (ebook)
Subjects: LCSH: Transportation geography.
Classification: LCC HE323. R63 2017 | DDC 388.01—dc23
LC record available at https://lccn.loc.gov/2016022173

ISBN: 978-1-138-66956-7 (hbk)
ISBN: 978-1-138-66957-4 (pbk)
ISBN: 978-1-315-61815-9 (ebk)

Typeset in Times New Roman
by RefineCatch Limited, Bungay, Suffolk
Printed in Great Britain by Ashford Colour Press Ltd

Contents

Photographs

Figures

Notes on contributors

The Editors

Dr Claude Comtois, Department of Geography, Université de Montréal, C.P. 6128, Succursale Centre Ville Montreal, Quebec, Canada, H3C 3J7.

Dr Jean-Paul Rodrigue is Professor in the Department of Geography and Global Studies at Hofstra University, New York. His research interests primarily cover issues related to freight transportation, logistics and globalization, particularly over North America, Latin American and the Caribbean and Pacific Asia. His recent work focuses on the integration of maritime and inland freight distribution systems through the setting of gateways and corridors and the impacts of containerization on freight distribution.

Dr Brian Slack, Department of Geography, Concordia University, 1400 de Maisonneuve West, Montreal, Quebec, Canada, H3G 1M8.

Contributors

Dr William Anderson, Department of Political Sciences, University of Windsor, Ontario, Canada, N9B 3P4.

Dr John Bowen, Department of Geography, Central Washington University, 400 East University Way, Ellensburg, WA, 98926 USA.

Dr Laetitia Dablanc, Institut Français des Sciences et Technologies, des Transports, de l'Aménagement et des Réseaux, SPLOTT Laboratory, 2 rue de la Butte Verte, Marne-la-Vallée, France.

Dr César Ducruet, CNRS (Centre National de la Recherche Scientifique), UMR 8504 Géographie-Cités, équipe P.A.R.I.S., 13 rue du Four, F-75006, Paris, France.

Dr Theo Notteboom, Maritime Institute, Faculty of Law, University of Ghent, Belgium.

Dr Shih-Lung Shaw, Department of Geography, University of Tennessee, Knoxville, Tennessee, 37996-0925 USA.

Preface

The Geography of Transport Systems is now into its fourth edition. Substantial efforts have been made to build on prior editions' success by improving the content and its structure. Like the previous editions, we have elected for a more synthetic writing style, instead of a narrative, where the goal is to provide a structured framework to the reader. Great care has been made to avoid factual information, so that the textbook can retain its relevance in spite of continuous and often unforeseeable changes in the transport industry. A large quantity of statistical information is available on the companion website, which is constantly updated.

In 2014 *The Geography of Transport Systems* was published in Chinese (China Communications Press). It is not that common for a textbook developed for the Western market to be translated for the Chinese market, underlining the international appeal of the textbook.

A driving force of the global economy resides in the capacity of transport systems to ship large quantities of freight and to accommodate vast numbers of passengers. The world has become interconnected at several scales. This new geographical dimension transcends a more traditional perspective of transportation mainly focused on the city or the nation, with a bias towards the transport of passengers. Further, a particular emphasis is placed on freight transportation, which conventional transport geography tended to cover superficially. At the beginning of the twenty-first century, the geography of transportation is thus fundamentally being redefined by global, regional and local issues.

Presenting these issues remains a challenging task. This book has specifically been designed with this in mind. Its origins are rather unusual, since it began in 1997 as an online initiative to provide material about transport geography and was simply titled "Transport Geography on the Web". The material was considerably revised and expanded over the years, often thanks to comments and queries we received, as the site gained a wider audience. It has already endured for almost 20 years the test of being exposed to the scrutiny of a global audience including practitioners, policy makers, educators and, most importantly, students.

Like the previous three editions, the textbook is articulated along two core approaches to transport geography, one conceptual and the other methodological. The conceptual parts present what we think are some of the most relevant issues explaining contemporary transport geography. In addition to the more conventional topics related to transport modes, terminals, as well as urban transportation, the book also substantially focuses on emerging issues such as globalization, supply chain management, energy and the environment. Many of these issues have been superficially covered, if at all, in the past, but their importance cannot be underestimated in a transport geography that involves an increasingly integrated world.

The methodological parts address how transportation information is used to assist transport operators to allocate their resources (investments, vehicles) or to influence public policy. This includes a wide array of methods ranging from qualitative to quantitative. Since transport is a field of application, the use of methodologies is particularly relevant, as they relate to real-world issues. The merging between methodologies and information technologies has led to many new opportunities, notably with the emergence of transportation geographic information systems (GIS-T). It has become a very active field of investigation and application.

It is our hope that the reader will have a better understanding of the nature, function, importance and challenges of contemporary transportation systems. The online companion site will insure that this book will not be a static endeavor and will be revised and updated as changes take place in this fascinating field which is transport geography.

Jean-Paul Rodrigue
New York, March 2016

1 Transportation and geography

Movements of people, freight and information have always been fundamental components of the economic and social life of societies. Contemporary economic processes have been accompanied by a significant increase in mobility and higher levels of accessibility. Although this trend can be traced back to the Industrial Revolution, it significantly accelerated in the second half of the twentieth century as trade was liberalized and with significant technological improvements. However, this requires the capacity to manage, support and expand movements of passengers and freight as well as their underlying information flows. Societies have become increasingly dependent on their transport systems to support a wide variety of activities ranging, among others, from commuting, tourism, supplying energy needs, to distributing parts and final goods. Developing transport systems has been a continuous challenge to satisfy mobility needs, to support economic development and to participate in the global economy.

Concept 1 – What is transport geography?

Core principles of transportation

In an ideal world, transportation would come at no effort in terms of cost and time and would have unlimited capacity and spatial reach. Under such circumstances, geography would not matter. Unfortunately, we do not live in an ideal world. In a real world, geography can be a significant constraint to transport, since it trades space for time and money.

The unique purpose of transportation is to overcome space, which is shaped by a variety of human and physical constraints such as distance, time, administrative divisions and topography. Jointly, they confer a friction to any movement, commonly known as the friction of distance (or friction of space). However, these constraints and the friction they create can only be partially circumscribed. The extent to which this is done has a cost that varies greatly according to factors such as the length of the trip, the capacity of modes and infrastructures and the nature of what is being transported. **Transport geography** is a subdiscipline of geography concerned about the mobility of people, freight and information. It seeks to understand the spatial organization of mobility by considering its attributes and constraints as they relate to the origin, destination, extent, nature and purpose of movements. Transport geography can be understood from a series of core principles:

1. Transportation is the **spatial linking of a derived demand**. It takes place because of other economic activities and is linking the spatial components of this demand. For instance, commuting is the spatial linking of labor flows resulting from the demand

for labor at one location (e.g. a commercial district) and its supply at another (e.g. a residential district). A market economy could not function without the capacity of transportation to link supply and demand.

2. Distance is a **relative concept** involving space, time and effort. How distance is perceived is a function of the amount of effort made to overcome it. These efforts can be assessed in terms of spatial distance, time distance or other effort measures such as cost or energy spent to overcome distance.

3. Space is at the same time the **generator, support and a constraint** for mobility. It is the formal context in which mobility takes place, so space can be a support for mobility as it will shape the nature and structure of the transport system. At the start, spatial differences in attributes such as resources, employment and demand act as generators and attractors of movements. How space acts as a constraint for transport is often relative and paradoxical. For instance, a river acts as a constraint for land transport systems such as roads and railways, but represents the support for fluvial transportation (if the river is navigable). At the same time that the atmosphere is the physical support for air transport operations, the weather can be a constraining factor under specific circumstances (e.g. snowstorms, thunderstorms, hurricanes). Further, transportation is a space by itself, an activity space, implying that during the transportation process, either in modes or at terminals, socioeconomic activities are taking place.

4. The relation between space and time can **converge or diverge**. Every form of transport involves the consumption of a unit of time in exchange for a given amount of space. Over time this process has mostly converged, implying that a greater amount of space can be reached with the same amount of time (or the same amount of space can be reached with a lesser amount of time). This is jointly the outcome of technological improvements as well as a better capacity and extent of transport infrastructures. The relation between space and time can also diverge when congestion starts to be significant and that each additional unit of movement results in additional delays.

5. A location can be a **central**, where it generates and attract traffic, or an **intermediate** element where traffic transits through. Locations are said to be central when they act as generators (origins) or attractors (destinations) of movements. Locations are labeled as intermediate when movements are passing (transiting) through them on their way to other locations. Ports and airports are often intermediate locations since they act as gateways or hubs within a complex transport network.

6. To overcome geography, transportation must **consume space**. Transportation infrastructures are important consumers of space, which include the pathways (e.g. roads and rail lines) as well as the terminals. The more extensive a transport system and the higher the level of mobility, the more extensive its consumption of space. Globalization has been linked with the setting of massive terminal facilities such as container ports and airports. While space consumed by road infrastructure is mostly linked with local and regional activities, the space consumed by rail, port and airport terminals is linked with activities taking place at a higher scale.

7. Transportation seeks **massification** but is constrained by **atomization** (Figure 1.1). Transport systems are the most effective when they develop economies of scale, particularly in terms of the loads (passengers or freight) they can carry. Massification involves conveyances with higher capacity and supported by larger terminals. However, more than often the first and last segments of a transport sequence require atomization, which implies that transport loads (passengers or freight) must be

consolidated and deconsolidated. So, the higher the level of massification, the more complex atomization becomes.

8. Velocity is a **modal, intermodal and managerial** effort. Velocity does not necessarily mean speed, but the time it takes for a passenger or a unit of freight to move across a complete transport sequence. For instance, the speed advantage of air transportation is undermined if a passenger is spending several hours between connecting flights. Therefore, the velocity of passengers or freight is a joint consideration of the effectiveness of the respective modes involved, as well as that of the intermodal operations connecting the modes. In addition, the complexity of transport systems requires an effective management of its operations, such as scheduling.

For transport modes, atomization represents the smallest load unit that can be effectively transported. The person is obviously the smallest load unit for passenger transportation, while a parcel or a part are the smallest load units for freight transportation. Atomization is less relevant for bulk, since the smallest load unit is a flexible concept; it can be subdivided without any changes in the characteristics of the product. Still, the smallest bulk trade transactions rarely go under a ton. Massification for transportation modes involves the growing capacity to move load units in a single trip. The relations between atomization and massification can be paradoxical, since individuals and customers tend to prefer the convenience of atomization while carriers are favoring massification and the economies of scale it confers.

For passenger transportation, the most massified land transportation mode is the passenger train which can carry about 1,000 passengers, while the Airbus A380, the largest operating passenger plane, has a standard configuration to carry about 550 passengers. The largest passenger conveyance is the cruise ship, with the biggest ships carrying about 6,000 passengers. For bulk transportation, tanker ships can carry up to 400,000 tons, while some bulk carriers have a capacity up to 350,000 tons. Containerization offers a unique advantage, since the container is a relatively small (atomized) load unit that can carry on average 20–25 tons, while containers can be massified on large containerships carrying up to the equivalent of 15,000 standard containers of 20 ft.

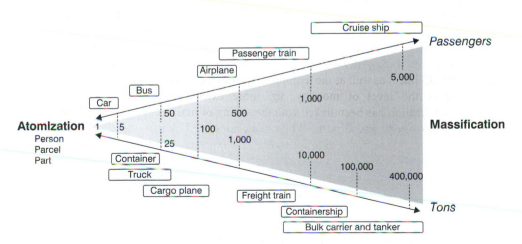

Figure 1.1 Atomization versus massification in transportation modes

The core principles of transport geography underline that there would be no transportation without geography and there would be no geography without transportation. The goal of transportation is thus to transform the **geographical attributes** of freight, people or information, from an origin to a destination, conferring them an **added value** in the process. The convenience at which this can be done varies considerably and is commonly labeled as **transportability**; the ease of movement of passengers, freight or information. It is related to transport costs as well as to the attributes of what is being transported (fragility, perishable, price). Political factors can also influence transportability such as laws, regulations, borders and tariffs. When transportability is high, activities are less constrained by distance.

The purpose of transportation

Transportation is not necessarily a science, but a field of application borrowing concepts and methods from a wide variety of disciplines. The specific purpose of transportation is to fulfill a demand for mobility, since transportation can only exist if it moves people, freight and information around. Otherwise, it has no purpose. This is because transportation is dominantly the outcome of a **derived demand** (Figure 1.2).

In economic systems what takes place in one sector has impacts on another; demand for a good or service in one sector is derived from another. For instance, a consumer

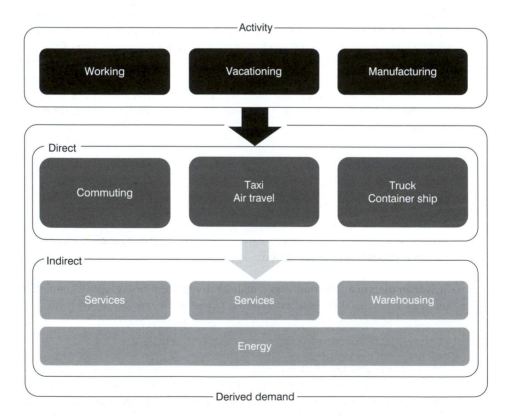

Figure 1.2 Transportation as a derived demand

buying a good in a store will likely trigger the replacement of this product, which will generate demands for activities such as manufacturing, resource extraction and, of course, transport. What is different about transport is that it cannot exist alone and a movement cannot be stored. An unsold product can remain on the shelf of a store until bought (often with discount incentives), but an unsold seat on a flight or unused cargo capacity in the same flight remain unsold and cannot be brought back as additional capacity later. In this case an opportunity has been missed, since the amount of transport being offered has exceeded the demand for it. The derived demand of transportation is often very difficult to reconcile with an equivalent supply, and actually transport companies would prefer to have some additional capacity to accommodate unforeseen demand (often at much higher prices). There are two major types of derived transport demand:

- **Direct derived demand**. Refers to movements that are directly the outcome of economic activities, without which they would not take place. For instance, work-related activities commonly involve commuting between the place of residence and the workplace. There is a supply of work in one location (residence) and a demand of labor in another (workplace), transportation (commuting) being directly derived from this relationship. For freight transportation, all the components of a supply chain require movements of raw materials, parts and finished products on modes such as trucks, rail or containerships. Thus, transportation is directly the outcome of the functions of production and consumption.
- **Indirect derived demand**. Considers movements created by the requirements of other movements. For instance, fuel consumption from transportation activities must be supplied by an energy production system requiring movements from zones of extraction, to refineries and storage facilities and, finally, to places of consumption. Warehousing can also be labeled as an indirect derived demand since it is a "non-movement" of a freight element. Warehousing exists because it is virtually impossible to move cargo instantly from where they are produced to where they are consumed.

Distance, a core attribute of transportation, can be represented in a variety of ways, ranging from a simple Euclidean distance – a straight line between two locations – to what can be called logistical distance; a complete set of tasks required to be done so that distance can be overcome (Figure 1.3).

Any movement must thus consider its geographical setting, which in turn is linked to spatial flows and their patterns. Three major representations can be used for distance and the friction it imposes on transportation:

- **Euclidean distance**. The most basic manner to represent distance as a simple function of a straight line between two locations where distance is expressed in geographical units such as kilometers. Commonly used to provide an approximation of distance, but rarely has a practical use.
- **Transport distance**. A more complex representation that accounts for the existing structure of the transport network. In a simple form involving only one mode, it is a routing exercise considering the shortest path between two points. In a more complex form, it concerns the set of physical activities related to transportation, such as loading, unloading and transshipment which are considered. On Figure 1.3, the transport distance between locations A and B includes pickup, travel by mode 1, transshipment,

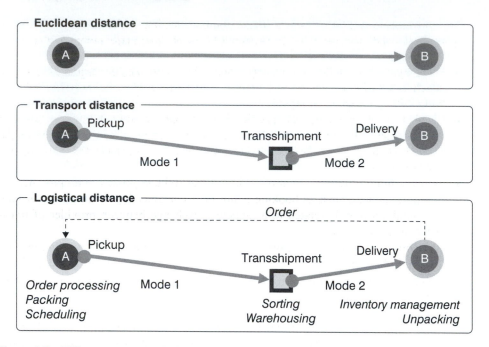

Figure 1.3   Different representations of distance

travel by mode 2 and, finally, delivery. The same applies to the circulation of people, although the involved activities will be different. For instance, someone using air travel between two locations will require going to an airport, may transit through an intermediate hub airport and will finally need to reach his or her destination from the airport terminal. Transport distance is jointly expressed in geographical units, in cost and in time.

- **Logistical distance**. A complex representation that encompasses all the tasks required so that a movement between two locations can take place. Logistical distance thus includes physical flows, but also a set of activities necessary for the management of these flows. For freight movements, among the most significant tasks are order processing, packing, sorting and inventory management. Geographical distance units are less relevant in this assessment, but the factors of costs and time are very significant. Time not only involves the delay related to management and circulation, but also how it is used to service the transport demand, namely the scheduling of pickups and deliveries. On Figure 1.3, the logistical distance between locations A and B includes an order from B, which is processed, packed and scheduled to be picked up. At the intermediate transshipment location, sorting and warehousing are performed and, finally, at the destination the delivery will be unpacked and used. For the transportation of passengers, logistical distance also concerns a specific array of tasks. Taking again an air travel example, a ticket would first need to be purchased, commonly several weeks in advance. Other common time and cost tasks concern checking in, security checks, boarding and disembarking and picking up luggage. Thus, a three-hour flight often requires to be planned several weeks in advance and its full realization can take twice as much time if all the related logistical activities are considered.

Any movement must thus consider its geographical setting, which in turn is linked to spatial flows and their patterns. The concept of flow has four major components:

- **Geographical**. Each flow has an origin and a destination and consequently a degree of separation. Flows with high degrees of separation tend to be more limited than flows with low degrees of separation.
- **Physical**. Each flow involves specific physical characteristics in terms of possible load units and the conditions in which they can be carried. Flows, depending on the transportation mode, can be atomized (smallest load unit) or massified (moving load units in batches).
- **Transactional**. The realization of each flow has to be negotiated with providers of transport services, such as booking a slot on a containership or an air travel seat. Commonly, a flow is related to a monetary exchange between provider of transportation and the user.
- **Distribution**. Flows are organized in sequences where the more complex are involving different modes and terminals. Many transport flows are scheduled and routed to minimize costs or maximize efficiency, often through intermediary locations.

Urbanization, multinational corporations and economic globalization are all forces shaping and taking advantage of transportation at different, but often related, scales. Consequently, the fundamental purpose of transport is geographic in nature, because it facilitates movements between different locations. Transport plays a role in the structure and organization of space and territories, which may vary according to the level of development. In the nineteenth century, the purpose of the emerging modern forms of transportation, mainly railways and maritime shipping, was to expand spatial coverage with the creation, expansion and consolidation of national markets. In the twentieth century, the objective shifted to selecting itineraries, prioritizing transport modes, increasing the capacity of existing networks and responding to the mobility needs, and this at a scale which was increasingly global, with its own space of flows. In the twenty-first century, transportation must cope with a globally oriented economic system in a timely and cost-effective way, but also with several local problems such as congestion and capacity constraints.

The importance of transportation

Transport represents one of the most important human activities worldwide. It is an indispensable component of the economy and plays a major role in supporting spatial relations between locations. Transport creates valuable links between regions and economic activities, between people and the rest of the world. It is composed of core components, which are the **modes**, **infrastructures**, **networks** and **flows**. These components are fundamental for transportation to take place, but they also underline that geography, in spite of significant technological, social and economic changes, remain a salient force shaping transportation. Transport is a multidimensional activity whose importance is:

- **Historical**. Transport modes have played several different historical roles in the rise of civilizations (Egypt, Rome and China), in the development of societies (creation of social structures) and also in national defense (Roman Empire, American road network). As such, transportation offers a valuable perspective to understand the history of a region or nation.

- **Social**. Transport modes facilitate access to healthcare, welfare and cultural or artistic events, thus performing a social service. They shape social interactions by favoring or inhibiting the mobility of people. Transportation thus supports and may even shape social structures.
- **Political**. Governments play a critical role in transport as sources of investment and as regulators. The political role of transportation is undeniable as governments often subsidize the mobility of their populations (highways, public transit, etc.). While most transport demand relates to economic imperatives, many communication corridors have been constructed for political reasons, such as national accessibility or job creation. Transport thus has an impact on nation building and national unity, but it is also a political tool.
- **Economic**. The evolution of transport has always been linked to economic development. It is an industry in its own right (car manufacturing, air transport companies, etc.). The transport sector is also an economic factor in the production of goods and services. It contributes to the value-added of economic activities, facilitates economies of scale, influences land (real-estate) value and the geographic specialization of regions. Transport is both a factor shaping economic activities and is also shaped by them.
- **Environmental**. Despite the manifest advantages of transport, its environmental consequences are also significant. They include air and water quality, noise level and public health. All decisions relating to transport need to be evaluated taking into account the corresponding environmental costs. Transport is a dominant factor in contemporary environmental issues, including sustainability and climate change.

Transportation studies are therefore multidisciplinary, and can involve hard (e.g. engineering) or soft sciences (e.g. economics) depending on the dimension being investigated such as infrastructure provision, operational management or planning. Substantial empirical evidence indicates that the importance of transportation is growing. The following contemporary trends can be identified regarding this issue:

- **Growth of the demand**. The years following World War II have seen a considerable growth of the transport demand related to individual (passengers) as well as freight mobility. This growth is jointly the result of larger quantities of passengers and freight being moved, but also the longer distances over which they are carried. Recent trends underline an ongoing process of mobility growth, which has led to the multiplication of the number of journeys involving a wide variety of modes that service transport demands.
- **Reduction of costs**. Even if several transportation modes are very expensive to own and operate (ships and planes for instance), costs per unit transported have dropped significantly over the last decades. This has made it possible to overcome larger distances and further exploit the comparative advantages of space. As a result, despite the lower costs, the share of transport activities in the economy has remained relatively constant in time.
- **Expansion of infrastructures**. The above two trends have obviously extended the requirements for transport infrastructures both quantitatively and qualitatively. Roads, harbors, airports, telecommunication facilities and pipelines have expanded considerably to service new areas and adding capacity to existing networks. Transportation infrastructures are thus a major component of the land use, notably in developed countries.

Facing these contemporary trends, an important part of the spatial differentiation of the economy is related to where resources (raw materials, capital, people, information, etc.) are located and how well they can be distributed. Transport routes are established to distribute resources between places where they are abundant and places where they are scarce, but only if the costs are lower than the benefits. Consequently, transportation has an important role to play in the conditions that affect global, national and regional economic entities. It is a strategic infrastructure that is so embedded in the socio-economic life of individuals, institutions and corporations that it is often invisible to the consumer, but always part of all economic and social functions. This is paradoxical, since the perceived invisibility of transportation is derived from its efficiency. If transport is disrupted or ceases to operate, the consequences can be dramatic such as workers unable to reach their workplace or parts not being delivered to factories.

Transportation in geography

The world is obviously not a place where features such as resources, people and economic activities are randomly distributed; there is a logic, or/and order, to spatial distribution. Geography seeks to understand the **spatial order of things** as well as their **interactions**, particularly when this spatial order is less evident. Transportation, being one element of this spatial order, is at the same time influenced by geography as well as having an influence on it. For instance, the path followed by a road is influenced by regional economic and physical attributes, but once constructed the same road will shape future regional developments.

Transportation is of relevance to geography for two main reasons. First, transport infrastructures, terminals, modes and networks occupy an **important place in space** and constitute the basis of a **complex spatial system**. Second, since geography seeks to explain spatial relationships, transport networks are of specific interest, because they are the main physical support of these interactions.

In the 1960s, transport costs were formalized as key factors in location theories and transport geography began to rely increasingly on quantitative methods, particularly over network and spatial interactions analysis. However, from the 1970s technical, political and economic changes challenged the centrality of transportation in many geographical and regional development investigations. The strong spatial anchoring effect of high transportation costs receded and decentralization was a dominant paradigm that was observed within cities (suburbanization), but also within regions. The spatial theory foundations of transport geography, particularly the friction of distance, became less relevant, or less evident, in explaining socioeconomic processes. As a result, transportation became underrepresented in economic geography in the 1970s and 1980s, even if the mobility of people and freight and low transport costs were considered as important factors behind the globalization of trade and production.

Since the 1990s, transport geography has received renewed attention with new realms of investigation. The issues of mobility, production and distribution became interrelated in a complex geographical setting where the local, regional and global became increasingly blurred through the development of new passengers and freight transport systems. For instance, suburbanization resulted in an array of challenges related to congestion and automobile dependency. Rapid urbanization in developing economies underlined the challenges of transport infrastructure investment for private as well as collective uses. Globalization supported the development of complex air and maritime transportation networks, many of which were supporting global supply chains and trade relations across long distances. The role of information and communication technologies was also being felt, often as a support or as an alternative to mobility. All of the above were linked with new and expanded mobilities of passengers, freight and information.

This "new transport geography" is based on the premise that transportation is a system supporting complex relationships between its core components, which are nodes, networks and demand (see Figure 1.4):

- **Transportation nodes**. Transportation primarily links locations, often characterized as nodes. They serve as access points to a distribution system or as transshipment/ intermediary locations within a transport network. This function is mainly serviced by transport terminals where flows originate, end or are being transshipped from one mode to the other. Transport geography must consider its places of convergence and transshipment.
- **Transportation networks**. Considers the spatial structure and organization of transport infrastructures and terminals. Transport geography must include in its investigation the structures (routes and infrastructures) supporting and shaping movements.
- **Transportation demand**. Considers the demand for transport services as well as the modes used to support movements. Once this demand is realized, it becomes an interaction which flows through a transport network. Transport geography must evaluate the factors affecting its derived demand function.

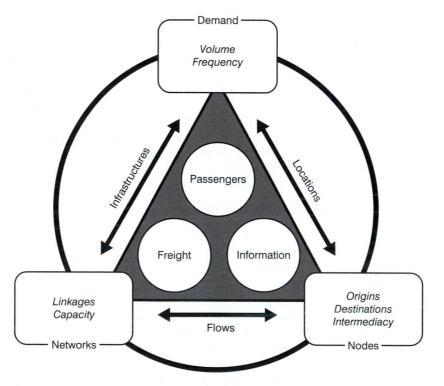

Figure 1.4 The transport system

The analysis of these concepts within transport geography relies on **methodologies** often developed by other disciplines such as economics, mathematics, planning and demography. For instance, the spatial structure of transportation networks can be analyzed with graph theory, which was initially developed for mathematics. Further, many models developed for the analysis of movements, such as the gravity model, were borrowed from physical sciences. **Multidisciplinarity** is consequently an important attribute of transport geography, as in geography in general, as each discipline provides a different dimension to transport geography. Transport geography must be systematic as one element of the transport system is linked with numerous others; transport systems are complex.

The role of transport geography is to understand the spatial relations that are produced by transport systems. This is essential to assist private and public actors involved in transportation to mitigate key transport problems, such as capacity, transfer, reliability and integration of transport systems. There are three basic geographical considerations relevant to transport systems:

- **Location**. As all activities are located somewhere, each location has its own characteristics conferring a potential supply and/or a demand for resources, products, services or labor. A location will determine the nature, the origin, the destination, the distance and even the possibility of a movement to be realized. For instance, a city provides employment in various sectors of activity in addition to consuming resources.
- **Complementarity**. Some locations have a supply of labor, resources, parts or final goods, while others have a deficit. The only way an equilibrium can be reached is by movements between locations having supply (or a surplus) and locations having a demand. For instance, a complementarity is created between a store (supply of goods) and its customers (demand of goods).
- **Scale**. Movements generated by complementarity are occurring at different scales, pending the nature of the activity. Scale illustrates how transportation systems are established over local, regional and global geographies. For instance, home-to-work journeys generally have a local or regional scale, while the distribution network of a multinational corporation is most likely to cover several regions of the world.

Consequently, transport systems consume land and support the relationships between locations at a scale that is increasingly global. Over this, transport geography provides a multidisciplinary perspective to understand the complexity of transportation and how space supports and hinders mobility.

Concept 2 – Transportation and space

Authors: Dr Jean-Paul Rodrigue and Dr Claude Comtois

Physical constraints

Transport geography is concerned with movements that take place over space and the physical features of this space impose major constraints on transportation systems, in terms of what mode can be used, the extent of the service, its costs, capacity and reliability. Three basic spatial constraints of the terrestrial space can be identified:

- **Topography.** Features such as mountains and valleys have strongly influenced the structure of networks, the cost and feasibility of transportation projects. The main land transport infrastructures are usually built where there are the fewest physical impediments, such as on plains, along valleys, through mountain passes or, when absolutely necessary, through the digging of tunnels. Water transport is influenced by water depths and the location of obstacles such as reefs. Coastlines exert an influence on the location of port infrastructure. Aircraft require airfields of considerable size for takeoff and landing. Topography can impose a natural convergence of routes that will create a certain degree of centrality and may assist a location in becoming a trade center as a collector and distributor of goods. Topography can complicate, postpone or prevent transport activities and investment. Physical constraints fundamentally act as absolute and relative barriers to movements. An absolute barrier is a geographical feature that entirely prevents a movement, while relative barriers impose additional costs and delays. Land transportation networks are notably influenced by the topography, as highways and railways tend to be impeded by grades higher than 3 percent and 1 percent respectively. Under such circumstances, land transportation tends to be of higher density in areas of limited topography.

- **Hydrology.** The properties, distribution and circulation of water play an important role in the transport industry. Maritime transport is influenced greatly by the availability of navigable channels through rivers, lakes and shallow seas. Several rivers such as the Mississippi, the St Lawrence, the Rhine, the Mekong or the Yangtze are important navigable routes into the heart of continents and historically have been the focus of human activities that have taken advantage of the transport opportunities. Port sites are also highly influenced by the physical attributes of the site where natural features (bays, sandbars and fjords) protect port installations. Since it is at these installations that traffic is transshipped, the location of ports is a dominant element in the structure of maritime networks. Where barriers exist, such as narrows, rapids, or land breaks, water transport can only overcome these obstacles with heavy investments in canals or dredging. Conversely, waterways serve as barriers to land transportation necessitating the construction of bridges, tunnels and detours.

- **Climate.** Its major components include temperature, wind and precipitation: their impacts on transportation modes and infrastructure ranging from negligible to severe. Freight and passenger movement can seriously be curtailed by hazardous conditions such as snow, heavy rainfall, ice or fog. Air transportation is particularly vulnerable to weather disruptions, such as during winter, when a snowstorm can create cascading effects of air services. Jet streams are also a major physical component that international air carriers must take into consideration. For an aircraft, the speed of wind can affect travel time and costs. Tailwind conditions can reduce scheduled flight time up to an hour for intercontinental flights. For instance, due to strong jet stream conditions during winter months, transatlantic flights between the American East Coast and Europe can gain between 30 to 45 minutes from the scheduled flight time eastbound. However, for westbound flights, unusually strong jet stream conditions will lengthen flight time and on occasion force a flight to do an unscheduled refueling stop in intermediary airports such as Gander (Newfoundland) or Bangor (Maine). Climate is also having an impact on transportation networks by influencing construction and maintenance costs. Even volcanic eruptions can have an impact, as was the case in 2010, when an eruption in Iceland released large amounts of ashes in the atmosphere, which forced the closing of most airports in northwestern Europe as well as the cancellation of many transatlantic flights out of concern that the ash could damage jet engines.

From a geometrical standpoint, the sphericity of the earth determines the great circle distance: the least distance line between two points on a sphere. This feature explains the paths followed by major intercontinental maritime and air routes. For instance, Figure 1.5 shows the shortest path between New York and Moscow (about 7,540 km). This path corresponds to an air transportation corridor. Air travel over the North Atlantic between North America and Europe follows a similar path.

Overcoming the physical environment

Rapid technological developments have enabled transportation to overcome the physical environment. Prior to the Industrial Revolution most road paths were adapted to topography. Since then, efforts have been made for paving roads, bridging rivers and

Figure 1.5 The great circle distance between New York, Moscow and Tokyo

cutting paths over mountain passes. Engineering techniques in terms of arch and vault used in Byzantine and Gothic church constructions in the twelfth century permitted bridge building across wider streams or deep river valleys. Road building thus has been at the core of technological efforts to overcome the environment since they are the support for local and even long-distance travel. From the efforts to mechanize road transport modes to the development of integrated multilane highways, road building has transformed the environment.

As level ground over long distance is important for increasing the efficiency of railway routes, the transport industry has come to modify the earth's features by building bridges and tunneling, by embanking and drainage. From the early steam engines to the first high-speed trains, increasing motive power has permitted physical obstacles to be overcome by rail.

Innovations in maritime transport can be found around the world. The earliest developments came in the transformation of waterways for transportation purposes through the development of canal locks coping with adverse natural gradients. Further improvements in navigation came with the cutting of artificial waterways. Some of the earliest examples can be found in the Dutch canals, the Martesana canals of Lombardy, the Canal de Briare in France or the Grand Canal of China. Further improvements in navigation technology are the nature of ships permitted to increase the speed, range and capacity of ocean transport. However, the increasing size of ships has resulted in excluding canals such as Panama and many ports from servicing the largest ships. Several port authorities have thus embarked in expansion programs.

Passages through the Arctic Ocean are being investigated with a view to create new international connections (Figure 1.6). If this trend continues, parts of the Arctic could be used more reliably for navigation, at least during summer months and for longer periods of time. The main trans-Arctic routes include:

- The **Northern Sea Route** along the arctic coast of Russia. This is the maritime route that is likely to be free of ice first and would reduce a maritime journey between East Asia and Western Europe from 21,000 km (using the Suez Canal) to 12,800 km, cutting transit time by 10–15 days. In 2009, two German ships, Beluga Fraternity and Beluga Foresight, completed with a Russian icebreaker escort the first commercial journey across the Northern Sea Route (or Northeast Passage) linking Busan to Rotterdam with several stopovers.
- The **Northwest Passage** crossing Canada's Arctic Ocean could become usable on a regular basis by 2020, lessening maritime shipping distances substantially. The maritime journey between East Asia and Western Europe would take about 13,600 km using the Northwest Passage, while taking 24,000 km using the Panama Canal. In 2007 the Northwest Passage was open during the summer months for the first time in recorded history, but it remains to be seen how stable this opening is.
- The **Arctic Bridge** linking the Russian port of Murmansk or the Norwegian port of Narvik to the Canadian port of Churchill could be used, mostly for the grain trade.
- The **Transpolar Sea Route** would use the central part of the Arctic to link the most directly the Strait of Bering and the Atlantic Ocean of Murmansk. This route is at this point hypothetical, as it involves ice-free conditions that are not yet observed.

The consideration of Arctic routes for commercial navigation purposes remains a very speculative endeavor, mainly for three reasons:

- First, it is uncertain to what extent the **receding perennial ice cover** is a confirmed trend or simply part of a long-term climatic cycle. Even if the Arctic routes became regularly open during the summer, the medium term underlines that that Arctic would still remain closed to commercial navigation during the winter months. As of 2010, the ice-free conditions of most Arctic shipping routes were only about 30 days. Since maritime shipping companies are looking for regular and consistent services, this seasonality has limited commercial appeal.

- Second, there is **very limited economic activity** around the Arctic Circle, implying that shipping services crossing the Arctic have almost no opportunity to drop and pick up cargo as they pass through. Thus, unlike other long-distance commercial shipping routes, there is limited revenue generation potential for shipping lines along the Arctic route, which forbids the emergence of transshipment hubs. Shipping in the Arctic is suitable for point-to-point services linking directly a source port and a destination port. This value proposition could improve if resources (oil and mining) around the Arctic are extracted in greater quantities, which would favor bulk shipping.

Figure 1.6 Polar shipping routes

Source: Adapted from the *New York Times*, 10 October 2005.

● Third, the Arctic remains a frontier in terms of weather forecast, charting and building a navigation system, implying **uncertainties and unreliability for navigation**. This implies that substantial efforts have to be made to insure that navigation can take place in a safe manner along well-defined and patrolled navigation routes. Ships also need to be certified to operate in Arctic conditions, which increases costs.

In view of all of the above, maritime shipping companies are not yet considering seriously the commercial potential of the Arctic as a navigation shortcut. Still, the rise in bunker fuel prices and slow steaming practices can be considered incentives for the development of niche services that could use the Arctic as a shortcut between major markets of the northern hemisphere. By doing so, shipping services would have the option to mitigate the distance advantage of the shorter Arctic routes with the option of slower speeds and their fuel consumption benefits.

The role of technology has been determinant in the development of the air transport sector. From the experiments of the Montgolfier brothers to the advent of jet aircraft, aerial crossing of rugged terrain over considerable distance became possible. Technical innovation in the aeronautic industry has permitted planes to avoid adverse atmospheric conditions, improve speed, increase range and raise carrying capacity. With the rapid rise in air passenger and freight transport demand, emphasis has been given to the construction of airport terminals and runways. As airports occupy large areas, their environmental footprint is important. The construction of Chek Lap Kok airport in Hong Kong led to leveling mountainous land for the airport site. Kansai airport, servicing Osaka, has been built on an artificial island.

Transportation and the spatial structure

The concepts of site and situation are fundamental to geography and to transportation. While the site refers to the geographical characteristics of a specific location, its situation concerns its relationships in regard to other locations. For instance, a port site relates to attributes such as the suitability of its harbor, while a port situation relates to its connectivity with its foreland (other ports) and hinterland (the inland market it serves). Thus, all locations are relative to one another, but situation is not a constant attribute as transportation developments change levels of accessibility, and thus the relations between locations. The development of a location reflects the cumulative relationships between transport infrastructure, economic activities and the built environment. The following factors are particularly important in shaping the spatial structure:

● **Costs**. The spatial distribution of activities is related to factors of distance, namely its friction. Locational decisions are taken in an attempt to minimize costs, often related to transportation.
● **Accessibility**. All locations have a level of accessibility, but some are more accessible than others. Thus, because of transportation, some locations are perceived as more valuable than others.
● **Agglomeration**. There is a tendency for activities to agglomerate to take advantage of the value of specific locations. The more valuable a location, the more likely agglomeration will take place. The organization of activities is essentially hierarchical, resulting from the relationships between agglomeration and accessibility at the local, regional and global levels.

Many contemporary transportation networks are inherited from the past, notably transport infrastructures. Even if, since the Industrial Revolution, new technologies have revolutionized transportation in terms of speed, capacity and efficiency, the spatial structure of many networks has not much changed. This **inertia** in the spatial structure of some transportation networks can be explained by two major factors:

- **Physical attributes**. Natural conditions can be modified and adapted to suit human uses, but they are a very difficult constraint to escape, notably for land transportation. It is thus not surprising to find that most networks follow the easiest (least cost) paths, which generally follow valleys and plains. Considerations that affected road construction a few hundred years ago are still in force today, although they are sometimes easier to circumscribe with civil engineering work.
- **Historical considerations**. New infrastructures generally reinforce historical patterns of exchange, notably at the regional level. For instance, the current highway network of France has mainly followed the patterns set by the national roads network built early in the twentieth century. This network was established over the royal road network, itself mainly following roads built by the Romans. At the urban level, the pattern of streets is often inherited from an older pattern, which itself may have been influenced by the pre-existing rural structure (lot pattern and rural roads).

While physical and historical considerations are at play, the introduction of new transport technology or the addition of new transport infrastructure may lead to a transformation of existing networks. Recent developments in transport systems such as container shipping, long-range aircrafts and the extensive application of information technology to transport management have created a new transport environment and a new spatial structure. These transport technologies and innovations have intensified global interactions and modified the relative location of places. In this highly dynamic context, two processes are taking place at the same time:

- **Specialization**. From a situation of diversification, linked geographical entities are able to specialize in the production of goods for which they have an advantage, and trading for what they do not produce. As a result, efficient transportation systems are generally linked with higher levels of regional specialization. Economic globalization clearly underlines this process as specialization occurs as long as the incurred savings in production costs are higher than the incurred additional transport costs.
- **Segregation**. The continuous evolution of transportation technology may not necessarily have expected effects on the spatial structure, as two forces are at play: concentration and dispersion. Linked geographical entities may see the reinforcement of one at the expense of others, notably through economies of scale. This outcome often contradicts regional development policies aiming at providing uniform accessibility levels within a region.

A common fallacy is to relate transportation solely as a force of dispersion, favoring the spatial diffusion of activities. This is not always the case. In numerous instances, transportation is a force of concentration and clustering, notably for business activities. Since transport infrastructures are generally expensive to build, they are established first to service the most important locations. For instance, even if it was a strong factor of dispersion, the automobile has also favored the clustering of several activities in a suburban setting.

Space/time relationships

One of the most basic relationships supported by transportation involves **how much space can be overcome within a given amount of time**. The faster the mode, the larger the distance that can be overcome within the same amount of time. Transportation, notably improvements in transport systems, changes the relationship between time and space. When this relationship involves easier, faster and cheaper access between places, the outcome is a space/time convergence because the amount of space that can be overcome for a similar amount of time increases significantly. It is, however, a spatially and socially uneven process since it will impact the accessibility of locations differently. For instance, infrastructure will not be laid up uniformly and segments of the population will experience a greater improvement in mobility because of their socioeconomic status. In spite of these uneven processes, significant regional and continental gains were achieved during the eighteenth and nineteenth centuries with the establishment of national and continental railway systems as well as with the growth of maritime shipping, a process which continued into the twentieth century with air and road transport systems. The outcome has been significant differences in space/time relationships, mainly between developed and developing countries, reflecting differences in the efficiency of transport systems.

At the international level, globalization processes have been supported by improvements in transport technology. The result of more than 200 years of technological improvements has been a space/time convergence of global proportions in addition to the regional and continental processes previously mentioned. This enabled the extended exploitation of the advantages of the global market, notably in terms of resources and labor. Significant reductions in transport and communication costs occurred concomitantly. There is thus a relationship between space/time convergence and the integration of a region in global trade. Five major factors are of particular relevance in this process:

- **Speed**. The most straightforward factor relates to the increasing speed of many transport modes, a condition that particularly prevailed in the first half of the twentieth century. More recently, speed has played a less significant role, as many modes are not going much faster. For instance, an automobile has a similar operating speed today than it had 60 years ago and a commercial jet plane operates at a similar speed than one 40 years ago.
- **Economies of scale**. Being able to transport larger amounts of freight and passengers at lower costs has improved considerably the capacity and efficiency of transport systems. For space/time convergence this implies that there is more capacity for a given quantity of passengers or freight being carried. Instead, the traffic can be handled with fewer trips implying that at the aggregate level it is moving faster.
- **Expansion of transport infrastructures**. Transport infrastructures have expanded considerably to service areas that were not previously serviced or were insufficiently serviced. A paradox of this feature is that, although the expansion of transport infrastructures may have enabled distribution systems to expand, it also increased the average distance over which passengers and freight are being carried.
- **Efficiency of transport terminals**. Terminals, such as ports and airports, have shown a growing capacity to handle large quantities in a timely manner. Thus, even if the speed of many transport modes has not increased, more efficient transport terminals and a better management of flows have helped reduce transport time.
- **Information technologies (IT)**. Enabled several economic activities to bypass spatial constraints in a very significant manner as IT supports complex management

structures. Electronic mail is an example where the transmission of information does not have a physical form (outside electrons or photons) once the supporting infrastructure is established. There is obviously a limit to this substitution, but several corporations are trying to use the advantages of telecommuting as much as they can because of the important savings involved.

Improvements in transport technology enabled a gradual space/time convergence of the global transport system (Figure 1.7). Before the Industrial Revolution, transport technology only permitted limited access to other regions of the world. Technological innovations in the domain of transportation were essentially used to increase the economic efficiency of European economies enabling them to have access to resources and markets. This began with mercantilism and gradually shaped the global economy with declining transport costs and the ability to move passengers and freight over longer distances. The global space/time convergence is, however, not spatially uniform, implying that some regions benefit more than others. For instance, space/time convergence in Western Europe and North America, and over the North Atlantic, has taken place at a faster rate than other regions of the world, such as Latin America or Africa. It can be assumed that, as economic and infrastructure development takes place around the world, space/time convergence is likely to become more uniform.

Circumnavigation is a good proxy for assessing space/time convergence. Prior to the introduction of the steamship in the mid-nineteenth century, circumnavigating the globe would take about one sailing year, a journey greatly delayed by rounding the Cape of Good Hope and the Strait of Magellan. The late nineteenth and early twentieth centuries provided a series of innovations that would greatly improve circumnavigation, notably the construction of the Suez (1869) and Panama (1914) canals as well as steam propulsion. Circumnavigation was reduced to about 100 days (the "Jules Vernes effect") at the beginning of the twentieth century and to 60 days by 1925 with fast liner services. The introduction of the jet plane in the second half of the twentieth century reduced circumnavigation to about 34 hours if two (or three) direct and connecting long-range flights can be booked (e.g. New York–Dubai, Dubai–Tokyo and Tokyo–New York).

Figure 1.7 Global space/time convergence: days required to circumnavigate the globe

Yet, space/time convergence does not occur in a ubiquitous manner. In time, some locations gain more accessibility than others particularly if they experience the accumulation of transport infrastructures. After centuries of transport developments and their impacts on geography, global accessibility reflects a heterogeneous geography. Space/time convergence can also be inverted under specific circumstances, which means that a process of space/time divergence takes place. For instance, congestion is increasing in many metropolitan areas, implying additional delays for activities such as commuting. Traffic in congested urban areas is moving at the same speed that it did 100 years ago on horse carriages.

Air transportation, despite having dramatically contributed to the space/time convergence is also experiencing growing delays. Flight times are getting longer between many destinations, mainly because of takeoff, landing and gate access delays. Airlines are simply posting longer scheduled flight times to factor in congestion. The termination of the Concorde supersonic jet service in 2003 can also be considered as a space/time divergence. More stringent security measures at airports have also imposed additional delays, which tends to penalize short distance flights. Additionally, direct transport services can be discontinued and replaced by a hub-and-spoke structure. The "last mile" can be the longest in many transport segments.

Concept 3 – Transportation and commercial geography

Authors: Dr Jean-Paul Rodrigue and Dr Claude Comtois

Trade and commercial geography

Trade, the exchange of goods and services over long distances, and commercial activities, the exchange of goods and services at specific markets, are core components of the economy. Trade and commerce have evolved in space and in time, from low volume and limited extent prior to the Industrial Revolution, to the extensive flows and transactions that characterize the contemporary global economy. Historically, wealth was dominantly related to agricultural output, implying that the largest economies were those with the largest populations, but these populations were mainly rural and with low income. As such, trade and commerce were marginal activities.

The Industrial Revolution irremediably changed trade and commerce with mechanization and its multiplying effects on production and consumption. Yet, in spite of substantial growth in production capabilities, economic systems remain based on trade and transactions, since specialization and efficiency require interdependency. People trade their labor for a wage, having to commute in the process, while corporations trade their output for capital, having to access markets. Trade is the transmission of a possession in return for a counterpart, generally money, which is often defined as a medium of exchange. This exchange involves a transaction and its associated flows of capital, information, commodities, parts or finished products. All these activities define **commercial geography**, which investigates the spatial characteristics of trade and transactions in terms of their nature, causes and consequences. It leans on the analysis of transactions, from a simple commercial transaction involving an individual purchasing a product at a store, to the complex network of transactions maintained between a multinational corporation and its suppliers. The scale and scope of commercial geography varies significantly.

Trade, in terms of its origins and destinations, has a **spatial logic**. It reflects the economic, social and industrial structure of the concerned markets, but also implies other factors such as transport costs, distance, trade agreements, exchange rates and the reciprocal economic advantages proponents get from trade. For trade to occur, several fundamental conditions must be met:

- **Availability**. Commodities, from coal to computer chips, must be available for trade and there must be a demand for these commodities. In other terms, a surplus must exist at one location and a demand in another, which implies a level of reciprocity. A surplus can often be a simple matter of investment in production capabilities, such as building an assembly plant, or can be constrained by complex geological and environmental factors like the availability of resources such as fossil fuels, minerals and agricultural products.
- **Transferability**. Transport infrastructures, in allowing goods to be moved from their origins to their destinations, support the transferability of goods. There are three major impediments to transferability, namely, regulatory barriers (tariffs, custom inspections, quotas), geographical barriers (time, distance) and transportation barriers (the simple capacity to move the outcome of a transaction). Distance often plays an important role in trade, as does the capacity of infrastructures to route and to transship goods.
- **Transactional capacity**. It must be legally possible to make a transaction. This implies the recognition of a currency for trading and legislations that define the environment in which commercial transactions are taking place, such as taxation and litigation. In the context of a global economy, the transactional environment is very complex, but is important in facilitating trade at the regional, national and international levels. The fundamental elements of a commercial transaction involving the transportation of a good are the letter of credit and the bill of lading. The transport terms have been regulated since 1936 by international commercial terms, which define the respective responsibilities and risks of the actors involved. Such terms are regularly updated and revised to reflect commercial and regulatory changes in global markets.

Once these conditions are met, trade is possible and the outcome of a transaction results in a flow (or interaction). Three particular issues relate to the concept of flow:

- **Value**. Flows have a negotiated value and are settled in a common currency. The American dollar, which has become the main global currency, is used to settle and/or measure many international transactions. Further, nations must maintain reserves of foreign currencies to settle their transactions. The relationship between the inbound and outbound flows of capital is known as the balance of payments. Although nations try to maintain a stable balance of payments, this is rarely the case; flows are commonly imbalanced.
- **Volume**. Flows have a physical characteristic, mainly involving a mass. The weight of flows is a significant variable when trade involves raw materials such as petroleum or minerals. However, in the case of consumption goods, weight has little significance relative to the value of the commodities being traded. With containerization, a new unit of volume has been introduced: the TEU (Twenty-foot Equivalent Unit), which can be used to assess trade flows.
- **Scale**. Flows have a range which varies significantly based on the nature of a transaction. While retailing transactions tend to occur at a local scale, transactions related to the operations of a multinational corporation are global in scale.

Cities are the world's major commercial centers, but the commercial importance of a city is relative to a number of factors, such as financial flows, the ease of doing business and transport infrastructure (Figure 1.8). Traditionally, commercial activities tended to develop where there was a physical break along transport chains. Cargo needed to be transferred from one mode to another and a new actor took over its ownership or its custody. The physical break imposed transactions, an important reason why most the world's most important financial centers tend to be port cities or major load break centers in the hinterland.

The most important consumer markets are also found in prominent commercial centers. The Worldwide Centers of Commerce Index evaluates 75 cities across seven dimensions (legal and political framework, economic stability, ease of doing business, financial flow, business centers, knowledge creation and information flow, and livability) consisting of 43 indicators. It underlines that city-specific data tends to be more relevant than country-level data. While Europe and North America continue to dominate the commercial landscape, the commercial relevance of centers in the Middle East, South Asia, Southeast Asia and East Asia is increasing.

Trends in commercial geography

The contemporary commercial setting is marked by increasing free trade and profound technological, industrial and geopolitical changes. The **liberalization of trade**, as confirmed by the implementation of the World Trade Organization, has given a strong impetus in the growth rate of world trade and industrial production. This has led to competitive pressures and shifting competitive advantages between regions. Even if in a true free trade environment, regulatory agencies would not be required, in spite of

Figure 1.8 Worldwide Centers of Commerce Index, 2008

attempts at deregulation, transactions and trade being prone to disputes, litigations and perceived imbalances concerning who benefits the most. Although these issues mainly apply to international trade, there are also situations where trade is constrained between jurisdictions (provinces, states) of a nation.

After decades of globalization and ongoing growth, much of the trade remains **dominantly regional**. An overview of world trade flows indicates that trade within regions is more significant than trade between regions, but long-distance trade has steadily been growing. This has been associated with an increasing share of East Asia, especially China, in world trade both in terms of exports and imports. Flows of merchandises have also been accompanied by a substantial growth in foreign direct investments. A remarkable reallocation of production capacities has taken place through outsourcing and offshoring following changes in comparative advantages around the world. This trend goes in tandem with mergers and acquisitions of enterprises that are increasingly global in scope. The analysis of international trade thus reveals the need to adopt different strategies to adapt to this new trading environment. As production is being relocated, there is a continuous shift in the structure of exports and imports among nations. The decline of manufacturing in its share of the global GDP is illustrative of the growing complexities that added value brings to the function of production. It masks a manufacturing sector that is embedded with service activities, such as logistics, and which is increasingly dependent on the generation of added value.

Major changes have occurred in the **organization of production**. There is a noticeable increase in the division of labor concerning the design, planning and assembly in the manufacturing process of the global economy. Interlocking partnerships in the structure of manufacturing have increased the trade of parts and the supply of production equipment around the world. One third of all trade takes place among parent companies and their foreign affiliates. A part of this dynamism resides in the adoption of standards, a process which began in the late nineteenth century to promote mass production. It permitted the rapid development of many sectors of activity, including railways (gauge), electricity (wattage), the automobile (safety) and the telecommunication industry more recently (communication protocols and electronic data formats). In the realm of globalization of economic activities, the International Standards Organization developed the ISO norms that serve as comparison between various enterprises around the world. These norms are applicable to the manufacturing and services industries and are a necessary tool for growth.

There are also indications that the trends that have supported globalization may be **receding**. The growth of the service sector, particularly its share of the GDP, involves economic activities that are more difficult to trade. Due to rising standards of living, countries are consuming a growing share of their manufacturing output, although this is not taking place uniformly. As a result, the commercial geography is influenced by the market size, the consumption level of an economy (often measured in GDP per capita), but also by the growth potential of different regions of the world. National GDP figures, however, do not reveal regional distributions well, particularly the prominence of a few large metropolitan areas.

At the global level, the bulk of the consumption remains concentrated in a limited number of countries, with the G7 countries alone accounting for two-thirds of the global Gross Domestic Product. Economic growth taking place in East and Southeast Asia has been one of the most significant force-shaping changes in the contemporary commercial environment. The commodification of the economy has led to significant growth in retail and wholesale and the associated movements of freight. As wages increase across the world, wage differences and their derived comparatives are less significant, implying that cheap labor becomes less relevant for competitiveness. While technical advances have benefited transportation, they are also conferring a growing level of automation to production. This implies that locational decision for production will tend to be more market-servicing-based than factors of production based.

Transportation and competitiveness

It is commonly assumed that regions compete over factors such a resources, labor and governance to provide the most suitable economic advantages. Transportation is considered to be a key factor for competitiveness, since it provides **accessibility to markets**, **labor** and **resources**. However, the true extent of how transportation can help improve competitiveness is often **unclear**, since transportation is embedded in many economic and social processes. The liberalization of trade was accompanied by a growth of transportation activities, since transactions involve movements of freight, capital, people and information. Developments in the transport sector are matched by global and regional interdependence and competition. Transportation – like commodities, goods and services – is traded, sometimes openly and subject to full market forces, but more often subject to a form of public control (regulation) or ownership. The core component of a transport-related transaction involves its costs, which either have to be negotiated between the provider of the service and the user, or are subject to some arbitrary decree (price setting such as public transit).

Since transportation can be perceived as a service to people, freight or information, its **commercialization** (how it is brought to the market) is an important dimension of its dynamics (Figure 1.9). Transport service providers tend to be private entities, particularly in the global freight sector. Local passenger transportation providers (transit) tend to be publicly owned. While transport companies have no specific location, as modes are allocated to fulfill demand, transportation assets have a deep spatial and locational imprint. Improving transportation is thus assumed to improve the competitiveness of regions.

Figure 1.9 The commercialization of transportation

Commercialization involving the extension of the operational scale of transport systems ensures that it reaches its optimal market potential for the passenger and freight markets. Although an optimal market size can never be attained, due to regulations preventing monopolies and differences in consumer preferences (e.g. modal choice), the trend to ensure maximal market exposure is unmistakable. Within transport systems, four distinct cyclic phases of extension and functional integration can be identified:

- **Introduction**. Initially, a transport system is introduced to service a specific opportunity in an isolated context. The technology is often "proprietary" and incompatible with other transport systems. Since they are not interconnected, this does not represent much of an issue.
- **Expansion and interconnection**. As the marketability and the development potential of a transport system becomes apparent, a phase of expansion and interconnection occurs. The size of the market serviced by these transport systems consequently increases as they become adopted in new locations and as new providers are created to service those markets. At some point, independently developed transport systems connect. This connection, however, is often subject to a function of transshipment between two incompatible transport systems.
- **Standardization and integration**. This phase often involves the emergence of a fully developed transport system servicing vast national markets. The major challenge to be addressed involves a standardization of modes and processes, further expanding the commercial potential. Modal flows are moving more efficiently over the entire network and are able to move from one mode to the other through intermodal integration. A process of mergers and acquisitions of transport providers often accompanies this phase for the purpose of rationalization and market expansion.
- **Integrated demand**. The most advanced stage of extension of a distribution system involves a system fully able to answer mobility needs of passengers and freight under a variety of circumstances, either predicted or unpredicted demand. As this system tends to be global, it commonly operates close to market potential. In such a setting, a transport system expresses an integrated demand where transport supply is tuned with the demand in an interdependent system.

One important component of the competiveness of transportation concerns investments in infrastructure, modes and terminals, as well as their marketing and financing. Financial activities have seen a concentration among major global financial centers. Investments are performed either to expand the geographical extent and/or the capacity of a transport system or to maintain its operating conditions. The public and private sectors have contributed to the funding of transport investments depending on economic, social and strategic interests. For obvious reasons, the private sector seeks transport investments that promise economic returns while the public sector often invests for social and strategic reasons. In many cases private transport providers have difficulties acting independently in formulating and implementing their transport investments. Various levels of government are often lobbied by transport firms for financial and/or regulatory assistance in projects that are presented as being of public interest and benefit. The consolidation of regional markets and the resulting increase in transborder traffic has led transport firms to seek global alliances and greater market liberalization in the transport and communication sector as a means to attract investments and to improve their productivity.

Deregulation and divestiture policy have also substantially changed the competitive environment in the transport industry and has led governments to withdraw from the management, operations and ownership of national carriers, ports and airports. This has given rise to a major reorganization of the international and national transport sectors with the emergence of transnational transport corporations that are governing the global flow of air, maritime and land trade and the management of airports, ports and railyards.

Competitiveness is not always a rational endeavor and behavioral issues could have an impact on the choice of modes, routes and terminals. There are a number of reasons behind this. First, decision makers could have incomplete or even inaccurate information about routing options. The range of options is therefore bounded, resulting in options that are not optimal. Second, existing relations between actors in a transport chain are commonly associated with informal commitments that may not be optimal. Third, there is an inertia in commercial decisions where actors are opting for the status quo, since changing existing structures would require an effort.

Logistics and supply chains

The development of logistics and the setting of global supply chains are substantially impacting commercial geography. A global economy with an acute **division between production and consumption** underlines the relevance of logistics as a commercial and spatial strategy to improve efficiency and reduce costs. Freight has commonly been managed by private interests, particularly in the maritime shipping segment. Similarly, the logistics industry is also prone to private commercial interests that own modes, terminals, distribution facilities and provide management services. The ownership and operation of supply chains is intensive in transactions, flows and information exchange. Logistics is, after all, the spatial and temporal management of freight flows and with globalization these flows are extensive and complex. As a commercial activity logistics involves a whole range of tasks, from the labor intensive (loading, packaging, unloading) to information management intensive (order processing, booking, routing). Still, the context in which logistics services are offered and managed has changed.

Freight transport services are increasingly being **outsourced** as many companies realize that transportation and warehousing are not part of their core business. Many companies are reducing the number of transportation suppliers to reduce costs and improve services. The development of the logistics industry has enabled many transport companies to take control of larger segments of the supply chain. With an increasing level of functional integration, many intermediate steps in the transport chain have been removed. Mergers and acquisitions have permitted the emergence of large logistics operators that control many segments of the supply chain. They are often labeled as third party logistics providers since they almost exclusively take care in the management and operation of logistics on behalf of their customers. Technology has also played a particular role in this process, namely in terms of information technology (control of the process) and intermodal integration (control of the flows).

Freight distribution promotes regional competitiveness and their integration in global supply chains and thus change the commercial geography of a region. Logistical capabilities are often equated with competitiveness over segments of the supply chain, ranging from resource extraction, manufacturing and retailing. Both public and private interests are now considering various infrastructure and activities related to logistics and supply chain management as high-priority projects for national investment and economic development. This often takes the form of logistics zones linked to intermodal terminal facilities, such as ports, railyards and barge terminals. Logistics is also linked with changes brought by e-commerce. For instance, the growth of online purchases is linked with a decline of the retail commercial footprint, but with the increase of warehousing and distribution (Figure 1.10).

The provision of goods to final consumers takes two channels: **retail-based,** where consumers travel to stores to purchase goods; and **distribution-based,** where the goods are delivered to the consumers' residences from distribution centers. Both have a footprint in terms of the amount of allocated space, since stores and distribution centers occupy land, but not necessarily at the same locations. However, for the same volume, retail-based activities have a larger footprint since goods are stacked on shelves, trying to maximize consumer visibility and access. In a distribution center, the goods are efficiently stored to minimize the warehousing space as well as make storage and retrieval an efficient process. In a retail-based system, accessibility to the final consumer is the dominant locational factor, while in a distribution-based system it is accessibility to freight distribution capabilities. Thus, retail tends to occupy central locations, while distribution tends to occupy more peripheral locations.

Historically, retail-based commercial activities dominated, particularly in central areas. Their footprint was related to the population of their market areas and the level of development, particularly in terms of income. Distribution-based commercial activities usually took the form of mail-order catalogs, but remained a marginal and niche activity that complemented retail. Goods were usually shipped either from a retail store or from a distribution center supplying stores. Demographic and income growth in developed economies in the later part of the twentieth century resulted in a substantial increase in the retail footprint, particularly in suburbia, where new commercial facilities such as shopping malls and megastores were built. Such a commercial landscape prevailed until the early twenty-first century and was adopted in many societies experiencing economic development.

The diffusion of information technologies, particularly online shopping, is shifting part of the commercial activities towards a distribution-based structure – the emergence of an "e-commercial" system. As more consumers adopt online shopping for a share of

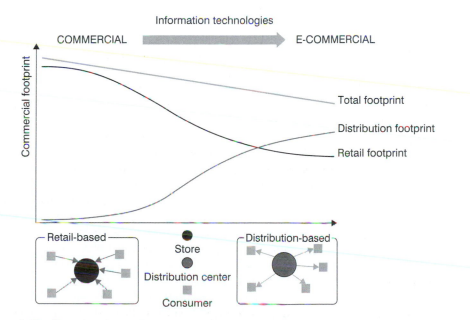

Figure 1.10 Footprint of retail-based and distribution-based commercial activities

their purchases, the outcome is a change in the nature of distribution and a decline in the total footprint of commercial activities in relation to the total sales volume. The transition is also dependent on the type of retail activity and consumer preferences. While the consumer electronics sector has a high potential to become substantially distribution-based, the grocery sector is less prone for such a transition, as consumers prefer to visually select their groceries. Under such circumstances, it can be expected to see a decline of the retail footprint in advanced economies as this footprint is partially replaced by a less intensive distribution footprint. At some point it could even be possible that distribution-based commercial activities become dominant and thus account for the largest share of the commercial footprint. Meanwhile a transition is still ongoing as online sales are taking a greater share of total retail sales.

An important geographical, commercial and logistical aspect of transportation is the issue of **empty movements**. Irrespective of the mode involved, the conveyance usually has to return to its location of origin. If part of the transport is done empty (without carrying goods or passengers), then the costs of these empty movements have to be assumed one way or the other, either directly by the carrier or indirectly by the customer. The main factors inducing empty movements are related to imbalanced flows (such as international trade), specialized transport equipment being able to carry only specific types of merchandises, short-range movements preventing a range of backhaul options and regulatory restrictions such as cabotage laws or the jurisdiction of operators.

Concept 4 – The geography of transportation networks

Authors: Dr Jean-Paul Rodrigue and Dr César Ducruet

Transport networks

Transportation systems are commonly represented using networks as an analogy for their structure and flows. Transport networks belong to the wider category of spatial networks because their design and evolution are physically constrained, as opposed to non-spatial networks such as social interactions, corporate organization and biological systems, which are usually constrained by other factors. The term **network** refers to the framework of routes within a system of locations, identified as nodes. A **route** is a single link between two nodes that are part of a larger network, which can refer to tangible routes such as roads and rails, or less tangible routes such as air and sea corridors.

The territorial structure of any region corresponds to a network of all its economic interactions. The implementation of networks, however, is rarely premeditated but the consequence of continuous improvements as opportunities arise, investments are made and conditions change. The setting of networks is the outcome of various strategies, such as providing access and mobility to a region, reinforcing a specific trade corridor or technological developments making a specific mode and its network more advantageous over others. A transport network denotes either a permanent track (e.g. roads, rail and canals) or a scheduled service (e.g. airline, public transit, train). It can be extended to cover various types of links between points along which movements can take place. The relevance of a network is related to its connectivity. Metcalfe's law states that the value of a network is proportional to the square of connected nodes.

In transport geography, it is common to identify several types of transport structures that are linked with transportation networks with key elements such as nodes, links, flows, hubs or corridors. Network structure ranges from centripetal to centrifugal in terms of the accessibility they provide to locations. A centripetal network favors a limited number of locations, while a centrifugal network tends not convey any specific locational advantages. The recent decades have seen the emergence of transport hubs, a strongly centripetal form, as a privileged network structure for many types of transport services, notably for air transportation. Although hub-and-spoke networks often result in improved network efficiency, they have drawbacks linked with their vulnerability to disruptions and delays at hubs, an outcome of the lack of direct connections. Evidence underlines that the emergence of hub-and-spoke networks is a transitional form of network development rationalizing limited volumes through a limited number of routes. When traffic becomes sufficient, direct point-to-point services tend to be established, as they better reflect the preference of users.

Hubs, as a network structure, allow a greater flexibility within the transport system, through a concentration of flows. For instance, on Figure 1.11, a point-to-point network involves 16 independent connections, each to be serviced by vehicles and infrastructures. By using a hub-and-spoke structure, only 8 connections are required. The main advantages of hubs are:

- Economies of scale on **connections** by offering a high frequency of services. For instance, instead of one service per day between any two pairs in a point-to-point network, four services per day could be possible.
- Economies of scale at the **hubs**, enabling the potential development of an efficient distribution system since the hubs handle larger quantities of traffic.
- Economies of scope in the use of **shared transshipment facilities**. This can take several dimensions, such as lower costs for the users as well as higher-quality infrastructures.

Many transportation services have adapted to include a hub-and-spoke structure. The most common examples involve air passenger and freight services that have developed global, national and regional hubs, like those used by parcel carriers such as UPS, FedEx and DHL. However, potential disadvantages may also occur, for example, additional transshipment as fewer point-to-point services are offered, which for some

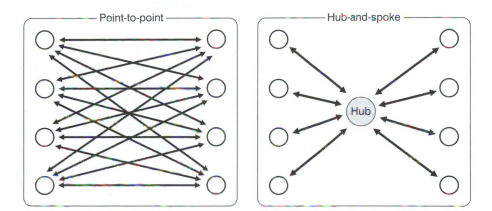

Figure 1.11 Point-to-point and hub-and-spoke networks

connections may involve delays and potential congestion as the hub becomes the major point of transshipment.

Transport networks are better understood by the usage level (e.g. number of passengers, tons, vehicles, capacity) than by their sole topology based on a binary state (i.e. presence or absence of links). Inequalities between locations can often be measured by the quantity of links between nodes and the related revenues generated by traffic flows. Many locations within a network have higher accessibility, which is often related to better opportunities. However, economic integration processes tend to change inequalities between regions, mainly through a reorientation of the structure and flows within transportation networks at the transnational level.

The efficiency of a network can be measured through **graph theory** and **network analysis**. These methods rest on the principle that the efficiency of a network depends partially on the layout of nodes and links. Obviously some network structures have a higher degree of accessibility than others, but careful consideration must be given to the basic relationship between the revenue and costs of specific transport networks. Rates thus tend to be influenced by the structure of transportation networks, since the hub-and-spoke structure, particularly, had a notable impact on transport costs, namely through economies of scale.

The topology and typology of networks

Transportation networks, like many networks, are generally embodied as a set of locations and a set of links representing connections between those locations. The arrangement and connectivity of a network is known as its topology. Each transport network has consequently a specific topology. The most fundamental elements of such a structure are the network geometry and the level of connectivity. Transport networks can be classified in specific categories depending on a set of topological attributes that describe them. It is thus possible to establish a basic typology of transport networks that relates to its geographical setting as well as its modal and structural characteristics.

There are many criteria that can be used to classify transportation networks (Figure 1.12). Its **level of abstraction** can be considered with tangible network representations closely matching the reality (such as a road map) while conversely an abstract network would only be a symbolization of the nodes and flows (such as the network of an airline). Since transportation networks have a geographical setting, they can be defined according to their **relative location** to main elements of a territory, such as a coastal network. Networks also have an **orientation** and an **extent** that approximates their geographical coverage or their market area. The **number of nodes and edges** is relevant to express the complexity and structure of transportation networks with a branch of mathematics, graph theory, developed to infer structural properties from these numbers.

Since networks are the support of movements, they can be considered from a **modal perspective**, their edges being an abstraction of routes (roads, rail links, maritime routes) and their nodes an abstraction of terminals (ports, airports, railyards). Specific modes can further be classified in terms **types of road** (highway, road, street, etc.) and **level of control** (speed limit, vehicle restrictions, etc.). Flows on a network have a **volume** and a **direction**, enabling links to be ranked by their importance and evaluate the general direction of flows (e.g. centripetal or centrifugal). Each segment and network has a **physical capacity** related to the volume it can support under normal conditions (traffic above capacity is labeled as congestion). The **load** (or volume to capacity) is the

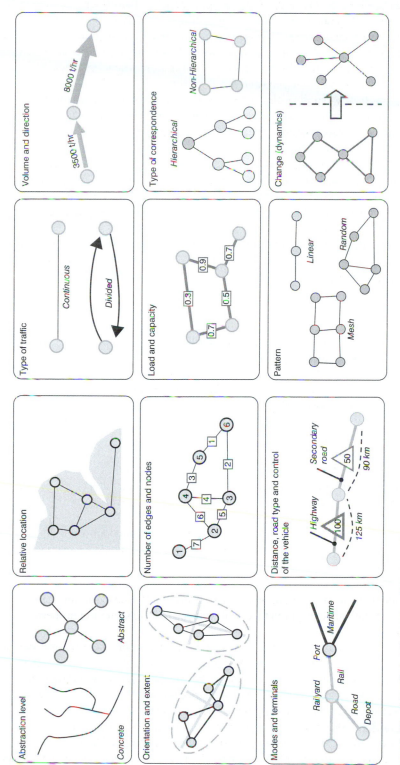

Figure 1.12 A typology of transportation networks

relation between the existing volume and the capacity. The closer a network is to its full load (a ratio of 1), the more congested it is. Since capacity is often a theoretical estimation, networks can operate above capacity. The **structure** of some networks imposes a hierarchy reflecting the importance of each of its nodes and a pattern reflecting their spatial arrangement. Finally, networks have a **dynamic** where both their nodes and links can change due to new circumstances.

The physical grounding of a network varies in relevance depending on the transport mode considered. Roads and railways are composed of track infrastructure, while maritime and air transports remain vaguely defined due to their higher spatial flexibility except for the terminals, whereas maritime networks remain more constrained than airline networks due to the necessity of bypassing coastline. River networks typically form basins and can be classified as trees or dendrograms. Therefore, there are three types of physical spaces on which transport networks are set and where each represents a specific mode of territorial occupation:

- **Clearly defined and delimited**. The space occupied by the transport network is strictly reserved for its exclusive usage and can be identified on a map. Ownership can also be clearly established. Major examples include road, canal and railway networks.
- **Vaguely defined and delimited**. The space of these networks may be shared with other modes and is not the object of any particular ownership, only of rights of way. Examples include air and maritime transportation networks.
- **Without definition**. The space has no tangible meaning, except for the distance it imposes, with nodes being the core structure. Little control and ownership are possible, but agreements must be reached for common usage. Examples are radio, television, WiFi and cellular networks, which rely on the use of specific frequencies granted by regulatory agencies.

Networks provide a level of transport service which is related to their costs. An optimal network would be a network servicing all possible locations but such a service would have high capital and operational costs. Transport infrastructures are established over discontinuous networks, since many were not built at the same time, by the same entity or with the same technology. Therefore, operational networks rarely service all parts of the territory directly. Some compromise must often be found among a set of alternatives considering a variety of route combinations and level of service. Networks are also labeled depending on their overall properties:

- **Regular network**. A network where all nodes have the same number of edges. In the same vein, a random network is a network that is formed by random processes. While regular networks tend to be linked with high levels of spatial organization (e.g. a city grid), random networks tend to be linked with opportunistic development opportunities such as accessing a resource.
- **Small-world network**. A network with dense connections among close neighbors and few but crucial connections among distant neighbors. Such networks are particularly vulnerable to catastrophic failures around large hubs.
- **Scale-free network**. A network having a strong hierarchical dimension, with few vertices having many connections and many vertices having few connections. Such networks evolve through the dynamic of preferential attachment by which new nodes

added to the network will primarily connect larger nodes instead of being connected randomly.

Investigating the interdependencies among different transport networks, notably when those are of different nature and structure, is challenging. Some crucial aspects and problems related with inter-network relations may be as follows:

- **Coevolution**. Different transport networks might follow similar or different paths based on spatial proximity and path-dependence of economic development, with a wider variety of networks at core regions than at remote regions.
- **Complementarity**. Some locations may be central in one network but peripheral in another, depending on their specialization and function and on the scale of analysis (terminal, city, region, country); the correlation between graphs can be measured based on the number of common nodes and links.
- **Interoperability and intermodal shifts**. Typically, cargo flows from a maritime network to a road network shift from a scale-free structure to a regular structure, thus following different topologies that are not easily combined; air and sea terminals remain few in the world due to the difficulty of combining and integrating technically air and sea networks physically at same locations.
- **Vulnerability**. How do changes in one network affect the other network, on a global level (entire network) or local level (single node or region)? This is particularly important for two networks sharing common nodes, such as global cities, logistics platforms and multilayered hubs. Such aspects are particularly relevant in the case of abrupt conjunctures (e.g. natural disasters, targeted attacks, labor disputes, security and geopolitical tensions), thus posing the problem of rerouting flows through alternative routes and locations.

Networks and space

Transportation networks underline the territorial organization of economic activities and the efforts incurred to overcome distance. These efforts can be measured in absolute (distance) or relative terms (time) and are proportional to the efficiency and the structure of the networks they represent. The relationships transportation networks establish with space are related to their **continuity**, their **topographic space** and the **spatial cohesion** they establish. The territory is a topological space having two or three dimensions depending on the transport mode considered (roads are roughly set over a two-dimensional space while air transport is set over a three-dimensional space). However, flows and infrastructures are linear, having one dimension since they conceptually link two points. The establishment of a network is thus a logical outcome for a one-dimensional feature to service a territory by forming a lattice of nodes and links. In order to have such a spatial continuity in a transport network, three conditions are necessary:

- **Ubiquity**. The possibility to reach any location from any other location on the network, thus providing a general access. Access can be a simple matter of vehicle ownership or bidding on the market to purchase a thoroughfare from one location to another. Some networks are **continuous**, implying that they can be accessed at any location they service. Roads are the most salient example of a continuous network. Other networks are **discrete**, implying that they can only be accessed at specific locations, commonly at a terminal. Rail, maritime and rail networks are considered discrete networks, since they can only be accessed through their terminals.

- **Fractionalization**. The possibility for a traveler or a unit of freight to be transported without depending on a group. It becomes a balance between the price advantages of economies of scale and the convenience of a dedicated service.
- **Instantaneity**. The possibility to undertake transportation at the desired or most convenient moment. There is a direct relationship between fractionalization and instantaneity, since the more fractionalized a transport system is, the more likely time convenience can be accommodated.

These three conditions are never perfectly met, as some transport modes fulfill them better than others. For instance, the automobile is the most flexible and ubiquitous mode for passenger transportation, but has important constraints such as low capacity and high levels of space and energy consumption. In comparison, public transit is more limited in the spatial coverage of its service, implies batch movements (bus loads, train loads, etc.) and follows specific schedules (limited instantaneity), but is more cost- and energy-efficient. Freight transportation also varies in its spatial continuity, ranging from massive loads of raw materials (oil and ores) that can be handled only in a limited number of ports, to highly flexible parcel movement. Containerization has been a remarkable attempt to address the issue of ubiquity (the system permits intermodal movements), fractionalization (each container is a load unit) and instantaneity (units can be loaded by trucks at any time of the day and containerships make frequent port calls).

An important cause of discontinuity is linked to the **spatial distribution of economic activities**, notably industrial and urban, which tend to agglomerate. Congestion may also alter those conditions. Road congestion in a metropolitan area may impair ubiquity, as some locations may be very difficult to reach since their accessibility is reduced. Fractionalization may also be reduced under such circumstances, as people would consider public transit and carpooling and would thus move as batches. Further, as commuters cope with increasing congestion, several trips may be delayed or cancelled altogether, reducing instantaneity.

Transportation networks have always been a **tool for spatial cohesion and occupation**. The Roman and Chinese empires relied on transportation networks to control their respective territories, mainly to collect taxes and move commodities and military forces. During the colonial era, maritime networks became a significant tool of trade, exploitation and political control, which was later on expanded by the development of modern transportation networks within colonies. In the nineteenth century, transportation networks also became a tool of nation building and political control. For instance, the extension of railways in the American hinterland had the purpose of organizing the territory, extending settlements and distributing resources to new markets. In the twentieth century, road and highways systems (such as the Interstate system in the United States and the *Autobahn* in Germany) were built to reinforce this purpose. In the later part of the twentieth century, air transportation networks played a significant role in weaving the global economy. For the early twenty-first century, telecommunication networks have become means of spatial cohesion and interactions abiding well to the requirements of global supply chains.

Network expansion

The co-evolution of roads, canals and ports during the Industrial Revolution in England reveals noticeable **interdependencies** among the different nodes and networks over time, based on spatial and functional proximity. Initial network developments are often done to support and complement an existing network, and then compete with the existing network by expanding geographically and topologically in ways unavailable to the prior network. As transport networks expand, existing transport infrastructures are being upgraded to cope with spatial changes. Airports and ports are being transformed, expanded or relocated. In the air transport sector, emphasis is being given to integrate airports within fully fledged **multimodal transport systems**, networking air with rail and road transport. In maritime transport, networks are also being modified with increasing attention paid to the expansion of the Panama and Suez canals, to the increasing traffic on inland waterways and to creating new inland passages between semi-enclosed or enclosed seas.

The growing competition between the sea and land corridors are not only reducing transport costs and encouraging international trade but prompting many governments to reassess their land-based connections and seek shorter transit routes. Existing land routes are also being extended. Passages through difficult terrain are being investigated with a view to create fully fledged land-based **continental connections**, notably through railways. These land network expansions are driven by economic globalization and interregional cooperation and eventually become multimodal transcontinental corridors for rail, road, pipelines and trunk telecommunications routes. But the impact of increasing world trade on land network expansion, notably over railways, is scale-specific. The expansion of railways has permitted inter- and intra-continental connections, namely landbridges (Figure 1.13).

Landbridges provide a level on continuity between maritime and long-distance inland transport networks. There are four main types of landbridges depending on the destination of the transoceanic cargo:

- **Landbridge**: Using a landmass as a link in a maritime transport chain involving a foreign origin and destination. This type of link is not highly used in the North American context as it is more convenient for Europe-bound cargo from Asia to use the maritime route instead or the emerging Eurasian landbridge for niche cargo.
- **Mini landbridge**: Using a landmass as a link in a transport chain involving a foreign origin and a destination at the end of the landmass.
- **Micro landbridge**: Using a landmass as a link in a transport chain involving a foreign origin and an inland destination. A common type of service for Asian cargo bound to an inland North American market.
- **Reverse landbridge**: Through a maritime detour reaching an inland destination by using the closest maritime facade instead of the landbridge. This type of landbridge has experienced remarkable growth with the usage of the Panama Canal to reach East Coast ports by an all-water route from Asia. The expansion of the Panama Canal is expected to increase the significance of this type of landbridge service.

In recent years, new rail routes in North America, Eurasia, Latin America and Africa have been developed or are being considered. There is scope for shippers to increase their trade through these new routes, particularly if rising insurance premiums, charter rates and shipping risks prompt them to opt for a land route instead of the sea route through the Suez or Panama canals. These developments linked to the integration of the regional economies to the world market are part of a rationalization and specialization process of rail traffic. But the success of these rail network expansions depends on the speed of movement and the unitization of general cargo by containerization. Railways servicing ports tend to consolidate container flows, which allows an increase in capacity

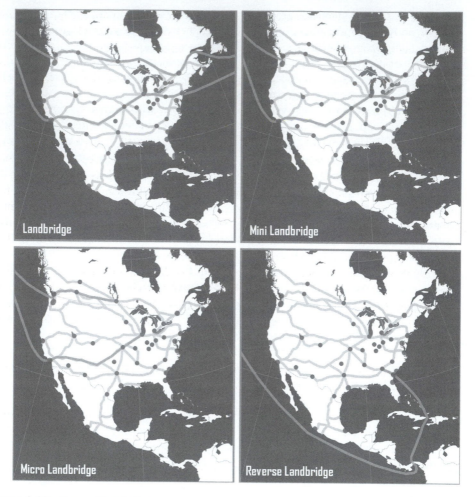

Figure 1.13 Types of landbridges

and the establishment of door-to-door services through a better distribution of goods among different transport modes.

New links are establishing and reshaping new trade flows, underpinning outward cargo movements and the distribution of goods. As some coastal gateways are emerging as critical logistics services centers that rationalize distribution systems to fit new trading patterns, the land network development and cross-border crossings throughout the world have far-reaching geopolitical implications.

CASE STUDY Strategic maritime passages

Authors: Dr Jean-Paul Rodrigue and Dr Theo Notteboom

Global maritime routes and chokepoints

Maritime transportation is the dominant purveyor of international freight distribution and evolves over a **global maritime space**. This space has its own constraints, such as the profile of continental masses and the detours and passages it creates. Maritime routes are spaces of a few kilometers wide, trying to avoid the discontinuities of land transport. They are a function of obligatory points of passage, which are almost all strategic places, physical constraints such coasts, winds, marine currents, depth, reefs, or ice and political boundaries where sovereignty may impede circulation. The majority of the maritime circulation takes place along coasts and three continents have limited fluvial trade (Africa; Australia; and Asia, except China).

International maritime routes are thus forced to pass through specific locations corresponding to passages, capes and straits (Figure 1.14). These routes are generally located between major markets such as Western Europe, North America and East Asia where an active system of commercial containerized trade is in place. The importance of these large manufacturing regions and their consumption markets are structuring the exchanges of semi-finished and finished goods. Also, major routes involve flows of raw materials, namely minerals, grains, food products and, most importantly, petroleum. The location of strategic oil and mineral resources shapes maritime routes for bulks, since they represent the most transported commodities. For instance, over 30 million barrels of oil per day are being shipped around the world.

Maritime routes draw arcs on the earth water surface as intercontinental maritime transportation tries to follow the great circle distance. Main shipping lanes are those supporting the most important commercial shipping flows servicing major markets. Secondary shipping lanes are mostly connectors between smaller markets. Figure 1.14 provides a simple taxonomy of the main strategic passages.

- **Primary passages**. The most important passages, since without them there would be limited cost-effective maritime shipping alternatives, which would seriously impair global trade.
- **Secondary passages**. Passages that have alternatives, but would still involve a notable detour.

The most important strategic maritime passages are known as chokepoints (or bottle-necks), due to:

- **Capacity constraints**. Chokepoints tend to be shallow and narrow, impairing navi-gation and imposing capacity limits on ships. For canals such as Panama and Suez, the capacity must effectively be managed with appointment and pricing systems.
- **Potential for disruptions or closure**. Disruption of trade flows through any of these export routes could have a significant impact on the world economy. Many choke-points are next to politically unstable countries, increasing the risk of compromising their access and use, such as with piracy. Closures are rare instances that have only taken place in situations of war as one proponent prevented another to access and use the chokepoint (e.g. Gibraltar and Suez during World War II). A closure of a mari-time chokepoint in the current global economy, even if temporary, would have important economic consequences with the disruption of trade flows and even the interruption of some supply chains (e.g. oil).

Changes in the technical and operational characteristics of transoceanic canals and passages can have substantial impacts on global trade patterns. The Panama Canal, the Suez Canal, the Strait of Malacca and the Strait of Hormuz account for the world's four most important strategic maritime passages in part because of the chokepoints they impose on global freight circulation and in part because of the economic activities and resources they grant more efficient access to. Their continuous availability for global maritime

Figure 1.14 Main maritime bottlenecks and shipping routes

circulation is challenging dominantly because the global trade system is highly reliant on their use. These potential risks and impacts are commonly used to justify military naval assets to protect sea lanes even if such benefits are difficult to demonstrate.

In addition to the transoceanic canals, "dry canals" have also been constructed or are under consideration. They are called dry canals because they replicate the role of regular canals, implying that they are relatively short overland corridors of rail, road and pipeline infrastructures connecting two ports where the cargo is transshipped. Several dry canals started as portage routes to be either discontinued as they lost their capability to compete, while others were complemented with a canal, such as for Panama. The main disadvantage of dry canals is the load break at both end, which adds costs and delays, as well as limited economies of scale on the overland route. Still, they represent routing options that can incite national imports and exports and the development of logistical activities. Such imprint on regional development is much less evident in canals, since they are simply points of passage.

The Suez Canal

The Suez Canal is an artificial waterway of about 190 km in length running across the Isthmus of Suez in northeastern Egypt, which connects the Mediterranean Sea with the Gulf of Suez, an arm of the Red Sea. The minimum width of the channel is 60 m and ships of a draft of 18 m (62 ft) can make the transit. The canal can accommodate ships as large as 220,000 deadweight tons fully loaded. The Suez Canal has no locks, because the Mediterranean Sea and the Gulf of Suez have roughly the same water level and it is thus the world's longest canal without locks. It acts as a shortcut for ships between both European and American ports and ports located in southern Asia, eastern Africa and Oceania. Because of obvious geographical considerations, the maritime route from Europe to the Indian and Pacific oceans must contour the Cape of Good Hope at the southernmost point of the African continent. There are a number of alternatives to the Suez Canal, but they involve either very long detours or have limited capacity.

The opening of the Suez Canal in 1869 brought forward a new era of European influence in Pacific Asia. The journey from Asia to Europe was considerably reduced by saving 6,500 km from the circum-African route. In 1874, Great Britain bought the shares of the Suez Canal Company and became its sole owner. According to the Convention of Constantinople signed in 1888, the canal was to be open to vessels of all nations in time of peace or in war. However, Great Britain claimed the need to control the area to maintain its maritime power and colonial interests (namely in South Asia). In 1936, it acquired the right to maintain defense forces along the Suez Canal, which turned out to be of strategic importance during World War II to uphold Asia–Europe supply routes for the Allies.

The second half of the twentieth century saw renewed geopolitical instability in the region, with the end of colonialism and the emergence of Middle Eastern nationalisms. In 1954, Egypt and Great Britain signed an agreement that superseded the 1936 treaty and provided for the gradual withdrawal of all British troops from the zone. All the British troops were gone by June 1956 as the canal was nationalized by Egypt. This triggered issues with Israel, as Israeli ships were not permitted to cross the canal. This threat was also extended to France and Britain, the former owners of the canal, because they refused to help finance the Aswan High Dam project, as initially promised. Israel, France and Britain thus invaded Egypt in 1956. Egypt responded by sinking ships in the canal, effectively closing it between 1956 and 1957. An agreement about the usage of the canal was then reached.

However, geopolitical problems persisted as tensions between Israel and neighboring Arab nations increased in the 1960s. The Six Day War between Israel and Egypt and the invasion of the Sinai Peninsula by Israel caused the closure of the Suez Canal between 1967 and 1975. The closure was so sudden and unexpected that several ships were caught stranded in the canal. The canal became the ceasefire line and saw again hostilities during the Yom Kippur War of 1973. The closure of the Suez Canal significantly destabilized international transportation and favored the development of ever larger tankers to use the long circum-Africa route. The canal was finally reopened in 1975 as Egypt agreed to let Israel use it. Significant improvements were made between 1976 and 1980, mainly the widening of the canal to accommodate very large crude carriers (VLCC) of about 200,000 tons supporting the oil trade between Europe and the Middle East. The current capacity of the canal, at 240,000 tons, means that ultra-large crude carriers (ULCC; tankers of more than 300,000 tons) cannot pass through the canal when fully loaded. A common practice is to unload a share of Mediterranean-bound ships and use the Sumed pipeline.

With additional deepening and widening projects, the depth of the canal reached 22.5 m in 2001 and 23.5 m in 2008. In 2014, a new expansion project that increased the capacity to about 100 transits per day took place. The "New Suez Canal" was inaugurated in August 2015 at a cost of over $8 billion. This expansion included a new 35 km section enabling the canal to transit ships in both directions at once. Prior to this expansion, convoys were organized since a section of the canal could only handle ships in one direction. All the existing sections of the canal will also be dredged to 24 m (78 ft). This expansion substantially improved the operational capabilities of the canal by reducing waiting and transit times in addition to improve capacity. The expanded Suez Canal has draft limitations similar to those of the Strait of Malacca.

The canal has the capacity to accommodate up to 25,000 ships per year (about 78 per day), but handled about 16,600 in 2013, on average 55 ships per day, which roughly account for 15 percent of the global maritime trade. Prior to its expansion in 2015 the canal could only handle unidirectional traffic, with crossings organized into convoys of about 10 to 15 ships. Three convoys per day, two southbound and one northbound, were organized. The transit time was about 17 hours. After the 2015 expansion, two simultaneous convoys per day were organized, since a longer section of the canal became bidirectional. Missing a convoy can incur supplementary delays to the point that, on occasion, maritime shipping companies (particularly for containers) would skip a port call to ensure that their ships arrive on time at the Suez Canal to be part of a daily convoy. A rail line also runs parallel to the canal.

The transit rates are established by the Suez Canal Authority (SCA). They are computed to keep the canal transit fees attractive to shippers. In fiscal year 2014, Egypt earned $5.3 billion in canal fees, making it the country's third largest revenue generator after tourism and remittances from expatriate workers. Container ships account for just under half of the canal's traffic and a slightly higher percentage of its net tonnage and revenues. The average canal transit fee per TEU (at 90 percent vessel utilization) amounts to $102 for a vessel of 1,000 TEU down to $56 for the largest container vessels. The Far East–Europe trade constitutes about 75 percent of the traffic handled by Suez. In recent years, services to the North American East Coast coming from Asia and transiting through the Suez Canal have increased to account for more than 15 percent of the traffic it handles. There are thus a number of alternatives to the Suez Canal (Figure 1.16).

Figure 1.15 Main routing alternatives between the Pacific and Atlantic

The Suez route is the main commercial artery between Asia and Europe and transits through locations such as the Strait of Malacca, Bab el-Mandab, the Suez Canal and the Strait of Gibraltar. It offers opportunities to pick up and drop cargo at major transshipment hubs such as Singapore, Colombo, Salalah, Suez, Gioa Tauro and Algeciras. These hubs act as collecting points for their respective regional cargoes as well as connectors to north/south routes. Because of the level of trade and the draft of the Suez Canal, maritime shipping companies have been able to allocate their largest ships along this route, with services including container ships with a capacity above 10,000 TEU. The Cape route is a shipping alternative involving a long detour through the southern tip of Africa, but represents an opportunity to handle African cargo as well as connect with routes bound to South America. Next to the Cape route, a number of other routing alternatives are being planned, or are in operation, to accommodate part of the trade volumes between Europe and Asia, but their market shares are expected to remain low compared to the Suez route, which offers substantial capacity, low costs and reliability.

- First there is the **Northern Sea Route**, a set of all-water shipping lanes between the Atlantic Ocean and the Pacific Ocean along the Russian coast of Siberia and the Far East. Future polar ice-cap reductions would open new possibilities for commercial shipping on this route. In cost terms the route today is still less favorable due to the need for ice-classed ships and ice-breaker assistance, non-regularity of the liner services, slower sailing speeds, navigation difficulties and Russian transit fees.
- Secondly, **North–South land corridors** could develop as landbridges from the Persian Gulf via Iran to Russia. However, geopolitical and infrastructure considerations forbid any serious consideration of this alternative in the medium term.
- Third, the **East–West rail corridors**, a set of railway lines connecting East Asia and the western part of Russia with the Eastern part of Russia, are becoming more commercially interesting. One of the main arteries is the Trans-Siberian Railway, which connects St Petersburg with the port of Vladivostok. Other primary rail connections are the Trans-Manchurian Railway, the Trans-Mongolian Railway and the Baikal Amur Mainline (BAM – opened in 1991). The "Trans-Siberian in Seven Days" program sets a target speed of 1,500 km a day, but is facing the problem of different rail gauges between the Chinese, Russian and Western European systems. Rail landbridges in principle offer lead time advantages to shippers, but capacities remain low compared to container liner services. They offer a niche potential for time-sensitive cargo.

The Panama Canal

The Panama Canal joins the Atlantic and Pacific oceans across the Isthmus of Panama, running from Cristobal on Limon Bay, an arm of the Caribbean Sea, to Balboa, on the Gulf of Panama. Its pre-expansion characteristics involve a length of 82 km, a depth of 12.5 m (39.5 ft), a width of 32 m (106 ft) and a length of 294 m (965 ft). Its construction ranks as one of the greatest engineering works of all time, as it prevents a long detour around South America, thus supporting the maritime flows of world trade (Figure 1.16). The Panama Canal is of strategic importance to the United States, as it serves to link the East and the West Coast more quickly, saving about 13,000 km (from 21,000 km to 8,000 km) for a maritime journey. It is composed of three main elements: the Gatun Locks (Atlantic Ocean access), the Gaillard Cut (continental divide) and the Miraflores/Pedro Miguel Locks (Pacific Ocean access).

Figure 1.16 Main routing alternatives between East Asia and Northern Europe

Source: Adapted from T. Notteboom and J.-P. Rodrigue (2011), "Emerging global networks in the container terminal operating industry," in T.Notteboom (ed.), *Current Issues in Shipping, Ports and Logistics*. Brussels: Academic & Scientific Publishers.

The Panama Canal is obviously the shortest operational route between the Atlantic and Pacific oceans. The maritime alternatives are the Magellan Route circumnavigating South America and the potential use of the Northwest Passage through the Arctic Ocean. The Magellan Route imposes a substantial detour, but offers the opportunity to pick up or drop off cargo along the way. The Northwest Passage is the shortest route between the North Pacific and the North Atlantic, but remains hazardous to navigation and does not offer any significant opportunity to pick up or drop off cargo. The landbridge alternatives are more numerous, with the North American landbridges composed of the Canadian, American and Mexican landbridges being operational realities. Still, their role is not necessarily to offer a substantial alternative to the Panama Canal, but options to shippers servicing North American supply chains. Other landbridges in Central or South America are simply projects of unknown market potential.

Since its completion in 1914, more than 1 million vessels transited the canal, carrying 11.17 billion tons of cargo (as of 2013). About 13,000 ships transit the canal every year,

Photo 1.1   Container ship and tanker ship entering the Miraflores locks

A containership and a tanker completes the transit through the Gaillard Cut, the part of the Panama Canal that slices through the Continental Divide. The ship mostly carries empty containers likely originating from the American East Coast and bound back to Asia. In the background is the Centennial Bridge, which opened in 2004 and which offers an additional crossing over the canal in addition to the Bridge of the Americas that was opened in 1962. Transits are usually organized in convoys using the dual locks in the same direction. For instance, crossings from the Atlantic to the Pacific usually cross the Gatun Locks in the morning, then wait on Lake Gatun until the ships cross to the Atlantic have transited through the Miraflores and Pedro Miguel locks. They will then cross these locks in the afternoon.

Source: Dr Jean-Paul Rodrigue, 2016.

with an average of 35 ships per day. However, the canal has the optimal capacity to handle 50 ships per day. Using the canal requires an average transit time of about 16.5 hours if the passage has been reserved in advance. With no reservations, the transit takes an average of 35 hours, due to the additional time spent waiting for a transit slot. Containers, grains and petroleum account for the dominant share of the cargo transited. The introduction of super-tankers at the beginning of the 1950s forced the reconsideration of its strategic importance as economies of scale in petroleum shipping are limited by the size of the canal. It is synonymous with a standard in maritime transport related to capacity, the **Panamax standard**, which equals to 65,000 deadweight tons, a draft of 12 m and a capacity of about 4,500 TEUs depending on the load configuration.

The canal handles about 5 percent of the global seaborne trade and about 12 percent of the American international seaborne trade. Under the control of the United States until 1979, its administration was entrusted to the State of Panama by the Panama Canal Treaty of 1977. In December 1999, the canal was reverted to Panama under the jurisdiction of the Panama Canal Authority. The authority generates revenue by collecting tolls on all ships crossing the canal and is responsible for the operation and maintenance of the facility. A loaded ship pays about $2.57 per net ton and the average toll is about $45,000. For container ships the toll (as of 2011) was $74 per TEU of capacity on laden containers and $65.60 per TEU of capacity on ships with empty containers. In 2008, $1.32 billion in tolls were collected, of which 54 percent was generated by container shipping.

In 1999, the Hong Kong terminal operator, Hutchison Port Holdings (HPH), got a 25-year concession for the operation of port terminals on both the Atlantic (Port of Cristobal) and Pacific (Port of Balboa) sides of the canal. This raised concerns within the American government, as it was perceived that the control of the canal was falling into foreign interests shortly after it was handed back to Panama. The rail line between the Atlantic and Pacific sides was reopened in 2002 to handle the growing containerized traffic. The Panama Canal Railway Company offers an alternative to the size limitations of the canal and supports transshipment activities between the Atlantic and the Pacific sides through double-stack services. The same rationale applies to oil circulation with the trans-Panama pipeline which resumed its operations in 2003, but the additional capacity this pipeline conveys is only about 1 Mb/d.

In spite of being a century old, the Panama Canal remains a critical bottleneck in global trade. The continuous growth of global trade since the 1990s has placed additional pressures on the Panama Canal to handle a growing number of ships in a timely and predictable manner. This raised concerns that the existing canal would reach capacity by the second decade of the twenty-first century. Because of these capacity limits, many shipping companies have changed the configuration of their routes. This became increasingly apparent as a growing share of the global containership fleet reached a size beyond the capacity of the Panama Canal, which came to be known as "post-Panamax" containerships. Through economies of scale, they offer significant operational cost advantages that cannot be exploited by the existing canal. The increasing usage of those ships along the Pacific Asia/Suez Canal/Mediterranean routes as well as the development of the North American rail landbridge have created a substantial competition to the canal as an intermediate location in global maritime shipping. There are thus a range of alternatives to the Panama Canal trade routes, with the North American landbridges being the most salient. Yet, concerns about the reliability of the landbridge connection incited the setting of "all-water routes" linking directly Pacific Asia and the American East Coast, particularly in light of the booming China–United States trade relation.

A decision to expand the Panama Canal was reached in 2006 by the Panamanian government. The expansion was a $5.25 billion project that involved building a new set of locks on both the Atlantic and Pacific sides of the canal to support a depth of 60 ft, a width of 190 ft and a length of 1,400 ft, which can accommodate ships up to 12,500 TEU depending on their load configuration. The dredging of access channels as well as the widening of several sections of the existing canal was required. This allows Aframax and Suezmax vessels to pass through the canal, thus permitting new opportunities for container shipping services such as the re-emergence of round-the-world services. Essentially, a new containership class will be created to add to the existing Panamax ship class. It will be dubbed New-Panamax (or Neo Panamax; NPX).

The new locks complement the existing lock systems, creating a two-tier service – one for the very large ships and the other for the Panamax, or smaller, ships. The outcome allows about 12 ships per day in the new lock system to be added to the existing capacity of about 45 ships per day in the existing locks. The additional capacity is, however, constrained by the fact that the new locks are unidirectional compared with the existing double locks. The new infrastructures became online in July 2016, after some delays (initially, the expansion was expected to be completed for 2014). However, this expansion is taking place in an environment of notable commercial changes such as a revision of sourcing strategies and the possibility of building a competing canal in Nicaragua. Further, the latest generation of containerships (such as the Triple E class) has reached sizes that are beyond the expanded locks. Within the foreseeable future the expanded Panama Canal will still be able to handle 95 percent of the global containership capacity. As a global intermediary location, Panama is shifting from being a point of transit towards being a logistics cluster and a trade platform for the Americas.

The Strait of Malacca

The Strait of Malacca is one of the most important strategic passages in the world because it supports the bulk of the maritime trade between Europe and Pacific Asia, which accounts for 50,000 ships per year. About 30 percent of the world's trade and 80 percent of Japan's, South Korea's and Taiwan's imports of petroleum transits through the strait, which involved approximately 15.2 Mb/d in 2013. It is the main passage between the Pacific and the Indian oceans, with the Strait of Sunda (Indonesia) being the closest alternative (Figure 1.17). It measures about 800 km in length, has a width between 50 km and 320 km (2.5 km at its narrowest point) and a minimal channel depth of 23 me (about 70 ft). It represents the longest strait in the world used for international navigation and can be transited in about 20 hours.

Traditionally, the Strait was an important passage point between the Chinese and the Indian worlds and was controlled at different points in time by Javanese and Malaysian kingdoms. From the fourteenth century, the region came under the control of Arab merchants who established several fortified trading towns, Malacca being the most important commercial center in Southeast Asia. Again, the control of the trade route shifted as the era of European expansion began in the sixteenth century. In 1511, Malacca fell to the Portuguese and this event marked the beginning of European control over the Strait. In 1867, England took control of the passage with Singapore as a main harbor and other important centers such as Malacca and Penang, forming the Strait Settlements. This control lasted until World War II and the independence of Malaysia in 1957. As the Pacific trade increased considerably after World War II, so did the importance of the passage. Singapore, located at the southern end of the Strait of Malacca is one of the most important ports in the world and a major oil refining center.

One of the main problems about the Strait of Malacca is that at some points it requires dredging, since it is barely deep enough to accommodate ships of about 300,000 deadweight tons. The Strait being between Malaysia, Indonesia and Singapore, an agreement is difficult to reach about how the dredging costs should be shared and how fees for its usage should be levied. Political stability and piracy are also major issues for the safety of maritime circulation, especially on the Indonesian side with the province of Aceh in a state a civil unrest.

The Strait of Malacca ends up in the South China Sea, another extremely important shipping lane and a region subject to contention since oil and natural gas resources are present. The Spartly and Paracel groups of islands are claimed in whole or in part by China, Vietnam, Malaysia, Indonesia, Brunei and the Philippines. The region has proven oil reserves estimated at about 7.0 Bb, with oil production accounting for 2.5 Mb/d.

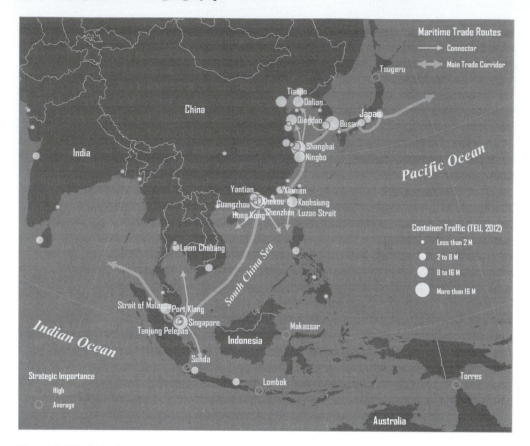

Figure 1.17   Shipping lanes and strategic passages in Pacific Asia

With the substantial economic growth taking place in the region, large flows of oil, liquefied natural gas and other raw materials (iron ore, coal) are transiting towards East Asia. About 25 percent of the global shipping fleet transits through the region each year, underlining the importance of the South China Sea as an extension of the Malacca chokepoint. Still, the potential for disruptions of trade routes in the South China Sea must take account of the high level of reliance China has on such routes and thus has limited interest in seeing them compromised.

Using the Kra Isthmus in Thailand as a shortcut between the Gulf of Thailand (Pacific Ocean) and the Andaman Sea (Indian Ocean) was considered as early as the seventeenth century. The Kra Canal project aims at building a 102-km-long canal along the narrowest segment of the Kra Isthmus. By avoiding a detour through the Strait of Malacca, the potential canal could reduce shipping distance by 1,200 km, which corresponds to about five shipping days (such figures do not take account of canal transit times). Although the project represents a shortcut, this benefit is rather marginal, particularly for long-distance shipping routes, and due to the importance of Singapore and Tanjung Pelepas as major transshipment hubs linking Asia/Oceania/Europe trade routes. The canal would mainly benefit Thailand, Burma, Cambodia and Vietnam, as they would see more significant shipping time and cost reductions for their maritime trade. China is pursuing this project for both commercial and strategic reasons, since it will give it an additional option to the usage of the Strait of Malacca.

The Strait of Hormuz

The Strait of Hormuz forms a strategic link between the oil fields of the Persian Gulf, which is a maritime dead end, the Gulf of Oman and the Indian Ocean. It has a width between 48 km and 80 km, but navigation is limited to two 3-km-wide channels, each exclusively used for inbound or outbound traffic. Circulation in and out of the Persian Gulf is thus highly constrained, namely because the sizable amount of tanker and containership traffic makes navigation difficult along the narrow channels. In addition, islands that ensure the control of the strait are contested by Iran and the United Arab Emirates.

The security of the strait has been often compromised and its commercial usage has been the object of contentions. Between 1984 and 1987 a "Tanker War" took place between Iran and Iraq (Iran–Iraq War of 1980–88), where each belligerent began firing on tankers, even neutrals, bound for their respective ports. Shipping in the Persian Gulf dropped by 25 percent, forcing the intervention of the United States to secure the oil shipping lanes. About 88 percent of all the petroleum exported from the Persian Gulf transits through the Strait of Hormuz, bound to Asia, Western Europe and the United States. Its importance for global oil circulation cannot be overstated. For instance, 75 percent of all Japanese oil imports transit through the strait. There are thus very few alternative outlets to oil exports if the traffic of about 14 million barrels per day going through Hormuz were compromised. In addition to geopolitics, the geography of the Middle East creates challenges for petroleum distribution. The first is the concentration of reserves around the Persian Gulf (Saudi Arabia, Kuwait, Iraq, Iran and United Arab Emirates), leaving the Strait of Hormuz as one of the only viable outlets to export oil using large oil tankers. The second is the constrained access to the main European markets through the Suez Canal, whereby a fully laden VLCC cannot transit through the canal and must round Africa.

While the Persian Gulf has conventionally been centered on the production and distribution of oil, the growth of container shipping has also expanded its commercial importance. For instance, Dubai ranked in 2014 as the world's ninth largest container port, with a traffic of 15.2 million TEU and can only be accessed through the Strait of Hormuz. It has become a major transshipment hub linking major Asian, Middle Eastern and East African trade routes. Consequently, compromising circulation through the Strait of Hormuz would impair global oil trade as well as commercial trade along Europe/Asia routes.

Bibliography

Banister, D. (2002) *Transport Planning*, 2nd ed. London: Spon Press.

Black, W. (2003) *Transportation: A Geographical Analysis*. New York: Guilford.

Goetz, A.R., T.M. Vowles and S. Tierney (2009) "Bridging the qualitative-quantitative divide in transport geography." *Professional Geographer*, 61(3): 323–335.

Harrington, R. (1999) "Transport: then, now, and tomorrow", *Royal Society of Arts Journal*, vol. 146(5488).

Hoover, E.M. (1948) *The Location of Economic Activity*. New York: McGraw-Hill.

Hoyle, B. and R. Knowles (eds) (1998), *Modern Transport Geography*, 2nd edition. London: Wiley.

Hugill, P.J. (1995) *World Trade since 1431*. Baltimore: Johns Hopkins University Press.

Keeling, D.J. (2007) "Transportation geography: new directions on well-worn trails." *Progress in Human Geography*, 31(2), 217–225.

Keeling, D.J. (2008) "Transportation geography – new regional mobilities." *Progress in Human Geography*, 32(2): 275–283.

Knowles, R.D. (2006) "Transport shaping space: the differential collapse of time/space." *Journal of Transport Geography*, 14(6): 407–425.

Knowles, R., J. Shaw and I. Docherty (eds) (2008) *Transport Geographies: Mobilities, Flows and Spaces*. Malden, MA: Blackwell.

Leinbach, T. (1976) "Networks and flows." *Progress in Human Geography*, 8: 179–207.

Newman, M. (2010) *Networks: An Introduction*. Oxford: Oxford University Press.

Rimmer, P. (1985) "Transport geography" *Progress in Human Geography*, 10: 271–277.

Rodrigue, J.-P., T. Notteboom and J. Shaw (eds) (2013) *The Sage Handbook of Transport Studies*. London: Sage.

Taaffe, E.J., H.L. Gauthier and M.E. O'Kelly (1996) *Geography of Transportation*, 2nd edition. Upper Saddle River, NJ: Prentice Hall.

Tolley, R. and B. Turton (1995) *Transport Systems, Policy and Planning: A Geographical Approach*. Burnt Mill, Harlow: Longman.

Urry, J. (2007) *Mobilities*. Cambridge: Polity Press.

US DOT – MARAD (2013) *Panama Canal Expansion Study, Phase I Report: Developments in Trade and National and Global Economies*, November. US Department of Transportation, Maritime Adminisiration.

2 Transportation and the spatial structure

Transportation has a strong influence on the spatial structure at the local, regional and global levels. An historical perspective on the evolution of transport systems underlines the impacts of technological innovations and how improvements in transportation were interdependent with economic, social and spatial changes. The current transport systems are thus the outcome of a long evolution marked by periods of rapid changes where new transport technologies were adopted. Following the Industrial Revolution in the nineteenth century, transportation systems were mechanized with the development of steam engine technology, which permitted the setting of networks servicing regions. This process was further expanded in the twentieth century with the setting of global air transport, container shipping and telecommunication networks. The impacts of transport on the spatial structure became multiscalar. Transportation systems are composed of a complex set of relationships between the demand, the locations they service and the networks that support movements. Such conditions are closely related to the development of transportation networks, both in capacity and in spatial extent. Future transportation systems will likely be shaped by the same forces as in the past but it remains to be seen which technologies will prevail and what will be their impacts on the structure.

Concept 1 – Historical geography of transportation: the emergence of mechanized systems

Transportation in the pre-industrial era (pre-1800s)

Transportation is closely linked with the process of globalization. Efficiently distributing freight and moving people has always been an important factor for maintaining the cohesion of economic systems from empires to modern nation states and economic blocs. With technological and economic developments, the means to achieve such a goal have evolved considerably with a series of historical revolutions and evolutions. It became possible to move people and cargoes faster, in greater volumes, over longer distances and more conveniently. This process is very complex and is related to the spatial evolution of economic systems and associated technical developments. It is possible to summarize this evolution, from the pre-industrial era to transportation in the early twenty-first century, in four major stages, each linked with specific technological innovations in the transport sector: the pre-industrial era, the Industrial Revolution, Fordism and post-Fordism (globalization).

Before the major technical transformations brought forward by the Industrial Revolution at the end of the eighteenth century, no forms of motorized transportation existed. Transport technology was mainly limited to harnessing animal labor for land transport and wind for maritime transport. The transported quantities were very limited and so was the speed at which people and freight were moving. The average overland speed by horse, which was domesticated around 2000 BCE, was around 8 km per hour and maritime speeds were barely above these figures. Also, a horse can only carry a load of about 125 kg while a camel can carry about 200 kg. Waterways were the most efficient transport systems available and cities next to rivers were able to trade over longer distances and maintain political, economic and cultural cohesion over a larger territory. It is not surprising to find that the first civilizations emerged along river systems for agricultural, but also for trading, purposes (Tigris-Euphrates, Nile, Indus, Ganges, Huang He). International trade did exist, but traded commodities were high-value (luxury) goods such as spices, silk, wine and perfume, notably along the **Silk Road** (Figure 2.1). Around the Mediterranean, the amphora permitted a form of intermodalism as an effective standard transport product of olive oil, grain or wine.

The Silk Road was the most enduring trade route in human history, being used for about 1,500 years. Its name is taken from the prized Chinese textile that flowed from Asia to the Middle East and Europe, although many other commodities were traded along the route. The Silk Road consisted of a succession of trails followed by caravans through Central Asia, about 6,400 km in length. Travel was favored by the presence of steppes, although several arid zones had to be bypassed such as the Gobi and Takla Makan deserts. Economies of scale, harsh conditions and security considerations required the organization of trade into caravans slowly trekking from one stage (town and/or oasis) to the other.

Although it is suspected that significant trade occurred for about 1,000 years beforehand, the Silk Road opened around 139 BCE once China was unified under the Han dynasty. It started at Changan (Xian) and ended at Antioch or Constantinople (Istanbul), passing by commercial cities such as Samarkand and Kashgar. It was very rare that

Figure 2.1 The Silk Road and Arab Sea routes (eighth to fourteenth centuries)

caravans traveled for the whole distance, since the trade system functioned as a cha.
Merchants with their caravans were shipping goods back and forth from one trade center
to the other. Major commodities traded included silk (of course), gold, jade, tea and
spices. Since the transport capacity was limited, over long distance and often unsafe,
luxury goods were the only commodities that could be traded. The Silk Road also served
as a vector for the diffusion of ideas and religions (initially Buddhism and then Islam),
enabling civilizations from Europe, the Middle East and Asia to interact.

The initial use of the sea route linking the Mediterranean basin and India took place
during the Roman Era. Between the first and sixth centuries, ships were sailing between
the Red Sea and India, aided by summer monsoon winds. Goods were transshipped
at the town of Berenike along the Red Sea and moved by camels inland to the Nile. From
that point, river boats moved the goods to Alexandria, from which trade could be undertaken with the Roman Empire. From the ninth century, maritime routes controlled
by the Arab traders emerged and gradually undermined the importance of the Silk
Road. Since ships were much less constraining than caravans in terms of capacity, larger
quantities of goods could be traded. The main maritime route started at Canton
(Guangzhou), passed through Southeast Asia, the Indian Ocean, the Red Sea and then
reached Alexandria. A significant feeder went to the Spice Islands (Moluccas) in today's
Indonesia. The diffusion of Islam was also favored through trade, as many rules of
ethics and commerce are embedded in the religion.

The Silk Road reached its peak during the Mongolian Empire (thirteenth century),
when China and Central Asia were controlled by Mongol Khans, who were strong
proponents of trade even if they were ruthless conquerors. At the same time relationships between Europe and China were renewed, notably after the voyages of Marco Polo
(1271–92). During the Middle Ages, the Venetians and Genoese controlled the bulk of
the Mediterranean trade which connected to the major trading centers of Constantinople,
Antioch and Alexandria. As European powers developed their maritime technologies
from the fifteenth century, they successfully overthrew the Arab control of this lucrative
trade route to replace it by their own. Ships being able to transport commodities faster
and cheaper marked the downfall of the Silk Road by the sixteenth century.

Because the efficiency of the land transport system of this era was poor, the
overwhelming majority of trade was **local in scope**. Economies based on autonomy
and basic subsistence could not generate much trade. Cities were located to take
advantage of the defensible or commercial advantage of a location. From the perspective
of regional economic organization, the provision of cities in perishable agricultural
commodities was limited to a radius of about 50 km, at most. The size of cities also
remained unchanged in time. Since people can walk about 5 km per hour and that they
are not willing to spend more than one hour per day walking, the daily space of interaction would be constrained by a 2.5 km radius, or about 20 sq km. Thus, most rural areas
centered around a village and cities rarely exceeded a 5 km diameter. The largest cities
prior to the Industrial Revolution, such as Rome, Beijing, Constantinople or Venice,
never surpassed an area of 20 sq km. Large cities above 100,000 were very rare and
those who exceed such a population did so because they were at the nexus of maritime
and land trade networks.

Prior to the Industrial Revolution, it was difficult to speak of an urban system, but
rather of a set of relatively self-sufficient economic systems with very limited trade. The
preponderance of city-states during this period can a priori be explained by transportation, in particular the difficulties of shipping goods (therefore to trade) from one place
to another. Among the most notable exceptions to this were the Roman and Chinese

empires, which committed extraordinary efforts at building transportation networks and consequently maintained control over an extensive territory for a long time period.

The transport system of the Roman Empire was a reflection of the geographical characteristics and constraints of the Mediterranean basin. The Mediterranean provided a central role to support trade between a network of coastal cities, the most important of the Empire (Rome, Constantinople, Alexandria, Carthage, etc.). These cities were serviced by a road network permitting trade within their respective hinterlands. Little fluvial transportation took place, since the major pan-European rivers, the Rhine and the Danube, were military frontiers, not the core of the Empire. The road served numerous functions, such as military movements, political control, cultural and economic (trade). To improve the traveling speed posthouses with fresh horses were laid every 15 km along the route and lodgings for travelers could be found about every 40 km. This 40 km corresponded to the average distance a traveler could cross each day. Courier services could travel twice that daily distance.

The Appian Way (Via Appia), about 560 km in length, was one of the first Roman roads (Viae) to be constructed (around 312 BCE) under the initiative of emperor Appius Claudius Caecus. It linked Rome to Brundisium (Brindisi). As the empire grew, this system was expanded to cover 80,000 km of first-class roads at the height of the Roman Empire (around AD 200). Most of the roads were constructed by soldiers, prisoners of war and slaves. The minimum requirement of a first-class road was a width of 5 m and a drained stone surface. The Romans also built the world's first dual carriageway, Via Portuensis, between Rome and its port Ostia at the mouth of the Tiber. The Roman road network covered most of the conquered provinces, with Rome as the focal point (thus the saying "All roads lead to Rome"). At the center of Rome was located the milliareum aureum (the golden milestone), from which the Roman roads radiated.

Figure 2.2 Roman Empire, c. AD 125

Maintenance was the responsibility of the inhabitants of the district through which the road passed by, but access was public. Waystations where travelers could rest and eat dotted the network. The system collapsed during the Middle Ages because of the lack of maintenance and plundering for construction material, but still, the remains of the Roman network provided transportation in Europe for a thousand years. Only small segments of this system are left today.

The economic importance and the geopolitics of transportation were recognized very early, notably for maritime transportation since before the Industrial Revolution, it was the most convenient way to move freight and passengers around. Great commercial empires were established with maritime transportation. However, long-distance maritime trade involved risk, which favored the setting of a financing and insurance industry. In Ancient Greece, merchants financed their commercial ventures through high-interest loans that acted at the same time as insurance since the loan would not be repaid if the ship sank. This model, known as "bottomry," was then copied by the Romans. It takes its origins in the Babylonian Code of Hammurabi around 1700 BCE stating repayment of a loan in case of a successful voyage. These early forms of financing and insurance permitted commercial activities that would not have taken place to the same extent otherwise.

By Medieval times, an extensive maritime trade network, the highways of the time, centered along the navigable rivers, canals and coastal waters of Europe (and also China) was established. Shipping was extensive and sophisticated using the English Channel, the North Sea, the Baltic and the Mediterranean, where the most important cities were coastal or inland ports (London, Norwich, Königsberg, Hamburg, Bruges, Bordeaux, Lyon, Lisbon, Barcelona and Venice). Trade of bulk goods, such as grain, salt, wine, wool, timber and stone, was taking place. By the fourteenth century galleys were finally replaced by full-fledged sailships (the caravel and then the galleon) that were faster and required smaller crews. 1431 marked the beginning of the European expansion with the discovery by the Portuguese of the North Atlantic circular wind pattern, better known as the trade winds. A similar pattern was also found on the Indian and Pacific oceans with the monsoon winds.

The fall of Constantinople, the capital of the Byzantium Empire (Eastern Roman Empire), to the Turks in 1453 disrupted the traditional land trade route from Europe to Asia. Europe was forced to find alternative maritime routes. One alternative, followed by Columbus in 1492, was to sail to the west, and the other alternative, followed by Vasco de Gama in 1497, was to sail to the east. Columbus stumbled upon the American continent, while Gama found a maritime route to India using the Cape of Good Hope. These events were quickly followed by a wave of European exploration and colonization, initially by Spain and Portugal, the early maritime powers, then by Britain, France and the Netherlands. The traditional trade route to Asia no longer involved Italy (Venice) and Arabia, but involved direct maritime connections from ports such as Lisbon and Amsterdam. European powers were able to master the seas with larger, better-armed and more efficient sailing ships and thus were able to control international trade and colonization. Private charter companies, such as the Dutch East India Company, were agents initially used to establish maritime trading networks that spanned the world. By the early eighteenth century, most of the world's territories were controlled by Europe, providing wealth and markets to their thriving metropolises through a system of colonial trade.

Figure 2.3 plots the density of a large sample of ship logs, which is indicative of the global trade network structure of the eighteenth century. Due to differences in the number of log entries geocoded, such as only 7,698 entries for French flagged ships as opposed to 83,036 entries for UK flagged ships, there are density variations that are

Figure 2.3 Density of ship log entries, 1750–1810

Source: Ship log data from CLIWOC Project. Data geocoded by David Hopp.

not necessarily reflective of the size of nationally flagged fleets and their level of commercial activity. Limited shipping is observed over the Pacific Ocean, mostly due to the yet limited scale of European involvement in this part of the world at that time. The second half of the nineteenth century will see an intensification of maritime trade to and across the Pacific, with the First Opium War of 1838–42 being the turning point. Prior to that, the China trade was mostly serviced by Portuguese flagged ships, which are not covered by the sample. The following observations can be made regarding the respective trade patterns of national flagged ships for the 1750 to 1810 period:

- **Spain**. The Spanish trade was mainly focused on their American colonies, particularly Mexico (which was linked to the transpacific trade through an overland route), Cuba and Hispaniola. The transatlantic triangular trade system follows the pattern of wind and sea currents that benefit the southern part of the North Atlantic for westbound travel and the northern part of the North Atlantic for eastbound travel. The second main component of the Spanish maritime trade network concerns the Argentinian trade. Less visible are the connections to Chile and Peru through the Strait of Magellan.
- **Netherlands**. The Dutch maritime trade network is mostly associated with the activities of the Dutch East India Company (VOC) with a long-distance network heading towards VOC's main trade ports of Batavia (Indonesia) and Galle (Sri Lanka) and using Cape Town as an intermediary staging point (a Dutch colony between 1652 and 1806). Dutch interests were also involved in the triangular transatlantic trade with their colonies of the Caribbean and Guyana (Dutch colony between 1616 and 1814).
- **United Kingdom**. Its trade network is the most extensive, as it reflects the emergence of the UK during that period as the world's dominant maritime power with

colonial interests in the Americas and South Asia. The Arctic trade segment is mainly related to the activities of the Hudson Bay Company established in 1670 for the fur trade around Rupert's Land.

- **France**. The trade network depicted by French flagged ships is the simplest and limited to the triangular trade structure between France, its Caribbean colonies (Haiti, Guadeloupe and Martinique) and New France (St Pierre and Miquelon after 1763).

Prior to the Industrial Revolution, the quantity of freight transported between nations was negligible by contemporary standards. For instance, during the Middle Ages, the totality of French imports via the Saint-Gothard Passage (between Italy and Switzerland) would not fill a freight train. The amount of freight transported by the Venetian fleet, which dominated Mediterranean trade for centuries, would not fill a modern container ship. The volume, but not the speed, of trade improved under mercantilism (fifteenth to eighteenth century), notably for maritime transportation. In spite of all, distribution capacities were very limited and speeds slow. For example, a stagecoach going through the English countryside in the sixteenth century had an average speed of 2 miles (1.3 km) per hour; moving one ton of cargo 30 miles (50 km) inland in the United States by the late eighteenth century was as costly as moving it across the Atlantic. The inland transportation system was thus very limited, both for passengers and freight. By the late eighteenth century, canal systems started to emerge in Europe, initially in the Netherlands and England. They permitted the beginning of large movements of bulk freight inland and expanded regional trade. Maritime and fluvial transportation were consequently the dominant modes of the pre-industrial era.

The Industrial Revolution and transportation (1800–70)

From the 1750s, a series of changes took place in Europe that would transform the global economic, political, social and technological landscape. This came to be known as the **Industrial Revolution**. The factors that have led to the remarkable changes brought by the Industrial Revolution are subject to debate in terms of their role and importance in the emergence of capitalism. Four of them appear to be prevalent and interdependent:

- **The scientific method**. Mostly the outcome of changes that took place in the seventeenth century, often dubbed the "Age of Reason," it triggered a rational approach to the laws of nature and formalized technical professions (physics, chemistry, engineering, etc.). This in turn fostered innovation and the application of these innovations.
- **Property rights**. The strengthening of democratic institutions leaning on the rule of law that guarantees and protects private ownership. Property owners had a greater representation in elected legislatures and capital accumulation could expand.
- **Capital markets**. Institutions such as banks able to gather capital pools and invest them in economic ventures. The process of capital accumulation and allocation became increasingly rational and institutionalized.
- **Communications and transport infrastructure**. The setting and development of mechanized transport systems supporting the distribution of resources and the setting of comparative advantages. Markets could interact more effectively.

At the scale of the world's economic history, the Industrial Revolution radically changed the foundations of economic systems and set in motion the emergence of the global economy. Most of the technical innovations that modified the way to produce and to transport took place in a short period, mainly between 1760 and 1800. It was during the Industrial Revolution that massive modifications of transport systems occurred in two major phases, the first centered along the development of **canal systems** and the second centered along **railways**. This period marked the development of the steam engine, an external combustion engine that converted thermal energy into mechanical energy, providing an important territorial expansion for maritime and railway transport systems. Much of the credit of developing the first efficient steam engine in 1765 is attributed to the British engineer Watt, although the first steam engines were used to pump water out of mines. It was then only a matter of time to see the adaptation of the steam engine to locomotion. In 1769, the French engineer Cugnot built the first self-propelled steam vehicle, and was also responsible for the first automobile accident ever recorded. The first mechanically propelled maritime vehicle was tested in 1790 by the American inventor Fitch as a mode of fluvial transportation on the Delaware River. By 1807, commercial steamboat services were inaugurated. This marked a new era in the mechanization of land and maritime transport systems alike.

From the perspective of land transportation, the early Industrial Revolution faced problems over bottlenecks, as inland distribution was unable to carry the growing quantities of raw materials and finished goods. Roads were commonly unpaved and could not be used to effectively carry heavy loads. Although improvements were made on road transport systems in the early seventeenth century, such as the Turnpike Trusts in Britain (1706) and the development of stagecoaches, this was not sufficient to accommodate the growing demands on freight transportation. The first coach services had speeds of about 5.5 miles per hour in the 1750s. By the 1820s turnpikes greatly improved overland transportation but roads were not profitable if used to haul anything except compact and valuable goods. In a horse-drawn era, road economics were clearly disadvantageous. Bulk products could be transported for about 100 miles, but in a slow, costly and inefficient manner. For instance, four horses could pull a wagon weight of one ton 12 miles a day over an ordinary road and 1.5 tons 18 miles a day over a well-maintained turnpike. Comparatively, four horses could draw a barge of 100 tons 24 miles a day on a canal.

From the 1760s a set of **freight shipping canals** were slowly built in emerging industrial cores such as England (e.g. Bridgewater Canal, 1761) and the United States (e.g. Erie Canal, 1825). These projects relied on a system of locks to overcome changes in elevation, and thus link different segments of fluvial systems into a comprehensive waterway system. Barges, many pulled by horses, became increasingly used to move goods at a scale and a cost that were not previously possible. Economies of scale and specialization, the foundation of modern industrial production systems, became increasingly applicable through fluvial canals. Physical obstacles made canal construction expensive, however, and the network was constrained in its geographical coverage. In 1830 there were about 2,000 miles of canals in Britain and, by 1850, there were 4,250 miles of navigable waterways. The canal era was, however, short-lived as a new mode would revolutionize and transform inland transportation emerged in the second half of the nineteenth century.

In the late eighteenth and particularly in the early nineteenth century the construction of canals was being considered to improve inland transportation in North America, which was limited to trails and coastal navigation. The setting of such canals was facing strong constraints as no navigable river system from the East Coast was reaching far inland, with the exception of the St Lawrence, which was navigable up to Montreal. The Appalachian Mountains limited the inland reach to just a few hundred miles, with navigation often blocked by rapids or waterfalls (the Fall Line). The Great Lakes offered a

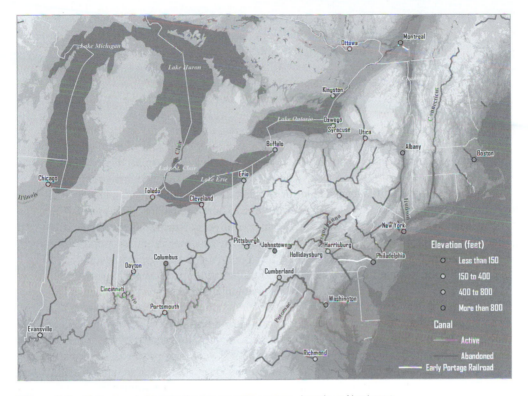

Figure 2.4 Major canals built in the nineteenth century, American Northeast

significant agricultural potential, but their access was blocked by the Lachine Rapids and the Niagara Escarpment. Segments between navigable waterways involved a portage where freight was carried by horses.

Canal construction closely followed the course of rivers, with some river segments being essentially canalized (replaced by the canal). Rivers provided water supply to be used in locks as well as a path of minimal impendence. The problem was that canals never followed a direct path. The exception was when a "cut" was needed, which was done with the straightest path possible, but at great expense. As the first major canals were being constructed in the 1820s and 1830s, they provided the first significant economies of scale for North American inland transportation. While a horse could carry one-eighth of a ton, a canal barge could carry 30 tons. Two canal systems emerged, one east of the Appalachians along the East Coast and one west of the Appalachians in the Midwest:

- The first canal system was an attempt to connect the interior from a set of coastal cities and go as far inland as technically possible. It took place from two main corridors. The first went from Montreal and along the St Lawrence to Lake Erie, with the completion of the Lachine Canal in 1825 and the Welland Canal in 1829, which overcame the Niagara Escarpment between Lake Ontario and Lake Erie. The second was the Erie Canal system, completed in 1825 and connecting Albany, Syracuse and Buffalo. A connection to Lake Ontario was provided to the Oswego branch, completed in 1828. Many other branch canals were built to carry coal from the Appalachian to the cities of the East Coast.

● The second canal system in the Midwest was mostly connecting the Ohio River to Lake Erie, enabling access to the agricultural resources of the region and to carry them back to the East Coast through the Erie Canal. The two most important canals were the Ohio and Erie Canal completed in 1833, linking Cleveland, Columbus and the Ohio River, and the Wabash and Erie Canal completed in 1853, linking Toledo to Evansville. A canal completed in 1848 between Chicago and the Illinois River was an important factor in the subsequent role of the city as the most important transportation hub in North America.

The first canals were constrained by several technical limitations related to their draft (4–10 ft) and the lift that locks could provide. Early locks could elevate a barge only by about 8–10 ft, implying that a climb of 100 ft required about 10 to 15 locks. For instance, the Chesapeake and Ohio Canal that linked Washington, DC to Cumberland, Maryland climbed 605 ft and required 74 locks (average of 8.2 ft per lock). By the late nineteenth century, improvement in lock technology permitted a single lift of 30–40 ft. For instance, a lock system at the town of Lockport climbing the Niagara Escarpment along the Erie Canal was modernized into one lock offering a lift of 40 ft, instead of five locks lifting 8 ft each. The first barges were propelled manually by pushing a pike and using a rudder (mostly downstream) or hauled by horses along the towpath (mostly upstream). Later, barges were motorized, but tended to be larger and used for canals having deeper drafts.

Paradoxically, the setting of canals also induced the construction of the first rail lines to compete with an existing transport market or for portage between unserviced segments. For instance, one of the first rail lines to be established in the United States in 1834, the Philadelphia and Columbia Railroad, was built to complement the Schuylkill and Union canals between Harrisburg and Philadelphia. Another important rail line completed the same year was the Allegheny Portage Railroad, which was the first railroad constructed through the Allegheny Mountains (part of the Appalachian Range), linking two canal cities; Johnstown (east of Pittsburgh) and Hollidaysburg (west of Harrisburg). The first railroad in Canada, the Champlain and St. Lawrence Railroad, completed in 1838 between La Prairie and St Jean-sur-Richelieu, was also built with the same rationale: a portage between the St Lawrence and Lake Champlain.

By the late nineteenth century the great majority of the canals were abandoned as they lost their commercial utility. Many had limited draft, had high upkeep and were no longer able to compete effectively with railways. Those that are left today, such as the Erie Canal, the Rideau Canal and the Champlain Canal, are used for recreational purposes and managed by state or federal governments as parks. Portions of some canals have been restored, again for recreational purposes. The only commercial exceptions are the Welland Canal, upgraded several times, which is now part of the St Lawrence Seaway that was completed in 1959, and the Illinois and Michigan Canal that links Chicago to the Illinois River and which has been supplemented by the Chicago Sanitary and Ship Canal in 1900. The canal era was short-lived as a new mode that would revolutionize and transform inland transportation emerging in the second half of the nineteenth century.

Steam railway technology initially appeared in 1814 to haul coal. It was found that using a steam engine on smooth rails required less power and could handle heavier loads. The first commercial rail line linked Manchester to Liverpool in 1830 (distance of 65 km). Shortly after, rail lines began to be laid throughout developed countries, leading to the setting of national systems. Speed improvements were significant as the first rail networks ran between 30 km and 50 km per hour, three times faster than stagecoach services. The capital costs to build railway networks were enormous and often left to the private sector, but with significant public involvements in terms of loans and land grants. They included rights of way, building, maintenance and operating costs. This was accompanied by a few railway manias (and their subsequent busts) with capital pouring in a sector that was perceived, at least by the general public, as limitless in possibilities. By the 1850s, railroad towns were being established and the railways were giving access to resources and markets of vast territories. 10,000 km of railways were then operating in England and railways were quickly being constructed in Western Europe and North America (Figure 2.5). The need to organize and schedule rail services incited the adoption of standard time (often labeled standard railroad time). England was the first to implement a standard time system in 1855, the Greenwich Mean Time, which became the global reference time.

In only 30 years after its introduction the American rail network totaled about 28,900 miles (46,500 km) on the eve of the Civil War (1861–5; Figure 2.5). Yet, the American rail network was composed of two systems, reflecting the sociopolitical division between the North (Union States) and the South (Confederate States). Outside the connection through Washington, the networks were not connected and serviced rather different economic

Figure 2.5 American rail network, 1861

Source: Railroads and the Making of Modern America, University of Nebraska, Lincoln (Rail Network). US Census Bureau (Urban Population).

systems. This lack of connectivity was compounded by the fact that railways servicing the same city were often not connected, requiring ferrying cargo from one terminal to the other and for passengers to spend a night to catch the train the next day (schedules were not effectively coordinated). The dominantly rural society of the South was mainly serviced by penetration lines seeking to connect the agricultural hinterland to ports where surpluses were exported (e.g. New Orleans and Charleston). As such, the network was not very cohesive. The more urbanized North developed a network based on interconnecting its main urban centers and agricultural regions in the Midwest in a complex lattice. At the end of the Civil War the expansion of the network would resume as well as its level of integration, since in 1869 the transcontinental line would be completed.

Railroads represented an inland transport system that was at the same time flexible in its spatial coverage and that could carry heavy loads. As a result, many canals fell into disrepair and were closed, as they were no longer able to compete with rail services. In their initial phase of development, railways were a point-to-point process where major cities were linked one at a time by independent companies. Thus, the first railroad companies bore the name of the city pairs or the region they were servicing (e.g. the Camden and Amboy Railroad Company chartered in 1830). From the 1860s, integrated railway systems started to cohesively service whole nations with standard gauges (made mandatory in the United States by the Interstate Commerce Act of 1887) and passenger and freight services. The journey between New York and Chicago was reduced from three weeks by stagecoach in 1830 to 72 hours by train in 1850. Many cities thus became closely interconnected, further favoring economic specialization and comparative advantages. The transcontinental line between New York and San Francisco, completed in 1869, represented a remarkable achievement in territorial integration made only possible by rail. It reduced the journey across the continent (New York to San Francisco) from six months to one week, thus opening for the Eastern part of the United States a vast pool of resources and new agricultural regions. This was followed by Canada in 1886 (Trans-Canada railway) and Russia in 1904 (Trans-Siberian railway).

In terms of international transportation, the beginning of the nineteenth century saw the establishment of the first regular maritime routes linking harbors worldwide, especially over the North Atlantic between Europe and North America. Many of these long-distance routes were navigated by fast clipper ships, which dominated ocean trade until the late 1850s. Another significant improvement resided in the elaboration of accurate navigation charts, where prevailing winds and sea currents could be used to the advantage of navigation (Figure 2.6).

Between 1842 and 1861 the navigator Matthew Fontaine Maury collected an extensive array of ship logs, which enabled him to chart prevailing winds and sea currents, as well as their seasonal variations. While mariners were well aware of specific regional conditions such as the Gulf Stream, Maury was the first to comprehensively tally oceanographic conditions at the global level. Many of this information appeared in *The Physical Geography of the Sea,* published in 1855, which many consider to be the first significant oceanography textbook. Such knowledge enabled sailing times to be considerably shortened, especially over long-distance travel. For instance, a journey from New York to Rio de Janeiro was reduced by 32 days, without any technical improvements on the ship, but by simply taking better advantage of winds and sea currents (Figure 2.6). Maury was also able to demonstrate that using the longer east-bound sailing route rounding Cape Horn from Australia to Europe or North America was actually faster than the shorter westbound sailing route rounding the Cape of Good Hope. The outcome was the creation of relatively well-defined navigation routes that

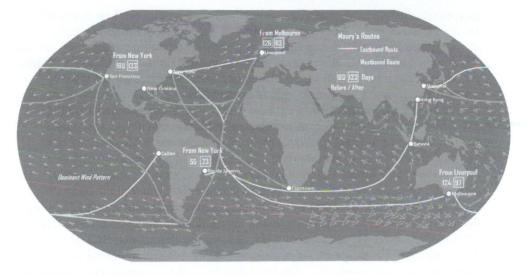

Figure 2.6 Impacts of Maury's navigation charts on sailing time, 1850s

Source: J. Leighly (ed.) (1963) *The Physical Geography of the Sea and its Meteorology by Matthew Fontaine Maury*, 8th edition. Cambridge, MA: Belknap Press. Cited by R.D. Knowles (2006) "Transport shaping space: the differential collapse of time/space." *Journal of Transport Geography* 14(6) 407–425.

followed dominant wind patterns. It represented a close to optimal use of routing for sailing which remained until steamships replaced sailships in the late nineteenth century.

Composite ships (mixture of wood and iron armature) then took over a large portion of the trade until about 1900, but they could not compete with steamships, which had been continually improving since they were first introduced a hundred years before. Regarding steamship technology, 1807 marks the first successful use of a steamship, Fulton's *North River/Clermont*, on the Hudson servicing New York and Albany. In 1820, the *Savannah* was the first steamship (used as auxiliary power) to cross the Atlantic, taking 29 days to link Liverpool to New York. The first regular services for transatlantic passenger transport by steamships was inaugurated in 1838, followed by the usage of the helix, instead of the paddle wheel, as a more efficient propeller in 1840. The gradual improvement of steam engine technology slowly but surely permitted longer and safer voyages, enabling steamships to become the dominant mode of maritime transportation by the late nineteenth century. Shipbuilding was also revolutionized by the usage of steel armatures (1860), which overcame the structural constraints of wood and iron armatures in terms of ship size. Iron armature ships were 30–40 percent lighter and had 15 percent more cargo capacity compared with wood armature ship of the same size.

The main consequence of the Industrial Revolution was a **specialization of transportation services** and the establishment of **large distribution networks** of raw materials and energy.

Emergence of modern transportation systems (1870–1920)

By the end of the nineteenth century, international transportation undertook a new growth phase, especially with improvements in **engine propulsion technology** of the steamship and a gradual shift from coal to oil in the 1870s. Although oil has been known for centuries for its combustion properties, its commercial use was only applied in the early nineteenth century. Inventors started experimenting with engines that could use the cheap new fuel. Oil increased the speed and the capacity of maritime transport. It also permitted the energy consumption of ships to be reduced by a factor of 90 percent relative to coal, the main source of energy for steam engines prior to this innovation. An equal size oil-powered ship could transport more freight than a coal-powered ship, reducing operation costs considerably and extending range. Also, coal refueling stages along trade routes could be bypassed. Global maritime circulation was also dramatically improved when infrastructures to reduce intercontinental distances, such as the Suez (1869) and the Panama (1914) canals, were constructed (Figure 2.7). With the Suez Canal, the far reaches of Asia and Australia became more accessible.

The Suez Canal represents, along with the Panama Canal, one of the most significant maritime "shortcuts" ever built. It brought a new era of European influence in Pacific Asia by reducing the journey from Asia to Europe by about 6,000 km by skipping a detour around the Cape of Good Hope. Asia became more commercially accessible and colonial trade expanded as a result of increased interactions because of a reduced friction of distance. Great Britain, the maritime power of the time, benefited substantially from this improved access. For instance, the Suez Canal shortened the distance on a maritime journey from London to Bombay by 41 percent and shortened the distance on a journey from London to Shanghai by 32 percent. The Panama Canal considerably shortened the maritime distances between the American East and West coasts by some 13,000 km.

The increasing size of ships, the outcome of advances in shipbuilding, imposed massive investments in port infrastructures such as piers and docks to accommodate them. Ship size grew dramatically, from the largest tonnage of 3,800 gross registered tons (revenue-making cargo space) in 1871 to 47,000 tons in 1914. Accordingly, ocean freight rates dropped by 70 percent between 1840 and 1910. The commercial demise of the sailship took place during that period as trade shifted to the steamship and expanded substantially. While sailships accounted for 85 percent of the total maritime tonnage in 1870, this share plummeted to 14 percent in 1910. 1878 appears to have been the last year where the sailship could compete effectively with the steamship for the China

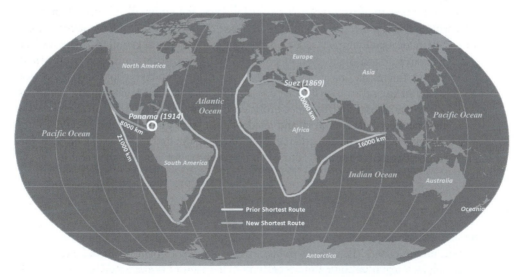

Figure 2.7 Geographical impacts of the Suez and Panama canals

trade. The harbor, while integrating production and transshipping activities, became an industrial complex around which agglomerated activities using ponderous raw materials. From the 1880s, liner services linked major ports of the world, supporting the first regular international passenger transport services, until the 1950s, when air transportation became the dominant mode.

The period between 1890 and 1925 underlines the dominance of the steamship as a support to global trade with its diffusion to ports across the world. 1890 marks the threshold where steamship services become competitive for distances above 16,000 km, placing Asia within its reach, particularly after the opening of the Suez Canal in 1869. Still, steamship services show for both periods a high level of concentration around industrialized clusters. While only two notable clusters are active around 1890, the North Sea and the American Northeast, by 1925 several additional clusters have emerged. One concerns the American West Coast that saw its industrialization expanded by the opening of the Panama Canal in 1914 and by an oil extraction boom. Another concerns Argentina, which at that time was going through a period of prosperity, including a phase of European immigration, and accounted for one of the world's highest GDP per capita. Buenos Aires at that time rivaled other metropolises such as Paris, London and New York. The activity in South Asia was linked with the British colonial trade. This also included Australia, which at that time was becoming an important exporter of agricultural goods. The fast industrialization of Japan as an outcome of the Meiji Revolution was also becoming apparent.

This period also marked the golden era of the development of railway transport systems as railway networks expanded tremendously and became the dominant land transport mode both for passengers and freight. As the speed and power of locomotives improved above 100 km per hour, and as the market expanded, rail services became increasingly specialized with trains entirely devoted to passengers or freight. Japan, the first Asian country to undertake its industrial revolution, saw its first train service in 1872. Rail systems reached a phase of maturity by the early twentieth century as, in most developed economies, the rail network reached its maximum extent in terms of total length.

Many European countries were undergoing a demographic transition, implying a rapid growth of their population and related urbanization and migration pressures. In such a context a significant technological change of this era involved urban transportation, which until then solely relied on walking and different types of carriages (mainly horse-drawn). The fast growth of the urban population favored the construction of the first public urban transport systems. **Electric energy** became widely used in the 1880s and considerably changed urban transport systems with the introduction of **tramways** (streetcars), notably in Western Europe and in the United States. They enabled the first forms of urban sprawl and the specialization of economic functions through a wider separation between place of work and residence. In large agglomerations, underground metro systems began to be constructed, London being the first in 1863. The **bicycle**, first shown at the Paris Exhibition of 1867, was also an important innovation, which changed commuting in the late nineteenth century. Initially, the rich used it as a form of leisure, but it was rapidly adopted by the working class as a mode of transportation to the workplace. Today, the bicycle is much less used in developed countries (outside recreational purposes), but it is still a major mode of transportation in developing countries, especially China.

This era also marked the first significant developments in **telecommunications**. The telegraph is considered to be the first efficient telecommunication device gaining wide market coverage. In 1844, Samuel Morse built the first experimental telegraph line in the United States between Washington and Baltimore, opening a new era in the transmission of information. By 1852, more than 40,000 km of telegraph lines were in service in the United States. In 1866, the first successful transatlantic telegraph line marked the inauguration of an intercontinental telegraphic network that was later dubbed the "Victorian Internet." The growth of telecommunications is thus closely associated with the growth of railways and international shipping. Managing a rail transport system, especially at the continental level, became more efficient with telegraphic communication. In fact, continental rail and telegraphic networks were often laid concomitantly. Telecommunications were also a dominant factor behind the creation of **standard times zones** in 1884. From a multiplicity of local times, zones of constant time with Greenwich (England) as the reference were laid. This improved the scheduling of passenger and freight transportation at national levels. By 1895, every continent was linked by telegraph lines, a precursor of the global information network that would emerge in the late twentieth century. Business transactions became more efficient as production, management and consumption centers could interact with delays that were in hours instead of weeks and even months.

Concept 2 – Historical geography of transportation: the setting of global systems

Transportation in the Fordist era (1920–70)

The Fordist era was epitomized by the adoption of the assembly line as the dominant form of industrial production, an innovation that benefited transportation substantially. The **internal combustion engine**, or four-stroke engine by Daimler (1889), which was a modified version of the Diesel engine (1885), together with the pneumatic tire (1885) by Dunlop, made road vehicles' operations faster and more comfortable. Compared with steam engines, internal combustion engines have a much higher efficiency and are using a lighter fuel: petrol. Petrol, previously perceived as an unwanted by-product of the oil refining process, which was seeking kerosene for illumination, became a convenient fuel. Initially, diesel engines were bulky, limiting their use to industrial and maritime propulsion, a purpose which they still fulfill today. The internal combustion engine permitted an extended flexibility of movements with fast, inexpensive and ubiquitous (door-to-door) transport modes such as automobiles, buses and trucks. Mass producing these vehicles changed the industrial production system considerably, notably by 1913, when Ford began the production of the Model T car using an assembly line. From 1913 to 1927, about 15 million Ford Model Ts were built, making it the second most produced car in history, behind the Volkswagen Beetle. Economies of scale realized along the assembly line were passed on to the consumer, which made the automobile even more affordable and popular. The rapid diffusion of the automobile marked an increased demand for oil products and other raw materials such as steel and rubber.

Economies of scale also improved transportation in terms of capacity, which enabled low-cost bulk commodities such as minerals and grain to be moved over long distances. The process was, however, slow to start, as cargo ships require large amounts of labor to be loaded and unloaded. This informally imposed a limit of 10,000 deadweight tons to break-bulk cargo ships that will remain as such until containerization began in the late 1950s. Still, the gradual growth of international trade and particularly World War II gave a strong impetus for shipbuilding. The end of the war left an ample supply of military cargo ships, namely Liberty Ships, which could be cheaply used for commercial purposes and became the workhorses of global trade until the 1960s. Oil tankers are a good example of the application of the principle of economies of scale to transport larger quantities of oil at a lower cost, especially in the postwar period, when global demand surged. Maritime routes were thus expanded to include tanker routes, notably from the Middle East, the dominant global producer of oil. The very long distances concerned in the oil trade favored the construction of larger tankers. In the 1960s, tanker ships of 100,000 tons became available, to be supplanted by VLCCs (very large crude carriers) of 250,000 tons in the 1970s and by the ULCCs (ultra-large crude carriers) of 550,000 tons at the end of the 1970s.

Economies of scale were also favored by **unitization** where batches of break-bulk cargo could be combined into one handling unit. In ancient times amphorae were used as load units, but had limitations for carrying goods. The pallet became the first effective load unit, particularly after the invention of the forklift in 1937. Pallets permitted a better handling of goods, as they could be more effectively managed and stored. By the early 1930s about three days were required to unload a rail boxcar containing 13,000 cases of unpalletized canned goods. With pallets and forklifts, a similar task could be done in about four hours. It was during World War II, however, that the massive adoption of pallets as the standard supply unit load became widely adopted by the US military, as it permitted fast handling of goods and turnaround of transport assets. This underlined the growing importance of efficient transportation systems in the competitiveness of nations, be it for commercial or military gain.

Although the first balloon flight took place in 1783, due to the lack of propulsion no practical applications for air travel were realized until the twentieth century. The first propelled flight was made in 1903 by the Wright brothers and inaugurated the era of air transportation. The initial air transport services were targeted at mail, since it was a type of freight that could be easily transported and, due to technical limitations in carrying capacity, initially proved to be more profitable than transporting passengers. 1919 marked the first commercial air transport service between England and France, but air transport suffered from limitations in terms of capacity and range. Several attempts were made at developing dirigible services with the Atlantic crossed by a Zeppelin dirigible in 1924. However, such technology was almost entirely abandoned in 1937 after the spectacular *Hindenburg* accident, in which the hydrogen-filled reservoirs burned. The 1920s and 1930s saw the expansion of regional and national air transport services in Europe and the United States with mass-produced propeller aircrafts such as the Douglas DC-3.

Through the first half of the twentieth century the Atlantic remained an important technical challenge for long-distance transportation modes, since it linked large markets in Europe and North America. The post-World War II period was the turning point for air transportation, as the range, capacity and speed of aircrafts increased as well as the average passengers' income. A growing number of people were thus able to afford the speed and convenience of air transportation. The application of the gas turbine principle led to the development of jet engines. 1952 marks the beginning of commercial jet services with the Comet, but a design flaw grounded the plane the following year. In 1958, the first successful commercial jet plane, the Boeing 707, entered into service and revolutionized international movements of passengers, marking the end of passenger transoceanic ships (liners) and replacing propeller planes for long-distance services. The jet plane enabled the setting of time-dependent trade relations between producers across the world (such as electronics), created a long-distance market for perishables (fruits, vegetables, flowers) and supported the development of mass tourism.

Basic telecommunications infrastructures, such as the telephone and the radio, were mass marketed during the Fordist era. However, the major change was the large **diffusion of the automobile**, especially from the 1950s as it became a truly mass consumption product when the first major highway systems, such as the American Interstate, began to be built. No other modes of transportation have so drastically changed lifestyles and the structure of cities, notably for developed countries. It created suburbanization and expanded cities to areas larger than 100 km in diameter in some instances. In dense and productive regions, such as the Northeast of the United States, Western Europe and Japan, the urban system became structured and interconnected by transport networks to the point that it could be considered as one vast **urban region**: the megalopolis.

A new context for transportation: the post-Fordist era (1970–)

Among the major changes in international transportation from the 1970s are the massive development of telecommunications, the globalization of trade, more efficient distribution systems through the application of logistics and the considerable development of air transportation.

Telecommunications enabled growing information exchanges, especially for the financial and service sectors. After 1970 telecommunications successfully merged with information technologies. As such, telecommunication also became a medium of doing business in its own right, in addition to supporting and enhancing other transportation modes. The **information highway** became a reality as fiber optic cables gradually replaced copper wires, multiplying the capacity to transmit information between computers. Global submarine cable networks, which have existed since the setting of telegraphs networks in the nineteenth century, were overhauled with fiber optics to become the backbone of the global telecommunication system, particularly the Internet (Figure 2.8).

The development of fiber optic transmission technology provided a substantial impetus in the setting of a **global telecommunication network,** since it permitted

Figure 2.8 Global submarine cable network

Source: Dataset encoded by Greg Mahlknecht.

significantly higher bandwidth and less signal degradation. Throughputs of hundreds of gigabytes of information per second became possible. The first transatlantic fiber optic cable (TAT-8) was laid in 1988 and over the years fiber optic cables were laid across the world, connecting economies and societies increasingly dependent on telecommunications. The Internet could not have existed otherwise. While initial submarine cables were laid on a point-to-point basis, technical advances permitted branching so that one cable could service a sequence of hubs (e.g. Africa and Latin America).

The global network is designed for redundancy as several cables are laid in parallel for major connections (transatlantic and transpacific), implying that a failure in one cable can be mitigated by rerouting traffic to the others. In recent years, Pacific Asia has seen significant submarine cable laying activities, as a support to its economic development. In 2012, a new route for submarine cable was being established with the setting of the first Arctic cables between London and Tokyo through the Northwest Passage. In addition to providing an additional redundancy to the global telecommunication network, it will shave about 60 milliseconds off the connection speed. Through lower latency (delay) levels, this would thus improve bandwidth-intensive telecommunications between Europe and Pacific Asia, such as financial transactions and videoconferencing. Another trend concerns the setting of large data centers in northern areas, namely Scandinavian countries. They benefit from cooler temperatures, which confers savings, as data centers generate a lot of heat. Because of hydroelectric potential, Nordic countries generally have lower electricity costs.

This growth was, however, dwarfed by the tremendous growth in processing power of personal computing devices, which are now fundamental components of economic and social activities across the world. A network of **satellite communication** was also created to support the growing exchanges of information, especially for television images, but remains of marginal use because of lower bandwidth. Out of this wireless technology emerged local cellular networks which expanded and merged to cover whole cities, countries, regions and then continents. Telecommunications have reached the era of individual access, portability and global coverage.

In a post-Fordist system, the **fragmentation of production**, organizing an international division of labor, as well as the principle of "just-in-time," increased the quantity of freight moving at the local, regional and international levels. This in turn required increasing efforts to manage freight and reinforced the **development of logistics**, the science of physical distribution systems. **Containers**, main agents of the modern international transport system, enabled an increased flexibility of freight transport, mainly by reducing transshipment costs and delays; handling a container requires about 25 times less labor than its equivalent in bulk freight. This increased the unitization trend brought forward by the pallet, particularly since pallets could be loaded into containers. Containers were introduced by the American entrepreneur Malcolm McLean, who initially applied containerization to land transport but saw the opportunity of using container shipping as an alternative to acute road congestion in the early 1950s before the construction of the first Interstate highways. The initial attempts at containerization thus aimed to reduce maritime transshipment costs and time. Before containerization, a cargo ship could spend as much time in a port being loaded or unloaded than it did at sea. Later on, the true potential of containerization became clear when interfacing with other modes became an operational reality, mainly between maritime, rail and road transportation.

The first **containership** (the *Ideal-X,* a converted T2 oil tanker) set sail in 1956 from New York to Houston and marked the beginning of the era of containerization. In 1960, the Port Authority of New York/New Jersey, foreseeing the potential in container trade, constructed the **first specialized container terminal** next to Port Newark: the Port Elizabeth Marine Terminal. The Sea-Land Company established the first regular maritime container line in 1965 over the Atlantic between North America and Western Europe. By the early 1980s, container services with specialized ships (cellular containerships, first introduced in 1967) became a dominant aspect of international and regional transport systems, transforming the maritime industry. However, for 20 years the size of those ships remained constrained by the size of the Panama Canal, which de facto became the **Panamax standard**. In 1988, the first **post-Panamax** containership was introduced, an indication of the will to further expand economies of scale in maritime container shipping. The container revolution was concomitant with globalization by supporting an increasingly complex system of trade involving parts, manufactured goods and even commodities. Few other transport innovations had such an impact on the global economic landscape.

Air and rail transportation experienced remarkable improvements in the late 1960s and early 1970s through massification and network developments. The first commercial flight of the Boeing 747 between New York and London in 1969 marked an important landmark for international transportation (mainly for passengers, but freight became a significant function in the 1980s). This giant plane could transport around 400 passengers, depending on the configuration. It permitted a considerable reduction of air fares through economies of scale and opened intercontinental air transportation to the mass market. Attempts were also undertaken to establish faster-than-sound commercial services with Concorde (1976; flying at 2,200 km per hour). However, such services proved to be unprofitable and no new supersonic commercial planes have been built since the 1970s. Concorde was finally retired in 2003. At the regional level, the emergence of **high-speed train systems** provided fast and efficient inter-urban services, notably in France (1981; speeds up to 300 km per hour) and in Japan (1964; Shinkansen; speeds up to 275 km per hour). More recently, high-speed train systems were constructed in China, Korea and Taiwan.

Major corporations making transportation equipment, such as car manufacturers, have become dominant players in the global economy. Even if the car is not an international transport mode, its diffusion has expanded global trade of vehicles, parts, raw materials and fuel (mainly oil). Car production, which used to be mainly concentrated in the United States, Japan and Germany, has become a global industry with a few key players being part of well-integrated groups such as Ford, General Motors and Toyota. Along with oil conglomerates, they have pursued strategies aimed at the diffusion of the automobile as the main mode of individual transportation. This has led to growing mobility but also to congestion and waste of energy. At the start of the twenty-first century, the automobile accounts for about 80 percent of the total oil consumption in developed countries.

Since the beginning of the modern era in the fifteenth century, transportation played a significant role in the development of the world economy (Figure 2.9). Like most technological innovations, transportation goes in waves that reflect the cumulative development of infrastructures. Although these cumulative development phases played out differently, developed economies such as Europe and the United States saw first the setting of canal systems, which were then complemented by rail transport systems. Later, the internal combustion engine supported the development of extensive road systems, and from the 1950s of air transport systems, that now span the globe.

Transport development tends to be a **cumulative process,** as each new transport technology adds to the capacity and mobility potential of the previous technologies.

Figure 2.9 Cumulative waves of transport development

Larger quantities of freight and more people can be moved more quickly and more efficiently. Developments in transport may also lead to the obsolescence and decline of prior technologies when they service similar markets. Since the modern era, five major waves of transport developments can be identified, each with a transport technology that had fundamental impacts on the mobility of passengers and freight:

- **First wave: sailships**. The mastery of high sea navigation in the mid-sixteenth and early seventeenth centuries led to the gradual setting of a global trade network supported by the emergence of colonial empires. Long-distance transportation became reliable.
- **Second wave: canals**. The early stages of the Industrial Revolution in the nineteenth century were accompanied by the setting of canals complementing existing rivers or linking them. They provided the first level of inland access with the economies of scale they were able to confer, but such accessibility was highly punctual, where canals could be built. Although canal systems have historically been set in other parts of the world (China being the most salient example), it is in Western Europe and North America that their impacts on economic development were the most significant. Even if canal systems were supplemented by railways for many commercial relations, they remained active transport modes, particularly in Europe, China and North America.
- **Third wave: railways and steamships**. The setting of rail systems in the second half of the nineteenth century permitted the first effective forms of inland accessibility and concomitantly of cohesive national transport systems, but interconnecting different rail systems took time. At the beginning of the twentieth century, rail systems were the dominant mode supporting passengers and freight flows. Although their relative importance has declined with the setting of highways, railways are far from being an obsolete technology with the setting of high-speed rail systems around the world as well as their conversion to intermodalism. On the maritime side, in the

late nineteenth century, the steamship would mark the demise of the sailship, but not of commercial maritime shipping networks that continued to expand to support more comprehensive international trade volumes and the long-distance mobility of passengers.

- **Fourth wave: highways**. The diffusion of the internal combustion engine and the availability of cheap oil supplies permitted an effective setting of individual or small load (truckload) mobility (national mobility systems). This, however, could not take place without the construction of national highway systems, such as the Interstate in the United States. Another important impact of the highways was lower density forms of urbanization, namely suburbs.

- **Fifth wave: airports and container ships**. The introduction of jet services in the late 1950s permitted for the first time the setting of true global mobility systems where locations can be reached within hours. Airports became important nodes in the national and global systems of passenger flows as well as freight flows. On the maritime side, the container ship, including the massification of bulk shipping, would strengthen global commercial relations to an unparalleled level through the setting of global distribution systems.

Concept 3 – Transport and spatial organization

The spatial organization of transportation

Geography imposes an organization to activities and consequently a spatial structure. The opposite also applies as the spatial structure influences geography. Spatial organization relies on two dimensions. The first relates to **spatial differentiation,** where attributes such as location, size and density are illustrative of the distribution inequalities of features such as resources and population. This differentiation is the outcome of a cumulative process as several elements of the spatial structure, such as urban areas, are the outcome of a long process of accumulation, which tends to change slowly. The second relates to **spatial interactions,** where the attributes of flows are also illustrative of inequalities of the origins and destinations.

Transportation not only favors economic development but also has an impact on the spatial organization. Throughout history, transport networks have structured space at different scales. The fragmentation of production and consumption, the locational specificities of resources, labor and markets generate a wide array of flows of people, goods and information. The structure of these flows in terms of origin, destination and routing is closely related to spatial organization. Space shapes transport as much as transport shapes space, which is a salient example of the reciprocity of transport and its geography. This **reciprocity** can be articulated over two points:

- **Reciprocity to locations**. This relationship concerns the transport system and the impact it has on locations. Since the transport system is composed of nodes and links as well as the flows they are supporting, the spatial organization of this system is a core defining component of the spatial structure. Transportation, by its physicality, shapes the spatial structure. Even if streets are not the city, they are shaping its organization in terms of locations and relations. The same applies for maritime shipping networks, which are not international trade but reflect the spatial organization of the global economy.

- **Reciprocity to demand**. This relationship concerns activities that are all dependent on transportation at different levels and at different scales. Since every single activity is based on a level of transport demand and mobility, the relationship they have with transportation is reflected in their spatial organization. While a small retail activity is conditioned by local accessibility from which it draws its customers, a large manufacturing plant relies on accessibility to global freight distribution for its inputs as well as its outputs.

The more interdependent an economy is, the more important transportation becomes as a support and a factor shaping this interdependence. However, it is also a reason why the importance of transportation can be neglected, as the interdependence will be noticed but its structural support less so. The effect is observed, while its cause is not. The relationship between transport and spatial organization can be considered from three major geographical scales: the global, the regional and the local (Figure 2.10).

While the major nodes structuring spatial organization at the global level are gateways supported by port, airport and telecommunication activities, at the local level, employment and commercial activities, which tend to be agglomerated, are the main structuring elements. Each of these scales is also characterized by specific links and relations, ranging from locally based commuting to global trade flows.

Figure 2.10   Scales of spatial organization for transportation

Global spatial organization

At the global level, transportation supports and shapes economic specialization and productivity through international trade. Improvements in transport are expanding markets and development opportunities, but **not uniformly**. The inequalities of the global economy are reflected in its spatial organization and the structure of international transport systems. The patterns of globalization have created a growth in spatial flows (trade) and increased interdependencies. Telecommunications, maritime transport and air transport, because of their scale of service, support the majority of global flows. The nature and spatial structure of these flows can be considered from two major perspectives that seek to explain global differences in growth and accessibility:

- **Core/periphery**. This basic representation assumes that the global spatial organization favors a few core areas that grow faster than the periphery. Differential growth creates acute inequalities in levels of development. For instance, global migration flows are illustrative of different levels of economic development, with flows from locations with lower development levels to higher development levels dominating. Transportation is thus perceived as a factor of polarization and unequal development. From this perspective, parts of the global economy are gaining, because they are more accessible, while others are marginalized and bound to dependency. However, this trend can be reversed if international transport costs are significantly reduced. This is evidenced by the substantial growth of many Pacific Asian countries that have opted for an export-oriented strategy which requires good access to global freight distribution. Consequently, the core/periphery relationship is flexible and relative.
- **Poles**. Transportation is perceived as a factor of articulation in the global economy where the circulation of passengers and freight is regulated by poles corresponding to a high level of accumulation of transport infrastructures, distribution and economic activities. These poles are subject to centrifugal and centripetal forces that have favored geographical concentration of some activities and the dispersion of others. The global economy is thus based on the backbone of freight distribution, which in turn relies on networks established to support its flows and on nodes that are regulating the flows within networks. Networks, particularly those concerning maritime shipping and air transportation, are flexible entities that change with the ebb and flow of commerce, while nodes are locations fixed within their own regional geography.

The global spatial organization is a priori conditioned by its nodality. Global flows are handled by **gateways** and **hubs**, each of which account for a significant share of the flows of people, freight and information. A **gateway** is a location offering accessibility to a large system of circulation of freight and passengers. Gateways reap the advantage of a favorable physical location such as highway junctions, the confluence of rivers, a good port site, and have been the object of a significant accumulation of transport infrastructures such as terminals and their links. A gateway is commonly an origin, a destination and a point of transit. It generally commands the entrance to and the exit from its catchment area. In other words, it is a pivotal point for the entrance and the exit in a region, a country or a continent, and often requires intermodal transfers. A **hub** is a central point for the collection, sorting, transshipment and distribution of goods for a particular area. This concept comes from a term used in air transport for passengers as well as for freight and describes collection and distribution through a single point such as the "hub-and-spoke" concept.

Gateways and hubs refer to rather similar elements of the spatial structure of flows (Figure 2.11). However, the concept of gateway tends to be more restrictive in its definition. While a hub is a central location in a transport system with many inbound and outbound connections of the same mode, a gateway commonly implies a shift from one mode to the other (such as maritime/land). A gateway is performing an intermodal function (between modes) while a hub is mostly transmodal (within a mode). Transport corridors are commonly linking gateways to the hinterland. Gateways also tend to be most stable in time, as they often have emerged at the convergence of inland transport systems, while the importance of a hub can change. For instance, a transport company such as a maritime shipping line or an air carrier may decide to use another hub. If this is the case, then the hub can lose its status. Also, a location can be a gateway and a hub at the same time.

Through the principle of economics of agglomeration and notable accessibility advantages, a region can accumulate several major intermodal infrastructures, namely port and airport terminals. When these nodes act as an interface they can be characterized as gateway systems (or regions) that play a substantial role in the global distribution of freight, connecting major systems of circulation. Gateways also act as bottlenecks in global freight distribution imposing capacity constraints because of capacity, infrastructure or supply chain management.

Services are following a spatial trend which appears to be increasingly different than that of production. As production disperses worldwide to lower cost locations, high-level services increasingly concentrate in a relatively few large metropolitan areas, labeled as world cities. They are centers for financial services (banking, insurance), head offices of major multinational corporations, nexuses for the arts and the seats of major governments. Thus, gateways and world cities may not necessarily correspond as locations, underlining the ongoing dichotomy between central places and transport places. This is particularly the case for containerized traffic which is linked with new manufacturing clusters and the usage of intermediary hubs.

The global system of freight circulation is articulated by major gateway regions (or gateway systems), often composed of a cluster of ports and airports within a metropolitan area (Figure 2.12). This does not mean that ports and airports are functionally integrated (they are not), but that the region they service is a major load center serviced by a variety of globally oriented supply chains, some using the ports, while others are using the airports. The Global Gateways Index represents the relative importance of a

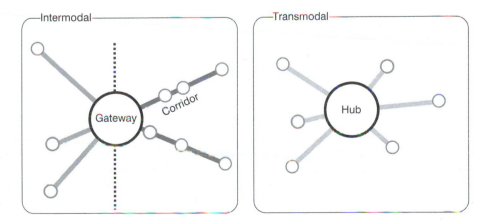

Figure 2.11   Gateways and hubs

Figure 2.12 The World Gateways Index, 2010

Note: The Global Gateways Index is the weighted sum of the global share of the container and air cargo traffic of a metropolitan area. It considers a sample of 198 cities that have either a significant container or significant air cargo traffic. The weight attributed to the container and air cargo components is related to their share of the value of global trade (85 percent and 15 percent respectively).

metropolitan area in the global container and air cargo transport system: two long-distance trade modes. The index does not include crossborder traffic, which would make cities such as Detroit rank much higher. Global gateways show a high concentration level, with the 25 largest gateways accounting for an index of 50 percent of the containerized and air freight activity and the 50 largest gateways with an index of 65 percent.

Gateway regions are groupings of gateways that are organized along a major corridor. The most important gateway region is the Pearl River Delta (Hong Kong, Shenzhen and Guangzhou), with a combined index of 10.5 percent of all the world's containerized and air cargo freight. Other significant gateway systems concern the Yangtze River Delta (8.4 percent), the Strait of Malacca (Singapore, 7.6 percent), the Rhine/Scheldt delta for Western Europe (e.g. Antwerp, Rotterdam, 3.9 percent) and Southern California (Los Angeles area, 2.6 percent) for the American West Coast. There are significant variations in the modal composition (and importance) of the gateways. While in the majority of cases containerized traffic dominates the gateway function, air cargo carries a high share in gateways such as Dubai, Seoul and Bangkok. Each of these are major air cargo hubs with an adjacent concentration of high-tech industries.

Services are following a spatial trend which appears to be increasingly different than of production. As production disperses worldwide to lower cost locations, high level services increasingly concentrate into a relatively few large metropolitan areas, labeled as world cities. They are centers for financial services (banking, insurance), head offices of major multinational corporations, nexuses for the arts and the seats of major governments. Thus, gateways and world cities may not necessarily correspond as locations, underlining the ongoing **dichotomy** between central places and transport places. This is particularly the case for containerized traffic which is linked with new manufacturing clusters and the usage of intermediary hubs.

Regional spatial organization

Regions are commonly organized along an interdependent set of cities forming what is often referred as an **urban system**. The key spatial foundation of an urban system is based on a series of market areas, which are a function of the level of activity of each center in relation to the friction of distance. The spatial structure of most regions can be subdivided into three basic components:

- A set of **locations of specialized industries,** such as manufacturing and mining, which tend to group into agglomerations according to location factors such as raw materials, labor and markets. They are often export-oriented industries from which a region derives the bulk of its basic growth.
- A set of **service industry locations**, including administration, finance, retail, whole-sale and other similar services, which tend to agglomerate in a system of central places (cities), providing optimal accessibility to labor or potential customers.
- A pattern of **transport nodes and links,** such as road, railways, ports and airports, which services major centers of economic activity.

Jointly, these components define the spatial order of a region, mostly its organization in a hierarchy of relationships involving flows of people, freight and information. More or less well-defined urban systems spatially translate such development. Many conceptual models have been proposed to explain the relationships between transport, urban systems and regional development, the core/periphery stages of development and the network expansion being among those. Three conceptual categories of regional spatial organization can be observed:

- **Central places/urban systems** models try to find the relationships between the size, the number and the geographic distribution of cities in a region. Many variations of the regional spatial structure have been investigated by the central place theory. The great majority of urban systems have a well-established hierarchy where a few centers dominate. Transportation is particularly important in such a representation, as the organization of central places is based on minimizing the friction of distance. The territorial structure depicted by central place theory is the outcome of a region seeking the provision of services in a (transport) cost-effective way.
- **Growth poles** where economic development is the structural change caused by the growth of new propulsive industries that are the poles of growth. The location of these activities is the catalyst of the regional spatial organization. Growth poles first initiate, then diffuse, development. It attempts to be a general theory of the initiation and diffusion of development models. Growth gets distributed spatially within a regional urban system, but this process is uneven, with the core benefiting first and the periphery eventually becomes integrated in a system of flows. In the growth poles theory transportation is a factor of accessibility which reinforces the importance of poles.
- **Transport corridors** represent an accumulation of flows and infrastructures of various modes and their development is linked with economic, infrastructural and technological processes. When these processes are involving urban development,

urbanization corridors are a system of cities oriented along an axis, commonly fluvial or a coastline, since historically they permitted cities to main transport and commercial relations. Many urban regions such as BosWash (Boston–Washington) or Tokaido (Tokyo–Osaka) share this spatial commonality. Corridors are also structured along articulation points that regulate the flows at the local, regional and global levels either as hubs or gateways. The development of high-speed train systems around the world takes place along major urban corridors and reinforces the existing regional spatial structure.

Local spatial organization

Although transport is an important element in rural spatial organization, it is at the urban level that transportation has the most significant local spatial impact. Urbanization and transport are interrelated concepts, particularly with transport shaping the size and extent of cities. Every city relies on a need for mobility of passengers (residence, work, purchases and leisure) and freight (consumption goods, food, energy, construction materials and waste disposal) and where the main nodes are employment zones. Urban demographic and spatial evolution is translated in space by the breadth and amplitude of movements. Employment and attraction zones are the most important elements shaping the local urban spatial organization:

- **Employment zones**. The growing dissociation between the workplace and the residence is largely due to the success of motorized transport, notably the private automobile. Employment zones being located away from residential zones have contributed to an increase in number and length of commuting trips. Before suburbanization, public transit was wholly responsible for commuting. Today, the automobile supports the majority of these trips. This trend is particularly prevalent in highly populated, industrialized and urbanized zones, notably in North America and Western Europe, but motorization is also a dominant trend in developing countries.
- **Attraction zones**. Attraction zones linked to transport modes are areas to which a majority of the population travels for varied reasons, such as shopping, professional services, education and leisure. As with central place theory, there is a certain hierarchy of services within an urban area, ranging from the central business district (CBD) offering a wide variety of specialized services to small local centers offering basic services such as groceries and personal banking.

The development of cities is conditioned by transport, and several modes, from urban transit to the automobile, have contributed to the creation of urban landscapes. Three distinct phases can be noted:

- **Conventional/classic city**. Constructed for pedestrian interactions and constrained by them, the historic city was compact and limited in size. The emergence of the first urban transit systems in the nineteenth century permitted the extension of the city into new neighborhoods. However, pedestrian movements still accounted for the great majority of movements and the local spatial organization remained compact. Many European and Asian cities still have a significant level of compactness today where urban transit remains a defining element of the spatial organization.
- **Suburbanization**. The advent of more efficient urban transit systems, and later of the automobile, permitted an increased separation between basic urban functions

(residential, industrial and commercial) and their spatial specialization. The rapid expansion of urban areas that resulted, especially in North America, created a new spatial organization, less cohesive than before but still relatively adjacent to the existing urban fabric. Although this process started in the early twentieth century, it accelerated after World War II.

- **Exurbanization**. Additional improvements in mobility favored urban expansion in the countryside, where urban and rural activities are somewhat intermixed. Many cities became extended metropolitan regions, with a wide array of specialized functions including residential areas, commercial centers, industrial parks, logistics centers, recreational areas and high-tech zones. These exurban developments have also been called "edge cities."

The automobile has clearly influenced contemporary spatial organization, but other socioeconomic factors have also shaped urban development such as gentrification and differential changes in land values. The diffusion of the automobile has led to an urban expansion relying on the mobility of individuals and permitting a disorderly growth and an allocation of space between often conflicting urban functions (residential, industrial, commercial). Still, distance decay remains a force shaping urban spatial organization, since suburban and exurban developments tend to occur along concentric rings within large metropolitan areas. Transport thus contributes to the local spatial organization; however, it must also adapt to urban morphologies. Transport networks and urban centers complement and condition each other.

Concept 4 – Transport and location

The importance of transport in location

The location of economic activities is fundamentally based on geographical concepts of the **site and its situation**. The site relates to the characteristics of a specific location, while the situation concerns the relationships of a location in relation to other locations. Historically, specific sites suitable for defense or commerce have been important factors in the location of cities. In addition to being a factor of spatial organization, transportation is linked with the location of economic activities, including retail, manufacturing and services. In a market economy, location is the outcome of a constrained choice where many issues are being considered, transportation being one of them. The goal is to find a suitable location that would maximize the economic returns for this activity. There is a long tradition within economic geography in developing location theories with a view to explain and predict the locational logic of economic activities by incorporating market, institutional and behavioral considerations.

The majority of location theories have an **explicit** or **implicit** role attributed to transport, since accessibility is an important factor in the location preferences of firms and individuals. As there are no absolute rules dictating locational choices, the importance of transport can only be evaluated with varying degrees of accuracy and based upon the context it takes place. At best, the following observations concerning transportation modes and terminals and their importance for location can be made:

- **Ports and airports**. Convergence of related activities around terminals, particularly for ports since inland distribution costs tend to be high. The location and the level of activity of ports and airports are reflective of global trade patterns.

- **Roads and railroads**. A structuring and convergence effect that varies according to the level of accessibility. For rail transport, terminals also have a convergence effect.
- **Telecommunications**. No specific local influence, but the quality of regional and national telecommunication systems tends to ease transactions.

Globalization has been associated with significant changes in business operations and markets. The whole scale of locational considerations has been expanded. Managing operations in such an environment has become increasingly complex, especially with the globalization of production and consumption. Manufacturing strategies tend to use different locations for each component of a product in order to optimize respective comparative advantages and reduce input costs. Transport requirements have proportionally increased to support and organize the related flows. The requirement of faster long-distance transport services has propelled the importance of air transport, especially for freight. Air terminals have thus become a significant location factor for globally oriented activities, which tend to agglomerate in the vicinity. Additionally, the surge in long distance trade has made logistical activities, namely transport terminals and distribution centers, at the forefront of locational considerations. Technological changes have also been linked with the relocation of industrial and even service activities. Global telecommunication facilities can favor the outsourcing of several services to lower cost locations.

Location factors

The location of economic activities is a priori dependent on the nature of the activity itself and on certain location factors such as the attributes of the site, the level of accessibility and the socioeconomic environment (Figure 2.13):

- **Site**. Specific micro-geographical (local) characteristics of the site, including the availability of land, basic utilities, visibility (for activities related to retail or prestige such as head offices), amenities (quality of life) and the level of access to local transportation (such as the proximity to a highway). These factors have an important effect on the costs associated with a location.

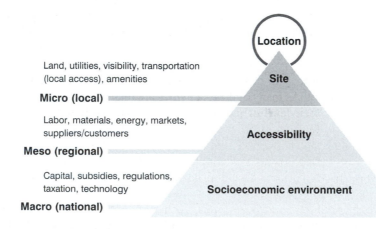

Figure 2.13 Basic location factors

- **Accessibility**. Include a number of opportunity factors related to a location, mainly labor (wages, availability, level of qualification), materials (mainly for raw materials-dependent activities), energy, markets (local, regional and global) and accessibility to suppliers and customers (important for intermediate activities). These factors tend to have a meso (regional) connotation.
- **Socioeconomic environment**. Specific macro-geographical characteristics that can to apply to jurisdictional units (nation, region, municipality). They consider the availability of capital (investment, venture capital), various subsidies and incentives, regulations, taxation and technology.

The role and importance of each factor depends on the nature of the activity and its locational behavior. Although each type of economic activity has its own set of location factors, some general factors can be identified by major economic sectors:

- **Primary economic activities**. Their dominant location factor is related to **environmental endowments**, such as natural resources. For instance, mining takes place where economically recoverable mineral deposits are found and agriculture is subject to environmental constraints such as soil fertility, precipitation and temperature (climate). Primary activities are thus characterized by the most basic location factors but have a strong reliance on transportation since their locations are rarely close to markets and they usually concern ponderous goods. Substantial investments in extraction and distribution infrastructures must thus be made before resources can be brought to markets. The capacity to transport raw materials plays a significant role in the possible development of extractive activities at a location.
- **Secondary economic activities**. Imply a complex web of location factors which, depending upon the industrial sector, relate to labor (cost and/or skill level), energy costs, capital, land, markets and/or proximity of suppliers. Location is thus an important **cost factor** and the general purpose is usually to minimize it. Considering the wide variety of industrial and manufacturing activities, understanding the rationale of each sector is a difficult task that has been subject to many investigations in economic geography. Globalization, recent developments in supply chain management and global production networks have made the situation even more complex with the presence of many intermediaries and significant locational changes. The industrialization of China has been supported by several strategies trying to multiply locational advantages, such as the setting of export-oriented special economic zones and large investment in transport infrastructure.
- **Tertiary economic activities**. Involve activities that are most bound to market proximity, since the capacity to distribute a product or service is their most important location requirement. As many of these activities are retail-oriented, consumer proximity (as well as their level of income) is essential and is directly related to sale levels. The main focus is to maximize sales revenues with location an important **revenue factor**. The retail industry has seen the emergence of large retail stores that maximize sales through economies of scale and local road accessibility. E-commerce also provides a new dynamic where niche retailing markets can be developed in a situation of high product diversity.
- **Quaternary economic activities**. Imply activities not linked to environmental endowments or access to a market, but to high-level services such as banking, insurance, education, research and development. This often relates to the high-technology

sector where innovation is a key commercial factor. With improvements in telecommunications, many of these activities can be located almost anywhere, as demonstrated by the trend to locate call centers offshore. There are still some strong locational requirements for high-technology activities that include proximity to large universities and research centers and to a pool of highly qualified workers (as well as cheap labor for supporting services), availability of venture capital, a high quality of life (cultural amenities) and access to excellent transportation and telecommunication facilities. The sector has shown a propensity at clustering as close inter-firm relations are a factor of innovation.

Each of these sectors thus has its own set of economies related to its relations with production, distribution and consumption. However, basic location strategies appear to be dominantly cost minimization or revenue maximization endeavors. Understanding location factors enables a better overview of the dynamics of the global economy and the associated territorial changes at the global, regional and local levels.

Accessibility and location economies

Since accessibility is predominantly the outcome of transportation activities, namely the capacity of infrastructures to support mobility, it presents the most significant influence of transportation on location. Hence, location (accessibility) and economic activities are interrelated. Accessibility plays an important role by offering more customers through an expanded market area, by making distribution more efficient (in terms of capacity, costs and time) or by enabling more people to reach workplaces (labor cost and qualification). While some transport systems have favored the dispersion of socioeconomic activities (e.g. automobiles and suburbanization), others have favored their concentration (e.g. airports and container terminals). All transport systems are bearers of spatial specialization and configuration.

Activities involved in production (manufacturing), distribution (transportation) and consumption (retail) are constantly seeking economies to improve their competitiveness and increase their market share (Figure 2.14). This is commonly done by opting for a specific location and type of facility:

- **Economies of transportation**. Relate to the benefits that lower transport costs may grant to specific activity sectors. For production, it relates to a location that minimizes total transport costs (accessibility to suppliers and customers) and thus lowers production unit costs. These considerations are at the core of classic industrial location theories where transport-dependent activities seek to minimize total transport costs. Economies of transportation in distribution consider the management of transport chains, often of several modes, to reduce total transport costs (modal and intermodal). Some are elements of transport costs in production, while others are elements of transport costs in consumption. Transport costs must be considered in a wider context where the quality and reliability of transport is of growing importance. It has been demonstrated that travel time, instead of distance, is the determining factor behind commuting ranges. For freight distribution, while cost factors are significant, there is a growing importance of the concept of reliability. Economies of transportation in consumption can be derived from economies in distribution as well as accessibility (proximity) to customers.

	Production	Distribution	Consumption
Economies of transportation	Lower unit costs through accessibility to suppliers and customers	Lower unit distribution costs through transport chains management	Lower unit output costs through accessibility to suppliers and customers
Economies of scale	Lower unit costs with larger plants	Lower unit transport costs through larger modes and terminals	Lower unit costs with larger retail outlets
Economies of scope	Lower unit output costs with more product types	Lower transport costs with bundling of different loads	Product diversification attracts more customers
Economies of agglomeration	Industrial and service linkages with manufacturing clusters	Lower input costs with clustering of distribution activities	Lower input costs with clustering of retail activities
Economies of density	Increased accessibility to labor (skills) with higher densities	Lower unit distribution costs with higher densities	Increased accessibility to goods and services with higher densities

Figure 2.14 Main types of economies in production, distribution and consumption

- **Economies of scale**. Relate to the benefits that scale may offer to activity sectors. For production, the larger the production plant, the lower the unit costs, since fixed costs (e.g. the factory) are spread over a larger quantity of units. For transportation, the principle involves unit costs reduction derived from larger modes (e.g. mega-ships), terminals and distribution centers: the massification of transportation. For consumption, larger retail outlets tend to reduce input costs, underlining the success of large megastore chains such as Wal-Mart. This concept also implies that **diseconomies of scale** can be reached after a certain size, particularly through growing complexity and management costs. Diseconomies vary substantially by the type of activity; steel production is prone to large economies of scale, while restoration much less so.
- **Economies of scope**. Relate to the benefits derived by expanding the range of goods and services. For production, they are commonly based on product diversification and flexible manufacturing systems able to produce a variety of products in view of changes in the demand. For distribution, economies of scope are very important and commonly achieved when a transporter is able to bundle several different loads into fewer loads. For instance, a container ship is able to bundle the loads (and offer economies of scale) for several customers in often completely different sectors of activity that are simply sharing a similar origin and destination. For consumption, activities offering a wider range of goods or services are usually able to attract more customers, since they have more choices. Economies of scale and economies of scope are highly related.
- **Agglomeration economies**. The benefits derived from locating in proximity to other activities, even if the location is suboptimal. Often referred to as the clustering effect

and involves the sharing of common infrastructures such as roads and utilities. Clustering continues to be a powerful force in location as the reduction in transport costs favors the agglomeration of retail, manufacturing and distribution activities at specific locations. For production, industrial and service linkages are offered as respective suppliers and customers benefit from close proximity and interactions. The outcome is a manufacturing cluster. A similar trend is observed in freight distribution as logistics activities tend to cluster and often co-locate next to an intermodal terminal. The distribution centers of parcels companies are commonly located directly adjacent to runways so that their air freight services can be tightly synchronized with the consolidation and deconsolidation of air parcels. For intermodal rail terminals, inland ports facilities are built over the principle of co-location. For consumption, commercial districts or shopping malls are common expressions of the benefits of agglomeration.

- **Economies of density**. The benefits derived from the increasing density of features on the costs of accessing them. For production, this could involve access to a larger labor pool (and skills) or resources (e.g. mining, agriculture). Higher market densities reduce distribution costs, as shorter distances service the same number of customers and the same freight volume. A similar rationale applies to consumption where higher market densities involve higher accessibility levels to goods and services. For instance, if the customer density is sufficient, a retailer can achieve several types of cost savings by locating its stores in proximity to one another. Such a structure reduces logistics and delivery costs by sharing a distribution center. High densities can also lead to diseconomies, particularly with congestion.

Because of the level of accessibility they provide, new transport infrastructures influence the setting of economic activities. It becomes a particularly strong effect when new infrastructures are added to an undeveloped (or underdeveloped) site and thus locational decisions tend to be simpler and unhindered by the existing spatial structure. The locational effects on activities are not always automatic or evident. They are important, however, when infrastructure is accompanied by social, economic and urban transformations. New infrastructures therefore play a catalytic role, because they are able to transform space through land use and mobility changes.

Concept 5 – Future transportation

Past trends and uncertain future

In 200 years of history since the introduction of forms of mechanized transportation, the capacity, speed, efficiency and geographical coverage of transport systems have improved dramatically. The goal to move passengers and freight faster, in greater quantities, safely and efficiently remains the core motivation to improve transport technology. Modes, terminals and networks alike have been subject to remarkable changes that come into two functional aspects:

- **Revolutionary changes**. Concerns a completely new technology that creates new markets and growth opportunities for transportation and the economy as well. It often marks the obsolescence of an existing transport mode as the new mode has substantial cost, capacity or time benefits. Revolutionary changes tend to be rare but profound, since they commonly involve the setting of entirely new networks. They commonly cannot be predicted, but once they occur it is possible to assess their potential impacts. Yet, in the early phase of their introduction, the potential of an innovation can be exaggerated.

- **Incremental (evolutionary) changes**. Concerns the stepwise improvement of an existing transport technology and operations. This leads to increases in productivity with more capacity, lower costs and better performance of the involved mode or terminal. Incremental changes are possible to extrapolate but the rate of change they bring is difficult to assess.

Considering these changes, the following observations can be made:

- Each mode, due to its geographical and technical specificities, was characterized by different technologies and different rates of innovation and diffusion. A transport innovation can thus be an additive/competitive force where a new technology expands or makes an existing mode more efficient and competitive. It can also be a destructive force when a new technology marks the obsolescence and demise of an existing mode often through a paradigm shift. Still, in many cases an older technology will endure because of its wide level of adoption, utilization and accumulated capital investment. This is commonly known as **path dependency**. Vested interests in an existing mode, particularly if publicly owned, may also delay or even prevent an innovation to take place.
- Technological innovation was linked with **faster and more efficient transport systems**. This process implied a space/time convergence where a greater amount of space could be exchanged with a lesser amount of time. The comparative advantages of space could thus be more efficiently used.
- Technological evolution in the transport sector has been linked with the phases of **economic development of the world economy**. Transportation and economic development are consequently interlinked, as one cannot occur without the other.

One of the pitfalls in discussing future trends is to look at the future as an **extrapolation of the past**. It is assumed that the future will involve a technology that already exists, but simply operating at an extended scale beyond what is currently possible. It can be seen as an incremental change bias. The parameters of such an extrapolation commonly involve a greater speed, mass availability, a higher capacity and/or a better accessibility, all of which imply similar or lower costs. Popular literature (such as *Popular Mechanics* or *Popular Science*) of the first half of the twentieth century is abundant with extrapolations and speculations, some spectacular, about how transportation technology would look like in the (their) future. Looking at such perspectives is labeled "paleo-futurology": how the past perceived the future.

At the start, the prediction of future outcomes must consider what is within the realm of forecasting, scenario building or speculation. Forecasting tries to evaluate near-term outcomes by considering that parameters do not change much, while scenario building tries to assess a series of possible outcomes based upon expected fluctuation in key parameters. A common failure of predictions is their incapacity to anticipate **paradigm shifts** brought by new technologies as well as economic and social conditions. Another flaw relates to the expectation of a massive diffusion of a new technology with profound economic and social impacts, and this over a short period of time (the "silver bullet effect"). This rarely takes place, as most innovations go through a cycle of introduction, adoption, growth, peak and then obsolescence, which can take several years, if not decades. Even in the telecommunication sector, which accounts for the fastest diffusion levels, the adoption of a technology takes place over a decade.

Any discussion about the future of transportation must start with the realization that much of what is being presented as plausible is unlikely to become a reality, more so if the extrapolation goes several decades into the future. Thus, as much as someone would have been unable at the beginning of the twentieth century to even dream of what transportation would look like half a century later (e.g. air transportation and the automobile), we may be facing the same limitations at the beginning of the twenty-first century. However, since substantial technological innovations took place in the twentieth century and the laws of physics are much better understood, we are likely better placed to evaluate which technological trends will emerge in the near future. Still, the socioeconomic impacts of new transport technologies and systems remain complex to assess and rarely lead to accurate assessment.

Automation and information technologies

Since the introduction of commercial jet planes, high-speed train networks and the container in the late 1960s, no significant technological changes have impacted passengers and freight transport systems, at least from a paradigm shift perspective. The early twenty-first century is an era of car and truck dependency, which tends to constrain the development of alternative modes of transportation, as most of the technical improvements aim to ensure the dominance of oil as a source of energy. However, with uncertainties about the future of oil production (in terms of price, capacity and availability), there is evidence that the end of the dominance of the internal combustion engine is approaching. In spite of significant fluctuations, energy prices are expected to continue their upward trend, triggering the most important technological transition in transportation since the introduction of the automobile.

The development of a set of information and communication technologies (ICT) to improve the speed, efficiency, safety and reliability of movements relies on complete or partial automation of the vehicle, transshipment (for freight) and control. These systems could involve the improvement of existing modes such as automated highway systems, or the creation of new modes and new transshipment systems such as for public transit and freight transportation (automated terminals). The diffusion of global positioning systems and mobile technology has already resulted in substantial benefits in terms of improved navigation and congestion mitigation.

On-demand car services are emerging, creating a hybrid operational model between the taxi and the private vehicle. With information technologies, fleets of cars can be managed and leased in real time, which should result in fewer vehicles being required to convey a similar level of mobility. In turn, less parking space is required, improving congestion in high-density areas. This also changes the ownership of vehicles, which have been predominantly private, towards a leasing system.

Driverless vehicles are a further evolution of the integration of ICT into transportation, but in an urban setting the large number of safety factors to consider makes such implementation more of a social than a technical constraint. There are other applications of the driverless technology, particularly in air transportation, which would raise many safety considerations. Therefore, remote-controlled airplanes are more likely to be initially applied to air cargo operations. A similar potential exists for maritime transportation, as recent decades have seen automation considerably reduce the crews required to man ships.

Driverless vehicles are also likely to improve the mobility of more marginal groups (e.g. elderly and people with disabilities), but, just as importantly, they would enable a more efficient use of vehicle assets. With fewer accidents, the social costs of using the automobile would drop, as well as insurance rates. This raises the question of the role of mass transit in such a context where users could have access to mobility almost on demand. This question is a particular relevance, since many transit systems are heavily subsidized. Many gains still remain to be achieved through the better management of existing infrastructures and vehicles. Yet the diffusion of ICT is influenced by the business models of the transport sectors in which it takes place.

Alternative modes and fuels

There is a range of modes that could replace but more likely complement existing modes, particularly for the transportation of passengers. Once such technology is Maglev, short for "magnetic levitation," which has the advantage of having no friction (except air friction), enabling operational speeds of 500–600 km per hour. Higher speeds are possible if the train circulates in a low pressure tube. This represents an alternative for passengers and freight land movements in the range of 75 to 1,000 km. Maglev improves on the existing technology of high-speed train networks, which face technical limitations at speeds higher than 300 km per hour. In fact, Maglev is the first fundamental innovation in railway transportation since the Industrial Revolution. The first commercial Maglev system opened in Shanghai in 2003 and has an operational speed of about 440 km per hour. There are further variations of the guided tube concept involving capsules circulating on air cushion (dubbed as "hyperloop").

Alternative fuels mainly concern existing mode but the sources of fuel, or the engine technology, are modified. For instance, **hybrid vehicles** involve the use of two types of motor technologies, commonly an internal combustion engine and an electric motor. Simply speaking, breaking is used to recharge a battery, which then can be used to power the electric motor. Although gasoline appears to be the most prevalent fuel choice, diesel has a high potential since it can also be made from coal or organic fuels. Diesel can thus be a fuel part of a lower petroleum dependency energy strategy. Hybrid engines have often been perceived as a transitional technology to cope with higher energy prices. There is also a possibility of greater reliance on **biofuels** as an additive (and possibly a supplement) to petroleum, but their impacts on food production must be carefully assessed.

Still, **electric car engines** are one of the most promising alternative technologies. In addition to having close to zero emissions, electric vehicles are less complex mechanically since they have fewer moving parts (no internal combustion engine and transmission). Such vehicles could be cheaper to build and maintain, increasing the range of manufacturing locations. The usage of electric vehicles continues to raise the question of the supply of electricity. Therefore, the diffusion of electric vehicles must include strategies for the supply of electric power, preferably from alternative sources such as solar or wind energy.

More far-reaching in terms of energy transition are **fuel cells**, which involve an electric generator using the catalytic conversion of hydrogen and oxygen. The electricity generated can be used for many purposes, such as supplying an electric motor. Current technological prospects do not foresee high output fuel cells, indicating they are applicable only to light vehicles, notably cars, or to small power systems. Nevertheless, fuel cells represent a low environmental impact alternative to generate energy. Additional challenges in the use of fuel cells involve hydrogen storage (especially in a vehicle) as well as establishing a distribution system to supply consumers.

Transportation modes can also be introduced to deal with specific transportation constraints that mainstream transportation modes are less able to accommodate. The use of a new generation of dirigibles to transport mostly freight in difficult-to-access areas (such as the Arctic) is such an example. On the other side of the mobility spectrum urban transportation shows some potential for a more effective use of alternative modes, such as greater reliance on cycling and walking, particularly in car-dependent cities, and this would be for passengers and freight transportation alike.

Economic and regulatory trends

Through recent history, there are few, if any, cases where a revolutionary transport technology was the outcome of a public endeavor. Still, the public sector came to play a growing role as transport innovations became more complex and required a concerted approach in infrastructure, management or regulation. For instance, the massive diffusion of the automobile in the twentieth century was associated with regulations concerning operations (e.g. speed limits), safety (e.g. seatbelts), emissions, as well as public investments in road infrastructures. While vehicle production came to be predominantly private, road infrastructures were perceived as a public good and provided as such. Similar processes took place for maritime transportation (port authorities), air transportation (national carriers and airport authorities), rail (national carriers), public transit (transit agencies) and telecommunications (frequencies). The complexity of transport systems, particularly with intermodalism, is likely to rise in the future – will this complexity be linked with additional public sector involvement?

Future transportation systems are also facing growing concerns related to energy, the environment, safety and security. Transport systems are either going to be developed to accommodate additional demands for mobility or to offer alternatives (or a transition) to existing demand. An important challenge relies in the balance between market forces and public policy, as both have a role to play in the transition. Since transportation is a derived demand, a core aspect of future transportation pertains to the **level of economic activity** and to what extent this level will be linked with specific passengers and freight volumes. In recent years, economic development and globalization have been important factors behind the surge in mobility. It remains to be seen to what extent this process will endure and if the global transportation system will become more globalized or regionalized:

- **Globalization**. Assumes affordable energy prices, growing accessibility and an enduring openness to trade. The exploitation of comparative advantages continues, leading to a more complex lattice of trade and transportation systems. In addition to active networks of regional transportation are superposed various transnational relations.
- **Regionalization**. Assumes higher energy prices and a commercial environment that is more prone to protectionism, all of which conveys more friction to long-distance interactions. The exploitation of comparative advantages is thus done on a more regional foundation. This environment does not forbid international trade, but the latter mostly concern goods and services that cannot be effectively substituted. It is also prone to the setting of more effective regional transport systems.

A fundamental component of future transport systems, freight and passengers alike, is that they must provide **increased flexibility** and **adaptability** to changing market circumstances (origins, destinations, costs, speed, etc.), some of which are unforeseen, while complying to an array of environmental, safety and security regulations. This cannot be effectively planned and governments have consistently been poor managers and slow to understand technological changes, often impeding them through regulations and preferences for specific modes or for specific technologies. Regulations have the tendency to **prevent technological innovations** and their potential positive impacts. This is often referred to as the **status quo bias,** where the dominant strategy of a public agency is to maintain existing conditions. Also, if a new mode or technology competes with a nationalized transport system, then it is likely that the government will intervene to prevent its emergence with regulations (e.g. permits) and delays (e.g. public safety hearings). Recent history indicates that it was when deregulation took place that the most significant changes and innovations resulted for transportation. One of the most salient examples is the Staggers Act (1980) in American rail transportation, which was linked with substantial productivity improvements and new investments.

It is thus likely that future transport systems will be the outcome of **private initiatives,** with the market (transport demand) the ultimate judge about the true potential of a new transport technology. Economic history has shown that market forces will always try to find and adopt the most efficient form of transportation available. Some transport systems or technologies have become obsolete and have been replaced by others that are more efficient and cost-effective based upon the prevailing input conditions such as labor, energy and commodities. This fundamental behavior is likely to endure in the setting of future transportation systems, which will reflect the level of abundance (or scarcity) of resources, energy, space and time.

The drivers of change for the transportation system come in six major categories; policy, demography and society, energy and environment, technology, economics and finance (Figure 2.15). Each plays a role individually and in conjunction. It is therefore virtually impossible to establish outcomes accurately, as there are too many interrelationships and uncertainties, particularly if a longer time frame is considered. It is, however, possible to identify trends that may impact each driver individually and try to assess how these trends will shape different components of the transport system:

- **Policy**. The inherent scale and complexity of transportation systems, particularly when they span multiple jurisdictions, will require novel approaches in governance. The role and impact of government policy is commonly subject to cycles of increasing commitments followed by different forms of retrenchment (e.g. privatization) as regulations lead to unproductive practices and unintended consequences. In spite of deregulation, the transportation is subject to many forms of regulations pertaining to safety, security and the environment. These regulations, as well as the taxation of transport activities, add to the management complexity and the cost burden.
- **Demography and society**. Population growth is expected to endure in many parts of the world until the mid-twenty-first century, a process which will be linked with demands in mobility and increased consumption. Yet, in other parts of the world, such as in Western Europe, North America and Japan, the rapid aging of the population and more people of retirement age will be associated with changes in mobility and lower levels of consumption per capita. Urbanization is expected to continue in many developing countries, underlining issues linked with the urban mobility of passengers and freight. As a greater share of the global population lives in urban

Figure 2.15 Drivers of change for future transportation

Source: Adapted from ICF International (2008) "Long range strategic issues facing the transportation industry," Final Future-Focused Research Framework, National Cooperative Highway Research Program, Project 20–80, Task 2.

areas, additional pressures are felt on terminal facilities, such as airports, railyards and ports, that find themselves with limited room for expansion. New sites are therefore located further away from existing activity centers. It also remains to be seen how changes in work patterns, such as a greater share of the population in the service sector, will be reflected in mobility.

- **Energy and environment**. Issues related to the availability of energy and raw materials, particularly fossil fuels, are likely to endure and become more acute. This will be reflected in higher energy prices and, since each mode has a different elasticity, the comparative advantages of modal options will change towards the most energy-efficient transport chains. A whole range of alternative fuels will be brought forward and transportation activities will increasingly be considered within a sustainability framework. Climate change is also an issue that may add to the sustainability of transport systems, particularly in terms of a more stringent regulatory framework.

- **Technology**. Technological innovation is a very difficult process to anticipate and its impacts even more complex to assess. For transportation, technological innovations either concern the management, the mode (or infrastructure) or the motion (engine). It is expected that information technologies (IT) are likely to transform mobility with an improved command of flows and supply chain management practices. This is commonly linked with a better utilization of existing assets and derived productivity gains. IT also has a high potential to contribute to trade facilitation through more efficient customs procedures as cargo information is standardized and exchangeable. Improvements in materials and engines are also highly possible with the expected benefits on modes and terminals, namely in terms of performance.

- **Economics**. Economic development and global trade have been significant vectors for the growth of mobility. Yet this process is subject to cycles of growth and recession and limits in credit-based consumption. The level of activity and the structure of national economies, as well as their trade patterns, are important influence on national and global transport systems. Economic integration is likely to endure, which will favor more comprehensive and seamless regional transport systems. The relative price of transportation is also linked with the viability of several supply chains and the comparative advantages they extract value from. As transportation costs are expected to rise on the medium term, namely due to fossil fuels, transport demand, from commuting to global supply chains, will be readjusted accordingly in volume but also in the locations they concern.
- **Finance**. Transportation projects, due to their size and technological complexity, are becoming increasingly capital intensive. In several cases, only the largest financial institutions, often in partnership with the public sector, can provide an adequate level of capitalization. The value of transportation assets and the revenue they generate are likely to be important factors behind their financing. Thus, a transport innovation cannot be adopted effectively if financing cannot be secured. Financial considerations are also linked with demographic issues, namely aging. An aging population tends to be more wealth-consuming as opposed to wealth-producing, which may undermine the availability of capital.

Anticipating future transport trends is very hazardous, since technology is a factor that historically created paradigm shifts and is likely to do so again in the future, with unforeseen consequences. For instance, in the late nineteenth century one of the major concerns about future transportation for London, England, was that by the mid-twentieth century the amount of horse manure generated by transport activities would become unmanageable . . .

CASE STUDY   Transport corridors

The spatial structure of corridors

Transport corridors are considered to be the backbones of transportation networks, linking major centers of articulation (e.g. gateways and hubs) and facing a convergence of freight and passenger flows. Most often, they lie at the intersection of economic, demographic and geographic processes, as they perform both market-serving and market-connecting functions. Thus, the corridor as a notion is neither temporally nor spatially immutable, but rather dynamic, contingent on such key factors as economic context (e.g. trade liberalization), investments in infrastructures, and technological changes (e.g. information corridors) and policies. Corridors come in two main categories:

- **Formal corridors**. These tend to be constructs trying to expand the planning and investment framework of public and private actors along them. On many occasions a form of governance, or at least a forum, has been set in place to address some of its challenges.
- **Functional corridors**. These represent an existing structure of flows along some infrastructure. The corridor is thus an operational reality.

The most structured corridors are obviously those that combine formal and functional characteristics. Transport corridors can also display physical variations on a modal basis as infrastructure layout becomes a determining factor. While airline flow configurations show greater autonomy, rail, road and maritime transport rely more on accessible physical infrastructures. Being fundamentally a spatial notion, transport corridors are observable throughout the entire spectrum of geographic scales: from an urban setting, to a regional level (e.g. Boston–Washington), to a national (e.g. the Interstate and the Trans-Canada Highway) and an international scale (e.g. the Trans-European transport network, the Eurasian landbridge).

As such, corridors are a fundamental structure shaping economic development. They involve exchange between firms in order to achieve greater efficiencies in their production systems and supply chains, a process commonly supported by various stakeholders, such as regional governments, promoting economic development. The main economic rationale underlining the economic efficiency of corridors is based on:

- The greater **capacity** of corridors in supporting trade volumes based upon the principle of **economies of scale** in transportation. This is likely to be the single most important factor behind the creation of corridors.
- Better **integration between production and distribution** due to cost and time efficiency along corridors. The corridor becomes an intermodal supply chain composed of gateways and inland ports.
- Greater **reliability of distribution** because of transport performance, but also because of a more coordinated governance (such as identifying critical infrastructure) and more efficient crossborder flows (for transnational corridors).

There is also a risk common to most corridors to reach various **diseconomies**. The most prevalent is congestion, as the heavy usage of infrastructures leads to capacity limits. Another concerns higher costs due to real-estate pressures, since the land along the corridor is more valuable because of its commercial potential. This can be an issue along high-density corridors in Asia (e.g. Tokaido in Japan), Western Europe or the Eastern Seaboard in North America.

The North American landbridge

Rail freight in North America, and in the United States in particular, has experienced a remarkable growth since deregulation in the 1980s. A significant share of this transformation concerns the emergence of long-distance rail freight corridors linking the two major gateway systems of North America: Southern California and New York/New Jersey via Chicago. The North American landbridge represents the most efficient landbridge in the world, which considerably reduces distances between the East and the West coasts, also includes a Canadian (Vancouver–Montreal–Halifax) and a Mexican section (Salina Cruz–Coatzacoalcos). Several connectors linking specific regions and networks are to be considered. As opposed to the Eurasian landbridge, the American landbridge has the advantage of providing a transcontinental link through a single country (Canada, USA or Mexico). Thus, the North American landbridge is mainly the outcome of growing transpacific trade and has undergone the containerized revolution; container traffic represented approximately 80 percent of all rail intermodal moves. Landbridges are particularly the outcome of a cooperation between rail operators eager to get lucrative long-distance traffic, maritime shippers eager to reduce shipping time

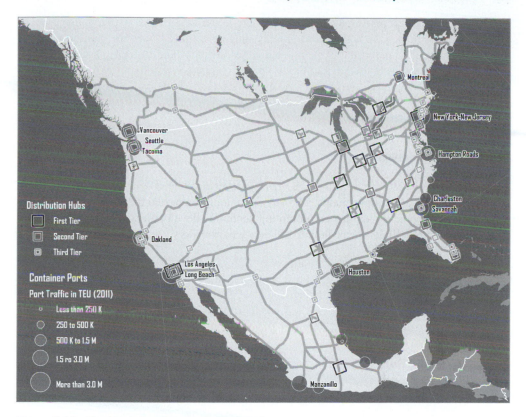

Figure 2.16 The North American landbridge

and costs, particularly from Asia, and freight forwarders looking at options to service the needs of their customers.

With the North American landbridge, an alternative to freight shipments across the Panama Canal is thus available. For instance, a container coming from Singapore takes 36 days to reach New York using the Panama Canal sea route (the average figure is about 21 days between Asia and the East Coast). The same journey takes 19 days if the landbridge is used (doublestack rail transport using the Seattle–Chicago–New York rail chain). On average, transport services between the East Coast of the United States and Pacific Asia are reduced from between 6 days and 2 weeks, depending on the case. The North American landbridge is also competing for a market share of the traffic between Europe and Asia. Maritime shippers require on average 5–6 weeks to service the harbors of Tokyo and Rotterdam. With the landbridge, this time is reduced to about 3 weeks with a 6-day railway journey across North America. Yet, this option is not much used as, post-Panamax, containership using the Suez Canal is the most cost-effective and reliable option to service European markets. It takes about 3.8 days to connect Los Angeles and Chicago and an additional 2.8 days to connect Chicago to New York. Alternatively, the Vancouver–Chicago connection takes about 6 days with the new Prince Rupert–Chicago link that can be done in about 4 days because of the lack of congestion, both at the port and along the long-distance rail corridor.

With the landbridge service, several maritime companies abandoned the Panama Canal and were able to shift to post-Panamax-class containerships for transpacific services. Their productivity increased and long-distance shipping costs were reduced proportionally as maritime shippers were able to use larger ships with a higher level of service frequency. A higher capacity can thus be achieved with the same number of ships. Yet, the landbridge is facing challenges, as labor and capacity issues along the West Coast have resulted in maritime shipping companies relying more on the all-water route to service East Coast ports. The expansion of the Panama Canal is also expected to impact the North American landbridge by making the use of East Coast ports to service the hinterland more cost-effective.

The Eurasian landbridge

The idea of linking the Far East and Europe by rail takes its origin from the construction of the Trans-Siberian Railway linking Moscow to Vladivostok, which was completed in 1916. With a length of 9,200 km it is the longest rail segment in the world. It was initially used solely as an inland rail link, but in the 1960s the Soviet Union started offering a landbridge service from Vladivostok using the Trans-Siberian to reach Western Europe. However, geopolitical considerations limited the adoption of this trade corridor by international shipping companies. In addition, the collapse of the Soviet Union in the early 1990s created a context of geopolitical instability within Russia and its former republics, as well as a lack of investments and maintenance over the existing rail and terminal facilities. The idea of using the corridor as a transcontinental and transnational route was abandoned.

The beginning of the twenty-first century has, however, brought renewed interest in a long-distance rail connection between Asia and Europe, especially with the booming

Figure 2.17 The Eurasian landbridge

Asian trade and increasing pressure to ship containerized freight in a time-sensitive manner over long distances. These connections came to be known as the Trans-Asian Railway, the Northern East–West corridor or the Eurasian landbridge (or the New Silk Road or the "One Belt, One Road" initiative). The main route uses the Trans-Siberian Railway, either branching to Vladivostok with connections to eastern China, branching to Kazakhstan, entering western China at Druzhba and then through the Lanzhou rail hub and onward to the coast of China; or branching in Mongolia to enter China at Erenhot and then to the main Beijing hub.

All the necessary infrastructure exists to ensure the setting and operations of the Eurasian landbridge, particularly along the Trans-Siberian, which is double-tracked and electrified. The question remains to improve some segments to ensure better integration of all the elements of this very complex multinational transport chain. Among the numerous challenges the corridor is facing are:

- **Multinational cooperation**. There are seven countries involved in rail land segment that are politically, economically and culturally very different. Unlike the North American landbridge, where rail segments are entirely contained within an individual nation (US, Canada or Mexico) and owned by large rail companies, the multitude of actors require a level of multinational cooperation. In 2006, the Trans-Asian Railway Network Agreement was signed by most of the countries the Eurasian landbridge is going through. This agreement tried to coordinate rail investments, customs procedures and the setting of long-distance rail corridors. However, a transport chain is as reliable as its weakest link. Kazakhstan, parts of Siberia (semi-autonomous administrative divisions) and even some parts of western China present some political risks. It is thus essential to ensure cargo security along the entire transport chain, as well as the continuity of rail operations.

- **Break of gauge**. The rail system operates on two gauges, standard (1.435 m: China and most of Western Europe) and broad (1.520 m: Russia and some Scandinavian countries), which imposes a technical challenge. It requires reloading or an adaptation of the equipment to gauge-change. Moving cargo between China and Germany would involve two gauge changes: a switch from the Chinese standard gauge to the Russian broad gauge; and a switch from the Russian broad gauge to the European standard gauge. At each gauge change, containers are transloaded from one train to the other, side by side, in a Thruport-like facility. Although containerization enables an efficient transfer of cargo, this still involves additional costs and delays.

- **Economics**. Long-distance rail services are facing several economic challenges undermining their commercial potential. This is particularly the case for the Eurasian landbridge. First, there are no double-stack services on the Eurasian landbridge, which significantly reduces the economic efficiency of rail. This is further exacerbated by the use of shorter trains. Second, the usual optimal distance for rail freight services is around 3,000 km (in North America it can easily go to 5,000–6,000 km for double-stack services), while the Eurasian landbridge involves three or four times that distance. It is thus very difficult to make these services profitable, because of the higher transport costs involved for such distances. The third challenge concerns transit time. While reaching European locations such as Germany from China takes about 15 days, going further inside Europe can take up to 21 days, which is close to the same time it takes for a maritime service to reach Europe from China. Servicing European locations in about 2 weeks has some commercial advantages for many goods, particularly those of high value, but once this threshold is exceeded maritime services start to make more sense, since they are much cheaper compared to the marginal additional time they imply. Fourth, we must look at the cargo itself. It can be difficult to find backhaul opportunities that would make the whole service more profitable. Since the Asia–Europe trade is highly imbalanced, the Eurasian land-bridge is facing a challenge similar to maritime transportation, such as the reposi-tioning of empty containers and equipment. It is also worth considering that, during winter times, the Eurasian landbridge is going through regions experiencing very low temperatures. This is not suitable for certain cargo types and would require temper-ature control equipment.

In spite of these challenges, the prospects of the Eurasian landbridge remain positive. For China, an opportunity to develop the interior provinces and avoid congestion at the coastal ports could also be partially fulfilled by the Eurasian landbridge. In January 2008 a long-distance service called the "Beijing–Hamburg Container Express" was inaugur-ated. The 10,000 km service takes 15 days to link the Chinese capital to the German port city, going through Mongolia, the Russian Federation, Belarus and Poland. The mari-time journey covering the same markets would take about 30 days. In 2014, the longest commercial rail service in the world was achieved when a train carrying 82 containers traveled from the city of Yiwu (a major manufacturing cluster in Zhejiang province) to Madrid, a journey of 12,800 km that took 21 days.

Bibliography

Ausubel, J.H. and C. Marchetti (2001) "The evolution of transportation." *Industrial Physicist* April/May: 20–24.

Bernstein, W.J. (2008) *A Splendid Exchange: How Trade Shaped the World*. New York: Atlantic Monthly Press.

Clark, G. (2008) *A Farewell to Alms: A Brief Economic History of the World*. Princeton: Princeton University Press.

Givoni, M. (2006) "Development and impact of the modern high-speed train: a review." *Transport Reviews* 26(5): 593–611.

Gottmann, J. (1961) *Megalopolis: The Urbanized Northeastern Seaboard of the United States*. New York: Twentieth Century Fund.

Harris, C. and E. Ullman (1945) "The nature of cities." *Annals of the American Academy of Political Science* 242: 7–17.

Henderson, J.V., Z. Shalizi and A.J. Venables (2000) "Geography and development." *Journal of Economic Geography* 1: 81–106.

Lundgren, N.G. (1996) "Bulk trade and maritime transport costs: the evolution of global markets." *Resources Policy* 22(1): 5–32.

McQuaid, R.W., et al. (2004) *The Importance of Transport in Business Location Decisions*. London: Department for Transport.

Rioux, J.-P. (1989) *La Révolution industrielle, 1780–1880*. Paris: Editions du Seuil.

Taaffe, E.J., H.L. Gauthier and M.E. O'Kelly (1996) *Geography of Transportation*, 2nd edition. Upper Saddle River, NJ: Prentice Hall.

US Department of Transportation (2015) *2015 OST-R Transportation Technology Scan: A Look Ahead*. Cambridge, MA: Volpe National Transportation Systems Center.

Weber, A. (1909; translation 1929) *Alfred Weber's Theory of the Location of Industries*. Chicago: University of Chicago Press.

3 Transportation, economy and society

Transport systems are closely related to socioeconomic changes. The mobility of people and freight and levels of accessibility are at the core of this relationship. Economic opportunities are likely to arise where transportation infrastructures are able to answer mobility needs and ensure access to markets and resources. From the Industrial Revolution in the nineteenth century to globalization and economic integration processes of the late twentieth and early twenty-first centuries, regions of the world have been affected differently by economic development. International, regional and local transportation systems alike have become fundamental components of economic activities. A growing share of the wealth is thus linked to trade and distribution. However, even if transportation has positive impacts on socioeconomic systems, there are also negative consequences such as congestion, accidents and mobility gaps. Transportation is also a commercial activity derived from operational attributes such as costs, capacity, efficiency, reliability and speed. Transportation systems are evolving within a complex set of relationships between transport supply – reflecting the operational capacity of the network – and transport demand – the mobility requirements of an economy.

Concept 1 – Transportation and economic development

Authors: Dr Jean-Paul Rodrigue and Dr Theo Notteboom

The economic importance of transportation

Development is related to improving the welfare of a society through appropriate social, political and economic conditions. The expected outcomes are quantitative and qualitative improvements in **human capital** (e.g. income and education levels) as well as **physical capital** such as infrastructures (utilities, transport, telecommunications). While in previous decades development policies and strategies tended to focus on physical capital, recent years have seen a better balance with the inclusion of human capital issues. Irrespective of the relative importance of physical versus human capital, development cannot occur without either: infrastructures cannot remain effective without proper operations and maintenance, while economic activities cannot take place without an infrastructure.

Because of its intensive use of infrastructures, the transport sector is an important component of the economy and a common tool used for development. This is even more so in a global economy where economic opportunities have been increasingly related to the mobility of people, goods and information. A relationship between the quantity and quality of transport infrastructure and the level of economic development is apparent. High-density transport infrastructure and highly connected networks are commonly associated with high levels of development. When transport systems are efficient, they provide

economic and social opportunities and benefits that result in positive multiplier effects, such as better accessibility to markets, employment and additional investments. When transport systems are deficient in terms of capacity or reliability, they can have an economic cost, such as **reduced or missed opportunities and lower quality of life**.

At an aggregate level, efficient transportation reduces costs in many economic sectors, while inefficient transportation increases these costs. In addition, the impacts of transportation are not always intended and can have unforeseen or unintended consequences. For instance, congestion is often an unintended consequence in the provision of free or low cost transport infrastructure to the users. However, congestion is also the indication of a growing economy where capacity and infrastructure have difficulties keeping up with the rising mobility demands. Transport carries an important social and environmental load, which cannot be neglected. Assessing the economic importance of transportation requires a categorization of the types of impacts it conveys. These involve core (the physical characteristics of transportation), operational and geographical dimensions (Figure 3.1):

- **Core**. The most fundamental impacts of transportation relate to the physical capacity to convey passengers and goods and the associated costs to support this mobility. This involves the setting of routes enabling new or existing interactions between economic entities. Transport developments are commonly associated with lower transport costs, implying that mobility becomes more affordable.
- **Operational**. Improvement in the time performance, notably in terms of reliability, as well as reduced loss or damage. This implies a better utilization level of existing transportation assets benefiting its users, as passengers and freight are conveyed more rapidly and with fewer delays.
- **Geographical**. Access to a wider market base where economies of scale in production, distribution and consumption can be improved. Increases in productivity from access to a larger and more diverse base of inputs (raw materials, parts, energy or labor) and broader markets for diverse outputs (intermediate and finished goods). Another important geographical impact concerns the influence of transport on the location of activities.

Figure 3.1 Economic impacts of transportation infrastructure

The economic importance of the transportation industry can thus be assessed from a macroeconomic and microeconomic perspective:

- At the **macroeconomic level** (the importance of transportation for a whole economy), transportation and the mobility it confers are linked to a level of output, employment and income within a national economy. In many developed countries, transportation accounts between 6 percent and 12 percent of the GDP.
- At the **microeconomic level** (the importance of transportation for specific parts of the economy) transportation is linked to producer, consumer and production costs. The importance of specific transport activities and infrastructure can thus be assessed for each sector of the economy. Transportation accounts on average between 10 percent and 15 percent of household expenditures while it accounts for around 4 percent of the costs of each unit of output in manufacturing, but this figure varies greatly according to subsectors.

The added value and employment effects of transport services usually extend beyond employment and added value generated by that activity; **indirect effects** are salient. For instance, transportation companies purchase a part of their inputs from local suppliers. The production of these inputs generates additional value added and employment in the local economy. The suppliers in turn purchase goods and services from other local firms. There are further rounds of local re-spending which generate additional value added and employment. Similarly, households that receive income from employment in transport activities spend some of their income on local goods and services. These purchases result in additional local jobs and added value. Some of the household income from these additional jobs is in turn spent on local goods and services, thereby creating further jobs and income for local households. As a result of these successive rounds of re-spending in the framework of local purchases, the overall impact on the economy exceeds the initial round of output, income and employment generated by passenger and freight transport activities. Thus, from a general standpoint the economic impacts of transportation can be direct, indirect and related (Figure 3.2):

- **Direct impacts**. The outcome of improved capacity and efficiency where transport provides employment, added value, larger markets as well as time and costs improvements. The overall demand of an economy is increasing.
- **Indirect impacts**. The outcome of improved accessibility and economies of scale. Indirect value added and jobs are the result of local purchases by companies directly dependent upon transport activity. Transport activities are responsible for a wide range of indirect value added and employment effects, through the linkages of transport with other economic sectors (e.g. office supply firms, equipment and parts suppliers, maintenance and repair services, insurance companies, consulting and other business services).
- **Induced impacts**. The outcome of the economic multiplier effects where the price of commodities, goods or services drops and/or their variety increases. For instance, the steel industry requires cost-efficient import of iron ore and coal for the blast furnaces and export activities for finished products such as steel booms and coils. Manufacturers and retail outlets and distribution centers handling imported containerized cargo rely on efficient transport and seaport operations.

Transportation links together the factors of production in a complex web of relationships between producers and consumers. The outcome is commonly a more efficient division

Figure 3.2 Socioeconomic benefits of transportation

of production by an exploitation of geographical comparative advantages, as well as the means to develop economies of scale and scope. The productivity of space, capital and labor is thus enhanced with the efficiency of distribution and personal mobility. Economic growth is increasingly linked with transport developments, namely infrastructures, but also with managerial expertise, which is crucial for logistics. Thus, although transportation is an infrastructure-intensive activity, hard assets must be supported by an array of soft assets, namely management and information systems. Decisions have to be made about how to use and operate transportation systems in a manner that optimizes benefits and minimizes costs and inconvenience.

Transportation and economic opportunities

Transportation developments that have taken place since the beginning of the Industrial Revolution have been linked to growing economic opportunities (Figure 3.3). At each stage of human societal development, a particular transport technology has been developed or adapted with an array of impacts. Each transport mode and technology is linked to a set of economic opportunities, notably in terms of **market areas**, the **types of commodities** that can be transported (including passengers) and **economies of scale**. All these issues are related to a scale and level of commercial geography that transport systems are supporting. Prior to the Industrial Revolution, economic opportunities were limited by the low capacity to move commodities over long distances, as most activities were much localized in scale and scope. The Industrial Revolution unleashed greater economic opportunities, initially with the development of inland canal systems, steamship services and then railway systems. Passenger and freight transportation expanded, as well as production and consumption, while new markets and resources became available. In many instances, the development of a transportation mode built on the opportunities developed by another mode, such as maritime and canal shipping. In other situations, the growth of a new mode of transportation benefited from the decline of others, such as the collapse of many inland canal networks in the late nineteenth century because of rail competition.

Figure 3.3 Cumulative modal contribution to economic opportunities

Source: Adapted from HOP Associates (2005) "Time, mobility and economic growth."

The development of the mass production system at the beginning of the twentieth century increasingly relied on the commercial opportunities introduced by road transportation, particularly the automobile. Later in the twentieth century, globalization benefited from the joint synergy of maritime shipping, roadways, railways, air and telecommunications, all of which supported integrated transport systems and supply chain management. Economic opportunities became global in scale and scope, particularly because of the capacity to maintain an intricate network of trade and transactions through transport systems. More recently, new opportunities arose with the convergence of telecommunications and information technologies, supporting a higher level of management of production, consumption and distribution, as well as a more efficient mobility of passengers. This process, building upon the advantages conferred by other transportation modes, is expected to account for a significant share of economic opportunities in the first half of the twenty-first century.

No single transport mode has been solely responsible for economic growth. Instead, modes have been linked with the economic functions they support and the geography in which growth was taking place. The first trade routes established a rudimentary system of distribution and transactions that would eventually be expanded by long-distance maritime shipping networks and the setting of the first multinational corporations managing these flows. Major flows of international migration that have occurred since the eighteenth century were linked with the expansion of international and continental transport systems that radically shaped emerging economies, such as in North America and Australia. Transport played a catalytic role in these migrations, transforming the economic and social geography of many nations.

Transportation has been a tool of territorial control and exploitation, particularly during the colonial era, when resource-based transport systems supported the extraction of commodities in the developing world and forwarded them to the industrializing nations of the time. The goal – to capture resource and market opportunities – was a strong impetus in the setting and structure of transport networks. More recently, port development, particularly container ports, has been of strategic interest as a tool of integration to the global economy, as illustrated by the case of China. There is a direct relation between foreign trade and container port volumes, so container port development is commonly seen as a tool to capture the opportunities brought by globalization.

Due to demographic pressures and increasing urbanization, developing economies are characterized by a mismatch between limited supply and growing demand for transport infrastructure. While some regions benefit from the development of transport systems, others are often marginalized by a set of conditions in which inadequate transportation plays a role. Transport by itself is not a sufficient condition for development. However, the lack of transport infrastructures can be seen as a constraining factor on development. In developing economies, the lack of transportation infrastructures and regulatory impediments are jointly impacting economic development by conferring higher transport costs, but also delays rendering supply chain management unreliable. A poor transport service level can negatively affect the competitiveness of regions and corporations and thus have a negative impact on the regional added value and employment. In 2007, the World Bank published its first ever report ranking nations according to their logistics performance, based on the Logistics Performance Index. Investment in transport infrastructures is thus seen as a tool of regional development, particularly in developing countries.

Transport investments also tend to have **declining marginal returns**. While initial infrastructure investments tend to have a high return, because they provide an entirely new range of mobility options, the more the system is developed, the more likely additional investment will result in lower returns. At some point, the marginal returns can be close to zero or even negative, implying a shift of transport investments from wealth-producing to wealth-consuming. A common fallacy is assuming that additional transport investments will have a similar multiplying effect than the initial investments had, which can lead to capital misallocation. The most common reasons for the declining marginal returns of transport investments are:

- **High accumulation of existing infrastructure**. In a context of high level of accessibility and transportation networks that are already extensive, further investments usually result in marginal improvements. This means that the economic impacts of transport investments tend to be significant when infrastructures were previously lacking and tend to be marginal when an extensive network is already present. Additional investments can thus have limited impact outside convenience.
- **Economic changes**. As economies develop, their function tends to shift from the primary (resource extraction) and secondary (manufacturing) sectors, towards advanced manufacturing, distribution and services. These sectors rely on different transport systems and capabilities. While an economy depending on manufacturing will rely on road, rail and port infrastructures, a service economy is more oriented towards the efficiency of logistics and urban transportation. In all cases transport infrastructures are important, but their relative importance in supporting the economy may shift.
- **Clustering**. Due to clustering and agglomeration, several locations develop advantages that cannot be readily reversed through improvements in accessibility. Transportation can be a factor of concentration and dispersion depending on the context. Less accessible regions thus do not necessarily benefit from transport investments if they are embedded in a system of unequal relations.

Therefore, each transport development project must be considered independently and contextually. Since transport infrastructures are capital-intensive fixed assets, they are particularly vulnerable to **misallocations** and **malinvestments**. The standard assumption is that transportation investments tend to be more **wealth-producing** as opposed to

wealth-consuming investments such as services. Still, several transportation investments can be wealth-consuming if they merely provide convenience, such as parking and sidewalks, or service a market size well below any possible economic return, with for instance projects labeled "bridges to nowhere." In such a context, transport investment projects can be **counterproductive** by draining the resources of an economy instead of creating wealth and additional opportunities. Since many transport infrastructures are provided through public funds, they can be subject to the pressures of special interest groups, which can result in poor economic returns. Efficient and sustainable transport markets and systems play a key role in regional development, although the causality between transport and wealth generation is not always clear.

Types of transport impacts

The relationship between transportation and economic development is **difficult to formally establish** and has been debated for many years. In some circumstances transport investments appear to be a **catalyst for economic growth**, while in others economic growth puts **pressures on existing transport infrastructures** and incites additional investments. In a number of regions around the world, transport markets and related transport infrastructure networks are seen as key drivers in the promotion of a more balanced and sustainable development, particularly by improving accessibility and the opportunities of less developed regions or disadvantaged social groups. To start with, there are different impacts on the **transport providers** (transport companies) and the **transport users**. There are several layers of activity that transportation can valorize, from a suitable location that experiences the development of its accessibility through infrastructure investment to better usage of existing transport assets through more efficient management. This is further nuanced by the nature, scale and scope of possible impacts:

- **Timing of the development**. The impacts of transportation can precede (lead), occur during (concomitantly) or take place after (lag) economic development. The lag, concomitant and lead impacts make it difficult to separate the specific contributions of transport to development. Each case appears to be specific to a set of timing circumstances that are difficult to replicate elsewhere.
- **Types of impacts**. They vary considerably, as the spectrum ranges from the positive to the negative. Usually transportation investments promote economic development, while in rarer cases they may hinder a region by draining its resources in unproductive transportation projects.

Cycles of economic development provide a revealing conceptual perspective about how transport systems evolve in time and space as they include the timing and the nature of the transport impact on economic development (Figure 3.4). This perspective underlines that, after a phase of introduction and growth, a transport system will eventually reach a phase of maturity through geographical and market saturation. There is also the risk of overinvestment, particularly when economic growth is credit-driven, which can lead to significant misallocations of capital. The outcome is a surplus capacity in infrastructures and modes creating deflationary pressures that undermine profitability. In periods of recession that commonly follow periods of expansion, transportation activities may experience a setback, namely in terms of lower demand and a scarcity of capital investment.

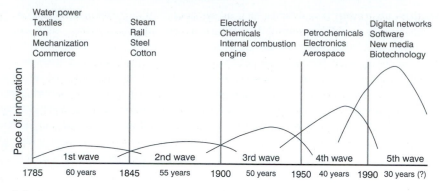

Figure 3.4 Long wave cycles of innovation

Source: Adapted from *The Economist*, 20 February 1999.

Technological innovation and economic growth are closely related and can be articulated within the concept of cycles or waves. Each wave represents a diffusion phase of a series of technological innovations creating entirely new economic sectors, and thus opportunities for investment and growth. Since the beginning of the Industrial Revolution in the late eighteenth century, five waves have been identified:

- **1st wave (1785–1845).** Leaned on innovations such as water power, textiles and iron. The beginning of the Industrial Revolution mainly focused on simple commodities such as clothes and tools. The conventional maritime technology relying on sailships was perfected, supporting the creation of large colonial/commercial empires, mainly by Great Britain, France, the Netherlands and Spain. Significant inland waterway systems were also constructed. The costs of production and transportation were significantly reduced.
- **2nd wave (1845–1900).** Involved the massive application of coal as a source of energy, mainly through the steam engine. This induced the development of rail transport systems, opening new markets and giving access to a wider array of resources. The steamship had a similar impact for maritime transportation and permitted expanded commercial opportunities in global trade. Also, the mass production of cotton substantially improved the opportunities of the textile industry.
- **3rd wave (1900–50).** Electrification was a major economic change as it permitted the usage of a variety of machines and appliances and permitted the development of urban transit systems (subways and tramways). Another significant improvement was the internal combustion engine, around which the whole automotive industry was created and expanded the mobility of passengers and freight.
- **4th wave (1950–90).** The post-World War II period represented significant industrial changes, with new materials such as plastics (petrochemicals) and new sectors such as electronics (television). The jet engine expanded the aviation industry towards the mass market, mobility could be realized globally and it created an active aerospace industry.
- **5th wave (1990–2020?).** The current wave mainly relies on information systems, which have tremendously modified the transactional environment with new methods of communication and more efficient forms of management of production and distribution systems (logistics). This has spawned new industries related to personal computing

devices, mainly computer manufacturing and software programming, but more recently e-commerce, as information processing converged with telecommunications.

These waves are related to the phases of development of the world economy. As time progressed, the lapse between each wave got shorter. For instance, the first wave lasted 60 years, while the fourth wave lasted 40 years. This reflects a growing potential for innovation and the capacity of economic systems to derive commercial opportunities from an innovation once it has been adopted. Innovations are no longer the result of individual efforts, but are organized and concerted actions whose results are rapidly diffused. Also, at the end of a cycle the rate of innovation usually declines, as most of the main innovations in the driving sector have already occurred and the industry has been captured by commercial and regulatory interests that focus more on rent seeking than innovation. It remains to be seen which innovations and technologies are going to support the next wave of economic development. Robotics, automation and sustainability are likely to be among the key drivers.

Transport, as a technology, typically follows a path of experimentation, introduction, adoption and diffusion and, finally, obsolescence, each of which has an impact on the rate of economic development. The most significant benefits and productivity gains are realized in the early to mid-diffusion phases, while later phases face diminishing returns. Containerization is a relevant example of such a diffusion behavior, as its productivity benefits were mostly derived in the 1990s and 2000s, when economic globalization was accelerating. Many technologies go through what can be called a "hype phase" with **unrealistic expectations** about their potential and benefits, and many are eventually abandoned as the technology proves ineffective at addressing market or operational requirements or is simply too expensive for the benefits it conveys. Since transportation is capital-intensive, operators tend to be cautious before committing to new technologies and the **significant sunk costs** they require. In addition, transport modes and infrastructures are **depreciating assets** that constantly require maintenance and upgrades. At some point, their useful lifespan is exceeded and the vehicle must be retired or the infrastructure rebuilt. Thus, the amortization of transport investments must consider the lifespan of the concerned mode or infrastructure.

Transportation as an economic factor

Contemporary trends have underlined that economic development has become less dependent on relations with the environment (resources) and more dependent on **relations across space**. While resources remain the foundation of economic activities, the commodification of the economy has been linked with higher levels of material flows of all kinds. Concomitantly, resources, capital and even labor have shown increasing levels of mobility. This is particularly the case for multinational firms that can benefit from transport improvements in two significant markets:

- **Commodity market**. Improvement in the efficiency with which firms have access to raw materials and parts as well as to their respective customers. Thus, transportation expands opportunities to acquire and sell a variety of commodities necessary for industrial and manufacturing systems.
- **Labor market**. Improvement in the access to labor and a reduction in access costs, mainly by improved commuting (local scale) or the use of lower cost labor (global scale).

Transportation provides market accessibility by linking producers and consumers so that transactions can take place. A common fallacy in assessing the importance and impact of transportation on the economy is to focus only on transportation costs, which tend to be relatively low: in the range of 5 to 10 percent of the value of a good. Transportation is an **economic factor of production** of goods and services, implying that it is fundamental in their generation, even if it accounts for a small share of input costs. This implies that irrespective of the cost, an activity cannot take place without the transportation factor. Thus, relatively small changes in transport cost, capacity and performance can have substantial impacts on dependent economic activities.

An efficient transport system with modern infrastructures favors many economic changes, most of them positive. The major impacts of transport on economic factors can be categorized as follows:

- **Geographic specialization**. Improvements in transportation and communication favor a process of geographical specialization that increases productivity and spatial interactions. An economic entity tends to produce goods and services with the most appropriate combination of capital, labor and raw materials. A region will thus tend to specialize in the production of goods and services for which it has the greatest advantages (or the least disadvantages) compared to other regions as long as appropriate transport is available for trade. Through geographic specialization supported by efficient transportation, economic productivity is promoted. This process is known in economic theory as **comparative advantages**.

- **Large-scale production**. An efficient transport system offering cost, time and reliability advantages permits goods to be transported over longer distances. This facilitates mass production through economies of scale because larger markets can be accessed. The concept of "just-in-time" in supply chain management has further expanded the productivity of production and distribution, with benefits such as lower inventory levels and better responses to shifting market conditions. Thus, the more efficient transportation becomes, the larger the markets that can be serviced and the larger the scale of production. This results in lower unit costs.

- **Increased competition**. When transport is efficient, the potential market for a given product (or service) increases, and so does competition. A wider array of goods and services becomes available to consumers through competition, which tends to reduce costs and promote quality and innovation. Globalization has clearly been associated with a competitive environment that spans the world and enables consumers to have access to a wider range of goods and services.

- **Increased land value**. Land which is adjacent or serviced by good transport services generally has greater value due to the utility it confers to many activities. Consumers can have access to a wider range of services and retail goods, while residents can have better accessibility to employment, services and social networks, all of which translates into higher land value. In some cases, transportation activities can lower land value, particularly for residential activities. Land located near airports and highways, near noise and pollution sources, will thus be impacted by corresponding diminishing land value.

Transport also contributes to economic development through job creation and its derived economic activities. Accordingly, a large amount of direct (freighters, managers, shippers) and indirect (insurance, finance, packaging, handling, travel agencies, transit operators) employment is associated with transport. Producers and consumers take economic decisions on products, markets, costs, location and prices, which are themselves based on transport services, their availability, costs and capacity.

Concept 2 – Transportation and society

Mobility and society

Transport systems are a fundamental component of societies since they support complex economic and social interactions. Mobility is one of the most fundamental and important characteristics of economic or social activities as it satisfies the basic need to go from one location to the other, a need shared by passengers, freight and information. Locations do not share the same level of mobility, as most are in a different stage in their mobility transition towards motorized forms of transport. Economies that possess greater mobility are often those with better opportunities to develop than those that have scarce mobility. Reduced mobility impedes development, while greater mobility is a catalyst for development. Mobility is thus a reliable indicator of development. Providing mobility is an industry that offers services to its customers, employs people and disburses wages, invests capital, generates income and provides taxation revenue. Mobility is therefore the recurrent aspect where transportation has its most significant societal impacts.

Mobility is a multidimensional concept, since it simultaneously expresses the **potential for a movement** and the movement itself. To start with, it is a choice to be exercised or not, depending on economic and social goals. For economic activities such as businesses, transportation enables access to a workforce, and the ability to reach suppliers and service customers. With improvements in transportation, interactions with the workforce are more effective and the costs of distribution usually decline with the derived competitive benefits. For individuals, transportation is the means to access employment, goods, services, leisure and social networks. Thus, a share of the societal consumption is allocated to satisfy mobility needs. Paradoxically, higher income levels are usually associated with a higher share of transportation in consumption, a trend particularly attributed to automobile ownership and air travel.

Mobility is an activity constrained by a number of factors. For an individual, time limits the number and length of possible daily trips. However, these constraints are technologically, socially and economically articulated, since more efficient transport modes are supportive of more extensive mobilities as well as higher incomes. Thus, an individual would have a mobility contingent on physical capabilities, available budget, transport supply and the spatial distribution of activities, such as residential, commercial and production areas. Furthermore, because of its impacts the social context of mobility is partially changing. Mobility can also be a factor in weaker social interactions, as individuals could be living further apart. At the same time, expanded mobility enables social interactions that were not effectively possible beforehand. This is particularly the case for long-distance interaction that has expanded with the growth of air transport.

Societal transportation challenges

While many of the social and economic impacts of transportation are positive, there are also significant societal challenges:

- **Mobility gaps.** Since mobility is one of the fundamental components of the economic benefits of transportation, its variations are likely to have substantial impacts on the opportunities of individuals. Mobility needs do not always coincide due to several factors, namely the lack of income, lack of time, lack of means and the lack of access. People's mobility and transport demands thus depend on their socioeconomic status. The higher the income, the higher the mobility, which may give rise to substantial mobility gaps between different population groups. Gender gaps exist in mobility, as women tend to have lower incomes. Mobility gaps are particularly prevalent for long-distance travel. With the development of air transport, a segment of the global population has achieved a very high level of mobility for their business and leisure activities, while the great majority of the global population has little mobility. This issue is expected to become more acute as the population of many advanced economies is aging rapidly, which implies that mobility will not be an income issue but an age issue. By 2020, about 10 percent of the global population (719 million) will be over 65, while by 2050 this share will reach 16 percent (1,492 million).

- **Costs differences**. Locations that have low levels of accessibility, such as land-locked countries, tend to have higher costs for many goods (sometimes basic necessities such as food), as most have to be imported, often over long distances. The resulting higher transport costs inhibit the competitiveness of such locations and limit opportunities. Consumers and industries will pay higher prices, impacting on their welfare (disposable income) and competitiveness.

- **Congestion**. With the increased use of transport systems, it has become common for parts of the network to be used above design capacity. Congestion is the outcome of such a situation, with its associated costs, delays and waste of energy. Distribution systems that rely upon on-time deliveries are particularly susceptible to congestion, as well as commuters seeking to arrive at work on time. As well as involving additional costs, congestion involves additional time, which is perceived to be increasingly valuable in advanced economies.

- **Accidents**. The use of transport modes and infrastructure is never entirely safe. Every motorized vehicle contains an element of danger and nuisance. Due to human errors and various forms of physical failures (mechanical or infrastructural) injuries, damage and even death occur. Accidents tend to be proportional to the intensity of use of transport infrastructures, which means that the more traffic there is, the higher the probability that an accident will occur. They have important socioeconomic impacts including healthcare, insurance, damage to property and the loss of life. The respective level of safety depends on the mode of transport and the speed at which an accident occurs. No mode is completely safe, but the road remains the most dangerous medium for transportation, accounting for 90 percent of all transport accidents on average. At the global level about 1.25 million people died in road accidents in 2010, in addition to 50 million injured. In developing economies, death rates are usually twice as high as those of developed countries. China has the world's largest number of fatalities – 250,000 in 2013 – a factor mainly due to a sharp growth in vehicle ownership in recent years, plus a lack of driver education.

- **Health**. The convenience of mobility, particularly through the diffusion of the automobile and its associated suburban lifestyle, is linked with rising obesity. Therefore, there can be a societal drawback to convenient mobility, since a population could be walking less and be not as involved in physical activities. Such a trend is complex to mitigate, and it has been advocated that the design of more walking- and cycling-friendly neighborhoods would convey some improved health benefits for residents.

All these issues underline the profound social implications of transportation in terms of opportunities, but also in terms of social exclusion. The most significant factors of social exclusion remain land use and housing policies, which tend to undermine access to employment, education, healthcare and other social activities. If this separation is not mitigated by efficient transportation, it becomes a factor of segregation.

Environmental transportation challenges

The emission of pollutants related to transport activities has a wide range of environmental consequences, which have a cost that has to be assumed by the users and society:

- **Air quality**. Atmospheric emissions from pollutants produced by transportation, especially by the internal combustion engine, are associated with air pollution and global climate change. Some pollutants (NO_2, CO, O_3, VOC, etc.) can produce respiratory troubles and aggravate cardiovascular illnesses. In urban regions, about 50 percent of all air pollution emanates from automobile traffic. Since pollution is a health issue, its societal impacts are perceived to be significant.
- **Noise**. A major irritant, noise can impact on human health and most often human welfare. Noise can be manifested in three levels depending on emissions intensity: psychological disturbances (perturbations, displeasure), functional disturbances (sleep disorders, loss of work productivity, speech interference) or physiological disturbances (health issues such as fatigue, and hearing damage). Noise and vibration associated with trains, trucks and planes in the vicinity of airports are major irritants and have commonly been associated with lower land values.
- **Water quality**. Accidental and nominal runoff of pollutants from transport, such as oil spills, are sources of contamination for both surface water and groundwater. In addition, paved surfaces are more prone to floods with intense rainfall.
- **Land take**. Transport is a large consumer of space when all of its supporting infrastructure and equipment are considered. This space is subject to competition between other activities and reflects societal values, particularly in terms of the space allocated to the automobile. Furthermore, the planning associated with transportation infrastructures does not always consider aesthetic values, as is often the case in the construction of urban highways. These visual impacts have adverse consequences on the quality of life of nearby residents.

Concept 3 – Transport costs

Authors: Dr Jean-Paul Rodrigue and Dr Theo Notteboom

Transport costs and rates

Transport systems face requirements to increase their capacity and to reduce the costs of movements. All users (e.g. individuals, enterprises, institutions, governments, etc.) have to **negotiate** or **bid** for the transfer of goods, people, information and capital because supplies, distribution systems, tariffs, salaries, locations, marketing techniques as well as fuel costs are changing constantly. There are also costs involved in gathering information, negotiating, and enforcing contracts and transactions, which are often referred to as the cost of doing business. Trade involves transaction costs that all agents attempt to reduce since transaction costs account for a growing share of the resources consumed by the economy.

Frequently, enterprises and individuals must take decisions about how to route passengers or freight through the transport system. This choice has been considerably expanded in the context of the production of lighter and high-value consuming goods, such as electronics, and less bulky production techniques. It is not uncommon for transport costs to account for 10 percent of the total cost of a product. This share also roughly applies to personal mobility, where households spend about 10 percent of their income for transportation, including the automobile, which has a complex cost structure. Thus, the choice of a transportation mode to route people and freight between origins and destinations becomes important and depends on a number of factors, such as the nature of the goods, the available infrastructures, origins and destinations, technology, and particularly their respective distances. Jointly, they define **transportation costs**, which are a monetary measure of what the **transport provider** must pay to produce transportation services. They come as fixed (infrastructure) and variable (operating) costs, depending on a variety of conditions related to geography, infrastructure, administrative barriers, energy, and on how passengers and freight are carried. Three major components, related to transactions, shipments and the friction of distance, impact on transport costs.

Transport costs have significant impacts on the structure of economic activities as well as on international trade. Empirical evidence underlines that raising transport costs by 10 percent reduces trade volumes by more than 20 percent and that the general quality of transport infrastructure can account for half of the variation in transport costs. In a competitive environment where transportation is a service that can be bidded on, transport costs are influenced by the respective **rates** of transport companies, the portion of the **transport costs charged to users**. They are the negotiated monetary cost of moving a passenger or a unit of freight between a specific origin and destination. Rates are often visible to the consumers, since transport providers must provide this information to secure transactions. They may not necessarily express the real transport costs.

The difference between costs and rates either results in a loss or a profit from the service provider. Considering the components of transport costs previously discussed, rate setting is a complex undertaking subject to constant change. For public transit, rates are often **fixed** and the result of a political decision where a share of the total costs is subsidized by the society. The goal is to provide an affordable mobility to the largest possible segment of the population, even if this implies a recurring deficit (public transit systems rarely make any profit). It is thus common for public transit systems to have rates that are lower than costs, and targeted at subsidizing the mobility of social groups such as students, the elderly or people on welfare.

For freight transportation and many forms of passenger transportation (e.g. air transportation) rates are subject to a competitive pressure. This means that the rate will be adjusted according to the demand and the supply. They either reflect costs directly involved with shipping (cost-of-service) or are determined by the value of the commodity (value-of-service). Since many actors are involved in freight transportation, private rates tend to vary, often significantly, but profitability is paramount.

Costs and time components

Transportation offers a spectrum of costs and level of services, which results in substantial differences across the world. The price of a transport service does not only include the direct out-of-the-pocket money costs to the user but also includes time costs and costs related to possible inefficiencies, discomfort and risk (e.g. unexpected delays).

However, economic actors often base their choice of a transport mode or route on only part of the total transport price. For example, motorists are biased by short-run marginal costs. They might narrow down the price of a specific trip by car to fuel costs only, thereby excluding fixed costs such as depreciation, insurance and vehicle tax. Many shippers or freight forwarders are primarily guided by direct money costs when considering the price factor in modal choice. The narrow focus on direct money costs is to some extent attributable to the fact that time costs and costs related to possible inefficiencies are harder to calculate and often can only be fully assessed after the cargo has arrived. Among the most significant conditions affecting transport costs and thus transport rates are:

- **Geography.** Its impacts mainly involve distance and accessibility. Distance is commonly the most basic condition affecting transport costs (Figure 3.5). The more difficult it is to trade space for a cost, the more the friction of distance is important. It can be expressed in terms of length, time, economic costs or the amount of energy used. It varies greatly, according to the type of transportation mode involved and the efficiency of specific transport routes. Landlocked countries tend to have higher transport costs, often twice as much, as they do not have direct access to maritime transportation. The impact of geography on the cost structure can be expanded to include several rate zones, such as one for local, another for the nation and another for exports.

There are four major categories of friction of distance functions – *no effects of distance* (1): economic activities on which distance has no effects are uncommon. However, the distance–cost function telecommunication networks and the virtual space of the Internet have such a cost structure. Telephone calls can be included in this category as well as postal fees and public transit fares. All those activities generally have a fixed cost that is not related to distance, but often to a service zone. Once a new zone is entered (such as for international phone calls), a new cost structure applies; *linear effects of distance* (2): transport costs increase proportionally to distance. Fuel consumption can be included in this category, since it is a direct function of the distance traveled. For reasons of simplicity, a stepwise approach is often used to establish transport rates by using administrative units as distance units; *non-linear effects of distance* (3): freight distribution costs

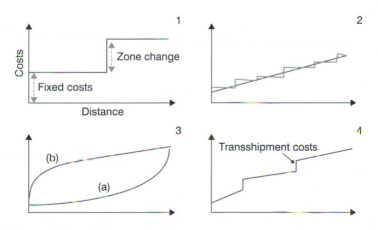

Figure 3.5   Different friction of distance functions

grow in a non-linear fashion with distance from the terminal or the distribution center, particularly because of empty backhauls (a). Inversely, international air transportation costs are not usually much higher than regional air transportation costs because long-haul planes have more capacity (b); and *multimodal transport chain* (4): a combination of linehaul and terminal costs where transshipment costs at terminals (e.g. ports and airports) increase the friction of distance, as efforts must be spent at loading or unloading when passing from one mode to another.

- **Type of product**. Many products require packaging, special handling, are bulky or perishable. Coal is obviously a commodity that is easier to transport than fruits or fresh flowers, as it requires rudimentary storage facilities and can be transshipped using rudimentary equipment. Insurance costs are also to be considered and are commonly a function of the value-to-weight ratio and the risk associated with the movement. As such, different economic sectors incur different transport costs as they each have their own transport intensity. With containerization the type of product plays little in the transport cost since rates are set per container, but products still need to be loaded or unloaded from the container. For passengers, comfort and amenities must be provided, especially if long-distance travel is involved.
- **Economies of scale**. Another condition affecting transport costs is related to economies of scale or the possibility to apply them as the larger the quantities transported, the lower the unit cost. Bulk commodities such as energy (coal, oil), minerals and grains are highly suitable for obtaining lower unit transport costs if they are transported in large quantities. A similar trend also applies to container shipping, with larger containerships involving lower unit costs.
- **Energy**. Transport activities are large consumers of energy, especially oil. About 60 percent of all the global oil consumption is attributed to transport activities. Transport typically accounts for about 25 percent of all the energy consumption of an economy. The costs of several energy-intensive transport modes, such as air transport, are particularly susceptible to fluctuations in energy prices.
- **Trade backhauls**. Many transport interactions involve empty backhauls since it is uncommon to have a perfect match between an inbound and a return trip. Commuting patterns involve imbalanced flows and empty return trips. For international trade, imbalances between imports and exports have impacts on transport costs. This is especially the case for container transportation since trade imbalances imply the repositioning of empty containers that have to be taken into account in the total transport costs. Consequently, if a trade balance is strongly negative (more imports than exports), transport costs for imports tend to be higher than for exports. Significant transport rate imbalances have emerged along major trade routes. The same condition applies at the national and local levels, where freight flows are often unidirectional, implying empty backhaul movements.
- **Infrastructures**. The efficiency and capacity of transport modes and terminals has a direct impact on transport costs. Poor infrastructures imply higher transport costs, delays and negative economic consequences. More developed transport systems tend to have lower transport costs since they are more reliable and can handle more movements.
- **Mode**. Different modes are characterized by different transport costs, since each has its own capacity limitations and operational conditions. When two or more modes are directly competing for the same market, the outcome often results in lower trans-

port costs. Containerized transportation permitted a significant reduction in freight transport rates around the world.

- **Competition and regulation**. Concerns the complex competitive and regulatory environment in which transportation takes place. Transport services taking place over highly competitive segments tend to be of lower cost than on segments with limited competition (oligopoly or monopoly). International competition has favored concentration in many segments of the transport industry, namely maritime and air modes. Regulations such as tariffs, cabotage laws, labor, security and safety impose additional transport costs, particularly in developing countries.
- **Surcharges**. Refer to an array of fees, often set in an arbitrary fashion, to reflect temporary conditions that may impact on costs assumed by the transporter. The most common are fuel surcharges, security fees, geopolitical risk premiums and additional baggage fees. The passenger transport industry, particularly airlines, has become dependent on a wide array of surcharges as a source of revenue.

Transport time is also an important dimension in the evaluation of transport costs, particularly since logistics concomitantly involves cost and time management. They include the transport time, the order time, the timing, the punctuality and the frequency (Figure 3.6):

- **Transport time**. Concerns the real duration of transport, which tends to be easily understood since it is commonly a proportional function of distance. Geographical constraints such as weather or technical limitations such as operational speed have a direct impact on transport time. Transport time on roads is technically limited to legal speed limits. For maritime and air, the limitation mainly concerns fuel economy and design speed. Although rail can accommodate a variety of speeds, tight schedules impose limited variations in operational speeds.
- **Order time** (not shown on Figure 3.6). Almost all transport requires a form of advance preparation, mainly to secure a capacity, an itinerary and a rate. In some cases, the order time is short and a matter of queuing on a first come, first served basis, while in other cases orders have to be secured months in advance.
- **Timing**. Involves the usage of a specific departure time, which depending on the mode can have a level of flexibility. While for air and rail travel timing is commonly tight due to fixed schedules and access to a terminal capacity (such as a gate and a takeoff time), commuters and trucking have more flexibility. If there is congestion either at the origin, destination or in between, trucking companies may elect to modify their schedule accordingly (earlier or later delivery).
- **Punctuality**. Represents the ability to keep a specified schedule, which can be represented as an average deviation from a scheduled arrival time. The longer the distance, the more likely potential disruptions that may affect schedule integrity will be. Some movements may have a level of tolerance to disruptions in punctuality, while others, such as heading to a business meeting or flows in a just-in-time supply chain, have limited tolerance.
- **Frequency**. The number of departures for a specific time range. The higher the frequency, the better the level of service. However, a high frequency ties up a larger quantity of vehicles. Distance is also a factor for lower frequency since transport demand tends to decline accordingly. Combining long-distance travel and high frequency is an expensive undertaking for transport providers as a greater number of vehicles must be assigned to a specific route, as in the case of maritime container shipping.

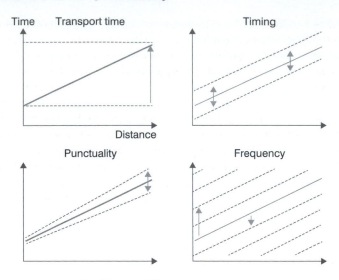

Figure 3.6 Different components of transport time

Srource: Adapted from J. Woxenius (2006) "Temporal elements in the spatial extension of production networks." *Growth and Change* 37(4): 526–549.

For instance, a maritime shipper may offer a container transport service between a number of North American and Pacific Asian ports. It may take twelve days to service two ports across the Pacific (transport time) and a port call is done every two days (frequency). In order to secure a slot on a ship, a freight forwarder must call at least five days in advance (order time). For a specific port terminal, a ship arrives at 8 a.m. and leaves at 5 p.m. (timing) with the average delay being two hours (punctuality).

Types of transport costs

Mobility is influenced by transport costs. Empirical evidence for passenger vehicle use underlines the relationship between annual vehicle mileage and fuel costs, implying that the higher the fuel costs, the lower the mileage. At the international level, doubling of transport costs can reduce trade flows by more than 80 percent. The more affordable mobility is, the more frequent the movements and the more likely they will take place over longer distances. Empirical evidence also underlines that transport costs tend to be higher in the early or final stages of a movement, also known as the first and the last mile. A wide variety of transport costs can be considered.

- **Terminal costs**. Costs that are related to the loading, transshipment and unloading. Two major terminal costs can be considered: loading and unloading at the origin and destination, which are unavoidable; and intermediate (transshipment) costs that can be avoided. For complex transport terminals, such as ports and airports, terminal costs can involve a wide array of components, including docking/gate fees, handling charges and pilotage/traffic control fees.
- **Linehaul costs**. Costs that are a function of the distance over which a unit of freight or passenger is carried. Weight is also a cost function when freight is involved. They include labor and fuel and commonly exclude transshipment costs.

- **Capital costs**. Costs applying to the physical assets of transportation – mainly infrastructures, terminals and vehicles. They include the purchase or major enhancement of fixed assets, which can often be a one-time event. Since physical assets tend to depreciate over time, capital investments are required on a regular basis for maintenance.

Transport providers make a variety of decisions based on their cost structure, a function of all the above types of transport costs. To simplify transactions and clearly identify the respective responsibilities specific commercial transportation terms have been set. **International Commercial Terms**, or Incoterms, are predefined commercial terms that are used to define the transport component and the share of costs and risks for international commercial transactions. They provide a consistent framework of the expected transport service to be provided, which removes uncertainty, and defines legally enforceable responsibilities across international jurisdictions. Although for many transactions it is either the seller's or the buyer's responsibility to carry the cargo, this task is often attributed to a shipper or a third party logistics provider that will act on their behalf. The most common Incoterms are (Figure 3.7):

- **EXW (Ex Works)**. The buyer virtually takes care of all the transport responsibilities and the only obligation of the seller is to have the cargo available at an agreed-upon time and premise (factory, distribution center). It often refers to the **factory price**, since it excludes all costs related to transportation, such as insurance and duties.
- **FCA (Free Carrier)**. The seller's responsibility is simply to provide the cargo that has been cleared for export at a specific delivery point.
- **FAS (Free Alongside Ship)**. Usually used for maritime bulk cargo where the seller provides the cargo at the dock, which is ready to be loaded on a ship. For instance, a grain seller would make available bulk grain at a dockside grain elevator and it would be the buyer's responsibility to charter a bulk cargo ship and load the cargo.
- **FOB (Free On Board)**. The seller provides, transports and loads the cargo on board a vessel, which is usually selected by the buyer. This is typical for containerized cargo.
- **CFR (Cost and Freight)**. The seller brings and unloads the cargo at a port of destination, but the buyer assumes the risk as soon as the cargo is loaded at the port of origin. The buyer has the responsibility of picking up the cargo.
- **CIF (Cost, Insurance and Freight)**. Same as above, but the seller also provides insurance for the cargo up to the port of destination. It usually applies to bulk cargo.
- **CIP (Carriage and Insurance Paid)**. Common in intermodal transport chains where the seller takes complete responsibility for bringing the cargo to the point of destination (e.g. the door of a distribution center) as well as providing insurance. The buyer is responsible for unloading the cargo at the point of destination.

While the transport price plays an important role in modal choice, firms using freight transport services are not always motivated by notions of cost minimization. They often show "satisficing behavior" whereby the transport costs need to be below a certain threshold combined with specific requirements regarding reliability, frequency and other service attributes. Such complexities make it more difficult to clearly assess the role of transport price in the behavior of transport users. The role of transport companies

Figure 3.7 Selected International Commercial Terms (Incoterms)

Source: Adapted from International Chamber of Commerce.

has sensibly increased in the general context of the global commercial geography. However, the nature of this role is changing as a result of a general reduction of transport costs but growing infrastructure costs, mainly due to greater flows and competition for land. Each transport sector must consider variations in the importance of different transport costs. While operating costs are high for air transport, terminal costs are significant for maritime transport. Several indexes, such as the Baltic Dry Index, have been developed to convey a pricing mechanism useful for planning and decision making.

Technological changes and their associated decline in transport costs have weakened the links with transport modes and their terminals. There is less emphasis on heavy industries and more importance given to manufacturing and transport services (e.g. warehousing and distribution). Indeed, new functions are being grafted to transport activities that are henceforward facilitating logistics and manufacturing processes. Relations between terminal operators and carriers have thus become crucial notably in containerized traffic. They are needed to overcome the physical and time constraints of transshipment, notably at ports.

The requirements of international trade gave rise to the development of **specialized and intermediary firms** providing transport services. These are firms that do not physically transport the goods, but are required to facilitate the grouping, storage and handling of freight as well as the complex paperwork and financial and legal transactions involved in international trade. Examples include freight forwarders, customs brokers, warehousing, insurance agents and banking. Recently, there has been a trend to **consolidate** these different intermediate functions, and a growing proportion of global trade is now being organized by multinational corporations that are offering door-to-door logistics services.

Concept 4 – Transport supply and demand

Authors: Dr Jean-Paul Rodrigue and Dr Theo Notteboom

The supply and demand for transportation

Each transport mode shares the common goal of fulfilling a derived transport demand, and each transport mode thus fills the purpose of supporting mobility. Transportation is a service that must be utilized immediately, since, unlike the resources it often carries, the transport service itself cannot be stored. Mobility must occur over transport infrastructures having a fixed capacity, providing a **transport supply**. In several instances, transport demand is answered in the simplest means possible, notably by walking. However, in some cases elaborate and expensive infrastructures and modes are required to provide mobility, such as for international air transportation.

Transportation is a market composed of suppliers of transport services and users of these services. Well-functioning transport markets should allow transport supply to meet transport demand so that transport needs for mobility are satisfied. An economic system including numerous activities located in different areas generates movements that must be supported by the transport system. Without movements infrastructures would be useless, and without infrastructures movements could not occur, or would not occur in a cost-efficient manner. This interdependency can be considered according to two concepts: transport supply and demand.

Transport supply is the capacity of transportation infrastructures and modes, generally over a geographically defined transport system and for a specific period of time. Supply is expressed in terms of infrastructures (capacity), services (frequency) and networks (coverage). Capacity is often assessed in static and dynamic terms, where static capacity represents the amount of space available for transport (e.g. terminal surface) and dynamic capacity is the improvement that can be made through better technology and management. The number of passengers, volume (for liquids or containerized traffic) or mass (for freight) that can be transported per unit of time and space is commonly used to quantify transport supply. **Transport demand** is the transport needs, even if those needs are satisfied, fully, partially or not at all. Similar to transport supply, it is expressed in terms of number of people, volume or tons per unit of time and space.

The supply side of the transport market can be divided into two categories:

- **Third-party transportation**. Transport companies offer transport services to users who require such services, often on open markets. Transport users pay for the services delivered according to the terms of the agreed contract. Examples include third-party trucking companies, container shipping lines, railway operators and bus companies. Competitiveness is a key advantage of third-party transportation as providers strive to offer better and lower cost services for their customers. There is also the risk of fluctuating prices due to changing market conditions and the fact that transport capacity may not be available when a customer requires it.
- **Own account transportation**. The transport user deploys his or her own transport means to move freight or to travel (e.g. motorists using private cars or large industrial companies owning a fleet of trucks or rail wagons). The transport user has a direct access to a known capacity, but at the risk of a lower level of asset utilization (e.g. empty movements or idle equipment).

Transport demand is generated by the economy, which is composed of persons, institutions and industries and which generates movements of people and freight. A distinction can be made between **consumptive** and **productive** transport needs. Productive transport needs have a clear economic focus. For example, the transport of semi-finished products from one production site to the final production or assembly site creates added value in the production process by benefiting from the locational advantages of each of the production sites. Consumptive transport needs to generate less visible added value. For example, a road trip does not really add value in a pure economic sense, but generates subjective utility and satisfaction to the users. A discussion on the functioning of transport markets is particularly relevant where it concerns the fulfillment of productive transport needs, but the consumptive dimension of transport must also be considered.

The location of resources, factories, distribution centers and markets is obviously related to freight movements. Transport demand can vary under two circumstances that are often concomitant: the quantity of passengers or freight increases, or the distance over which these passengers or freight are carried increases (Figure 3.8). Geographical considerations and transport costs account for significant variations in the composition of freight transport demand between countries. For the movements of passengers, the location of residential, commercial and industrial areas says a lot about the generation and attraction of movements.

The realized transport demand, expressed in passenger or ton-km, can increase for two reasons. The first is obviously that more passengers or freight are being carried. This is an outcome of growth in population, production, consumption and income. The second is a growth in the average distance over which passengers or freight loads are being carried. Outsourcing, offshoring, economic specialization (factors linked with globalization) and suburbanization are relevant factors behind this trend. These two factors are often occurring concomitantly, creating multiplying effects on the transport demand.

Supply and demand functions

Transport supply and demand have a **reciprocal but asymmetric** relation. While a realized transport demand cannot take place without a corresponding level of transport

Figure 3.8 Growth factors in transport demand

supply, a transport supply can exist without a corresponding transport demand. This is common in infrastructure projects that are designed with a capacity fulfilling an expected demand level, which may or may not materialize, or may take several years to do so. Scheduled transport services, such as public transit or airlines, offer a transport supply that runs even if the demand is insufficient. Infrastructures also tend to be designed at a capacity level higher than the expected base scenario in case that demand turns out to be higher than anticipated. In other cases, the demand does not materialize, often due to improper planning or unexpected socioeconomic changes.

Transport demand that is met by a supply of transport services generates traffic (trucks, trains, ships, airplanes, buses, bicycles, etc.) on the corresponding transport infrastructure networks. The traffic capacity is generally larger than the actual transport demand, since the average utilization degree of vehicles rarely reaches 100 percent – for instance, empty hauls of trucks, an underutilized container ship capacity sailing on a shipping route characterized by imbalanced container flows, an underutilized off-peak bus service and the one person, per car situation in commuter traffic. There is a simple statistical way to measure transport supply and demand for passengers or freight. The **passenger-km** (or passenger-mile) is a common measure expressing the realized passenger transport demand, as it compares a transported quantity of passengers with a distance over which it gets carried. The **ton-km** (or ton-mile) is a common measure expressing the realized freight transport demand. Although both the passenger-km and ton-km are most commonly used to measure realized demand, the measure can equally apply for transport supply.

There are several factors impacting the capacity of transport infrastructure, from the physical characteristics of the network, how it is funded, operated and maintained, to the presence of bottlenecks. Transport supply can be simplified by a set of functions representing the main variables influencing the capacity of transport systems. These variables are different for each mode. For road, rail and telecommunications, transport supply is often dependent on the capacity of the routes and vehicles (**modal supply**), while for air and maritime transportation transport supply is strongly influenced by the capacity of the terminals (**intermodal supply**).

Transport demand tends to be expressed at specific times that are related to economic and social activity patterns. In many cases, transport demand is stable and recurrent, which allows a good approximation in planning services. In other cases, transport demand is unstable and uncertain, which makes it difficult to offer an adequate level of service. For instance, commuting is a recurring and predictable pattern of movements, while emergency response vehicles such as ambulances are dealing with an unpredictable demand that can be expressed as a probability. Transport demand functions vary according to the nature of what is to be transported:

- **Passengers**. For the road and air transport of passengers, demand is a function of demographic attributes of the population such as income, age, standard of living, race and sex, as well as modal preferences.
- **Freight**. For freight transportation, demand is a function of the nature and the importance of economic activities (GDP, commercial surface, number of tons of ore extracted, etc.) and of modal preferences. Freight transportation demand is more complex to evaluate than passengers.
- **Information**. For telecommunications, demand can be a function of several criteria including the population (telephone calls) and the volume of financial activities (stock exchange). The standard of living and education levels are also factors to be considered.

Supply/demand relationships

Relationships between transport supply and demand continually change, but they are mutually interrelated. From a conventional economic perspective, transport supply and demand interact until an equilibrium is reached between the quantity of transportation the market is willing to use at a given price and the quantity being supplied for that price level (Figure 3.9).

The demand curve assumes that if transport costs are high, demand is low, as the consumers of a transport service (either freight or passengers) are less likely to use it. If transport costs are low, the demand would be high, as users would get more services for the same cost. The supply curve behaves inversely. If costs are high, transport providers would be willing to supply high quantities of services, since high profits are likely to arise under such circumstances. If costs are low, the quantity of transport services would be low, as many providers would see little benefits operating at a loss. The equilibrium point represents a compromise between what users are willing to pay and what providers are willing to offer. Under such circumstances, an amount of traffic T1 would flow at an operating cost C1. If because of an improvement a larger amount of service is possible for the same cost (the supply curve moves from S1 to S2), a new equilibrium will be reached with a quantity of traffic T2 at a price C2. Elasticity refers to the variation of the demand in accordance to the variation of the price. The higher it is, the more the traffic in a transport system is influenced by cost variations.

Price changes not only affect the level of transport demand, but can also lead to shifts of demand to other routes, alternative transport modes and/or other time periods. In the medium or long term, structural changes in the pricing of transport can affect location decisions of individuals and businesses. However, several considerations are specific to the transport sector, which make supply/demand relationships more complex:

- **Entry costs**. These are the costs incurred to operate at least one vehicle in a transport system. In some sectors, notably maritime, rail and air transportation, entry costs are very high, while in others, such as trucking, they are very low. High entry costs imply that transport companies will consider seriously the additional demand before adding new capacity or new infrastructures (or venturing into a new service). In a situation of low entry costs, the number of companies fluctuates with the demand. When

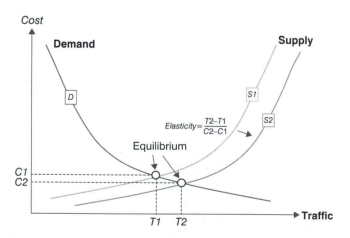

Figure 3.9 Classic transport demand/supply function

entry costs are high, the emergence of a new player is uncommon, while dropping out is often a dramatic event linked to a large bankruptcy. Consequently, transport activities with high entry costs tend to be oligopolistic, while transport activities with low entry costs tend to have many competitors.

- **Public sector**. Few other sectors of the economy have seen such a high level of public involvement than transportation, which creates many disruptions in conventional price mechanisms. The provision of transport infrastructures, especially roads, was massively funded by governments, namely for the sake of national accessibility and regional equity. Transit systems are also heavily subsidized to provide accessibility to urban populations and more specifically to the poorest segment, judged to be deprived in mobility. As a consequence, transport costs are often considered as partially subsidized. Government control (and direct ownership) was also significant for several modes, such as rail and air transportation, in a number of countries. Recent years have, however, been characterized by privatization and deregulation.

- **Elasticity**. The notion of price elasticity is at the core of transport demand and refers to the variation of demand in response to a variation of cost. For example, an elasticity of -0.5 for vehicle use with respect to vehicle operating costs means that an increase of 1 percent in operating costs would imply a 0.5 percent reduction in vehicle mileage or trips. Variations of transport costs have different consequences for different modes, but transport demand has a tendency to be inelastic. While commuting tends to be inelastic in terms of costs, it is elastic in terms of time. For economic sectors where freight costs are a small component of the total production costs, variations in transport costs have limited consequences on the demand. For air transportation, especially the tourism sector, price variations have significant impacts on the demand. There are thus differences among the obtained price elasticities, which raises questions about the transferability of the results to other locations and or other time periods. Hence, each case is characterized by a specific local environment in terms of modal choice options, budget/income of the transport user, spatial planning, price levels, etc. All these factors combined can make the behavior of transport users somewhat different across regions and settings.

As transport demand is a derived demand from individuals, groups and industries, it can be desegregated into series of partial demands fulfilled by the adaptation and evolution of transport techniques, vehicles and infrastructures to changing needs. Moreover, the growing complexity of economies and societies linked with technological changes forces the transport industry to constant changes. This leads to growing congestion, a reduction in transport safety, a degradation of transport infrastructures and concerns about environmental impacts.

Transportation yield management

Transport demand tends to be variable in time and space, whereas transport supply is fixed. When demand is lower than supply, transit times are stable and predictable, since the infrastructures are able to support their load. When transport demand exceeds supply for a period in time, there is congestion, with significant increases in transit times and higher levels of unpredictability. A growth of the transport demand increases the load factor of a transport network until transport supply is reached. Speed and transit times drop afterwards. The same journey can thus have different durations according to the time of the day.

Conventionally, congestion tended to have limited impacts on the fare structure, as many transport operators were state owned or highly regulated. With deregulation, transport companies were able to establish a level of service reflecting market forces, as well as being able to expand, or rationalize, their capacity. Subsidies were removed, implying that the fare structure would be the dominant source of income to provide for operating and capital costs of the transport service. A common issue is that, while the transport supply is relatively well-known, often a scheduled service, the transport demand remains predictable but subject to volatility. Many transport providers, particularly airline companies, have responded to the complexity of predicting transport demand with **yield management** approaches. It involves managing the usage price of a transport asset, such as the fare paid by users, in view of continuous changes in the demand. The goal of such an approach is to maximize profit in the context where the transport supply is fixed.

Yield management leans on three conditions:

- **A fixed transport capacity**, implying that transport demand is the only function that can effectively vary. For instance, the capacity of a scheduled flight or of a container ship is fixed (known value) and cannot be readily changed without serious impacts on the quality of service. An exception to this rule concerns on-demand taxi services, where peak hours often lead to surges in fares, encouraging additional drivers to become available during that time period.
- **Unused transport capacity loses all of its utility**, implying that transport suppliers cannot store for another time the services that have not been used. Once an aircraft or a ship has departed, its transport capacity is lost for the concerned airport or port. Any unused capacity is therefore a loss of potential revenue.
- Transport users are willing to **pay different rates for the same capacity or service**, implying that they value transportation differently based upon their priorities and time preferences. For instance, a business traveler who needs to attend a meeting values differently the same airplane seat than a tourist would. The former would be willing to pay a high price to secure a seat on a specific flight, while the latter tends to seek discounted values and would be unwilling to bid above a certain price threshold. Also, time-dependent users of cargo services (e.g. electronics) are willing to pay more for the same capacity than those who are less time-dependent.

Under such circumstances, transport operators may constantly change their rates to reflect the temporal and spatial fluctuations in demand. For instance, in the United States, between the time seats are made available and when the flight is scheduled to depart domestic airfares are adjusted on average 92 times on a specific flight.

CASE STUDY The cruise industry

Authors: Dr Jean-Paul Rodrigue and Dr Theo Notteboom

Emergence of the cruise industry

From the mid-nineteenth century liner services supported long-distance passenger transportation between continents, particularly between Europe and North America. The need to accommodate a large number of passengers of different socioeconomic status for at least a week led to the emergence of specific ship designs radically different from cargo ships, where speed and comfort (at least for the elite) were paramount. The emergence of the cruise industry can be traced to the **demise of the ocean liner** in the 1960s, as it was replaced by fast jet services with which it could not compete. The last liners became the first cruise ships, as it took more than a decade to see the complete demise of liner services with the final realization that long-distance travel was now to be assumed by air transport. The availability of a fleet of liners whose utility was no longer commercially justifiable prompted their reconversion to form the first fleet of cruise ships.

For instance, one of the last purposely designed liners, the SS *France*, operating between 1961 and 1974, was mainly used for the conventional transatlantic service between Le Havre and New York. With rising oil prices and more efficient jet liners, including the 747 (introduced in 1970), the liner was no longer able to effectively compete over the transatlantic route. While a jet plane could link Paris or London to New York in about eight hours, it took about four days for a liner to cross the Atlantic, excluding a train segment between London and Southampton (or Paris and Le Havre). Considering one round trip per day, a 747 could carry about 3,200 passengers across the Atlantic in the time it took the SS *France* to carry 2,000 passengers on a single journey. Unable to generate enough revenue to justify its operating costs the SS *France* was mothballed in 1974 and purchased by Norwegian Cruise Line (and renamed the SS *Norway*). Its final commercial years between 1980 and 2003 were spent as a **cruise ship**. However, liners were not particularly suitable to the requirements of the emerging cruise industry. For instance, since many liners were designed to operate on the North Atlantic throughout the year for scheduled passenger services, their outdoor amenities such as boardwalks and swimming pools were limited. Additionally, they were built for speed (which was their trademark) with the related high levels of fuel consumption.

The modern cruise industry began in the late 1960s and early 1970s with the founding of Norwegian Cruise Line (1966), Royal Caribbean International (1968) and Carnival Cruise Lines (1972), which have remained the largest cruise lines. The early goal of the cruise industry was to **develop a mass market** since cruising was up till then an activity for the elite. A way to achieve this was through economies of scale, as larger ships are able to accommodate more customers as well as create additional opportunities for **on-board sources of revenue**. The first dedicated cruise ships began to appear in the 1970s and could carry about 1,000 passengers. By the 1980s, economies of scale were further expanded with cruise ships that could carry more than 2,000 passengers. The current large cruise ships have a capacity of about 6,000 passengers. The market for the cruise industry was by then established and recognized as a fully fledged touristic alternative directly competing with well-known resort areas such as Las Vegas or Orlando.

Cruise ships tend to have a low draft, since they do not carry cargo; they are more volume than weight. This confers the advantage of being able to **access a large number of ports**, and therefore multiplying itinerary options, since the setting of a pure cruise port leans on criteria that are different from commercial ports. Cruise ports tend to be located close to either city centers (cultural and commercial amenities) or to natural amenities (e.g. a protected beach). These sites do not have on average very deep drafts and dredging would be socially or environmentally unacceptable. For instance, ships of the Oasis class, which as of 2016 accounted for the largest cruise ship class, have a draft of 31 ft. Comparatively, a containership of 2,500 TEUs requires a draft of 33 ft, while a sovereign class container ship of 8,400 TEUs requires a draft of 46 ft. Draft issues that have plagued container ports are a much more marginal constraint for cruise shipping.

Additionally, cruise ships have the option to anchor and use **tendering service**s, which opens a wide array of ports of call.

Market dynamics

The global cruise industry offers a combination of local destinations accessible through the cruise port and on-board amenities offered by the cruise ship. It carried about 22.2 million passengers in 2015, up from 7.2 million in 2000. The global growth rate of the cruise industry has been enduring and stable, at around 7 percent per year in spite of economic cycles of growth and recession. For instance, the financial crisis of 2008–9 has not impacted the demand for cruises. Three major trends have particularly shaped the cruise market since its emergence:

- **Amenities**. The cruise ship has become an important part of the cruise experience since it also represents a destination in itself. An increasing number of amenities are being offered, both on the ships and as shore experiences.
- **Massification**. The principle of economies of scale and the development of a wider customer base has prompted the deployment of larger cruise ships. While in the 1990s cruise ships rarely exceeded 2,000 passengers, by the 2010s ships of 6,000 passengers were being deployed. Also, larger ships are able to support a wider range of amenities.
- **Concentration**. The industry has a high level of ownership and market concentration. Carnival and Royal Caribbean are the two main cruise lines and account for 73 percent of the market. The Caribbean and the Mediterranean account for about 70 percent of the global annual deployment of cruise capacity.

These trends underline that the industry has so far been fundamentally **supply-based**; the ships are built and the customers are found to fill them through various marketing and discounting strategies. The possibility for cruise ship operators to successfully follow a supply push strategy makes the cruise industry quite different from other shipping markets, such as container shipping. This is also in contradiction to the tourism sector in general, which is highly demand driven and thus sensitive to the general economic context. Hence, in most shipping markets the shipping activity is a clear derived activity of trade and demand is rather price inelastic. As mentioned earlier, demand in the cruise business is created through pricing, branding and marketing. Cruise operators are challenged to develop competitive cruise packages which involve a high-quality stay onboard, an array of shore-based activities offering access to a variety of cultures and sites, and easy transfers to/from the vessel. Most cruise lines have a logistics office that is responsible for supplying ships, particularly in terms of food – a core amenity. Variation in preferences are observed depending on the itinerary, and the composition of passengers, including factors such as origin and age.

The construction of cruise ships tends to take place in cycles where several ships are ordered and enter the market within a short time frame. Since the cruise industry is a relatively small segment of the touristic sector, it has so far been very successful in **finding customers to fill a greater number of ever larger ships**. The cruise product has become diversified to attract new customers and to respond to the preferences of a wide array of customer groups. In view of fulfilling the desires of its guests, the cruise industry has innovated through the development of new destinations, new ship designs, new and diverse on-board amenities, facilities and services, plus wide-ranging shoreside activities. Most cruise ship operators work around specific cruise themes, and voyage lengths can vary to meet the changing vacation patterns of customers. Its highest level of market penetration is in North America, with about 3 percent of the population taking a cruise each year. This includes people who may take more than one cruise in a year, so actual figures are actually lower.

The market drivers of the cruise industry are similar to those that have fostered the growth of tourism after World War II, particularly the rising affluence of the global population and the growing popularity of exotic and resort destinations. The general aging of the population is also a factor in favor of cruise shipping, as the main market remains older adults, although customers are getting significantly younger. While in 1995 the average age of a cruiser was about 65 years, this figure dropped to 45 years by 2006. What is novel with cruising is that the ship represents in itself the **destination**, essentially acting as a floating hotel (or a theme park) with all the related facilities (bars, restaurants, theaters, casinos, swimming pools, etc.). This permitted cruise lines to develop a captive market within their ships as well as for shore-based activities (e.g. excursions or facilities entirely owned by subsidiaries of the cruise line).

Networks and ports of call

The cruise industry sells **itineraries**, not destinations, implying a greater flexibility in the selection of ports of call. Cruise ports fall into two major categories: **turn ports** (or hub ports) where passengers begin and end their cruises; and **ports of call** that are visited along an itinerary. The selection of an itinerary is the outcome of several commercial considerations, including potential revenue generation, distance between ports of call (cruise ships can cover 200 nautical miles per night), brand positioning (exotic ports of call for premium services), guest satisfaction (customer-oriented industry), economic trends and market research, such as evaluating changes in disposable incomes and the demographics of the customer base. Ships are constantly moving between ports of call and shore leaves are of low duration: 4.3 hours on average in the Caribbean. A standard cruise itinerary is a loop, beginning and ending at a hub port (also called a turn port or port of embarkation) and typically lasting seven days with three to five ports of call depending on their respective proximity. Cruises of 10 to 21 days are also offered, but they tend to have lower profit margins, as customers are inclined to spend less as the cruise progresses.

The global cruise port system shows a high level of concentration and clustering (Figure 3.10). The observed destination patterns are clearly underlining the prominence of port visits around the Caribbean and the Mediterranean, in line with the operational characteristics of seven- day cruises calling at three to five ports. Other clusters of significant activity concern the US Northeast and Atlantic Canada, Alaska, Hawaii, Hanseatic ports and the coast of Norway. Limited cruise activity takes place in East and Southeast Asia, despite the significant economic development processes that have occurred in the region in recent decades. Therefore, the geography of cruise and commercial ports is completely different in terms of the dominant ports and the regions being serviced. It is also indicative that new cruising clusters may emerge to serve a latent demand from a growing middle and upper class in Asia, the Middle East and South America.

Three main types of itineraries can be found:

- **Perennial**. The region covered by the itinerary is serviced throughout the year as the demand remains resilient, which is associated with stable (subtropical) weather conditions as well as stable itineraries. There may be significant seasonal variations in the number of ships deployed, but the market remains serviced throughout the year. The Caribbean is the foremost perennial cruise market (summer low season), but the Mediterranean is also serviced year-round with a winter low season.
- **Seasonal**. Weather is the dominant factor explaining seasonality, implying that some regions have a market potential only during a specific period or season. This is particularly the case for Baltic, Norwegian, Alaskan and New England cruises that are serviced during summer months. Inversely, South American and Australian itineraries are serviced during the winter months.
- **Repositioning**. Because of the seasonality of the cruise industry, the repositioning of ships between seasons is required. Cruise companies are increasingly using this opportunity to offer customers lower cost cruises for the inconvenience of having to book air travel arrangements for the return trip, since the beginning and end ports of call are not the same. This mainly takes place across the Atlantic as ships move from the winter Caribbean peak season to the summer Mediterranean peak season (and vice versa). The beginning and the end of the Alaska season are also combined with a Hawaiian cruise as ships get repositioned. Barcelona and Dubai are emerging repositioning hubs, since the Mediterranean (3.10) and the Indian Ocean are growing faster than the conventional Caribbean market.

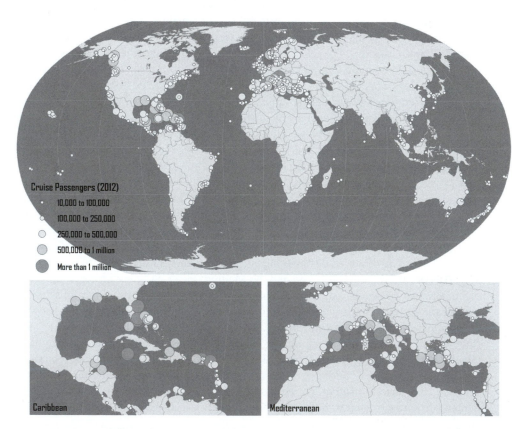

Figure 3.10 The global cruise port system

Source: Data adapted from Cruise Market Watch.

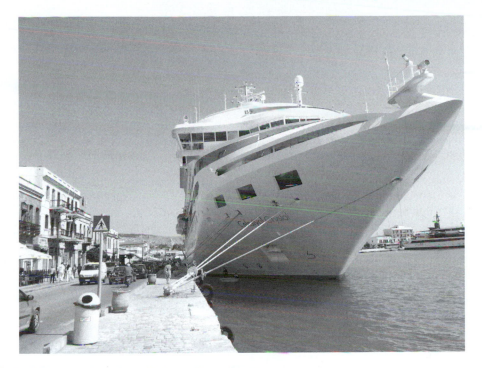

Photo 3.1 Large ships in small places, Chios, Greece

Cruise ships often call in on relatively small ports since they represent attractive venues in the cruise experience; a sense of exclusiveness. However, depending on the local amenities, such as docks, they can have a disruptive impact on local communities. The above cruise ship, the *Celestyal Crystal*, is docked at the port of Chios, an island in the Aegean Sea in Greece. The town has a population of about 32,000. Initially used as a ferry, the ship was rebuilt in 1992 as a fully fledged 1,000-passenger cruise ship. Although this ship is relatively small, the docking facilities are directly adjacent to the main commercial street. To ensure safe boarding and onboarding, one street lane has to be closed, which impedes local circulation. However, such impacts are minor compared to what communities such as Venice and Santorini are facing, since they have several cruise ships docked (or anchored) at once. The thousands of daily cruise passengers are placing acute pressures on the tourist amenities of these high-profile destinations. Two days after the above photo was taken, the *Celestyal Crystal* collided with a tanker off the coast of Gallipoli in Turkey. No injuries were reported and the ship was slightly damaged at the bow.

Photo: Dr Jean-Paul Rodrigue, 2015.

Bibliography

Berry, B.J.L. (1967) *Geography of Market Centers and Retail Distribution*. Englewood Cliffs, NJ: Prentice Hall.

Berry, B.J.L. (1991) *Long-wave Rhythms in Economic Development and Political Behavior*. Baltimore: Johns Hopkins University Press.

Brueckner, K. (2003) "Airline traffic and urban economic development." *Urban Studies* 40(8): 1455–1469.

Button K. (2010) *Transport Economics*, 3rd edition. Aldershot: Edward Elgar.

Button, K. and A. Reggiani (eds) (2011) *Transportation and Economic Development Challenges*. Cheltenham: Edward Elgar Publishing.

Dowling, R.K. (ed.) (2006) *Cruise Ship Tourism*. Cambridge, MA: CAB International.

European Conference of Ministers of Transport (2001) *Transport and Economic Development*. Paris: OECD.

Goodbody Economic Consultants (2003) *Transport and Regional Development*. Ballsbridge, Dublin: GEC/Department of Urban & Regional Planning UCD/Oscar Faber Transportation.

Harrington, J.W. and B. Warf (1995) *Industrial Location: Principles, Practice & Policy*. London: Routledge.

Henckel, T. and W. McKibbin (2010) *The Economics of Infrastructure in a Globalized World: Issues, Lessons and Future Challenges*. Washington: The Brookings Institution.

Henderson, J.V., Z. Shalizi and A.J. Venables (2000) "Geography and Development." *Journal of Economic Geography* 1: 81–106.

Hickman, R., M. Givoni, D. Bonilla, and D. Banister (eds) (2015) *Handbook on Transport and Development*. Cheltenham: Edward Elgar Publishing.

Lakshmanan, T.R. (2011) "The broader economic consequences of transport infrastructure investments." *Journal of Transport Geography* 19(1): 1–12.

MacKinnon, D., G. Pine and M. Gather (2008) "Transport and economic development, in R. Knowles, J. Shaw and I. Docherty (eds), *Transport Geographies: Mobilities, Flows and Spaces*. Oxford: Blackwell, pp. 10–28.

Pred, A. (1977) *City Systems in Advanced Economies: Past Growth, Present Processes and Future Development Options*. New York: Wiley.

Rodrigue, J.-P. and T. Notteboom (2013) "The geography of cruises: itineraries, not destinations." *Applied Geography* 38: 31–42.

United Nations Development Programme (2009) *Human Development Report 2009, Overcoming Barriers: Human Mobility and Development*. New York: Palgrave Macmillan.

Vickerman, R. (2012) *Recent Developments in the Economics of Transport*. Cheltenham: Edward Elgar Publishing.

4 Transportation modes

Transportation modes are an essential component of transport systems since they are the means by which mobility is supported. Geographers consider a wide range of modes that may be grouped into three broad categories based on the medium they exploit: land, water and air. Each mode has its own requirements and features, and is adapted to serve the specific demands of freight and passenger traffic. This gives rise to marked differences in the ways the modes are deployed and utilized in different parts of the world. Recently, there is a trend towards integrating the modes through intermodality and linking the modes ever more closely into production and distribution activities. At the same time, however, passenger and freight activity is becoming increasingly separated across most modes.

Concept 1 – Transportation modes, modal competition and modal shift

A diversity of modes

Transport modes are the means by which people and freight achieve mobility. They fall into one of three basic types, depending on over what surface they travel – land (road, rail and pipelines), water (shipping) and air. Each mode is characterized by a set of technical, operational and commercial characteristics (see Figure 4.1 and Figure 4.2).

Telecommunications are a special case as they cover a gray area in terms of whether they can be considered as a transport mode since, unlike true transportation, telecommunications often do not have a physicality. Yet, they are structured as networks with a practically unlimited capacity with very low constraints, which may include the physiography and oceanic masses that may impair the setting of cables. They provide for the instantaneous movement of information (speed of light in theory). Wave transmissions, because of their limited coverage, often require substations, such as for cellular phone and wireless data networks. Satellites often use a geostationary orbit which is getting crowded. High network costs and low distribution costs characterize many telecommunication networks, which are linked to the tertiary and quaternary sectors (stock markets, business to business information networks, etc.). Telecommunications can provide a substitution for personal movements in some economic sectors.

Modal competition

Each transportation mode has key operational and commercial advantages and properties. However, contemporary demand is influenced by **integrated transportation**

Figure 4.1 Main passenger modal options

Figure 4.2 Main freight modal options

Source: Adapted from W.J. DeWitt, "Freight transport and modes in global logistics and supply chains" (2000).

systems that require maximum flexibility. As a result, modal competition exists at various degrees and takes several dimensions. Different transportation modes have different cost functions according to the serviced distance (Figure 4.3). Road, rail and maritime transport have, respectively, C1, C2 and C3 cost functions. While road has a lower cost function for short distances, its cost function increases faster than rail and maritime cost functions. At a distance D1, it becomes more profitable to use rail transport than road transport, while from a distance D2, maritime transport becomes more advantageous. Point D1 is generally located between 500 km and 750 km from the point of departure, while D2 is nearer 1,500 km away. Although the explication above is rather straightforward, it does not fit reality well, mainly for the following reasons:

- It assumes that modal options are **interchangeable**. For many origins and destinations, modal options such as rail or maritime may not be present.
- Since rail and maritime transportation are discrete networks **only accessible through a terminal**, most locations will involve a road transportation segment, which changes the cost structure.

Modes can **compete or complement one another** in terms of cost, speed, accessibility, frequency, safety, comfort, etc. There are three main conditions that ensure that some modes complement each other:

- **Different geographical markets**. It is clear that if different markets are involved, modes will permit a continuity within the transport system, particularly if different scales are concerned, such as between national and international transportation. This requires an interconnection, commonly known as a gateway, where it is possible to transfer from one mode to the other. Intermodal transportation has been particularly relevant to improving the complementarity of different geographical markets.
- **Different transport markets**. The nature of what is being transported, such as passengers or freight, often indicates a level of complementarity. Even if the same

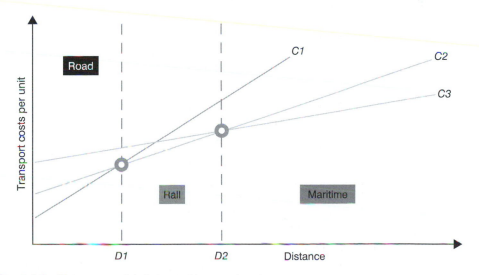

Figure 4.3 Distance, modal choice and transport costs

market area is serviced, it may not be equally accessible depending on the mode used. Thus, in some markets rail and road transportation can be complementary, as one may be focusing on passengers and the other on freight.

- **Different levels of service**. For a similar market and accessibility, two modes that offer a different level of service will tend to complement another. The most prevailing complementarity concerns costs versus time.

Thus, there is modal competition when there is an **overlap** in geography, transport and level of service. Cost is one of the most important considerations in modal choice. Because each mode has its own price/performance profile, the actual competition between the modes depends primarily upon the distance traveled, the quantities that have to be shipped and the value of the goods. While maritime transport might offer the lowest variable costs, over short distances and for small bundles of goods road transport tends to be most competitive. A critical factor is the terminal cost structure for each mode, where the costs (and delays) of loading and unloading the unit impose fixed costs that are incurred independent of the distance traveled.

With increasing income levels, the **propensity for people to travel rises**. At the same time, international trade in manufactured goods and parts has increased. These trends in travel demand act differentially upon the modes. Those that offer the faster and more reliable services gain over modes that might offer a lower cost, but slower, alternative. For passenger services, rail has difficulty in meeting the competition of road transport over short distances and aircraft for longer trips, for freight, rail and shipping have suffered from competition from road and air modes for high-value shipments. While shipping, pipelines and rail still perform well for bulkier shipments, intense competition over recent decades has seen road and air modes capture an important market share of the high revenue-generating goods. Road transport clearly dominates.

Although intermodal transportation has opened many opportunities for a complementarity between modes, there is intense competition as companies are now competing over many modes in the transport chain. A growing paradigm thus involves supply chain competition, with the modal competition component occurring over three dimensions:

- **Modal usage**. Competition that involves the comparative advantage of using a specific or a combination of modes. Distance remains one of the basic determinants of modal usage for passenger transportation. However, for a similar distance, costs, speed and comfort can be significant factors behind the choice of a mode.
- **Infrastructure usage**. Competition resulting from the presence of freight and passenger traffic on the same itineraries linking the same nodes.
- **Market area**. Competition experienced between transport terminals for using new space (terminal relocation or expansion) or capturing new markets (hinterland).

It is generally advocated that a form of **modal equality** (or modal neutrality) should be part of public policy where each mode would compete based upon its inherent characteristics. Since different transport modes are under different jurisdiction and funding mechanisms, modal equality is conceptually impossible, as some modes will always be more advantageous than others. Modal competition is influenced by public policy where one mode could be advantaged over the others. This particularly takes place over government funding of infrastructure and regulation issues. Roads are usually provided by the public sector, while many other transport infrastructures are financed by the operators using them. This is the case for rail, air and maritime transportation.

Modal shift

The technological evolution in the transport industry aims to adapt the transport infrastructures to growing needs and requirements. When a transport mode becomes more advantageous than another over the same route or market, a modal shift is likely to take place. A modal shift involves the growth in the demand of a transport mode at the expense of another, although a modal shift can involve an absolute growth in both of the concerned modes. The comparative advantages behind a modal shift can be in terms of costs, convenience, speed or reliability. For passengers, this involved a transition in modal preferences as incomes went up, such as from collective to individual modes of transportation. For freight, this has implied a shift to faster and more flexible modes when possible and cost-effective, namely trucking and air freight.

There are important **geographical variations in modal competition**. The availability of transport infrastructures and networks varies enormously. Some regions possess many different modes that in combination provide a range of transport services that ensure an efficient commercial environment. Thus, in contrast to the situation in the European Union, rail freight transport occupies a more important market share in North America but passenger rail has a negligible share. In many parts of the world, however, there are only limited services, and some important modes such as rail may be absent altogether. This limits the choices for passengers and shippers, and acts to limit accessibility. People and freight are forced to use the only available modes that may not be the most effective to support their mobility. Areas with limited modal choices tend to be among the least developed. Advanced economies, on the other hand, possesses a wide range of modes that can provide services to meet the needs of society and the economy.

Since 2000, fuel prices have increased significantly as well as their volatility, illustrated by significant price declines in 2009 and 2015. All modes are affected by fuel price volatility, from the individual car owner to the corporation operating a fleet of hundreds of aircraft or ships. Different pricing mechanisms are used, namely direct rate adjustments, as in the case of shipping, or indirect adjustments as in the case of airlines, with the reliance on fuel surcharges when energy prices increase.

Concept 2 – Road transportation

The setting of road transport systems

Road transportation and its infrastructures are large consumers of space, with the lowest level of physical constraints among transportation modes. However, physiographical constraints are significant in road construction with substantial additional costs to overcome features such as rivers or rugged terrain. While historically road transportation was developed to support non-motorized forms of transportation (walking, domestication of animals and cycling at the end of the nineteenth century), it is motorization that has shaped its development the most since the beginning of the twentieth century. Road transportation has an average operational flexibility as vehicles can serve several purposes but are rarely able to move outside roads. It offers a range of motorized and non-motorized options for short-distance movements that a user may opt for depending on affordability, convenience, availability and comfort. The automobile has emerged as a preferred form of passenger transportation, as it offers flexibility and convenience, but also contributes to the dominant share of the congestion of roads, particularly in urban areas.

Road transport systems have **high maintenance costs**, both for the vehicles and infrastructures. They are mainly linked to light industries where rapid movements of freight in small batches are the norm. Yet, with containerization, road transportation has become a crucial link in freight distribution. Trucks are highly flexible vehicles able to carry almost every type of cargo over short to medium distances. Package trucks are commonly used in urban freight distribution since they carry a variety of cargo (in boxes or pallets) servicing a fluctuating demand. Less-than-truckload (LTL) carriers usually consolidate and deconsolidate loads coming from different customers, which is common in the parcel-carrying business. Truckload (TL) transportation carries large volumes that have been broken down into the largest possible truckload unit; several truckloads are required to fulfill an order. The variety of modal options is related to the technical requirements to carry specific cargoes such as bulk, liquids or containers. Trucks using chassis are able to carry domestic (usually 53 ft in North America) and ISO containers (20 ft and 40 ft).

Road development accelerated in the first half of the twentieth century. By the 1920s, the first all-weather transcontinental highway, the Lincoln Highway, spanned over 5,300 km between New York and San Francisco. The Germans, however, were the first to build the modern highway (*Autobahn*) in 1932 with specifications such as restricted access, overpasses and road separation that would eventually become common characteristics of highway systems. The post-World War II era represented a period of rapid expansion of road transportation networks worldwide. The most remarkable achievement is without doubt the American **Interstate highway system**, initiated in 1956. Its strategic purpose was to provide a national road system servicing the American economy and also able to support troop movements and act as airstrips in case of an emergency. About 56,000 km was built from the 1950s to the 1970s, but between 1975 and 2006 only 15,000 km were added to the system, underlining growing construction costs and diminishing returns. Overall, about 70,000 km of four-lane and six-lane highways were constructed, linking all major American cities, coast to coast. A similar project took place in Canada with the Trans-Canada Highway, completed in 1962. By the 1970s, every modern nation had constructed a national highway system, which in the case of Western Europe resulted in a pan-European system. This trend now takes place in many industrializing countries.

An overview of the growth of the American and the Chinese highway systems underlines different growth sequences and rates (Figure 4.4). From its inception, the American Interstate highway system expanded substantially, but at a declining rate as the system neared its planned size (74,000 km). By 1991, after more than three decades of construction, the system was considered completed, with a total cost of about $129 billion. Between 1954 and 2001, $370 billion were invested by the federal government in the construction and the maintenance of the system. Close to three-quarters of the financing came from fuel taxes, which created a positive feedback loop as the more Interstate roads were available, the more fuel consumption and thus tax collection. However, the Interstate is facing diminishing returns due to high construction and maintenance costs, which is forcing many state governments to consider privatization of several highway segments. Construction costs went from $4 million per mile in 1959 to $20 million in 1979. Still, the system has returned more than $6 in economic productivity for each $1

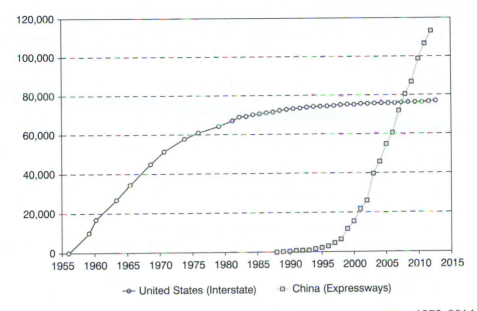

Figure 4.4 Length of the Interstate highway system and Chinese expressway system, 1959–2014 (in km)

Source: Federal Highway Administration and National Bureau of Statistics of China.

it cost, placing it at the core of American economic productivity gains in the second half of the twentieth century.

The Chinese expressway system was developed later, but at a much faster rate. Prior to 1989, there were no highways in China, but as the economy opened up, the development of a national system of expressways was seen as a priority. To facilitate the fast construction of the system, almost all expressways are toll roads financed by private companies under contract from provincial governments, commonly as public–private partnerships. Debt contracted for expressway construction is expected to be recovered through toll collection. Unlike the United States, China did not implement a national fuel tax road financing mechanism. This mode of financing thus differs from the publicly funded highway systems built in Europe and North America. A significant landmark was achieved in 2011, when the length of the Chinese expressway system surpassed that of the American interstate system. The planned length of the expressway system was set at 85,000 km, but was exceeded since the system surpassed 100,000 km in 2013. The construction of new expressways will likely slow down afterward, underlining that at this point China will have achieved an important step in its motorization transition. It remains to be assessed in light of the significant urban population, rising levels of national production and consumption, and the fast growth of car ownership, to what extent the national expressway network will be sufficient to effectively support China's mobility needs.

The spatial impacts of road transportation

Road transportation is the mode that has expanded the most over the last 50 years, both for passengers and freight transportation. This represents a dramatic change in the built environment, with the massive addition of road infrastructures. The spatial cover of road transportation is extensive. Growth in road freight transport has been fueled largely by trade liberalization, as modal shares of trade within the European Union and North American Free Trade Agreement (NAFTA) suggest. This is the result of growth of the loading capacity of vehicle and an adaptation of vehicle to freight (e.g. perishables, fuel, construction materials) or passengers (e.g. school bus) demand for speed, autonomy and flexibility. Problems, such as a significant growth of fuel consumption, increasing environmental externalities, traffic congestion and safety (accidents) have also emerged.

Roads have a **functional hierarchy** depending on the role they play in the network. At the top of the hierarchy are freeways (highways), which are limited access roads with no intersections. There are also arterials that are roads that have traffic signals at intersections, forcing vehicles to stop. These arterials are fed by collectors and local roads, which have the main purpose of connecting specific activities (residences, retail stores, industries). Put together, this network enables point-to-point services, a notable advantage the road transport has over other transport modes. Road transport modes have **limited potential to achieve economies of scale**. This is due to size and weight constraints imposed by governments and also by the technical and economic limits of engines. In most jurisdictions, trucks and buses have specific weight and length restrictions which are imposed for safety reasons.

Road transport, however, possesses significant advantages over other modes:

- The **capital cost** of vehicles is relatively small, which makes it comparatively **easy for new users to gain entry**. This helps ensure that the trucking industry, for example, is highly competitive. Low capital costs also ensure that innovations and new technologies can diffuse quickly through the industry.
- Another advantage of road transport is the **high relative speed** of vehicles, the major constraint being government-imposed speed limits.
- One of its most important attributes is the **flexibility of route choice**, once a network of roads is provided. Road transport has the unique opportunity of providing door-to-door service for both passengers and freight.

These multiple advantages have made cars, buses and trucks the modes of choice for a large number of trip purposes, and have led to their market dominance for short-distance trips. The success of cars and trucks has given rise to a number of serious problems. Road congestion has become a feature of most urban areas around the world. In addition, the mode is behind many of the major environmental externalities linked to transportation. Addressing these issues is becoming an important policy challenge at all levels of jurisdiction, from the local to the global. A symbiosis between types of roads and types of traffic with specialization (reserved lanes and hours) is to be expected.

Infrastructures and investments

Road infrastructures are **moderately expensive** to provide, but there is a wide divergence of costs, from a gravel road to a multi-lane urban expressway. Because vehicles have the means to climb moderate slopes, physical obstacles are less important than for some other land modes, namely rail. Most roads are provided as a **public good** by governments, while the vast majority of vehicles are owned privately. Capital costs, therefore, are generally assumed by the society, and do not fall as heavily on one source as is the case for other modes. Unlike many transport infrastructures where the network is paid for by the user through a pricing mechanism, 95 percent of the financing of road infrastructure is covered by the public sector, leaving the reminder covered by tolls.

Road transportation thus has a unique characteristic where several costs are externalized. This is an indirect form of mobility subsidy.

The public offering of free road infrastructure conveys several advantages to the private sector, but can also lead to serious problems. The main advantage is clear: the users of roads commonly **do not bear the full operating costs**, implying that road transportation tends to be below real market price. For road freight transportation, this can be seen as a subsidy, as road maintenance is not part of the operating costs but is indirectly present with taxes and tolls. As long as there is spare road capacity this situation works for the benefit of the users. However, when congestion starts to arise, users have limited, if any, influence on the construction of new and improved infrastructure to mitigate the problem, since they do not own the infrastructure and are using it for free. Lobbying public entities to receive public road infrastructure investments can be a very long process, subject to constant delays and changes. Road users thus become trapped in a situation they can do little to change since it is provided free of charge. This can be labeled as the "**free roads curse.**" An entity owning and operating its own network has the advantage of directly implementing improvements with its own capital if congestion arises on a segment of its network. It is thus better placed to cope with congestion.

In many cases governments have been inefficient custodians of road infrastructure, as it is tempting to delay road maintenance or improvements because of the high costs involved. Budgetary problems are also prompting the sale of assets to increase revenue and reduce expenses. Consequently, a growing number of roads have been **privatized** and companies specializing in road management have emerged, particularly in Europe and North America. This is only possible on specific trunk roads that have important and stable traffic. Private enterprises usually have vested interests to see that the road segments they manage are maintained and improved, since the quality of the road will be directly linked with revenue generation. The majority of toll roads are highways linking large cities or bridges and tunnels where there is a convergence of traffic. Most roads are not economically profitable but must be **socially present**, as they are essential to service populations.

Concept 3 – Rail transportation

Rail transportation and rail lines

Rail transportation is composed of a traced path on which vehicles are bound. They have an average level of physical constrains linked to the types of locomotives and a low gradient is required, particularly for freight. Rail transportation is characterized by a high level of economic and territorial control since most rail companies are operating in situation of **monopoly**, as in Europe, or **oligopoly**, as in North America where seven large rail freight carriers control and operate large networks. Operating a rail system involves using regular (scheduled), but rigid, services. Rail transportation, like roads, has an important relationship with space, since it is the transport mode the most constrained by the physiography. Gauges, however, vary around the world, often complicating the integration of rail systems. The global rail network, which is mostly a collection of unlinked national rail systems, is an overlay of three main types of rail lines (Figure 4.5):

- **Penetration lines.** Their main purpose is to link a port city with its hinterland, particularly in order to access natural resources such as minerals, agricultural products and wood products. The purpose of a penetration line is to convey large amounts of materials in a manner that would be prohibitive for road transport. It also represented one of the initial stages of rail development, notably in the United States, which later became regional networks linked by transcontinental lines. Penetration lines are today mainly found in developing countries (Africa and Latin America) and were partially the result of the colonial era. Such areas have several gauges and limited crossborder connectivity and thus offer limited competitiveness with trucking.

- **Regional networks**. These service high-density population areas of developed countries with the goal to support massive shipment of freight and passengers. Regions with the highest rail density are Western Europe, the northeastern part of North America, coastal China and Japan.
- **Transcontinental lines**. These lines were mainly established to improve territorial accessibility and for the setting of national sovereignty. The most relevant examples are in the United States, Canada, Russia and Australia, which have built rail systems of this scale, such as between New York and Los Angeles, across Eurasia (between Dalian and Moscow), across Southern Australia (Perth and Adelaide) or across South America (Buenos Aires and Valparaiso). More recently, transcontinental rail lines have seen a renewal in interest by their capability to attenuate the discontinuity of maritime transportation by transporting containers such as over the North American landbridge and the Eurasian landbridge. They are a chain in the global intermodal transport system.

Other factors that inhibit the movement of trains between different countries include signaling and electrification standards. These are particular problems for the European Union where the lack of interoperability of the rail systems between the member states is a factor limiting the wider use of the rail mode. There is also a trend where the passenger and freight markets are being separated.

Figure 4.5 World rail network and rail systems

The spatial economy of rail transportation

The ability of trains to haul large quantities of goods and significant numbers of people over long distances is the mode's primary asset. Overall, rail transportation is more efficient than road transportation, although its main drawback is flexibility, as traffic must follow fixed routes and transshipment must be done at terminals. Once the cars have been assembled or the passengers have boarded, trains can offer a high-capacity service at a reasonable speed (with some high-speed systems). It was this feature that in the nineteenth century led to the train's pre-eminence in opening up the interior of the continents, and this is still its major asset.

With containerized unit trains, economies of scale can readily be achieved, while roads have limited ability to benefit from this advantage. Each additional container carried by road involves the same marginal cost increase, while for rail there is a declining marginal cost per additional container until the unit train size is reached. The same applies to passengers for road transportation: an additional movement usually involves an additional vehicle, while for rail there are declining marginal costs as a passenger train gets filled. Passenger service is thus effective where population densities are high. Freight traffic is dominated by bulk cargo shipments – agricultural and industrial raw materials in particular. Rail transport is a greener inland mode, in that its consumption of energy per unit load per kilometer is lower than road mode.

The initial **capital costs of rail are high** because the construction of rail tracks and the provision of rolling stock are expensive. Historically, investments have been made by the same source (either governments or the private sector). These expenditures have to be made before any revenues are realized and thus represent important entry barriers that tend to limit the number of operators. It also serves to delay innovation, compared with road transport, since rail rolling stock has a service life of at least 20 years. This can also be an advantage, since rolling stock is more durable and offers better opportunities to amortize. On average, rail companies need to invest about 45 percent of their operating revenues each year in capital and maintenance expenses of their infrastructure and equipment. Capital expenditures alone account for about 17 percent of revenue, while this share is around 3 to 4 percent for manufacturing activities.

Since the end of the 1950s, railway systems in advanced economies have faced **increasing competition from road transport**, with varying results. In all cases, the break-even distance, which is the threshold above which rail becomes most cost-effective than road, changed to the advantage of road transport. The more efficient road transport became, the higher its break-even distance. In the current context, the break-even distance between intermodal rail and truck is 600–800 miles (950–1,300 km). Under 500 miles (800 km), drayage costs from the terminal usually account for 70 percent of total costs.

In several countries, such as China, India and Japan, rail transportation accounts for the majority of interurban passenger transportation. Among developed countries, there are acute geographical differences in the economic preference of rail transportation. For Europe, China and Japan rail transportation is still very important, mainly for passenger transportation, but has declined over the last decades. High-speed passenger rail projects, however, are improving its popularity, but the competition was mainly felt on air transportation services rather than road transport. For North America, rail transportation is strictly related to freight, with passengers playing a marginal role only along a few major urban corridors. Passenger trains are even getting delayed because priority is given to freight.

Rail freight services are also facing the challenge of improving their reliability, which leads to a fragmentation of the types of services being offered. For conventional rail freight markets such as coal, grain, forest products or chemicals, the priority has consistently been the provision of high-capacity and low-cost forms of transportation. However, these services were unreliable but could be easily accommodated by stock-piling, a strategy common in the resource sector (e.g. power plants, grain elevators). An emerging freight market for rail mostly concerns intermodal services that require a much higher level of reliability, similar to what is expected in trucking.

Rail transportation in the twenty-first century

Although railways are a product of the Industrial Revolution, they have been affected by continuous innovations, technical, regulatory and commercial changes which have improved their capacity and efficiency. Rail transportation is thus as important in the twenty-first century as it was in the late nineteenth century. One innovation relates to the quality of the rail infrastructure, particularly rail tracks (e.g. better steel, concrete ties), which determines the operational characteristics of their use such as speed, permitted weight, maintenance and resilience to the environment. Increasing **electrification** and **automation** also improve the efficiency of rail transportation, passenger and freight alike. A few new rail lines are being built, but mainly in developing countries. Railway speed records have constantly improved with the introduction of high-speed rail systems. However, freight trains run at a considerably lower speed, in the range of 30–35 km per hour. In some cases, as the rail system gets used more, operational speed may decline because of congestion.

Rail transport has comparative advantages in carrying heavy bulk traffic on specific itineraries over long distances. For instance, a 10-car freight train can carry as much cargo as 600 trucks. Aside from its emphasis on safety and reliability, rail transport favors the fast commuting of suburbanites during peak hours and has become an important mode supporting passenger movements in large cities.

The global trend involves the closure of unprofitable lines as well as the elimination of several stops. Over the last 50 years, with downsizing of rail transportation while traffic was moving to other modes, rail companies abandoned lines (or sold them to local rail companies), removed excess terminals and warehousing capacity and sold off property. The process of rationalization (deregulation) of the rail network is now completed in a number of countries, such as in the United States. This has implied significant labor savings with the reduction of train crews, more flexible working hours and the usage of subcontractors for construction and maintenance. In addition to energy-efficient and lighter equipment, the usage of double-stack cars has revolutionized rail transportation, with additional fuel efficiency and cost reductions of about 40 percent. Depending on the service and type of commodity carried, rail can be 1.9 to 5.5 times more energy efficient than trucking. Unit trains, carrying one commodity type only, allow scale economies and efficiencies in bulk shipments, and double-stacking has greatly promoted the advantages of rail for container shipments.

Trends concerning cargo transport using trailers on flat cars (TOFC) and containers on flat cars (COFC) well illustrate the increasing adoption of intermodal transport. Still, TOFC services are being phased down and COFC increasingly dominates. Due to its great versatility, the container is highly favored as such a means of cargo transport: loading trailers onto rail cars is prone to inefficiencies, particularly a much lower load factor than containers. Double-stack rail technology is a major challenge for the rail transport system, as it is effective for long distances where additional terminal costs are compensated by lower transport costs. North America has a notable advantage over Europe on this issue since a full double-stacked unit train can carry between 400 and

600 TEU (200 to 300 containers) and can have a length exceeding 10,000 ft (about 3,000 m). The average intermodal train length in the United States is around 6,500 ft (about 2,000 m). European trains are generally limited to 750 m and can carry 80 TEU of single-stacked containers, while some rail segments can accommodate 850 m.

Further, most railroads were constructed early in the twentieth century and have an overhead clearance that is inadequate for the usage of double-stack trains. This is notably the case for tunnels and bridges. Even if improving clearance is a major investment, several rail companies, notably in North America, have invested massively on double-stacking projects. The economies and improved capacity of double-stacking have justified investments of raising the clearance from 5.33 m (17 ft 6 in) to 8.1 m (20 ft 6 in) along major long-distance rail corridors. Europe is less advanced in this process because most of its rail facilities were built in the middle of the nineteenth century. Clearance thus forbids the usage of double-stacking on most European rail corridors.

The emergence of **high-speed rail networks** and increasing rail speed had significant impacts on passenger transportation, especially in Europe and Japan. High-speed passenger trains require special lines, but can also use the existing lines at a lower speed. In many cases it permitted a separation between rail passenger traffic rolling at high speed and freight traffic using the conventional rail network. The efficiency of both the passenger and freight rail network was thus improved significantly. Since high-speed trains require some time to accelerate and decelerate, the average distance between stations has increased significantly, bypassing several centers of less importance. Over average distances, they have proved to be able to compete effectively with air transportation. Other strategies include improving the speed of existing passenger services without building a high-speed corridor. This involves upgrading the equipment and improving the infrastructure at specific locations along the corridor. The benefits of offering a passenger rail service above 120 km per hour can substantially improve the quality and efficiency of intercity services in high-density urban regions.

Pipelines

Pipelines represent a completely separate system of freight distribution where liquids (particularly oil) and gases can be pumped over long distances. Pipeline routes are practically unlimited, as they can be laid on land or under water. Two main products dominate pipeline traffic – oil and gas – although locally pipelines are significant for the transport of water, and in some rare cases for the shipment of dry-bulk commodities, such as coal in the form of slurry. The longest gas pipeline links Alberta to Sarnia (Canada), which is 2,911 km in length. The longest oil pipeline is the Transiberian, extending over 9,344 km from the Russian Arctic oilfields in eastern Siberia to Western Europe. Physical constraints are low and include the landscape and permafrost in Arctic or sub-Arctic environments. Pipeline construction costs vary according to the diameter and increase proportionally with the distance and with the viscosity of fluids (gas, low viscosity – oil, high viscosity). The Trans-Alaskan pipeline, which is 1,300 km long, was built under difficult conditions and has to be above ground for most of its path. Pipeline terminals are very important, since they correspond to refineries and harbors.

Pipelines are almost everywhere designed for a **specific purpose** only: to carry one commodity from a location to another. They are built largely with private capital and, because the system has to be in place before any revenues are generated, represent a significant capital commitment. They are effective in transporting large quantities of products where no other feasible means of transport (usually water) is available. Pipeline routes tend to link isolated areas of production to major refining and manufacturing centers in the case of oil, or to major populated areas, as in the case of natural gas. Pipelines can even be used to carry small quantities of freight, such as in pneumatic tubes, but this use remains marginal and for short distances.

The routing of pipelines is largely indifferent to terrain, although environmental concerns frequently delay approval for construction. In sensitive areas, particularly in Arctic/sub-Arctic areas where the pipes cannot be buried because of permafrost, the impacts on migratory wildlife may be severe, and be sufficient to deny approval, as was the case of the proposed McKenzie Valley pipeline in Canada in the 1970s. Geopolitical factors play a very important role in the routing of pipelines that cross international boundaries. Pipelines from the Middle East to the Mediterranean have been routed to avoid Israel, and new pipelines linking Central Asia with the Mediterranean are being routed in response to the ethnic and religious mosaic of the republics in the Caucasus.

Pipeline construction costs vary according to the diameter and increase proportionally with the distance and with the viscosity of fluids (needed for pumping stations). Operating costs are very low, however, and as mentioned earlier pipelines represent a very important mode for the transport of liquid and gaseous products. One major disadvantage of pipelines is the inherent inflexibility of the mode. Once built (usually at great expense), expansion of demand is not easily adjusted to. There are specific limits to the carrying capacity. Conversely, a lessening of supply or demand will produce a lowering of revenues that may affect the viability of the system. A further limit arises out of geographical shifts in production or consumption, in which a pipeline having been built from one location to another may not be able to easily adjust to changes.

Concept 4 – Maritime transportation

Maritime geography and routes

Maritime transportation, similar to land and air modes, operates in its own space, which is at the same time **geographical** by its physical attributes, **strategic** by its control and **commercial** by its usage. While geographical considerations tend to be constant in time (with the exception of the seasonality of weather patterns), strategic and especially commercial considerations are much more dynamic. The physiography of maritime transportation is composed of two major elements: rivers and oceans. Although they are connected, each represents a specific domain of maritime circulation (Figure 4.6). The notion of maritime transportation rests on the existence of regular itineraries, better known as **maritime routes**.

Maritime routes are corridors of a few kilometers in width trying to avoid the discontinuities of land transport by linking ports, the main elements of the maritime/land interface. Maritime routes are a function of obligatory points of passage, which are strategic places, of physical constraints (coasts, winds, marine currents, depth, reefs, ice) and of political borders. As a result, maritime routes draw arcs on the earth's surface as intercontinental maritime transportation tries to follow the great circle distance. Maritime routes link maritime ranges representing main commercial areas, between and within which maritime shipping services are established.

Even if maritime transportation has experienced remarkable improvements in its safety and reliability, maritime routes are still hindered by dominant winds, currents and general weather patterns. The North Atlantic and the North Pacific are subject to heavy wave activity during the winter that sometimes impairs navigation, and may cause ships

Figure 4.6   Domains of maritime circulation

Source: Shipping density data adapted from National Center for Ecological Analysis and Synthesis, "A global map of human impacts to marine ecosystems" (2015)

to follow routes at lower latitudes, thereby increasing route lengths. During the summer monsoon season (April to October), navigation may become more hazardous on the Indian Ocean and the South China Sea.

About 50 countries have an inland navigation network of more than 1,000 km. Rivers may not be useful for commercial navigation if their orientation does not correspond to the directions of transport demand. Thus, many of the major rivers of Russia flow north–south, while the main trade and passenger flows are east–west. Shallow draft and extensive obstacles, such as rapids, may also limit navigation. However, many rivers, such as the Rhine or the Chang Jiang, are significant arteries for water transport because they provide access from the oceans to inland markets.

The majority of maritime circulation takes place along coastlines and three continents have limited fluvial trade: Africa, Australia and Asia (with the exception of China). There are, however, large fluvial waterway systems in North America, Europe and China over which significant fluvial circulation takes place. Despite regular services on selected fluvial arteries, such as the Yangtze, the potential of waterways for passenger transport remains limited to fluvial tourism (river cruises). Most major maritime infrastructures involve maintaining or modifying waterways to establish more direct routes (navigation channels and canals). This strategy, however, is very expensive and undertaken only when absolutely necessary. Significant investments have been made in expanding transshipment capacities of ports, which is also very expensive, as ports are heavy consumers of space.

Not every region has direct access to the ocean and maritime transport. As opposed to coastal countries, maritime enclaves (**landlocked countries**) are such countries that have difficulties undertaking maritime trade, since they are not directly part of an oceanic domain of maritime circulation. This requires agreements with neighboring countries to have access to a port facility through a highway, rail line or river. However, being landlocked does not necessarily imply an exclusion from international trade, but substantially higher transport costs that may impair economic development. Furthermore, the concept of being landlocked can be relative, since a coastal country could be considered as relatively landlocked if its port infrastructures were not sufficient to handle its maritime trade or if its importers or exporters were using a port in a third country.

Maritime traffic

Maritime transportation is dominantly focused on freight since there are no other effective alternatives to the long-distance transportation of large amounts of freight. Before the era of intercontinental air transportation, transcontinental passenger services were assumed by liner passenger ships, dominantly over the North Atlantic. Long-distance passenger movements are now a marginal leisure function solely serviced by cruise shipping. Still, several oceanic ferry services are also in operation over short distances, namely in Western Europe (English Channel, Baltic Sea), Japan and Southeast Asia (Indonesia and the Philippines). The systematic growth of maritime freight traffic has been fueled by:

- **Absolute advantages**. Linked with the geographical distribution of resources, implying that the places of production are usually different from the places of consumption. Large quantities of cargo therefore need to be carried over long distances. The growth in mineral and energy trades, the dominant cargoes carried by maritime shipping, is the outcome of both conventional demands from developed countries as well as new demands from developing economies. For instance, coal is mainly used for energy generation and steelmaking, activities that grew substantially in the developing world.
- **Comparative advantages**. Concerns cargoes that under ideal circumstances would likely not be carried, but because of cost and capabilities differentials substantial shipping flows are generated. The international division of production and trade liberalization, commonly referred to as globalization, prompted a large number of parts and finished goods to be carried over long distances, which has supported growth in container shipping. Therefore, such cargoes can be temporary and subject to changes in their origins and destinations.
- **Technical improvements**. Ships and maritime terminals have become more efficient in terms of their throughput and their ability to handle several types of cargo (e.g. containers, natural gas, refrigerated goods), enabling the support of long-distance trade.
- **Economies of scale**. The growth in the size of ships permitted maritime transportation to become increasingly cost-effective, a trend which has been strengthened by containerization.

Maritime traffic is commonly measured in **deadweight tons**, which refers to the amount of cargo that can be loaded on an "empty" ship without exceeding its operational design limits. This limit is often identified as a loadline, which is the maximal draft of the ship and does not account for the weight of the ship itself but includes fuel and ballast water. Maritime freight is conventionally considered in two main markets:

- **Bulk cargo**. Refers to freight, both dry and liquid, that is not packaged, such as minerals (oil, coal, iron ore, bauxite) and grains. It often requires the use of specialized ships such as oil tankers as well as specialized transshipment and storage facilities. Conventionally, this cargo has a single origin, destination and client and is prone to economies of scale. Services tend to be irregular, except for energy trades, and part of vertically integrated production processes (e.g. oil field to port to refinery). The dynamics of the bulk market are mainly attributed to industrialization and economic development, creating additional demand for resources and energy.

- **Break-bulk cargo**. Refers to general cargo that has been packaged in some way with the use of bags, boxes, drums and particularly containers. This cargo tends to have numerous origins, destinations and clients. Before containerization, economies of scale were difficult to achieve with break-bulk cargo, as the loading and unloading process was very labor- and time-consuming. The dynamics of the break-bulk market are related to manufacturing and consumption.

The global maritime shipping industry is serviced by about 22,000 vessels, falling into four broad types:

- **Passenger vessels** historically played an important role since they were the only mode available for long-distance transportation. In a contemporary setting, passenger vessels can be divided into two categories: passenger ferries, where people are carried across relatively short bodies of water (such as a river or a strait) in a shuttle-type service; and cruise ships, where passengers are taken on vacation trips of various durations, usually over several days. The former tend to be smaller and faster vessels; the latter are usually very large capacity ships having a full range of amenities. In 2014, about 21.5 million passengers were serviced by cruise ships, underlining an industry with much growth potential, since it services several seasonal markets where the fleet is redeployed to during the year.

- **Bulk carriers** are ships designed to carry specific commodities, and are differentiated into liquid bulk and dry bulk vessels. They include the largest vessels afloat. The largest tankers, the Ultra-Large Crude Carriers (ULCC) are up to 500,000 dead-weight tons (dwt), with the more typical size being between 250,000 and 350,000 dwt; the largest dry bulk carriers are around 400,000 dwt, while the more typical size is between 100,000 and 150,000 dwt. The emergence of liquefied natural gas (LNG) technology enabled the maritime trade of natural gas with specialized ships.

- **General cargo** ships are vessels designed to carry non-bulk cargoes. The traditional ships were less than 10,000 dwt, because of extremely slow loading and offloading. Since the 1960s these vessels have been replaced by container ships because they can be loaded more rapidly and efficiently, permitting a better application of economies of scale. Like any other ship class, larger container ships require larger drafts, with the current largest ships requiring a draft of 15.5 m.

- **Roll-on/roll-off (RORO)** vessels, which are designed to allow cars, trucks and trains to be loaded directly onboard. Originally appearing as ferries, these vessels are used on deep-sea trades and are much larger than the typical ferry. The largest are the car carriers that transport vehicles from assembly plants to their main markets.

The distinctions in vessel types are further differentiated by the kind of services on which they are deployed. Bulk ships tend to operate both on a regular schedule between two ports or on a voyage basis to reflect fluctuations in the demand. This demand may be seasonal, as for grain transport, or niche, such as for project cargo (e.g. carrying construction material). General cargo vessels operate on liner services, in which the vessels are employed on a regular scheduled service between fixed ports of call, or as tramp ships, where the vessels have no schedule and move between ports based on cargo availability.

Maritime economics

An important feature of the economics of shipping relates to its capital costs, which requires financing. Because of their size, ships represent a significant capital outlay. Cruise ships represent the most expensive class of vessels, with an Oasis class cruise ship costing $1.2 billion, but even container ships of the largest class represent an initial capital outlay of $190 million. The annual cost of servicing the purchase of these vessels represents the largest single item of operating expenditures, typically accounting for over half of the annual operating costs. Container shipping requires the deployment of many vessels to maintain a regular service (14 ships in the case of a typical Far East–Europe service), which is a severe constraint on the entry of new players. On the other hand, older secondhand vessels may be purchased for much smaller amounts, and sometimes the purchase price can be easily covered by a few successful voyages. In some regards, therefore, the shipping industry is quite open and historically has provided opportunities for entrepreneurs to accumulate large fortunes. Many of the largest fleets are in private hands, owned by individuals or by family groups.

The main advantage of maritime transportation is obviously its economies of scale, making it the cheapest per unit of all transport modes, which fits well for heavy industrial activities. On the other hand, maritime transportation has one of the highest entry costs of the transport sector. This is part of the maritime life cycle that includes building, registration, operations and the final scrapping of the ship. Typically, a ship has an economic life between 15 and 20 years, and thus represents a significant investment that must be amortized. For instance, a Panamax container ship can cost $50,000 per day to operate, with most of the expenses related to fuel and port charges. The operation of the maritime transport system requires financing that can come from two sources:

- **Public**. The public sector is commonly responsible for guidance infrastructures (beacons and charts), public piers, dredging, security and, in several cases, the administration of ports (under the umbrella of port authorities).
- **Private**. The private sector is mostly concerned about specific facilities such as piers, transshipment infrastructures and ships, which are commonly owned by private maritime companies.

In the past, governments have intervened, often massively, in the maritime sector to fulfill different goals such as economic development, national defense, prestige, balance of payments and the protection of the national industry. To reach those goals, governments relied on methods such as regulations, subsidies, national fleets, preference of cargo and ports of entry. **Cabotage regulations** have been one of the privileged measures to protect the national maritime transportation industry. Under such circumstances, each nation reserves for its national carriers the right to move domestic freight or passenger traffic.

Shipping services and networks

The shipping industry has a very **international character**, particularly in terms of ownership and flagging. The ownership of ships is very broad. While a ship may be owned by a Greek family or a Japanese corporation, it may be flagged under another nationality. There are two types of registers – national registers and open registers– which are often labeled as "flags of convenience." The use of flags of convenience is a means by which shipowners can obtain lower registration fees, lower operating costs and fewer restrictions. The maritime industry is now more deregulated than before because of technical changes, mainly containerization and open registry ships operating under fiscal shelters. As of 2013, about 73 percent of the global tonnage was registered under a flag of convenience, with Panama and Liberia being the most prevalent.

An important historic feature of oceanic liner transport is the operation of **conferences**. These are formal agreements between companies engaged on particular trading routes. They fix the rates charged by the individual lines – operating, for example, between Northern Europe and the East Coast of North America, or eastbound between Northern Asia and the West Coast of North America. Over the years, in excess of 100 such conference arrangements have been established. While they may be seen as anti-competitive, the conference system has always escaped prosecution from national anti-trust agencies. This is because they are seen as a mechanism to stabilize rates in an industry that is inherently unstable, with significant variations in supply of ship capacity and market demand. By fixing rates exporters are given protection from swings in prices, and are guaranteed a regular level of service provision. Firms compete on the basis of service provision rather than price.

A new form of inter-firm organization has emerged in the container shipping industry since the mid-1990s. Because the costs of providing ship capacity to more and more markets are escalating beyond the means of many carriers, many of the largest shipping lines have come together to form **strategic alliances** with former competitors. They offer joint services by pooling vessels on the main commercial routes. In this way they are each able to commit fewer ships to a particular service route, and deploy the extra ships on other routes that are maintained outside the alliance. The alliance services are marketed separately, but operationally involve close cooperation in selecting ports of call and in establishing schedules. The alliance structure has led to significant developments in route alignments and the economies of scale of container shipping. The consequences have been a concentration of ownership, particularly in container shipping.

The 20 largest carriers controlled 26 percent of the world slot capacity in 1980, 42 percent in 1992, 58 percent in 2003 and 81 percent in 2013. The level of concentration is causing concerns among various national regulatory bodies, which see such developments as potentially unfair competitive practices. For instance, in 2013 a large alliance dubbed P3 was being planned between the world's three largest carriers, Maersk, MSC and CMA CGM, to help mitigate overcapacity along several major trade routes, particularly between Asia and Europe. However, in 2014 the Chinese government rejected the alliance with the rationale that it was creating an undue level of concentration and the possibility of unfair competition with its own carriers. Therefore, Maersk and MSC decided to form a smaller alliance called M2 that began operations in 2015. Further CMA CGM, China Shipping Container Lines and United Arab Shipping Company (UASC) formed their own alliance called Ocean Three.

Carriers have the responsibility to establish and maintain profitable routes in a competitive environment. This involves three major decisions about how such a maritime network takes shape:

- **Frequency of service**. Frequency is linked with more timely services, since the same port will be called at more often. A weekly call is considered to be the minimum level of service but, since a growing share of production is time-dependent, there is a pressure from customers to have a higher frequency of service. A trade-off between the frequency and the capacity of service is commonly observed. This trade-off is often mitigated on routes that service significant markets since larger ships can be used with the benefits of economies of scale.

- **Fleet and vessel size**. Due to basic maritime economics, large ships, such as post-Panamax container ships, offer significant advantages over long distances. Shipping lines will obviously try to use this advantage over their long-distance routes, keeping smaller ships for feeder services. In addition, a large enough number of ships must be allocated to ensure a good frequency of service. To keep their operations consistent, shippers also try to have ships of similar size along their long-distance pendulum routes. This is not an easy undertaking, since economies of scale force the introduction of ever larger ships which cannot be added all at once due to extensive financial requirements and the capacity of shipbuilders to provide them. So each time a bigger ship is introduced on a regular route, the distribution system must adapt to this change in capacity.
- **Number of port calls**. A route that involves fewer port calls is likely to have lower average transit times in addition to requiring a lower number of ships. Conversely, too few port calls could involve difficulties for the cargo to reach inland destinations remote from the serviced ports. This implies additional delays and potentially the loss of customers. An appropriate selection of port calls along a maritime facade will help ensure access to a vast commercial hinterland.

A global maritime freight transport system has been established since the late nineteenth century and expanded with containerization. It includes east–west and north–south routes and locations enabling interconnectivity between these systems of circulation. Figure 4.7 illustrates the structure this system is likely to take in the coming years. The main components are:

- **Circum-equatorial route**. With the expansion of the Panama Canal, a relative parity exists for the first time between the Panama and Suez canals. In such a setting, maritime shipping companies may elect to establish circum-equatorial routes in both directions with the usage of high-capacity (8,000 to 14,000 TEU) container ships. This high-frequency "conveyor belt" could support a significant share of global east–west freight movements in a cost-effective way. This does not imply a homogenous service, as several different configurations of ports of call are possible along this route, particularly if a 300 nautical mile deviation is considered. This enables different circum-equatorial network configurations.
- **North–south pendulum connectors**. These connectors reflect existing commercial relations, namely for raw materials (oil, minerals, agricultural goods), such as South America/North America, Africa/Europe or Australia/Asia. For container shipping, they are mostly based on the rationale that there is not enough volume to support transoceanic services, so cargo is collected/delivered along a latitudinal sequence of ports. This conventional network will be expanded with transshipment opportunities with the circum-equatorial route.
- **Transoceanic pendulum connectors**. Connect a series of ports along ranges of large oceanic masses. The three main transoceanic connectors are transpacific, Asia–Europe (through the Indian Ocean) and transatlantic. The industrialization of Asia (China in particular) has made the Asia–Europe and the transpacific connectors

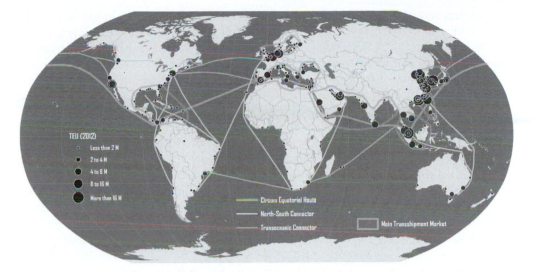

Figure 4.7 Emerging global maritime freight transport system

particularly important. The emergence of a new connector in the southern hemisphere between the east coast of South America, the Cape of Good Hope and to Southeast Asia is also observed.

- **Transshipment markets**. They connect regional port systems to transoceanic and circum-equatorial routes, mainly through hub-and-spoke services. The intersection and relay functions between long-distance shipping services performed by those markets is also significant. The most important are Southeast Asia, the Mediterranean and the Caribbean. They are referred to as markets because the transshipment function can be substituted to another port. Therefore, a group of ports in a transshipment market are vying to attract port calls, as this type of traffic is difficult to anchor. The development of circum-equatorial routes is thus likely to expand the opportunities for transshipment.

- **Polar routes**. Consider the usage of circum-polar routes as shortcuts to link East Asia, Western Europe and North America (both East and West Coasts). Even if the distance advantages of these polar routes appear significant, they are subject to the uncertainties of climate change and niche market opportunities.

Concept 5 – Air transport

Author: Dr John Bowen, Department of Geography, Central Washington University, contributed to this section

The rise of air transportation

By the eve of World War II, air travel was quite literally taking off, borne aloft by important advances in technology. Particularly important was the Douglas DC-3, the first airliner that could fly profitably. The 21-seat DC-3 was a long-range aircraft for its time, able to fly across the US, stopping just three times. By 1941, 80 percent of all commercial aircraft in the USA were DC-3s. The DC-3 was a landplane, but on longer-haul, inter-continental routes, flying boats remained common through World War II. Flying boats, like the double-deck Boeing 314, were the largest commercial aircraft until the building of the B747. They could fly very long distances but their slow speeds undercut their profitability. The market for long-haul travel was very small, partly because of the extraordinarily high cost. Many of the long-haul air services were to colonies and dependencies. Only the elite or government officials were able to afford air travel.

It was only after World War II that air transportation became the dominant mode of long-haul passenger travel in developed countries. In 1956, more people traveled on intercity routes by air than by Pullman car (sleeper) and coach-class trains combined in the USA. In 1958, airlines carried more passengers than ocean liners across the Atlantic for the first time. Even more momentous, in October 1958, the Boeing 707 took its maiden commercial flight with a Pan American World Airways route linking New York and Paris, with a refueling stop in Gander, Newfoundland. The B707 was not the first jetliner, but it was the first successful one. The B707 and other early jets, especially the Douglas DC-8, doubled the speed of air transportation and radically increased the productivity of airlines, which enabled fares to fall. Just a few years after the B707's debut, jet service had been extended to most major world markets.

In the years since the beginning of the Jet Age, commercial aircraft have advanced markedly in capacity and range. Just 12 years after the debut of the B707, the B747 made its maiden flight. Not coincidentally, it too premiered on a transatlantic route from New York City. The entry of dozens of B747s into the market around the same time that the Arab Oil Embargo triggered a worldwide recession led to a torrent of red ink for early Jumbo enthusiasts like Pan Am; but the longer-term effect was to push real airfares ever downward, thereby democratizing aviation beyond the so-called "Jet Set." The B747, particularly the longer-range B747–400 version introduced in the late 1980s, has been nicknamed the "Pacific Airliner" because of its singular significance in drawing Asia closer to the rest of the world and because Asia-Pacific airlines have been major B747 customers. However, by the 2010s, the majority of the B747s were being retired and replaced by longer-range and more fuel-efficient aircrafts such as the B777, the B787 and the A380. Three major categories of passenger jet planes may be recognized:

- **Short-range aircraft**. Bombardier's CRJ series and Embraer's ERJs are examples of planes with relatively small capacities (30–100 passengers) that travel over relatively short distances. They are usually referred to as regional jets that serve smaller markets and feed hub airports. They also provide high-frequency point-to-point services between large city pairs.
- **Medium-range aircraft**. The airbus A320 and its Boeing equivalent, the B737, are designed to service destinations within a continent with a range around 5,000 km for the later generation models. From New York, most of North America can be serviced. This range can also be applied to the European continent, South America, East Asia and Africa. This type of aircraft is the workhorse of high-demand regional services where low-cost air carriers compete (Photo 4.1).
- **Long-range aircraft**. There are a variety of aircraft capable of crossing the oceans and linking together the continents. Early variants such as the B707 have evolved into planes offering high capacity, such as the B747 series, which have then evolved into extra-long-range abilities, such as the B777 series (14,500 km range) or the A350 series (14,350 km range). Fuel efficiency was a major criterion in the design of the B787, which has a slightly shorter range of 13,600 km.

Photo 4.1   Boarding a Ryanair flight

Ryanair is a salient example of a low-cost airline business strategy relying on the usage of one type of aircraft (B737–800) and of secondary airports for hubs (e.g. Charleroi, Dublin) for lower gate fees. The booking is done online with the pricing system based on yield management, implying that prices vary constantly based on the availability of seats. Carry-on luggage is limited to one piece weighing up to 9 kg and any additional luggage is on a fee basis. Baggage policy is strictly enforced to ensure revenue generation, as the pricing system is much higher if booking options are changed at the airport (e.g. boarding pass, additional luggage). Ryanair does not use sky-bridges, accelerating the boarding sequence, which is done by using both the front and the back doors of the plane. A 737 can thus be boarded in less than 15 minutes, which can take twice a much time if a sky-bridge is used. This ensures fast turnaround times and a higher level of asset utilization. Passengers seat themselves with no pre-assigned seat, underlining the importance of priority boarding for customers wishing better seats and thus a source of revenue that comes at no cost for the airline. The 737s have a high-density seat configuration, with no reclining and seat pockets (no documentation or magazines). All inboard services are fee-based, with merchandising common (e.g. duty-free, phonecards, advertising on the overhead bins).

Photo: Dr Jean-Paul Rodrigue, 2011.

Economic and spatial impacts

The capacity of air transportation to dramatically lower the cost (friction) of distance has been instrumental in **fostering globalization**. Manufacturers, especially those producing high-value electronics, are heavily reliant upon air transport to tie together spatially disaggregated operations. Relatively inexpensive air transport has also been crucial to the **growth of tourism**. It is no coincidence that the five major Disney theme parks are all located near one of the world's 30 busiest airports: Disneyworld near Orlando International Airport, Disneyland near Los Angeles International Airport, Disneyland Paris near Paris-Charles de Gaulle, Tokyo Disneyland near Tokyo-Haneda, and the newest park in Hong Kong, which shares Lantau island with the most expensive airport in history.

Air transportation is overwhelmingly dominant in transcontinental and intercontinental travel and is becoming more competitive for shorter trips in many regional markets. In the USA, for instance, air travel is the most important mode for trips more than about 1,100 km. In developing countries low-cost carriers are proliferating as well, bringing airfares lower and attracting more passengers, particularly because of the poor quality of land transportation. Therefore, the world's busiest air routes are not long-haul flights, but **short-range flights** between cities less than 1,000 km apart (Figure 4.8).

The world's busiest air route is between Seoul and the resort island of Jeju, located just 450 km apart. It accounted for 10.16 million passengers in 2012. Short-haul air routes take different configurations depending on the region they serve. East Asia has experienced a fast growth in its air travel industry. Japan accounts for the busiest routes, even if the national urban system has extensively been linked with a high-speed train system. The routes involved are beyond the two-hour service time frame for high-speed rail, or not serviced (Okinawa). The Hong Kong–Taipei segment emerged because direct flights between Taiwan and mainland China were not permitted until 2014. Although the European air transport network is extensive, it does not figure predominantly among the world's busiest air routes. One reason is that for many of the largest city pairs that used to represent important air routes, the development of high-speed rail has captured a significant amount of the traffic. The large number of airports within Europe confers an extensive air transport network, but few large-scale airports. The corridors that still rank among the world's busiest involve city pairs not well serviced by train services, such as Paris–Toulouse, Paris–Nice and Madrid–Barcelona. North America has the longest routes, where many of the busiest routes involve more than two-hour flights. The most significant route, New York–Miami, jointly reflects business and touristic purposes. Other routes are short-distance hauls between two

Figure 4.8 The world's busiest air transport routes, 2012

major cities, such as between Johannesburg and Cape Town in South Africa, between Melbourne and Sydney in Australia and between Rio de Janeiro and São Paulo in Brazil.

Both passenger and cargo traffic have grown rapidly and have outpaced the growth of the broader global economy. By 2012, approximately one million people were airborne on scheduled flights somewhere in the world at any given time. This is compared to an annual traffic of 2.4 billion passengers that traveled over 33,000 scheduled flight routes, underlining the enduring growth of air travel. This accounted for about 25 percent of the global population, but a much smaller share are actually air travelers, as individuals who use air transportation usually do so several times per year. The propensity to fly is therefore highly uneven. North America and Europe alone accounted for 44.3 percent of all passenger-km in 2015, a share that has been declining in light of the growth in other regions of the world. As of 2015, the Chinese domestic market accounted for 12.7 percent of the world's passenger-km.

Air transportation's share of world trade in goods is only 2 percent measured by weight, but **more than 40 percent by value**. For the international operations, freight can account for 45 percent of the revenue of a regular airline. Typically, air cargo relates to time-sensitive, valuable or perishable freight carried over long distances. This is particularly suitable in supporting "just-in-time" production and distribution strategies with low inventory levels. Air cargo has also a niche market for emergency situations where the fast delivery of supplies prevails over cost issues. For regular passenger airlines, cargo usually accounts for less than 5 percent of total revenues. The air freight market is serviced by five types of operations:

- **Dedicated cargo operators** maintaining a fleet or cargo-only aircrafts and offering regular scheduled services between the airports they service. They also offer charter operations to cater to specific needs.
- **Combination services** where an airline company will maintain a fleet of both specialized and passenger aircrafts able to carry freight in their bellyhold. Most of the cargo operations involve long-haul services.
- **Passenger operators** that will offer the freight capacity in the bellyhold of their aircrafts. For these operators, freight services are rather secondary and represent a source of additional income. However, low-cost airlines usually do not offer air cargo services.
- **Air freight integrators** commonly operating hub-and-spoke freight services that reconcile short- and long-haul flights. They offer comprehensive services that are usually door-to-door and can support the logistics requirements of their customers.
- **Specialized operators** fulfilling niche services that cater to specific cargo requirements (e.g. heavy loads) that do not fit the capabilities of standard cargo aircrafts.

Efficient and affordable air freight has contributed to changes in diet by making available new products or products in seasons during which they would not be available; to changes in retailing; and correspondingly to changes in manufacturing. Examples abound, such as fresh produce grown on the southern hemisphere available in the northern hemisphere during winter, or merchandise purchased online and shipped promptly by air transport or a computer manufacturer depending on the global shipment of various components in the manufacturing and assembly processes. The increased importance of **time-based competition** ensures that air cargo augurs well for the future growth of air transportation.

The geography of airline networks

Theoretically, air transport enjoys **greater freedom of route choice** than most other modes. Yet, while it is true that the mode is less restricted than land transport to specific rights of way, it is nevertheless much more constrained than what might be supposed. Early in the history of aviation, physical obstacles such as the Rocky Mountains and the great gap of the North Atlantic limited the articulation of air transport networks. While those limitations have fallen, physical geography still affects the geography of intercity air transportation. Weather events such as snowstorms and thunderstorms can temporarily create major disruptions. Aircraft seek, for instance, to exploit (or avoid) upper atmospheric winds, in particular the **jet stream**, to enhance speed and reduce fuel consumption. Volcanic eruptions may also impede air travel by releasing ash in the atmosphere, which can damage and even shoot down turbo-fan engines. Such occurrences are, however, rare and specific, with the exception of April 2010, when a volcanic eruption in Iceland forced the closing down of airports in most of Europe, as well as several North Atlantic routes. This represented the largest natural disruption of air travel in history.

Yet the limitations that structure air transportation are mainly human creations. First, in the interest of air safety, air traffic is channeled along specific corridors so that only a relatively small portion of the sky is in use. China faces significant air capacity constraints, not because its airports are congested but mostly because a large segment of its airspace is regulated by the military and not available for commercial use.

Strategic and political factors have also influenced route choice. For example, the flights of South African Airways were not allowed to overfly many African nations during the apartheid period, and Cubana Airlines has been routinely prohibited from overflying the USA. Even more significant was the opening up of Siberian airspace to Western airlines after the Cold War. The new freedom permitted more direct routes not only between cities like London and Tokyo or New York and Hong Kong, but also between transpacific city pairs like Vancouver and Beijing. Few large areas of airspace forbidden to carriers on political grounds now remain. However, the intervention of the state in airline networks remains pervasive. From its infancy, air transport was then seen as a public service and as an industry that should be regulated and protected. In many parts of the world, government intervention in the industry took the form of state-owned airlines. During early 1970s, Air Canada, Air France, British Airways, Japan Airlines, Qantas and most other flag carriers throughout the world were fully state-owned. In the United States, the government did not own any airlines but strongly impacted the industry's development via the regulation of fares, in-flight service, routes and mergers.

Beginning in the 1970s, the relationship between the airline industry and the state changed, although the timing of **liberalization** (a term which refers to both deregulation and privatization) and its extent has varied among the world's main markets. Across the globe, dozens of airlines have been at least partially privatized, and many airline markets have been deregulated. In the United States, the Air Deregulation Act of 1978 opened the industry to competition. The results have been significant. Once-hallowed names like TWA, Pan Am and Braniff sank into bankruptcy (though Pan Am has been reborn as a much smaller carrier along the Atlantic coast) and many new players emerged. Most lasted only a short time, but some have had a profound, enduring effect on the industry and air transportation more generally. In Europe, deregulation came after 1997 with the opening of the European market to all European carriers. The Chinese market has also been subject to deregulation, from state-owned airlines servicing predefined regional markets to reforms in 2005 that led to private ownership (many airlines remain owned by public interests) and a consolidation of carriers.

Geographically, a key outcome of airline deregulation has been the emergence of hub-and-spoke networks centered on a major airport where a single carrier is often dominant. Such networks existed before deregulation to some degree, but the Civil Aeronautics Board hampered the expansion of airlines and the rationalization of networks. United Airlines, for instance, was allowed to add only one city to its network between 1961 and 1978. Hub-and-spoke systems rely on the usage of an intermediate airport hub. They can either connect a domestic (or regional) air system if the market is large enough (e.g. United States, China, European Union) or international systems through longitudinal (e.g. Dubai, Reykjavik) (Figure 4.9) or latitudinal (Panama City) intermediacy. An important aspect of an intermediate hub concerns the maintenance of schedule integrity, since the majority of passengers are using connecting flights. Airports that are prone to delays due to congestion are not effective hubs, since they compromise the schedule integrity.

Icelandair is a small airline company that carried around 2.6 million passengers in 2014. Because of the convenient intermediary location of Reykjavik along the trans-atlantic great circle route, the airline has been successful in establishing a pure long-distance hub-and-spoke system servicing mostly Northern Europe and nine North American cities. Scandinavian airports using Reykjavik to reach North America have a particularly low deviation. The same applies to western North American airports (Seattle, Denver and Minneapolis) having a low deviation to Western European airports. Additionally, Scandinavian countries may not generate enough traffic to justify regular direct services to American airports and using congested European hubs such as London, Paris or Amsterdam involves higher deviation and the risk of delays. Therefore, the consolidation of traffic at Reykjavik becomes an effective business proposition.

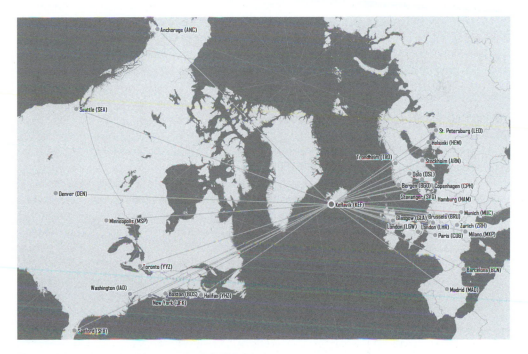

Figure 4.9   Longitudinal intermediacy: Icelandair

Iceland is the only effective location for such a pan-Atlantic network as there are no other significant airports in the North Atlantic. It is expected that, with the growth of economic activity along the Arctic Circle, Iceland's role as an intermediary hub will be reinforced.

Copa Airlines is a medium-sized Panamanian company operating from its major hub in Panama City (Tocumen International Airport – PTY). Panama City is strategically located as the intermediate location of the Americas; the main reason why the airline labels its hub as "Hub of the Americas in Panama." This hub services two ranges: the circum-Caribbean through a standard hub-and-spoke network structure; and a latitudinal intermediacy connecting medium-/long-distance destinations in the northern and southern hemisphere. Panama has historically been a small player in the Latin American airline industry. The national economy did not generate a large amount of air traffic and, because of the small size of the country, there is almost no domestic market to develop on, unlike countries like Mexico, Brazil and Colombia, which support significant and fast-growing domestic markets. With a traffic of 8.5 million passengers and 110,000 tons of air cargo in 2014, Tocumen ranked as the first airport in Central America,

Figure 4.10 Latitudinal intermediacy: Copa Airlines

Source: Network from Copa Airlines website.

but only the twentieth largest Latin American airport. Still, airports such as Mexico City, Bogotá (a major hub) and Lima are handling two to four times as much traffic as Panama City, in large part because of their substantial local populations. The growth of Tocumen and of Copa, however, indicates that Panama will play a larger role in Latin America by connecting the circum-Caribbean, North and South American air transport systems.

Concept 6 – Intermodal transportation and containerization

The nature of intermodalism

History as well as competition between modes has tended to produce a transport system that was **segmented and unintegrated**. Each mode, particularly the carriers that operated them, has sought to exploit its own advantages in terms of cost, service, reliability and safety. Carriers try to retain business and increase revenue by maximizing the line haul under their control. All the modes saw the other modes as competitors, and were viewed with a level of suspicion and mistrust. The lack of integration between the modes was also accentuated by public policy that has frequently barred companies from owning firms in other modes (as in the United States before deregulation), or has placed a mode under direct state monopoly control (as in Europe). **Modalism** was also favored because of the difficulties of transferring goods from one mode to another, thereby incurring additional terminal costs and delays, mainly because the load unit needs to be changed, which is common for bulk transportation.

Since the 1960s major efforts have been made to integrate separate transport systems through intermodalism, which took place in several stages. What initially began as improving the productivity of shipping evolved into an integrated supply chain management system across modes. This involves the use of at least two different modes in a trip from an origin to a destination through an intermodal transport chain (Figure 4.11).

Four major functions define an intermodal transport chain:

- **Composition**. The process of assembling and consolidating freight at a terminal that offers an intermodal interface between a local/regional distribution system and a national/international distribution system. It is commonly referred to as the "first mile." Ideally, loads of freight coming from different suppliers are assembled at distribution centers so they can be forwarded to high-capacity modes such as rail and maritime shipping. The dominant mode for such a process is trucking, as it offers flexibility and door-to-door services. Activities such as packaging and warehousing are also included in the composition process, which is closely linked with the **function of production**.
- **Connection (transfer)**. Involves a consolidated modal flow, such as a freight train or a containership (or even fleets of trucks), between at least two terminals, which takes place over national or international freight distribution systems. The efficiency of a connection is mainly derived from economies of scale, such as double-stacking or post-Panamax container ships, coupled with an adequate frequency of service.
- **Interchange**. The major intermodal function takes place at terminals whose purpose is to provide an efficient continuity within a transport chain. Those terminals are

Figure 4.11 Intermodal transport chain

dominantly within the realm of national or international freight distribution systems, with ports (transshipment hubs) being the most notable example.

- **Decomposition**. Once a load of freight has reached a terminal close to its destination, it has to be fragmented and transferred to the local/regional freight distribution system. Commonly referred as the "last mile," it often represents one of the most difficult segments of distribution. This function, which is linked with the function of consumption, dominantly occurs within metropolitan areas and involves unique distribution problems also known as urban logistics.

Intermodality enhances the economic performance of a transport chain by using modes in the most productive manner. Thus, the line-haul economies of rail may be exploited for long distances, with the efficiencies of trucks providing flexible local pickup and delivery. The key is that the entire trip is seen as a whole, rather than as a series of legs, each marked by an individual operation with separate sets of documentation and rates. From a functional and operational perspective, two components are involved in intermodalism:

- **Intermodal transportation**. The movements of passengers or freight from one mode of transport to another, commonly taking place at a terminal specifically designed for such a purpose.
- **Transmodal transportation**. The movements of passengers or freight within the same mode of transport. Although "pure" transmodal transportation rarely exists and an intermodal operation is often required (e.g. ship to dockside to ship), the purpose is to ensure continuity within the same modal network.

Figure 4.12 illustrates two alternatives to freight distribution. The first is a conventional point-to-point multimodal network where origins (A, B and C) are independently linked to destinations (D, E and F). In this case, two modes (road and rail) are used. The second alternative involves the development of an integrated intermodal transport network with

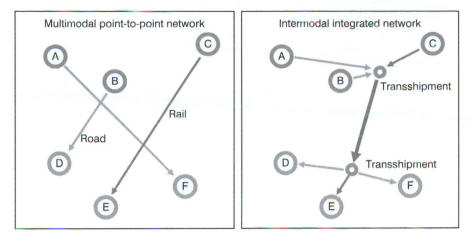

Figure 4.12 Intermodal transportation as an integrative force

common load units (containers). Traffic converges at two transshipment points, rail terminals, where loads are consolidated. This can result in higher load factors and/or higher transport frequency, especially between terminals. Under such circumstances, the efficiency of such a network mainly resides in the transshipment capabilities of transport terminals.

What initially began as improving the productivity of shipping evolved into an integrated supply chain management system across modes and the development of **intermodal transportation networks**. This involves the use of at least two different modes in a trip from an origin to a destination through an intermodal transport chain, which permit the integration of several transportation networks. Intermodality enhances the economic performance of a transport chain by using modes in the most productive manner. Thus, the line-haul economies of rail may be exploited for long distances, with the efficiencies of trucks providing flexible local pickup and deliveries. The key is that the entire trip is seen as a whole, rather than as a series of legs, each marked by an individual operation with separate sets of documentation and rates. This is organized around the followings concepts:

1. The **nature and quantity** of the transported cargo. Intermodal transportation is usually suitable for intermediate and finished goods in load units of less than 25 tons.
2. The **modes of transportation** being used. Intermodal transportation is organized as a sequence of modes, often known as an intermodal transport chain. The dominant modes supporting intermodalism are trucking, rail, barges and maritime. Air transportation usually only requires intermodalism (trucking) for its "first and last miles" and is not used in combination with other modes. Additionally, load units used by air transportation are not readily convertible with other modes.
3. The **origins and destinations**. Distances play an important role as, the longer the distance, the more likely an intermodal transport chain will be used. Distances above 500 km (longer than one day of trucking) usually require intermodal transportation.
4. Transportation **time and costs**. Intermodalism tries to use each mode according

to their respective time and cost advantages so that total transport costs are minimized.

5. The **value of the cargo**. Suitable for intermediate cargo values. Low- and high-value shipments are usually less suitable for intermodal transportation. High-value shipments will tend to use the most direct options (such as air cargo), while low-value shipments are usually point-to-point and relying on one mode, such as rail or maritime.

6. The **frequency of shipments**. Intermodalism functions well when cargo flows need to be continuous and in similar quantities.

Forms of intermodalism

The emergence of intermodalism has been brought about in part by technology and requires **management units** for freight such as containers, swap bodies, pallets or semi-trailers. In the past, pallets were a common management unit, but their relatively small size and lack of protective frame made their intermodal handling labor-intensive and prone to damage or theft. Better techniques and management units for transferring freight from one mode to another have facilitated intermodal transfers. Early examples include piggyback (TOFC: trailers on flat cars), where truck trailers are placed on rail cars, and LASH (lighter-aboard-ship), where river barges are placed directly onboard seagoing ships.

While handling technology has influenced the development of intermodalism, another important factor has been changes in public policy. Deregulation in the United States in the early 1980s liberated firms from government control. Companies were no longer prohibited from owning across modes, which developed a strong impetus towards intermodal cooperation. Shipping lines in particular began to offer **integrated rail and road services** to customers. The advantages of each mode could be exploited in a seamless system, which created multiplying effects. Customers could purchase the service to ship their products from door to door, without having to concern themselves with modal barriers.

The most important feature of intermodalism is the provision of a service with **one ticket** (for passengers) or **one bill of lading** (for freight). With one bill of lading clients can obtain one through-rate, despite the transfer of goods from one mode to another. This has necessitated a revolution in organization and information control. At the heart of modern intermodalism are data handling, processing and distribution systems that are essential to ensure the safe, reliable and cost-effective control of freight and passenger movements being transported by several modes. Electronic Data Interchange (EDI) is an evolving technology that is helping companies and government agencies (customs documentation) cope with an increasingly complex global transport system.

Intermodal transport is transforming a growing share of the medium- and long-haul freight flow across the globe where large integrated transport carriers provide door-to-door services, such as the high degree of integration between maritime and rail transport in North America. In Europe rail intermodal services are becoming well-established between the major ports, such as Rotterdam, and southern Germany, and between Hamburg and Eastern Europe. Rail shuttles are also making their appearance in China. While rail intermodal transport has been relatively slow to develop in Europe, there are extensive interconnections between barge services and ocean shipping, particularly on the Rhine. Barge shipping offers a low-cost solution to inland distribution where navigable waterways penetrate to interior markets. The limits of intermodality are imposed by factors of space, time, form, pattern of the network, the number of nodes and linkages, and the type and characteristic of the vehicles and terminals.

Containerization

The driver of intermodal transportation has undoubtedly been the container, which permits easy handling between modal systems. While intermodalism could take place without the container, it would be very inefficient and costly. To start with, a distinction is necessary between containerization and the container. The **container** is a large standard-size metal box into which cargo is packed for shipment aboard specially configured transport modes. It is designed to be moved with common handling equipment, enabling high-speed intermodal transfers in economically large units between ships, rail cars, truck chassis and barges using minimal labor. The container, therefore, serves as the load unit rather than the cargo contained therein. The reference size is the 20 ft box, 20 ft long, 8 ft 6 in high and 8 ft wide, or 1 Twenty-foot Equivalent Unit (TEU). Since the great majority of containers are now 40 ft long, the term "Forty-foot Equivalent Unit" (FEU) is also used, but less commonly. "Hi-cube" containers are also common and they are 1 ft higher (9 ft 6 in) than the standard. **Containerization** refers to the increasing and generalized use of the container as a support for freight transportation. It involves processes where the intermodal container is increasingly used because it either substitutes cargo from other conveyances, is adopted as a mode supporting freight distribution or is able to diffuse spatially as a growing number of transport systems are able to handle containers.

Containers are made either of steel (the most common for maritime containers) or aluminum (particularly for domestic routes) and their structure confers flexibility and hardiness. Another factor behind the diffusion of the container is that an agreement about its base dimensions and latching system was reached through the International Standards Organization (ISO) within 10 years of its introduction. From this standard, a wide variety of container sizes and specifications have been put in use. The most prevalent container size, however, is the 40 ft box (2,400 cubic ft), which carries on average 22 tons of cargo. However, transporting cargo in a 20 ft container is usually 20 percent cheaper than transporting cargo in a 40 ft container. Irrespective of the size, a 20 ft container requires the same number of intermodal movements even if it takes about half the space during transport and at terminals. There are five main types of container:

- **Standard container**. Container designed to carry a wide variety of general cargo. They are often labeled as dry containers because they carry dry goods either in breakbulk (most common) or bulk (less common) form. Cargo is loaded and unloaded through a double door, which marks the "back side" of the container.
- **Tank container**. Container designed to carry liquids (chemicals or foodstuffs). It is composed of a tank surrounded by a structure, making it the same size as a standard 20 ft container, including its four latching points.
- **Open top container**. A container with an open roof and designed to carry cargo that is too large to be loaded through standard container doors, such as machinery. The container is loaded from the top, with a tarpaulin used to cover its contents.
- **Flat container**. Container with an open roof and sides designed to carry heavy and oversized cargo. The cargo transported is left exposed to outdoor conditions.
- **Refrigerated container**. Also known as a "reefer." Container designed to carry

temperature-controlled cargo, often around or below freezing point. It is insulated and equipped with a refrigeration plant that maintains a constant temperature.

The development of intermodal transportation and containerization are mutually inclusive, self-strengthening and rely on a set of driving forces linked with technology, infrastructures and management. One of the initial issues concerned the different sizes and dimensions of containers used by shipping lines, which were a source of much confusion in compiling container shipping statistics. A lift could involve different volumes, since different box sizes were involved. As a result, the term TEU (Twenty-foot Equivalent Unit) was first used by Richard F. Gibney in 1969, who worked for the *Shipbuilding & Shipping Record*, as a comparative measure. Since then, the TEU remains the standard measure for containerized traffic, and an agreement about its base dimensions and latching system was reached through the ISO, as mentioned earlier,

The use of containers shows the complementarity between freight transportation modes by offering a higher fluidity to movements and a standardization of loads. The container has substantially contributed to the adoption and diffusion of intermodal transportation, which has led to **profound mutations in the transport sector**. Through reduction of handling time, labor costs and packing costs, container transportation allows considerable improvement in the efficiency of transportation. Thus, the relevance of containers is not what they are – simple boxes – but what they enable: intermodalism. Globalization could not have taken its current form without containerization.

While it is true that the maritime container has become the workhorse of international trade, other types of containers are found in certain modes, most notably in the **airline industry**. High labor costs and the slowness of loading planes, which require a very rapid turnaround, made the industry highly receptive to the concept of a loading unit of standard dimensions designed to fit the specific shape of the bellyhold. The maritime container was too heavy and did not fit the rounded configuration of a plane's fuselage, and thus a box specific to the needs of the airlines was required. The major breakthrough came with the introduction of wide-bodied aircraft in the late 1970s. Lightweight aluminum boxes, called unit load devices, could be filled with passengers' baggage or parcels and freight, and loaded into the holds of the planes using tracking that requires little human assistance.

Most North American double-stack rail corridors can handle two stacked hi-cube containers, creating an additional multiplying effect in terms of total capacity per rail car (Photo 4.2). The 53 ft hi-cube container, which is the maximum length permitted on the American Interstate highway system, is a load unit that would enable the carriage of even more low weight cargo (42 percent more volume than a 40 ft hi-cube container). However, it is not commonly used, since it can only be stacked in the upper section of container ships and does not fit into their bellyhold, designed to accommodate 40 ft containers.

Globalization and containerization are closely interrelated. According to UNCTAD, between 1970 and 1990 trade facilitation measures accounted for 45 percent of the growth in global trade, while membership of a global trade organization such as GATT/WTO accounted for another 285 percent. The container accounted for an **additional 790 percent**, exceeding all the other trade growth factors put together. The diffusion and adaptation of transport modes to containerization is an ongoing process, which will eventually reach a level of saturation. Containers have thus become the most

Photo 4.2   40 ft containers double-stacked on a rail car

Double-stacking rail services were first introduced in North America in 1984, multiplying the productivity of inland container transportation. The advantages are obvious, since two 40 ft containers (or four 20 ft) can be stacked on a rail car, essentially doubling the capacity of a unit train. The drawback is a more complex loading or unloading procedure and a higher clearance requirement, so that double-stacked cars can fit under bridges and tunnels – as shown here in the port of Vancouver, Canada. Until recently, North America remained the only region of the world where double-stacking services were possible. In April 2004, double-stack container train services using 40 ft boxes between Shanghai and Beijing were launched. Both cities can be serviced in about 38 hours. There is also the possibility of using double-stacked trains on the Betuweroute, a 160 km rail segment between Rotterdam and the German border, but no such trains are currently using the corridor.

Photo: Dr Jean-Paul Rodrigue, 2012.

important component for rail and maritime intermodal transportation. The challenge remains in choosing the modes in an intermodal transport chain, as well as minimizing the costs and delays related to moving containers between modes.

The advantages of containerization

Among the numerous advantages related to the success of containers in international and hinterland transport, it is possible to note the following (Figure 4.14):

- **Standard transport product**. A container can be manipulated anywhere in the world as its dimensions are an ISO standard. Indeed, transfer infrastructures allow all elements (vehicles) of a transport chain to handle it with relative ease. Standardization is a prevalent benefit of containerization as it conveys a ubiquity to access the distribution system and reduces the risks of capital investment in modes and terminals. The rapid diffusion of containerization was facilitated by the fact that its initiator, Malcolm McLean, purposely did not patent his invention. Consequently, all segments of the industry, competitors alike, had access to the standard. It necessitated the construction of specialized ships and of lifting equipment, but in several instances existing transport modes can be converted to container transportation.

- **Flexibility of usage**. A container can transport a wide variety of goods ranging from raw materials (coal, wheat), manufactured goods and cars to frozen products. There are specialized containers for transporting liquids (oil and chemical products) and perishable food items in refrigerated containers (called "reefers," which now account for 50 percent of all refrigerated cargo being transported). About 2.3 million TEUs of reefers were being used by 2013. Discarded containers are often used as storage, housing, office and retail structures.

- **Management**. The container, as an indivisible unit, carries a unique identification number and a size type code enabling transport management, not in terms of loads, but in terms of unit. This identification number is also used to ensure that it is carried by an authorized agent of the cargo owner and is verified at terminal gates. Computerized management enables the considerable reduction of waiting times and the ability to know the location of containers (or batches of containers) at any time. It allows the assignation of containers according to priority, destination and available transport capacities. Transport companies book slots in maritime or railway convoys, which they use to distribute containers under their responsibility. As such, the container has become a production, transport and distribution unit.

- **Economies of scale**. Relative to bulk, container transportation reduces transport costs considerably – about 20 times over. While before containerization maritime transport costs could account between 5 and 10 percent of the retail price, this share has been reduced to about 1.5 percent, depending on the goods being transported. The main factors behind cost reductions reside in the speed and flexibility incurred by containerization. Similar to other transportation modes, container shipping benefits from economies of scale with the usage of larger container ships. The 6,000 TEUs landmark was surpassed in 1996 with the *Regina Maersk*, and in 2006 the *Emma Maersk* surpassed the 12,000 TEU landmark. By 2013, ships of more than 18,000 TEU became available. A 5,000 TEU container ship has operating costs per container 50 percent lower than a 2,500 TEU vessel. Moving from 4,000 TEU to 12,000 TEU reduces operating costs per container by a factor of 20 percent, which is very significant considering the additional volume involved. System-wide the outcome of containerization use has been cost reductions of about 35 percent.

- **Speed**. Transshipment operations are minimal and rapid, which increase the utilization level of the modal assets and port productivity. A modern container ship has a monthly capacity of three to six times more than a conventional cargo ship. This is notably attributable to gains in transshipment time, as a crane can handle roughly 30 movements (loading or unloading) per hour. Port turnaround times have thus been reduced from an average of three weeks in the 1960s to less than 24 hours, since it is uncommon for a ship to be fully loaded or unloaded along regular container shipping routes. It takes on average between 10 and 20 hours to unload 1,000 TEUs, compared to between 70 and 100 hours for a similar quantity of bulk freight. With larger container ships, more cranes can be allocated to transshipment; three or four cranes can service a 5,000 TEU container ship, while ships of 10,000 TEU can be serviced by five or six cranes. This suggests that larger ship sizes do not have many differences in loading or unloading time, but this requires more yard equipment. A regular freighter can spend between half and two-thirds of its useful life in ports. With less time in ports, container ships can spend more time at sea. Since a ship generates revenue while at sea, container ships are more profitable. Furthermore, container ships are on average 35 percent faster than regular freighter ships (19 knots versus 14 knots). Put all together, it is estimated that containerization has reduced travel time for freight by a factor of 80 percent.

- **Warehousing**. The container limits damage risks for the goods it carries, because it is resistant to shocks and weather conditions. The packaging of goods it contains is therefore simpler, less expensive and can occupy less volume. This reduces insurance costs, since cargo is less prone to be damaged during transport. Besides, containers fit together, permitting stacking on ships, trains (double-stacking) and on the ground. It is possible to superimpose three loaded and six empty containers on the ground. The container is consequently its own warehouse.

- **Security**. The contents of the container are anonymous to outsiders as it can only be opened at the origin, at customs and at the destination. Thefts, especially those of valuable commodities, are therefore considerably reduced. This was a serious issue at ports before containerization, as longshoremen had ready access to cargo.

The challenges of containerization

Despite the numerous advantages in the usage of containers, some challenges are also evident (Figure 4.13):

- **Site constraints**. Containerization implies a large consumption of terminal space. To fully load or unload a containership of 5,000 TEU a minimum of 12 hectares of stacking space is required. Conventional port areas are often not adequate for the location of container transshipment infrastructures, particularly because of draft issues as well as

Figure 4.13 Advantages and drawbacks of containerization

required space for terminal operations. Many container vessels require a draft of at least 14 m (45 ft) and the later generation of larger ships require at least 15 m (50 ft). A similar challenge applies to container rail terminals, and many have been relocated at the periphery of metropolitan areas. Consequently, major container handling facilities have new location criteria where suitable sites are only found at the periphery.

- **Infrastructure costs**. Container handling infrastructures, such as gantry cranes, yard equipment, road and rail access, represent important investments for port authorities and load centers. For instance, costs of a modern container crane (portainer) are in the range of $4–10 million depending on the size. Several developing countries, as well as smaller ports, face the challenge of finding capital for these infrastructure investments.

- **Stacking**. The arrangement of containers, both at terminals and on modes (container-ships and double-stack trains), is a complex problem. At the time of loading, it becomes imperative to make sure that containers that must be taken out first are not below the pile. Furthermore, container ships must be loaded in a way to avoid any restacking along its numerous port calls where containers are loaded and unloaded (Photo 4.3).

- **Thefts and losses**. While many theft issues have been addressed because of the freight anonymity a container confers, it remains an issue for movements outside terminals where the contents of the container can be assessed based upon its final destination. It is estimated that about 10,000 containers per year are lost at sea when they fall overboard container ships. Rough weather is the major cause, but improper container stacking also plays a role (distribution of heavy containers). Yet, the loss rate remains very low, since five to six million containers are being transported at any given time.

- **Empty travel**. Maritime shippers need containers to maintain their operations along the port networks they service. The same number of containers brought into a market must thus eventually be relocated, regardless of whether they are full or empty. On average containers will spend about 56 percent of their 10- to 15-year lifespan idle or being repositioned empty, which is not generating any income but convey a cost that is part of the shipping rates. Either full or empty, a container takes the same amount of space on the ship or in a storage yard and takes the same amount of time to be transshipped. Due to a divergence between production and consumption, it is uncommon to see an equilibrium in the distribution of containers. About 2.5 million TEUs of empty containers are stored in yards and depots around the world, under-lining the issue of the movement and accumulation of empty containers. They represent about 20 percent of the global container port throughput and of the volume carried by maritime shipping lines. Most container trade is imbalanced, and thus containers "accumulate" in some places and must be shipped back to locations where there are deficits (mostly locations having a strong export function). This is particu-larly the case for American container shipping. As a result, shipping lines waste substantial amounts of time and money in repositioning empty containers.

- **Illicit trade**. By its confidential character, the container is a common instrument used in the illicit trade of counterfeit goods, drugs and weapons. Concerns have also been raised about containers being used for terrorism. These fears have given rise to an increasing number of regulations aimed at counteracting illegal use of containers. In 2003, following US inspection requirements, the International Maritime Organization (IMO) introduced regulations regarding the security of port sites and the vetting of workers in the shipping industry. The USA itself established a 24-hour rule, requiring

Photo 4.3   Stacked container ship

Stacking containers on a ship is a complex operation involving a close interaction between the container yard, drayage operations between the ship and the yard and crane operations. This photo depicts a typical stacking configuration of different container sizes and types taking place on a Panamax container ship (13 container rows) at the port of Veracruz in Mexico (ICAVE terminal operated by HPH). Each row (more likely, several rows) generally contains containers bound to a specific port. This is done to facilitate crane operations, since cranes are designed to quickly move along a row but require the entire crane to be displaced laterally to access another row. Since a ship is usually serviced by several cranes, they can all operate at once on their ship section without impeding one another. This also enables distribution of the weight across several sections of the ship. The empty rows are likely to be loaded at another port of call. 20 ft and 40 ft containers are usually loaded in separate rows to facilitate stacking and loading/unloading efficiency. Container loads bound for a single large customer are usually bundled together, as evidenced by the 20 ft tanker containers. Specialized and oversized containers are stacked on top of the pile, since their structure forbids the stacking of container on top of them. In this case top-loaded containers are used to carry oversized cargo, with some of them covered with a tarpaulin.

all shipments destined for the USA to receive clearance from US authorities 24 hours prior to the departure of the vessel. In 2008, the US Congress passed a regulation requiring all US-bound containers to be electronically scanned at the foreign port of loading, prior to departure. Needless to say, these measures incur additional costs and delays that many in the industry oppose.

Yet, the advantages of containerization have far outweighed its drawbacks, transforming the global freight transport system and, along with it, the global economy.

CASE STUDY   High-speed rail systems

Existing high-speed networks

High-speed rail (HSR) refers to passenger rail systems running at operational speed between 200 km and 300 km per hour, and above in some cases. The HSR era originates from Japan with the Tokaido line, bridging Tokyo and Osaka, which entered into service in 1964, in time for the Tokyo Olympics. Japan presented several suitable conditions for the setting of a HSR system, particularly a high population density and closely inter-connected large cities. It simply became a matter of overlapping the HSR network over this spatial structure. Today, HSR is perceived as an **efficient alternative to highway and airport congestion**. Evidence underlines that rail travel time is essentially cut in half when a high-speed service is established between two city pairs.

The setting of high-speed rail systems has accelerated around the world over the last two decades, particularly in China, where since 2000 several high-speed rail corridors have been rapidly set, reaching 19,000 km in 2016, so making it the longest in the world. Several countries, including the United States, are also planning for high-speed rail corridors, but these projects tend to take decades to implement, in part due to funding issues, the limited importance of existing passenger rail services, as well as the domin-ance of air and road transportation. Dedicated high-speed postal trains are used in Europe (e.g. France and Sweden) on a daily basis, but the relative decline of postal use leaves such endeavors with questionable growth potential. High-speed rail currently functions under two discrete technologies:

- **Improvement of conventional rail**. The first type uses existing conventional rail systems and its great velocity is primarily the result of considerable improvements in locomotive performance and train design. They may not be considered as a pure high-speed trains per se. England (London–Edinburgh), Sweden (Stockholm–Gothenburg), Italy (Rome–Florence and Rome–Milan) and the United States (Boston–Washington) are examples of this type of technology. Trains can reach peak speeds of approximately 200 km per hour in most cases and up to 250 km per hour in Italy. The principal drawback from using this system, however, is that it must share existing lines with regular passengers and freight services, which limits the slots available to HSR.
- **Exclusive high-speed networks**. In contrast, the second category of high-speed train runs on its own exclusive and independent tracks. In Japan, trains can attain speeds of 240 km per hour, but ongoing projects to raise peak speeds at 300 km per hour aim to maintain competitiveness of rail passenger transport versus air. In France, the TGV Sud-Est (Train à Grande Vitesse) reaches speeds of 270 km per hour, while the TGV Atlantique can cruise at speeds of 300 km per hour. One of the key advantages of such a system is, since passenger trains have their exclusive tracks, that the effi-ciency of rail freight transport increases as it inherits the almost exclusive use of the conventional rail system.

The first high-speed rail networks were built to service national systems, mostly in a linear fashion along main corridors. In the case of Europe, this development has reached a phase where integration between different national high-speed systems takes place. This notably involves Eurostar (Paris–Lille–London) and Thalys (Paris–Brussels–Antwerp–Rotterdam–Amsterdam). The setting of high-speed rail networks consequently must take into consideration the following constraints:

- **Commercial potential**. High-speed rail is particularly suitable in a system of large metropolitan areas in close proximity. The existence of thriving short-haul air services is an indication of an existing market of passengers valuing fast services.
- **Distance between stations**. A distance of 50 km is often considered a minimum, leaving enough for trains to accelerate and reach cruising speed. Servicing too many stations undermines the rationale of high-speed systems, which is to service large urban agglomerations in a fast and continuous manner.
- **Right of way separation from other rail systems**. This is mainly the case in and out of metropolitan areas, where high-speed trains are forced to use the standard rail network so that they may connect to central rail stations.
- **Availability of land, both for terminals and high-speed lines**. This problem can be mitigated by using existing central rail stations. The development of new HSR stations has often required the use of suburban greenfield sites.

High-speed rail (HSR) systems are built to **reinforce accessibility and functional relations** within well-developed regional urban systems (many which are mega-urban regions) by filling a gap between short-range mobility provided by cars and buses and medium-range mobility provided by air transport. As of 2016 there were more than 34,800 km of operational HSR lines in the world, with an additional 24,800 km under construction (Figure 4.14). These lines were initially set as corridors between city pairs and their growth eventually led to integrated systems spanning extended regions, such as for Japan, coastal China and Western Europe. While services remain designed along corridors, nodes where it is possible to effectively switch from one corridor to the other are emerging. Like air transport, a good frequency of high-speed services enables these interconnections to occur effectively.

HSR systems are mainly found in three regions of the world, where they have contributed to structuring intercity mobility:

- In **Asia**, the urban density factor is the most suitable for the development of HRS systems, with most cities well above 5,000 people per square kilometer. Japan was the innovator, and from 1964 a national integrated HSR system was built along dedicated lines to service the major cities and three of the four main islands of the Japanese territory. Both South Korea and Taiwan have built HSR to service a corridor between their two largest cities. China has embarked on an ambitious plan to build a national HSR system that shows a growing level of integration. The Chinese HSR system has grown rapidly and is already the world's most extensive, with 19,000 km being operational as of 2016. For instance, the world's longest HSR service between Beijing and Guangzhou was inaugurated in December 2012, taking approximately eight hours to link both cities. It is expected that, by 2020, China's HSR system will total 30,000 km. For China the development of a HSR system was seen as a national priority because of growing mobility demands, the lack of transport infrastructure and highly congested standard rail and air transport routes. India has several high-speed corridors planned, but high capital requirements and securing rights of way are serious challenges.
- In **Europe**, urban density is average, with cities usually above 3,000 people per square kilometer. The setting of HSR systems has gradually permitted a growing level of integration, particularly between the highly urbanized regions of France, Belgium, the Netherlands and Germany. The completion of the Eurotunnel in 1994

Figure 4.14 World high-speed rail systems, 2014

enabled London to link to the European HSR system. Northern European countries (Norway, Sweden and Finland) have mostly developed their HSR system through the reconversion of existing lines, a strategy that reflects the relatively short distances involved and lower population densities. As the 6,600 km European system is getting more integrated, HSR hubs connecting different corridors are emerging, notably Brussels.

● In **North America**, urban density is low, commonly below 2,000 people per square kilometer. Only one high-speed rail corridor is in operation in the high-density Boston–Washington corridor, but technical requirements limit the speed along several segments (the New York–Washington segment can be considered high speed). The setting of HSR corridors linking regional urban systems has been debated for more than two decades, with many corridor projects clearly identified and advocated (e.g. San Francisco–San Diego, Quebec–Toronto, Miami–Orlando–Tampa or Vancouver–Seattle–Eugene). Yet, the prominence and relatively low cost of road and air transport have been factors playing against the development of HSR. The density of North American cities, including their central areas, is low and it remains debatable whether this density is sufficient to justify large-scale HSR projects. Another important impediment to the development of HSR systems in North America is the dominance of freight, with the rail network owned and operated by private companies. This leads to right-of-way conflicts in the vicinity of major metropolitan areas, which also have important intermodal and bulk terminal facilities.

Benefits and challenges

HSR provides a number of **economic, social and environmental benefits** for the corridors they service. The most salient are:

- **Capacity and reliability**. HSR corridors have the capacity to move a large number of passengers in a safe and reliable manner. They can mitigate congested road and air infrastructure, particularly for short- to medium-distance trips. They are also much less impacted by adverse weather conditions (e.g. storms) than road and air transport.
- **Energy and environment**. HSR systems consume less energy per passenger-km than road and air transport. They are perceived to provide a more sustainable mobility, with electric power and denser land use structures associated with rail-oriented developments.

High-speed rail systems can have substantial impacts on other transport modes, even freight transport systems. One of the most apparent is on air transportation services between cities along the high-speed rail corridor, particularly the most distant ones. High-speed rail is able to compete successfully with short- to medium-distance air transport services, as it conveys the advantage of servicing downtown areas and has much lower terminal time, mainly because of fewer security constraints. For city pairs closer than 500 km, the introduction of high-speed rail services will, in the majority of cases, remove commercial air services as they cease to be competitive. Flights on routes that are over 1,500 km are usually little impacted. This can have a very important impact on air transportation, since the world's most active air routes are all short hauls of less than 1,000 km. Still, low-cost air services are able to compete with HSR on specific segments.

Another emerging trend concerns a **complementarity** between HSR and air transportation, which involves cooperation between a national air and rail carrier. For instance, Lufthansa and Deutsche Bahn, as well as Air France and SNCF, offer single fares and tickets for selected routes where a high-speed rail segment is offered instead of a flight. There is thus a balance between competition and complementarity for HSR and air transportation services, particularly when there is congestion in the air transport system. In this situation the complementarity may help release airport gate slots that can be used to support more revenue-generating (longer-distance) flights or to reduce congestion.

Rail stations with high-speed rail services are also increasingly becoming **transport hubs** with the associated demands on urban transport systems, particularly public transit. Regarding high-speed rail stations, two dynamics have emerged:

- The **reconversion** and usage of central railway stations. Such facilities benefit from high accessibility levels due to their central locations and can thus grant a significant customer base for HSR services. This is particularly the case for the European system that is using existing tracks to access the central train station (e.g. Paris, Frankfurt, Munich), which avoided expensive development projects such as new stations or the building of tunnels (Photo 4.4).
- The setting of **new facilities** in suburbia. In this case, the HSR station represents an opportunity to create a new node of activity (growth pole) within a metropolitan area.

For freight transportation, there are several potential impacts, mostly indirect. The most straightforward is that, since high-speed rail uses its own right of way, the separation between passenger and freight systems **promotes the efficiency and reliability of both**

Photo 4.4   Antwerp Centraal train station

Antwerp train station, completed in 1905, is considered to be among the world's most architecturally impressive. However, due to increased ridership, as well as the setting of a high-speed train system along the Paris–Brussels–Amsterdam corridor (Thalys), the station became increasingly inadequate. Renovations of the train station, completed in 2007, allowed them to address two issues: a shortage of boarding platforms, which was expanded by providing three levels (two underground) with a total of 16 quays; and the fact that Antwerp was a dead-end spur with bay platforms, suggesting that trains had to reverse back to the mainline to continue intercity services, so creating additional delays. A tunnel servicing the lowest level was constructed, and through-platforms enabled a continuous intercity service along the high-speed rail corridor.

Photo: Dr Jean-Paul Rodrigue, 2008.

networks. The main reason is that passengers and freight have different operational characteristics, namely in terms of speed and frequency of service. For each passenger car that is removed from regular rail lines, an additional three freight rail cars can be accommodated by the new slot. The setting of high-speed networks may also prompt additional investments in rail freight infrastructure, particularly in metropolitan areas, plus better signaling technologies and cost-sharing initiatives. Although there have been discussions about the potential of using high-speed rail to move freight, these have not yet led to concrete realizations. There are plans to have a high-speed rail cargo network in Europe, which would link major air cargo hubs such as Paris, Liege, Amsterdam, London and Frankfurt. The goal is to provide an alternative to short-haul air cargo routes as well as the possibility to move cargo between the hubs and improve their long-distance air cargo connectivity.

However, HSR do not have the far-reaching impacts on passenger mobility that its proponents suggest, at least in the medium term. Although HSR in Europe is considered to be successful, its implementation required massive subsidies and its profitability remains difficult to achieve. For Spain, the world's second most extensive system in terms of length, the process has particularly been a political one, with the purpose of linking regional capitals with the national capital (Madrid). For developing countries, low fares are the dominant factor in mode selection, implying that HSR is not affordable for the great majority of the population. The location of stations remains a salient issue, as suburban locations are advantageous from an availability of land perspective. However, suburban locations tend not to be well connected to the local transport system and are remote from central areas, which is commonly the destination for most passenger traffic. The impacts of new HSR stations as poles for urban growth and development so far remain elusive.

In addition to present technologies, an entirely new technological paradigm has been under development in Japan and Germany since the late 1970s. The new technology is known as **Maglev** (magnetic levitation), which uses magnetic forces to uplift trains, guide them laterally and to propel them, relying upon highly efficient electromagnetic systems. The first commercial Maglev rail system was inaugurated in Shanghai in 2003. Maglev systems have experienced some constraints on widespread commercialization, however, such as difficulties with integration in established rail corridors and perceptions of high construction costs.

Bibliography

Allaz, C. (2005) *History of Air Cargo and Airmail from the 18th Century*. London: Christopher Foyle Publishing.

Bowen, J. (2010) *The Economic Geography of Air Transportation: Space, Time, and the Freedom of the Sky*. London: Routledge.

Brooks M. (2000) *Sea Change in Liner Shipping*. New York: Pergamon.

Comtois, C. and B.P.Y. Loo (2015) *Sustainable Railway Futures: Issues and Challenges*, Transport and Mobility Series. London: Ashgate.

Cullinane, K. and M. Khanna (2000) "Economies of scale in large containerships." *Journal of Transport Economics and Policy* 33: 185–207.

Feigenbaum, B. (2013) *High-Speed Rail in Europe and Asia: Lessons for the United States*. Reason Foundation, Policy Study 418, 13 May. Available at http://reason.org/news/show/1013398.html Accessed: 01 July 2016.

Fremont, A. (2007) *Le Monde en boîtes. Conteneurisation et mondialisation*. Paris: Les Collections de l'Inrets.

Goetz, A.R. and L. Dudd (eds) (2014) *The Geographies of Air Transport*, Transport and Mobility Series. Farnham, Surrey: Ashgate.

Givoni, M. (2006) "Development and Impact of the modern high-speed train: a review", *Transport Reviews* 26(5): 593–611.

Graham B. (1995) *Geography and Air Transport*. Chichester: Wiley.

Hayuth, Y. (1987) *Intermodality: Concept and Practice*. London: Lloyds of London Press.

Kaluza, P., A. Kölzsch, M.T. Gastner and B. Blasius (2010) "The complex network of global cargo ship movements." *Journal of Royal Society Interface* 7(48): 1093–1103.

Levinson, M. (2006) *The Box: How the Shipping Container Made the World Smaller and the World Economy Bigger*. Princeton: Princeton University Press.

Mokhtarian, P. L. (2009) "If telecommunication is such a good substitute for travel, why does congestion continue to get worse?" *Transportation Letters* 1(1): 1–17.

Notteboom, T. (2012) "Container shipping." in W. Talley (ed.), *The Blackwell Companion to Maritime Economics*. New York: Wiley-Blackwell Publishing, pp. 230–262.

Notteboom, T. and J.-P. Rodrigue (2009) "The future of containerization: perspectives from maritime and inland freight distribution." *Geojournal* 74(1): 7–22.

O'Connell, J.F. and G. Williams (2013) *Air Transport in the Twenty-First Century: Key Strategic Development*. Farnham, Surrey: Ashgate.

Stopford, M. (2009) *Maritime Economics*, 3rd edition. London: Routledge.

van Klink, A. and G.C. van den Berg (1998) "Gateways and intermodalism." *Journal of Transport Geography* 6(1): 1–9.

5 Transportation terminals

All spatial flows, with the exception of personal vehicular and pedestrian trips, involve movements between terminals. Transport modes require assembly and distribution of their traffic, both passenger and freight. For example, passengers have to go to bus terminals and airports first in order to reach their final destinations, and freight has to be consolidated at a port or a railyard before onward shipment. Terminals are, therefore, essential links in transportation chains, with many representing substantial infrastructure and capital investments. The goal of this chapter is to examine the spatial and functional characteristics of transport terminals. They occupy specific locations and they exert a strong influence over their surroundings. At the same time, they perform specific economic functions and serve as clusters of specialized activities.

Concept 1 – The function of transport terminals

Authors: Dr Jean-Paul Rodrigue and Dr Brian Slack

The nature of transport terminals

A terminal may be defined as any facility where passengers and freight are **assembled or dispersed**. Both cannot travel individually, but in batches. Passengers have to go to bus terminals and airports first, where they are "assembled" in busloads or planeloads to reach their final destinations where they are dispersed. Freight has to be consolidated at a port or a railyard before onward shipment. Terminals may also be points of interchange involving the same mode of transport. Thus, a passenger wishing to travel by train from Paris to Rotterdam may have to change trains in Brussels, or an air passenger wishing to fly between Montreal and Los Angeles may have to change planes in Toronto. Terminals may also be points of interchange between different modes of transportation, so that goods being shipped from the American Midwest to the Ruhr in Germany may travel by rail from Cincinnati to the port of New York, be put on a ship to Rotterdam, and then placed on a barge for delivery to Duisburg. Transport terminals, therefore, are central and intermediate locations in the movements of passengers and freight.

A **terminal** is any location where freight and passengers either originate, terminate or are handled in the transportation process. Terminals are central and intermediate locations in the movements of passengers and freight. They often require specific facilities and equipment to accommodate the traffic they handle. Terminals may be **points of interchange** within the same modal system, and which ensure a continuity of the flows. This is particularly the case for modern air and port operations with hubs connecting parts of the network. Terminals, however, are also very important **points of transfer** between modes. Buses and cars deliver people to airports, trucks haul freight to rail terminals, and rail brings freight to docks for loading on ships. One of the main attributes of transport terminals, international and regional alike, is their **convergence function**. They are indeed obligatory points of passage, having invested in their geographical location, which is generally **intermediate** to commercial flows. Thus, transport terminals are either created by the centrality or the intermediacy of their respective locations. In some cases, large transport terminals, particularly ports, confer the status of gateway or hub to their location, since they become obligatory points of transit between different segments of the transport system.

Three major attributes are linked with the importance and the performance of transport terminals:

- **Location**. The major locational factor of a transport terminal is obviously to serve a large concentration of population and/or industrial activities, representing a terminal's market area. Specific terminals have specific locational constraints, such as port and airport sites. New transport terminals tend to be located outside central areas to avoid high land costs and congestion.
- **Accessibility**. Accessibility to other terminals (at the local, regional and global scale), as well as how well the terminal is linked to the regional transport system, is of importance. For instance, a maritime terminal has little relevance if it is efficiently handling maritime traffic but is poorly connected to its market areas through an inland transport system (rail, road or barge).
- **Infrastructure**. The main function of a terminal is to handle and transship freight or passengers, since modes and passengers or cargo are physically separated. They have a nominal capacity, which is related to the amount of land they occupy and their level of technological, labor and managerial intensity. Infrastructure considerations are consequently important, as they must accommodate current traffic and anticipate future trends and also technological and logistical changes. Modern terminal infrastructures consequently require massive investments and are among the largest structures ever built. A utilization rate of 75 to 80 percent is considered to be the optimal, since above this level congestion starts to rise, undermining the reliability of the terminal facility.

A transport terminal is composed of a set of intermodal infrastructures taking advantage of a geographical location, conferring a higher level of accessibility to local, regional and global markets. Depending on the mode being considered, terminals are bound to various degrees to the site. For instance, maritime transportation terminals are particularly dependent on local conditions, especially for large port activities, which can be accommodated in a limited number of locations. Airport terminals are more flexible in their locations, but still bound to specific locational constrains. Terminals fulfill three general functions within transport systems (Figure 5.1):

- **Connectivity**. Transport terminals provide connectivity within a transport network, as they are the only locations where a network can be entered or exited. For instance, subway stations are the connecting nodes of a transit network, while ports and airports are the connecting nodes of maritime and air networks.
- **Interface**. Transport terminals provide an interface between transport modes enabling passengers and cargo to transit. A port or an airport is a point of interface between maritime or air and land transport systems.
- **Buffer**. Transport terminals provide a buffer between the different capacity and frequency of the transport modes they connect, such as a port does for the maritime

Figure 5.1 The functions of transport terminals

and land transportation systems. A containership may call a port once every two days while trucks carrying containers may come in and out of the terminal every few minutes. A similar analogy applies to airports that act as buffers between the various levels of service of land transport systems and the scheduling of air services.

The time a vehicle (bus, truck, train, or ship) is allowed to load or unload passengers or freight at a terminal is usually referred as **dwell time**. For freight terminals dwell time refers to the amount of time cargo stays in a terminal yard or storage area while waiting to be loaded. Dwell time can be **operational**, which reflects the performance of terminal infrastructures and management, including the scheduling and availability of transport services. It can also be **transactional**, which is usually linked with the performance of clearance procedures (such as customs). Finally, dwell time can be **storage-related**, implying that the owner or the carrier of the cargo deliberately leaves the cargo at the terminal as part of a transport or supply chain management strategy. Intermodalism has prompted new relations between transport terminals, which are becoming nodes in integrated transport chains. This is particularly the case between port, rail and barge terminals. New forms of integration are also emerging, such as between ports and airports.

Passenger terminals

With one exception, passenger terminals require relatively little specific equipment. This is because individual mobility is the means by which passengers access buses, ferries or trains. Certainly, services such as information, shelter, food and security are required, but the layouts and activities taking place in passenger terminals **tend to be simple**. They may appear congested at certain times of the day, but the flows of people can be managed successfully with good design of platforms and access points, and with appropriate scheduling of arrivals and departures. The amount of time passengers spend in such terminals tends to be brief. As a result, bus terminals and railway stations tend to be made up of simple components, from ticket offices and waiting areas to limited amounts of retailing.

Airports are of a completely different order. They are among the **most complex of terminals**. Moving people through an airport has become a very significant problem, not least because of security concerns. Passengers may spend several hours transiting, with check-in and security checks on departure, and baggage pickup and in many cases customs and immigration on arrival. Planes may be delayed for a multitude of reasons, which involves a complex management of gates and scheduling of flights. The result is that a **wide range of services** have to be provided for passengers not directly related to

Photo 5.1   Modern airport terminal, Barajas, Madrid

Barajas terminal in Madrid, which opened in 2006, is typical of a modern airport terminal design. Very high ceilings convey an impression of spaciousness, which has a calming effect on passengers. Since the linear design conveys long distances between gates, mechanized walkways are a common feature. The growing size of planes has also prompted the provision of larger waiting areas at the gate.

the transfer function, including restaurants, bars, stores, hotels, in addition to the activities directly related to operations, such as check-in halls, passenger loading ramps and baggage handling facilities (Photo 5.1). At the same time airports have to provide the very specific needs of the aircraft, from runways to maintenance facilities, from fire protection to air traffic control.

Measurement of activities in passenger terminals is generally straightforward. The most common indicator is the number of passengers handled, sometimes differentiated according to arrivals and departures. **Transfer passengers** are counted in the airport totals even though they do not originate there, so airports that serve as major transfer facilities inevitably record high passenger totals. This is evident in airports such as Atlanta and Chicago, where in-transit passengers account for over 50 percent of the total passenger movements. High transfer passenger activity has been enhanced by the actions of many of the leading airlines adopting hub-and-spoke networks. This results in many passengers being forced to change planes at the hub airports. By selecting certain airports as hubs, the carriers are able to dominate activity at those airports, thereby controlling most landing and departure slots and the best gates, thus fending off rival airlines. In this way they are able to extract monopoly profits.

A further measure of airport activity is the number of aircraft movements, a figure that must be used with some caution because it pays no regard to the capacity of planes. A 50-seat regional jet and a 300-seat wide-body aircraft both count as one movement.

High numbers of aircraft movements thus may not be highly correlated with passenger traffic totals. Still, the number of aircraft movements is an important variable, as it indicates the level of usage of the runways as aircraft take about the same landing or take-off capacity, irrespective of their size.

Freight terminals

Freight handling requires **specific loading and unloading equipment**. In addition to the facilities required to accommodate ships, trucks and trains (berths, loading bays and freight yards respectively), a very wide range of handling gear is required that is determined by the kinds of cargoes handled. Freight transport terminals have a set of characteristics linked with core (terminal operations) and ancillary activities (added value such as distribution). The result is that terminals are **differentiated functionally** both by the mode involved and the commodities transferred. A basic distinction is that between bulk, general cargo and containers:

- **Bulk** refers to goods that are handled in large quantities that are unpackaged and are available in uniform dimensions. Liquid bulk goods include crude oil and refined products that can be handled using pumps to move the product along hoses and pipes. Relatively limited handling equipment is needed, but significant storage facilities may be required. Dry bulk includes a wide range of products, such as ores, coal and cereals. More equipment for dry bulk handling is required, because the material may have to utilize specialized grabs and cranes and conveyor-belt systems.
- **General cargo** refers to goods that are of many shapes, dimensions and weights, such as machinery, processed materials and parts. Because the goods are so uneven and irregular, handling is difficult to mechanize. General cargo handling usually requires a lot of labor.
- **Containers** are standard units that have had a substantial impact on terminal operations. Container terminals have minimal labor requirements and perform a wide variety of intermodal functions. However, they require a significant amount of storage spaces, that is, simple paved areas where containers can be stacked and retrieved with intermodal equipment (cranes, straddlers and holsters). Depending on the intermodal function of the container terminal, specialized cranes are required, such as portainers (container cranes; Photo 5.2). Intermodal terminals and their related activities are increasingly seen as agents of added value within supply chains.

A feature of most freight activity is the **need for storage**. Assembling the individual bundles of goods may be time-consuming and thus some storage may be required. This produces the need for terminals to be equipped with specialized infrastructures such as grain silos, storage tanks and refrigerated warehouses, or simply space to stockpile, such as for containers. Containerization, because of its large volumes, has forced a significant modal and temporal separation at terminals and thus the need for a buffer in the form of storage areas. In addition, a variety of transloading activities can take place in the vicinity of terminals, particularly if long-distance inland transportation is involved. Transloading, when suitable, enables the reduction of transportation and inventory costs.

Measurement of freight traffic through terminals is more complicated than for passengers. Because freight is so diverse, standard measures of weight and value are **difficult to compare and combine**. Because bulk cargoes are inevitably weighty,

Photo 5.2   Portainer, APM Terminal, Port Newark, New York

Container cranes, also known as portainers, require a high level of capital equipment, such as the above post-panamax crane at the APM terminal (Maersk) at the port of New York (Newark facilities). It was manufactured by ZPMC (Shanghai Zhenhua Port Machinery Company), which is the world's largest gantry crane supplier and accounts for about 60 percent of the world's manufactured cranes.

terminals specializing in such cargoes will record higher throughputs measured in tons than others more specialized in general cargoes. This is evident for the world's two leading ports, Singapore and Rotterdam, which are dominated by petroleum. The reverse may be true if the measure employed is value of commodities handled. The problem of measurement involving weight or volumes becomes very difficult when many types of freight are handled, because one is adding together goods that are inherently unequal. Care must be taken in interpreting the significance of freight traffic totals, therefore. For container terminals a common measure of productivity concerns the number of lifts per container gantry crane-hour, which are usually 25–40 moves per hour for quay cranes and 40–60 for rail cranes.

Terminal costs

Because they jointly perform **transfer and consolidation** functions, terminals are important economically because of the costs incurred in carrying out these activities. The traffic they handle is a source of employment and benefit regional economic activities, notably by providing accessibility to suppliers and customers. Terminal costs represent an **important component of total transport costs**. They are fixed costs that are incurred regardless of the length of the eventual trip, and vary significantly between modes. They can be considered as:

- **Infrastructure costs**. Include construction and maintenance costs of structures such as piers, runways, cranes and facilities (warehouses, offices, etc.).
- **Transshipment costs**. The costs of loading and unloading passengers or freight.
- **Administration costs**. Many terminals are managed by institutions such as port or airport authorities or by private companies (e.g. terminal operators). In both cases administration costs are incurred.

Because ships have the largest carrying capacities, they incur the **largest terminal costs**, since it may take many days to load or unload a vessel. Conversely, a truck or a passenger bus can be loaded much more quickly, and hence the terminal costs for road transport are the lowest. Terminal costs play an important role in determining the competitive position between the modes. Because of their high freight terminal costs, ships and rail are generally unsuitable for short-haul trips.

Competition between the modes is frequently measured by **cost comparisons**. Efforts to reduce transport costs can be achieved by using more fuel-efficient vehicles, increasing the size of ships and reducing the labor employed on trains. However, unless terminal costs are reduced as well, the benefits would not be realized. For example, in water transportation, potential economies of scale realized by ever larger and more fuel-efficient vessels would be negated if it took longer to load and offload the jumbo ships.

Over the last decades, very significant steps to reduce terminal costs have been made. These have included introducing **information management systems** such as EDI (Electronic Data Interchange) that have greatly speeded up the processing of information and removing delays typical of paper transactions. The most significant development has been the mechanization of loading and unloading activities. Mechanization has been facilitated by the use of units of standard dimensions such as the pallet and, most importantly, the container. The container, in particular, has revolutionized terminal operations. For the mode most affected by high terminal costs, ocean transport, ships used to spend as much as three weeks in a port undergoing loading and unloading. The much larger ships of today spend less than a couple of days in port. A modern container ship requires approximately 750 man-hours to be loaded and unloaded. Prior to containerization it would have required 24,000 man-hours to handle the same volume of cargo. The rail industry too has benefited from the container, which permits trains to be assembled in freight yards in a matter of hours instead of days.

Reduced terminal costs have had a major impact on transportation and international trade. Not only have they reduced overall freight rates, and thereby reshaping competition between the modes, but they have had a profound effect on transport systems. Ships spend far less time in port, enabling ships to make many more revenue-generating trips per year. Efficiency in the airports, rail facilities and ports greatly improves the effectiveness of transportation as a whole.

Activities in transport terminals represent not just exchanges of goods and people, but constitute an **important economic activity**. Employment of people in various terminal operations represents an advantage to the local economy. Dockers, baggage handlers, crane operators and air traffic controllers are examples of jobs generated directly by terminals. In addition, a wide range of activities exist that are linked to transportation activity at the terminals. These include the actual carriers (airlines, shipping lines, etc.) and intermediate agents (customs brokers, freight forwarders) required to carry out transport operations at the terminal. It is no accident that centers performing major airport, port and rail functions also important economic poles.

Concept 2 – The location of terminals

Authors: Dr Brian Slack, Dr Jean-Paul Rodrigue and Dr Theo Notteboom

The relative location of terminals

Geographers have long recognized situation, or relative location, as an important component of location. It refers to the position of places in relation to other places. **Accessibility is relative**, because the situation of places changes over time with the fluctuations in trade and growth opportunities. For example, ports in the Mediterranean used to be at the core of the Western world during the Greek and Roman eras, and Genoa and Venice prospered during the Middle Ages. The emergence of the Americas, particularly the United States, as an economic power focused on Atlantic ports and the Mediterranean became more marginal. The opening of the Suez Canal in the nineteenth century refocused the relative location of the Mediterranean again with increased interactions with Asia.

Although "terminal" implies a final **destination**, because they are transfer points terminals in fact are typically **intermediate locations** in the global flows of passengers and freight. Landlocked countries do not have direct access to port terminals and an intermediary country must be used. Differences in the nature, composition and timing of transfer activities give rise to significant differentiations in the form and function between terminals. A basic distinction is between passenger and freight transfers, because in order to carry out the transfer and bundling of each type, specific equipment and infrastructures are required. Passenger and freight terminals are consequently referring to substantially different entities and often have different locational attributes.

Spatial relationships between terminals are a vital element in competition, particularly for ports and rail terminals, and a number of concepts to explore these locational features have been developed. One of particular interest concerns the function of centrality and intermediacy performed by transport terminals. **Centrality** focuses on the terminal as a point of origin and destination of traffic. Thus, centrality is linked with the generation and attraction of movements, which are related to the nature and the level of economic activities within the vicinity of the concerned terminal. The function of centrality also involves a significant number of intermodal activities.

One of the most enduring concepts in urban geography is the central place theory, with its emphasis on centrality as a feature of the urban hierarchy. Cities more centrally located to markets are larger, with a wider range of functions. Transport accessibility is equated with size, and thus many large terminals arise out of centrality. Examples include Heathrow Airport, London, whose traffic preeminence is related to the city's location in the heart of the most developed part of Britain, as one of the world's most important financial center, as well as Britain's functional centrality to its former empire to a lesser degree. The port of New York owes its preeminence in part to the fact that it is at the heart of the largest market area in the USA: the Boston–Washington corridor. A similar observation applies to the port of Shanghai, serving a large market, industrial and manufacturing base.

Intermediacy focuses on the terminal as an intermediate point in the flows of passengers or freight. This term is applied to the frequent occurrence of places gaining advantage because they are between other places. The ability to exploit transshipment has been an important feature of many terminals.

Anchorage, Alaska, for example, was a convenient airport located on the great circle of air routes between Asia and Europe and continental USA and Asia. For many years passengers alighted here while the planes refueled. The growth of long-haul jets has made this activity diminish considerably, and Anchorage now joins the list of once important airports, such as Gander, Newfoundland, that have seen their relative locations change because of technological improvements. It should be noted, however, that Anchorage continues to fulfill its intermediacy role for air freight traffic. Other examples include Chicago, the dominant US rail hub, which is not only a major market area in its own right (centrality) but also lies at the junction of the major eastern and western railroad networks. Ports too can exploit advantages of intermediate locations. One of the largest container ports in the Mediterranean, Gioia Tauro, is located on the toe of Italy. A few years ago the port did not exist, but because of its location close to the main East–West shipping lanes through the Mediterranean it has been selected as a hub, where the large mother ships can transfer containers to smaller vessels for distribution to the established markets in the northern Mediterranean – a classic hub-and-spoke network.

The concept of centrality is straightforward, as the vicinity of the terminal is either the origin or the destination of the movement, which in turn is linked with the level of economic activity. The extent of this vicinity remains to be fully assessed, but a range of about 100 km appears suitable, as it corresponds to a commuting or drayage range. Intermediacy, however, is a multifaceted concept that relates to a number of issues (Figure 5.2):

- **Range**. This is more a conventional aspect of intermediacy that tends to be of lesser importance in the contemporary situation. Due to technical limitations of the modes, such as the range of an aircraft or the need to refuel a coal-powered ship, intermediate locations were used as stages to overcome the range gap as two locations could not be reached in a single trip. Although range plays a more limited role for air passenger transportation, particularly with long-range aircrafts, it is still prevalent for air freight transportation, as the range of freight aircrafts is more limited due to heavier loads. Therefore, transpacific air cargo routes commonly involve a stop at Anchorage, while Asia–Europe routes will have a stop at a Middle Eastern airport such as Dubai. To a lesser extent, intermediate locations are used for long-distance trucking since rest periods are required for drivers, but the required facilities are very basic.
- **Gateway**. It connects two systems of circulation and thus represents an intermediate location imposed by geographical constraints. Thus, in order to reach its final destination, a movement must use an intermediate location, often implying a transfer from one mode to the other. Many gateways have also a significant centrality component as they represent industrial zones and large urban agglomerations.
- **Hub (interception)**. A location nearby, or at, the convergence of several long-distance routes can develop an intermediacy by "intercepting" some of the traffic. This is notably the case for intermediate hub terminals located along major long-distance maritime corridors, such as Algeciras (Spain) or Singapore.
- **Hub (transcalar)**. A location is specifically used to serve as a connection between different scales of a transport system. Air transportation is a notable example with the emergence of hub-and-spoke network structures where the hub is an intermediate location between regional and international flights. Freight distribution, particularly cross-docking distribution centers, also rely on the usage of intermediate location to service specific market segments often supplied by distant sources.

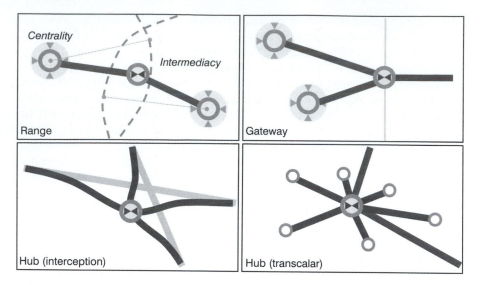

Figure 5.2 Centrality and intermediacy

Hinterlands and forelands

One of the most enduring concepts in transport geography is the **hinterland**, which is a land space over which a transport terminal, such as a port, sells its services and interacts with its clients. It accounts for the regional market share that a terminal has relative to a set of other terminals servicing a region. It regroups all the customers directly bounded to the terminal and the land areas from which it draws and distributes traffic. The terminal, depending on its nature, serves as a place of convergence for the traffic coming by roads, railways or by sea/fluvial feeders.

Two types of hinterlands are often noted (Figure 5.3). The term main or **fundamental hinterland** refers to the market area for which a terminal is the closest. It is assumed that traffic will normally pass through the terminal, because of proximity and the lack of competitive alternatives. The **competitive hinterland** (or competitive margin) is used to describe the market areas over which the terminal has to compete with others for business. Transport terminals are elements of transport chains that include the notions of foreland and hinterland binding imports and exports activities. The concept of **foreland** is a mirror image of the hinterland. It refers to the other terminals it is connected to. For a port, this would represent the other ports it is linked to through maritime shipping services. The foreland of an airport would represent all the connected airports accessible through regular air services.

The main nature of a hinterland is commercial, and its importance is linked with the **level of economic activity** as well as the **level of competition** from other modes not linked to the terminal. Hinterlands vary significantly for the same location if the flows concern passengers or freight. For airports, like most passenger terminals, the hinterland is well delimited and corresponds to a commuting range where customers can access the terminal within a couple of hours. The level of activity is proportional to the population density, the level of income and the prominence of tertiary activities. For ports, like most freight terminals, the level of activity corresponds to the dynamics of the land they are connected to, which is subject to changes in the nature of its activities and in the

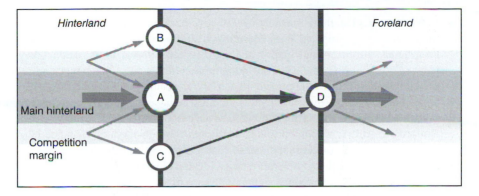

Figure 5.3 Port foreland and hinterland

level of accessibility. Any change implies either new opportunities to generate additional port traffic, a decline, or a change in the nature and composition of the traffic. Inbound hinterland traffic tends to be consumption-based, except in the case where commodities and parts are involved in the fabrication of a product, while outbound hinterland traffic is an outcome of extraction or production. Hinterlands can further be discriminated by the type of commodity, as each is part of a specific supply chain with its own spatial relationships:

- **Bulk products** (minerals, chemicals, raw materials, wood, grain, etc.). In this case distance is one of the most important factors shaping hinterlands. Due to the nature of the products and the high transport costs involved, hinterlands tend to be small and serviced by high-capacity corridors to the direct location of extraction or production.
- **Parts and manufactured goods**. Mostly concerns containerized traffic. Improvements in intermodal transportation and globalization have considerably expanded the hinterland for this type of traffic. In many cases, the hinterland can encompass large economic regions, particularly if transport corridors are involved.

With the emergence of feeder services and hub ports, the concept of foreland has been expanded, as a port can service a hinterland through a maritime link. In recent years the validity of the hinterland concept has been questioned, especially in the context of contemporary containerization. The mobility provided by the container has greatly facilitated market penetration, so that many ports compete over the same market areas for business. Therefore, hinterland may be **overlapping**. The notion of discrete hinterlands with well-defined boundaries is questionable, since many hinterlands have become discontinuous, a process facilitated by the development of **corridors and inland terminals**. The extension and strengthening of hinterlands follows a vertical or horizontal integration process depending if the port establishes more effective functional linkages with inland intermodal terminals (vertical) or other maritime terminals (horizontal). Nevertheless, the concept of hinterland is still widely employed, and port authorities continue to emphasize their port's centrality to hinterland areas in their promotional literature.

The hinterlands of three major economic regions can be synthetically represented in terms of their intensity and the importance of gateways and corridors that service them (Figure 5.4):

- In **North America**, there is a high level of concentration of economic activities along the coastal areas (East and West coasts) with significant resource and manufacturing hinterlands. From coastal gateways long-distance rail corridors, often taking the form of a landbridge, are servicing a continental hinterland. This hinterland is articulated by major transportation and industrial hubs such as Chicago.
- In **Western Europe**, the hinterland is the most intense in the interior, notably along the Rhine river system. This hinterland is accessed from coastal gateways, such as Rotterdam, Antwerp, Hamburg and Le Havre, through medium-distance corridors involving a variety of combinations of road, barge and rail services. Almost all the major European capitals are interior cities located along rivers.
- In **East and Southeast Asia**, a significant share of the economic activity takes place along the coast, with a few high population density interior hinterlands, such as in China. Hinterland access is commonly problematic, linked to the fact that a large share of the accumulation of new economic activities has taken place in the vicinity of major gateways. There is thus a strong contrast between coastal gateways equipped with modern (container) terminals and hinterlands usually poorly serviced by rail freight services.

The provision of services to a wide range of markets around the world is considered to be an advantage. With the growth in maritime traffic and congestion in proximity of port terminal facilities, several port authorities have become more involved in the development of strategies aiming at better servicing their hinterland. Such strategies and the stakeholders involved are dependent on the direction of the flows since import- and export-based flows usually involve different concerns. The foreland and hinterland should be seen as a **continuum**, rather than separate and distinct elements. The emergence of door-to-door services and networks, where the port is seen as one link in through transport chains, underlines this continuum. In such a context, the port becomes one element of the maritime/land interface which ensures the continuity of global freight circulation.

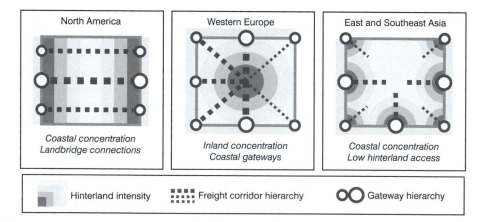

Figure 5.4 Hinterland setting and major economic regions

Source: Adapted from S.W. Lee, D.W. Song and C. Ducruet (2008) "A tale of Asia's world ports: the spatial evolution in global hub port cities." *Geoforum* 39: 373–385.

Concept 3 – Port terminals

Ports and port sites

Ports are points of convergence between two geographical domains of freight circula-tion (sometimes passengers); the **land and maritime domains**. While the maritime domain can involve substantial geographical coverage related to global trade, the land domain is related to the port's region and locality. The term "port" comes from the Latin *portus*, which means "gate" or "gateway." Historically, many ports emerged as safe harbors for fishing and those with convenient locations became trade hubs, many of which with free access and designed to protect trade. As such, they became nexuses of urbanization, with many becoming the first port cities to play an important role in the economic welfare of their regions. Today, many of the most important cities in the world owe their origin to their port location. The port is a multidimensional entity, anchored within geography, but also dependent on its operations, governance structure and embedded within supply chains (Figure 5.5).

Four main dimensions help define the role and function of a port:

- **Place**. A port is at start a location that has physical characteristics (such as a protected bay) and thus supports a more effective interface between the maritime and land domains than many other locations. This marks the difference between a good and a less suitable port site. Although the location of a port does not change, the site can be improved through dredging and land reclamation. However, this comes at the expense of substantial capital investment. The situation of a port can also change, since it is relative to large zones of production and consumption.
- **Operations**. A port has some operational characteristics in terms of the type of traffic it can handle and related volumes. This is contingent upon the infrastructure (e.g. berths) and the superstructure (e.g. cranes and yard equipment) linking the port fore-land (the ports it is connected to) and the port hinterland (its inland market area). With capital investments and training the operational efficiency of a port can be improved.
- **Administrative unit**. A port is a well-defined administrative unit that involves land ownership and a jurisdiction (what a port can legally do). The port authority is a common administrative framework for a port and in many cases the management and operations of many terminals is leased to private companies. Port authorities usually have the right to spearhead port development projects.
- **Value chain**. A port is the support of transport and supply chains and thus adds value. Historically, heavy industrial activities such as steel mills and petrochemical plants had a propensity to locate within or nearby ports, a process that is still going on and being complemented by a large array of freight distribution activities.

As terminals, ports handle the largest amounts of freight, more than any other types of terminals combined. To handle this freight, port infrastructures jointly have to accom-modate transshipment activities both on ships and inland, and thus facilitate conver-gence between land transport and maritime systems. In many parts of the world, ports are the points of convergence from which inland transport systems, particularly rail, were laid. Considering the operational characteristics of maritime transportation, the location of ports is constrained to a limited array of sites, mostly defined by geography. Most ports, especially those that are ancient, owe their initial emergence to their site, as

Place	Operations	Administrative unit	Value chain
	Foreland | Hinterland		
Site and situation	Operational capacity and efficiency	Governance and management	Added economic value

Figure 5.5 The dimensions of a port

the great majority of harbors are taking advantage of a natural coastline or a natural site along a river. Many port sites are constrained by:

- **Maritime access,** which refers to the physical capacity of the site to accommodate ship operations. It includes the tidal range, which is the difference between the high and low tide, as normal ship operations cannot handle variations of more than 3 m. Channel and berth depths are also very important to accommodate modern cargo ships. A standard Panamax ship of 65,000 deadweight tons requires more than 12 m (40 ft) of depth. However, about 70 percent of world ports have depths of less than 10 m and are unable to accommodate ships of more than 200 m in length. In view of the construction of larger ships, namely tankers and container ships, many port sites found themselves unable to provide maritime access to modern cargo operations. Since container terminals were constructed much more recently, they have a better nautical profile, as depth and available space were fundamental factors in site selection. There is thus a pressure to increase channel depth where possible, but this is a costly and environmentally controversial endeavor. Berths and channel depth have become important constraints for maritime operations in light of growing ship size. Many ports are also impacted by sedimentation, particularly ports in river deltas. This requires continuous dredging, which adds to the costs of port operations. Some river ports may be impacted by periods of flooding and drought, while other ports may be impeded or closed during winter because of icy conditions.
- **Maritime interface**. Indicates the amount of space that is available to support maritime access, namely the amount of shoreline that has good maritime access. This attribute is very important since ports are linear entities. Even if a port site has an excellent maritime access, namely deep-water waterways, there may not be enough land available to guarantee its future development and expansion. Containerization has expanded the land consumption requirements of many ports. It is therefore not surprising to see that modern port expansion projects involve significant capital investments to create artificial port facilities.
- **Infrastructures and equipment**. The site, to be efficiently used, must have infrastructures such as piers, basins, stacking or storage areas, warehouses and equipment such as cranes, all of which involve high levels of capital investment. In turn, these infrastructures consume land, which must be available to ensure port expansion. Keeping up with the investment requirements of modern port operations has become a challenge for many ports, particularly in light of containerization, which requires substantial amounts of terminal space to operate. Many terminals are also becoming

increasingly automated, particularly for stacking areas that can be serviced by automated cranes and vehicles.

- **Land access**. Access from the port to industrial complexes and markets ensures its growth and importance. This requires efficient inland distribution systems, such as fluvial, rail (mainly for containers) and road transportation. The land access to ports located in densely populated areas is facing increasing congestion. For instance, the ports of Los Angeles and Long Beach have invested massively to develop the Alameda rail corridor in an attempt to promote inland access and reduce truck congestion. A similar trend has taken place in Europe, where ports such as Rotterdam and Antwerp have been involved in the setting of inland barge and rail shuttle services.

There is also an array of problems related to port infrastructures. Ports along rivers are continuously facing **dredging problems** and the width of rivers is strongly limiting their capacity since it provides constraints to navigation. Rarely a port along a river has the capacity to handle a new generation of giant ships, namely post-Panamax container ships, which have put additional pressures on port infrastructures to accommodate the transshipment generated by these ships. Ports next to the sea are commonly facing a **lateral spread** of their infrastructures. Several ports have growth problems that force them to spread their infrastructures far from the original port sites. Since ports are generally old, and in several cases were responsible for urban growth, they are located nearby central areas. This is creating congestion problems where the transport network has the least capacity to be improved.

The city and the port are often **competing for the same land**, which can create prioritization problems. Ports thus have a complex set of relationships, sometimes conflicting, with the cities they service, often a function of the port and city size. While ports are sources of employment of commercial interactions, they also generate externalities such as noise and congestion near their access points. The pressure of many ports on their sites is even more demanding than those of airports, because they have to be adjacent to deep water. Such sites are very limited, and may give rise to conflicts with the city that sees waterfront land as potential high-value residential and commercial areas, park space, or as environmentally sensitive. Many ports are now constrained by urban and environmental pressures, which did not exist when the initial facilities were developed.

Port functions and traffic

The main function of a port is to supply **services to freight** (warehousing, transshipment, etc.) and **ships** (docking, refueling, repairs, etc.). Consequently, it is misleading to consider a port strictly as a maritime terminal since it acts concomitantly as a land terminal where inland traffic originates or ends. Ports are primarily cargo-oriented facilities. To this significant cargo-related function, many ports are also involved in other activities such as fishing, ferries, cruises (a growing activity) and recreation (e.g. marinas).

Ports are becoming increasingly regional in their dynamics, which represents a new development from their traditional local function, namely as industrial complexes. For instance, the port of Hong Kong owes its wealth to its natural site and its geographical position of a transit harbor for southern China. A similar function is assumed by Shanghai for central China with the Yangtze river system. Singapore, for its part, has been favored by its location at the outlet of the strategic Strait of Malacca and is therefore a point of convergence of Southeast Asian transportation. More than 90 percent of the traffic it handles is strictly transshipments. New York has traditionally acted as the

Figure 5.6 Tonnage handled by the world's major ports, 2013

gateway of the North American Midwest through the Hudson/Erie Canal system, a function which Western European ports such as Rotterdam or Antwerp perform with their access to the Rhine system.

A port throughput is linked to a variety of local and regional industrial activities, as the largest ports in the world are all gateways to massive industrial regions (Figure 5.6). However, comparing ports on a tonnage basis requires caution, as it does not indicate the nature and the value of the cargo. For instance, a mineral port (e.g. iron ore), an energy port (e.g. coal or oil) and a commercial port (containers) could handle a similar tonnage but significantly different value levels.

The geography of the world's major ports, as measured in tonnage, obviously shares some commonality with traffic figures measured in TEU, but very large port facilities are found in areas that have limited commercial activity. For instance, Port Hedland in northwestern Australia is the world's largest exporter of iron ore, and handled 372 million tons of cargo in 2013, which is more than three times the amount handled by Los Angeles/Long Beach (129 million tons), the largest commercial gateway of North America. Two general patterns are observed:

- Major **commercial gateways** (polyfunctional ports) that are clustered around East Asia and the European northern range. Although many are large industrial and manufacturing complexes generating large quantities of bulk cargo, they are also major centers of containerized trade. They tend to have a high value-to-weight ratio.
- **Resource ports** (monofunctional ports) that are in different clusters than main commercial gateways, since the majority of them do not handle significant container traffic. Of particular relevance are Australian, Brazilian and American Gulf Coast ports that are linked with mineral, petrochemical and grain trade. They have a low value-to-weight ratio.

About commercial 4,600 ports are in operation worldwide, but only less than 100 ports have a global importance. There are about 500 container ports with 180 handling traffic of more than half a million TEU (Figure 5.7). Maritime traffic thus has a high level of concentration in a limited number of large ports, a process mainly attributed to constraints related to maritime access and infrastructure development. Major ports have established themselves as gateways of continental distribution systems and have access to high-capacity inland freight distribution corridors, notably rail. Such a position is very difficult to challenge unless a port is facing acute congestion forcing maritime shipping companies to seek alternatives.

Container ports are reflective of the world's **commercial geography,** particularly since they dominantly handle finished and intermediate goods. Commodities are becoming more prevalent, but they still remain a niche market. Prior to the 1990s, the world's most important ports were North American (e.g. New York) and Western European (e.g. Rotterdam). Globalization, supported by containerization, completely changed the world's commercial geography with the emergence of new port locations reflecting changes in the global geography of production, distribution and consumption. This geography indicates a high level of traffic concentration around large port facilities, notably Pacific Asian ports along the Tokyo–Singapore corridor. As export-oriented economic development strategies took shape, the number of containers handled in Pacific Asian ports, notably Chinese ports, surged. The comparative size of ports requires caution, as several ports can be considered more statistical agglomerations than functional entities. For instance, the port of Shenzhen in the Pearl River Delta is composed of several large port facilities (e.g. Yantian, Chiwan, Shekou) that act as distinct entities within their operations and are even servicing different hinterlands. The same observation applies to Guangzhou and Shanghai, which are multiport (and multi-terminal) entities.

Figure 5.7 World's major container ports, 2012

The world's largest container ports underline the intricate relationships between export-oriented ports (e.g. Shanghai and Hong Kong), import-oriented ports (e.g. Los Angeles/Long Beach) and intermediary hubs (e.g. Singapore and Dubai). The world container port system is characterized by a high level of traffic concentration, with the 20 largest container ports handling more than 49 percent of global traffic in 2012. There is also an emerging geography of container ports involving a specialization between container ports acting as gateways and container ports acting as intermediate hubs. Gateway ports command the access of large manufacturing or market regions and are the spearhead of long-distance corridors. Hong Kong, Los Angeles and Rotterdam are notable examples of ports that command access to a vast and complex hinterland. Intermediate hub ports (or offshore hubs) act as intermediary locations where containers are transshipped between different segments of the global maritime transport system in a manner similar to hubs in air transportation. Singapore and Dubai are among the most prominent transshipment hubs, each servicing a specific transshipment market (Southeast Asian and the Middle East/South Asia respectively).

The world container throughput is the summation of all containers handled by ports, either as imports, exports or transshipment. In 2014, about 677 million TEU were handled by container ports, with a notable growth in containers transshipped at intermediate locations as well as the repositioning of empty containers. This means that a container is at least counted twice; as an import and as an export, but also each time it is handled at the ship-to-shore interface, such as at a transshipment hub, where it will be counted when unloaded and reloaded. Empty containers, most of them being repositioned, account for about 20 percent of the world's throughput. Thus, throughput should ideally be counted in container moves, but for basic commercial and strategic reasons, both port authorities and terminal operators prefer to communicate throughput figures in TEU. The world container traffic is the absolute number of containers being carried by sea, excluding the double counts of imports and exports as well as the number of involved transshipments. The throughput reflects the level of transport activity, while the traffic reflects the level of trade activity.

Port authorities and port holdings

Due to the growing level of complexity of port operations, **public port authorities** were created at the beginning of the twentieth century. For instance, the London Port Authority, the world's first, was established in 1908 by consolidating all the existing harbor facilities. Such a management structure became a standard that was adapted to many other ports. For North America, in 1921, the states of New York and New Jersey created the Port Authority of New York and New Jersey, which has become one of the world's most diversified port authority, with a portfolio including port facilities, bridges, airports and public transit systems. Administratively, port authorities are regulating infrastructure investments, its organization and development and its relationships with customers using its services.

The main rationale behind the setting of many port authorities was their **ability to manage more efficiently port facilities as a whole** rather than privately owned and operated terminals. Since port facilities were becoming more complex and more capital-intensive, it was perceived that public agencies would be better placed to raise investment capital and mitigate the risk of such investments. Port authorities tend to be vertically integrated entities as they are involved in most of the activities related to port operations, from the construction and maintenance of infrastructure to the marketing and management of port services. Yet, their activities were limited within their jurisdictions, an attribute that became increasingly at odds with the transformation of the maritime shipping industry through globalization.

Occasionally, terminals were leased to private companies, but throughout the greater part of the twentieth century public ownership and operation of ports was dominant. Privatization marks a reversal in this trend, since many became inefficient, unable to cope with market expectations (performance, reliability and quality of service) and provide adequate financing for infrastructure and equipment becoming increasingly capital-intensive. As public agencies, many port authorities were seen by governments as a source of revenue and were mandated to perform various non-revenue-generating community projects, or at least provide employment.

The emergence of specialized and capital-intensive container terminals servicing global trade has created a new environment for the management of port terminals, both for the port authorities and the terminal operators. Port authorities are gradually prompted to look at a new array of issues related to the governance of their area and are increasingly acting as cluster managers. For port operations that have conventionally been assumed by port authorities, a significant trend has been an increase in the role of private operators, where major port holdings have emerged with the purpose of managing a wide array of terminals, the great majority of which are containerized. As of 2013, port holdings accounted for over 58 percent of the world's container port capacity (Figure 5.8).

Since terminal operators have various stakes depending on the concerned terminal, **equity-based throughput** is commonly used to measure the respective amount of containerized traffic they handle. For instance, two terminal operators may have respective stakes in a terminal of 75 percent and 25 percent. If that terminal handles 100,000 TEU per year, then 75,000 TEU will be attributed to one terminal operator and 25,000 TEU to the other. By using such a measure, the Port of Singapore Authority (PSA) is the world's largest terminal operator, even if Hutchison Port Holdings (HPH), Dubai Ports World (DPW) and A.P. Moller Group (APM) have respectively more terminals in their portfolio. Actually, PSA owns a 20 percent stake in HPH, which from

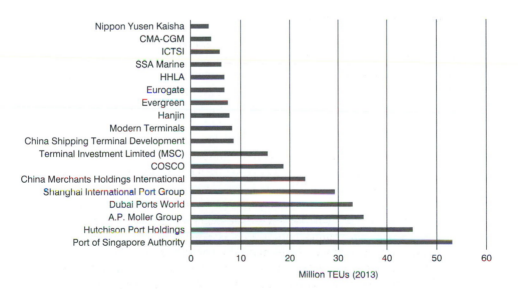

Figure 5.8 Largest global container terminal operators by equity-based throughput, 2013

an equity-based throughput perspective conveys traffic handled by another terminal operator. The four largest terminal operators are highly internationalized, with assets in several countries and regions of the world. However, the fifth largest, Shanghai International Port Group (SIPG), is almost exclusively locally focused around the Shanghai area, where it handles substantial volumes.

Concept 4 – Rail terminals

Location dynamics

The use of the transport capacity offered by rail transportation requires **purposely designed terminals** where passengers can embark and disembark and where freight can be transferred. Rail terminals, while not quite as space-extensive as airports and ports, suffer less from site constraints. This involves two major issues:

- **Location**. An important distinction concerns passengers and freight rail terminals, which commonly involve very different locations. Many rail terminals were established in the nineteenth century during the heyday of rail development. While sites may have been on the edge of urban areas at the time, decades of urban development, including residential and industrial areas, have surrounded older rail terminals, leaving limited opportunities for expansion. Passenger terminals tend to occupy central locations and are commonly the defining element of urban centrality, while freight terminals have seen a growing separation from central locations, with new facilities often built in an exurban location, particularly for high-speed train stations.
- **Setting**. Because of the linear characteristic of the mode they serve, rail terminals are predominantly rectangular-shaped facilities. Their capacity is a function of the number of track spurs available, which is a characteristic difficult to change once the terminal has been built. Individually rail terminals may not be as extensive as airports or ports, but cumulatively the area of all the rail sites in a city may exceed those of the other modes. For example, in Chicago the combined area of rail freight yards exceeds that of the airports.

Rail terminals can be categorized by the passenger and freight markets they service, with the function of shunting accounting for an intermediary form (Figure 5.9). Passenger and freight terminals can also be differentiated by their locational setting:

- **Passenger terminals**. The intercity rail terminal, often taking the form of a central station, is the standard passenger terminal and a distinctive urban landmark, since many have been present for decades and have helped defined urban centrality. Commuter rail covers metropolitan areas with stations of a simpler design and function, since waiting time is of short duration. Urban transit systems are also serviced by rail, namely subway and light rail, and depending on density levels are shape urban dynamics through their network structure. There is a whole hierarchy of rail stations depending on their size and the passenger traffic they handle, ranging from a simple quay along a commuter line to large central stations that are hubs for intercity, commuter and urban transit rail systems. A much more recent type of rail terminal involves high-speed rail stations, which has either required the adaptation of existing central stations to provide spurs connected to the high-speed rail network or the construction of new dedicated terminals in suburban areas that can act as new poles of urban development. The growth of air transportation has conferred new opportunities for rail, with the airport becoming a hub for intercity, commuter and urban transit. In some instances, a high-speed rail station is part of the airport terminal complex.

- **Freight terminals.** For bulk, rail freight terminals tend to be commodity-specific with dedicated facilities for either loading or unloading (both activities rarely take place at the same terminal). Roll-on/roll-off terminals (RORO) are even simpler, since a simple ramp is required to load or unload the equipment, but a large amount of parking space is needed. Break-bulk rail terminals concern a wide variety of activities where the loading and unloading often take place at small privately owned facilities serviced by rail spurs. It is the intermodal terminal that has seen the most development with the setting of facilities handling international and domestic containers. The locational setting of rail freight terminals is usually centered along port terminals, fluvial terminals (less common) or inland locations providing accessibility to markets or resources.

- **Shunting (switching) terminals.** While shunting yards are not necessarily a terminal, since they do not handle passengers or cargo, they are a fundamental element of rail operations. The shunting of passenger rail cars is important but less frequent and often takes place at maintenance yards or at yards near central stations (also known as coach yards). For freight, particularly non-intermodal cars, shunting has an important function in assembling, sorting and breaking down train units based on a variety of cargoes, origins and destinations.

Rail terminals have significant structuring and agglomeration effects that have had an impact on urban land markets since their introduction. This involved related activities, such as retail, restaurants and hotels for passenger terminals or distribution centers for freight terminals. This is in part due to the **accessibility they provide** and in part because of the **traffic they generate**. Before the prominence of the automobile and trucking, economic activities tended to cluster around their respective rail terminals. Whole urban districts emerged around rail terminals. However, as the trucking industry matured and highway infrastructure was expanded and improved, rail terminals lost a great deal of their primacy. Even if rail transportation is generally more fuel-efficient than other modes, the mobility of passengers and freight quickly responded to the availability of the ubiquitous highway infrastructure.

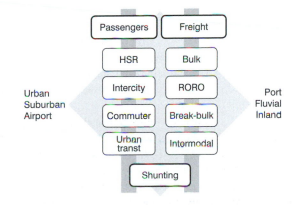

Figure 5.9 Types of rail terminals

Rail terminals were initially developed to complement the shortcomings of other modes, particularly to service gaps in fluvial (canal) and maritime transportation. In the second half of the twentieth century, as rail passenger traffic declined, the need for many rail stations diminished, particularly in North America. A rationalization has resulted in the conversion of many stations to other uses, sometimes with striking effects, such as the Musée d'Orsay in Paris and Windsor Station in Montreal. Railyard conversion has been less spectacular, partly because the sites are less interesting from an architectural standpoint, but nonetheless important. Many former downtown freight facilities have been completely redeveloped in residential developments or commercially. Indeed, the CN Tower-Skydome complexes in Toronto are on former rail land. In other cases, yards can be converted to related activities such as warehouses or even urban logistics centers.

The current setting of rail systems underlines an almost **complete separation between rail passenger and freight terminals**. Although they can share access to the same rail network, they service completely different mobility requirements. Any proximity between passengers and freight terminals tends to be coincidental.

Passenger terminals

Passenger rail terminals tend to be **functionally simple facilities,** and in their most basic form they include a quay for passengers to embark or disembark and a common area for ticket purchase, waiting and for activities servicing large volumes of passengers (e.g. retail and restoration). While some are along a line that requires a stop of a few minutes so that passengers can embark or disembark, others are terminal locations at the head of an intercity corridor. Like any other terminal facility, rail terminals have a size and complexity directly related to the number of passengers they service. The hierarchy of the importance of passenger rail terminals is illustrated in the rail network structure, ranging from simple stops with only a platform available for passengers to embark or disembark, to central rail stations composed of enclosed facilities with multiple piers and amenities.

Central railway stations are typically in the heart of downtown cores and primary elements of national or regional passenger rail systems. At one time their sites may have been on the edge of the pre-industrial city, as is the case for London and Paris's urban growth, and the shift of commercial and business activity have conferred many with an important central function. These stations are typically imposing buildings, reflecting the power and importance represented by the railway in the nineteenth and twentieth centuries. For many cities, railway stations are the key elements of urban centrality and activity, representing an impressive architectural achievement unmatched in any other type of transportation terminal and occupying a large amount of real estate. Notable examples include the Grand Central Station in New York, St Pancras station in London, the Gare de Lyon in Paris or the Shinjuku train station in Tokyo, which is the world's busiest with more that 3.5 million people per day. Since many central rail stations handle large numbers of commuters, that also tend to be the nexus of public transit systems, as subway stations are directly connected to the terminal facility. Even if in several cases, particularly in North America, the long-distance function has subsided, the imprint of passenger rail terminals on the structure of urban transit systems has endured.

Still, the development of high-speed rail systems has offered new opportunities for rail terminals with the renovation of existing facilities, many of which are central railway stations, or the construction of new facilities in suburban areas. The centrality of rail stations became a positive factor in the development of high-speed rail systems as it confers a direct accessibility to core business activities. In many cases the high-speed rail station has become a new nexus of activity with co-located real-estate development such as office buildings, retail stores, hotels and parking facilities. An additional level of integration concerns the design of airport terminals with high-speed train stations, such as the case of Charles de Gaulle (Paris), Schiphol (Amsterdam) and Pudong (Shanghai), which enable connecting long-distance air travel with regional accessibility. Over specific corridors in France, Spain and Germany, high-speed rail stations are effectively competing with airports. Some air carriers such as Air France and Lufthansa are starting to offer services that include a rail segment, so that the train station becomes a proxy for the airport. In some instances, such as Hong Kong, a centrally located public transit station services an airport terminal with a rail connection (light or heavy rail) and offers ticket and luggage check-in services. A better integration between passenger rail and air transportation therefore enables **substitution** of air travel and the possibility of using **satellite airport terminals**. This is linked with new forms of airport competitiveness.

Freight terminals

Unlike passenger terminals, rail freight yards did not have to be quite so centrally located, and because they required a great deal of space for multiple tracks for marshaling they were more likely to be located on entirely greenfield sites than passenger terminals. However, railyards tended to attract manufacturing activities able to use the distribution capabilities of rail, and thus became important industrial zones. When dealing with bulk commodities, rail terminals will locate close to the source as they are the main means for these commodities to be shipped to markets. They also vary in complexity because of the different freight markets they service (e.g. grain, coal, cars, containers), which requires specialized loading/unloading facilities and equipment. Rail freight terminals perform four major functions:

- **Bulk**. These rail terminals are linked with extractive industries such as agriculture, mining and wood products. Terminals are generally designed to be commodity-specific. For instance, grain elevators are bulk terminals commonly used to store, mix and load grain into rail cars. Another important characteristic of bulk rail terminals is their unidirectional flows, implying that they are designed specifically to either load or unload bulk. Rail terminals doing both are uncommon. This is reflective of the nature of bulk trades.
- **Roll-on/roll-off**. Used to transport vehicles such as cars, trucks or construction equipment where the vehicles are rolled in a rail car using a ramp. Such terminals commonly require a large amount of parking space to store vehicles, particularly if they concern cars bound for retail outlets, and many serve as storage facilities supplying regional markets.
- **Break-bulk**. Involves the handling of various cargoes that can be bagged, in drums, rolls or crates. They are commonly related to a specific activity such as a manufacturing plant or a warehouse handling break-bulk cargo and serviced by dedicated rail spurs. Containerization has reduced the need for break-bulk terminals.
- **Intermodal**. The function of loading and unloading unitized freight from rail cars. Containerization has greatly expanded the intermodal productivity of rail terminals since it permits quick loading and unloading sequences, but at the expense of more trackside space available. Depending on the type of operation, specific intermodal

equipment will be used. Intermodal terminal can be part of a port facility (on-dock or near-dock facilities) or a standalone inland terminal.

● **Shunting**. The function of assembling, sorting and breaking of freight trains. Since trains can be composed of up to about 100 rail cars (even more in North America), often of various nature, origin and destination, shunting can be a complex task performed on several occasions. Comparatively, unit trains which carry the same commodity, such as coal, cars or containers, require less shunting. Bailey yard in North Platte, Nebraska, operated by Union Pacific, is the largest classification yard in the world and handles 10,000 rail cars per day.

The first forms of intermodal application to rail appeared in the late nineteenth century with practices dubbed "circus trains" because lorries were rolled in on flatcars using a ramp, a practice that was pioneered by circuses (Barnum in 1872). This simple ramp-based technique enabled many rail terminals to become "intermodal" by offering "piggyback" services. By the end of the twentieth century many of the industries around rail freight yards had relocated or disappeared, and in many cities these former industrial parks have been targets of urban revitalization. At the same time, new intermodal practices emerged, notably lifting trailers or containers directly onto a flatcar. However, this required capital investments in intermodal equipment as well as paved terminal surfaces for storage. Only terminals with sufficient size and volume could be profitable. This has been accompanied by closure of some of the railyards, either because they were too small for contemporary operating activities, or because of a reduction of the local traffic base. In spite of a growth of intermodal traffic, the number of intermodal terminals declined, each covering an extensive market area of about one day of trucking.

In North America and Europe, many older rail freight yards have been converted into intermodal facilities because of the burgeoning traffic involving containers and road trailers, a process which started in the 1960s. The ideal configuration for these terminals is different from the typical general freight facility, with their need for multiple spurs to permit the assembling of wagons to form train blocks. The loading and unloading of wagons tended to be a manual process, often taking days, tying up terminal rail capacity. Retrofitting conventional railyards for contemporary intermodal operations proved problematic. Intermodal trains tend to serve a more limited number of cities and are more likely to be dedicated to one destination. They offer the notable advantage of being able to be quickly loaded or unloaded, thus tying up less terminal rail capacity. They, however, need fewer but longer rail spurs. The configuration typically requires a site over 3 km in length and over 100 hectares in area. In addition, good access to the highway system is a requisite, as well as a degree of automation to handle the transshipment demands of modern intermodal rail operations.

One of the important growth factors of rail transportation has been its closer integration with maritime shipping. This is particularly the case at port terminals with new on-dock container rail facilities. The term "on-dock" can itself be misleading, since a direct ship-to-rail transshipment actually rarely takes place. A dray carries the container from alongside the ship to alongside the rail track (and vice versa), but frequently the containers are brought back and forth from a stack. Transloading, the practice of transferring loads between truck and rail transportation, has also experienced a remarkable growth in recent years. As long-distance trucking is getting increasingly expensive due to growing energy costs and congestion, many shippers see the advantages of using rail transportation to a location in the vicinity of their markets. At this location, freight loads are broken down into LTL and then shipped by short-distance trucks to their final destinations.

Former rail terminals and port sites have been among the most important redevelopment areas in most major urban centers. The redevelopment of old port sites, because of their scale (very large), location (adjacent to downtown) and sites (waterfront), have been at the forefront of the process. Their renovation has had a major influence on the surrounding regions. Many cities have experienced significant benefits from waterfront redevelopment in downtown revitalization and economic revival. Similar experiences have occurred in the United States (Boston, New York, Baltimore, San Francisco, Seattle) and Europe (London, Manchester, Bristol, Liverpool, Rotterdam).

Concept 5 – Airports

Author: Dr John Bowen, Department of Geography, Central Washington University, contributed to this section.

Airports: global reach, local impacts

The rapid expansion of air passengers and air freight flows fostered by globalization is supported by the setting of an **extensive system of airports**. They are bigger in the volumes of traffic they handle, their sizes and the distances that separate them from the cities they serve, their costs and economic impacts, their social importance, their environmental externalities and the political controversies they engender. The very importance of airports globally has exacerbated the local conflicts they provoke in terms of required land, surrounding commercial and manufacturing developments, the land traffic they generate and the noise of approaching and departing aircrafts. Indeed, a fundamental feature of airports is the degree to which they are embedded at several scales:

- **Regional/national/global**. Airports are the articulation points of the circulatory system of the global economy. They mediate currents of people and goods. The importance of an airport in this regard is a function of its centrality and its intermediacy. The former term refers to a node's role as an origin and destination gateway to a surrounding region, and the latter term refers to the degree to which a node serves as an interchange between different regions. The most important passenger and freight airports enjoy either centrality within one of the world's foremost city-regions, intermediacy among key markets, or both. Global outsourcing and offshoring has increased the importance of intermediacy on a global scale. For example, one factor propelling the growth of Dubai as an air transport hub is the fact that with ultra-long-range aircraft like the B777 and the A340 any two locations on earth can be linked via a stop in Dubai.
- **Local**. Airports, especially large ones, are defining features of the communities in which they are set. A large airport generates thousands of jobs directly and thousands more via forward and backward linkages. For Amsterdam's Schiphol Airport it is estimated that 60,000 people were employed at the airport itself and that for every person employed directly, two more were employed in the Greater Amsterdam area by firms linked to the airport (e.g. tourist attractions). Airports are not just features of a community's economic geography, however. An airport the size of Schiphol is a critically important source of noise pollution and other local environmental effects, a large consumer of land, and a signature piece of the built environment. Indeed, the newest airport terminals feature extremely long roofs and are impressive architectural achievements.

Passenger air travel is linked with the level of economic development and the structure of the regional urban system. There are three major concentrations of airports around which the world's air traffic is articulated: North America, Western Europe and East Asia (Figure 5.10). The key airports of these platforms, or rather the main airport cities since they count more than one airport, are New York, London and Tokyo. They correspond to the world's most prominent cities and the most important financial centers. Yet, this supremacy is being challenged by new hubs of activity such as Beijing and Dubai. There is thus a direct relationship between the level of air passenger traffic and the primacy of a city in the world urban system. In some cases, the level of passenger activity is related to a pronounced touristic or resort function of an area (e.g. Las Vegas, Orlando, Cancun, Venice, Palma de Mallorca).

Global air freight activity is clustered around East Asia, the American Midwest and Western Europe (Figure 5.11). Other clusters are around the Middle East and Southeast Asia. The level of air freight activity is usually related to airports servicing important consumption markets or manufacturers of high-value goods, or to a hub in a national or international distribution system. Another factor concerns load centers in developing countries exporting perishables (e.g. produce, flowers) to developed countries, such as for many Latin American airports. Because cargo planes have less range than passenger planes, two airports play a notable intermediate role: Anchorage (Pacific Asia–North America traffic) and Dubai (Pacific Asia–Western Europe traffic). The largest freight airports are usually the hubs of global air freight integrators.

The global and local character of airports cannot be looked at separately. For instance, the location of large corporate headquarters has a pronounced tendency to **cluster in cities with good international air accessibility**. A global city is commonly serviced by several

Figure 5.10 Passenger traffic at the world's largest airports, 2010

Source: Airport Council International. Includes airports with an annual passenger volume above 5 million.

Figure 5.11   Freight traffic at the world's largest airports, 2010

Source: Airport Council International. Includes airports with an annual cargo volume above 25,000 metric tons.

large airports within its metropolitan area. There is a strong correlation, for instance, between the number of headquarters and the number of airline passengers in US metropolitan areas. To some degree, the link between accessibility and headquarters underlines a reciprocity between the concentration of headquarters jobs in a city, so generating the traffic that prompts airlines to increase the number of connecting flights, and the influence of better air accessibility in attracting headquarters jobs. The relationship works in both directions, but it appears that the second direction (i.e. accessibility drawing jobs) is stronger. The success of cities such as Atlanta and Dallas in attracting headquarters from other, smaller cities substantiates that finding. Cities with high air accessibility thus have a higher propensity to attract activities related to the information economy.

Airport sites

Airports require very large sites – they need space for runways, for terminal buildings, maintenance hangars and for parking. The **runway** remains one of the most vital elements of air transportation, as it dictates the capacity of the system. While there are considerable variations in the scale of different airports, minimum sizes in excess of 500 hectares represent enormous commitments of urban land. Thus, airports are sited at the periphery of urban areas because it is only there that sufficient quantities of land are available. Many airports built in the 1940s and 1950s at the periphery of cities eventually found themselves surrounded by subsequent metropolitan developments. New site development, in North America and Europe at least, is becoming very difficult, because available sites are frequently so far from the urban core that, even if planning permission could be obtained, it would lead to very significant diseconomies because of the distance from business and demographic cores. It is significant that there have been few new large-scale airport developments in North America since the 1980s, and the examples of Denver (new airport located far from the city center) and Montreal (second airport that was eventually abandoned) illustrate how difficult and contentious such developments have become. The result has been that most airports have to adjust to their existing sites, by reconfiguring runways and renovating existing terminal facilities.

Suburbanization in general is the main factor why it has become more difficult to place major airports with each passing decade, leading to paradoxes. On the one hand, suburbanization implies that a greater share of the metropolitan population lives in peripheral sites, potentially with better accessibility to the airport. On the other, the land use argument of suburbanization leaves fewer options available for airport developments. Local site requirements are extremely important for air terminals for its two major components: the airfields and the terminals. Airport site location involves a wide variety of considerations:

Air transportation forecasts demand. Forecasted demand strongly affects the number and length of runways and the size of airport terminals, and therefore the physical size of the airport itself. Larger aircraft generally require longer runways. For example, the largest commercial planes, such as the A380, require about 3,300 m (10,000 ft) to take off.

- **Runway configuration**. About 30 to 60 movements (landings and take-offs) per hour are possible on a commercial runway, depending on the type of plane and weather conditions. Landings take about 60 seconds, from the moment that the plane has touched touch down and cleared the runway, while take-offs take between 40 to 60 seconds. However, where runways intersect, capacity is significantly reduced and this type of configuration is considered obsolete for modern airport operations. Thus, the trend for the largest airports is to have parallel runways permitting simultaneous take-offs and landings. Parallel runway configurations generally demand more space than crossing runways.
- **Altitude**. At higher altitude, a longer runway is required to achieve the same lift, because the air density is lower. 60 percent of all commercial airports are at an altitude of less than 500 ft (150 m).
- **Meteorological conditions**. Local variations in precipitation, prevailing wind, turbulences, visibility, etc. must be taken into account. Oakland's less fog-bound airport has gained some business, especially from low-cost carriers, at the expense of San Francisco International.
- **Topography**. The land upon which runways is built must be flat, with no more than a 1 percent slope. Hilly land can be flattened and swampy land filled, of course, but at a cost.
- **Environmental considerations**. Airports have significant effects on local waterways, wildlife and air quality. An important aspect of London Heathrow's new Terminal 5 project is the diversion of two rivers around the site.
- **Adjacent land uses**. Concerns about noise and other airport impacts have encouraged the setting aside of buffer areas much larger than runways and the supporting terminals, taxiways and other infrastructure would require. The new Denver International Airport, for instance, occupies a parcel of land twice the size of Manhattan. In other cases, such as Dun Huang in China, specific geographical constraints had to be respected, namely that the airport could not consume scarce agricultural land.

- **Local accessibility**. At the same time, however, an airport must be accessible to the communities it serves, making its location relative to highways and passenger rail lines (both intercity and metro) important. The integration of airports with passenger rail (e.g. Charles de Gaulle, Schiphol, Hong Kong, Shanghai, New York) is intended to link the airport terminal with the regional market it serves, thus reinforcing its function as a pole in the regional economy.
- **Obstructions**. Beyond the airport perimeter, the proximity of mountains, hills and/ or heavily built-up areas (as in the case of Hong Kong's old airport at Kai Tak) complicates airport operations. If approach corridors pass over residential zones, pressures can emerge to restrict operating hours.
- **Other airports**. Nearby airports, especially in the same metropolitan area, may limit the available airspace and constrain new airport operations. This is particularly the case in New York, where the respective airspace of three major airports, John F. Kennedy, Newark and LaGuardia, are impeding one another.

Many cities around the world are serviced by **more than one airport**, usually within a range of 100 to 150 km. Cities such as London, San Francisco, Paris, New York, Seoul, Tokyo, Shanghai or Washington all have more than one airport within commuting range. The increasing physical size of airports and the difficulty of fitting in with neighboring land uses have encouraged the development of airports at increasingly remote locations. Indeed, the more recently an airport was constructed, the more likely it is to have been located far from the center of the metropolitan area it services (Figure 5.12). In the most extreme cases, land has been reclaimed from the sea to make space for airports. Chek Lap Kok (Hong Kong) and Changi (Singapore) are likewise built on land reclaimed from the sea.

Asia is, in fact, home to several of the most extreme examples of airport "terra-forming." More distinctive than Kansai's roof, for instance, is its location on a man-made island in Japan's Inland Sea. The island, which was a prime contributor to the stratospheric cost of Kansai, is an extreme example of the lengths to which airport

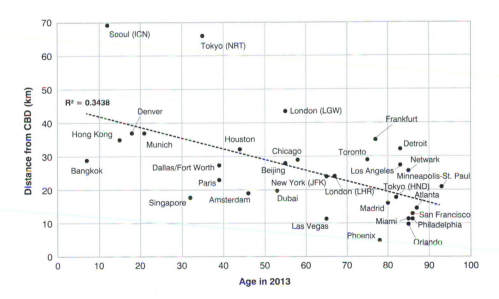

Figure 5.12 Distance from CBD and age of the world's largest airports

builders have had to go to meet the spatial requirements of key hub airports. Overall, the four most expensive new airports in the world (Chek Lap Kok, Osaka-Kansai, Nagoya-Central Japan, and Seoul-Incheon) share three characteristics: their location in fast-growing Asia, the proximity to densely populated metropolitan areas and their construction atop land reclaimed from the sea. The Asian airport-building boom has a long way yet to run as air transport demand in the region continues to increase. Conversely, few new airports have been built in North America or Europe recently.

Keeping pace: airports and delay

About 6,000 passengers per minute are taking off from a runway across the world, underlining the intensity of these terminal facilities. There are two main types of delays experienced by air transport. There are **runway delays,** related to the capacity to have flights take off and land under various weather conditions. During peak hours this capacity is strained and may require putting some inbound flights into a waiting pattern for an available landing slot. There are also **land delays,** where planes are impaired by taxiing time and the unavailability of gates. Nevertheless, the expansion of air traffic ensures that the building of new runways, new terminals and new airports will continue. There are a variety of ways – other than new runways and terminals – to meet the needs of the future, including better use of information technology, such as **air traffic control systems**. It seems inevitable that for many airports physical expansion will need to take place. China probably represents the most acute situation. With a limited number of airports and traffic growing rapidly, terminals are hard pressed to handle additional demand.

Failing to keep pace with demand will mean worsening congestion and the risk of delay in many parts of the global airline industry, prompting many airlines to adapt their schedule. Expansion projects will help, but the lack of additional capacity in many parts of the system (e.g. LaGuardia, where almost every available take-off and landing slot is scheduled for use) means that there are many chokepoints from which delays can propagate. This has become a particular vulnerability within air transportation, notably in systems strongly developed around the hub-and-spoke structure. Delays at highly congested hub airports **quickly propagate within the whole system**. For instance, if a congested airport is forced to shut down for a short period of time due to meteorological conditions (e.g. thunderstorm), delays increase exponentially. Once the airport reopens, the priority is to land the inbound flights that were waiting in standby patterns (some may be getting low in fuel), which delays outbound flights. The outbound queue can become so substantial that gate access for inbound flights can be impaired, which again exacerbates delays, since delayed inbound flights will become delayed (or cancelled) outbound flights. The point is that the lost capacity cannot be effectively recovered. The matter obviously gets worse when a longer weather disruption, such as a blizzard, impairs whole systems with across-the-board cancellations if a hub shuts down. Additionally, airport labor, such as baggage handlers, is often unionized and disruptive strikes can be used to pressure for additional benefits and compensation.

It remains to be stressed that, like international trade, the growth pattern in air transportation is cyclical and subject to phases of growth and even decline. Commercial and industrial location may change, airlines may decide to change their hubbing strategies and the price of fuel may rise. Assumptions that were made in terms of traffic expectation may thus not be realized. Since air transportation has experienced half a century of almost continuous growth, it is assumed that this process will endure.

CASE STUDY   Mega airport projects

Mega airports in a global world

The substantial growth of air travel has been associated with the demand for new airport terminal facilities, particularly in the context where an existing airport terminal is no longer able to handle current or forecasted traffic. Expectations about future passenger volumes are prompting the consideration of large airports consuming a significant amount of land that has to be found, secured and developed. This has led to the siting and setting of **mega airport complexes** including large terminals, hangars, parking facilities, runways and space for adding new runways, as well as space for ancillary activities such as hotels, offices and distribution centers. The airport has become a miniature city.

Large airport facilities (terminals, runways, parking areas, hangars, etc.) require a substantial amount of land, which in itself often leads to a dilemma between proximity to central areas and the availability of land. Figure 5.13 depicts the world's largest airport facilities in terms of hectares. This does not imply that the whole land is occupied, but that land may have been secured for future expansion, namely for new runways. Several American airports occupy large tracks of land, with Dallas/Fort Worth remaining the world's largest airport in terms of surface. However, many mega airport terminal facilities have been established in developing economies, such as Dubai, Bangkok and Shanghai/Pudong. Mega airport terminal facilities have also a density of utilization, which can be measured in passengers per hectare. The size of the airport does not necessarily correspond to a level of passenger density, but none of the largest airports have a density of more than 35,000 passengers per hectare and the majority are under 15,000 passengers per hectare. Evidence from more than 33 mega airports stresses that at around 25,000 passengers per hectare an airport is starting to face congestion problems.

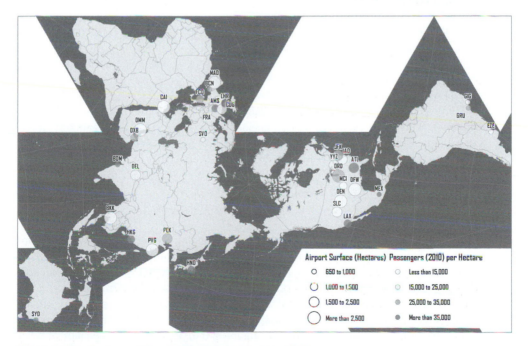

Figure 5.13   Surface of the world's largest airport terminals

The drivers of mega airport projects fall into two major categories. First, **regional economic development** will incite organic traffic growth, both for passengers and freight. Second, major airlines can decide to use airports as their **main hubs**, involving a growth in transit traffic. In a high-growth context, this places acute pressures to expand airport infrastructure to cope with significant expected future traffic levels. Both these drivers can be subject to contention, since on one side economic growth expectations may not materialize to their full extent, while on the other side airlines can change their network strategies and elect for other hubs (or use the existing hub less extensively). The most successful mega airport projects are thus those that jointly gain from regional economic development as well as the additional traffic that hubbing generates.

Mega airports are such large projects that they are usually set into **development phases**. These phases either expand the airport real estate with additional runways, or add terminals or ancillary activities such as commercial and logistics real estate. The major challenge remains financing, since airports are usually publicly funded and require substantial capital investment locked for long periods of time and with uncertain returns. They are rarely profitable but often marketed as symbols of economic success.

Dallas/Fort Worth

Dallas/Fort Worth (DFW) Airport is the seventh largest airport in the world in terms of passenger traffic, but the **largest in terms of surface** (about 4,360 hectares). It opened in 1974 and represents one of the first examples of a mega airport terminal project located in a new site: halfway between two important urban agglomerations, about 28 km from the respective city centers of Dallas and Fort Worth, Texas. DFW Airport therefore benefits from the air traffic generated by these two major cities.

The airport was built in an era of high traffic growth and high expectation about future growth prospects. The Texan economy was booming, in part through the petro-chemical sector, as well as with new industries such as electronics. Air cargo transportation has also become an increasingly relevant dimension of DFW's operations, with nearby Mexico and Latin America an important factor for this strong growth in cargo traffic. The airport is composed of seven runways, four of which can accommodate the largest commercial planes in existence. When it opened, DFW was an innovative layout designed to accommodate considerable expansion.

DFW, like many mega airports, has had substantial economic impacts on the local economy, with some estimates stating an income of over $16 billion annually and a contribution of about 160,000 jobs in the Dallas/Fort Worth area. Texas benefits from its intermediary location between the eastern and western coasts of the United States and of its proximity to Latin America. It thus competes with Miami for this market. Every major city within the United States, Canada and Latin America is within four hours of DFW. In fact, more than 60 percent of all the traffic at the airport is related to connecting flights going elsewhere.

Although DFW is a strong consumer of space, the airport design allows for future expansion with much larger traffic levels. Many new airports designed in the 1970s expected strong growth levels and secured land and developed infrastructure accordingly. Five new terminals can be added to the existing five, therefore increasing the total capacity to accommodate more than 120 million passengers annually. In the mega project development plans, it was estimated that, by 2010, 100 million passengers would transit through the airport. Traffic figures for 2010 were just over half of what was expected. There was thus a large overestimation of the market potential of the airport, but traffic has been steadily increasing since 2010 to reach 63.5 million passengers in 2014.

Kansai International Airport (Osaka)

With 19.3 million passengers handled in 2014, Kansai International Airport does not figure among the world's largest airports. It is particularly remarkable in the sense that it was the first airport project entirely constructed on an artificial island. The construction of airports in Japan has faced serious space constraints due to the obvious lack of available flat land near to major metropolitan areas. For instance, when the construction of a new airport in Tokyo (Narita) was announced in the 1960s, it led to massive protests because of the expropriation of scarce agricultural land. Therefore, when a new airport facility was required in the Osaka metropolitan area, a decision was made to locate the new airport on an artificial island exclusively built for such a purpose. The goal – to avoid political and social fallouts of a mega airport project – thus led to additional construction costs and engineering challenges.

Construction of the artificial island started in 1987, followed by the airport terminal in 1991. The airport opened in 1994, an impressive time achievement for such a complex project. Because of the unique geographical constraints of Japan, the airport was built with strong engineering requirements to be able to withstand earthquakes and typhoons. The resiliency of this engineering was soon tested with the 1995 Kobe earthquake, which left the airport undamaged. Another important engineering challenge that contributed substantially to construction costs was the gradual sinking of the airport due to the geological conditions of Osaka Bay. While it was predicted that the island would sink by about 6 m, by 2000 it had sunk by over 9 m. The airport still continues to sink, but at a lower rate. Linking the airport to the mainland also required the construction of a 3.7 km bridge, which was also a major project. Kansai International Airport thus became a pioneering mega engineering project that set the stage for other similar projects, such as Centrair International Airport in Nagoya and Chek Lap Kok in Hong Kong.

Chek Lap Kok (Hong Kong)

Hong Kong is a major financial center and a **strategic commercial gateway** commanding access to the Pearl River Delta, one of the world's most significant manufacturing clusters. In 2014, Chek Lap Kok handled 63.3 million passengers, making it the tenth largest in the world, but the **first in the world in terms of freight** being handled. The original commercial airport of Hong Kong, Kai Tak, was established in 1925 and went through a series of expansions, mostly through land reclamations over Victoria Harbor. By the late 1980s and early 1990, Kai Tak was facing capacity constraints in addition to being at a site not well suited to airport operations. The airport only had one runway, limiting operations, and its approach required a complex series of turns. Still, it had the advantage of being located very close to the central areas of Hong Kong (Kowloon). Once the new airport of Chek Lap Kok was built, the old airport site was converted for other uses, such as residential and commercial activities and a cruise terminal.

The construction of Hong Kong's new airport terminal, which opened in July 1998, represented a unique geographical and engineering challenge. Since not enough flat land was available in the territory of Hong Kong, a 1,250 hectare island had to be reclaimed. Road and rail connections, including a number of bridges, were also built to connect the airport to Kowloon and Hong Kong island, located about 34 km from the new airport. A light-rail transit system (LRT) links the airport terminal to downtown Hong Kong in about 23 minutes. In addition, ferry services also directly call in at the airport (SkyPier), which represents a rather **unique form of airport connectivity**.

The airport site, with additional expansions, was designed to jointly handle freight and passengers and could ultimately accommodate about 87 million passengers per year, but its current capacity is about 70 million passengers per year. Two significant expansions have taken place so far. This first was the North Satellite Concourse, which opened in 2009, adding 10 gates used by narrow-body aircrafts. The second is the Midfield Concourse, which opened in 2016, adding 20 gates. Land for logistics and cargo facilities were also provided directly adjacent to runways. The mega project thus significantly contributed to maintaining the commercial position of Hong Kong and helped support thriving air cargo operations linked with the development of the electronics sector in the Pearl River Delta.

Bibliography

Bowen, J. (2010) *The Economic Geography of Air Transportation: Space, Time, and the Freedom of the Sky*. London: Routledge.

Bowen, J.T. and J.L. Cidell (2011) "Mega-airports: the political, economic, and environmental implications of the world's expanding air transportation gateways," in S.D. Brunn (ed.), *Engineering Earth: The Impacts of Megaengineering Projects*. Dordrecht, The Netherlands: Kluwer Academic Publishers, pp. 867–887.

Dempsey, P.S., A.R. Goetz and J.S. Szyliowicz (1997) *Denver International Airport: Lessons Learned*. New York: McGraw-Hill.

De Langen, P.W. (2004) "Analysing seaport cluster performance," in D. Pinder and B. Slack (eds), *Shipping and Ports in the Twenty-first Century*. London: Routledge, pp. 82–98.

De Neufville, R. and A.R. Odoni (2013) *Airport Systems: Planning, Design and Management*, 2nd Edition, New York: McGraw-Hill.

Ducruet, C. and S.W. Lee (2006) "Frontline soldiers of globalization: port–city evolution and regional competition." *GeoJournal* 67(2): 107–222.

Federal Aviation Administration (2007) *Capacity Needs in the National Airspace System, 2007–2025*. Washington: FAA.

Fleming, D.K. and Y. Hayuth (1994) "Spatial characteristics of transportation hubs: centrality and intermediacy." *Journal of Transport Geography* 2(1): 3–18.

Fremont, A. (2007) "Global maritime networks: the case of Maersk." *Journal of Transport Geography* 15(6): 431–442.

Hoyle, B.S. (1989) "The port–city interface: trends problems and examples." *Geoforum* 20: 429–435.

Kasarda, J.D. and G. Lindsay (2011) *Aerotropolis: The Way We'll Live Next*. New York: Farrar, Straus & Giroux.

McCalla, R.J. (2004) "From 'anyport' to 'superterminal'," in D. Pinder and B. Slack (eds), *Shipping and Ports in the Twenty-First Century*. London: Routledge, pp. 123–142.

Notteboom, T. and J.-P. Rodrigue (2005) "Port regionalization: towards a new phase in port development." *Maritime Policy and Management* 32(3): 297–313.

Olivier, D. and B. Slack (2006) "Rethinking the port." *Environment and Planning A* 38: 1409–1427.

Slack, B. and A. Fremont (2005) "Transformation of port terminal operations: from the local to the global." *Transport Reviews* 25(1): 117–130.

6 International trade and freight distribution

Globalization, trade and freight transportation are interrelated and concern a mobility scale that spans nations and often continents. This transnational mobility is subject to many geopolitical considerations, such as who controls trade routes and what forms of competition and cooperation have emerged with expanded trade relations. Processes related to economic integration, the fragmentation of production systems due to outsourcing and offshoring are interdependent and have favored the setting of global commodity chains, from the extraction of raw materials, manufacturing, to final consumption. This requires an understanding of logistics and the growing level of integration between production, distribution and consumption.

Concept 1 – Transborder and crossborder transportation

Co-author: Dr William Anderson, Director of Cross-Border Transportation Centre (CBTC), Ontario Research Chair in Cross-Border Transportation Policy, Department of Political Sciences, University of Windsor, Ontario, Canada.

International transportation

The growth of the amount of freight being traded as well as a great variety of origins and destinations promotes the **importance of international transportation** as a fundamental element supporting the global economy. Economic development in Pacific Asia and in China in particular has been the **dominant factor behind the growth of international transportation** in recent years. Since the trading distances involved are often considerable, this has resulted in increasing demands on the maritime shipping industry and on port activities. As its industrial and manufacturing activities develop, China is importing growing quantities of raw materials and energy and exporting growing quantities of manufactured goods. The ports in the Pearl River Delta in Guangdong province now handle as many containers as all the ports in the United States combined.

International transportation systems have been under increasing pressures to support **additional demands in freights volume** and the **distance at which this freight is being carried**. This could not have occurred without considerable technical improvements permitting the transport of larger quantities of passengers and freight, and this more quickly and more efficiently. Few other technical improvements other than **containerization** have contributed to this environment of growing mobility of freight. Since containers and their intermodal transport systems improve the efficiency of global distribution, a growing share of general cargo moving globally is containerized.

Consequently, transportation is often referred to as an **enabling factor** that is not necessarily the cause of international trade, but a condition without which globalization could not have occurred. A common development problem is the inability of international transportation infrastructures to support flows, undermining access to the global market and the benefits that can be derived from international trade. International trade also requires **distribution infrastructures** that can support trade between several partners.

About half of all global trade takes place between locations that are more than 3,000 km apart. Because of this geography, most international freight movements involve several modes, since it is impossible to have physical continuity in freight flows. **Transport chains** must thus be established to service these flows, reinforcing the importance of intermodal transportation modes and terminals at strategic locations (Figure 6.1).

The physical realization of international trade requires a transport chain that is a series of logistical activities organizing modes and terminals, such as railway, maritime and road transportation systems, and thus the continuity along the supply chain through a set of stages along an intermodal transport chain. In the operational reality of modes and terminals, international trade is a series of physical flows that may not necessarily use the most direct path, but the path of least resistance. The existence of inland corridors where economies of scale are more effective shapes the structure of freight flows as well as the selection of the port of exit. On the maritime side, transshipment hubs have become strategic intermediary locations helping to consolidate maritime flows and connecting different maritime systems of circulation. In such a setting, the container has become the fundamental element facilitating transfers between modes and supporting international trade flows. Distribution centers play an important role in physical flows, since they can act as a buffer helping to reconcile the temporal and spatial requirements of demand.

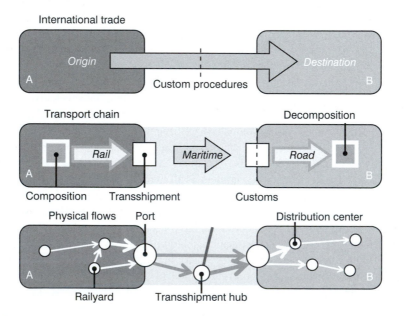

Figure 6.1 International trade, transportation chains and flows

Source: J.–P. Rodrigue (2012) "Supply chain management, logistics changes and the concept of friction," in P.V. Hall and M. Hesse (eds), *Cities, Regions and Flows*. London: Routledge.

Among the numerous transport modes, two are specifically concerned with international trade:

- **Ports and maritime shipping**. The importance of maritime transportation in global freight trade in unmistakable, particularly in terms of tonnage, as it handles about 90 percent of the global trade. Thus, globalization is the realm of maritime shipping, with containerized shipping at the forefront of the process. The global maritime transport system is composed of a series of major gateways granting access to major production and consumption regions. Between those gateways are major hubs acting as points of interconnection and transshipment between systems of maritime circulation.
- **Airports and air transport**. Although in terms tonnage air transportation carries an insignificant amount of freight (0.2 percent of total tonnage) compared with maritime transportation, its importance in terms of the total value is much more significant: 15 percent of the value of global trade. International air freight is about 70 times more valuable than its maritime counterpart and about 30 times more valuable than freight carried overland, which is linked with the types of goods it transports (e.g. electronics). The location of freight airports corresponds to high-technology manufacturing clusters as well as intermediary locations where freight planes are refueled and/or cargo is transshipped.

Road and railway modes tend to occupy a more marginal portion of international transportation, since they are above all modes for national or regional transport services. Their importance is focused on their role in the "first and last miles" of global distribution. Freight is mainly brought to port and airport terminals by trucking or rail. There are, however, notable exceptions in the role of overland transportation in international trade. A substantial share of the NAFTA trade between Canada, United States and Mexico is supported by trucking, as well as a large share of the Western European trade. In spite of this, these exchanges are a priori regional by definition, although intermodal transportation confers a more complex setting in the interpretation of the geographical scale of these flows.

International transportation and geopolitics

The basic features of international transportation are constrained by its geography, which involves **geopolitical considerations**. In the past, many wars have been started to gain control over trade routes, to gain control over mineral or energy deposits, to gain colonial control over untapped regions or to set trade routes via existing ocean ports. This has been particularly important for maritime nations seeking to support the existing trade, to expand it and to secure its circulation. Through history, passages were subject to many conflicts that generally aimed to assure control of a strategic location. International transport infrastructures, such as ports, airports and canals, were also subject to geopolitical considerations as they can provide access to strategic resources or key markets. The geopolitics of international transportation can be considered from five perspectives:

- **Conquest**. Transport technology was initially a mean to control and conquer oceans, territories and resources. European powers were the first to improve significantly the maritime technology in terms of military potential and were thus able to establish maritime trading roads and colonies all over the world, particularly from the middle of the nineteenth century. This period of early globalization was thus characterized by the usage of military advantages of European colonial powers to access markets and resources to their advantage. The railroad was also a means to achieve territorial conquest, notably in North America (nation building) and in Africa (colonialism).

- **Competition**. International transportation is a means of competing on the global economy. Traditionally, through cabotage regulations, many nations reserved the right to carry national passengers and freight to national transport companies. For freight, this is often associated with empty flows on the return trip. Although cabotage regulations are still prevalent for air (air freedoms) and maritime transportation (Jones Act), competition has become a prevalent force in shaping modern transportation systems. For several countries, the development of their international transport system has favored exports and transport-related activities such as shipbuilding, trade and insurance. Several newly established maritime nations in East Asia, such as South Korea, Taiwan and now China, have grown using this strategy. A new form of international transport competition is related to the usage of flags of convenience, where a maritime company can significantly reduce its costs by using the fiscal advantages of another country.

- **Jurisdiction**. All sovereign nations have the jurisdiction over their territories, including internal water bodies such as lakes and rivers if they do not act as a boundary with another nation. Any international transportation entering, exiting or going through this jurisdiction is subject to national regulations. This jurisdiction also applies to the maritime segment. The United Nations Convention on the Law of the Sea in 1982 formally defined the different levels of jurisdiction a nation can have over its adjacent sea. The territorial sea, a buffer of 12 nautical miles (22 km) from the coast, is considered as sovereign territory, both for the above airspace and the seabed. Foreign ships are, however, allowed passage, but by doing so are subject to national regulations. This jurisdiction is partially extended to the Exclusive Economic Zone (EEZ), over which a state has rights to the exploration and use of marine resources (e.g. fishing, oil extraction). By convention, it extends to 200 nautical miles (370 km) but a state cannot prevent free passage through the EEZ.

- **Cooperation**. Although international transportation mostly involves competition, common interests obviously favor agreements over different aspects involving access to infrastructures or setting standards. By 1792, most countries along the Rhine agreed to free navigation. From 1871, Canada and the United States started a long process of negotiation and common management of the St Lawrence River that would eventually lead to the development of the St Lawrence Seaway in 1954. International trade within Europe was enhanced by the adoption of a rail gauge standard (1,435 mm). International air transportation is subject to regulations over security, access to specific gateways (air freedoms) and prices. Furthermore, the emergence of economic blocs such as the European Union and the North American Free Trade Agreement leans on common rules about transport standards and prices. The emergence of continental landbridges, such as the Eurasian landbridge, represents a new and complex form of collaboration.

- **Security**. The control of strategic places is also an important part of international transportation, mainly to reduce vulnerability to disruptions and to improve national security. As the global economy becomes more interdependent, economies are becoming vulnerable to supplies of raw materials, energy and food. For instance, as the United States became more dependent on external supplies of oil, its foreign policy shifted to secure strategic locations in oil trade, predominantly in the Middle East.

Boundaries and borders

Globalization implies increasing flows of people and goods **across international borders**. Thus, an increasing proportion of personal and freight transportation operations must cope with borders as impediments to movement. At a time when tariff barriers are falling and technologies for identification and surveillance are proliferating, this might seem to be no great problem, as borders are more easily crossed than in the past. However, concerns with issues of international terrorism and illegal immigration have led some states to exercise ever more scrutiny at their borders. Therefore, crossing borders remains one of the greatest challenges in global transportation for both passengers and freight.

A boundary is an abstract line separating the territories over which two states have sovereignty. Since the boundary is a legal entity, its precise location must be determined in a treaty between the two states. This means that for a state to have precisely defined territory it must have boundary treaties with all contiguous states. Even where such treaties exist, the boundary may be delineated on paper but not demarcated on the ground, which means its exact location cannot be found without surveying. The border is a more broadly defined geographical entity, comprising elements of the natural and built environment that define the boundary and control passage across it.

Sometimes the distinction between the boundary and the border is one of precision; for example, one might say that a river defines the border between two countries, while the boundary is a precise line located somewhere on the river. The main point is that the border includes a set of things that facilitate (roads, bridges, ferries), prevent (fences, military installations), monitor (cameras, motion detectors) and control (border crossing facilities) movement across the boundary. Borders also have the effect of creating bottlenecks in transportation networks, which are commonly associated with a concentration of crossborder flows along a **limited number of gateways**.

While boundaries have become more clearly delineated and immutable, it might appear that borders – or, more specifically, border functions – are **declining in importance**. At one time, the most important border function was defense. Since territory increasingly defined the state, defending territory was critical to preserving sovereignty. To some extent, the territorial integrity norm has reduced the importance of border defense. But changes in the technology of warfare that undermine the importance and even the possibility of defending lines on the ground have also reduced the defensive function of borders. After defense, the main functions of borders are **customs and immigration control**. With the reduction of tariffs and the application of information and communications technology to both customs and immigration, one might expect that borders as impediments to the movement of goods and people would be a matter of declining importance. Yet, a "borderless world" is far from being a reality, and in some places, such as North America, border impediments have actually increased in recent years, particularly along the US–Mexico border. The border thus remains an important element impacting transportation activities and flows.

Crossborder transportation

Crossborder transportation concerns the activities, infrastructures and flows that ensure the passage of passengers and freight across an international border. Crossborder transportation can be facilitated, monitored, controlled and even prevented. Unless all goods are unloaded and transferred at the border, crossborder freight movement involves some trade in transportation services. For example, if an American trucking company moves a consignment from a US origin to a Canadian destination, it is providing transportation services in a foreign country as soon as it crosses the border. This brings up two types of problems:

- The first is **compliance with technical standards** for transportation operators, which may vary between the two states.
- The second is **cabotage restrictions** that limit the ability of transportation providers to sell their services in a foreign country.

The classic problem of technical standards occurs when national rail systems have inconsistent track gauges, making it impossible to link networks across borders. While most gauge inconsistencies have been resolved with adoption of the standard gauge (1,435 mm), some still exist, for example between countries of the former Soviet Union that use the 1,520 mm Russian gauge and neighboring EU countries using standard gauge. Crossborder transportation is also influenced by trade imbalances, as it implies different freight volumes depending on the direction of the border crossing as well as empty cargo flows.

Cabotage refers to the provision of transportation service between two points within the same country by a foreign firm. Cabotage is restricted under NAFTA in the sense that a Canadian truck could move loads from a Canadian origin to a US destination or from US origin to a Canadian destination, but not between a US origin and US destination, since it would be considered as cabotage. The problem with cabotage restrictions is that they lead to frequent empty backhauls, especially at crossings where crossborder flows are imbalanced. Cabotage restrictions reflect the fact that NAFTA does not extend to free trade in transportation services. In the case of the European Union, cabotage restrictions have been lifted, but only after many years of negotiation and legal challenge.

Despite trade liberalization, new technologies for communication and surveillance, and improved border procedures, crossing borders remains one of the principal challenges in global transportation. The border effects on freight distribution remains salient (Figure 6.2), even in areas where levels of economic integration are high.

Economic integration processes such as trade agreements and customs unions have greatly contributed to the growing fluidity of freight flows across borders, notably in

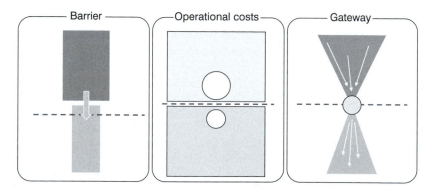

Figure 6.2   The effect of a border on freight distribution

Europe and North America. Still, border effects have not disappeared and they continue to influence the structure of hinterlands and freight distribution processes. The three most common border effects are:

- **Barrier**. Relates to a conventional border effect where a change in jurisdiction imposes a sudden friction effect. It mostly involves customs procedures and duties, delays at border crossing and also physical differences in transport infrastructures, such as capacity. Rail gauges are an example of capacity change taking place at a border (e.g. between Europe and Russia). Therefore, the border usually marks a change in the efficiency of freight distribution and is related to a different transport rate structure.
- **Operational costs differences**. As borders mark a change in jurisdiction, those jurisdictions commonly have differences in operational costs such as labor, land value, energy and taxation levels. This can be linked to different levels of economic development, such as borders between developed and developing countries (e.g. United States and Mexico) or also to subsidies and economic development policies (e.g. Europe). In a setting where there are notable operational cost differences, freight distribution activities will tend to locate where operational costs are lower and use the proximity offered by border regions to service jurisdictions having higher operational costs.
- **Gateway**. Transport networks are often constrained to use specific gateways to go from one jurisdiction to another. This creates a convergence effect on networks and flows where the border represents an opportunity to consolidate or deconsolidate shipments. It also prompts the setting of high-capacity corridors, which can reinforce the border convergence effect. While this structure is common in maritime shipping and air transportation, it also takes place at land gateways.

Increased concern about clandestine transnational actors (drugs, illegal immigration, terrorism) has led to a new regime of enhanced scrutiny that has offset many of the institutional and technological changes that once promised to make borders irrelevant. While the threat of international terrorism is very real, the intensification of scrutiny is reinforced by public opinion that is more aware of the benefits of security than of the benefits of trade. Especially in the United States, the strategy of interdiction takes priority over trade facilitation.

Concept 2 – Transportation, globalization and international trade

The flows of globalization

In a global economy, no nation is self-sufficient. Each is involved at different levels in trade to sell what it produces, to acquire what it lacks and also to produce more efficiently in some economic sectors than its trade partners. International trade is an exchange of goods or services across national jurisdictions. Inbound trade is defined as imports and outbound trade is defined as exports, and both are subject to the regulatory oversight and taxation of the involved nations, namely through customs. As supported by conventional economic theory, trade promotes economic efficiency by providing a wider variety of goods, often at lower costs, notably because of specialization, economies of scale and the related comparative advantages. The main theoretical foundations of international trade include:

- **Mercantilism**. A trade system where a nation tries to impose a positive trade balance (more exports than imports, particularly value-wise) on other nations to favor the accumulation of wealth. This system was prevalent during the colonial era and often undertaken by charter companies receiving a monopoly on trade. Mercantilism represents the antithesis of free trade, since trade relations are controlled and aligned to benefit one partner at the expense of the other. Still, mercantilism established the foundations of a global trading system, albeit an unequal one.

- **Neomercantilism**. A more recent trade system, which like mercantilism leans on establishing a positive trade balance to meet economic development goals. Export-oriented strategies can be considered a form of neomercantilism, particularly if a government establishes an incentive and subsidy system (e.g. free trade zones), which confers additional advantages to the factors of production. Neomercantilism can also be a response by some governments to the competitive and disruptive consequences of free trade, particularly if the trade partners are engaged in neomercantilist strategies. The outcome is tariff and non-tariff measures regulating trade and protecting national commercial sectors that are perceived to be subject to unfair competition. Therefore, neomercantilist strategies can be controversial and subject to contention.

- **Absolute advantages**. Based on a nation (or a firm) able to produce more effectively in an economic sector while using fewer resources (e.g. capital, labor). It therefore has an absolute advantage over its competitors. Global efficiency can thus be improved with trade, as a nation can focus on its absolute advantages, trade its surplus and import what it lacks. The drawback of this perspective is that in theory nations that have no absolute advantages should not be involved in trade.

- **Comparative advantages**. Even if a nation (or a firm) has absolute advantages over a wide array of economic sectors, it can focus on the sectors where it has the highest comparative advantages (the difference of its production costs and those of its competitors) and import goods in sectors where it has fewer comparative advantages. The comparative productivity increases the total production level, since even if a nation (or a firm) has no absolute advantages it can focus on sectors where the total productivity gains are the most significant.

- **Factor endowments**. Expands the comparative advantages perspective by under-lining that trade is related to the factor endowments of a nation. The most basic endowments are capital, land and labor. A nation will export goods to which it has notable factor endowments and import goods in which it has scarce factor endowments. As such, nations that have low-cost labor available will focus on labor-intensive activities while nations having high capital endowments will focus on capital-intensive activities. Factor endowments can be improved through capital and human resources investments.

The **globalization of production** is concomitant with the **globalization of trade** as one cannot function without the other. Even if international trade (or long-distance trade since there were no nations in the modern sense) has taken place for centuries, as ancient trade routes such as the Silk Road can testify, trade has occurred at an ever increasing scale over the last 600 years to play an even more active part in the economic life of nations and regions. This process has been facilitated by significant technical changes in the transport sector. The scale, volume and efficiency of international trade have all continued to increase since the 1970s. As such, space/time convergence was an ongoing process that implied a more extensive market coverage that could be accessed with a smaller amount of time. It has become increasingly possible to trade between parts of the

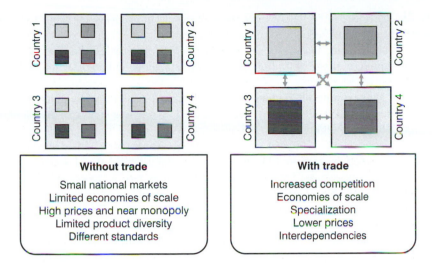

Figure 6.3 Economic rationale of trade

world that previously had limited access to international transportation systems. Further, the division and the fragmentation of production that went along with these processes also expanded trade. Trade thus contributes to **lower manufacturing costs** (Figure 6.3).

Without international trade, few nations could maintain an adequate standard of living. With only domestic resources being available, each country could only produce a **limited number of products** and shortages would be prevalent. Global trade allows for an enormous variety of resources – from Persian Gulf oil, Brazilian coffee to Chinese labor – to be made more widely accessible. It also facilitates the distribution of a wide range of manufactured goods that are produced in different parts of the world to global markets. Wealth becomes increasingly derived through the regional specialization of economic activities. This way, production costs are lowered, productivity rises and surpluses are generated, which can be transferred or traded for commodities that would be too expensive to produce domestically or would simply not be available. As a result, international trade decreases the overall costs of production worldwide. Consumers can buy more goods from the wages they earn, and standards of living should, in theory, increase.

International trade demonstrates the extent of globalization with increased spatial interdependencies between elements of the global economy and their level of integration. These interdependencies imply numerous relationships where flows of capital, goods, raw materials and services are established between regions of the world. International trade is also subject to much contention, since it can at times be a disruptive economic and social force as it changes the conditions in which wealth is distributed within a national economy, particularly due to changes in prices and wages.

The setting of the contemporary global trade system

International trade, both in terms of value and tonnage, has been a growing trend in the global economy. It is important to underline when looking at the structure of global trade that it is not nations that are trading, but mostly **corporations** with the end products consumed in the majority by **individuals**. The nation is simply a regulatory unit where data is collected, since freight movements crossing boundaries are subject to customs oversight and tabulated as trade flows. Inter- and intra-corporate trade that takes place across national jurisdictions is counted as international trade. The emergence of the current structure of global trade can mainly be articulated within three major phases:

- **First phase (immobile factors of production)**. Concerns a conventional perspective on international trade that prevailed until the 1970s where factors of production were much less mobile. Prior to the end of World War I, global trade was mainly structured by colonial relations, but was fairly unregulated. There was a limited level of mobility of raw materials, parts and finished products. After World War I, international trade became fairly regulated with impediments such as tariffs, quotas and limitations to foreign ownership. Trade mainly concerned a range of specific products, namely commodities (and very few services) that were not readily available in regional economies. Due to regulations, protectionism and fairly high transportation costs, trade remained limited and delayed by inefficient freight distribution. In this context, trade was more an exercise in coping with scarcity than promoting economic efficiency.
- **Second phase (mobility of factors of production)**. From the 1980s, the mobility of factors of production, particularly capital, became possible. The legal and physical environment in which international trade was taking place led to a better realization of the comparative advantages of specific locations. Concomitantly, regional trade agreements emerged and the global trade framework was strengthened from a legal and transactional standpoint (GATT/WTO). In addition, containerization provided the capabilities to support more complex and long-distance trade flows, as did the growing air traffic. Due to high production (legacy) costs in old industrial regions, activities that were labor-intensive were gradually relocated to lower cost locations. The process began as a national one, then went to nearby countries when possible and subsequently became a truly global phenomenon. Thus, foreign direct investments surged, particularly towards new manufacturing regions, as multinational corporations became increasingly flexible in the global positioning of their assets.
- **Third phase (global production networks)**. There is a growth in international trade, now including a wide variety of services that were previously fixed to regional markets and a surge in the mobility of the factors of production. Since these trends are well established, the priority is now shifting to the geographical and functional integration of production, distribution and consumption with the emergence of global production networks. Complex networks involving flows of information, commodities, parts and finished goods have been set, which in turn demands a high level of command of logistics and freight distribution (see Concept 3, p. 221). In such an environment, powerful actors have emerged which are not directly involved in the function of production and retailing, but mainly take the responsibility of managing the web of flows.

The global economic system is thus characterized by a growing level of integrated services, finance, retail, manufacturing and (nevertheless) distribution, which in turn is mainly the outcome of **improved transport and logistics**, a more efficient exploitation of regional **comparative advantages** and a **transactional environment** supportive of the legal and financial complexities of global trade. The volume of exchanged goods and services between nations takes a growing share of the generation of wealth, mainly by offering economic growth opportunities in new regions and by reducing the costs of a wide array of manufacturing goods. By 2007, international trade surpassed 50 percent of global GDP for the first time, a twofold increase in its share since 1950.

Trade costs and facilitation

The **facilitation of trade** involves how the procedures regulating international movements of goods can be improved so that actors involved in international trade have more efficient formalities. For regulatory authorities, trade facilitation improves their effectiveness as well as reducing the risk of custom duty evasion. It depends on the reduction of the general costs of trade, which considers **transaction, tariff, transport and time costs**, often labeled as the "Four Ts" of international trade. These trade costs are derived from two main sources:

- **Separation factors**. These are usually exogenous factors separating two trade partners such as distance, transportation costs, travel time, as well as common attributes shared by trade partners. These usually involve being part of an economic agreement (e.g. a free trade zone), which is facilitated when partners have a common boundary.
- **Country-specific factors**. Relates to endogenous factors that are either related to the origin or the destination of trade. This usually involves customs procedures (tariffs and non-tariffs), the overall performance of the national transport and logistic sector and how well an economy is connected to the international transport system through its gateways (mostly ports and airports).

United Nations estimates have underlined that for developing countries a 10 percent reduction in transportation cost could be accompanied with a growth of about 20 percent in international and domestic trade. Thus, the ability to compete in a global economy is dependent on the transport system as well as a trade facilitation framework:

- **Distribution-based**. A multimodal and intermodal freight transport system composed of modes, infrastructures and terminals that spans across the globe. It insures a physical capacity to support trade and its underlying supply chains.
- **Integration-based**. Customs procedures, tariffs, regulations and handling of documentation. They ensure that trade flows abide to the rules and regulations of the jurisdictions they cross. Crossborder clearance, particularly in developing countries, can be a notable trade impediment, with border delays, bottlenecks and long customer clearance times.
- **Transaction-based**. Banking, finance, legal and insurance activities where accounts can be settled and risk mitigated. They ensure that the sellers of goods and services receive an agreed upon compensation and that the purchasers have legal recourse if the outcome of the transaction is judged unsatisfactory or is insured if a partial or full loss incurs.

The quality, cost and efficiency of these services influence the trading environment as well as the overall costs linked with the international trade of goods. Many factors have been conductive to trade facilitation in recent decades, including integration processes, standardization, production systems, transport efficiency and transactional efficiency:

- **Integration processes**, such as the emergence of economic blocks and the decrease of tariffs at a global scale through agreements, promoted trade as **regulatory regimes** were harmonized. One straightforward measure of integration relates to customs delays, which can be a significant trade impediment since it adds uncertainty in supply chain management. The higher the level of economic integration, the more likely the concerned elements are to trade. International trade has consequently been facilitated by a set of factors linked with growing levels of economic integration, the outcome of processes such as the European Union or the North American Free Trade Agreement. The transactional capacity is consequently facilitated with the development of transportation networks and the adjustment of trade flows that follows increased integration. Integration processes have also taken place at the local scale with the creation of free trade zones where an area is given a different governance structure in order to promote trade, particularly export-oriented activities. In this case, the integration process is not uniform as only a portion of a territory is involved. China is a salient example of the far-reaching impacts of the setting of special economic zones operating under a different regulatory regime.

- **Standardization** concerns the setting of a common and ubiquitous frame of reference over information and physical flows. Standards facilitate trade, since those abiding by them benefit from reliable, interoperable and compatible goods and services, which often results in lower production, distribution and maintenance costs. Measurement units were among the first globally accepted standards (metric system) and the development of information technologies eventually led to common operating and telecommunication systems. It is, however, the container that is considered to be the most significant international standard for trade facilitation. By offering a load unit that can be handled by any mode and terminal with the proper equipment, access to international trade is improved.

- Production systems are more **flexible and embedded**. It is effectively productive to maintain a network of geographically diversified inputs, which favors exchanges of commodities, parts and services. Information technologies have played a role by facilitating transactions and the management of complex business operations. Foreign direct investments are commonly linked with the globalization of production as corporations invest abroad in search of lower production costs and new markets. China is a leading example of such a process, which went on a par with a growing availability of goods and services that can be traded on the global market.

- **Transport efficiency** has increased significantly because of innovations and improvements in the modes and infrastructures in terms of their capacity and throughput. Ports are particularly important in such a context since they are gateways to international trade through maritime shipping networks. As a result, the transferability of commodities, parts and finished goods has improved. Decreasing transport costs does more than increasing trade; it can also help change the location of economic activities. Yet, transborder transportation issues still need to be better addressed in terms of capacity, efficiency and security.

- **Transactional efficiency**. The financial sector also played a significant role in integrating global trade, namely by providing investment capital and credit for international commercial transactions. For instance, a letter of credit may be issued based upon an export contract. An exporter can thus receive a payment guarantee from a bank until its customer finalizes the transaction upon delivery. This is particularly important, since the delivery of international trade transactions can take several weeks due to the long distances involved. During the transfer, it is also common that the cargo is insured in the event of damage, theft or delays, a function supported by insurance companies. Also, global financial systems permit currency conversions according to exchange rates that are commonly set by market forces, while some currencies, such as the Chinese Yuan, are set by policy. Monetary policy can thus be a tool, albeit contentious, used to influence trade.

All these measures are expected to promote the level of economic and social development of the concerned nations since trade facilitation relies on the expansion of human, infrastructure and institutional capabilities.

Global trade flows

The nature of what can be considered international trade has changed, particularly with the emergence of **global value chains** and the trade of intermediary goods they involve. This trend obviously reflects the strategies of multinational corporations positioning their manufacturing assets in order to lower costs and maximize new market opportunities. International trade has thus grown at a faster rate than global merchandise production, with a growing complexity of distribution systems supported by supply chain management practices. The structure of global trade flows has shifted, with many developing economies having a growing participation in international trade with an increasing share of manufacturing activities.

Globalization has been accompanied by growing flows of manufactured goods and their increasing share of international trade. The trend since the 1950s involved a relative decline in bulk liquids (such as oil) and more dry bulk and general cargo being traded. Recently, the share of fuels in international trade has increased, mainly due to rising energy prices. Another emerging trade flow concerns the increase in the imports of resources from developing economies, namely energy, commodities and agricultural products, which is a divergence from their conventional role as exporters of resources. This is indicative of an economic diversification as well as increasing standards of living. There are, however, significant **fluctuations in the growth rates of international trade** that are linked with economic cycles of growth and recession, fluctuations in the price of raw materials, as well as disruptive geopolitical and financial events.

The geography of international trade remains dominated by a few **large economic blocs**, mainly in North America, Europe and East Asia (coastal China, Japan, South Korea and Taiwan), which are commonly referred to as the triad. Alone, the United States, Germany and Japan account for about a quarter of all global trade, with this supremacy being seriously challenged by emerging economies. Further, G7 countries account for half of the global trade, a dominance which has endured for over 100 years. A growing share is being accounted for by the developing countries of Asia, with China accounting for the most significant growth, both in absolute and relative terms. Those geographical and economic changes are also reflected over transoceanic trade with transpacific trade growing faster than transatlantic trade.

Neo-mercantilism is reflective of global trade flows as several countries have been actively pursuing **export-oriented economic development policies** using infrastructure development, subsidies and exchange rates as tools. This strategy has been followed by developing economies and is associated with growing physical and capital flow imbalances in international trade. This is particularly reflective in the American container trade structure, which is highly imbalanced and has acute differences in the composition of imports and exports. Still, these imbalances must be looked at with caution, as products are composed of parts manufactured in several countries with assembly often taking place in a low cost location and they are then exported to major consumption markets. In international trade statistics, a location assumes the full value of finished goods imported elsewhere while it may have only contributed to a small share of the total added value. Electronic devices are illustrative of this issue.

Regionalization has been one of the dominant features of global trade as the bulk of international trade has a regional connotation, promoted by proximity and the establishment of economic blocs such as NAFTA and the European Union. The closer economic entities are, the more likely they are to trade, due to lower transport costs, fewer potential delays in shipments, common customs procedures and linguistic and cultural affinities. The most intense trade relations are within Western Europe and North America, with a more recent trend involving trade within Asia, particularly between Japan, China, Korea and Taiwan, as these economies are getting increasingly integrated.

Global trade at a threshold?

The flows of globalization at the beginning of the twenty-first century have been shaped by four salient trends (Figure 6.4):

- An ongoing **growth of international trade**, both in absolute terms and in relation to global national income. From 1970 to 2010 the value of exports grew by a factor of 48, if measured in current dollars, while GDP increased 22 times and population increased 1.8 times.
- A substantial level of **containerization**, often complete, of commercial flows. Containerization tends to grow at a faster rate than trade and GDP growth.
- A higher relative **growth of trade in Pacific Asia,** as many economies developed an export-oriented development strategy that has been associated with imbalances in commercial relations.
- The growing role of **multinational corporations** as vectors for international trade, particularly in terms of the share of international trade taking place within corporations and the high level of concentration of their head offices.

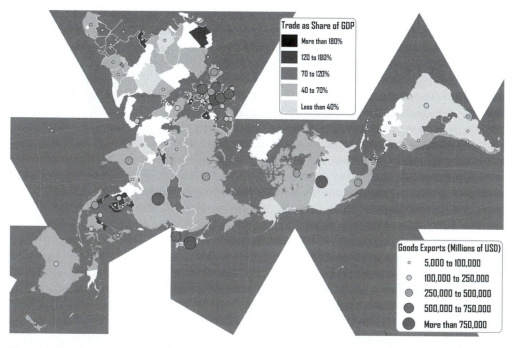

Figure 6.4 Global trade, 2013

Source: World Trade Organization.

Geographically, global trade takes place around three major poles; North America, Europe and Pacific Asia (the Japan, Korea and China triad). Trade volumes are not necessarily correlated with trade as a share of GDP. Some countries, like the United States, have significant trade volumes, but this volume accounts for a relatively small share of the national economy (about 25 percent). Inversely, countries having a strong export component, such as the Netherlands, China and Canada, have a higher dependence on international trade. Countries having a very high share of trade in relation to GDP (above 100 percent) usually focus on natural resources exports (e.g. Middle East, Southeast Asia, Africa), which can lead to a situation of dependence. Landlocked countries tend to have a higher share of trade over their GDP, which is in part reflective of their higher trade costs.

Still, many challenges are impacting future developments in international trade and transportation, mostly in terms of demographic, supply chain, energy and environmental issues. While the global population and its derived demand will continue to grow and reach around 9 billion by 2050, demographic changes such as the aging of the population, particularly in developed countries, will **transform consumption patterns** as a growing share of the population shifts from wealth-producing (working and saving) to wealth-consuming (selling saved assets). Demographic trends in North America, Europe and East Asia (e.g. Japan, South Korea, Taiwan) may not place them as drivers of global trade, a function they have assumed in recent decades. The demographic dividend in terms of peak share of working age population that many countries benefited from, particularly China, will recede.

As both maritime and air freight transportation depend on petroleum, international trade remains influenced by fluctuations in energy prices. The paradox has become that periods of high energy prices usually impose a rationalization of international trade and its underlying supply chains, However, periods of low or sharply declining energy prices, which should benefit international transportation, are linked with economic recessions. Environmental issues have also become more salient, with the growing tendency of the public sector to regulate components of international transportation that are judged to have negative externalities. Also, international trade enables several countries to **mask their energy consumption and pollutant emissions** by importing goods that are produced elsewhere and where environmental externalities are generated. Thus, international trade has permitted a shift in the international division of production, but also a division between the generation of environmental externalities and the consumption of the goods related to these externalities.

Concept 3 – Freight transportation and value chains

Contemporary production systems

As the fourth industrial revolution is unfolding, production and consumption are the two core components of economic systems and are both interrelated through the conventional supply/demand relationship. Basic economic theory underlines that what is being consumed has to be produced and what is being produced has to be consumed. Any disequilibrium between the quantity being produced and the quantity being consumed can be considered as a market failure. On one side, insufficient production involves shortages and price increases, while on the other, overproduction and overcapacity involve waste, storage and price volatility. It is mainly through the corporation and its perception of market potential that a set of decisions are made about how to allocate scarce resources, reconciling production and consumption. The realization of production and consumption cannot occur without flows of freight within a complex system of distribution that includes modes, terminals, but also facilities managing freight activities, namely distribution centers.

Contemporary production systems are the outcome of significant changes in production factors, distribution and industrial linkages:

- **Production factors**. In the past, the three dominant factors of production – land, labor and capital – could not be effectively used at the global level. For instance, a corporation located in one country had difficulties taking advantage of cheaper inputs (e.g. labor and land) in another country, notably because regulations would not permit full (and often dominant) ownership of a manufacturing facility by foreign interests. This process has also been strengthened by economic integration and trade agreements. The European Union established a structure that facilitates the mobility of production factors, which in turn enabled a better use of the comparative productivity of the European territory. Similar processes are occurring in North America (NAFTA), South America (Mercosur) and in Pacific Asia (ASEAN) with various degrees of success. Facing integration processes and massive movements of capital coordinated by global financial centers, factors of production have an **extended mobility**, which can be global in some instances. To reduce their production costs, especially labor costs, many firms have relocated segments (sometimes the entire process) of their manufacturing activities to new locations.
- **Distribution**. In the past, the difficulties of overcoming distances were related to constraints in physical distribution as well as to telecommunications. Distribution systems had limited capabilities to transport merchandises between different parts of the world and it was difficult to manage fragmented production systems due to inefficient communication systems. In such a situation, freight alone could cross borders, while capital flows, especially investment capital, had more limited ranges. The tendency was to trade finished goods, since it was more complex to trade intermediate goods. Trade could be international, but production systems were dominantly regionally focused and mainly built through regional agglomeration economies with industrial complexes as an outcome. With improvements in transportation and logistics, the efficiency of distribution has reached a point where it is possible to manage large-scale production and consumption.
- **Industrial linkages**. In the past, the majority of relationships between elements of the production system took place between autonomous entities, which tended to be smaller in size. As such, those production networks tended to be rather uncoordinated. The emergence of multinational corporations underlines a higher level of linkages within production systems, as many activities that previously took place over several entities are now occurring within the same corporate entity. While in the 1950s the share of the global economic output attributable to multinational corporations was in the 2–4 percent range, by the early twenty-first century this share has surged to the 25–50 percent range. About 30 percent of all global trade occurs within elements of the same corporation, with this share climbing to 50 percent for trade between advanced economies.

The development of global transportation and telecommunication networks, ubiquitous information technologies, the liberalization of trade and multinational corporations are all factors that have substantially impacted production systems. Products are getting

Figure 6.5 Disconnection of global production and distribution

increasingly sophisticated, requiring a vast array of skills for their fabrication. One key issue is the array of corporate expansion strategies available in a global economy, including horizontal and vertical integration, as well as outsourcing. In many cases, so-called "platform companies" have become new paradigms where the function of manufacturing has been removed from the core of corporative activities (Figure 6.5). Corporations following this strategy, particularly mass retailers, have been active in taking advantage of the "China effect" in a number of manufacturing activities. Yet, this advantage is being eroded with rising input costs, prompting a process of re-shoring where activities that were offshored are brought back to locations they were initially offshored from. This underlines that locational decisions are constantly being reassessed in light of changes in global input costs. Additionally, the attention of public policy is shifting from the promotion of competitiveness to the development of capabilities. The main rationale is that competitiveness tends to focus on decreasing different input costs, while capabilities are focusing on increasing added value provided by the manufacturing sector.

A growing disconnection is being observed between the manufacturing base and what can be called the "core base," which mainly includes R&D, distribution and marketing/retail. The term "platform corporation" has been used to describe a variety of multinational corporations that have removed the manufacturing component from their core activities, or never had manufacturing in the first place. They have done so by focusing on activities that provide the most added value, and have outsourced or offshored the manufacturing of the products they design. Their core activities include research and development, finance, marketing, retail and distribution. Many of them own globally recognized brand names and are actively involved in the development of new products.

The net worth of a platform corporation is thus more a function of their brand names and capacity at innovation than from tangible assets (like factories), outside those heavily involved in mass retailing, where commercial real-estate assets can be very significant. Low margin work is usually outsourced, leading to a very flexible supplier base. This is reminiscent of the cottage production system that took place in the early phases of the Industrial Revolution, where many labor-intensive activities (especially in garments) were subcontracted to households looking for additional income.

Commodity and value chains

Commodities are resources that can be consumed. They can be accumulated for a period of time (some are perishable while others can be virtually stored for centuries), exchanged as part of transactions or purchased on specific markets (such as the futures market). Some commodities are fixed, implying that they cannot be transferred, except for the title. This includes land, mining, logging and fishing rights. In this context, the value of a fixed commodity is derived from the utility and the potential rate of extraction. Bulk commodities are commodities that can be transferred, which includes, for instance, grains, metals, livestock, oil, cotton, coffee, sugar and cocoa. Their value is derived from utility, supply and demand, which is established through major commodity markets involving a constant price discovery mechanism.

The global economy and its production systems are highly integrated, interdependent and linked through **value chains**, which are functionally integrated networks of production, trade and service activities that cover all the stages in a supply chain, from the transformation of raw materials, through intermediate manufacturing stages, to the delivery of a finished good to a market (Figure 6.6). The chain is conceptualized as a series of nodes, linked by various types of transactions, such as sales and intra-firm transfers. Each successive node within a commodity chain involves the acquisition or organization of inputs for the purpose of added value.

A value chain is articulated through several stages, which in large part are conditioned by the location and availability of raw materials, production costs and the location of main consumption markets. Value chains are also integrated by a transport chain routing goods, parts and raw materials from extraction and transformation sites to markets. Obviously, the nature of what is being produced and the markets where it is consumed will correspond to a unique geography of flows. Three major stages can be considered within a value chain:

- **First stage (raw materials)**. The availability of raw materials often imposes sourcing at the international level, a process which has accelerated in recent years. It dominantly concerns the procurement of commodities that are stored in large stockpiles. The flows occurring at this stage are mainly supported by international transportation systems relying on bulk shipping. Distribution tends to involve high volumes (economies of scale) and low frequency. This system is also being impacted by the containerization of several commodity markets.
- **Second stage (manufacturing and assembly)**. Mainly concerns intermediate goods. Globalization has shown an impressive flexibility in the sourcing of various manufacturing tasks. The output of this stage are commonly stored in warehouses either near the place of production or close to customers and will be delivered upon the specific synchronism of the concerned value chain. Flows are either containerized or on pallets, with average volumes and rather high frequencies, notably for value chains relying on timely deliveries.
- **Third stage (distribution)**. Distribution of final goods mainly takes place on the national market, although globally-oriented distribution implies that a national market is serviced from a major gateway. Depending on the scale of the distribution

Figure 6.6 The value chain (or commodity chain)

(international, national or regional), flows can be coordinated by distribution centers having each their own market areas. Flows are actively managed, often in low volumes (less than truckload; LTL), but with a high frequency since they are related to retailing. Since the final consumption markets are in urban areas, a fair amount of distribution involves city logistics.

The setting of global value chains and their related commodity flows has led to a growing importance of the concept (activities behind the creation of a good) and logistics (activities making goods available on markets) segments. This leads to new forms of competition, as different segments of the value chain require different capabilities (Figure 6.7).

Therefore, a value chain offers three main dimensions over which competition may take place:

- **Competition over concepts**. In a global production and consumption market, R&D, branding and design (creating a product) can be a significant component of the competitiveness and added value of a commodity chain. This requires specific scientific, technical and design (aesthetical) capabilities. This is also known as pre-fabrication services.
- **Competition over processes**. The manufacturing function (or fabrication) of many corporations has been hollowed out by the process of globalization, in which manufacturing accounts for one of the least added value activities, particularly if it takes place within an outsourcing and offshoring framework. This enables conventional input costs such as labor and raw materials to be lowered. The massive entry of low-cost manufacturers led to a high level of competitiveness in fabrication, reducing profit margins as well as its overall level of contribution to added value. Still, fabrication remains functionally the most important process within a value chain and is influenced by production and location factors.
- **Competition over markets**. The growing complexity of products and market imperatives has reinforced the importance of the logistics segment (making a specified product available on markets). It includes distribution, marketing and sales/after-sales services (such as customer support), activities that are generating significant added value. This is also known as post-fabrication services.

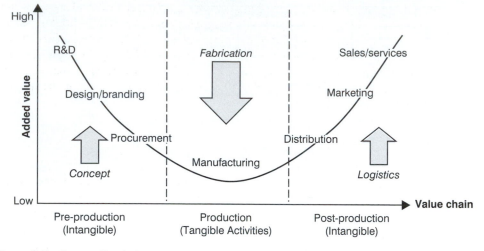

Figure 6.7 Commodity chains and added value

Source: Adapted from the Stan Shih "Smile Curve" concept.

Value chains are thus a sequential process used by corporations within a production system to **gather resources**, **transform** them in parts and products and, finally, **distribute** manufactured goods to markets. Each sequence is unique and dependent on product types, the nature of production systems, the location where added value activities are performed, markets requirements, as well as the current stage of the product life cycle. Value chains enable a sequencing of inputs and outputs between a range of suppliers and customers, mainly from a producer and buyer-driven standpoint. They also offer adaptability to changing conditions, namely an adjustment of production to adapt to changes in price, quantity and even product specification. This means that value chains are constantly upgraded to fit technological, cost and market changes. The flexibility of production and distribution becomes particularly important, with a reduction of production, transaction and distribution costs as the logical outcome. The three major types of value chains involve:

- **Raw materials**. The origin of these goods is linked with environmental (agricultural products) or geological (ores and fossil fuels) conditions. The flows of raw materials (particularly ores and crude oil) are dominated by a pattern where developing countries export towards developed countries. Transport terminals in developing countries are specialized in loading, while those of developed countries unload raw materials and often include transformation activities next to port sites. Industrialization in several developing countries has modified this standard pattern with new flows of energy and raw materials.
- **Semi-finished products**. These goods already had some transformation performed, conferring them with an added value. They involve metals, textiles, construction materials and parts used to make other goods. Depending on the labor-intensiveness and comparative advantages, segments of the manufacturing process have been offshored. The pattern of exchanges is varied in this domain. For ponderous parts, it is dominated by regional transport systems integrated to regional production systems. For lighter and high-value parts, a global system of suppliers tends to prevail.

- **Manufactured goods**. These include goods that are shipped towards large consumption markets and require a high level of organization of flows to fulfill the demand. The majority of these flows concerns developed countries, but a significant share is related to developing countries, especially those specializing in export-oriented manufacturing. Containerization has been the dominant transport paradigm for manufactured goods, with production systems organized around terminals and their distribution centers.

Integration in value chains

Transport chains are being **integrated into production systems**. As manufacturers are spreading their production facilities and assembly plants around the globe to take advantage of local factors of production, transportation becomes an ever more important issue. The integrated transport chain is itself being integrated into the production and distribution processes. Transport can no longer be considered as a separate service that is required only as a response to supply and demand conditions. It has to be built into the entire supply chain system, from multi-source procurement, to processing, assembly and final distribution. Supply Chain Management (SCM) has become an important facet of international transportation. As such, the container has become a transport, production and distribution unit.

A significant trend has thus been a growing level of embeddedness between production, distribution and market demand. Since interdependencies have replaced relative autonomy and self-sufficiency as the foundation of the economic life of regions and firms, high levels of freight mobility have become a necessity. The presence of an efficient distribution system supporting global value chains (the term "global production networks" is also often used) is sustained by:

- **Functional integration**. Its purpose is to link the elements of the supply chain in a cohesive system of suppliers and customers. A functional complementarity is then achieved through a set of supply/demand relationships, involving flows of freight, capital and information. Functional integration relies on distribution over vast territories where "just-in-time" and "door-to-door" strategies are relevant examples of interdependencies created by new freight management strategies. Intermodal activities tend to create heavily used transshipment points and corridors between them, where logistical management is more efficient.
- **Geographical integration**. Large resource consumption by the global economy underlines a reliance on supply sources that are often distant, as, for example, crude oil and mineral products. The need to overcome space is fundamental to economic development and the development of modern transport systems has increased the level of integration of geographically separated regions with a better geographical complementarity. With improvements in transportation, geographical separation has become less relevant, as comparative advantages are exploited in terms of the distribution capacity of networks and production costs. Production and consumption can be more spatially separated without diminishing economies of scale, even if agglomeration economies are less evident.

The level of customization of a product can also be indicative of how commodity chains are integrated. For products requiring a high level of customization (or differentiation), the preference is usually to locate added-value components relatively close to the final market. For products that can be mass-produced and that require limited customization, the preference leans on locating where input costs (e.g. labor) are the lowest.

Freight transport and value chains

As the range of production expanded, transport systems adapted to the new operational realities of local, regional and international freight distribution. Freight transportation offers a whole spectrum of services catering to cost, time and reliability priorities and has consequently taken an increasingly important role within value chains. Improvements in freight transportation are therefore associated with more efficient value chains. Among the most important factors are:

- Improvements in transport efficiency facilitated an **expanded territorial range of commodity chains**.
- A reduction of telecommunication costs and the development of information technologies, enabling corporations to establish a **better level of control over their commodity chains**. Information technologies have a wide array of impacts on the management of freight distribution systems.
- Technical improvements, notably for intermodal transportation, enabled a more efficient **continuity** between different transport modes (especially land/maritime) and thus within commodity chains.

The results have been an improved velocity of freight, a decrease of the friction of distance and a spatial segregation of production. This process is strongly embedded with the capacity and efficiency of international and regional transportation systems, especially maritime and land routes. It is uncommon for the production stages of a good to occur at the same location. Consequently, the **geography of value chains is integrated with the geography of transport systems**. Among the main sectors of integration between transportation and commodity chains are:

- **Agricultural commodity chains**. They include a sequence of fertilizers and equipment as inputs and cereal, vegetable and animal production as outputs. Several transportation modes are used for this production system, including rail cars, trucks and grain ships. Since many food products are perishable, modes often have to be adapted to these specific constraints. Agricultural shipments tend to be highly seasonal with the ebb and flows of harvest seasons. Ports play an important role as points of warehousing and transshipment of agricultural commodities such as grain. A growing share of the international transportation of grain is getting containerized. In 2007, 100 million tons of grain were carried on bulk ships, while an additional 10 million tons were carried by container.
- **Energy commodity chains**. Include the transport of fuels (oil, coal, natural gas, etc.) from where they are extracted to where they are transformed and finally consumed, for example, for international oil transportation. They are linked to massive flows of bulk raw materials, notably by railway and maritime modes, but also by pipeline when possible. They tend to be very stable and consistent commodity chains since a constant energy supply is required with some seasonal variations.
- **Metal commodity chains**. Similar to energy commodity chains, these systems include the transport of minerals from extraction sites, but also of metals towards the industrial sectors using them such as shipbuilding, car making, construction materials, etc.

- **Chemical commodity chains**. Include several branches such as petrochemicals and fertilizers. This commodity chain has linkages with the energy and agricultural sectors, since it is at the same time a customer and a supplier.
- **Wood and paper commodity chains**. Include collection over vast forest zones, namely Canada, Northern Europe, South America and Southeast Asia, towards production centers of pulp and paper and then to consumers.
- **Construction industry**. Implies movements of materials such as cement, sand, bricks and lumber, many of which are local in scale.
- **Manufacturing industry**. Involves a much-diversified set of movements of finished and semi-finished goods between several origins and destinations. These movements will be related to the level of functional and geographical specialization of each manufacturing sector. Such flows are increasingly containerized.

Most value chains are linked to regional transport systems, but with globalization, international transportation accounts for a growing share of flows within production systems. The usage of resources, parts and semi-finished goods by value chains is an indication of the type of freight being transported. Consequently, transport systems must adapt to answer the needs of value chains, which incites diversification. Within a value chain, freight transport services can be categorized by:

- **Management of shipments**. Refers to cargo transported by the owner, the manufacturer or by a third party. The tendency has been for corporations to subcontract their freight operations to specialized providers who provide more efficient and cost-effective services.
- **Geographical coverage**. Implies a wide variety of scales ranging from intercontinental, within economic blocs, national, regional or local. Each of these scales often involves specific modes of transport services and the use of specific terminals.
- **Time constraint**. Freight services can have a time element ranging from express, where time is essential, to the lowest cost possible, where time is secondary. There is also a direct relationship between transport time and the level of inventory that has to be maintained in the supply chain. The shorter the time, the lower the inventory level, which can result in significant savings.
- **Consignment size**. Depending on the nature of production, consignments can be carried in full loads, partial loads (less than truckload; LTL), as general cargo, as container loads or as parcels.
- **Cargo type**. Unitized cargo (containers, boxes or pallets) or bulk cargo requires dedicated vehicles, vessels and transshipment and storage infrastructures.
- **Mode**. Cargo can be carried on a single mode (sea, rail, road or air) or in a combination of modes through intermodal transportation.
- **Cold chain**. A temperature controlled supply chain linked to the material, equipment and procedures used to maintain specific cargo shipments within an appropriate temperature range. Commonly relates to the distribution of food and pharmaceutical products.

Globalization also concomitant – a by-product – of a post-Fordist environment where just-in-time (JIT) and synchronized flows are becoming the norm in production and distribution systems. International transportation is shifting to meet the increasing needs of organizing and managing its flows through logistics. In spite of the diversity of transport services supporting various value chains, containerization is adaptable enough to cope with a variety of cargo and time constraints.

Concept 4 – Logistics and freight distribution

The nature of logistics

The growing flows of freight have been a fundamental component of contemporary changes in economic systems at the global, regional and local scales. These changes are not merely quantitative with more freight in circulation, but also structural and operational. **Structural changes** mainly involve manufacturing systems with their expanded geography of production, while operational changes mainly concern freight transportation with its geography of distribution, namely intermodal transport systems. As such, the fundamental question does not necessarily reside in the nature, origins and destinations of freight movements, but **how this freight is moving**. New modes of production are concomitant with new modes of distribution, which brings forward the realm of logistics – the science of physical distribution.

Logistics involves a wide set of activities dedicated to the transformation and distribution of goods, from raw material sourcing to final market distribution, as well as the related information flows. Derived from Greek *logistikos* (responsible for counting), the word is polysemic. In the nineteenth century the military referred to it as the art of combining all means of transport, revictualing and sheltering of troops. Today it refers to the set of operations required for goods to be made available on markets or at specific locations.

The application of logistics enables a **greater efficiency of movements** with an appropriate choice of modes, terminals, routes and scheduling. The implied purpose of logistics is to make available goods, raw materials and commodities, fulfilling four major requirements related to order, delivery, quality and cost fulfillment (Figure 6.8).

Figure 6.8 Logistics goals and operations

Logistics aims at the fulfillment of four basic requirements:

- **Order fulfillment**. Implies that the transaction between the supplier and the customer is being satisfied with the specified product provided in the agreed quantity.
- **Delivery fulfillment**. The order must also be delivered at the right location and at the right time. Both involve the scheduling of transportation and freight distribution activities.
- **Quality fulfillment**. The order must be provided intact (in good condition), implying that any form of damage must be avoided during transport and delivery. This is particularly important for products that are fragile, perishable or sensitive to temperature fluctuations.
- **Cost fulfillment**. The final costs of the order, including manufacturing and distribution costs, must be competitive. Otherwise, other options will be considered.

All operations related to logistics aim at ensuring that a demand is satisfied (fulfilling goals), be it a part made available to a manufacturer or a good present on a store's shelf. There are three major categories of logistics operations:

- **Purchase order processing**. Operations related to the transactional procurement of goods.
- **Stock management**. Operations related to the physical procurement of goods.
- **Transportation**. Operations related to the physical distribution of goods.

Logistics is thus a multidimensional value-added activity including production, location, time and control of elements of the supply chain. It thus enables a better managerial level of space–time relations and as such is an important aspect of transport geography. Logistics acts as the material and organizational support of globalization requiring a complex set of decisions to be made concerning an array of issues, such as the location of suppliers, the transport modes to be used and the timing and sequencing of deliveries.

Logistics and supply chain management are becoming increasingly blurred and are often used interchangeably. Previously, logistics tended to focus on transportation and warehousing aspects, while supply chain management would consider sourcing as well as final distribution. In recent years the meaning of both has converged. Thus, we consider logistics and supply chain management as similar. Activities comprising logistics include physical distribution; the derived transport segment, and materials management; and the induced transport segment.

Physical distribution is the collective term for the range of activities involved in the movement of goods from points of production to final points of sale and consumption. It must ensure that the mobility requirements of supply chains are entirely met. Physical distribution includes all the functions of movement and handling of goods, particularly transportation services (trucking, freight rail, air freight, inland waterways, marine shipping and pipelines), transshipment and warehousing services (e.g. consignment, storage, inventory management), trade, wholesale and, in principle, retail. Conventionally, all these activities are assumed to be derived from materials management demands.

Materials management considers all the activities related to the manufacturing of commodities in all their stages of production along a supply chain. It includes production and marketing activities such as production planning, demand forecasting, purchasing and inventory management. Materials management must ensure that the requirements of supply chains are met by dealing with a wide array of parts for assembly and raw materials, including packaging (for transport and retailing) and, ultimately, recycling discarded commodities. All these activities are assumed to induce physical distribution demands.

The close integration of physical distribution and materials management through logistics is blurring the reciprocal relationship between the derived transport demand function of physical distribution and the induced demand function of materials management. This implies that distribution, as always, is derived from materials management activities (namely production), but also that these activities are coordinated within distribution capabilities. The functions of production, distribution and consumption are difficult to consider separately, thus recognizing the integrated transport demand role of logistics. **Distribution centers** (DCs) are the main facilities from which logistics are coordinated. They are a facility or a group of facilities that perform consolidation, warehousing, packaging, decomposition and other functions linked with handling freight. Their main purpose is to provide value-added services to freight, which is stored for relatively short periods of time (days or weeks). Distribution centers are often in proximity to major transport routes or terminals. They can also perform light manufacturing activities such as assembly and labeling. A **warehouse** is a facility designed to store goods for longer periods of time. Therefore, a distribution center tends to focus on the demand, while a warehouse is more driven by the supply.

Since it would be highly impractical to ship goods directly from producers to retailers, distribution centers essentially act as a buffer where products are assembled, sometimes from other distribution centers, and then shipped in batches. Distribution centers are established in part to deal with different forms of asynchronisms in freight distribution (Figure 6.9).

Freight distribution is characterized by an asynchronous behavior, implying that supply and demand are never perfectly matched in time and space. A temporary buffer is thus required to bring a level of synchronism, particularly in light of the four main forms of asynchrony that challenge freight distribution:

- **Production and consumption**. Both the supply and the demand can experience substantial fluctuations depending on the related supply chains. While large-scale manufacturing processes are designed to provide a stable output, consumption is often characterized by daily, weekly or seasonal fluctuations. Conversely, food production is commonly seasonal, while demand is relatively stable. A distribution center can thus accommodate the fluctuations of production with the fluctuations of consumption. In recent decades the manufacturing sector has shown a growing level of agility, being able to cope with higher levels of fluctuations in consumption. As such, inventories tend to spend less time in a distribution center.
- **Shipment size**. Because of economies of scale and intermodal integration, there is a tendency towards the massification of shipments to reduce transportation costs, particularly over long distances. Distribution centers are able to cope with the asynchrony of shipment sizes by being able to consolidate or deconsolidate shipments. Transloading is an example of an activity focusing on using a distribution center to change shipment size.
- **Supply and demand**. Contemporary sourcing strategies, the complexity of products and the variety of retail inventories often imply a diversity of suppliers, many of which are located abroad (offshoring). The distribution center thus enables the

Figure 6.9 Asynchronism and distribution centers

reconciliation of the temporal and geographical asynchrony of suppliers and customers. For instance, a cross-docking distribution center is designed to synchronize a variety of suppliers and regional retail outlets. There are also uncertainties in supply and demand that require a buffer to deal with temporary disruptions in supply chains.

- **Market area**. Distribution centers are supplied by different supply chains of various geographical extents (local, regional, global). Many distribution centers located at gateways reconcile the flows of global supply chains through inbound maritime and air cargoes with regional flows. Alternatively, some distribution centers act as consolidation points of regional output, which is then distributed on global markets. They are thus a way to reconcile freight distribution systems at different geographical scales.

The wide array of activities involved in logistics, from transportation to warehousing and management, have respective costs. Once compiled, they express the **burden that logistics impose on distribution systems and the economies** they support, which is known as the total logistics costs. Costs are, however, not the only consideration in supply chain management, since supply chains can also be differentiated by time, reliability and risk level. The nature and efficiency of distribution systems is strongly related to the nature of the economy in which they operate. Worldwide logistics expenditures represent about 10–15 percent of the total world GDP. In economies dependent on the extraction of raw materials, logistical costs are comparatively higher than for service economies, since transport costs account for a larger share of the total added value of goods. For the transport of commodities, logistics costs are commonly in the range of 20 to 50 percent of their total costs.

The emergence of logistics in contemporary supply chains is based upon continuous improvements in transport and inventory management costs, leading to lower cycle and lead times. **Cycle time** is the amount of time required from the receipt of an order to when this order is completed (assembled) and ready for delivery. Often labeled as the completion rate, it is mostly linked with the function of production in the manufacturing sector: its level of responsiveness. **Lead time** is the time it takes for an order to be fulfilled, which includes preparation, packing and delivery to a designed location. Often labeled as the arrival rate, it is mostly linked with the function of distribution, mainly its efficiency and reliability: its level of responsiveness.

Before the emergence of online purchases, customers were rarely exposed to the concepts of cycle and lead times, since goods were directly purchased at a store. The customer saw the outcome of cycle and lead times, but not the process. An online transaction, particularly if it concerns a complex and customizable good (e.g. a computer), commonly involves the time it takes for the order to be ready for shipment and the delivery time from the distribution center to the customer's address.

Driving forces in supply chain management

Lean supply chains, as a managerial concept, are often labeled as seminal in the emergence of modern supply chains, where inventory levels are kept at a minimum and where a large share of the inventory is in constant circulation. Typically, the manufacturing sector has 6–8 inventory turns per year. In the electronics sector, this can be even more frequent, with 10–20 inventory turns per year. During the 1980s, the application of **flow control** enabled the reduction of inventories in time-sensitive manufacturing activities from several days to several hours. Much of these efforts initially took place within the factory, while supply and output flowed as batches from suppliers and to distributors. In the 1990s, with the convergence of logistics and information and communication technologies (ICT), this principle was increasingly applied to the whole supply chain, particularly to the function of distribution.

Another important requirement was **containerization**, which conferred substantial flexibility to production systems, in addition to the container being its own storage unit. The expansion of standard transport infrastructure such as highways, terminals and airports was also essential for the development of modern logistics. Logistics and integrated transport systems are therefore related, particularly because of the container, which has concomitantly become a unit of load (transport), production and distribution. The technological dimension of logistics can thus be considered from six perspectives:

- **Transportation modes**. Modes have been the object of very limited technological changes in recent decades. In some cases, modes have adapted to handle containerized operations such as road and rail (e.g. double-stacking). It is maritime shipping that has experienced the most significant technological change, requiring the construction of an entirely new class of ships and the application of economies of scale to maritime container shipping.
- **Transportation terminals**. The technological changes have been very significant with the construction of new terminal facilities operating on a high turnover basis. Better handling equipment led to improvements in the velocity of freight at the terminals, which are among the most significant technological changes brought by logistics in materials movements. In such a context, the port has become one of the most significant terminals supporting global logistics. Port facilities are increasingly being supported by an array of inland terminals connected by high-capacity corridors.
- **Distribution centers and distribution clusters**. Technological changes impacted over the location, design and operation of distribution centers: the facilities handling the requirements of modern distribution. They serve different purposes depending on the combination of fabrication, storage and distribution functions they perform within their supply chains. Modern distribution centers tend to consume more space, both from the site they occupy and the building area. From a locational standpoint,

distribution centers mainly rely on trucking, implying a preference for suburban locations with good road accessibility supporting a constant traffic. They service regional markets with a 48-hours service window (lead time) on average, implying that replenishment orders from their customers are met within that time period. They have become one-floor facilities designed more for throughput than for warehousing, with specialized loading and unloading bays and sorting equipment. Cross-docking distribution centers represent one of the foremost expressions of a facility that handles freight in a time-sensitive manner. Automation is also pushing forward the productivity level of distribution centers. For instance, it is possible to fully automate the sorting, storing and palletizing processes in a distribution center. Another trend has been the setting of freight distribution clusters where distribution activities agglomerate to take advantage of shared infrastructures and accessibility. This tends to expand the added value performed by logistics.

- **Load units**. Since logistics involves improving the efficiency of flows, load units have become particularly important. They are the basic physical management unit in freight distribution and take the form of pallets, swap bodies, semi-trailers and containers. Containers are the privileged load unit for long-distance trade, but the growing complexity of logistics required a more specific level of load management. The use of bar codes and increasingly of RFID (radio-frequency identification devices) enables a high level of control of the load units in circulation.
- **Information technologies**. Consider the vast array of information processing changes brought by logistics. The commodity chain is linked with physical flows as well as with information flows, notably through Electronic Data Interchange (EDI). Producers, distributors and consumers are embedded in a web of reciprocal transactions. Standardization of Internet-based applications enabled corporations to establish interfaces with their customers. While these transactions mostly take place virtually, their outcomes are physical flows. The commercial diffusion of Global Positioning Systems (GPS) now allows for the identification and routing of vehicles and therefore a better utilization of these assets. The outcome is often more efficient production and distribution planning, with the additional convenience of tracking modes, shipments and inventories, thus giving a greater visibility for customers.
- **E-commerce**. E-commerce offers advantages for the whole commodity chain, from consumers being exposed to a wider range of products to manufacturers and distributors being able to adapt quickly to changes in demand. E-commerce generates a lot of home delivery parcel movements that are carried by conventional postal services as well as specialized parcel carriers. In the United States, about 70 percent of home deliveries are made by the United States Postal Services, while the remaining 30 percent is carried by private parcel companies. Fulfillment (warehousing, packaging) costs account for 10–12 percent of the revenue of e-commerce, while shipping and delivery costs added another 10 percent. E-commerce is also prompting shifts in retail freight distribution with the setting of new fulfillment and sortation centers. As retail sales get partially replaced by online sales, the need for conventional retail space declines while the footprint occupied by distribution centers increases.

Freight distribution is within a paradigm shift from inventory-based logistics (push) to replenishment-based logistics (pull). Demand, particularly in the retail sector, is very difficult to anticipate accurately. A closer integration between supply and demand enables a more efficient production system with less waste in terms of unsold inventory. Logistics is thus a fundamental component of efficiency improvements in a market economy.

Figure 6.10 The evolution of retail logistics

Source: adapted from Jones Lang Lassalle (2013) E-commerce boom triggers transformation in retail logistics: Driving a global wave of demand for new logistics facilities.

The retail sector has experienced a notable evolution of its logistics in recent decades, with globalization and e-commerce being the factors having the most significant impact. This evolution has involved new and more effective forms of distribution and can be summarized in four phases:

- **Direct replenishment (1970s).** Up to the 1970s, most of the sourcing was domestic and provided either directly by suppliers (manufacturers) or by wholesalers specializing in specific categories of retail goods (e.g. toys, apparel, shoes). These suppliers had their own warehouses supplying their customers directly. Each store also maintained its own inventory and ordered directly from its suppliers, many of them within the region.
- **Rationalization (1980s).** During the 1980s the emergence and expansion of large retail chains such as Wal-Mart prompted the rationalization of logistics, where many retailers built distribution centers in peripheral areas. They acted as warehousing and sorting facilities between the suppliers and several stores, often within the same region (regional distribution centers). A streamlined and high-throughput form of distribution center took shape as a cross-docking facility.
- **Global sourcing (1990s).** Outsourcing and offshoring expanded the spatial reach of sourcing strategies, which involved a growing number of overseas suppliers and more long-distance transportation. As an important share of retail imports became containerized, import centers emerged near to container port facilities. These centers destuffed import containers and arranged shipments for domestic distribution. Transloading is a common activity performed by import centers.
- **E-commerce (2000s).** The growth of web-based retail sales triggered the development of new logistics structures. Since the majority of the online retail purchases are shipped as parcels, this distribution structure saw the emergence of e-fulfillment

centers, which are large facilities assembling individual orders that are shipped through parcel services. The parcels are then moved to hubs that consolidate shipments or sortation centers that arrange shipments according to their regional/local destinations. The parcels will then reach a delivery center, where they will be placed on specific local delivery routes. In large urbanized areas local depots can also be used for urban deliveries using small vehicles such as vans ("last mile logistics"). The final destination is either the residence of the customer, a collection point (such as an urban freight station or an urban pickup location) or a delivery point (such as postal box or even the lobby of a residential building).

It is important to stress that each of these phases in the evolution of retail logistics did not completely replace the previous ones, but more than often added to them. For instance, there are still direct deliveries from suppliers to stores, but this strategy is less prevalent. E-commerce has obviously not replaced standard retailing activities supplied by national or regional distribution centers, but added new distribution channels that at times compete with existing retailing, but also can be complementary when a retailer is jointly involved in conventional retail and e-commerce.

Distribution systems

In a broader sense distribution systems are embedded in a changing macro- and micro-economic framework, which can be roughly characterized in terms of flexibility and globalization:

- **Flexibility** implies a highly differentiated, strongly market- and customer-driven mode of creating added value. Contemporary production and distribution is no longer subject to single-firm activity, but increasingly practiced in networks of suppliers and subcontractors. The supply chain bundles together all this by information, communication, cooperation and, last but not least, by physical distribution.
- **Globalization** means that the spatial frame for the entire economy has been expanded, involving the spatial expansion of the economy, more complex global economic integration and an intricate network of global flows and hubs.

The flow-oriented mode affects almost every single activity within the entire process of value creation. The core component of materials management is the supply chain, the time- and space-related arrangement of the whole goods flow between supply, manufacturing, distribution and consumption. Its major parts are the supplier, the producer, the distributor (e.g. a wholesaler, a freight forwarder, a carrier), the retailer, the end consumer, all of whom represent particular interests. Compared with conventional freight transport systems, the evolution of supply chain management and the emergence of the logistics industry are mainly characterized by three features:

- **Integration**. A fundamental restructuring of goods merchandising by establishing integrated supply chains with integrated freight transport demand. According to macroeconomic changes, demand-oriented activities are becoming predominant. While traditional delivery was primarily managed by the supply side, current supply chains are increasingly managed by the demand.
- **Time mitigation**. Whereas transport was traditionally regarded as a tool for overcoming space, logistics is concerned with mitigating time. Due to the requirements

of modern distribution, the issue of time is becoming increasingly important in the management of commodity chains. Time is a major issue for freight shipping, as it imposes inventory holding and depreciation costs, which becomes sensitive for tightly integrated supply chains.

● **Specialization**. This was achieved by shifts towards vertical integration, namely subcontracting and outsourcing, including the logistical function itself. Logistics services become complex and time-sensitive to the point that many firms are now subcontracting parts of their supply chain management to what can be called third-party logistics providers (3PL; asset-based). More recently, a new category of providers, called fourth-party logistics providers (4PL; non-asset-based) have emerged.

While many manufacturing corporations may have own account transportation, increasingly the complex needs of the supply chain are being contracted out to third parties. Depending on the strategy and costs, corporations can outsource in whole or in part their transport and supply chain operations. Third-party logistics providers (3PL) have emerged from traditional intermediaries such as the forwarders, or from transport providers such as FedEx or Maersk. Both groups have been at the forefront of the inter-modal revolution that is now assuming more complex organizational forms and importance. By offering door-to-door services, the customer is no longer aware or necessarily concerned with how the shipment gets to its destination, namely the modes used and the routing selected (Photo 6.1). The preoccupation is with cost, reliability and level of

Photo 6.1   Third-party less-than-truckload service, FedEx

Many freight transport companies offer less-than-truckload (LTL) services to their customers. Such shipments are generally composed of items of various sizes filling up specific orders that are usually not recurrent. Here, a FedEx (second largest LTL carrier in the United States) truck is picking up cargo at a concrete foundation mold manufacturer in Kansas City. This shipment is likely bound for a specific construction project.

service. This produces a paradox: that for the customer of intermodal services geographic space becomes meaningless, but for the intermodal providers routing, costs and service frequencies have significant geographical constraints. The effectiveness of intermodal transport systems is thus masking the importance of transportation to its users.

Geography of freight distribution

Logistics has a distinct geographical dimension, which is expressed in terms of flows, nodes and networks within the supply chain. Space/time convergence, a well-known concept in transport geography where time was simply considered as the amount of space that could be traded within a specific length of time, including travel and trans-shipment, is being transformed by logistics. Activities that were not previously considered fully in space/time relationships, such as distribution, are being integrated. This involves an organization and synchronization of flows through nodes and network strategies.

The traditional arrangement of **goods flow** included the processing of raw materials to manufacturers, with a storage function usually acting as a buffer (Figure 6.11). The flow continued via wholesaler and/or shipper to retailer, ending at the final customer. Delays were very common on all segments of this chain and accumulated as inventories in warehouses. There was a limited flow of information from the consumer to the supply chain, suggesting that the producers were not well informed (often involving a time lag) about the extent of consumption of their outputs. This procedure is now changing, mainly by eliminating one or more of the costly operations in the supply chain organization. Reverse flows are also part of the supply chain, namely for recycling and product returns. An important physical outcome of supply chain management is the concentration of storage or warehousing in one facility, instead of several. This facility is increasingly being designed as a flow- and throughput-oriented distribution center, instead of a warehouse holding cost-intensive large inventories.

Due to new corporate strategies, a concentration of logistics functions in certain facilities at strategic locations is prevalent. Many improvements in freight flows are

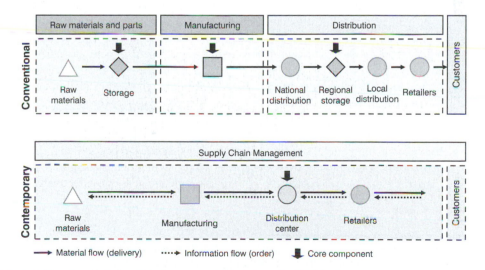

Figure 6.11 Conventional and contemporary arrangement of goods flow

achieved at terminals. Facilities are much larger than before, the locations being characterized by a particular connection of regional and long-distance relations. Traditionally, freight distribution has been located at major places of production – for instance, in the manufacturing belt at the North American East Coast and in the Midwest – or in the old industrialized regions of England and continental Europe. Today, particularly the large-scale goods flows are directed through major **gateways and hubs**, mainly large ports and major airports, also highway intersections with access to a regional market. The changing geography of manufacturing and industrial production has been accompanied by a changing geography of freight distribution taking advantage of intermediary locations.

The spatial structure of contemporary **transportation networks** is the expression of the spatial structure of distribution. The setting of networks leads to a shift towards larger distribution centers, often serving significant transnational catchments. However, this does not mean the demise of national or regional distribution centers, with some goods still requiring a three-tier distribution system, with regional, national and international distribution centers. The structure of networks has also adapted to fulfill the requirements of an integrated freight transport demand, which can take many forms and operate at different scales. Most freight distribution networks, particularly in retailing, are facing the challenge of the "last mile," which is the final leg of a distribution sequence, commonly linking a distribution center and a customer (store).

Since cities are at the same time zones of production, distribution and consumption, the realm of city logistics is of growing importance. This issue is made even more complex by a growing dislocation between production, distribution and consumption, brought on by globalization, global production networks and efficient freight transport systems and logistics. This dislocation has prompted a growing emphasis on issues related to supply chain integration so that, in spite of acute geographical separation, physical and managerial processes have minimal friction. Logistical costs in developing countries tend to be higher, which undermines economic development for these main reasons:

- The **regulatory complexity** of distributing goods in developing countries involves higher logistic costs and is inciting distributors to maintain higher inventory levels to cope with uncertainty. Custom regulations are complex and prone to delays and road transportation can be subject to arbitrary tolls and inspections. This is reflected in higher final goods or component prices that are assumed directly or indirectly by consumers.
- **Labor and infrastructure productivity** in developing countries tend to be lower, which in many cases doubles logistics costs. The advantages of cheap labor can often be counterbalanced by lower levels of productivity. This also impacts the reliability of freight distribution with unreliable lead times and deliveries.
- **Modal and intermodal capacity** is inconsistent. While several terminal facilities, particularly ports, are modern with capacity on par with global standards, hinterland transportation can be problematic with road segments unable to effectively handle trucks of standard capacity.

In such a context, reforms have been advocated to promote the effectiveness of logistics services and therefore break a vicious cycle in which several developing countries are entangled. This involves a series of reform, pending the capacity to overcome political constraints and the inertia (and commonly rent-seeking behavior) of established stakeholders, concerning service providers, infrastructure investment, as well as the administrative and regulatory environment.

CASE STUDY   Inland ports and logistics zones

Co-author: Dr Theo Notteboom, Chair Professor "Port of Ghent," Maritime Institute, Faculty of Law, University of Ghent.

Freight facilities

Logistics tend to **agglomerate (cluster) at specific locations**, mainly because of the accessibility they confer, the availability of land, as well as benefiting from being close to one another. There is also a wide array of benefits to be derived from improved logistics capabilities. The development of logistics zones has been an important component of globalization, since the growth in international trade and the related material flows requires activities supporting their consolidation, deconsolidation, transloading and light transformation. Freight facilities are punctual, fixed infrastructures used to support freight transportation and come in a wide variety of shapes, sizes and functions (Figure 6.12). They serve a combination of three standard functions, each having a respective degree of importance:

- **Fabrication**. Involves assembling goods out of parts, making the parts themselves or performing a task changing the physical characteristics of a good (packaging, labeling, etc.). This is usually a transformation-related function.
- **Storage**. Holding goods in inventory for an extended period of time and releasing them on demand. This is usually a buffer-related function and related to intermediate goods.
- **Distribution**. Consolidating, deconsolidating, sorting a cargo load or changing the load unit. This is usually a throughput-related function involving final goods.

Figure 6.12 Types of freight facilities

The main difference between the storage and distribution functions relates to the time the inventory spends within the facility: usually less than a few days, and less than 48 hours in high-throughput facilities. Based upon these three functions (fabrication, storage and distribution), freight facilities are of five main types:

- **Manufacturing facilities**. A pure fabrication facility is essentially considered as a factory, which always has an associated storage function. While the main purpose of manufacturing facilities is fabrication, light manufacturing systems are usually more integrated to supply chains (e.g. just-in-time inventory management), suggestng that they rely on distribution capabilities to effectively operate. This requires the goods to spend some time in the manufacturing plant's warehouse with some parts being stored before assembly. Heavy manufacturing tends to have more storage-based inventory management, mainly because of the ponderous characteristics of their inputs and outputs.
- **Terminal facilities**. Terminal facilities are freight facilities as well. Outside their standard role of transferring cargo from one mode to another, they also act as a buffer in the transport chain with a significant storage function. While for a container terminal this function is subject to dwell-time considerations (usually less than seven days for a port), for a bulk terminal storage is part of the services offered by the facility and last much longer. A transloading facility such as an automobile terminal is also highly storage-dependent. Therefore, terminal facilities are balancing the buffer and throughput functions, with the container terminal more a throughput facility and the bulk terminal more a buffer facility.
- **Storage facilities**. The purpose of a storage facility is to hold inventory for a period of time. Bulk warehouses are usually single-purpose facilities for storing bulk materials (sometimes in break-bulk form, e.g. stored in bags or drums), such as grain or fertilizers. For a standard warehouse, different types of storage models exist, such as racks and pallets, which are related to the goods they are storing. For instance, rack-supported warehouses are pure storage facilities with the rack system being the basic structural support for the building. They offer a high storage density along with a comparatively low land use footprint, many of which are automated. The most general warehouse is the multitenant facility, a general-purpose facility usually rented through short- to medium-term leases and where the tenant uses the facility depending on their respective supply chain requirements. When users reach a critical mass, they tend to build and operate their own facilities, since they fit their operations better (custom designed). Still, an active warehouse-leasing market remains, and even large enterprises rely on it when it fits their strategies.
- **Distribution facilities**. These facilities are more based on the concept of throughput of the inventory they carry, implying a much higher level of integration within supply chains. For instance, a distribution center temporarily holds the inventory for the market area it services, suggesting that some storage will take place and on occasion light manufacturing activities will be performed such as inspection, packaging and labeling. Still, the main purpose of distribution center is its ability to fulfill a variety of orders in a timely manner. A cross-docking distribution center is a good example of a pure distribution facility with no (or very little) storage function. Due to the perishable nature of many goods being shipped, such as food, cold-storage facilities (mostly refrigerated warehouses) are jointly able to perform fabrication (e.g. packaging before final delivery) and distribution functions. The urban logistics depot is also a facility mostly focusing on distribution, with the main purpose of

deconsolidating cargo loads (mostly parcels) for urban deliveries (which usually use adapted vehicles).

- **Parcel facilities**. While parcel delivery services have been around for close to a century, the surge brought by the growth of e-commerce has expended parcel facilities substantially, to the point that many are solely dedicated to e-commerce supply chains. First, the e-fulfillment center is a facility designed to handle a large amount of online orders to be mostly put in parcels. Such a facility is storage-based (holding a very high range of goods), but also relies on a high level of throughput because of the timely nature of online orders. Sortation centers, particularly large parcel hubs, are facilities designed on the cross-docking principle, with the main purpose of sorting parcels to a wide array of destinations, usually as part of a hub-and-spoke distribution system.

Consequently, there is a wide variety of freight facilities, each servicing a specific role depending on the nature, operations and constraints of the supply chains they are supporting. These facilities are usually developed as clusters.

A new role for inland logistics

In many places around the world bimodal and trimodal inland terminals have become an intrinsic part of the transport system, particularly in gateway regions having a high reliance on trade. Transport development is gradually **shifting inland** after a phase that focused on the development of port terminals and maritime shipping networks. The complexity of modern freight distribution, the increased focus on intermodal and comodal transport solutions and capacity issues appear to be the main drivers behind a renewed focus on hinterland logistics. While trucking tends to be sufficient in the initial phase of the development of inland freight distribution systems, at some level of activity, diminishing returns such as congestion, energy consumption and empty movements become strong incentives to consider the setting of inland terminals as the next step in regional freight planning. Also the massification of flows in networks, through a concentration of cargo on a limited set of ports of call and associated trunk lines to the hinterland, have created the right conditions for nodes to appear along and at the end of these trunk lines.

The evolution of inland freight distribution can be seen as a cycle in the ongoing developments of containerization and intermodal transportation. The geographical characteristics linked with modal availability, capacity and reliability of regional inland access have an important role to play in shaping this development. As maritime shipping networks and port terminals become better integrated, the focus shifted on inland transportation and the inland terminal as a fundamental component of this strategy. Thus, after a phase that relied on the development of port terminals and maritime shipping networks, the integration of maritime and inland freight distribution systems has favored the setting of **inland ports**. An inland port is a rail or a barge terminal that is linked to a maritime terminal with regular inland transport services. An inland port has a level of integration with the maritime terminal and supports a more efficient access to the inland market both for inbound and outbound traffic. This implies an array of related logistical activities linked with the terminal, such as distribution centers, depots for containers and chassis, warehouses and logistical service providers.

There seems to be no consensus on the terminology, resulting in a wide range of terms including dry ports, inland terminals, inland ports, inland hubs, inland logistics centers, inland freight villages. The reason for this lies in the multiple shapes, functions and network positions these nodes can have. A similar issue applies to the inclusion of airport terminals, mainly the freight component, as an element of an inland port. A whole array of transport terminal infrastructures is therefore often presented as a dry port. Regardless of the terminology used, three fundamental characteristics are related to an inland node:

- An **intermodal terminal**, either rail or barge that has been built or expanded.
- A **connection with a port terminal** through rail, barge or truck services, often through a high-capacity corridor.
- An array of **logistical activities** that support and organize the freight transited, often co-located with the intermodal terminal.

The functional specialization of inland terminals has been linked with **cluster formation** of logistical activities. Inland terminals in many cases have witnessed a clustering of logistics sites in the vicinity, leading to a process of logistics polarization and the creation of logistic zones. They have become excellent locations for consolidating a range of ancillary activities and logistics companies. In recent years, the dynamics in logistics networks have created the right conditions for a large-scale development of such logistics zones.

Driving forces

Each inland port remains the outcome of the considerations of a transport geography pertaining to modal availability and efficiency, market function and intensity, as well as the regulatory framework and governance. Their emergence underlines some deficiency in conventional inland freight distribution that needed to be mitigated. This mitigation includes:

- **Input costs**. Land and labor costs are among the most significant logistics costs. Many deep-sea terminal facilities have limited land available for expansion, involving higher land costs, while inland locations tend to have land available. Many port areas are also facing higher labor costs since they are located within large metropolitan areas. High input costs favor the intensification of activities at the main terminal and the search of lower value locations supporting less intensive freight activities.
- **Capacity and congestion**. Capacity issues appear to be the main driver of inland port development, since a system of inland terminals increases the intermodal capacity of inland freight distribution. While trucking tends to be sufficient in the initial phase of the development of inland freight distribution systems, at some level of activity diminishing returns such as congestion, energy and empty movements become strong incentives to consider the setting of inland terminals as the next step in regional freight planning.
- **Hinterland market**. Through long-distance transport corridors, inland ports confer a higher level of accessibility because of lower distribution costs and improved capacity. These high-capacity inland transport corridors allow ports to penetrate the local hinterland of competing ports and thus to extend their cargo base. In such a setting, the inland port becomes a commercial and trade development tool that jointly increases imports, exports and intermodal terminal use. It is thus better placed to support regional and international trade patterns.

- **Supply chain management**. An inland port is a location actively integrated within supply chain management practices, particularly in view of containerization. It is reflective of the level of vertical integration between the port and hinterland actors, for example, transport companies and supply chain managers. This takes many forms, such as the agglomeration of freight distribution centers, custom clearance, container depots and logistical capabilities. The inland terminal can also become a buffer in supply chains, acting as a temporary warehousing facility.
- **Policy and regulations**. Economic development strategies, land use policy, and financial incentives by port authorities and economic development agencies can lead to the development of inland ports. This can be supported by policies related to foreign trade zones and customs procedures, enabling a transfer of functions that were previously taking place at the port to an inland location. This is commonly a significant hurdle, since many national trade regulations only enable containers to be cleared for imports or exports at a port. A similar trend applies to cargo safety and security procedures, where the inland port becomes a component of a chain of cargo integrity.

The growth of hinterland traffic, if only supported by drayage (truck) operations, leads to increasing diseconomies such as congestion. The level of disorder in the transport system involves higher transport costs and unreliability in freight distribution. The formation of an inland load center network therefore aims to cope with these diseconomies through a massification of several inland flows (Figure 6.13). It involves a series of inland terminals (IT) linked to the port facilities by high-capacity rail or barge corridors. Also, a supporting land use structure needs to be established, mostly concerning the clustering of logistics activities (e.g. distribution centers) and often in co-location with the terminal facilities.

Inland load center network formation and logistics

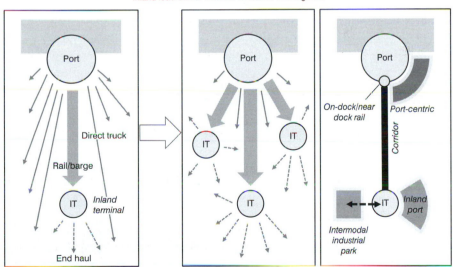

Figure 6.13 The massification of transportation in inland systems

Source: J.-P. Rodrigue and T. Notteboom (2011) "Port regionalization: improving port competitiveness by reaching beyond the port perimeter." *Port Technology International* 52: 11–17.

For instance, **port-centric logistics zones** support freight distribution activities related to maritime shipping and have a dominant international trade orientation. Port authorities tend to be proactive in this type of development, since it supports and provides added value to port activities.

The geographical characteristics linked with modal availability and the capacity of regional inland access have an important role to play in shaping the emergence and development of inland ports. Each inland market has its own potential requiring different transport services. Thus, there is **no single strategy** for an inland port in terms of modal preferences, as the regional effect remains fundamental. In developed countries, namely North America and Europe, which tend to be at the receiving end of many containerized supply chains, a number of inland ports have been developed with a focus on inbound logistics (Photo 6.2).

The setting of global supply chains and the strategy of Pacific Asian countries around the export-oriented paradigm have been powerful forces shaping contemporary freight distribution. Indirectly, this has forced players in the freight transport industry to examine supply chains as a whole and to identify legs where capacity and reliability were an issue. Inland terminals have evolved from simple intermodal locations to their incorporation within logistic zones. Rail terminals in particular have historically been locations from which specific market coverage was achieved. Containerization has impacted this coverage through the selection of terminals that serviced a wider market area. This spatial change also came with a functional change, as intermodal terminals began to experience a specialization of roles based on their geographical location but also based on their function within supply chains.

Photo 6.2 Terminal Intermodal Logistica de Hidalgo (TILH)

TILH is an inland port facility (owned and operated by Hutchison Port Holdings Ltd) which opened in 2012. It is located in the southern part of the state of Hidalgo, 50 km north of Mexico City, which is one of the world's largest metropolitan areas, with a population of more than 21 million people.

Bibliography

Arvis, J.-F., M.A. Mustra, L. Ojala, B. Shepherd and D. Saslavsky (2012) *Connecting to Compete 2012 Trade Logistics in the Global Economy*. Washington, DC: The World Bank.

Bernstein, W.J. (2008) *A Splendid Exchange: How Trade Shaped the World*. New York: Atlantic Monthly Press.

Braudel, F. (1982) *The Wheels of Commerce. Civilization and Capitalism 15th–18th Century*, vol. 2. New York: Harper & Row.

Brooks, M. (2008) *North American Freight Transportation: The Road to Security and Prosperity*. Cheltenham: Edward Elgar.

Daniels, J.D., L.H. Radebaugh and D. Sullivan (2012) *International Business: Environments and Operations*, 14th edition. New York: Prentice Hall.

Dicken, P. (2011) *Global Shift: Mapping the Changing Contours of the World Economy*, 6th edition. New York: The Guilford Press.

Hesse, M. (2008) *The City as a Terminal: The Urban Context of Logistics and Freight Transport*. Aldershot: Ashgate.

Hesse, M. and J.-P. Rodrigue (2004) "The transport geography of logistics and freight distribution." *Journal of Transport Geography* 12(3): 171–184.

Hummels, D. (2001) *Time as a Trade Barrier*, GTAP Working Paper No. 18.

Mangan, J.C. Lalwani, T. Butcher and R. Javadpour (2011) *Global Logistics and Supply Chain Management*, 2nd edition. New York: Wiley.

O'Connor, K. (2010) "Global city regions and the location of logistics activity." *Journal of Transport Geography* 18(3): 354–362.

Rodrigue, J.-P. and T. Notteboom (2012) "Dry ports in European and North American intermodal rail systems: two of a kind?" *Research in Transportation Business & Management* 5: 4–15.

Sheffi, Y. (2012) *Logistics Clusters: Delivering Value and Driving Growth*. Cambridge, MA: MIT Press.

Waters, D. and S. Rinsler (2014) *Global Logistics: New Directions in Supply Chain Management*. London: Kogan Page.

7 Urban transportation

Urbanization has been one of the dominant contemporary processes, as a growing share of the global population lives in cities. Considering this trend, urban transportation issues are of foremost importance to support the passengers and freight mobility requirements of large urban agglomerations. Transportation in urban areas is highly complex because of the modes involved, the multitude of origins and destinations and the amount and variety of traffic. Traditionally, the focus of urban transportation has been on passengers, as cities were viewed as locations of utmost human interactions with intricate traffic patterns linked to commuting, commercial transactions and leisure/cultural activities. However, cities are also locations of production, consumption and distribution, activities linked to movements of freight. Conceptually, the urban transport system is intricately linked with urban form and spatial structure. Urban transit is an important dimension of mobility, notably in high-density areas.

Concept 1 – Transportation and the urban form

Global urbanization

No discussion about the urban spatial structure can take place without an overview of **urbanization**, which has been one of the dominant trends of economic and social change of the twentieth century, especially in the developing world. Urbanization is the process of transition from a rural to a more urban society. Statistically, urbanization reflects an increasing proportion of the population living in settlements defined as urban, primarily through net rural to urban migration. The level of urbanization is the percentage of the total population living in towns and cities, while the rate of urbanization is the rate at which it grows.

This transition is expected to go on well into the second half of the twenty-first century, a trend reflected in the growing size of cities and in the increasing proportion of the urbanized population. Cities also dominate the national economic output as they account for the bulk of the production, distribution and consumption. Urban mobility problems have increased proportionally (and in some cases exponentially) with urbanization since mobility demands are concentrated over a specific area. Since 1950, the world's urban population has more than doubled, to reach nearly 3.8 billion in 2014, about 54 percent of the global population. This is the outcome of three main demographic trends:

- **Natural increase**. It is simply the outcome of more births than deaths in urban areas, a direct function of the fertility rate as well as the quality of healthcare systems (lower mortality rates, particularly for infants). Phases in the demographic transition are commonly linked with urbanization rates. Although this factor played an important role in the past, it is of much lesser importance today, as fertility rates in many developed countries have dropped significantly, in some cases, like Western Europe, Japan and South Korea, below replacement rate.

- **Rural to urban migrations**. This has been a strong factor of urbanization, particularly in the developing world, where migration accounted for between 40 and 60 percent of the urban growth. Such a process has endured since the beginning of the Industrial Revolution in the nineteenth century, first in the developed world and then in the developing world. The reasons for urban migration are numerous and may involve the expectation to find employment, improved agricultural productivity, which frees rural labor, or even political and environmental problems where populations are constrained to leave the countryside.

- **International migration**. The growth in international migration has been an important factor in the urbanization of major gateway cities, such as Los Angeles, Miami, New York, London and Paris. This process has a tendency to take place in the largest cities, but there is a trickle down to cities of smaller size.

Current global trends indicate a growth of about 50 million urbanites each year, roughly a million a week. More than 90 percent of that growth occurs in developing countries, which places intense pressures on urban infrastructures, particularly transportation, to cope. By 2050, 6.4 billion people, about two-thirds of humankind, are likely to be urban residents. What can be considered as urban includes a whole continuum of urban spatial structures, ranging from small towns to large urban agglomerations. This also brings up the question of optimal city size, since technical limitations (road, utilities) are not much of an impediment when building very large cities. Many of the world's largest cities can

Figure 7.1 World's largest cities, 2010

be labeled as dysfunctional, mainly because, as city size increases, the rising complexities are not effectively coped with by managerial expertise.

Global urbanization and the emergence of large cities has been a significant process with far-reaching economic and social impacts:

- Urbanization involves a much higher level of **concentration** of the global population, which used to be more dispersed. Higher levels of concentration are easier to service from a market perspective, but are also prone to congestion and diseconomies.
- Several **mega-cities** of more than 8 million have emerged. These cities command a large share of the global wealth creation and dominate their respective national economies. Many act as global cities.
- **Urban residents** have different activities, lifestyles and levels of consumption than rural residents, particularly in developing countries.

The urban form

Demographic and mobility growth have been shaped by the capacity and requirements of urban transport infrastructures, such as roads, transit systems or simply walkways. Consequently, there is a wide variety of urban forms, spatial structures and associated urban transportation systems. The **urban form** refers to the spatial imprint of an urban transport system as well as the adjacent physical infrastructures. Jointly, they confer a level of spatial arrangement to cities. The **urban spatial structure** refers to the set of relationships arising out of the urban form and its underlying interactions of people, freight and information. It tries to evaluate to what extent specific urban structures can be achieved with specific transport systems.

In light of transport developments, the urban spatial structure can be categorized by its level of centralization and clustering (Figure 7.2):

- **Centralization**. Refers to the setting of activities in relation to the whole urban area. A centralized city has a significant share of its activities in its center, while a decentralized city does not. Large employers such as financial institutions are the main drivers of centralization.
- **Clustering**. Refers to the setting of activities in relation to a specific part of the urban area. A cluster of activities is therefore a concentration around a specific focal point, which tend to be transport infrastructures such as a highway interchange, a transit terminal or a smaller town that has been absorbed by the expansion of the metropolis.

The urban spatial structure can be characterized by its level of centralization and clustering of value-added activities such as retail, management, fabrication and distribution. Centralization refers to the preponderance the central part of the city has on the organization of urban activities. It is mainly derived from accessibility. Clustering refers to the overall respective proximity that urban activities maintain, and is mainly derived from the benefits of agglomeration. A centralized and clustered setting (Type A) implies that most of the value-added activities are located around the central area of a city and are also in close proximity to another. Although these four types of urban spatial structures are possible, the two most significant trends that have impacted urban spatial structures have been decentralization, but this decentralization took place while maintaining a high level of clustering (Type C). This is reflective of a multicentric city.

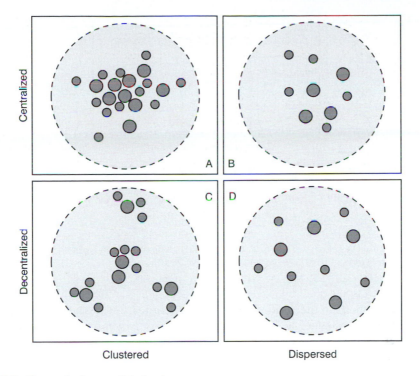

Figure 7.2 Types of urban spatial structures

Even if the geographical setting of each city varies considerably, the urban form and its spatial structure are articulated by two structural elements:

- **Nodes**. These are reflected in the centrality of urban activities, which can be related to the spatial accumulation of economic activities or to the accessibility to the transport system. Terminals, such as ports, train stations, railyards and airports, are important nodes around which activities agglomerate at the local or regional level. Nodes have a hierarchy related to their importance and contribution to urban functions, with high-order nodes such as management and retailing and lower-order nodes such as production and distribution.
- **Linkages**. These are the infrastructures supporting flows from, to and between nodes. The lowest level of linkages includes streets, which are the defining elements of the urban spatial structure. There is a hierarchy of linkages moving up to regional roads and railways and international connections by air and maritime transport systems.

Depending on their nature, urban nodes and linkages provide for a functional connectivity, implying interdependent urban functions related to trade, production and telecommunications. Urban transportation is thus associated with a spatial form which varies according to the modes being used. What has not changed much is that cities tend to opt for a **grid street pattern**. This was the case for many Roman cities built in the first century, as it was for American cities built in the twentieth century. The reasons behind this permanence are relatively simple: a grid pattern jointly optimizes accessibility and available real estate. Obviously, many cities are not organized as a grid.

Conventional grid
pattern (c. 1900)

Curvilinear loop pattern and
beginning of cul-de-sacs
(1930–1950)

Conventional
cul-de-sac pattern
(since 1950)

——— Arterial road ------ Local street

Figure 7.3 Street network types

Source: Adapted from W.E. Marshall and N.W. Garrick (2010), "Street network types and road safety." *Urban Design International*, 10.1057/udi.2009.31, 21 April 2010.

They correspond to older cities, many former fortified towns, as well as cities which grew from a constrained location, such as an island or a river junction. Local geographical and historical characteristics remain important influences on the urban form.

In an age of motorization and personal mobility, an increasing number of cities are developing a spatial structure that increases reliance on motorized transportation, particularly the privately owned automobile. This has incited a shift from a grid pattern towards curvilinear and cul-de-sac patterns that are commonly found in suburban areas (Figure 7.3).

The conventional street grid is mostly the outcome of the streetcar suburbs that emerged in the early part of the twentieth century. It conferred optimal accessibility and use of available space. The diffusion of the automobile was a driver in the shift in the street network towards a more curvilinear pattern. This implied a reduction in the level of connectivity as well as the density of land use. This was part of a paradox where, while the automobile was becoming the dominant support of urban mobility, it was also being increasingly associated with local disturbances. Planners responded by developing cul-de-sac suburban patterns with the goal to reduce and even eliminate through-movements on a large number of residential streets and having them taking place on main arterials. By the 1950s, the conventional cul-de-sac pattern became prevalent in suburban developments. Although this pattern minimizes non-local circulation, it also generates more movements and energy consumption.

Dispersion, or urban sprawl, is taking place in many different types of cities, from dense, centralized European metropolises such as Madrid, Paris (Photo 7.1), and London, to rapidly industrializing metropolises such as Seoul, Shanghai and Buenos Aires, to those experiencing recent, fast and uncontrolled urban growth, such as Mumbai and Lagos. Recent urban expansion is consequently almost all geared towards the automobile.

Therefore, there are significant differences in the density of cities across the world (Figure 7.4). Urban density is reflective of the mode of habitation elected by the population, with high-density cities characterized by apartment buildings (or crowded slums), while lower-density cities have low-rise habitation units and even single family homes in the suburbs. It is also reflective of the reliance on collective forms of urban transportation, with high-density cities more prone to have a high modal split in favor of public transit. However, higher densities are less suitable for urban freight distribution, since

Photo 7.1 High-density structured urban form, Paris

Paris, like many European cities, has a prominent core, high land use density and high levels of accessibility to urban transit. Still, it remains highly motorized with limited parking space.

Figure 7.4 Population density of the world's largest metropolitan areas, 2012

Source: *Demographia World Urban Areas*, 9th annual edition, no. 3 (2013). Belleville, IL: Demographia.

delivery trucks, which usually support most urban deliveries, have difficulties performing deliveries in high-density areas.

There is a clear geographical distribution of urban population densities among metropolitan areas of more than 1 million inhabitants across the world. While most metropolitan areas have an total density of between 4,500 and 8,000 people per square kilometer, a high number of cities with a density of less than 3,000 people per square kilometer can be found. There is also a number of very high-density cities, most of them in South Asia. North American and Australian cities are among those with the lowest densities, followed by European cities. The rest of the world has on average much higher densities, usually above 5,000 people per square kilometer.

Evolution of transportation and urban form

Urbanization and urban developments occur in accordance to the development of urban transport systems, particularly in terms of their capacity and efficiency. Historically, movements within cities tended to be restricted to walking, which made medium- and long-distance urban linkages rather inefficient and time-consuming. Thus, activity nodes tended to be **agglomerated** and urban forms **compact**. Many modern cities have inherited an urban form created under such circumstances, even though they are no longer prevailing. The dense urban cores of many European, Japanese and Chinese cities, for example, enable residents to make between one third and two-thirds of all trips by walking and cycling. At the other end of the spectrum, the dispersed urban forms of most Australian, Canadian and American cities, which were built recently, encourage automobile dependency and are linked with high levels of mobility. Many major cities are also port cities, with maritime accessibility playing an enduring role not only for the economic vitality but also in the urban spatial structure, with the port district being an important node. Airport terminals have also played a growing role in the urban spatial structure as they can be considered as cities within cities.

The evolution of transportation has generally led to changes in urban form. The more radical the changes in transport technology have been, the more the alterations on the urban form. Among the most fundamental changes in the urban form is the emergence of new clusters expressing new urban activities and new relationships between elements of the urban system. In many cities, the **central business district** (CBD), once the primary destination of commuters and serviced by public transportation, has been changed by new manufacturing, retailing and management practices. Whereas traditional manufacturing depended on centralized workplaces and transportation, technological and transportation developments rendered modern industry more flexible. In many cases, manufacturing relocated in a suburban setting, if not altogether to entirely new low-cost locations offshore. Retail and office activities are also suburbanizing, producing changes in the urban form. Concomitantly, many important transport terminals, namely port facilities and railyards, have emerged in suburban areas following new requirements in modern freight distribution brought in part by containerization. The urban spatial structure shifted from a nodal to a multinodal character, involving new forms of urban development and new connections to regional and global economic processes (Figure 7.5).

The urban spatial structure basically considers the location of different activities as well as their relationships. **Core activities** are those of the highest order in the urban spatial structure, namely tertiary and quaternary activities involved in management (finance and insurance) and consumption (retailing). **Central activities** are concerned by production and distribution with activities such as warehousing, manufacturing,

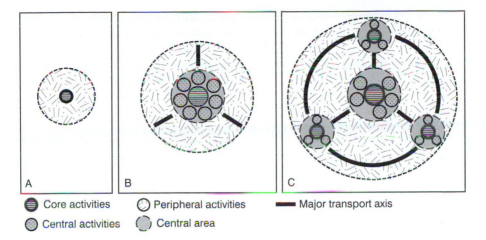

Core activities   Peripheral activities   ▬▬ Major transport axis
Central activities   Central area

Figure 7.5 Evolution of the spatial structure of a city

wholesaling and transportation. Peripheral activities are dominantly residential or servicing local needs. A central area refers to an agglomeration of core and/or central activities within a specific location. The emergence of a CBD (Central Business District; the central area of a city) is the result of an historical process, often occurring over several centuries (depending on the age of a city), that has changed the urban form and the location of economic activities. Obviously, each city has its own history, but it is possible to establish a general common process:

- **Pre-industrial era**. For cities that existed before the Industrial Revolution, the CBD was limited to small section of the city, generally nearby the waterfront, the market and/or a site of religious or political importance. These were locations where major transactions took place and thus required financial, insurance, warehousing and wholesale services.
- **Industrial Revolution**. With the Industrial Revolution came mass production and mass consumption. This permitted the emergence of a distinct retailing and wholesaling part of the CBD, while manufacturing was located outside the core. Major terminal facilities, such as ports and railyards, were also located in proximity to the city core. Managing these expanding activities also created an increasing need for office space that located nearby traditional places of financial interaction. As the Industrial Revolution matured, major transportation axis spurred from the central area towards the periphery.
- **Contemporary era**. After World War II, industries relocated massively away from central areas to suburban areas, leaving room for the expansion of administrative and financial activities. The CBD was thus the object of an important accumulation of financial and administrative activities, particularly in the largest cities, as several corporations became multinational enterprises. These activities were even more willing to pay higher rents than retailing, thereby pushing some retail activities out of the CBD. New retailing subcenters emerged in suburban areas because of road accessibility and because of the need to service these new areas. Warehousing and transportation, no longer core area activities, have also relocated to new peripheral locations close to modern terminal facilities such as container terminals and airports. The spatial structure of many cities became increasingly multinodal (or multicentric).

Initially, suburban growth mainly took place adjacent to major road corridors, leaving plots of vacant or farm land in between. Later, intermediate spaces were gradually filled up, more or less coherently. Highways and ringroads, which circled and radiated from cities, favored the **development of suburbs** and the emergence of **important subcenters** that compete with the CBD for the attraction of economic activities. As a result, many new job opportunities have shifted to the suburbs (if not to entirely new locations abroad) and the activity system of cities has been considerably modified. Different parts of a city have a different dynamism depending on its spatial pattern. These changes have occurred according to a variety of geographical and historical contexts, notably in North America and Europe, as each subsequent phase of urban transportation developments led to different spatial structures. Sometimes, particularly when new modern urban road infrastructures are built, the subsequent changes in the urban form can be significant.

Although transportation systems and travel patterns have changed considerably over time, one enduring feature remains that most people travel between 30 and 40 minutes in one direction. Globally, people are spending about 1.2 hours per day commuting, wherever this takes place in a low- or a high-mobility setting. Different transport technologies, however, are associated with different travel speeds and capacity. As a result, cities that rely primarily on non-motorized transport tend to be different to auto-dependent cities. Transport technology thus plays a very important role in defining urban form and the spatial pattern of various activities. Still, the evolution of the urban form is **path-dependent**, suggesting that the current spatial structure is obviously the outcome of past developments, but that those developments were strongly related to local conditions involving the setting, physical constraints and investments in infrastructures and modes.

The spatiality of urban transportation

The amount of urban land allocated to transportation is often correlated with the level of mobility. In the pre-automobile era, about 10 percent of the urban land was devoted to transportation which was simply roads for a predominantly pedestrian traffic. As the mobility of people and freight increased, a growing share of urban areas was allocated to transport and the infrastructures supporting it. Large variations in the spatial imprint of urban transportation are observed between different cities, as well as between different parts of a city, such as between central and peripheral areas. The major components of the spatial imprint of urban transportation are:

- **Pedestrian areas**. Refer to the amount of space devoted to walking. This space is often shared with roads, as sidewalks may use between 10 percent and 20 percent of a road's right of way. In central areas, pedestrian areas tend to use a greater share of the right of way and in some instances whole areas are reserved for pedestrians. However, in a motorized context, most pedestrian areas are for servicing people's access to transport modes, such as parked automobiles.
- **Roads and parking areas**. Refer to the amount of space devoted to road transportation, which has two states of activity: moving or parked. In a motorized city, on average 30 percent of the surface is devoted to roads, while another 20 percent is required for off-street parking. This implies, for each car, about two off-street and two on-street parking spaces. In North American cities, roads and parking lots account for between 30 and 60 percent of the total surface.
- **Cycling areas**. In a disorganized form, cycling simply shares access to pedestrian and road space. However, many attempts have been made to create spaces specifically for bicycles in urban areas, with reserved lanes and parking facilities (Photo 7.2).

Photo 7.2 Bicycle pool, Paris

The pooling of vehicles for short-term rent is an option that is increasingly being considered and applied. This photo shows the "Velib" (*Velo Libre*) initiative in Paris, France, where bicycles are offered for rental for less than 24 hours, and ideally for less than two hours. The system comprises 1,250 bicycle rental stations spaced at average intervals of 300 m, with a pool of 18,200 bicycles. It turned out to be a very popular pooling system, but also had some problems – notably a high level of vandalism and the need to reposition bicycles every night because of commuting patterns.

The Netherlands has been particularly proactive over this issue, with biking paths very much part of the urban transport system: 27 percent of the total amount of commuting is accounted by cycling.

- **Transit systems**. Many transit systems, such as buses and tramways, share road space with automobiles, which often impairs their respective efficiency. Attempts to mitigate congestion have resulted in the creation of road lanes reserved for buses either on a permanent or temporary (during rush hour) basis. Other transport systems such as subways and rail have their own infrastructures and, consequently, their own rights of way.
- **Transport terminals**. Refer to the amount of space devoted to terminal facilities such as ports, airports, transit stations, railyards and distribution centers. Globalization has increased the mobility of people and freight, both in relative and absolute terms, and consequently the amount of urban space required to support those activities. Many major terminals are located in the peripheral areas of cities, which are the only locations where sufficient amounts of land are available.

The spatial importance of each transport mode varies according to a number of factors, density being the most important. If density is considered as a gradient, rings of mobility represent variations in the spatial importance of each mode with regard to providing urban mobility. Further, each transport mode has unique performance and space consumption characteristics. The most relevant example is the automobile. It requires space to move around (roads) but it also spends 98 percent of its existence stationary in a parking space. Consequently, a significant amount of urban space must be allocated to accommodate the automobile, especially when it does not move and is thus economically and socially useless. In large urban agglomerations, close to all the available street parking space in areas of average density and above is occupied throughout the day. At an aggregate level, measures reveal a significant spatial imprint of road transportation among developed countries. In the United States, more land is thus used by the automobile than for housing. In Western Europe, roads account for between 15 and 20 percent of the urban surface, while for developing countries this figure is about 10 percent (6 percent on average for Chinese cities, but this is growing fast due to motorization).

Concept 2 – Urban land use and transportation

The land use–transport system

Urban land use comprises two elements: the **nature of land use** which relates to which activities are taking place where, and the **level of spatial accumulation**, which indicates their intensity and concentration. Central areas have a high level of spatial accumulation and corresponding land uses, such as retail, while peripheral areas have lower levels of accumulation. Most economic, social or cultural activities imply a multitude of functions, such as production, consumption and distribution. These functions take place at specific locations and are part of an activity system. Some are routine activities, because they occur regularly and are thus predictable, such as commuting and shopping. Others are institutional activities that tend to be irregular, and are shaped by lifestyle (e.g. sports and leisure) or by special needs (e.g. healthcare). Others are production activities that are related to manufacturing and distribution, whose linkages may be local, regional or global. The behavioral patterns of individuals, institutions and firms have an imprint on land use in terms of their locational choice.

At the global level, cities consume about 3 percent of the total landmass. Although figures can vary considerably depending on the city, residential land use is the most common, occupying between 65 and 75 percent of the surface of a city. Commercial and industrial land uses occupy 5–15 percent and 15–25 percent of the surface respectively. Land use, both in formal and functional representations, implies a set of relationships with other land uses. For instance, commercial land use involves relationships with its supplier and customers. While relationships with suppliers will dominantly be related with movements of freight, relationships with customers would include movements of people. Thus, a level of accessibility to both systems of circulation must be present. Since each type of land use has its own specific mobility requirements, transportation is a factor of activity location, and is therefore associated intimately with land use.

Within an urban system each activity occupies a suitable, but not necessarily optimal location, from which it derives rent. Transportation and land use interactions mostly consider the retroactive relationships between activities, which are land-use-related, and accessibility, which is transportation-related. These relationships have often been described as a classic "chicken-and-egg" problem since it is difficult to identify the triggering cause of change: do transportation changes precede land use changes or vice versa? There is a **scale effect** at play, as large infrastructure projects tend to precede and trigger land use changes while small-scale transportation projects tend to complement the existing land use pattern. Further, the expansion of urban land uses takes place over various circumstances such as infilling (near the city center) or sprawl (far from the city center) and where transportation plays a different role in each case.

Urban transportation aims at supporting transport demands generated by the diversity of urban activities in a **diversity of urban contexts**. A key for understanding urban entities thus lies in the analysis of patterns and processes of the transport/land use system. This system is highly complex and involves several relationships between the transport system, spatial interactions and land use:

- **Transport system**. Considers the set of transport infrastructures and modes that support urban movements of passengers and freight. It generally expresses the level of accessibility.
- **Spatial interactions**. Consider the nature, extent, origins and destinations of the urban movements of passengers and freight. They take into consideration the attributes of the transport system as well as the land use factors that are generating and attracting movements.
- **Land use**. Considers the level of spatial accumulation of activities and their associated levels of mobility requirements. Land use is commonly linked with demographic and economic attributes.

Urban activities such as retail or manufacturing have spatial locations from which a land use pattern is derived and influenced by the existing urban form and spatial structure (Figure 7.6). This form is strongly related to the types of activities that can roughly be divided in three major classes:

- **Routine activities** occur regularly and are thus predictable. They involve journey to work (residential to industrial/commercial/administrative) and shopping (residential to retailing). The land use pattern generated is thus stable and coherent. Generally, these activities are zonal and links are from areas to areas.

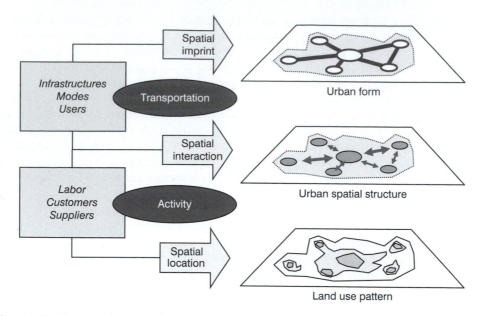

Figure 7.6   Transportation, activity systems and land use

- **Institutional activities**. Most institutions are located at specific points and generally have links with individuals. This activity system is linked to an urban environment where links occur irregularly and according to the lifestyle (students, sports, leisure, etc.) or special needs (health).
- **Production activities** involve a complex network of relationships between firms, such as control, distribution, warehousing and subcontracting. This activity system can be linked to a specific urban environment, but also to a region, nation or even the world. Some activities are strongly linked to the local urban area, while others are far more linked to the global economy. The land use pattern of an activity may thus be linked to an external (international) process.

A conundrum concerns the difficulties of **linking a specific mode of transportation with specific land use patterns**. While public transit systems tend to be associated with higher densities of residential and commercial activities, and highways with lower densities, the multiplicity of modes available in urban areas, including freight distribution, conveys an unclear and complex relationship.

Urban land use models

The relationships between transportation and land use are rich in theoretical representations that have contributed much to regional sciences. Since transportation is a distance–decay altering technology, spatial organization is assumed to be strongly influenced by the concepts of **location** and **distance**. Several descriptive and analytical models of urban land use have been developed over time, with increased levels of complexity. All involve some consideration of transport in the explanations of urban land use structures.

Von Thunen's regional land use model is the oldest representation based on a **central place, the market town and its concentric impacts** on surrounding land uses (Figure 7.7). It was initially developed in the early nineteenth century (1826) for the analysis of agricultural land use patterns in Germany. It used the concept of economic rent to explain a spatial organization where different agricultural activities compete for the usage of land. The underlying principles of this model have been the foundation of many others where economic considerations, namely land rent and distance–decay, are incorporated. The core assumption of the model is that agricultural land use is patterned in the form of concentric circles around a market that consumes all the surplus production, which must be transported. The relative costs of transporting different agricultural commodities to the central market determined the agricultural land use around a city. The most productive activities will thus compete for the closest land to the market, and activities not productive enough will locate further away. The relationships between agricultural land use and market distance are very difficult to establish in the contemporary context. However, a strong relationship between the transport system and regional agricultural land use patterns can be acknowledged at the continental level in North America.

Burgess's concentric model was among the first attempts to investigate spatial patterns at the urban level (1925). Although the purpose of the model was to analyze social classes, it recognized that transportation and mobility were important factors behind the spatial organization of urban areas (Figure 7.8). The formal land use representation of this model is derived from commuting distance from the CBD, creating concentric circles. Each circle represents a specific socioeconomic urban landscape. This model is conceptually a direct adaptation of the Von Thunen's model to urban land use since it deals with a concentric representation. Even close to one century after the

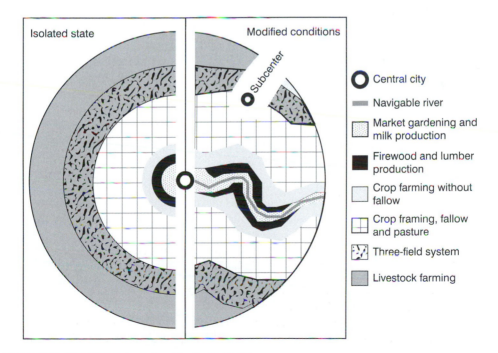

Figure 7.7 Von Thunen's regional land use model

Figure 7.8 Burgess's urban land use model

concentric urban model was designed, spatial changes in Chicago are still reflective of such a process.

Sector and multiple nuclei land use models were developed to take into account numerous factors overlooked by concentric models, namely the influence of transport axis (Hoyt, 1939) and multiple nuclei (Harris and Ullman, 1945) on land use and growth. Both representations consider the emerging impacts of motorization on the urban spatial structure. Such representations also considered that transportation infrastructures, particularly terminals such as rail stations or ports, occupy specific locations and can be considered as land uses.

Moving further, **hybrid models** are an attempt to include the concentric, sector and nuclei behavior of different processes in explaining urban land use. They are an attempt to integrate the strengths of each approach since none of these appear to provide a completely satisfactory explanation. Thus, hybrid models consider the concentric effect of central locations (CBDs and sub-centers) and the radial effect of transport axis, all overlain to form a land use pattern. Also, hybrid representations are suitable to explain the evolution of the urban spatial structure as they combine different spatial impacts of transportation on urban land use, let them be concentric or radial, and this at different points in time.

Land rent theory was also developed to explain land use as a market where different urban activities are competing for land usage at a location. It is strongly based in the market principle of spatial competition where actors bid to secure and maintain their presence at a specific location. The more desirable a location is, the higher its rent value (Figure 7.10). By overlapping the bid rent curves of all the urban economic activities, a concentric land use pattern is created with retailing in the CBD, industry/commercial on the next ring, apartments farther on and then single houses. This representation considers

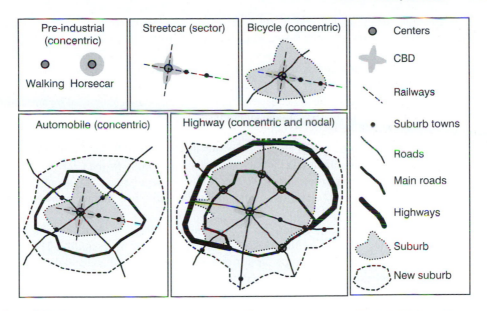

Figure 7.9 The hybrid land use model: transportation and the formation of urban landscapes

Source: Adapted from E.J. Taaffe, H.L. Gauthier and M.E. O'Kelly (1996) *Geography of Transportation*, 2nd edition. Upper Saddle River, NJ: Prentice Hall.

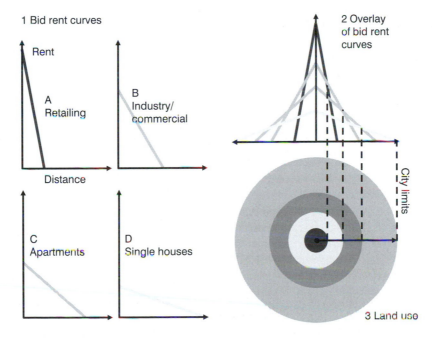

Figure 7.10 Land rent and land use

an isotropic space. In the real world a set of physiographic (waterfront, hills, etc.), historical (tourism) and social (race, crime, perception) attributes will influence bid rent curves.

Transportation, through accessibility and distance–decay, is a strong explanatory factor on the land rent and its impacts on land use. However, conventional representations of land rent leaning on the concentric paradigm are being challenged by structural modifications of contemporary cities, including:

- The downtown area is **not necessarily the most accessible location**. The rapid extension of metropolitan areas involves new locations far from the CBD, notably in suburbia. This has favored the emergence of subcenters having a concentration of retailing, commercial, distribution and industrial activities, mainly aimed at servicing a growing population.
- Improvements in transportation and telecommunications have made several activities **far more tolerant to distance**, but still dependent on accessibility. The urban land use pattern thus tends to be far less coherent, more specialized and dispersed.
- A significant share of the land, notably nearby central areas, is captured and **not available on real-estate markets**. Governments, institutions, parks, industries and transport infrastructures occupy a large part of most central areas and this ownership can last for several decades (if not several centuries for historical landmarks). This caused an imbalance in the price fixing mechanism in central areas with less land available (thus higher prices) that has favored urban sprawl.

Cellular automata are dynamic land use models developed on the principle that space can be represented as a grid where each cell is a discrete land use unit (Figure 7.11). Cell states thus symbolize land uses and transition rules express the likelihood of a change

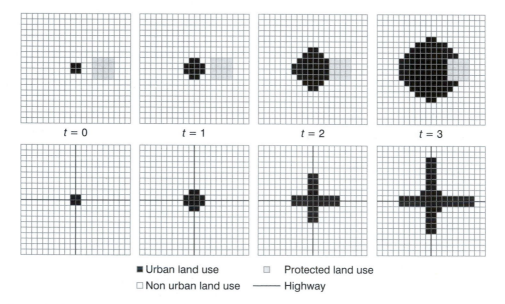

Urban land use   Protected land use
Non urban land use   ——— Highway

Figure 7.11 Cellular automata land use dynamics

Source: Adapted from D. Kim and M. Batty (2011) "Calibrating cellular automata models for simulating urban growth: comparative analysis of SLEUTH and Metronamica." UCL Center for advanced Analysis, Paper 176.

from one land use state to another. Because cells are symbolically connected and inter-related (e.g. adjacency), models can be used to investigate the dynamics, evolution and self-organization of cellar automata land use systems. The cellular approach enables the achievement of a high level of spatial detail (resolution) and realism, as well as to link the simulation directly to visible outcomes on the regional spatial structure. They are also readily implementable since Geographic Information Systems are designed to work effectively with grid-based spatial representations.

Cellular automata paradigms improve upon most transportation – land use models that are essentially static as they explain land use patterns, but they do not explicitly consider the processes that are creating or changing them. The applicability and dynamics of land use models is related to issues such as the age, size and the locational setting of a city. For instance, concentric cities are generally older and of smaller size, while polycentric cities are larger and relate to urban development processes that took place more recently. While most of the conceptual approaches related to transportation and land use relationships have been developed using empirical evidence related to North America and Western Europe, this perspective does not necessarily apply to other parts of the world. A **dualism** in land uses has been observed in cities in developing countries, where on the one hand processes such as economic development and motor-ization create an urban landscape which is common in advanced economies, and on the other hand, an informal landscape of shantytowns represents a land use structure that is not effectively captured by conventional land use models. It remains to be seen to what extent globalization will favor a convergence of land use patterns across the world's cities.

Transportation and urban dynamics

Both land use and transportation are part of a dynamic system that is subject to external influences. Each component of the system is constantly evolving due to changes in tech-nology, policy, economics, demographics and even culture or values. As a result, the interactions between land use and transportation are played out as the outcome of the many **decisions made by residents, businesses and governments**. The field of urban dynamics has expanded the scope of conventional land use models, which tended to be descriptive, by trying to consider relationships behind the evolution of the urban spatial structure. This has led to a complex modeling framework including a wide variety of components. Among the concepts supporting urban dynamics representations are retro-actions, whereby one component changes its influence on others. The changes will influ-ence the initial component back, either positively or negatively. The most significant components of urban dynamics are:

- **Land use**. This is the most stable component of urban dynamics, as changes are likely to modify the land use structure over rather a long period of time. This comes as little surprise since most real estate is built to last at least several decades. The main impact of land use on urban dynamics is its function as a generator and attractor of movements.
- **Transport network**. This is also considered to be a rather stable component of urban dynamics, as transport infrastructures are built for the long term. This is particularly the case for large transport terminals and subway systems that can operate for a very long period of time. For instance, many railway stations are more than 100 years old. The main contribution of the transport network to urban dynamics is the provision

of accessibility. Changes in the transport network will impact accessibility and movements.

- **Movements**. The most dynamic component of the system, since movements of passengers or freight reflect changes almost immediately. Movements thus tend more to be an outcome of urban dynamics than a factor shaping them.
- **Employment and workplaces**. They account for significant inducement effects over urban dynamics since many models often consider employment as an exogenous factor. This is specifically the case for employment that is categorized as basic, or export-oriented, which is linked with specific economic sectors such as manufacturing. Commuting is a direct outcome of the number of jobs and the location of workplaces.
- **Population and housing**. They act as the generators of movements, because residential areas are the sources of commuting. Since there is a wide array of incomes, standards of living, preferences and ethnicity, this diversity is reflected in the urban spatial structure.

The issue about how to articulate these relations remains, particularly in the current context of interdependency between local, regional and global processes. **Globalization** has substantially blurred the relationships between transportation and land use as well as its dynamics. The main paradigm is concerned with some factors once endogenous to a regional setting that have become **exogenous**. Consequently, many economic activities that provide employment and multiplying effects, such as manufacturing, are driven by forces that are global in scope and may have little to do with regional dynamics. For instance, capital investment could come from external sources and the bulk of the output could be bound to international markets. In such a context it would be difficult to explain urban development processes taking place in coastal Chinese cities, or in a region such as the Pearl River Delta, since export-oriented strategies are among the most significant driving forces. Looking at the urban dynamics of such a system from an endogenous perspective would fail to capture driving forces that are dominantly exogenous.

Concept 3 – Urban mobility

Urban mobility and its evolution

Urban transportation is organized in three broad categories of **collective**, **individual** and **freight** transportation. While passenger movements are the outcome of numerous individual decisions based on different rationales, freight movements are decided in tandem between the cargo owners (procurers and customers) and the transportation service providers. In several instances, passengers and freight movements are complementary to one another, but sometimes they may be competing for passengers, the usage of available land and transport infrastructures:

- **Collective transportation** (public transit). The purpose of collective transportation is to provide publicly accessible mobility over specific parts of a city. Its efficiency is based upon transporting large numbers of people and achieving economies of scale. It includes modes such as tramways, buses, trains, subways and ferryboats.
- **Individual transportation**. Includes any mode where mobility is the outcome of a personal choice and means such as the automobile, walking, cycling and the motorcycle. The majority of people walk to satisfy their basic mobility, but this number

varies according to the city considered. For instance, walking accounts for 88 percent of all movements inside Tokyo, while this figure is only 3 percent for Los Angeles.

- **Freight transportation**. As cities are dominant centers of production and consumption, urban activities are accompanied by large movements of freight. These movements are mostly characterized by delivery trucks moving between industries, distribution centers, warehouses and retail activities, as well as from major terminals such as ports, railyards, distribution centers and airports. The mobility of freight within cities tends to be overlooked.

Rapid urban development occurring across much of the globe implies **increased quantities of passengers and freight moving within urban areas**. Movements also tend to involve longer distances, but evidence suggests that commuting times have remained relatively similar through the last 100 years, approximately 1 to 1.2 hours per day. This means that commuting has gradually shifted to faster transport modes and consequently greater distances could be traveled using the same amount of time. Different transport technologies and infrastructures have been implemented, resulting in a wide variety of urban transport systems around the world. In developed countries, there have been three general eras of urban development, each of which is associated with a different form of urban mobility:

- **The walking–horsecar era (1800–90)**. Even during the Industrial Revolution, the dominant means of getting around was on foot. Walking cities were typically less than 5 km in diameter, making it possible to walk from the downtown to the city edge in about 30 minutes. Land use was mixed and density was high (e.g. 100 to 200 people per hectare). The city was compact and its shape was more or less circular. Still, the Industrial Revolution brought additional populations through rural to urban migrations, improved construction techniques, allowing for higher densities and new forms and locations of employment. The development of the first public transit in the form of omnibus service extended the diameter of the city but did not change the overall urban structure. The railroad facilitated the first real change in urban morphology. New developments, often referred to as trackside suburbs, emerged as small nodes that were physically separated from the city itself and from one another. The nodes coincided with the location of rail stations and stretched out a considerable distance from the city center, usually up to a half-hour train ride. Within the city proper, rail lines were also laid down and horsecars introduced mass transit.

- **The electric streetcar or transit era (1890–1920s)**. The invention of the electric traction motor created a revolution in urban travel. The first electric trolley line opened in 1888 in Richmond, Virginia. The operating speed of the electric trolley was three times faster than that of horse-drawn vehicles, and nor did it generate waste. The streetcar city was able to spread outward 20–30 km along the streetcar lines, creating an irregular, star-shaped pattern. The urban fringes became areas of rapid residential development. Trolley corridors became commercial strips that would come to characterize the structure of the main commercial areas of cities. The city core was further entrenched as a mixed-use, high-density zone. Land use patterns reflected social stratification where suburban outer areas were typically middle class, while the working class continued to concentrate in the central city. As street congestion increased in the first half of the twentieth century due to the diffusion of the automobile, the efficiency of streetcar systems deteriorated as cars used their right of way. Further, many cities had ordinances that prevented fare increases, meaning that many streetcar systems were unprofitable, leading to a lack of maintenance and investment in additional services. These factors contributed to the demise of many streetcar systems.

- **The automobile era (1930s–50s)**. The automobile was introduced in European and North American cities in the 1890s, but only the wealthy could afford this innovation. From the 1920s, ownership rates increased dramatically, with lower prices made possible by Henry Ford's revolutionary assembly-line production techniques. As automobiles became more common, land development patterns changed. Developers were attracted to greenfield areas located between the suburban rail corridors, and the public was attracted to these single-use zones, thus avoiding many inconveniences associated with city – mainly pollution, crowding and lack of space. Still, this phase usually represented the peak share of public transit in urban mobility as suburban developments did not yet account for a large share of the urban landscape and cities were still high density and transit-dependent.

- **The freeway era (1950s onward)**. After World War II, the massive diffusion of the automobile, as well as the construction of highway networks, had substantial impacts on urban mobility. Highways were built to connect the central business district to outlying areas and in many cases complete or partial ring roads were built. The personal mobility offered by the automobile represented a paradigm shift in terms of lifestyle, consumption patterns as well as residential areas. The automobile reduced the friction of distance considerably, which led to urban sprawl. The emergence of the suburb created a new landscape in which public transit did not fit well. Transit ridership fell and such companies ran into financial difficulties and eventually services throughout North America and Europe became subsidized, publicly owned enterprises. As time went on, commercial activities also began to suburbanize, creating additional mobility systems of passengers and freight. Within a short time, the automobile became the dominant mode of travel in all cities of North America, and from the 1970s in a growing number of developed and developing economies. A similar process took place in China on a massive scale in the 2000s.

In many areas of the world where urbanization is more recent, the above synthetic phases did not take place. In the majority of cases fast urban growth led to a scramble to provide transport infrastructure in an inadequate fashion. Each form of urban mobility, be it walking, the automobile or urban transit, has a level of suitability to fill mobility needs. Motorization and the diffusion of personal mobility has been an ongoing trend linked with substantial declines in the share of public transit in urban mobility.

A taxonomy of urban mobilities

Movements are linked to specific urban activities and their land use. Each type of land use involves the generation and attraction of a particular array of movements. This relationship is complex, but is linked to factors such as recurrence, income, urban form, spatial accumulation, level of development and technology. Urban movements are either **obligatory**, when they are linked to scheduled activities (such as home-to-work movements), or **voluntary**, when those generating it are free to decide their scheduling (such as leisure). The most common types of urban movements are:

- **Pendulum movements**. These are obligatory movements involving commuting between locations of residence and work. They are highly cyclical since they are predictable and recur on a regular basis, most of the time a daily occurrence, hence the term "pendulum."

- **Professional movements**. These are movements linked to professional, work-based, activities such as meetings and customer services, predominantly taking place during work hours.
- **Personal movements**. These are voluntary movements linked to the location of commercial activities, which includes shopping and recreation.
- **Touristic movements**. Important for cities having historical and recreational features they involve interactions between landmarks and amenities such as hotels and restaurants. They tend to be seasonal in nature or occur at specific moments. Major sports events such as the World Cup or the Olympics are important generators of urban movements during their occurrence.
- **Distribution movements**. These are concerned with the distribution of freight to satisfy consumption and manufacturing requirements. They are mostly linked to transport terminals, distribution centers and retail outlets.

The consideration of urban movements involves their generation, the modes and routes used and their destination:

- **Trip generation**. On average, an urban resident undertakes between three and four trips per day. Moving in an urban area is usually done to satisfy a purpose such as employment, leisure or access to goods and services. Each time a purpose is satisfied, a trip is generated. Important temporal variations in the number of intentional trips are observed, with the most prevalent pattern being commuting. Similar temporal variations are observed for freight movements, with the majority of movements taking place in the morning when goods are delivered to retail outlets. This often leads to conflicts with passenger transport, since vehicles share the same road infrastructure, which in urban areas is the object of capacity constraints.
- **Modal split**. Refers to the use of a series of transportation modes for urban trips, which is the outcome of a **modal choice**. This choice depends on a number of factors such as cost, technology, availability, preference, travel time (distance) and income. Therefore, walking, cycling, public transit, the automobile or even telecommuting are going to be used either as a choice or as a constraint (lack of choice). For instance, locations within five minutes of walking are considered to be readily accessible to pedestrians. Urban freight distribution can also use a variety of modes, but the van and the truck tend to dominate.
- **Trip assignment (routing)**. Involves which routes will be used for journeys within the city. Passenger trips usually have a stable routing. For instance, most of the time a commuter driving a car has a fixed route between his residence and place of work. This route may be modified if there is congestion or if another activity (such as shopping) is linked with that trip – a practice often known as **trip chaining**. The routing of freight distribution is dependent on the types of deliveries involved. For large retail outlets, direct deliveries are the norm, while for smaller stores and parcel deliveries, vehicles will accommodate flexible routing. Several factors influence trip assignment, the three most important being transport **costs**, **time** and **congestion levels**.
- **Trip destination**. Changes in the spatial distribution of economic activities in urban areas have caused important modifications to the destination of movements, notably those related to work. Activity-based considerations are important since each

economic activity tends to be associated with a level of trip attraction. Retail, public administration, entertainment and restoration are the activities that attract the most movements per person employed. For freight movements, manufacturing, transport terminals and retail are the activities attracting the most movements. The **central city** used to be a major destination for movements, particularly passengers, but its share has substantially declined in most areas and **suburbs** now account for the bulk of urban movements.

Mobility is also a social equity issue. The share of the automobile in urban trips varies in relation to location, social status, income, quality of public transit and parking availability. Mass transit is often affordable, but several social groups, such as students, the elderly and the poor, are a **captive market**. There are important variations in mobility according to age, income, gender and disability. The gender gap in mobility is the outcome of socioeconomic differences, as access to individual transportation is predominantly a matter of income. Within households, differences in role and income are related to the respective activity range and mobility of its members. Consequently, in some instances modal choice is more a **modal constraint linked to economic opportunities**.

Central locations generally have the most urban mobility options because private and public transport facilities are present. However, this does not mean that mobility is easier, since central areas are congested. In locations outside the central core, a share of the population not having access to the automobile faces a level of isolation, or at least a more limited access to amenities and employment opportunities. Limited public transit and high automobile ownership costs have created a class of spatially constrained (mobility deprived) people.

Urban transit

Transit is almost exclusively an urban transportation mode, particularly in large urban agglomerations. The urban environment is particularly suitable for transit because it provides conditions fundamental to its efficiency, namely **high-density** and significant **short-distance mobility demands**. Since transit is a **shared service**, it potentially benefits from economies of agglomeration related to high densities and from economies of scale related to high-mobility demands. One key advantage of public transit is, the higher the demand, the more effectively public transit services can be offered. Lower densities are linked with lower demand and a greater likelihood of public transit systems operating at a loss and requiring subsidies. In fact, most public transit systems are not financially sound and have to be subsidized. Transit systems are made up of many types of services, each suitable to a specific set of market and spatial context. Different modes are used to provide complementarity services within the transit system and in some cases between the transit system and other transport systems.

- **Bus transit**. One of the most common forms of urban transit that includes vehicles of various sizes (from small vans to articulated buses) offering seating and standing capacity along scheduled routes and services. They usually share roadways with other modes and are therefore susceptible to congestion. Bus rapid transit systems offer permanent or temporary rights of way and have the advantage of unencumbered circulation.
- **Rail transit**. Vehicles with fixed guideways that usually have their own right of way. Light rail systems are composed of streetcars that can share rights of way,

particularly in central areas. Heavy rail systems are commonly called subways or metro, since many operate underground (Figure 7.12). Another type of rail transit concerns commuter rail systems that usually service central business districts and peripheral areas along specific corridors.

- **Taxi systems**. Usually private for hire vehicles such as automobiles, jitneys or rickshaws to offer point-to-point services. Recent technological developments have enabled car sharing services and expanded the availability of on-demand transit.
- **Alternative transit**. Refer to transit systems that were developed to cope with specific conditions (or niche markets) using alternative modes. Ferries are the most common form of alternative transit as they service cities that have waterways separating different urban districts. Funiculars are also prevalent in locations that have a steep incline and enough traffic to justify their construction. Aerial lifts are also used in some settings to connect locations difficult to access.

There are approximately 200 subway (metro) systems in operation around the world, with several carrying more than 1 billion passengers per year (Figure 7.12). The construction and setting of subway systems has accelerated in recent years, particularly in cities in developing economies where mass transit becomes a clear strategy to improve urban mobility and mitigate congestion. The level of ridership is linked with several geographical and economic considerations. Some cities with high ridership, such as Moscow, Beijing and Shanghai, have a tradition of subsidized public transportation and transit-oriented urban planning. Many high-density cities have a level of subway ridership proportional to their population (London, Hong Kong, Osaka, Paris, Seoul and

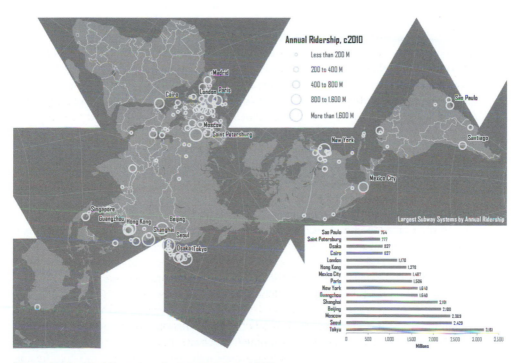

Figure 7.12 World's main subway systems, c. 2010

Source: Adapted from Metrobits.org, World Metro Database.

Tokyo), indicating a consistent level of ridership where public transit accounts for between 25 and 50 percent of commuting. Cities where ridership is proportionally less than the population either have a significant portion of their population who are too poor to afford subway (São Paulo and Mexico) or who are wealthy enough to prefer the automobile (New York).

Contemporary transit systems tend to be **publicly owned**, suggesting that many decisions related to their development and operation are politically motivated. This is in sharp contrast to what took place in the past, as most transit systems were private and profit-driven initiatives. With the fast diffusion of the automobile in the 1950s, many transit companies faced financial difficulties, and the quality of their service declined; in a declining market there were limited incentives to invest. Gradually, they were purchased by public interests and incorporated into large agencies, mainly to continue providing mobility. As such, public transit often serves more a social function, of public service and a tool of social equity, than having an economic role. Transit has become dependent on government subsidies, with little if any competition permitted as wages and fares are regulated. As a result, they tend to be disconnected from market forces and subsidies are constantly required to keep a level of service. With suburbanization transit systems tend to have even fewer relationships with economic activities.

Government-owned public transit systems are facing financial difficulties for three main reasons. The first is that they are often designed to service taxpayers, not necessarily potential customers. Because of the funding base, transit systems may be spread into neighborhoods that do not provide a significant customer base. The second is that transit unions were able to extract significant advantages in terms of wages and social benefits, increasing labor costs. The third concerns a technology fixation which pushes investment in high-cost transit (e.g. light rail), while low-cost solutions (buses) would have been sufficient to many transit systems, particularly in lower density areas.

Reliance on urban transit as a mode of urban transportation tends to be high in Asia, intermediate in Europe and low in North America. Since their inception in the early nineteenth century, comprehensive urban transit systems had significant impacts on the urban form and spatial structure, but this influence is receding. Three major classes of cities can be found in terms of the relationships they have with their transit systems (Figure 7.13):

- **Adaptive cities**. Represent true transit-oriented cities where urban form and urban land use developments are coordinated with transit developments. While central areas are adequately serviced by a metro system and are pedestrian-friendly, peripheral areas are oriented along transit rail lines.
- **Adaptive transit**. Represent cities where transit plays a marginal and residual role and where the automobile accounts for the dominant share of movements. The urban form is decentralized and of low density.
- **Hybrids**. Represent cities that have sought a balance between transit development and automobile dependency. While central areas have an adequate level of service, peripheral areas are automobile-oriented.

Contemporary **land development tends to precede the introduction of urban transit services**, as opposed to concomitant developments in earlier phases of urban growth. Thus, new services are established once a demand is deemed to be sufficient, often after being the subject of public pressures. Transit authorities operate under a service warrant and often run a recurring deficit, as services are becoming more

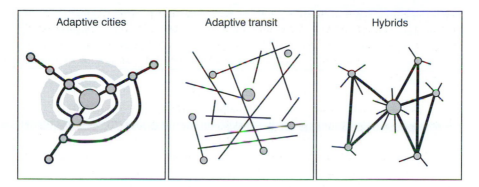

Figure 7.13 Transit and urban form

Source: Adapted from R. Cervero (1998) *The Transit Metropolis*. Washington, DC: Island Press.

expensive to provide. This has led to a set of considerations aimed at a higher integration of transit in the urban planning process, especially in North America, where such a tradition is not well established. Still, in spite of decades of investment, North American public transit ridership has remained roughly the same throughout the 1980s and 1990s, but has increased since then, leading to expectations that they may become more profitable.

From a transportation perspective, the potential benefits of a better **integration between transit and local land uses** are reduced trip frequency and increased use of alternative modes of travel (i.e. walking, biking and transit). Evidence is often lacking to support such expectations, since the relative share of public transit ridership is declining across the board. Community design can consequently have a significant influence on travel patterns. Local land use impacts can be categorized in three dimensions of relationships and are influenced by levels of use. Land use initiatives should be coordinated with other planning and policy initiatives to cope with automobile dependence. However, there is a strong bias against transit in the general population because of negative perceptions, especially in North America, but increasingly globally. As personal mobility is a symbol of status and economic success, the users of public transit are perceived as the least successful segment of the population. This bias may undermine the image of transit use within the general population.

Concept 4 – Urban transport problems

Challenges facing urban transportation

Cities are locations that have a high level of accumulation and concentration of economic activities and are complex spatial structures that are supported by transport systems. The larger the city, the greater its complexity and the potential for disruptions, particularly when this complexity is not effectively managed. The most important transport problems are often related to urban areas and take place when transport systems, for a variety of reasons, cannot satisfy the numerous requirements of urban mobility. Urban productivity is highly dependent on the efficiency of its transport system to move labor, consumers and freight between multiple origins and destinations. Additionally, important transport terminals such as ports, airports and railyards are located within urban areas, contributing to a specific array of problems. Some problems are ancient, like congestion (which plagued cities such as Rome), while others are new, like urban freight distribution or environmental impacts. Among the most notable urban transport problems are:

- **Traffic congestion and parking difficulties**. Congestion is one of the most prevalent transport problems in large urban agglomerations, usually above a threshold of about 1 million inhabitants. It is particularly linked with motorization and the diffusion of the automobile, which has increased the demand for transport infrastructures. However, the supply of infrastructures has often not been able to keep up with the growth of mobility. Since vehicles spend the majority of the time parked, motorization has expanded the demand for parking space, which has created space consumption problems particularly in central areas; the spatial imprint of parked vehicles is significant. Congestion and parking are also interrelated, since looking for a parking space (called "cruising") creates additional delays and impairs local circulation. In central areas of large cities cruising may account for more than 10 percent of the local circulation, as drivers can spend 20 minutes looking for a parking spot. This practice is often judged more economically effective than using a paying off-street parking facility, as the time spent looking for a free (or low cost) parking space is compensated by the monetary savings. Also, many delivery vehicles will simply double-park at the closest possible spot to unload their cargo.
- **Longer commuting**. On par with congestion people are spending an increasing amount of time commuting between their residence and workplace. An important factor behind this trend is related to residential affordability, as housing located further away from central areas (where most of the employment remains) is more affordable. Therefore, commuters are trading time for housing affordability. However, long commuting is linked with several social problems, such as isolation, as well as poorer health (obesity).
- **Public transport inadequacy**. Many public transit systems, or parts of them, are either over- or underused. During peak hours, crowdedness creates discomfort for users as the system copes with a temporary surge in demand. Low ridership makes many services financially unsustainable, particularly in suburban areas. In spite of significant subsidies and cross-financing (e.g. tolls), almost every public transit system cannot generate sufficient income to cover its operating and capital costs. While in the past deficits were deemed acceptable because of the essential service that public transit was providing for urban mobility, its financial burden is increasingly controversial.
- **Difficulties for non-motorized transport**. These difficulties are either the outcome of intense traffic, where the mobility of pedestrians, bicycles and vehicles is impaired, but also because of a blatant lack of consideration for pedestrians and bicycles in the physical design of infrastructures and facilities.
- **Loss of public space**. The majority of roads are publicly owned and free of access. Increased traffic has adverse impacts on public activities that once crowded the streets, such as markets, agoras, parades and processions, games and community interactions. These have gradually disappeared, to be replaced by automobiles. In many cases, these activities have shifted to shopping malls, while in other cases they have been abandoned altogether. Traffic flows influence the life and interactions of residents and their usage of street space. More traffic impedes social interactions and street activities. People tend to walk and cycle less when traffic is high.

- **High maintenance costs**. Cities with an aging transport infrastructure are facing growing maintenance costs as well as pressures to upgrade to more modern infrastructure. In addition to the involved costs, maintenance and repair activities create circulation disruptions. Delayed maintenance is rather common, since it conveys the benefit of keeping current costs low, but at the expense of higher future costs and on some occasion the risk of infrastructure failure. The more extensive the road and highway network, the higher the maintenance cost and the financial burden.
- **Environmental impacts and energy consumption**. Pollution, including noise, generated by circulation has become a serious impediment to the quality of life and even the health of urban populations. Further, energy consumption by urban transportation has dramatically increased and so also has the dependency on petroleum. Yet, peak oil considerations are increasingly linked with peak mobility expectations, with higher energy prices inciting a shift towards more efficient and sustainable forms of urban transportation, namely public transit.
- **Accidents and safety**. Growing traffic in urban areas is linked with a growing number of accidents and fatalities, especially in developing countries. Accidents account for a significant share of recurring delays. As traffic increases, people feel less safe to use the streets.
- **Land consumption**. The territorial imprint of transportation is significant, particularly for the automobile. Between 30 and 60 percent of a metropolitan area may be devoted to transportation, an outcome of the over-reliance on some forms of urban transportation. Yet, this land consumption also underlines the strategic importance of transportation in the economic and social welfare of cities.
- **Freight distribution**. Globalization and the materialization of the economy have resulted in growing quantities of freight moving within cities. As freight traffic commonly shares infrastructures with the circulation of passengers, the mobility of freight in urban areas has become increasingly problematic. City logistics strategies can be established to mitigate the variety of challenges faced by urban freight distribution.

Many dimensions to the urban transport challenge are linked with the **dominance of the automobile**.

Automobile dependency

Automobile use is obviously related to a variety of **advantages** such as on-demand mobility, comfort, status, speed, and convenience. These advantages jointly illustrate why automobile ownership continues to grow worldwide, especially in urban areas. When given the choice and the opportunity, most individuals will prefer using an automobile. Several factors influence the growth of the total vehicle fleet, such as sustained economic growth (increase in income and quality of life), complex individual urban movement patterns (many households have more than one automobile), more leisure time and suburbanization. Therefore, rising automobile mobility can be perceived as a positive consequence of economic development. The acute growth in the total number of vehicles also gives rise to congestion at peak traffic hours on major thoroughfares, in business districts and often throughout the metropolitan area.

Cities are important generators and attractors of movements, which have created a set of geographical paradoxes that are self-reinforcing. For instance, specialization leads to additional transport demands, while agglomeration leads to congestion. Over time, a state of automobile dependency has emerged which results in a diminution in the role of other modes, thereby limiting still further alternatives to urban mobility. In addition to the factors contributing to the growth of driving, two major factors that contribute to automobile dependency are:

- **Underpricing and consumer choices**. Most road infrastructures are subsidized, as they are considered a public service. Consequently, drivers do not bear the full cost of automobile use. Like the "Tragedy of the Commons," when a resource is free of access (road), it tends to be overused and abused (congestion). This is also reflected in consumer choice, where automobile ownership is a symbol of status, freedom and prestige, especially in developing countries. Single home ownership also reinforces automobile dependency.
- **Planning and investment practices**. Planning and the ensuing allocation of public funds aim towards improving road and parking facilities in an ongoing attempt to avoid congestion. Other transportation alternatives tend to be disregarded. In many cases, zoning regulations impose minimum standards of road and parking services and de facto impose a regulated automobile dependency.

Among the most relevant indicators of automobile dependency are the level of vehicle ownership, per capita motor vehicle mileage and the proportion of total commuting trips made using an automobile. A situation of high automobile dependency is reached when more than three-quarters of commuting trips are done using the automobile. For the United States, this proportion has remained at around 88 percent over the recent decades. Automobile dependency is also served by a cultural and commercial system promoting the automobile as a symbol of status and personal freedom, namely through intense advertising and enticements to purchase new automobiles. Not surprisingly, many developing countries perceive motorization as a condition for development. Even if the term "automobile dependency" is often negatively perceived and favored by market distortions such as the provision of roads, its outcome reflects the choice of individuals who see the automobile more as an advantage than an inconvenience.

There is a growing body of evidence underlining that a **peak level of car mobility** is unfolding, at least in developed countries. Higher energy prices, congestion, fewer economic prospects and the general aging of the population are all countervailing forces to car dependency. For instance, since 2006 the number of vehicle-miles traveled in the United States has peaked, a process associated with higher energy prices and an economic recession. There are many alternatives to automobile dependency, such as intermodality (combining the advantages of individual and collective transport), carpooling (strengthened by policy and regulation by the US government) or non-motorized transportation (walking and cycling). These alternatives can only be partially implemented, as the automobile remains, in the short and medium term, the prime choice for providing urban mobility.

Congestion

Congestion occurs when **transport demand exceeds transport supply** at a specific point in time and in a specific section of the transport system. Under such circumstances, each vehicle impairs the mobility of others. Congestion can be perceived as an unavoidable consequence of the usage of scarce transport resources, particularly if they are not priced. The last decades have seen the extension of roads in urban areas, most of them free of access. Those infrastructures were designed for speed and high capacity, but the growth of urban circulation occurred at a rate higher than often expected. Investments came from diverse levels of government with a view to provide accessibility to cities and regions. There were strong incentives for the expansion of road transportation by providing high levels of transport supply. This has created a vicious circle of congestion which supports the construction of additional road capacity and automobile dependency. Urban congestion mainly concerns two domains of circulation, often sharing the same infrastructures:

- **Passengers**. In many regions of the world incomes have significantly increased; one automobile or more per household is becoming common. Access to an automobile conveys flexibility in terms of the choice of origin, destination and travel time. The automobile is favored at the expense of other modes for most trips, including commuting. For instance, automobiles account for the bulk of commuting trips in the United States. The majority of automobile-related congestion is the outcome of time preferences in the usage of vehicles (during commuting hours) as well as a substantial amount of space required to park vehicles. About 95 percent of the time an automobile is idle.
- **Freight**. Several industries have shifted their transport needs to trucking, thereby increasing the usage of road infrastructure. Since cities are the main destinations for freight flows (either for consumption or for transfer to other locations), trucking adds to further congestion in urban areas. The "last mile" problem remains particularly prevalent for freight distribution in urban areas. Congestion is commonly linked with a drop in the frequency of deliveries tying additional capacity to ensure a similar level of service.

It is important to underline that congestion in urban areas is predominantly caused by **commuting patterns** and little by truck movements. On average, infrastructure provision was not able to keep up with the growth in the number of vehicles, even more with the total number of vehicle-km. During infrastructure improvement and construction, capacity impairment (fewer available lanes, closed sections, etc.) favors congestion. Important travel delays occur when the capacity limit is reached or exceeded, which is the case in almost all metropolitan areas. In the largest cities, such as London, road traffic is actually slower than it was 100 years ago. Marginal delays are thus increasing and driving speed becomes problematic as the level of population density increases. Once a population threshold of about 1 million is reached, cities start to experience recurring congestion problems. This observation must be nuanced by numerous factors related to the urban setting, modal preferences and the quality of existing urban transport infrastructures.

Another important consideration concerns parking, which consumes large amounts of space and provides limited economic benefit. In automobile-dependent cities, this can be very constraining, as each land use has to provide an amount of parking space proportional to their level of activity. Parking has become a land use that greatly inflates the demand for urban land (Photo 7.3).

Urban mobility also reveals congestion patterns. Daily trips can be either "mandatory" (workplace–home) or "voluntary" (shopping, leisure, visits). The former is often performed within fixed schedules, while the latter complies with variable and discretionary schedules. Correspondingly, congestion comes in two major forms:

- **Recurrent congestion**. The consequence of factors that cause regular demand surges on the transportation system, such as commuting, shopping or weekend trips. However, even recurrent congestion can have unforeseen impacts in terms of its duration and severity. Mandatory trips are mainly responsible for the peaks in circulation flows, suggesting that about half the congestion in urban areas is recurring at specific times of the day and in specific segments of the transport system.
- **Non-recurrent congestion**. The other half of congestion is caused by random events such as accidents and unusual weather conditions (rain, snowstorms, etc.), which are unexpected and unplanned. Non-recurrent congestion is linked to the presence and effectiveness of incident response strategies. As far as accidents are concerned, their randomness is influenced by the level of traffic, as the higher the traffic on specific road segments, the higher the probability of accidents.

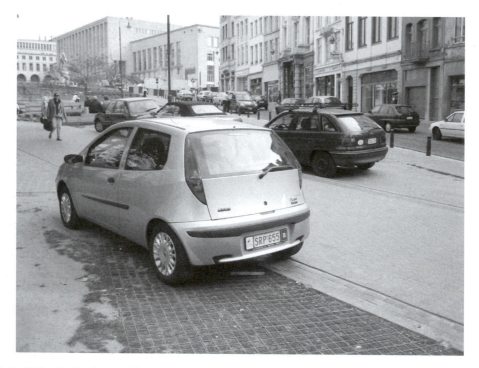

Photo 7.3 Parking in a public park, Brussels

Many cities are facing acute difficulties providing parking space, especially in central areas. This problem is also prevalent in Western Europe. In North American cities, suburbanization has often resulted in the abandonment of buildings in central areas. Many of these facilities have been torn down and converted into parking space (either as a vacant lot or as a dedicated multistoried facility), while awaiting a better use. This process did not much take place in Western Europe, where the real estate of most central areas has remained relatively unchanged and includes real estate of historical and architectural significance. To provide parking space, many European cities have been forced to build underground facilities that are expensive and rarely able to provide for the demand. This photo was taken in downtown Brussels, where motorists desperate for parking space have parked their vehicles along a walkway in a public space, which has been severely degraded.

Behavioral and response time effects are also important as, in a system running close to capacity, simply braking suddenly may trigger what can be known as a **backward traveling wave**. It implies that, as vehicles are forced to stop, the bottleneck moves up the location in which it initially took place, often leaving drivers puzzled about its cause. The spatial convergence of traffic causes a surcharge on transport infrastructures up to the point where congestion can lead to the total immobilization of traffic. Not only does the massive use of the automobile have an impact on traffic circulation and congestion, but it also leads to the **decline in public transit efficiency** when both are sharing the same roads.

The urban transit challenge

As cities continue to become more dispersed, the **cost of building and operating public transportation systems increases**. For instance, as of 2015 about 201 urban agglomerations had a subway system, the great majority of them being in developed countries. Furthermore, dispersed residential patterns characteristic of automobile-dependent cities makes public transportation systems less convenient to support urban mobility. In many cities additional investments in public transit did not result in significant additional ridership. Unplanned and uncoordinated land development has led to rapid expansion of the urban periphery. Residents, by selecting housing in outlying areas, restrict their potential access to public transportation. Overinvestment (when investments do not appear to imply significant benefits) and underinvestment (when there is a substantial unmet demand) in public transit are both complex challenges.

Urban transit is often perceived as the most efficient transportation mode for urban areas, notably large cities. However, surveys reveal a stagnation of public transit systems, especially in North America. The economic relevance of public transit is being questioned. Most urban transit developments had **little, if any, impacts to alleviate congestion** in spite of mounting costs and heavy subsidies. This **paradox** is partially explained by the spatial structure of contemporary cities that are oriented along servicing the needs of the individual, not necessarily the needs of the collectivity. Thus, the automobile remains the preferred mode of urban transportation. In addition, public transit is publicly owned, suggesting that it is a politically motivated service that provides **limited economic returns**. Even in transit-oriented cities, transit systems depend massively on government subsidies. Little or no competition is permitted, as wages and fares are regulated, undermining any price adjustments to changes in ridership. Thus, public transit often serves the purpose of a social function ("public service"), as it provides accessibility and social equity, but with limited relationships with economic activities. Among the most difficult challenges facing urban transit are:

- **Decentralization**. Public transit systems are not designed to service low density and scattered urban areas that are increasingly dominating the landscape. The greater the decentralization of urban activities, the more difficult and expensive it becomes to serve urban areas with public transit. Additionally, decentralization promotes long-distance trips on transit systems, causing higher operating costs and revenue issues for flat fare transit systems.
- **Fixity**. The infrastructures of several public transit systems, notably rail and subway systems, are fixed, while cities are dynamical entities, even if the pace of change

can take decades. This implies that travel patterns tend to change and that a transit system built for servicing a specific pattern may eventually face "spatial obsolescence."

- **Connectivity**. Public transit systems are often independent from other modes and terminals. It is consequently difficult to transfer passengers from one system to the other. This leads to a paradox between the preference of riders to have direct connections and the need to provide a cost-efficient service network that involves transfers.
- **Automobile competition**. In view of cheap and ubiquitous road transport systems, public transit faced strong competition and loss of ridership in relative terms and in some cases in absolute terms. The higher the level of automobile dependency, the more inappropriate the public transit level of service. The public service being offered is simply outpaced by the convenience of the automobile.
- **Financing and fare structures**. Historically, most public transit systems have abandoned a distance-based fare structure for a simpler flat fare system. This had the unintended consequence of discouraging short trips, for which most transit systems are well suited, and encouraging longer trips that tend to be costlier per user than the fares they generate. Information systems offer the possibility for transit systems to move back to a more equitable distance-based fare structure, particularly with the usage of smartcards that facilitate charging according to the point of entry and exit within the public transit system.
- **Legacy costs**. Most public transit systems employ unionized labor that has consistently used strikes (or the threat of a strike), and the acute disruptions they create, as leverage to negotiate favorable contracts, including health and retirement benefits. Since public transit is subsidized these costs were not well reflected in the fare systems. In many transit systems, additional subsidies went into compensation or to cover past debt, not necessarily into performance improvements or additional infrastructure. As most governments are facing stringent budgetary constraints because of social welfare commitments, public transit agencies are being forced to reassess their budgets through an unpopular mix of higher fares, deferred maintenance and the breaking of labor contracts.
- **Self-driving vehicles**. Development in information technologies let us anticipate the availability of self-driving vehicles in the coming years. Such a development would entail point-to-point services by on-demand vehicles and a much better utilization level of such assets. This system could compete directly with transit systems due to its convenience, comfort and likely affordability.

Public transit systems are therefore challenged to **remain relevant to urban mobility** or to **increase its market share**. The rise in petroleum prices since 2006 has increased the cost of vehicle ownership and operation, but it still remains affordable. A younger generation perceives the automobile as a less attractive proposition than prior generations and is more willing to use public transit and live in higher-density areas. Electronic fare systems also makes the utilization of public transit more convenient. A recent trend concerns the usage of incentives, such as point systems (e.g. air miles with purchase of a monthly pass) to further promote the use of public transit and to influence consumer behavior. Yet, evidence underlines that the inflation-adjusted cost of using public transit is increasing, implying that the cost advantage of public transit over the automobile is not changing in a significant way.

CASE STUDY   City logistics

Authors: Dr Jean-Paul Rodrigue and Dr Laetitia Dablanc

Freight and the city

Freight transportation maintains a set of core relations with urban areas, since a city is an entity where production, distribution and consumption activities are using and competing for scarce land (Figure 7.14). Elements of the urban landscape such as commercial districts are important **generators and attractors of freight movements**. Further, freight distribution often shares the same road infrastructure as many passenger transport modes, with their activity patterns corresponding to periods of peaks and troughs. The global urban and economic system has also become functionally specialized, permitting a global division of production and its associated freight volumes. Urban freight concerns the transportation of goods by or for commercial entities taking place in an urban area. City logistics, as a strategy ensuring efficient freight movements and innovative responses to urban customer and business demands, is an emerging field of investigation that was created by the challenges of the commodification and massification of production and consumption.

The functions of consumption, production and distribution are associated with various types of material flows, each representing a form of city logistics. For instance, retailing relies on urban deliveries originating from distribution centers, which themselves are likely to have been supplied through terminal haulage. The intensity level of urban freight distribution is usually clustered around large specialized generators, which come in four major types:

- **Terminals**, such as ports, airports and railyards, are highly localized entities with access points often supporting high traffic levels. Since terminals handle a wide variety of freight, it can be expected that it will enter urban areas as bulk, containers, full truckloads (TLs) and less than truckloads (LTLs). The market area of transport terminals is defined as the hinterland, which can involve destinations (logistics zones and manufacturing districts) within the city itself or flows having to transit through urban areas on their way to other destinations. The impact of a transport terminal on city logistics is obviously related to the intensity of the terminal activity, the supply chain it services and the extent of its hinterland.
- **Logistics zones** include warehouses, sometimes associated with clustered distribution and light manufacturing activities. Higher consumption levels and global supply chains have been a driving force in the setting and expansion of logistics zones. Co-location with a terminal facility has been a driving force, implying more efficient interactions because of proximity; freight has less propensity to enter urban areas. High land prices near terminals and central areas have also prompted the development of greenfield logistics zones in peripheral areas, sometimes far away.
- **Manufacturing districts**. In the contemporary setting many production activities are related to global processes and elements of global value chains since they may produce finished goods, but more likely intermediate goods (e.g. parts). They are generators of producer-related urban freight movement involving all possible forms of road transport. Manufacturing districts are commonly found in association with transport terminals, particularly for heavy industry. Still, manufacturing and logistics activities are often mixed, as pure manufacturing or logistics areas are rare; standard

Figure 7.14 City functions and urban distribution

manufacturing activities are common in logistics areas. The distinction between a logistics and a manufacturing zone can therefore on occasion be blurred. For instance, many logistics zones were developed as industrial zones that attracted distribution centers instead.

● **Commercial districts**. Core component of the urban centrality and the destination of the bulk of urban passenger flows. They concern consumer-related freight movements, mostly through retail activities usually supplied through LTLs (e.g. delivery vans and trucks). The clustering of office towers and large institutions (seats of government, universities, museums, etc.) is also a large generator of freight demand such as parcels. Some central business districts also involve adjacent freight-intensive activities such as railyards and even port terminals, particularly in older cities or in cities having an important gateway function. As cities are increasingly polycentric, several commercial districts such as urban subcenters have emerged.

Store inventory levels have shrunk and businesses are increasingly supplied on a **just-in-time basis**. The number of different products sold has increased considerably, and inventories change several times a year. With the rise of the service economy, the demand for express transport and courier services is also soaring. These factors have made urban economies more dependent on transportation systems, with more frequent and customized deliveries. All this brings a greater intensity and frequency of urban freight distribution and correspondingly improved forms, organization and management. Accurate figures are difficult to come by but urban goods movements account for 20 to 30 percent of all vehicle-km. There is a complex relationship between the spatial and functional structure of city logistics, where the organization and density of land uses interact with various forms of transport infrastructure influences on the location of logistics activities.

Therefore, although city logistics appears to be an issue taking place at the local (metropolitan) level, a comprehensive understanding of its drivers and dynamics requires the following:

- **Global supply chains**. A salient issue relates to urban freight distribution in the context of global supply chains, as global processes are imposing local forms of adaptation to ensure that freight is delivered in a timely and reliable fashion. Offshoring has also contributed to the setting of supply chains where freight distribution activities taking place within an urban area cannot be effectively explained by the regional economic structure.
- **Global freight distribution**. Since the distances involved in supporting global supply chains have increased, the function of distribution has taken on a new significance, particularly with the setting of large terminal facilities such as ports, airports, railyards and distribution centers. They are handling movements originating from, bound to or simply passing through a metropolitan area. With containerization as a tool supporting the bulk of international trade, intermodal terminals have become a notable element of the urban landscape. With the growth of valuable cargo carried over long distances, airports are also active nodes interacting with urban freight distribution. Along with their attached freight distribution facilities (e.g. transloading facilities and warehouses), large terminals form a fundamental element of the interface between global distribution and city logistics.
- **Urbanization**. Global urbanization is compounding the challenges of city logistics. since the share and the level of concentration of the global population living in cities is increasing. Historically, the production and consumption of freight has predominantly taken place in cities, but with the Industrial Revolution and then globalization, this share has increased. Cities also present a variety of forms and levels of density, each associated with specific city logistics patterns. Socioeconomic factors, such as rising income and consumer preferences, should also not be neglected.

Most of the early applications of city logistics were undertaken in Japan and Western Europe as these cities were more constrained by the lack of available land and had an established tradition pertaining to urban planning. Up to the twenty-first century the consideration of urban freight distribution within the planning discipline remained **limited**. This implies that urban planning generally does not pay much attention to issues related to urban freight distribution. Yet these issues are linked with externalities and growing concerns by private and public interests to address them:

- **Private concerns**. Actors directly involved in urban freight distribution are mainly concerned with its constraints, such as congestion, since it imposes additional costs and delays in their operations. Also, restrictions on street access by trucks, as well as for pickups and deliveries, provide additional challenges. Urban logistics becomes a competitive factor that needs to be addressed, since it impairs the cost and efficiency of the "last (or first) mile" of global supply chains.
- **Public concerns**. Actors involved in the oversight of urban freight distribution, as well as urban residents in general, are concerned by its externalities. Congestion and noise impacts residents, particularly their commuting and social interactions, as well as the general livability of a city. Passengers and freight flows are therefore subject to conflicts. Environmental concerns such as air pollution are recurrent in many cities. City logistics is becoming a salient urban sustainability issue.

The diversity of urban freight distribution

A city is supplied by an impressive variety of supply chains servicing a wide array of economic activities such as grocery stores, retail, restaurants, office supplies, raw materials and parts, construction materials and wastes. Each of these activities is associated with a specific **freight profile** – the freight that it attracts, consumes and generates. The level of economic development is linked with the level of urban freight activity, as income and consumption levels are interdependent. Because of the divergence in built environments and the diversity of urban economic activities, each city around the world has different freight transport and logistics activities and level of intensity. This rasies the question about the specific size threshold after which urban freight distribution problems, such as delays and congestion, become more prevalent, which requires a concerted approach. Using the United States as evidence, congestion starts to be a serious issue once a threshold of about 1 million inhabitants is reached. For cities of less than 1 million, city logistics is less likely to be a problem and may be localized to specific areas, such as the downtown or the port or other terminal areas.

The unique and often non-replicable conditions of each city influence the nature and intensity of congestion in its urban freight distribution system. The share of public transit use, land use pattern and density and income levels are common factors relatively unique to each city. Considering the growing level of material intensiveness related to the functions of production, distribution and consumption, cities above 4 million inhabitants should have planning and circulation management schemes where urban freight distribution is preeminent. Cities of smaller size can also proactively be involved in mitigating specific and localized urban freight distribution activities.

The intensity of urban freight distribution depends on local economic, geographic and cultural characteristics, which leads to different objectives and preoccupations in urban freight distribution. For instance, each world city has a diverse array of concerns:

- **Paris** aims to limit the environmental footprint of freight distribution so that the quality of life of its residents can be maintained and improved. The city's status as one of the world's leading cultural and touristic hubs has a notable impact on the strategies and priorities accorded to urban freight distribution to support the city's image.
- **Mexico** tries to cope with the contradictory demands related to the dual presence of both modern (motorized) and traditional forms of urban distribution in terms of infrastructure provision and regulations. Modern logistics services are as vital to the urban economies of developing countries as the more basic freight activities serving street vendors or home-based manufacturing workshops.
- **Chicago** aims at maintaining its role as a major rail hub and freight distribution platform for North America with concentration on distribution and manufacturing activities. The metropolitan area is the point of convergence of the rail lines of the Class I carriers, but the different terminal facilities are in separate parts of the city and not well connected. This involves truck congestion, as containers need to be carried from one terminal to the other.
- **Los Angeles** is facing congestion and environmental issues such as noise and air pollution. The city is also facing conflicts between its function as a major commercial gateway for the East Asian trade and other functions linked with touristic and cultural activities. Recent initiatives concern trucking associated with the main port facilities as well as nearby major import-based distribution centers.

- **Shanghai** has become the largest cargo port in the world and acts as the main transport hub supporting China's export-oriented strategies. A significant share of the freight circulating within the city is therefore linked with global distribution processes. Rising standards of living imply growing consumption levels and the setting of city logistics challenges common in advanced economies.
- **Istanbul** is coping with rapid urbanization and economic growth, along with unique geographical constraints, namely a scarcity of flat land and the division of the city by the Strait of Bosphorus. Its commercial function is being strengthened by its role as a platform between Middle Eastern, European and Black Sea commercial interactions. The outcome has been severe constraints for freight circulation in an environment of accelerated economic and urban growth. The city is embarking in large infrastructure projects, with a new mega airport and the relocation of manufacturing activities to exurban locations.

Forms of urban freight distribution

All urban freight distribution systems involve a wide array of supply chains, each of varying importance depending on the urban setting and the level of development, but coming into two main functional classes and associated with specific freight flows. The first involves what can be called **consumer-related distribution**:

- **Independent retailing**. Urban areas have a notable variety of retailing activities, many of which define the commercial and social character of neighborhoods. More than often they are small single owner stores and, in developing countries, these retailing activities are often complemented by informal street markets and stalls. This form of retailing usually relies on a variety of suppliers that tend to rely on their own account delivery vehicles.
- **Chain retailing**. In the contemporary commercial landscape chain retailing (stores directly affiliated to a common brand or franchised from this brand) have become an important element. Like independent retailing, chain retailing covers an extensive array of goods that are supplied by manufacturers that have extensively relied on global sourcing. Chain retail outlets are located in central areas (and are a defining element of urban centrality), as well as in suburban and periurban areas (such as "big-box" stores). Shopping malls, many quite large, are set on the principle of economies of agglomeration and the provision of ample parking space. Chain retailing tends to rely on the expertise of third-party logistics service providers to mitigate urban freight distribution challenges, but mostly to organize complex multinational sourcing strategies for mass retailers. Large stores are commonly accessed through dedicated delivery bays, where they are resupplied on a daily basis through their own regional warehousing facilities.
- **Food deliveries**. Since most food products are perishable, a specialized form of urban distribution has been set to supply outlets such as grocery stores and restaurants. A large grocery store can receive 15 to 30 deliveries per day from different suppliers. The outdoor market (central markets offer enclosed facilities) also takes an important role in supplying urban populations with perishables, particularly in developing countries. This may be linked with informal forms of distribution where food producers deliver their production to urban markets. Limited information is available

about urban food consumption levels, but high levels of spoilage are observed, in the range of 50 percent of all the food consumed. Since food deliveries commonly involve perishable goods, the reliable transport of refrigerated goods (often referred to as cold chain logistics) is an important component in improving this relatively poor performance.

- **Parcel and home deliveries**. Globalization and the setting of advanced services such as insurance, finance or corporate management (head or regional offices) are linked with a growth in the movement of parcels. While some are serviced by local companies, large parcel carriers have established services covering the majority of the world's main commercial cities. They maintain a network of strategically located distribution centers where shipments are consolidated or deconsolidated. International shipments are often taken care of by parent companies, namely air freight integrators. Online shopping (for retail goods, but also for groceries) has grown significantly, a trend which is associated with the growth of home deliveries.

The second functional class of city logistics is related to **producer-related distribution**:

- **Construction sites**. Urban infrastructures, from roads, residences to office and retail spaces, are constantly been constructed, renovated and repaired. Such activities are intensive in material use and must be supplied on an irregular basis, both in terms of the time and location of the deliveries.
- **Waste collection and disposal**. Urban activities generate large quantities of waste, namely paper, paperboard, food, plastics, metals and glass. These materials must be collected and carried to recycling or disposal sites. In particular, recycling has become an important activity that takes place in urban areas and involves specialized vehicles and dedicated pickup tours. As standards of living are increasing across the world, the amount of waste generated by cities has grown accordingly.
- **Industrial and terminal haulage**. Cities are zones of production as well as gateways for the circulation of goods. Large transportation terminals such as ports, airports and railyards are dominant elements of the urban landscape, including logistics zones where freight is distributed to extensive markets. Transport terminals and logistics zones are also generators of goods movements that may impact urban circulation ("the last mile"). Gate access at large intermodal terminals such as ports can lead to congestion (queuing) and local disruptions.

Two actors, private and common carriers, hande commercial freight transportation. **Private carriers** are at the same time beneficial cargo owners (manufacturers or retailers) using their own transportation assets (fleet and workforce). They can also subcontract this function to an independent carrier. **Common carriers** service any customer on a contractual basis, which also leads to the opportunity to consolidate cargo and deliveries. The share of private carriers is dominant for urban freight distribution in developing countries, while in developed countries common carriers account for about half of urban deliveries.

Bibliography

Batty, M. and Y. Xie (1994) "From cells to cities." *Environment and Planning* B, 21: 531–548.

Browne, M., J. Allen, A. Woodburn and M. Piotrowska (2007) *Urban Freight Transport – Literature Review*, London: Transport Studies Group, University of Westminster.

Camagni, R., M.C. Gibelli and P. Rigamonti (2002) "Urban mobility and urban form: the social and environmental costs of different patterns of urban expansion." *Ecological Economics* 40: 199–216.

Carter, H. (1995) *The Study of Urban Geography*, 4th edition. London: Arnold.

Cervero, R. (1998) *The Transit Metropolis: A Global Inquiry*. Washington, DC: Island Press.

Dablanc, L. (2009) *Freight Transport for Development Toolkit – Urban Transport*. Washington, DC: International Bank for Reconstruction and Development/World Bank.

Gwilliam, K. (ed) (2001) *Cities on the Move: A World Bank Urban Transport Strategy Review*, Strategy Paper. Washington, DC: World Bank.

Hanson, S. and G. Giuliano (eds) (2004) *The Geography of Urban Transportation*, 3rd edition. New York: The Guilford Press.

Harris, C. and E. Ullman (1945) "The nature of cities." *Annals of the American Academy of Political Science* 242: 7–17.

Harvey, J. and E. Jowsey (2003) *Urban Land Economics*, 6th edition. Gordonsville: Palgrave Macmillan.

Hesse, M. (2008) *The City as a Terminal: The Urban Context of Logistics and Freight Transport*. Aldershot: Ashgate.

Hoyt, (1939) *The Structure and Growth of Residential Neighborhoods in American Cities*. Washington, DC: Federal Housing Association.

Kaplan, D. and S. Holloway (2014) *Urban Geography*, 3rd edition. New York: Wiley.

Litman, T. (2015) *Evaluating Transportation Land Use Impacts: Considering the Impacts, Benefits and Costs of Different Land Use Development Patterns*. Victoria, BC, Canada: Victoria Transport Policy Institute.

Meyer, M.D. and E.J. Miller (2000) *Urban Transportation Planning: A Decision-Oriented Approach*. New York: McGraw-Hill.

Moore, T. and P. Thorsnes (2007) *The Transportation/Land Use Connection,* Report 448/449. Washington, DC: American Planning Association.

Rodrigue, J.-P. (2013) "Urban goods transport," in *Planning and Design for Sustainable Urban Mobility: Global Report on Human Settlements 2013*. London: Earthscan/United Nations Human Settlements Programme.

8 Transport, energy and environment

Transportation systems are linked with a wide range of environmental considerations at all geographical scales, from the global to the local. The nature of these environmental impacts is related to the transport modes themselves, their energy supply systems, their emissions and the infrastructures over which they operate. While consuming large quantities of energy, especially oil, vehicles also emit numerous pollutants such as carbon dioxide and nitrogen oxide, as well as noise and transport infrastructures, which have damaged many ecological systems. Several of the environmental impacts of transport systems have been externalized, implying that the benefits of mobility are realized by a few, while the costs are assumed by the whole society. The spatial structure of economic activities, notably their land use, is also increasingly linked with environmental impacts. The sustainability of transport systems has become one core issue in the provision of mobility.

Concept 1 – The environmental impacts of transportation

The issue of transport and the environment

The issue of transportation and the environment is paradoxical in nature since transportation conveys substantial socioeconomic benefits, but at the same time it is impacting environmental systems. From one side, transportation activities support increasing mobility demands for passengers and freight, while on the other, transport activities are associated with growing levels of **environmental externalities**. The growth of personal and freight mobility in recent decades has expanded the role of transportation as a source of emission of pollutants and their multiple impacts on the environment. These impacts fall within three categories:

- **Direct impacts**. The immediate consequence of transport activities on the environment where the cause and effect relationship is generally clear and well understood. For instance, noise and carbon monoxide emissions are known to have direct harmful effects.
- **Indirect impacts**. The secondary (or tertiary) effects of transport activities on environmental systems. They are often of higher consequence than direct impacts, but the relationships involved are often misunderstood and more difficult to establish. For instance, particulates are mostly the outcome of incomplete combustion in an internal combustion engine and are indirectly linked with respiratory and cardiovascular problems, since they contribute among other factors to such conditions.
- **Cumulative impacts**. The additive, multiplicative or synergetic consequences of transport activities. They take into account the varied effects of direct and indirect

impacts on an ecosystem, which are often unpredicted. Climate change, with its complex causes and consequences, is the cumulative impact of several natural and anthropogenic factors, in which transportation plays a role. 15 percent of global CO_2 emissions are attributed to the transport sector.

The complexities of the problems have led to much **controversy** in environmental policy, the role of transportation and mitigation strategies. The transportation sector is often subsidized by the public sector, especially through the construction and maintenance of road infrastructure, which tend to be free of access. Sometimes, public stakes in transport modes, terminals and infrastructure can be at odds with environmental issues. If the owner and the regulator are the same (different branches of the government), then there is a risk that regulations will not be effectively complied with.

Total costs incurred by transportation activities, notably environmental damage, are generally not fully assumed by the users. The lack of consideration of the **real costs of transportation** could explain several environmental problems. Yet, a complex hierarchy of costs is involved, ranging from internal (mostly operations), compliance (abiding to regulations), contingent (risk of an event such as a spill) to external (assumed by the society). For instance, external costs account on average for more than 30 percent of estimated automobile costs. If environmental costs are not included in this appraisal, car use is consequently subsidized by the society and costs accumulate as environmental pollution. This requires due consideration as the number of vehicles, especially automobiles, is steadily increasing.

The transport–environment link

The relationships between transport and the environment are **multidimensional**. Some aspects are unknown and some new findings may lead to drastic changes in environmental policies, as it did with regards to acid rain and chlorofluorocarbons (CFCs) in the 1970s and 1980s. The 1990s were characterized by a realization of **global environmental issues**, epitomized by the growing concerns between anthropogenic effects and climate change. Transportation also became an important dimension of the concept of **sustainability**, which has become a core focus of transport activities, ranging from vehicle emissions to green supply chain management practices. These impending developments require a deep understanding of the reciprocal influence between the physical environment and transport infrastructures, and yet this understanding is often lacking. The main factors considered in the physical environment are geographical location, topography, geological structure, climate, hydrology, soil, natural vegetation and animal life. The environmental dimensions of transportation sequentially involve (Figure 8.1):

- **Causes**. Two major factors contribute to the level of transport activities. Economics refers to the general level of development, income and transport supply. An advanced economy is likely to generate more transportation activities per capita than a developing economy. Land use refers to the spatial structure and location of the transport demand, which indirectly influence travel distance and the modes used to support spatial interactions generated by economic activities.
- **Activities**. Involve a wide array of factors expressing the usage of transportation infrastructures and all the related services to support the transport system, particularly operations. All these activities have environmental outputs.

Figure 8.1 Environmental dimensions of transportation

Source: EPA.

- **Outputs**. The first outcome of transportation activities are emissions of all sorts (carbon monoxide, nitrogen oxides, particulates, etc.). According to the geographical characteristics of the area where emissions are occurring (e.g. wind patterns), ambient pollution levels are created. Once these levels are correlated with population density and levels of activity, a level of exposure to harmful pollutants can be calculated. This exposure is likely to have consequences.
- **End results**. They include all the health, environmental and welfare effects of the exposure to emissions from transportation activities, which are very difficult to measure.

Establishing linkages between environmental dimensions is a difficult undertaking. For instance, to what extent are carbon dioxide emissions linked to land use patterns? Furthermore, transportation is embedded in environmental cycles, notably over the carbon cycle, where carbon flows from one element of the biosphere, like the atmosphere, to another, like the ecosphere, where it can be accumulated (permanently or temporarily) or passed on. The relationships between transport and the environment are also complicated by two observations:

- **Level of contribution**. Transport activities contribute, among other anthropogenic and natural causes, directly, indirectly and cumulatively to environmental problems. In some cases, they may be a dominant factor, while in others their role is marginal and difficult to establish.
- **Scale of impact**. Transport activities contribute at different geographical scales to environmental problems, ranging from local (noise and CO emissions) to global (climate change), not forgetting continental/national/regional problems (smog and acid rain).

Establishing environmental policies for transportation thus has to take into account the level of contribution and the geographical scale; otherwise some policies may just move the problems elsewhere and have unintended consequences. A noted example are environmental policies in advanced economies that prompt the relocation of some activities with high environmental externalities (e.g. steelmaking) in developing economies. This transfers the problem from one location to another. Still, such a transfer usually involves new equipment and technologies that are usually less impactful. Even if an administrative division (municipality, county, state) has adequate environmental enforcement policies, the geographical scale of an environmental impact (notably air pollutants) goes beyond established jurisdictions.

The structure of the **transport network**, the **modes** used and **traffic levels** are the main factors of environmental impact of transportation. Networks influence the spatial distribution of emissions (e.g. centralized versus diffuse networks), while modes relate to the nature of the emissions and the intensity of these emissions. In addition to these environmental impacts, economic and industrial processes sustaining the transport system must be considered. These include the extraction and production of fuels, vehicles and construction materials, some of which are very energy-intensive (e.g. aluminum), and the disposal of vehicles, parts and the provision of infrastructure. They all have a life cycle timing their production, utilization and disposal. Thus, the evaluation of the link between transport and the environment without considering cycles in the environment, and also in the product life, is likely to convey a limited overview of the situation and may even lead to incorrect appraisal, policies and mitigation strategies.

Environmental dimensions

Transportation activities support increasing mobility demands for passengers and freight, notably in urban areas. But transport activities have resulted in growing levels of motorization and congestion. As a result, the transportation sector is becoming increasingly linked to environmental problems. The most prominent concerns **climate change**. The activities of the transport industry release several million tons of gases each year into the atmosphere. These include lead (Pb), carbon monoxide (CO), carbon dioxide (CO_2; not a pollutant), methane (CH_4), nitrogen oxides (NOx), nitrous oxide (N_2O), chlorofluorocarbons (CFCs), perfluorocarbons (PFCs), silicon tetrafluoride (SiF_4), benzene and volatile components (BTX), heavy metals (zinc, chrome, copper and cadmium) and particulate matters (ash, dust). There is an ongoing debate as to what extent these emissions are linked to climate change, but the debate relates more to the extent of these impacts than their nature. Some gases, particularly nitrous oxide, also participate in depleting the stratospheric ozone (O_3) layer, which naturally screens the earth's surface from ultraviolet radiation. Climate change also has a significant impact on transportation systems, particularly infrastructure (e.g. floods) and operations (changes in weather).

Concerning **air quality**, highway vehicles, marine engines, locomotives and aircraft are the sources of pollution in the form of gas and particulate matters emissions that affect air quality, causing damage to human health. Toxic air pollutants are associated with cancer, cardiovascular, respiratory and neurological diseases. Carbon monoxide (CO) when inhaled reduces the availability of oxygen and can be extremely harmful. Nitrogen dioxide (NO_2) emissions from transportation sources reduce lung function, affect the respiratory immune defense system and increase the risk of respiratory problems. The emissions of sulfur dioxide (SO_2) and nitrogen oxides (NOx) in the atmosphere form various acidic compounds that, when mixed in cloud water, create acid rain. Acid precipitation has detrimental effects on the built environment, reduces agricultural crop yields and causes forest decline. Smog is a mixture of solid and liquid fog and smoke particles formed through the accumulation of carbon monoxide, ozone, hydrocarbons, volatile organic compounds, nitrogen oxides, sulfur oxide, water, particulates and other chemical pollutants. The reduction of visibility caused by smog has a number of adverse impacts on the quality of life and the attractiveness of tourist sites. Particulate emissions in the form of dust emanating from vehicle exhaust, as well as from non-exhaust sources such as vehicle and road abrasion, have an impact on air quality. The physical and chemical properties of particulates are associated with health risks such as respiratory problems, skin irritations, eye inflammations, blood clotting and various types of allergies.

Noise represents the general effect of irregular and chaotic sounds on people as well as animal life. Basically, noise is an undesirable sound. Long-term exposure to noise levels above 75 decibels (dB) seriously hampers hearing and affects human physical and psychological wellbeing. Noise emanating from the movement of transport vehicles and the operations of ports, airports and railyards affects human health, through an increase in the risk of cardiovascular diseases. Ambient noise is a frequent result of road transportation in urban areas, which is the cumulative outcome of all the noise generated by vehicles (ranging from 45 to 65 db), which impairs the quality of life and thus property values. Falling land values near acute noise sources such as airports are often noted.

Transport activities have an impact on hydrological conditions and **water quality**. Fuel, chemical and other hazardous particulates discarded from aircraft, cars, trucks and trains or from port and airport terminal operations can contaminate hydrographic systems. Because demand for maritime shipping has increased, marine transport emissions represent the most important segment of water quality impact of the transportation sector. The main effects of marine transport operations on water quality predominantly arise from dredging, waste, ballast waters and oil spills. Dredging is the process of deepening harbor channels by removing sediments from the bed of a body of water. Dredging is essential to create and maintain sufficient water depth for shipping operations and port accessibility. Dredging activities have a twofold negative impact on the marine environment. They modify the hydrology by creating turbidity that can affect the marine biological diversity. The contaminated sediments and water raised by dredging require spoil disposal sites and decontamination techniques. Waste generated by the operations of vessels at sea or at ports cause serious environmental problems, since they can contain a very high level of bacteria that can be hazardous for public health as well as marine ecosystems when discharged in waters. Besides, various types of garbage containing metals and plastic are not easily biodegradable. They can persist on the sea surface for long periods of time and can be a serious impediment for maritime navigation in inland waterways and at sea, also affecting berthing operations. Ballast waters are required to control ships' stability and draft and to modify their center of gravity in relation to cargo carried and the variance in weight distribution. Ballast waters acquired in a region may contain invasive aquatic species that, when discharged in another region, may thrive in a new marine environment and disrupt the natural marine ecosystem. Invasive species have resulted in major changes in nearshore ecosystems, especially in coastal lagoons and inlets. Major oil spills from oil cargo vessel accidents are one of the most serious problems of pollution from maritime transport activities.

The environmental impact of transportation on **soil quality** consists of soil erosion and soil contamination. Coastal transport facilities have significant impacts on soil erosion. Shipping activities modify the scale and scope of wave actions, leading to damage in confined channels such as riverbanks. Highway construction or lessening surface grades for port and airport developments have led to important loss of fertile land. Soil contamination can occur through the use of toxic materials by the transport industry. Fuel and oil spills from motor vehicles are washed up on roadsides and enter the soil. Chemicals used for the preservation of wooden railroad ties may enter into the soil. Hazardous materials and heavy metals have been found in areas contiguous to railroads, ports and airports.

Transportation also influences **biodiversity**. The need for construction materials and the development of land-based transportation has led to deforestation. Many transport routes have required draining land, thus reducing wetland areas and driving out water plant species. The need to maintain road and rail right-of-way or to stabilize slopes along transport facilities has resulted in restricting growth of certain plants or has produced changes in plants with the introduction of new species different from those which originally grew in the areas. Many animal species are becoming endangered as a result of changes in their natural habitats and reduction of ranges.

Environmental externalities

Externalities are an economic concept that refers to activities of a group that have **consequences**, positive or negative, intended or unintended, on other groups. Those consequences, particularly if they are negative, are **not assumed by those causing them**. The impacts are therefore externalized. A common example of a positive externality concerns technology, since it obviously benefits the innovative firm but also the whole economy through various productivity improvements or improved convenience. Negative externalities have a lot of relevance for environmental issues, since many of the negative consequences of pollution are assumed by the whole society.

The environmental externalities of transportation include the consideration of physical measures of environmental damage and the evaluation of involved costs for society. The main fallacy underlined by externalities is that the costs attributed to a few sources (e.g. users of cars) must be burdened by many (users and non-users alike). Knowing the sources of environmental externalities is a relatively easy undertaking, while the evaluation of damage and other costs has not yet reached comparative standards among governmental and non-governmental agencies. The challenge resides over three issues:

- **Relationships**. The nature and extent of the relationships between transport and the environment has to be considered. This is particularly complex, as most environmental relationships tend to be indirect and cumulative.
- **Quantification**. Relationships have to be quantified and also a value to environmental externalities should be appraised. This is highly challenging as only general figures, much subject to debate, can be assessed. The quantification of economic, social and environmental costs are therefore subject to much contention.
- **Mitigation.** The level and extent of corrective actions that can be taken to alleviate environmental externalities linked to transportation, usually in a manner where those contributing bear the consequences of their activities. In view of the two above points, attempts at regulation, particularly if they involve a comprehensive framework (multinational and multisector), have not reached a significant consensus. Alternatively, a consensus may be reached about the nature of an environmental externality, but not about its mitigation.

The costs of environmental externalities can be considered from **economic**, **social** and **environmental** dimensions. The basic types of transportation externalities attributed to the environment fall within air pollution, water pollution, noise and hazardous materials. **Establishing and quantifying environmental externalities** is a complex undertaking. Quantification is only at its preliminary stage and many have used this argument to defer the application of several environmental policies by lobbying governments (e.g. acid rain, CFCs and, most importantly, climate change). Additionally, the wider the geographical scale, the more complex the environmental problem becomes, since it involves cross-jurisdictional issues. Recent attempts to reach a consensus about climate change have underlined the complexity of multilateral environmental agreements.

The sources/emitters of pollutants **rarely bear the consequences of their impacts**. This has several implications. First, when specific sources are concerned, like road transportation, users only take account of the direct costs of modal ownership like a car (vehicle, fuel, insurance, etc.). Ownership is often the only entry and utilization cost for several transportation modes. Society generally assumes the role of providing and maintaining infrastructure and other indirect costs like damage to structures and infrastructure, losses in productivity, clean-up, health services and damage to ecosystems. Second, the geographic separation between sources and recipients is often acute. Acid rain and climate change are obvious examples. On a local level, a community may be affected by noise levels well over its own contribution (notably near major highways), while another (e.g. in the suburbs) may be affected in a very marginal way and still significantly contribute to noise elsewhere during commuting.

There is a tendency towards a shift from **direct** to **indirect consequences for environmental externalities**, in terms of total costs involved. For instance, the absolute levels of air pollutants emissions have considerably dropped in developed countries. The problem of source reduction by vehicles was addressed because it was a straightforward cause of air pollutants emissions. This has tended to displace problems elsewhere and developed new types of externalities. Thus, the relative share of air pollution impacts is lessening, but not the number of vehicles, investment in infrastructure or noise levels, which have their own externalities. Reductions in the relative importance of one type of externality redirect the focus on to other types that were less addressed, but probably as important in the overall impacts of transport over the environment.

Transfers and additions of costs are very common attributes of environmental externalities. Trying to lessen economic costs will either lessen or worsen social and environmental costs, depending on the externality. In the context of limited resources, the distribution of economic, social and environmental costs takes on an important role in what type of damage is most acceptable and in what proportions. It is clear from past strategies that several economic costs have been minimized, notably for producers and users, while social and environmental consequences were disregarded. This practice is less applicable, since society is less willing to bear the costs and consequences of externalities for various reasons (public awareness, quality of life considerations, high health costs, etc.).

Concept 2 – Transportation and energy

Energy

Human activities are closely dependent on the usage of several forms and sources of energy to perform work. Energy is the potential that allows movement and/or the modification of matter (e.g. making steel by combining iron and carbon). The energy content of an energy source is the available energy per unit of weight or volume, but the challenge is to effectively extract and use this energy (Figure 8.2). Thus, the more energy consumed, the greater the amount of work realized and it comes as no surprise that economic development is correlated with greater levels of energy consumption.

Different fuels have different levels of energy content and Figure 8.2 relates to energy released through combustion. The higher the energy content, the higher the quality of the fuel, which is inversely proportional to its chemical complexity. High-quality fuels are gases while low-quality fuels are solids, with liquids in between. The fuel with the highest energy content is hydrogen, which is also the simplest chemical component in existence. Gasoline, which is derived from refining crude oil, contains much more energy than coal (twice than the lower grade bituminous) or wood (three times). Liquid natural gas is almost entirely composed of methane, while natural gas has about 85 percent of its mass accounted for by methane. Jet A-1 is the standard fuel used by commercial jet planes and is mostly composed of kerosene and a number of additives (antifreeze, anti-oxidant and antistatic) since the fuel must meet very strict specifications, as it will be exposed to high altitudes and low temperatures. Conversely, Bunker C fuel, which is the main fuel used for maritime shipping, can be considered as one of the lower-quality fuels in liquid form, but suitable for vast ship engines. Although methane and hydrogen both have higher energy content than gasoline, their gaseous form creates storage difficulties. Furthermore, hydrogen must be synthesized, which requires energy. One of the most efficient energy storage devices, the lithium battery, can only hold about the equivalent of 0.5 MJ per kilogram, underlining the challenge of developing electric vehicles.

There are enormous reserves of energy able to meet the future needs of mankind. Unfortunately, one of the main contemporary issues is that many of these reserves are not necessarily available at competitive costs, such as solar energy, or are unevenly

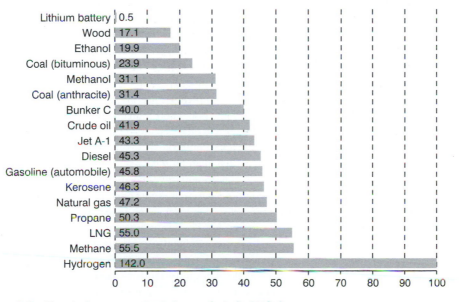

Figure 8.2 Chemical energy content of some fuels (in MJ/kg)

Source: Adapted from C. Ronneau (2004) *Energie, pollution de l'air et développement durable*. Louvain-la-neuve: Presses Universitaires de Louvain.

distributed around the world, such as oil. Still, the competitiveness of an energy source can improve with technological development and, even if some energy sources are extracted far from where they are consumed, the massification of transportation enables their movement. Since the Industrial Revolution, efforts have been made for work to be performed by machines, which considerably improved industrial productivity. The development of the steam engine and the generation and distribution of electric energy over considerable distances have also altered the spatial pattern of manufacturing industries by liberating production from a direct connection to a fixed power system. While in the earlier stages of the Industrial Revolution factories located close to sources of energy (a waterfall or a coal field) or raw materials, mass conveyances and new energy sources (electricity) enabled a much greater locational flexibility.

Industrial development places large demands on fossil fuels. At the turn of the twentieth century, the invention and commercial development of the internal combustion engine, notably in transport equipment, made possible the efficient movement of passengers and freight and prompted the development of a global trade network. With globalization, transportation accounts for a growing share of the total amount of energy spent for implementing, operating and maintaining the international range and scope of human activities. Energy consumption has a strong correlation with the level of development. Among developed countries, transportation now accounts for between 20 and 25 percent of the total energy being consumed. The benefits conferred by additional mobility, notably in terms of a better exploitation of comparative advantages, have so far compensated for the growing amount of energy spent to support it. At the beginning of the twenty-first century, the transition reached a stage where fossil fuels, notably petroleum, are dominant.

Transportation and energy consumption

Transportation and energy is a standard physics application where giving momentum to a mass (people, vehicles, cargo, etc.) requires a proportional amount of energy. The relationship between transport and energy is a direct one, but subject to different interpretations since it concerns different transport modes, each having their own utility and level of performance. There is often a compromise between speed and energy consumption, related to the desired economic returns (Figure 8.3).

Within the transport sector there are significant differences between speed, energy costs, mode and type of loads (freight and passengers). Since economies of scale play a crucial role in freight transportation, this is reflected in its lower levels of energy consumption. Overall, transport operators try to seek a compromise between speed (returns in overcoming distance) and energy (costs in overcoming distance). The lowest energy consumption levels are associated with bulk freight traveling at slow speed (like oil), while high levels of energy consumption correspond to passengers or merchandises being carried at high velocities. The first corresponds to a compromise of energy over speed, while the second is a compromise of speed over energy. The compromise for supersonic planes was so disadvantageous that commercial services (Concorde) were abandoned in 2003.

Passengers and high-value goods can be transported by fast but energy-intensive modes, since the time component of their mobility tends to have a high value, which conveys the willingness to use more energy. Economies of scale, mainly those achieved by maritime transportation, are linked to low levels of energy consumption per unit of mass being transported, but at a lower speed. This fits relatively well for freight transport imperatives, particularly for bulk. Comparatively, air freight has high energy

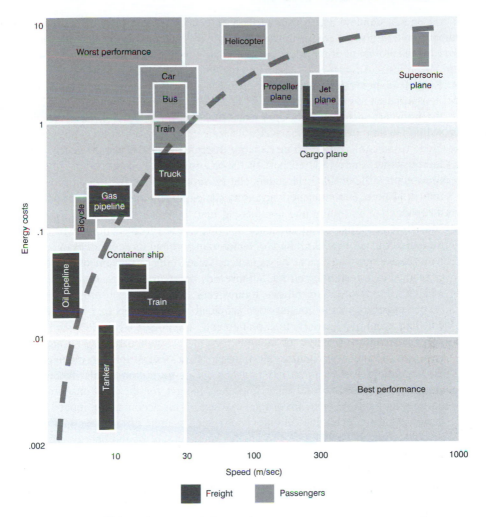

Figure 8.3 Energy efficiency by transportation mode

Source: Adapted from J.D. Chapman (1989) *Geography and Energy: Commercial Energy Systems and National Policies.* New York: Longman Scientific & Technical.

consumption levels linked to high-speed services. Transportation markets are particularly impacted by these three energy issues:

- The **price level** and **volatility** of energy sources which are dependent on the processes used in their production. Stable energy sources are obviously preferred.
- Technological and technical changes in the level of **energy performance** of transport modes and terminals. An important goal is thus to improve this energy performance.
- **Environmental externalities** related to the use of specific modes and energy sources and the goal to reduce them.

A trend that emerged since the 1950s concerns the growing share of transportation in the world's total oil consumption; transportation accounts for approximately 25 percent of world energy demand and for about 61.5 percent of all the oil used each year. The impacts of transport on energy consumption are diverse, including many that are necessary for the provision of transport facilities:

- **Land transportation** accounts for the great majority of energy consumption. Road transportation alone is consuming on average 85 percent of the total energy used by the transport sector in developed countries. This trend is not, however, uniform within the land transportation sector itself, as road transportation is almost the sole mode responsible for additional energy demands over the last 30 years. Despite a falling market share, rail transport, on the basis of 1 kg of oil equivalent, remains four times more efficient for passengers and twice as efficient for freight movement as road transport. Rail transport accounts for 6 percent of global transport energy demand.
- **Maritime transportation** accounts for 90 percent of crossborder world trade as measured by volume. The nature of water transport and its economies of scale make it the most energy-efficient mode, since it uses only 7 percent of all the energy consumed by transport activities, a figure way below its contribution to the mobility of goods. For terminal operations, figures vary, but a container terminal usually has 70 percent of its energy consumption provided by fossil fuels (e.g. yard equipment) and 30 percent by electricity (e.g. portainers).
- **Air transportation** plays an integral part in the globalization of transportation networks. The aviation industry accounts for 8 percent of the energy consumed by transportation. Air transport has high energy consumption levels, linked to high speeds. Fuel is the second most important budget for the air transport industry, accounting for 13–20 percent of total expenses. This accounts for about 1.2 million barrels per day. Technological innovations, such as more efficient engines and better aerodynamics, have led to a continuous improvement of the energy efficiency of each new generation of aircrafts.

Further distinctions in the energy consumption of transport can be made between passenger and freight movement:

- **Passenger transportation** accounts for 60–70 percent of energy consumption from transportation activities. The private car is the dominant mode but has a poor energetic performance, although this performance has seen substantial improvements since the 1970s, mainly due to growing energy prices and regulations. Only 12 percent of the fuel used by a car actually provides momentum. There is a close relationship between rising income, automobile ownership and distance traveled by vehicle. The United States has one of the highest levels of car ownership in the world, with one car for every two people. About 60 percent of all American households owned two or more cars, with 19 percent owning three or more. Another trend has been the increasing rise in ownership of minivans, sport utility vehicles (SUVs) and light-duty trucks for personal use and the corresponding decline in fuel economy. Fuel consumption, however, is impacted by diminishing returns, meaning that higher levels of fuel efficiency involve declining marginal gains in fuel consumption. Also, the growth of vehicle-miles traveled is correlated with changes in energy prices and is entering a phase of maturity in several developed countries.
- **Freight transportation** is dominated by rail and maritime shipping, the two most energy-efficient modes. Coastal and inland waterways also provide an

energy-efficient method of transporting passengers and cargoes. A towboat moving a typical load of 15 barges in tow holds the equivalent of 225 rail carloads or 870 truckloads. The rationale for favoring coastal and inland navigation is based on lower energy consumption rates of shipping and the general overall smaller externalities of water transportation.

Figure 8.4 depicts the respective share of energy consumption by type of fuel, transportation mode, type of transport (passenger or freight) and the level of energy efficiency. It also depicts the main energy flows between sectors. Oil-related fuels accounted for 94 percent of the energy used by transportation modes, with gasoline being the most used fuel (42.5 percent), followed by diesel (34.5 percent), heavy oil, biofuels and kerosene (34.9 percent). Electricity and gases (e.g. LNG) account for a marginal use as fuels. Gasoline is mostly used for light road vehicles (cars and vans) for passenger transportation. Diesel is the prevalent fuel for heavy road vehicles for freight transportation. Water transportation relies on heavy oils, and the great majority of the fuel is used for freight transport. For air transport, kerosene is the main fuel, mostly used to carry passengers. The energy conversion level for the transport sector is around 32 percent, a figure which is higher for freight transport than for passenger transport.

Transportation and alternative fuels

All other things being equal, the energy source with the lowest cost will always be preferred. The dominance of petroleum-derived fuels is a result of the relative simplicity with which they can be stored and efficiently used in the internal combustion engine vehicle. Other fossil fuels (natural gas, propane and methanol) can be used as transportation fuels as well, but require a **more complicated storage system**. The main issue concerning the large-scale uses of alternative vehicle fuels is the large

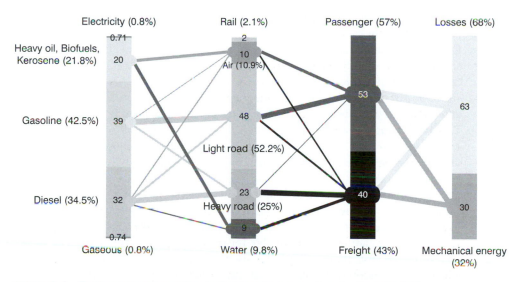

Figure 8.4 Final energy consumption by fuel type by transport sector (in exajoules)

Source: Adapted from Intergovernmental Panel on Climate Change (2014) *Climate Change 2014: Mitigation of Climate Change*.

capital investments required in distribution facilities as compared with conventional fuels. Another issue is that in terms of **energy density**, these alternative fuels have lower efficiency than gasoline and thus require greater volume of on-board storage to cover the equivalent distance as a gasoline propelled vehicle if performance is kept constant.

Alternative fuels in the form of non-crude oil resources are drawing considerable attention as a result of the non-renewable character of fossil fuels and the need to reduce emissions of harmful pollutants. The most prevalent alternatives being considered are:

- **Biofuels** such as ethanol, methanol and biodiesel can be produced from the fermentation of food crops (sugarcane, corn, cereals; often called first generation biofuels) or the biomass (such as wood and grasses; called second generation biofuels). Their production, however, requires large harvesting areas that may compete with other types of land use. This limit is related to the capacity of plants to absorb solar energy and transform it through photosynthesis. This low productivity of the biomass does not meet the energy needs of the transportation sector. Besides, the production of ethanol is an energy-intensive process. Biodiesel can also be obtained from a variety of crops. The choice of biomass fuel will largely depend on the sustainability and energy efficiency of the production process.

- **Hydrogen** is often mentioned as the energy source of the future. The steps in using hydrogen as a transportation fuel consist in producing hydrogen by electrolysis of water or by extracting it from hydrocarbons, then compressing or converting hydrogen into liquid form and storing it on-board a vehicle, and finally using fuel cells to generate electricity on demand from the hydrogen to propel a motor vehicle. Hydrogen fuel cells are more efficient than gasoline and generate near-zero pollutants. But hydrogen suffers from several problems, particularly since a lot of energy can be wasted in its production, transfer and storage. Hydrogen manufacturing requires electricity production. Besides, hydrogen has a very low energy density and requires very low temperature and a very high-pressure storage tank, adding weight and volume to a vehicle. This suggests that liquid hydrogen fuel would be a better alternative for ship and aircraft propulsion.

- **Electricity** is being considered as an alternative to petroleum fuels as an energy source. A pure battery electric vehicle is considered a more efficient alternative to hydrogen fuel-propelled vehicle, as there is no need to convert energy into electricity since the electricity stored in the battery can power the electric motor. Besides an all-electric car is easier and cheaper to produce than a comparable fuel-cell vehicle. The main barriers to the development electric cars are the lack of storage systems capable of providing driving ranges and speed comparable to those of conventional vehicles. The low energy capacity of batteries makes the electric car less competitive than internal combustion engines using gasoline. The current technological level of electric cars has a range of around 430 km, which is steadily increasing. As technology improves, the energy and cost-effectiveness of batteries is getting better. For instance, between 2010 and 2015, the cost of lithium-ion batteries fell by 65 percent. Electric vehicles are eminently suitable for urban transportation for both passenger and freight because of the lower ranges involved.

- **Hybrid vehicles** consisting of propulsion system using an internal combustion engine supplemented by an electric motor and batteries, which provides opportunities to combine the efficiency of electricity with the long driving range of an internal combustion engine. A hybrid vehicle still uses liquid fuel as the main source of energy but the engine provides the power to drive the vehicle or is used to charge the battery via a generator. Alternatively, the propulsion can be provided by the electricity generated by the battery. When the battery is discharged, the engine starts automatically without intervention from the driver. The generator can also be fed by using the braking energy to recharge the battery. Such a propulsion design greatly contributes to overall fuel efficiency. Given the inevitable oil depletion, the successful development and commercialization of hybrid vehicles appears in the medium term the most sustainable option to conventional gasoline-engine-powered vehicles.

The diffusion of non-fossil fuels in the transportation sector has **serious limitations**. While the price of oil has increased over time, it has been subject to significant fluctuations. The comparative costs of alternative energy sources to fossil fuels are higher in the transportation sector than in other types of economic activities. This suggests higher competitive advantages for the industrial, household, commercial, electricity and heat sectors to shift away from oil and to rely on solar, wind or hydropower. Transportation fuels based on renewable energy sources might not be competitive with petroleum fuels unless significant price increases occur.

Concept 3 – Transport and sustainability

Sustainable development

An issue that has triggered concerns over the recent decades relates to the capacity of the global economy to accommodate an enduring demographic, economic and resource consumption growth. Since the 1970s, many statements have been made asserting that the world would be unable to sustain such growth without a possible socioeconomic and environmental breakdown. While these perspectives have been demonstrated to be inaccurate, since resource availability and the quality of life have increased, there are enduring concerns that at some point a threshold will be reached, particularly in regard to climate change. Under such conditions, an emphasis on sustainable development has been advocated as a priority for future social and economic development.

Sustainable development is, however, a complex concept that is subject to numerous interpretations, since it involves interdisciplinary and numerous interconnections. It is not surprising that the subject is prone to confusion in terms of its nature, consequences and appropriate response, but it is generally agreed that a sustainable society favors conditions that benefit the environment, the economy and the society without compromising the welfare of future generations. Still, as history clearly demonstrates, the conditions of future societies will largely depend on the legacy of current societies on resources and the environment. All forms of assets (capital, real estate, infrastructures, resources) passed on to the next generation should be at least of equal value (utility) per capita.

Societies do not contribute to environmental problems at the same level. Sustainability can be thus expressed at two spatial levels:

- **Global**. Long-term stability of the earth's environment and availability of resources to support human activities.
- **Local**. Localized forms often related to urban areas in terms of jobs, housing and environmental pollution.

Figure 8.5 Sustainable urban passenger travel, selected cities

Source: Urban population data from United Nations, *World Urbanization Prospects: The 2007 Revision Population Database*; J. Kenworthy and F. Laube (2001) *The Millennium Cities Database for Sustainable Transport*. International Union of Public Transport (UITP), Brussels and Institute for Sustainability and Technology Policy (ISTP), Perth.

Since a growing share of the global population is urbanized, sustainability has increasingly become focused on urban areas (Figure 8.5). Major cities are requiring a vast array of supporting infrastructures including energy, water, sewers and transport. A key to urban sustainability issues is linked with the provision and maintenance of a wide range of urban infrastructure. Every city has specific infrastructure and environmental problems. For instance, many cities in developing countries have chronic deficiencies in the provision of the most basic infrastructure while their environmental conditions are deteriorating.

Figure 8.5 provides a typology of the sustainability level of urban passenger transportation systems from a sample of 64 cities across the world. The classification is mainly based on the assumption that a high level of reliance on the automobile, coupled with low density levels, is less sustainable than lower levels of automobile dependency and higher densities. Five major classes can be identified:

- **Class A**. Comparatively most sustainable transport. Very low automobile dependency, with public transport, walking and cycling more prominent than cars, which involves very low gasoline use per capita.
- **Class B**. Comparatively more sustainable transport. Low automobile dependency, public transport, walking and cycling equal with cars, low gasoline use.
- **Class C**. Comparatively sustainable transport. Moderate automobile dependency, important role for public transport, walking and cycling, moderate gasoline use.

- **Class D**. Comparatively less sustainable transport. High automobile dependency, minor role for public transport (important support for peak hour movements), walking and cycling, high gasoline use.
- **Class E**. Urban passenger transport systems that are comparatively the least sustainable. They involve a very high level of automobile dependency, a very limited role for public transit, walking and cycling, as well as very high gasoline use.

The typology has a distinct geography. North American and Australian cities are dominantly in class E, with a few of the denser cities (e.g. New York, Toronto) in class D. This is mostly related to automobile dependency. European cities rank higher on the sustainable passenger transportation scale, mainly due to the higher role of public transit and denser urban settings. This characteristic is also shared with many Latin American cities. East Asian cities are generally on top of the urban passenger sustainability scale. However, rapid development and motorization in the majority of large Chinese cities (e.g. Beijing and Shanghai) has resulted in a relative decline of their sustainability level. Southeast Asian cities with a high level of automobile dependence, such as Bangkok and Saigon, are in a similar situation.

Efficient and productive cities are not necessarily linked with high levels of energy consumption per capita. The first three classes of cities (A, B and C) are characterized by high densities and rely on public transit for mobility, while the last two classes (D and E) have lower densities and rely on the automobile for most urban movements. A shortcoming of the above classification is that it considers **only one dimension of urban transportation**: the mobility of passengers. Cities are also subject to intense flows of goods, since they are locations of production, consumption and distribution. **Freight distribution** should thus be considered an important component of urban sustainability.

Sustainable transportation

Transportation, as a core component supporting the interactions and the development of socioeconomic systems, has also been the object of much consideration about to what extent it is sustainable. Sustainable transportation can be defined as the capacity to support the mobility needs of people, freight and information in a manner that is the least damageable to the environment (Figure 8.6).

The concept of sustainable transportation is intricately linked with the development of sustainable transport modes, infrastructures and logistics. Three major dimensions are considered for such a purpose:

- **Environment**. A reduction of the environmental impacts of transportation is a likely strategy for sustainability. Transportation significantly contributes to harmful emissions, noise and to climate changes. However, vehicles are becoming more environmentally efficient but there are more of them around. An improvement of the land use impacts of transportation, especially the impacts of infrastructure construction and maintenance, is also a strategic goal to achieve. The transportation system is also a generator of waste (vehicles, parts, packaging, etc.) that must be reduced.
- **Economy**. Transportation is a factor of economic growth and development. A sustainable strategy would aim to efficiently use transportation for the purpose of growth and for the creation of jobs. Transportation should also have a fair pricing strategy, meaning that users are bearing the full costs (direct and indirect) of their

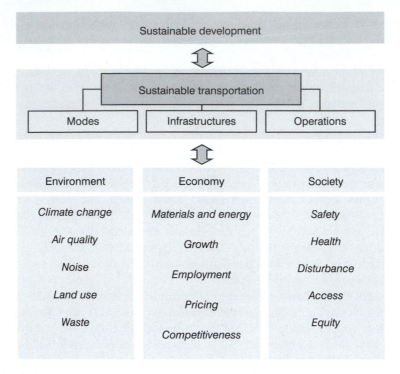

Figure 8.6 Sustainable transportation

Source: Adapted from UK Department of the Environment, Transport and the Regions (1999) *Indicators of Sustainable D evelopment.*

usage of the transport system. A transport system where competition is fair and open is likely to promote modal choice and efficiency. In a system where transport is a public or private monopoly, price distortions and misallocations of capital are created, which in the long run are likely to render the system unsustainable.

● **Society**. Sustainable transportation should benefit society. It should be safe, should not impair human health and should minimize disturbance on communities. Access and equity are also two important principles, as transportation should promote the access to goods and services for as many people as possible.

The matter is often that reconciling all these principles, which individually appear logical and straightforward, leads to transportation systems that are unsustainable because they are too costly and regulated.

Sustainable development applied to transport systems requires the promotion of linkages between environmental protection, economic efficiency and social progress. Under the environmental dimension, the objective consists in understanding the reciprocal influences of the physical environment and the practices of the industry and that environmental issues are addressed by all aspects of the transport industry. Under the economic dimension, the objective consists of orienting progress in the sense of economic efficiency. Transport must be cost-effective and capable of adapting to changing demands. Under the social dimension, the objective consists in upgrading standards of living and quality of life.

Automobile dependence is a situation that is often related to an unsustainable urban environment. However, such an observation is at odds with the mobility choice and preferences of the global population where the automobile is rapidly adopted when income levels reach a certain threshold. Other transport alternatives commonly do not measure up to the convenience of the automobile. Automobile dependency is thus the outcome of **market forces,** expressed as consumer preferences and national manufacturing policies. Private and flexible forms of transportation, such as the automobile, are thus fundamental to urban mobility and should not be discarded as options for the sake of sustainability.

Recent advances in **car sharing technologies** and the potential for **self-driving vehicles** underline a much more sustainable usage of car assets that could remove up to 90 percent of the vehicles from the streets. This is in contradiction with the bias observed in the transport community towards an emphasis for public transit and non-motorized transportation as the dominant, if not sole, strategy towards sustainable transportation. Yet, almost all public transit systems are financially unsustainable, imposing burdens on society. Freight transportation must also be considered in this process considering the substantial growth of raw materials and goods being traded in a global economy. In fact, freight transportation relies on much more environmentally sound modes such as rail and maritime transport.

Measures to promote transport sustainability have their limits. Indeed, the built environment, transport infrastructures and even modes cannot change quickly enough to solve the bulk of problems related to unsustainable transport. Most of the investment that is already in place will remain in place for 50 years or more and new investments (in additional or improved infrastructure) will not represent much more than a few percentage points change in terms of reducing traffic congestion and its negative externalities. While policies, rules and regulations expect compliance, users tend to instinctively react to price signals and discard modes that are becoming costly (unsustainable) and find loopholes. Transportation and sustainability for both passengers and freight must also contend with mitigation versus adaptation issues:

- **Mitigation** concerns the improvement of productivity and efficiency of existing modes, terminals and managerial approaches so that environmental externalities are reduced. They tend to be short- to medium-term strategies.
- **Adaptation** is a change in the level of use and the market share of respective modes to better reflect a long-term trend, such as higher energy prices and stricter environmental regulations.

There is a wide range of responses to environmental sustainability, with different local, national and international regulations. This involves a variety of costs in transport operations that must be built into the price of providing transport facilities and services. Environmental sustainability represents a growing **area of responsibility** for the providers of transport services, inciting them to acquire expertise in environmental management. The most important challenge is to implement environmentally sustainable transport within competitive market structures leaning on coping with changes in transport demand while improving transport supply. The issue of sustainable transport thus remains elusive, since to start with any economic activity, including transportation, has negative environmental impacts. The matter remains as to whether these activities are taking place at a level exceeding the environmental and social carrying capacity.

CASE STUDY   Green logistics

Greenness and logistics

Most considerations in sustainable transportation focus on passengers, leaving freight issues somewhat marginalized. **Logistics** are at the heart of the operation of modern transport systems and implies a degree of organization and control over freight movements that only modern technology could have brought into being. It has become one of the most important developments in the transportation industry. **Greenness** has become a code word for a range of environmental concerns, and is usually considered positively. It is employed to suggest compatibility with the environment, and thus, like logistics, is something that is perceived as beneficial. When put together the two words suggest an environmentally friendly and efficient transport and distribution system.

The loosely defined term of green logistics covers several dimensions related to production planning, materials management and physical distribution, opening the door to a wide array of potential applications of environmentally friendly strategies along supply chains (Figure 8.7).

Since logistics are related to all the activities involved in making goods available to the final consumers, including all the stages related to procurement and distribution, the green applications of logistics are numerous and cover three main dimensions:

- **Product design and production planning**. Developing products that have a lower environmental footprint, including their production process. This can involve opting for suppliers that are closer (near sourcing) or that are abiding to more stringent environmental standards (sustainable sourcing). However, this strategy runs the risk of offering goods and services that are less competitive.
- **Physical distribution**. Ensuring that the mobility of freight related to logistics operations is performed in a sustainable and environmentally friendly manner. This can involve a wide array of strategies, such as a better consolidation of loads to avoid

Figure 8.7   Logistic activities and their green dimensions

sub-optimal use of transportation (from LTL to FTL), as well as alternative modes (modal shift) or fuels (technological improvements).

- **Materials management**. Moving towards more efficient forms of materials use, including packaging (Photo 8.1) and recycling so that what used to be an output can become an input. Optimally, a much higher level of recycling should be part of the inputs of the manufacturing sector.

All these dimensions can be individually or jointly applied. Since they involve different actors, concerted efforts are uncommon as each element of the supply chain pursues strategies that are judged to be the most effective along their respective channels. The **conventional forward channel** in freight distribution is well understood, with raw materials, parts and finished goods flowing from suppliers to producers, distributors and, finally, to consumers. In many cases, there is also a **reverse channel** where wastes, packages and defective/obsolete products are "climbing back" up the supply chain. In some instances, such as for a defective product, distributors will take back the merchandise, but in other instances a specialized segment of the distribution industry

Photo 8.1   Packed memory foam mattresses

The global furniture distributor and retailer Ikea commits to making substantial efforts when designing its products. A fundamental design element relates how can each product be optimally packed in a limited footprint and preferably in a box. This involves the design of the shape of the parts as well as the selection of materials they are made from. For instance, here a twin-size mattress is rolled into a vacuum-sealed pack. The growing prevalence of memory foam technology, which is replacing standard spring-based designs, offers a product that can be packed, compressed and rolled without damaging its properties. This substantially reduces transport and inventory costs, in addition to being convenient for customers, who can easily carry the product away on their own.

Photo: Dr Jean-Paul Rodrigue, 2016.

aims at collecting and then recycling goods and parts. Thus, reverse logistics (or reverse distribution) is concerned about the movements of previously shipped goods from customers back to manufacturers or distribution centers due to repairs, recycling or returns. There are several variants:

- An important segment is **customer-driven**, where domestic waste is set aside by home dwellers for recycling. This has achieved wide popularity in many communities, notably because the public became involved in the process.
- A second type is where non-recyclable waste, including hazardous materials, is transported for disposal to designated sites. As landfills close to urban areas become scarce, waste has to be transported greater distances to disposal centers.
- A different approach is where reverse distribution is a continuous embedded process in which the organization (manufacturer or distributor) takes responsibility for the delivery of new products as well as their take-back. This means environmental considerations for the **whole life cycle of a product** (production, distribution, consumption and recycling/disposal).

Different stakeholders could be applying different strategies, all of which are labeled as green logistics. One corporation could be focusing on product packaging, while another on alternative fuel vehicles; both are undertaking green logistics. However, a closer inspection at the concept and its applications raises a great many **paradoxes** and **inconsistencies**, which suggest that its application may be more difficult than initially expected. Although there has been much debate about what green logistics truly entails, the transportation industry has developed very narrow and specific interests about the issue. If transportation costs are reduced and assets such as vehicles, terminals and distribution centers better utilized, the assumption is that green logistics strategies are being implemented.

Green logistics and its paradoxes

An overview of the standard characteristics of logistical systems reveals several inconsistencies with regards to the mitigation of environmental externalities. The purpose of logistics is to **reduce costs**, notably transport costs. While the former remain the most salient logistics cost, inventory-carrying costs come second. In addition, economies of time and improvements in service reliability, including flexibility, are further objectives. Corporations involved in the physical distribution of freight are highly supportive of strategies that enable them to cut transport costs in a competitive setting. Economies of scale in transportation as well as higher load densities are common cost-saving strategies that concomitantly lead to environmental benefits in terms of lower fuel consumption per ton-km. On some occasions, the cost-saving strategies pursued by logistic operators can be at variance with environmental considerations, which become externalized. This means that the benefits of logistics are realized by the users and eventually to the consumer if the benefits are shared along the supply chain. However, the environment assumes a wide variety of burdens and costs, which form a hierarchy ranging from costs internal to the supply chain to externalized costs. Society is becoming less willing to accept these costs, and pressure is increasingly being put on governments and corporations to include greater environmental considerations in their activities. A salient example concerns food supply chains that have been impacted by lower transport costs, enabling a diversification of the suppliers and longer transport chains. The concept of food-miles has been developed in an attempt to capture the full costs of food distribution by using the distance that food is carried as a proxy.

In logistics, **time is often the essence**. By reducing the time of flows, the velocity of the distribution system is increased and, consequently, its efficiency. This is achieved in the main by using the most polluting and least energy-efficient transportation modes. The significant increase of air freight and trucking is partially the result of time constraints imposed by logistical activities. The time constraints are themselves the result of an increasing flexibility of industrial production systems and of the retailing sector. Logistics offers door-to-door (DTD) services, mostly coupled with just-in-time (JIT) strategies. Other modes cannot satisfy the requirements such a situation creates as effectively. This leads to a vicious circle; the more DTD and JIT strategies are applied, the further the negative environmental consequences of the traffic it creates. The slow steaming strategy pursued by maritime shipping companies is further challenging time management within long-distance supply chains.

At the heart of logistics is the overriding importance of **service reliability**. Its success is based upon the ability to deliver freight on time with the least breakage or damage. Logistics providers often realize these objectives by utilizing the modes that are perceived as being most reliable. The least polluting modes are generally regarded as being the least reliable in terms of on-time delivery, lack of breakage and safety. Ships and railways have inherited a reputation for poor customer satisfaction. For instance, the schedule reliability of container shipping is around 50 percent, implying that about half the time a container ship will not arrive at a port terminal at the scheduled day. Lower reliability levels are linked with lower levels of asset utilization and higher inventory levels, which is wasteful and indirectly damaging to the environment. The reliability of the logistics industry is built around air and truck shipments, which are the two least environmentally friendly modes.

Modern logistics systems economies are based on the reduction of inventories, as the speed and reliability of deliveries removes the need to store and stockpile. Consequently, a reduction in **warehousing demands** is one of the advantages of logistics. This means, however, that inventories have been transferred to a certain degree to the transport system, especially to roads but also to terminals. Inventories are actually in transit, contributing still further to congestion and pollution. The environment and society, not the logistical operators, are assuming the external costs. Not all sectors exhibit this trend, however. In some industrial sectors – computers, for example – there is a growing trend for vertical disintegration of the manufacturing process, in which extra links are added to the supply chain. Intermediate plants where some assembly is undertaken have been added between the manufacturer and consumer. While facilitating the customization of the product for the consumer, it adds an additional external movement of products in the production line.

Information technologies have led to new dimensions in retailing. One of the most dynamic markets is e-commerce. This is made possible by an integrated supply chain with data interchange between suppliers, assembly lines and freight forwarders. Even if for the online customers there is an appearance of a movement-free transaction, the distribution online transactions create may consume more energy than other retail activities. The distribution activities that have benefited the most from e-commerce are parcel-shipping companies such as UPS, FedEx or DHL, who rely solely on trucking and air transportation. Information technologies related to e-commerce applied to logistics can obviously have positive impacts. So, once again, the situation may be seen as paradoxical.

It can be argued that the paradoxes of green logistics make it challenging for the logistics industry to become significantly greener. The internal inconsistencies between the goal of environmental sustainability and an industry that gives undue preference to road and air transport can be seen as being **irreconcilable**. Yet internal and external pressures promoting a more environmentally friendly logistics industry appear to be inexorable. How the logistics industry has responded to the environmental imperatives is not unexpected, given its commercial and economic imperatives, particularly in view of the paradoxes it is facing. By overlooking significant environmental issues, such as pollution, congestion, resource depletion, means that the logistics industry is still not very green. Green logistics remains an indirect outcome of policies and strategies aimed at improving the cost, efficiency and reliability of supply chains. A key aspect of more environmentally friendly freight distribution systems concerns city logistics where the "last mile" in freight distribution takes place as well as a large share of reverse logistics activities. Still, even in this context the driving force is not directly environmental issues, but factors linked with costs, time, reliability, warehousing and information technologies.

Bibliography

Banister, D. (2008) "The sustainable mobility paradigm." *Transport Policy* 15(2): 73–80.

Black, W.R. (2010) *Sustainable Transportation: Problems and Solutions*. New York: The Guilford Press.

Davis, S., S. Diegel and R. Boundy (2009) *Transportation Energy Data Book*, edition 28. US Department of Energy, ORNL-6984. Knoxville, TN: Oak Ridge National Laboratory.

Gilbert, R. and A. Perl (2008) *Transport Revolutions: Moving People and Freight without Oil*. London: Earthscan.

Intergovernmental Panel on Climate Change (2014) *Climate Change 2014: Mitigation of Climate Change*. Cambridge: Cambridge University Press.

IEA/OECD (2009) *Transport, Energy and CO2: Moving Toward Sustainability*. Paris: International Energy Agency.

McKinnon, A., M. Browne and A. Whiteing (eds) (2013) *Green Logistics: Improving the Environmental Sustainability of Logistics*, 2nd edition. London: Kogan Page.

Newman, P. and J.R. Kenworthy (1999) *Sustainability and Cities: Overcoming Automobile Dependence*, New York: Island Press.

OECD (2015) *Urban Mobility System Upgrade: How Shared Self-driving Cars Could Change City Traffic*, Corporate Partnership Board Report. Paris: OECD.

Rodrigue, J.-P., B. Slack and C. Comtois (2001) "Green logistics," in A.M. Brewer, K.J. Button and D.A. Hensher (eds), *The Handbook of Logistics and Supply-Chain Management*, Handbooks in Transport 2. London: Pergamon/Elsevier, pp. 339–351.

Ryley, T.J. and Chapman, L. (eds) (2012) *Transport and Climate Change*. Bingley: Emerald.

Schiller, P.L., E.C. Bruun and J.R. Kenworthy (2010) *An Introduction to Sustainable Transportation*. London: Earthscan.

Tolley, R. (ed) (2003) *Sustainable Transport: Planning for Walking and Cycling in Urban Environments*. New York: CRC Press.

UN-Habitat (2009) *Planning Sustainable Cities, Global Report on Human Settlements 2009*, United Nations Human Settlements Programme. London: Earthscan.

US Environmental Protection Agency (2000) *The Lean and Green Supply Chain: A Practical Guide for Materials Managers and Supply Chain Managers to Reduce Costs and Improve Environmental Performance*, Environmental Accounting Project, EPA 742-R-00-001. Washington, DC: US-EPA.

World Energy Council (2007) *Transport Technologies and Policy Scenarios*. London: World Energy Council.

9 Transport planning and policy

Since transportation is such an important component of contemporary society, capable of producing significant benefits, yet giving rise to many negative externalities, appropriate policies need to be devised to maximize the benefits and minimize the inconveniences. At the same time, the allocation, design and construction of transport infrastructure and services must be subject to careful planning, both by public and private agencies. A distinction must be drawn between policy and planning, since the former usually relates to the strategies and goals, while the latter refers to concrete actions. Because they both have to reflect the fundamental changes in society and contemporary issues and problems, policies and planning are constantly changing. For instance, the changing orientation of public policy led to deregulation in many transport sectors. Among the core policy issues, transport safety and security have come to the forefront. Natural and man-made disasters are also serious challenges for transport planning.

Concept 1 – The nature of transport policy

Authors: Dr Brian Slack, Dr Theo Notteboom and Dr Jean-Paul Rodrigue

Policy and planning

The terms "policy" and "planning" are used very loosely and are frequently interchangeable in many transport studies. Mixing them together is misleading. Policy and planning represent separate parts of an overall process of intervention. There are circumstances where **policy may be developed without any direct planning implications**, and **planning is frequently undertaken outside any of direct policy context**. However, precise definitions are not easy to come by. **Transport policy** deals with the development of a set of constructs and propositions that are established to achieve particular objectives relating to social, economic and environmental development, and the functioning and performance of the transport system. **Transport planning** deals with the preparation and implementation of actions designed to address specific problems.

The goal of transport policy is to make effective decisions concerning the allocation of transport resources, including the management and regulation of existing transportation activities. Thus, transport policy can be concomitantly a **public** and **private endeavor**, but governments are often the most involved in the policy process, since they either own or manage many components of the transport system and have levels of jurisdiction on all existing transportation modes. Governments also often perceive that it is their role to manage transport systems due to the important public service they provide in addition to imposing a regulatory framework. Yet, many transport systems, such as maritime and air transportation, are privately owned. There are, however, substantial geographical variations in ownership, with the United States having an history of private involvement, while Europe, China, India and Japan have more relied on public owner-ship and operations. The common rule is that the public sector usually provides trans-port infrastructure and the regulatory framework, while the private sector assumes the operations of many modes.

With globalization and deregulation, the private sector has much leverage into the policy process through its asset allocation decisions, which is reflected in new public transport policy paradigms. **Public policy** is the means by which governments attempt to reconcile the social, political, economic and environmental goals and aspirations of society with reality. These goals and aspirations change as the society evolves, and thus a feature of policy is its changing form and character. Policy has to be dynamic and evolutionary.

A major distinction between the planning and policy is that the latter has a much **stronger relation with legislation**. Policies are frequently, though not exclusively, incorporated into laws and other legal instruments that serve as a framework for devel-oping planning interventions. Planning does not necessarily involve legislative action, and is more focused on the means of achieving a particular goal, often within the existing regulatory framework.

The relevance of transport policy

Transport policies arise because of the extreme importance of transport in virtually every aspect of economic, social and political activities of nation states. Transport is taken by governments of all inclination, from those that are interventionalist to the most liberal, as a vital factor in economic development. Transport is seen as a key mechanism in promoting, developing and shaping the national economy. Many regional develop-ment programs, such as the Appalachia Project in the USA in the 1960s and the contem-porary Trans-European Networks (TENs) policy in the EU, are transport-based. Governments and international institutions such as the World Bank also seek to promote transportation infrastructure and services where private capital investment or services may not be forthcoming. Paradoxically, the links between transport and economic development are at times questionable.

Transport frequently is an issue in **national security**. Policies are developed to establish sovereignty or to ensure control over national space and borders. The Interstate Highway Act of 1956, which provided the United States with its network of expressways, was formulated on the grounds of national security. Security was at the heart of the more recent impositions regarding passengers or freight clearance taking place at the port of departure in addition to conventional clearance occurring at the port of entry.

Transport raises many questions about **public safety** and **the environment**. Issues of public safety have for a long time led to the development of policies requiring driving licenses, limiting the hours of work of drivers, imposing equipment standards, estab-lishing speed limits, mandating highway codes, seatbelts and other accident controls. More recently, environmental standards and control measures are being instituted, in response to the growing awareness of the environmental impacts of transport. Examples include banning leaded gasoline and mandating catalytic converters in automobiles.

Transport policy has been developed to prevent or control the inherent **monopolistic tendency** of many transport modes. Unrestrained competition commonly leads to market dominance by a company, thereby achieving monopoly power. Such dominance brings into question many issues affecting the public interest such as access (smaller actors prevented to access infrastructure), availability (smaller markers being less service or services being discontinued) and price (the monopolist being in a position to charge high prices). Other reasons for policy intervention include the desire to **limit foreign ownership** of such a vital industry over concerns that the system would be side-tracked to service more foreign than national interests.

In recent years, four trends have had significant consequences over the context in which transport policy takes place:

- **Globalization** increased interactions at the international level, both for freight and passengers. This led to the emergence of large actors managing a portfolio of modes and infrastructures across international jurisdictions and therefore dealing with a variety of transport policies.
- **Deregulation and privatization** have been ongoing in many transport markets. This has enabled the transfer of ownership and operation of many transport modes to the private sector and favored the entry of new actors.
- A **broader focus** of policies, particularly in light of intermodalism and multi-modalism. This has enabled a better coordination of investments improving the efficiency of interconnected transportation networks.
- A move towards **social and political issues** behind transport projects as opposed to technical and engineering issues. Policy is becoming more responsive towards public concerns over issues such as environmental externalities and social equity. However, this has also been linked with additional costs, delays and controversy of many large transportation projects.

Policy instruments

Governments have a large number of instruments at their disposal to carry out transport policy. Some are direct, such as public ownership, but the majority are indirect, such as safety standards. An extremely important instrument is **public ownership**. The direct control by the state of transportation infrastructure, modes or terminals is very wide-spread. Most common is the provision by public agencies of transport infrastructure such as roads, ports, airports and canals. Public ownership also extends to include the operation of transport modes. In many countries airlines, railways, ferries and urban transit are owned and operated by public agencies.

Subsidies represent an important instrument used to pursue policy goals. Many transport modes and services are capital-intensive, and thus policies seeking to promote services or infrastructure that the private sector are unwilling or unable to provide may be made commercially viable with the aid of subsidies. Indirect subsidies were offered to the air carriers of many countries in the early years of commercial aviation through the awarding of mail contracts. Dredging of ship channels and the provision of other marine services, such as pilotage and navigation aids, are subsidies to facilitate shipping. Both public ownership and subsidies represent instruments that require the financial involvement of governments. Revenue generation is becoming an increasingly important instrument in transport policy.

Regulatory control represents a means of influencing the shape of transportation that is very widely employed. By setting up public agencies to oversee particular sections of the transport industry, governments can influence the entire character and performance of the industry. The agencies may exert control on entry and exit, controlling which firms can offer transportation services, at what prices, to which markets. Thus, while the actual services may be offered by private firms, the regulator in fact plays a determining role.

Many governments are major promoters of **research and development (R&D)** in transportation. Government research laboratories are direct products of state investments in R&D, and much university and industry R&D is sustained by government contracts and programs. The outcomes of this research are extremely important to the industry. It is a vital source for innovation and the development of new technologies such as intelligent vehicles and intelligent highway systems. In addition, educational institutions that are commonly funded by public resources provide managers and analysts for the private transport sector.

Labor regulations pertaining to conditions of employment, training, and certification may not be directed purposefully at influencing transport, but as a policy they may exert a significant effect over the industry. **Safety and operating standards**, such as speed limits, may have a similar effect. The restrictions on limiting the number of hours a truck driver may work may be instituted for safety reasons and for enhancing the working conditions of drivers, but they shape the economics of truck transport. In the same fashion speed limits help fix the distance of daily trips that one driver may undertake, thereby shaping the rate structure of the trucking industry.

Trends in policy development

Public policies reflect the **interests of decision makers** and their approaches to solving transport problems. These interests and approaches are both place-specific (they apply to a particular area of jurisdiction) and time-specific (they are established to reflect the conditions of transport and the intended solutions at a point in time). Policies change and evolve as conditions change and as new problems are recognized; they are dynamic. The dynamic nature of policy is reflected in the way the policy instruments have been employed over the years. In the nineteenth century, when many of the modern transport systems were being developed, the prevailing political economy was one of laissez-faire, in which it was believed that the private sector should be the provider of transport services and infrastructure. Examples of private transport provision include:

- **Turnpikes**. The first British modern roads in the eighteenth century were the outcome of private trusts aiming to derive income from tolls on roads they built and maintained. It was likely the first massive private involvement in transport infrastructure provision.
- **Canals**. Many of the earliest canals were built with private capital. One of the first canals that helped spark the Industrial Revolution in Britain was the Bridgewater Canal, built by the Duke of Bridgewater between 1761 and 1765 to haul coal from his mines to the growing industrial city of Manchester.
- **Urban transit**. In most North American cities public transit was operated by private firms. The earliest examples were horsecars that followed rail lines laid out on city streets. With electrification at the end of the nineteenth century, the horsecars were converted to streetcars and the network was greatly expanded. In the twentieth century, buses were introduced by private companies operating on very extensive route systems.

- **Ships**. Most maritime shipping companies were private enterprises. Many were family businesses, some of which became large companies, such as the Cunard Line in the UK, MSC in Switzerland or Maersk in Denmark. The main government involvement concerns military navies and ferries.
- **Railways**. Railways were developed by private companies during the nineteenth century, including companies such as Canadian Pacific and Union Pacific. In North America this has continued to the present day.

Many segments of the private transport sector were eventually captured by the government. In addition to the public ownership of transport modes, a growing amount of **regulatory control** emerged in the twentieth century. The belief in liberal markets with little public interference was seriously reconsidered after the crash of 1929 and the economic downturn of the early 1930s. From that moment on, governments were encouraged to extend the scope of their responsibilities. The public sector was an important trigger for the reconstruction of Europe in the aftermath of World War II (e.g. the Marshall Plan), for the modernization of the industrial structure and for economic growth. Economic and social measures were directed towards the creation of the welfare state. The period from the 1940s to the 1970s was characterized by nationalization when socialist ideology was put into practice throughout the world. For example, the European transport industry saw the emergence of large national companies in public transport, freight rail, ferry services, deep-sea shipping and the airline industry. These large nationalized companies could mobilize new sources and technologies, thereby contributing to the national objectives of economic growth and full employment.

While centrally planned economic systems (such as the Soviet Union, Eastern Europe and China) involved a complete control by the public sector, governments in Western Europe and North America were also major players in the market through market control systems up to the full nationalization of industries considered to be of strategic importance to economic development and external trade. The airline and the trucking industries saw entry limited by permits, and routes and rates were fixed by regulatory boards that had been set up to control the industries. At the same time greater safety regulations were being imposed and working conditions were increasingly being shaped by labor legislation.

By the 1960s, therefore, transportation had come under the sway of public policy initiatives that exerted an enormous influence on the industries and their spatial structures. At the same time, there was also a growing body of evidence that indicated that public ownerships and regulation were not always in the public interest. Transportation costs that were fixed by the regulatory authorities were maintained at higher levels than were necessary. Research demonstrated that many regulatory boards had been "captured" by those they were supposedly regulating, so that they were frequently acting to protect the industries rather than the public. At the same time there was a crisis of public finances in many countries, where the costs of operating the state-owned transportation industry were seen to be unsustainable. The **theory of contestability** repudiated traditional economic theory concerning monopoly power by arguing that the threat of entry of a new actor was sufficient to thwart a monopolist's ability to impose monopoly pricing. The key, therefore, is to relax entry thresholds, by allowing new firms to start up, a process that regulatory boards were impeding.

Deregulation and privatization policies have spread, unequally, to many other parts of the world. New Zealand has perhaps the most open transport policy, but many others, such as Canada and Australia, have made significant steps in this direction. In the EU, the pace of deregulation and privatization is proceeding unevenly. Subsidies to state-owned transport companies have been terminated and many airlines have been privatized. The government-owned railroads still exist in France, Germany, Italy and Spain, but the tracks have been separated from the traction and rail service operations, and have been opened up to new service providers. In Latin America, most of the state-owned transport sector has been deregulated. While the former centrally planned states have had to make the furthest adjustments to a more open market economy, several, such as China, have opened up large sections of the transport industry to joint ventures with foreign private enterprises. In China, many new highways and most of the major ports are being developed with private capital. Thus, at the beginning of the twenty-first century, transportation is under less direct government economic control worldwide than at any period over the last 100 years.

Changing nature of policy interventions

The recent trends in transport policy towards liberalization and privatization have not necessarily weakened government interventions. Government policy orientations have changed, however. Governments are beginning to exert greater control over environmental and security concerns, issues that are replacing former preoccupations with economic matters. For instance, because of biofuel policies aiming at ethanol production using corn, the unintended consequence was a surge on global food prices as more agricultural land was devoted for energy production instead of food production. The environment is becoming a significant issue for government intervention. Coastal zone legislation has made it increasingly difficult for ports to develop new sites in the USA. Air quality is a major factor influencing the allocation of US federal funds for urban transport infrastructure. In Europe, environmental issues are having an even greater influence on transport policy. The EU Commission is promoting rail and short sea shipping as alternatives to road freight transport. Projects are assessed on the basis of CO_2 reduction. All transportation projects are subject to extensive environmental assessments, which may lead to a rejection of proposals, despite strong economic justification. As a major source of atmospheric pollution and environmental degradation, the transportation industry can anticipate many further government environmental policy interventions.

Safety has always been a policy issue. Legislation imposing speed limits, mandating seatbelts, and other measures, have sought to make travel safer. These continue to proliferate. However, it is the area of security that the most recent set of policy initiatives have been drawn. Screening of people and freight has become a major concern since 9/11. Both the US government and international organizations such as the International Maritime Organization (IMO) and the International Civil Aviation Organization (ICAO) have instituted new measures that impact on operations, and represent additional costs to the transport industry.

While there may have been some reduction of policy involvement involving economic regulations, the influence of public policy on transport overall is still powerful but contentious at times. It must be acknowledged that capital investment by government in transport infrastructure commonly follows **multiple and sometimes conflicting policy goals**. For instance, short-terms policy goals of job creation are usually incompatible with long-term goals such as economic growth and energy efficiency. The usual outcome is that projects with multiple policy goals reduce their economic benefit.

Concept 2 – Transport planning

Authors: Dr Brian Slack and Dr Jean-Paul Rodrigue

The traditional transport planning process

Transport planning focuses upon the public provision and financing of transportation assets, particularly roads and public transit systems. It usually addresses specific problems or broad transport concerns at a local level and has been traditionally a preoccupation of lower tier governments. Because of this fact, transport planning is **most developed in the urban sphere**, and it is there where most experience has been gathered. The planning process, however, has a number of similarities with the policy process. Identifying a problem, seeking options and implementing the chosen strategy are essential steps in planning too. Because it tends to deal with localized problems, the solutions adopted in transport planning tend to be much more exact and specific than policy directives.

The common perspective is that planning is the realm of the public sector, although the private sector owns and operates substantial transportation assets. For a long time, planning was a field dominated by traffic engineers who gave it a distinctly mechanistic character, in which the planning process was seen as a series of rigorous steps undertaken to measure likely impacts and to propose engineering solutions. There were four major steps: trip generation, trip distribution, modal split and route selection. They involved the use of mathematical models, including regression analysis, entropy-maximizing models and critical path analysis. There are many reasons why the results of these models should be treated with caution:

- They are only **as good as the data they manipulate** and many times the data is inaccurate or incomplete.
- They are based on assumptions that the mathematical relationships between variables **remain constant**.
- They can be **manipulated** to produce the outcome that the analyst knows the client prefers.
- Because the predictions were **rarely subjected to subsequent evaluation**, their validity is largely questioned, and the modeler is happy to predict the future since projections rarely question the validity of the methodology.

The predictions of future traffic flows produced by the four-stage sequence are then used to identify planning options. Since the most common prediction of the modeling is that present capacities will be unable to cope with traffic growth, the tendency has been to produce planning solutions that call for an **expansion of capacity**. This has been referred to as predict and accommodate. It is the solution that typified so much urban transport planning from the 1940s to the 1980s. It has given rise to the enormous expansion of highway construction that reinforces the dominance of the automobile. Rarely are there post mortems of the prediction models and, as has been learned by empirical observation, the issue of induced demand has distorted the actual traffic.

Forecasting is contingent upon **predictability** where a result is expected to be consistently observed and **uncertainty**, which is the level of potential deviation from expected results (Figure 9.1). The prediction of a future outcome such as the traffic level (e.g. port or airport terminal, transit ridership) logically experiences a decline in

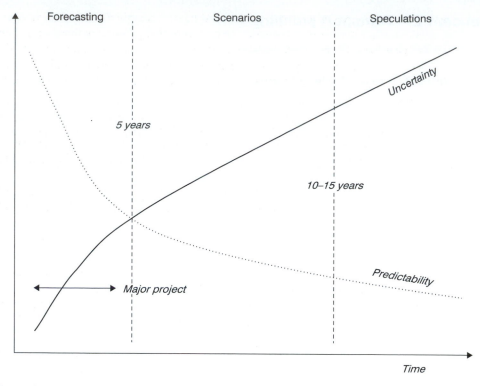

Figure 9.1   The prediction of future outcomes

predictability and a proportional increase in uncertainty as longer time frames are being considered. This exercise falls into three main dimensions:

- **Forecasting**. Commonly uses a trend of past observations and tries to infer this trend into the future. It assumes that the parameters related to an outcome remain constant and, as such, that its extrapolation is a relatively simple exercise using time series methods (e.g. moving average and compounded annual growth). These models also express uncertainty as growing confidence intervals. Once uncertainly reaches a level that is higher than predictability, forecasting ceases to be a relevant exercise, which requires scenario building. Depending on the level of predictability of what is being forecasted (some trends are more volatile than others) a time frame of five years is usually considered within the realm of reasonable forecasting. In addition, forecasting is subject to biases that can under- or overestimate trends.
- **Scenario building**. Tries to predict future outcomes by changing an array of parameters, with each change part of a specific scenario. A common strategy is to present the future within the realm of low, medium and high growth scenarios and apply these scenarios to forecasting by changing the annual growth rate. Scenario building does not remove uncertainty, but may improve predictability by considering a set of possibilities. There is no formal time frame for scenario building, but 10 to 15 years can be considered acceptable.
- **Speculations**. At some point the level of uncertainty is such that any prediction enters the realm of speculation. Quantitative methods lose much of their relevance

and under such circumstances the future must be seen mainly as a speculative exercise about what may or may not take place. A common problem is that forecasting often makes predictions within a speculative time frame, using a quantitative methodology to claim a high level of predictability, although this predictability is very low. Any forecast looking more than 10 years into the future should be considered as a speculation.

Scale has an important impact on predictability, as forecasting traffic for a single terminal is much more uncertain than for a region. Some outcomes are obviously easier to forecast than others as they have shown a greater level of stability and predictability in the past. For instance, demographic trends tend to be stable, shifting slowly and not subject to radical changes. An important challenge resides in the planning time frame of mega projects such as port or airport infrastructure. The delay between the decision to go ahead with the construction and the beginning of operations can easily last five years or longer. During that time, traffic expectations assumed by forecasting may have substantially changed.

Forecasting may not only provide inaccurate estimates, but may also support flaws, leading to incorrect interpretations. When forecasting is used to support investment decisions for infrastructure developments, these flaws can be far-reaching in consequence, such as fewer returns on investment than expected. The goal is obviously to be able to provide a capacity in line with the expected traffic level.

Figure 9.2 illustrates three conventional flaws in forecasting, particularly when such an exercise takes place within a standard cyclical growth pattern that includes introduction, acceleration, peak growth and maturity:

- **Underestimation bias**. Forecasting usually uses a reference year from which future trends are extrapolated. In the short term there are likely to be limited differences between the forecasted and actual traffic, leading to the impression that the trend is accurate. However, as the growth enters a phase of acceleration, a negative forecasting gap emerges where the level of activity is higher than expected. These biases are common at the beginning of business cycles and are the outcome of a lack of understanding of the growth potential, mostly because of uncertain market conditions. When the forecasting gap becomes too acute, congestion and capacity shortages take place. New forecasting attempts are usually made, which often leads to an overestimation bias.
- **Overestimation bias**. During phases of acceleration and peak growth positive outcomes are expected in the long term concerning the continuation of this growth. However, as growth enters a phase of maturity, a positive gap emerges, leading to less activity than expected. The overestimation bias is usually the most far-reaching in consequences since it often leads to an overinvestment in capacity. It is supported by the enthusiastic perception by managers and planners.
- **"Return to normal" bias**. On occasion, forecasts are made in a low growth context but assuming a growth trend that took place during peak growth. Such an approach is more a cognitive dissonance issue, with a refusal to see the existing context because it is contradictory to institutional or stakeholder interests.

The identified flaws are difficult to avoid since, as always, forecasting involves assessing future trends based upon incomplete information and uncertain market developments. Yet, recognizing that there are biases may lead to a more pragmatic view of how forecasting fits transportation infrastructure planning.

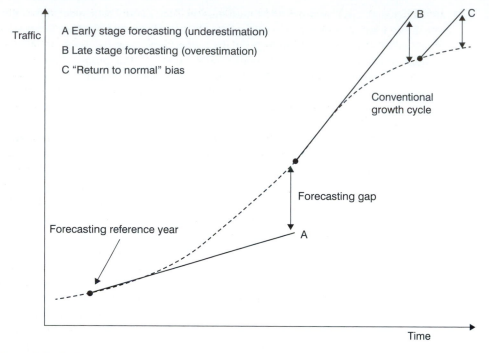

Traffic

A Early stage forecasting (underestimation)

B Late stage forecasting (overestimation)

C "Return to normal" bias

B

C

Conventional growth cycle

Forecasting gap

Forecasting reference year

A

Time

Figure 9.2 Common flaws in forecasting

Contemporary transport planning

In cities traffic problems have increased significantly since the 1970s, despite a great deal of urban transport planning. There is a growing realization that perhaps planning has failed and that the wrong questions have been asked. Rather than estimate traffic increases and then provide capacity to meet the expected growth, it is now accepted that what is required is **better management of the transport system**, particularly maintenance, through new approaches to planning. Just as urban planning requires the inputs of many specialists, transport planning is beginning to utilize multidisciplinary teams in order to broaden the scope of the planning process. Planning is still a multistep process, but it has changed considerably:

- **Goals and objectives**. While the goal of traditional transport policy, improving accessibility, is still useful, it has to be considered in the context of other desirable goals. For instance, improving safety and health, reducing emissions from vehicles, improving equity, enhancing economic opportunities, improving community livability and promoting mobility are all valid. But the prioritization of goals results in a very different planning process. Defining goals becomes a much more complicated stage in contemporary planning. Increasingly, goals have turned to consider managing demand rather than trying to build capacity.
- **Options**. Given the possible range of goals that transport planners have to consider, it becomes necessary to provide a set of possible options. Several objectives may be desirable, and thus it is important to consider what they imply. Several scenarios may have to be considered, and they must become important components of the planning process.

- **Identification of actors, institutions, stakeholders**. Given that transport planning has the potential to influence so many elements of society, it is important that those affected by the transport problem and its potential resolution should be identified so that they can be engaged. This would be a much wider list of affected parties than simply those involved in transportation activity itself, and requires recognizing a role for citizen participation. Failure to do so runs the risk of a project to meet significant opposition from stakeholders perceiving that they have been left out or that can be negatively impacted.

- **Predicting outcomes, identifying benefits and assessing costs**. The stage of predicting the outcomes for each of the options is a critical step in the process. Models continue to play an important role, but whereas the traditional models were based on the number of trips, increasingly modeling is becoming more activity-based. Transport is seen in the context of scheduling household decisions in time and space. Demographic and social data are used extensively, and mathematical models have become more sophisticated. Nevertheless, there are roles for other types of analyses, including non-objective forecasts. The predicted outcomes must then be assessed as to their benefits and costs. These may be expressed in monetary terms, but many transport planning situations call for measurement in other terms, such as visual impacts, environmental dislocations and employment impacts.

- **Choosing course of action**. Evaluation of the scenarios has to consider the costs and benefits from the frequently conflicting perspectives of the stakeholders and actors. Extensive public consultation may be required. The information has to be disseminated and explained so that an informed public can participate in the debate. Ultimately it will be the politicians who decide, but they are swayed by the strength of the arguments presented by the transport professionals, and in publicly contentious cases by pressure brought to bear by citizen groups.

Transport demand management and pricing

In rejecting the former paradigm of building capacity, transport planners have turned increasingly to **managing both demand and the transport system**. Building roads has produced a car-oriented society in which the other modal alternatives have little opportunity to coexist. Car ownership is beyond the ability of the transport planner to control directly and the question remains if it should. But car use and ownership is affected by land use and density, both elements that planners can affect. High population densities, in particular, favor walking, bicycling and public transit use. It is for this reason that a great deal of attention in planning is being paid to **densification and integration**. This includes concentrating development along well-served transport corridors (transit-oriented development) and increasing densities in areas undergoing rehabilitation.

While planning interventions may have a positive cumulative effect in shaping transport demand, some economists suggest that a more direct approach involving the imposition of more stringent cost measures on car users is necessary. It is widely accepted that car users pay only a small proportion of the actual costs of their vehicle use. Economists argue that the external costs should be borne by the users. As intuitively rational as this argument may be, there are several problems with its application:

- First, there are **difficulties in measuring externalities**, with considerable variations in estimates between different studies. Different types of use, speeds, engines, vehicle weight, or driving conditions, make it difficult to produce broadly accepted values.

Decision makers have difficulty agreeing to impose charges when there is a diversity of evidence about external costs.

- Second, there are **practical difficulties in collecting these costs**. One of the easiest and most widely used methods is a gasoline tax. It is a crude approach, however, because it imperfectly distinguishes between driving conditions and engine type. A fuel-efficient vehicle may have just as high consumption in heavy urban traffic as a less efficient vehicle in a rural setting.
- Third is the political difficulty of **imposing such additional costs on the public**. In North America in particular, free access to roads is regarded as a right, and it is intensely unpopular to propose any new forms of revenue generation that hints at additional taxation.

The effectiveness of economic controls is evident by the experience of Hong Kong, where, despite high incomes, car ownership and use remains at a very low level. This is due in the main to the high cost of parking. An even more drastic example is Singapore, where extreme measures limiting car purchases, high vehicle licenses, electronic tolls on highways and **cordon pricing** in the downtown area have restrained car use. The use of pricing mechanisms may be less in other countries, but the trend towards greater application of some forms of tolling is accelerating. Cordon pricing has been applied in a number of jurisdictions where access to certain areas, usually the CBD, is tolled. The most famous application was the decision to charge private vehicles for entry into Central London in early 2003, a program that has proved to be successful, despite a great deal of opposition.

Another form of pricing is congestion or "fair" pricing. Here certain lanes of a highway are tolled, but at variable rates. When traffic is moving freely, the charges for the tolled lanes are nil. But as traffic builds up and speeds are reduced, the costs of using the reserved lanes increase. Collection of the tolls is electronic, and drivers are informed of the current charges by large signs. Drivers are given a choice, therefore, to stay in the slower lanes for free, or move to the tolled lanes at a cost that is proportionate to the speed on the congested lanes.

Freight planning

The vast preponderance of transport planning, certainly at the urban level, has been devoted to passengers. The automobile and public transit issues have preoccupied planners, since individual mobility can be a highly political issue (drivers are also voters). Yet, freight traffic represents a **significant part** of many problems that planning seeks to address. The models and data inputs used in transportation planning are of little relevance when applied to freight movements. For example, demographic data, such as household size, the backbone of passenger analysis, are irrelevant for freight. The bipolar daily peak of traffic movements applies only to passengers, freight movements being distributed in a different profile over a 24-hour period.

While trucks account for approximately 10 percent of vehicles on the road, their size, low maneuverability, noisiness and high pollution output make their presence particularly objectionable. Truck pickup and delivery in city centers is particularly problematic because of limited parking. At the same time **trucks are vital to the economy** since they provide critical supplies. Commerce is dominated by trucking, and the logistics industry in particular is dependent on road transport for pickup and delivery. Garbage pickup, snow removal and fire protection are among many essential services that are truck-oriented.

Planning for freight movements, such as **city logistics**, is still in its infancy. As a largely private sector activity it is difficult to control, and many of the decisions that affect trucking are made by the industry itself. The emergence of large distribution centers on the outer fringes of metropolitan areas is taking place without much public control or oversight. In Europe, some attempts to manage such development by establishing publicly promoted freight villages had only limited success.

Several cities are seeking to limit trucking as pressures keep mounting. In many jurisdictions limits on heavy trucks in urban areas are in place, and there are restrictions on the times of delivery and pickup, which in some European cities extend to the exclusion of all trucks in the urban core during daytime hours. The question remains as to the extent that constraining urban freight circulation impairs the economy.

All these steps signify the beginning of the emergence of a more comprehensive freight planning process. In many cities there are limited data on freight traffic, so that planning takes place on an ad hoc basis. A much greater focus on freight planning is required, since freight distribution is an important component of urban mobility and activities.

Concept 3 – Transport safety and security

Authors: Dr Brian Slack and Dr Jean-Paul Rodrigue

A new context in transport security

While issues of safety and security have been before transport planners and managers for many years, it is only recently that physical security has become an overriding issue. In the past, concerns were already being raised, but the tragic events of 9/11 thrust the issue of physical security into public domain as never before and set in motion responses that are reshaping transportation in unforeseen ways. In addition, threats to health, such as the spread of pandemics, present significant challenges to transport planning and operations. Because of the nature of transport systems, safety and security issues concern the modes and the terminals. Each involves a different set of issues.

As locations where passengers and freight are assembled and dispersed, terminals have particularly been a focus of concern about security and safety. Because railway stations and airports are some of the most densely populated sites anywhere, crowd control and safety have been issues that have preoccupied managers for a long time. Access is monitored and controlled, and movements are channeled along pathways that provide safe access to and from platforms and gates. In the freight industry security concerns have been directed in two areas: worker safety and theft. Traditionally, freight terminals have been dangerous workplaces. With heavy goods being moved around yards and loaded onto vehicles using large mobile machines or manually, accidents are systemic. Significant improvements have been made over the years, through worker education and better organization of operations, but freight terminals are still comparatively hazardous. The issue of thefts has been one of the most severe problems confronting all types of freight terminals, especially where high-value goods are being handled. Docks, in particular, have been seen as places where organized crime has established control over local labor unions. Over the years, access to freight terminals has been increasingly restricted, and the deployment of security personnel has helped control thefts somewhat.

In light of the emergence of global supply chains the emphasis on freight transport security is gradually shifting into a more comprehensive but complex approach, including several dimensions and potential measures:

- **Dimensions**. Particularly concern the integrity of the cargo, the route and the information systems managing the supply chain.
- **Measures**. The set of procedures that can be implemented to maintain the integrity of the cargo, namely inspections, the security of facilities and personnel as well as of the data.

The expected outcomes of these measures include:

- **Reduced risk of disruptions of trade** in response to security threats.
- **Improved security against theft and diversion of cargo**, with reductions in direct losses (cargo and sometimes the vehicle) and indirect costs (e.g. higher insurance premiums).
- **Improved security against illegal transport of goods** such counterfeits, narcotics and weapons, and of persons.
- Reduced risk of **evasion of duties and taxes**.
- Increased **confidence in the international trading system** by current and potential shippers of goods.
- **Improved screening process** (cost and time) and simplified procedures.

Still, in spite of the qualitative benefits, the setting and implementation of security measures come at a cost that must be assumed by the shippers and eventually by the consumers. It has been estimated that an increase of 1 percent in the costs of trading internationally would cause a decrease in trade flows in the range of 2 to 3 percent. Security-based measures could increase total costs between 1 and 3 percent. Additionally, the impacts are not uniformly assumed, as developing countries, particularly export-oriented economies, tend to have higher transport costs. Security measures can affect them in a greater fashion.

Physical security of passengers

Airports have been the focus of security concerns for many decades. Hijacking aircraft came to the fore in the 1970s, when terrorist groups in the Middle East exploited the lack of security to commandeer planes for ransom and publicity. Refugees fleeing dictatorships also found taking over aircraft a possible route to freedom. In response, the airline industry and the international regulatory body, ICAO, established **screening procedures for passengers and bags**. This process seems to have worked, in the short run at least, with reductions in hijackings, although terrorists changed their tactics by placing bombs in unaccompanied luggage and packages, as for example in the Air India crash off Ireland in 1985 and the Lockerbie, Scotland, crash of Pan Am 103 in 1988 (Figure 9.3).

The growth in passenger traffic and the development of hub-and-spoke networks placed a great deal of strain on the security process. There were wide **disparities in the effectiveness of passenger screening** at different airports, and because passengers were being routed by hubs the numbers of passengers in transit through the hub airports grew significantly. Concerns were raised by some security experts, but the costs of improving

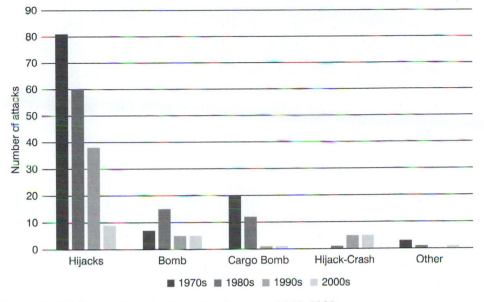

Figure 9.3 Worldwide attacks inside an aircraft by type, 1970–2009

screening and the need to process ever larger numbers of passengers and maintain flight schedules caused most carriers to oppose tighter security measures.

The situation was changed irrevocably by the events of 11 September 2001. The US government created the Department of Homeland Security, which in turn established a Transportation Security Authority (TSA) to oversee the imposition of strict new security measures on the industry. Security involves many steps, from restricting access to airport facilities, fortifying cockpits, the setting of no-fly lists, to the more extensive security screening of passengers. Screening now involves more rigorous inspections of passengers and their baggage at airports, including restrictions on what can be personally carried in airplanes such as gels and liquids. For foreign nationals, inspection employs biometric identification, which at present involves checking fingerprints, but in the future may include retinal scans and facial pattern recognition. A new system, the Computer Assisted Passenger Prescreening System (CAPPS II) was introduced. It required more personal information from travelers when they book their flights, which is used to provide a risk assessment of each passenger. Passengers considered as high risk were further screened. However, this program was cancelled in 2004, mostly because it created too many false positives, and replaced by the **Secure Flight** program, working under similar principles but entirely managed by the TSA. From 2009, all flights originating, bound to or flying over the United States had their list of passengers cross-referenced by a central no-fly list managed by the TSA.

The imposition of these measures has come at a considerable cost, which was estimated to be more than $7.4 billion annually by IATA. A significant factor has been the screening of passengers with the hiring and training of a workforce, the purchase of improved screening machines and the redesigning of airport security procedures. Further, aircraft design and operations have been changed, including the introduction of reinforced cabin doors. These measures also had an impact on passenger throughputs, with an estimated 5 percent decline attributed to security measures. Clearing security has become the most important source of delays in the passenger boarding process.

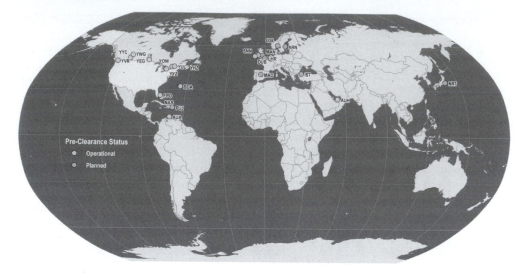

Figure 9.4 Customs pre-clearance airports for the United States

Passengers are now expected to arrive two hours before departure at the terminal in order to clear security.

Security issues have had a negative effect on the air transport industry as costs increased, with delays and inconveniences to passengers increasing as well. Business travel, the most lucrative submarket for the regular airlines, has suffered particularly sharp declines. Anecdotal evidence suggests that these passengers are switching to other modes for shorter trips so as to avoid the time delays and aggravation caused by the security process, and to executive jets for longer trips. However, these delays and inconveniences are now considered **part of contemporary air travel** with passengers accustomed to security requirements. The burden that security and customs procedures impose at major ports of entry have also prompted the expansion of customs pre-clearance programs (Figure 9.4).

A customs pre-clearance involves a traveler (and his/her belongings) clearing customs procedures in a third country before arriving in the destination country. It is the outcome of a bilateral agreement where the locations and the conditions (facilities, security, personnel) for pre-clearance to occur are set. Although pre-clearance can be used for many transportation modes, it is the most common for air transportation where each traveler undergoes immigration, customs, and agriculture inspection prior to boarding a direct flight to the destination country. Pre-clearance involves an airport setting a facility solely reserved for this purpose, such as a wing including a number of gates. The procedures and the facility must meet the criteria set by the pre-clearance agreement. This also incurs additional costs assumed by the airport, which are reflected in airfares (often as additional fees). However, passengers are commonly willing to assume these costs because of the convenience of not having to clear customs at the destination airport. About half a million passengers per year is deemed to be the threshold for pre-clearance to be economically justified. The main advantages of customs pre-clearance are:

● **Improved control**. By "pushing the border" outside its national boundary, a country is usually able to cope more effectively with immigration and security concerns. A traveler can be denied admission in a third country, without incurring deportation costs (holding and travel costs).

- **More destination choices**. An airline can use a pre-clearance airport to service any destination airport in a third country, even if these airports do not have customs facilities. This can substantially improve commercial opportunities through a wider set of destinations.
- **Less congestion at national gateways**. Customs pre-clearance can remove a significant number of passengers handled at national ports of entry. This can help mitigate congestion and overburdened customs facilities and improve international travel time at the aggregate level. The pre-clearance takes time before boarding, which is more flexible than time taken after disembarking.

The world's most significant pre-clearance agreement is between Canada and the United States, which involves eight Canadian airports (Calgary, Toronto, Edmonton, Halifax, Montreal, Ottawa, Vancouver and Winnipeg). Pre-clearance began in 1952 at Toronto Airport and by 1974 a formal agreement was reached. Since then the agreement has been revised and expanded. Although the agreement is bilateral, allowing pre-clearance to take place in both countries, pre-clearance only takes place in Canada. The structure of transborder airflows means that it is not conductive to have Canadian pre-clearance taking place in the United States, since the network involves a few Canadian airports connected to many American airports. Pre-clearance agreements also exist with Ireland (Dublin and Shannon), Aruba, the Bahamas (Freeport and Nassau), Bermuda and the United Arab Emirates (Abu Dhabi). As of 2014, more than 16 million passengers bound to the United States were handled through pre-clearance agreements (including Canada).

In light of the increasing growth of international passenger flows and the congestion of major American ports of entry, the pre-clearance program is being expanded. An additional 10 airports are being considered. They include Belgium (Brussels), the Dominican Republic (Punta Cana), Japan (Tokyo Narita), the Netherlands (Amsterdam Schiphol), Norway (Oslo), Spain (Madrid Barajas), Sweden (Stockholm Arlanda), Turkey (Istanbul Ataturk) and the United Kingdom (London Heathrow and Manchester). Collectively these airports handled about 20 million passengers bound to the United States in 2014. This is likely to further reinforce the hub function of these airports within international and regional air transport systems.

Freight security

Security in the freight industry has always been a major problem. Illegal immigrants, drug smuggling, custom duty evasion, piracy, and the deployment of substandard vessels (higher propensity to accidents) have been some of the most important concerns. However, as in the air passenger business, the events of 9/11 highlighted a new set of security issues. The scale and scope of these problems in freight is of an even greater magnitude. The **less regulated** and **greater international dimensions** of the shipping industry in particular have made it vulnerable to security breaches. The large number of ports, the vast fleet of global shipping and the range of products carried in vessels, and the difficulty of detection, has made the issue of security in shipping an extremely difficult one to address. For ports, vulnerabilities (unauthorized access to cargo and facilities) can both be exploited from the land side as well as on the maritime side. The container, which has greatly facilitated globalization, makes it extremely difficult to identify illicit and/or dangerous cargoes. In the absence of scanners that can scan the entire box, manual inspection becomes a time-consuming and virtually impossible task considering the large volumes involved. **Hubbing** compounds the problem, as large numbers of containers are required to be handled with minimum delays and inconvenience.

In the USA the response was to enact the Maritime Transportation and Security Act in 2002. The basic elements of this legislation were adopted by the International Maritime Organization (IMO) in December 2002 as the International Ship and Port Security code (ISPS). There are three important features of these interventions. First is the requirement of an **Automated Identity System** (AIS) for all vessels between 300 and 50,000 dwt. AIS requires vessels to have a permanently marked and visible identity number, and there must be a record maintained of its flag, port of registry and address of the registered owner. Second, each port must undertake a **security assessment**. This involves an assessment of its assets and facilities and an assessment of the effects of damages that might be caused. The port must then evaluate the risks, and identify its weaknesses to its physical security, communication systems, utilities, etc. Third, all cargoes destined for the USA must **receive customs clearance prior to the departure of the ship**. In addition, it is proposed that biometric identification for seafarers is to be implemented and that national databases of sailors are to be maintained.

The ISPS code is being implemented in ports around the world. Without certification, a port would have difficulty in trading with the USA. Security is thus becoming a **factor in a port's competitiveness**. The need to comply with ISPS has become an urgent issue in ports large and small around the world. The costs of securing sites, of undertaking risk assessments and of monitoring ships all represent an additional cost of doing business, without any commercial return. US ports have been able to tap funding from the Department of Homeland Security, but foreign ports have to comply or risk the loss of business. In 2008, legislation in the USA required that all containers being shipped to the USA undergo screening. Foreign ports were expected to purchase very expensive gamma-ray and x-ray scanners, and undertake screening of all US-bound containers, regardless of the degree of security threat. This is a further financial and operational complication that foreign ports have to contend with.

Like its passenger counterpart, the airline freight industry is facing stringent security requirements. Since 2010, a TSA regulation requires the screening of all cargo carried by air within the United States or internationally, and this before being loaded. The **Certified Cargo Screening Program** (CCSP) forces airlines, freight forwarders and shippers to assume the costs of these security measures in an attempt to establish a secure air freight transport chain. The measure imposed additional costs, delays and disruptions, undermining the operational effectiveness of air cargo. Still, the air freight industry has adapted to these measures.

Concept 4 – Transportation and disasters

Transportation and national security

Transportation systems are designed to operate under normal conditions. Yet, disruptions such as those caused by an accident or by a storm are rather common and well mitigated. On occasion, a disruption at a much higher scale takes place to the extent that the safety or security of a whole region or nation is compromised. A **disaster** involves extensive damage to people and physical infrastructure that is unforeseen in nature, scale and extent. It often implies that their risk of occurrence has not been properly assessed and a large share of the damage is the outcome of a lack of preparedness.

Transportation is often considered a **critical infrastructure,** since a disruption in one of its components can have a significant impact on the economic and social well-being of a region of a nation. An effective way to assess how critical an infrastructure is would be to consider the impacts its removal would have on the flows and activities it services. From an economic standpoint, the impacts of disasters are dependent on three factors: the nature and level of incidence of disasters; the level of exposure of populations and infrastructures; and the level of vulnerability of populations and infrastructures. There are several drivers that have an impact on the threats and risk level of disasters on transportation systems:

- **Increased mobility**. The mobility of passengers (for commuting, tourism, business and migration) and freight has increased notably around the world, including the crossing of international boundaries. Air and maritime transportation are particularly illustrative, since their growth implies more vehicles and cargo in circulation. This trend has also been strengthened by trade agreements and reductions in tariffs promoted by organizations such as the World Trade Organization. There are more economic opportunities, but some risks, such as infectious diseases, can spread faster and more extensively.

- **Infrastructure and economic interdependency**. Infrastructures are increasingly interdependent, particularly transportation and energy infrastructures, so a disruption in one will have an effect on others. This interdependency is also economic, as global or regional trade is based upon mutual specialization. Some parts and components are provided by a limited number of suppliers, which can be prone to risks in case of disruptions. In several sectors, supply chains are relatively rigid, implying that there are limited options for substitution. The same applies to resources such as oil that require a continuous supply with limited margins to accommodate major disruptions.

- **Centralization and concentration of distribution**. The principle of economies of scale often leads to a centralization of network structures and a concentration of economic activities. Most transportation systems are organized in hub-and-spoke networks, particularly for air transportation, but this characteristic is also prevalent in maritime shipping. Global trade is articulated by major gateways where a few control a large share of the commercial flows. At the more basic geographical level, strategic passages impose bottlenecks for global maritime freight circulation.

- **Urbanization**. The emergence of large cities has led to acute concentrations of populations, a pattern significantly different than the more dispersed settlements that prevailed in rural societies. Concentration of population equates with a concentration of risk. Thus, any disaster affecting an urban area is compounding its impacts on a par with the population and infrastructure density. It is also worth underlining that many of the world's largest cities are located in coastal areas, exposing them to an additional array of risks linked with hurricanes and storm surges.

The transport industry has responded to these drivers with massive investments in infrastructure and facilities that have expanded the capacity and efficiency of transportation systems, at both the domestic and international levels. Added flows and capacities have in turn created increased demands on the management of physical distribution systems, which includes activities such as transportation, transshipment, warehousing, insurance and retailing. These are all of strategic importance to national economies. With the increasing reliance on distribution systems, any failure of transportation, due to intentional or non-intentional causes, can have very disruptive consequences and can compromise national security over four major issues:

- **Transportation supply**. Ensuring that transportation modes, routes, terminals and information systems are able to satisfy national security needs such as troop deployment and emergency relief.
- **Transportation readiness**. Maintaining the readiness of transportation to face time-sensitive national security needs.
- **Transportation vulnerability**. Reducing the vulnerability of the transportation modes, terminals and users to intentional harm or disruption from natural events.
- **Illegal use of transportation**. Reducing the trade of restricted or illegal goods (e.g. drugs, endangered species) and illegal immigration.

Potential threats and risks

The disruptions caused by disasters take place over complex transportation systems and are consequently difficult to evaluate. Particularly, the non-linearity character of complex systems implies that a disruption can have multiplying and feedback effects, many unforeseen. A disaster of high severity is likely to trigger a phase transition where the resulting transport conditions are very different to those before the event. The **resilience** of a transport system is its capability to resume operations at a level similar to that before a disruption occurred. A simple taxonomy of disasters reveals that they are natural or man-made in origin. **Natural disasters** come in four main categories.

Many **weather events** such as storms and blizzards occur regularly and tend to have minimal impacts on transport systems with delays, partial closures or diversions. Others, such as floods, cyclones (hurricanes), tornadoes and droughts, can be of disastrous proportions. Tropical cyclones (hurricanes) are particularly harmful, since they cover wide areas (a midsized cyclone can cover an area of 500 km in diameter), are moving slowly (25 km per hour) and are associated with high winds and rainfalls. Regional air transport and public transit systems are usually shut down and land transportation can be seriously impaired. For instance, Hurricane Sandy, which struck the New York/New Jersey coasts in 2012, caused the preemptive shut down of all the airports, ports and public transit systems of the region. Due to flooding and power outages, it took several days for the system to be brought back to normal operating conditions, which had substantial impacts on commuting. There are concerns that climate change may be linked with more recurrent extreme weather events. Beyond this debate the fact remains that extreme weather events will continue to occur, but their frequency and scale is uncertain.

Tectonic activity is the source of the most serious **geophysical disasters**. Earthquakes are salient forms of geophysical threats since they are difficult to predict. Tsunamis are also considered an emerging risk as a growing number of people live along coastal areas. The 2011 Tohoku earthquake in Japan is among the five largest in recorded history. While the damage by the earthquake was significant, it is the associated tsunamis that caused the most extensive damage to Japanese transport infrastructure. Further, the earthquake had significant impacts on global supply chains as the Japanese automobile production fell by 50 percent in the following months, mostly because of disruptions in supply chains. Although areas of high earthquake occurrence are readily identified, the specific location and scale of an event remains a probability that is often difficult to conceptualize in the planning of transport infrastructure. While volcanoes have always been localized and easily identifiable risks, the ash clouds they release have recently been a source of concern. For instance, the ash cloud released by the 2010 eruption of the Eyjafjallajökull volcano in Iceland forced the shutdown of most of the European and transatlantic air transport systems for close to a week, stranding millions of passengers. Since air transportation is an extremely recent phenomenon in geological times, the probability and extent of ash cloud events remains uncertain. For instance, an event of the scale of the Krakatau 1883 eruption taking place today would be have profound ramifications for the global maritime and air transport systems.

Geomagnetic storms concern disturbances in the earth's magnetic structure, mostly the outcome of solar activity where the frequency of geomagnetic storms varies accordingly. Geomagnetic storms can impair power grids and have a higher probability of taking place around the north and south poles. Still, they are a less known and often underestimated risk. The largest geomagnetic storm in history took place in 1859, but since back then electrical systems were rudimentary, its impacts on human activities were marginal. Such an event taking place today would be heavy in consequences (e.g. hundreds of millions losing electric power) and would qualify as a disaster.

Potential **rises in sea levels** attributed to anthropogenic causes (global warming) qualify as a natural disaster. There is a variety of scenarios about potential sea level rises, but evidence suggests the near certainty of a 1 m rise by the year 2100 (compared to a 2000 baseline). If the sea level rise accelerates, this 1 m scenario could even be reached by 2050. Irrespective of the timing, sea level rise places critical transport infrastructures such as ports and airports at risk of damage and discontinuity in operations. For instance, a port terminal or an airport could not be directly impaired by sea level rise, but its access roads could be, compromising its commercial viability. Sea level rise would also amplify the impacts of extreme weather events, namely storm surges.

The second class of disasters concern those that are **man-made,** and they can be intentional or unintentional. **Accidents** are the outcome of technical failures or human errors and where modes, infrastructure or terminals can be damaged, even destroyed, which includes injuries, the loss of life and property damage. Small-scale accidents occur very frequently, particularly over road transportation systems. However, transportation-related accidents are rarely considered as disasters because they are mostly very isolated events not related to a massive loss of life and damage. There are notable exceptions. An aircraft crash with a complete loss of life can be considered a disaster. With improved airline safety these events are, however, increasingly uncommon, particularly in relation to the growing number of passenger-km flown each year around the world (Figure 9.5). Industrial accidents related to the release of hazardous cargo (particularly fuel and chemicals) that takes place in an urban area, either during transport or at a transport terminal, are also an issue for concern.

Like all modes of transportation, air transport is subject to accidents that can be due to human (67 percent) or technical (20 percent) causes, and rarely due to atmospheric conditions (6 percent). Since air accident statistics started to be systematically compiled, 54 percent of all accidents took place less than 10 km from an airport, whereas 50 percent and 21 percent of all accidents occurred during the landing and take-off phases respectively. The evolution of the yearly number of fatalities is quite revealing. Up to the early 1970s the number of fatalities increased with some proportionality with the growth of air traffic. By the 1970s, in spite of substantial growth levels of air traffic, fatalities took a downward trend. This is jointly the outcome of better aircraft designs, improved pilot training, better navigation and control systems, as well as comprehensive accident management aiming to identify the causes and then possible mitigation strategies.

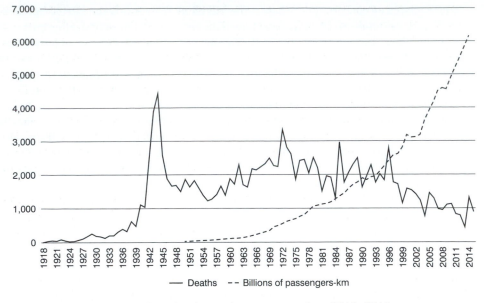

Figure 9.5 Number of yearly fatalities due to air transport crashes, 1918–2015

Source: Aircraft Crashes Record Office, Geneva.

For instance, on 2 August 1985 Delta Flight 191 from Fort Lauderdale ran into a developing thunderstorm and wind shear conditions on its final approach to Dallas/Fort Worth Airport (DFW). The strong and unstable winds forced the plane, a Lockheed L-1011, to hit the ground before the runway, resulting in 135 fatalities. An investigation into the cause of the accident prompted substantial revisions in airport emergency procedures and upgrades in weather detection equipment. On 1 June 2009, Air France Flight 447 from Rio de Janeiro to Paris crashed in the Atlantic Ocean off the coast of Brazil. In this case temporarily defective air sensor speed readings, due to ice accumulation and pilot error, caused an aerodynamic stall that crashed the plane, resulting in 228 fatalities. After the investigation, it was recommended that staff received better training concerning stall recovery at high altitudes, and that planes be retrofitted with heated air speed sensors. The safety record of air transportation therefore continues to improve.

Transportation infrastructure can fail due to a lack of (or deferred) maintenance, design flaws or handling more traffic than they are designed for. Bridges and other similar structures are particularly vulnerable, especially from a system-wide perspective where aging (or poorly maintained) infrastructure can impact many components within a similar time frame.

Conflicts such as wars and civil unrest often result in the damaging of infrastructure, with transportation commonly a voluntary or involuntary target. Due to the importance of global trade and the structure of maritime shipping networks, bottlenecks (strategic passages) are subject to risk of partial or complete closure. **Terrorism** has been a disruptive issue that came to the forefront over the last two decades. For instance, the disruptions caused by the 11 September 2001 events can clearly be considered a disaster because of their scale and scope, such as the closing of the North American air transport system. The surge in global trade in the second half of the twentieth century created an environment where **piracy** is on the rise. Shipping lines are forced to pass through constrained areas, chokepoints, namely straits such as Malacca and Bab el-Mandab along the heavily used Asia–Europe maritime routes, which make the interception of ships more feasible within a delimited area. The outcome of piracy on global supply chains has been small but not negligible, as ships have changed their routing and insurance surcharges are being levied for cargo transiting through areas prone to piracy.

Economic and political shocks are likely to play a growing role in the future, particularly financial issues, as most developed nations have accumulated a staggering amount of debt that is likely to be defaulted on. Such an event would be associated with a lack of capital available for infrastructure construction, maintenance and oversight, rendering elements of the transport system more prone to risks, such as accidents and infrastructure failure.

At the intersection of natural (biological) and man-made causes (people are vectors and a virus could be mutated by anthropogenic causes), a **pandemic** is an event of potential profound ramifications. Yet, the risk of the event itself is extremely difficult to assess. Although a pandemic would not directly damage transportation systems, transportation is intractably linked with such a disaster, as it will act as a vector for its diffusion (particularly air transportation) and a shutting down of transportation services in the wake of a pandemic would compromise supply chains (food, energy, medical supplies).

As the freight transportation dimension is getting increasingly globalized and complex, supply chain risks are salient. Developing countries are particularly vulnerable to an array of disasters because infrastructure, including transportation, tends to be of lower quality and thus less resilient to disruptions. A fundamental element in addition to the risk is who bears the responsibility for it. International commercial transactions underline that the actor assuming the liability depends on the type of terms. Therefore, depending on the terms of the contract, the same event may imply a different allocation of liability.

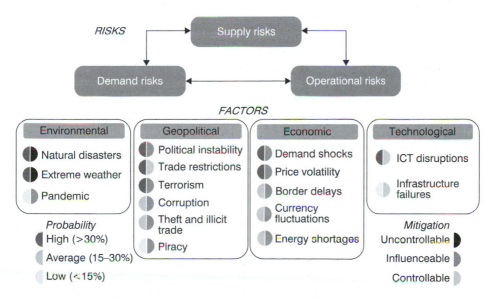

Figure 9.6 Risks in global supply chains

Source: Adapted from World Economic Forum (2012) *New Models for Addressing Supply Chain and Transport Risk.*

The complexity of supply chains requires an assessment of the types of risks involved and the related factors that may cause them. The risks are interrelated:

- **Supply risks**. Impacts elements of inbound supply, implying that a supply chain is unable to meet the demand in terms of quantity and quality of parts and finished goods. The outcome is labeled as a supply disruption.
- **Demand risks**. Impacts elements of the outbound supply chain where the extent or fluctuation of the demand are unexpected. This is labeled as demand disruption.
- **Operational risks**. Impacts elements within a supply chain, impairing its ability to supply services, parts or finished goods within the standard requirements of time, cost and quality. Transportation is one of the most salient operational risks.

The most significant factors impacting supply chain risks are environmental, geopolitical, economic and technological. Each factor has a probability of causing disruptions within global supply chains, ranging from high to low. There is also a level of mitigation associated with each factor, ranging from uncontrollable, where an actor has no influence on an event and must thus simply assume the consequences, to controllable, where an actor has a good level of influence on the event itself and may thus be able to mitigate more effectively some of its aspects. The main factors are:

- **Environmental**. Considered to be the factors that have among the highest probability of occurrence and that can be the least effectively mitigated, since they tend to be uncontrollable. Natural disasters (e.g. earthquakes) and extreme weather are within this category, including potential sea level rises. Pandemics are also a possibility, but their probability and mitigation remains uncertain.
- **Geopolitical**. Several geopolitical factors tend to have a high probability, namely conflicts and trade restrictions, but supply chain actors have a level of influence on the outcome.
- **Economic**. The most significant economic factors relate to demand shocks, often associated with political or economic sudden changes. Price volatility is also a concern since it has an important impact on input costs. Like geopolitical factors, supply chain actors have a level of influence on the outcome. For instance, trade restrictions arbitrarily imposed by governments can have important impacts, but the industry is able either to comply or to put pressures to have these restrictions changed if they are judged to be unacceptable.
- **Technological**. Transport infrastructure failures are fairly rare, so the most salient technological concern involves ICT disruptions. As supply chain management increasingly relies on information technologies for its management and operations, any information system failure has important ramifications.

Transportation disaster planning

Although a potential disaster can never be effectively planned, and even anticipated in some instances, there are a series of steps, known as **Disasters Risk Management**, which could reduce disruptions:

- **Risk assessment**. The likelihood of an event and its potential impacts should be comprehensively assessed, such as low to high probability over a defined time frame and over a specific area (e.g. a city). This should provide a prioritization of risks, but it remains a very uncertain process.

- **Preparedness**. In light of the potential risks, a level of preparedness should be considered in terms of potential responses. This can involve the warehousing and positioning of relief material, such as fuel, parts and equipment, and the training of the labor force in emergency situations.
- **Mitigation**. Concerns the immediate reaction to the event and can involve the shutting down of transport systems (particularly public transit), the evacuation of populations and the mobilization of first response resources, namely distributing emergency relief (food, medical supplies). The goal is to control and attenuate the disruptions caused by the disaster.
- **Response**. Once the disaster has been mitigated, steps are implemented to bring back capacity with existing infrastructure. If a mode has been impaired, the usage of alternative modes and infrastructure has to be considered. The goal is to keep operational as many elements of the transport system as possible.
- **Recovery**. Concerns all the steps necessary to recover the transport capacity that was lost during the disaster. It can involve repairs, the restarting services that were discontinued, as well as investments in new and improved infrastructures, modes and terminals. The goal is to bring back the capacity and level of service to pre-disaster conditions. With the lessons learned from the disaster, more resilient infrastructure and networks are a likely outcome.

The reconstruction time of transportation infrastructure tends to be slower than other infrastructure. Evidence from the 1995 Kobe earthquake underlines that electric power and telecommunications are first restored in a matter of weeks. Road and rail infrastructure can take several months, while for port infrastructure it can be a matter of years. Transport infrastructures, particularly terminals, are much more capital-intensive than utilities and require specialized and heavy equipment for their repair or construction. Highway and rail services can run at lower capacity and on alternative routes. If a port is shut down, other ports can generally be used (the same applies for air travel). While this is less efficient, as it involves longer routes for imports or exports, it remains in most cases economically feasible.

CASE STUDY   Information technologies and mobility

Information technologies and transportation

The emergence and diffusion of information and telecommunication technologies (ICT) have several economic and social impacts, notably on functions related to information processing and diffusion. First, it is important to underline that information technologies **do not lead to a dematerialization of an economy**. They enable a better management and organization of existing material assets. With the emergence of an information society, the transactional structures of the economy have changed drastically towards a networked organizational form to which ICT support improved, and more intensive interactions. These interactions involve three major spheres:

- **Personal**. ICT enables individuals to maintain contact through additional mediums (e.g. email). This may lead to more interactions. The diffusion of mobile personal computing devices (e.g. laptops, smartphones and tablet computers) has also enabled

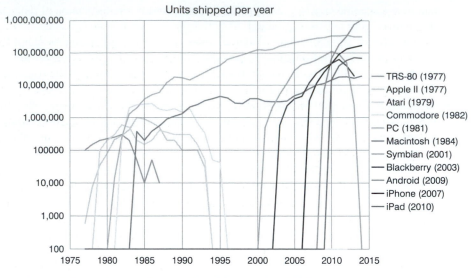

Figure 9.7 Diffusion of personal computing devices, 1977–2014

Source: pre-2000 data compiled by H. Dediu and J. Reiner. Recent data from Gartner, Inc.

individuals to enrich their mobility by enabling them to perform various tasks while in transit or outside a conventional office setting (Figure 9.7). Several applications, such as Global Positioning Systems (GPS), enable individuals to better manage their mobility.

- **Customer/retailer**. Online retailing has opened a whole new array of commercial opportunities as a complement or a substitution to conventional shopping. It does not necessarily imply that there would be more consumption, but that a growing share of retailing transactions takes place online, resulting in parcels to be delivered.
- **Business to business**. The increasing scale and intensity of business transactions is commonly linked with new efficiencies, particularly through supply chain management.

Personal computing devices, enabling its user to execute customizable programs, started to become available in the late 1970s and became mass-market products by the mid-1980s. By 2014, more than 315.9 million PC platform devices alone were sold around the world – a slight decline from 335.4 million units sold in 2011. The diffusion of personal computing undertook three distinct phases:

- **The setting of standards**. By the late 1970s several different platforms using different standards and operating systems were being introduced. Interoperability was close to being nonexistent, suggesting that each platform required its own hardware and software. The main contenders were Apple (Apple II), Commodore (64 and Amiga), Atari (400/800) and Tandy (TRS-80). The introduction of the IBM PC in 1981 marked the downfall of competing standards with the adoption of the MS-DOS operating system from which the PC platform would evolve. In 1984, MacOS, the first graphical user interface available for a home computer, would carve a niche on which the Macintosh platform would evolve. By the late 1980s, non-PC and MacOS devices were disappearing from the market.

- **Performance, interface and interconnectivity**. From 1985, the two prevailing platforms, with the PC dominating (selling 8–10 times more platforms than Macintosh), undertook a massive diffusion in the consumer and corporate markets. Performance in terms of processing, memory and storage capacity was growing exponentially (Moore's law), while costs were declining. Graphical user interfaces became the standard (e.g. Windows), enabling users to operate complex applications in a relatively easy fashion. By the late 1990s, the development of the Internet opened an entirely new range of services to personal computing devices, such as telecommunications (e.g. email), e-commerce, information access and entertainment. Portable computing devices (laptops) also became widely available.

- **Mobile computing**. By 2005, cellular phones, which emerged as mass-market products in the mid-1990s, saw their integration with features that were previously only available to desktop and laptop computers or to specialized devices such as digital cameras or GPS receivers. The cellular phone evolved from being solely a telecommunication device (with basic features such as an address book, a clock and a calendar) to a true mobile personal computing device offering a wide range of customizable features (apps). The most salient platforms were Symbian (Nokia), Blackberry, iPhone and Android. Their massive diffusion was helped by the ubiquity of wireless networks in developed and developing countries alike. Similar to what happened in the early stages of commercial computing, two mobile telephone platforms dominate (Android and iPhone), while Symbian was discontinued in 2014 and Blackberry has seen its user base substantially decline. In 2013, Android device sales exceeded 1 billion units, making this platform the most dominant personal computing device in the world. With the introduction of the iPad in 2010, new forms of personal portable computing devices became available, which created new niches (e.g. ebooks) that are more complementing than competing with conventional personal computing devices such as the PC. The latter reached peak market diffusion with sales stabilizing and new competitors introducing tablet products.

One of the ongoing tenets is that ICT can offer a form of substitution for physical mobility. Particularly, it can be expected that work-related movements can be mitigated through **telecommuting**, that is, using information and telecommunication technologies to perform work at a location away from the traditional office location and environment. Commuting is thus substituted and it is implied that it takes place remotely instead. There are obviously various degrees of telecommuting, ranging from a partial substitution where a worker may spend one day per week performing work at another location, to a complete substitution, where the work is performed elsewhere, such as in an offshore call center. The latter is much less likely, as the great majority of work tasks tend to be collaborative and require face-to-face meetings.

ICT and mobility

The ICT potential impacts on mobility either involve a modification, a substitution or a generation of a movement. Such outcome is contingent upon the socioeconomic and geographical context in which it is taking place. ICT technologies continue to push the centrifugal forces that have shaped the physical structure of metropolitan areas around the world outward. **Reducing automobile use** is one of the primary expected benefits of telecommuting, as it is assumed that corresponding home-to-work trips will not be made. Telecommuters usually eliminate two trips per day when they work at home. If this commuting was done in a car, the reduction of trips obviously has environmental benefits, including reduced emissions of pollutants and reduced fossil fuel use.

Telecommunications, like the automobile, has become a **force shaping land use and transportation** in urban areas. Cheaper space in the suburbs is an important requirement for newer and smaller firms that are users of new telecommunications technologies. The growing capability of telecommunications allows businesses and other organizations to locate operations more flexibly, but this may be perceived as paradoxical, as ICT may be supporting an **energy-inefficient spatial structure**. The intensity and scheduling of mobility can become highly interactive with ICT, as users are able to coordinate their mobility in the light of real-time changes and events such as congestion.

Having said all this, telecommuting has often failed to meet expectations and its share of total commuting movements remains low and relatively unchanged: 3–5 percent of the total workforce can be telecommuting at least once a month. There are many reasons for this enduring low share, ranging from activities that cannot be easily substituted to a loss of direct control from management. One major factor is that if a job has the potential to be complemented by telecommuting, it is also a target for **relocation to a low-cost location either through outsourcing or offshoring**. There is thus a large amount of telecommuting that took place as offshoring instead. Also, many workers use forms of telecommuting to work overtime and carry extra work at home. Therefore, telecommuting allows employers to impose longer work hours, as well as ensure a higher level of availability of employees to work on an on-call basis outside regular working hours.

ICT and economic activities

In addition to substitution and mobility issues, ICT have an impact on the location and the operations of economic activities. **Location and larger building sizes** have dominated retailing and offices since World War II. Indeed, newer and larger stores overtook smaller rivals and established new distribution structures based on mass retailing. The standard 2,000 square ft market of the 1950s became the 20,000 square ft supermarket in the 1960s, and evolved into the 50,000 square ft superstore of the 1990s. Following a similar trend, the small office of a company has become several floors in a skyscraper located in downtown areas, and in time the amount of space devoted to administrative functions has increased significantly.

Competition and technological changes are forcing corporations to recognize real estate as an undermanaged asset as occupancy cost is the second largest corporate expense after wages. Telecommunications advances may lead to a change in the space needs of several corporations, as more services can be performed with less office and branch space. Telecommuting workers also tend to be more productive, as they systematically spend more time working, mainly because they are not spending that time commuting but also ICT makes them more available to perform tasks.

Most corporations see ICT **as a way to reduce costs**, not necessarily to promote the welfare of their office employees, even if they are doing both at the same time. The costs of providing office space to employees are very high, far more than just the cost of leasing or building the space and maintaining it. It also concerns, for instance, parking, which tends to be more expensive in high-density areas often related with office activities. In some cases, it can run as high as 20–30 percent of disbursed salaries per employee. A common outcome is to outsource or offshore the job instead of focusing on telecommuting.

The expected impacts of ICT on economic activities and on the general urban environment can be summarized by the following:

- **Travel substitution**. The rapid proliferation of ICT, such as mobile phones, intranets and teleconferencing, promotes new forms of mobility mostly in the form of travel substitutions such as telecommuting. Yet, substitution remains relatively marginal.
- **Efficiency improvements**. The outcome of better management of vehicles, routes and assets. This is particularly the case with freight distribution with the application of logistics. It also increasingly applies to individual mobility where smartphones and GPS provide navigation assistance and real-time information about traffic conditions, as well as the opportunity to synchronize one's mobility with others.
- **Organizational structure**. Organizational structures are being transformed from a hierarchy to a network of collaborators. This commonly results in management which is more flexible and able to adapt to market changes, including new sourcing strategies.
- **Retail structure**. ICT is changing the retailing sector by rendering some location structures obsolete and by minimizing inventory costs. The impacts of e-commerce are particularly salient since the permitted new forms of distribution and new forms of retailing.
- **Locational flexibility**. ICT improves the flexibility of office activities by offering a wider array of locational choices. This helps lower office space requirements by decentralizing a set of tasks to a lower cost environment, such as the suburbs or at home, or by permitting their complete offshoring to low-cost locations. ICT are therefore a corporate strategy to improve the productivity of labor.

Bibliography

Baumol W.J. (1984) "Deregulation and the theory of contestable markets." *Yale Journal on Regulation* 1: 111–137.

Flyvbjerg, B. (2009) "Survival of the unfittest: why the worst infrastructure gets built – and what we can do about it." *Oxford Review of Economic Policy* 25(3): 344–367.

Gillen, D. and W.G. Morrison (2015) "Aviation security: costing, pricing, finance and performance." *Journal of Air Transport Management* 48: 1–12.

Goetz A.R. (2002) "Deregulation, competition, and antitrust implications in the US airline industry." *Journal of Transport Geography* 10: 1–19.

Hogwood, B. and L.A. Gunn (1984) *Policy Analysis for the Real World*. Oxford: Oxford University Press.

Kappenman, J. (2012) "A perfect storm of planetary proportions." *IEEE Spectrum*, February.

Luke, T.C. and J.-P. Rodrigue (2008) "Protecting public health and global freight transportation systems during an influenza pandemic." *American Journal of Disaster Medicine* 3(2): 99–107.

OECD (2011) *Future Global Shock – Improving Risk Governance*. Paris: OECD Publishing.

Osterholm, M.T. (2005) "Preparing for the next pandemic." *Foreign Affairs*, July/August: 24–37.

Stopher, P. and J. Stanley (2014) *Introduction to Transport Policy*. Northampton, MA: Edward Elgar Publishing.

van Wee, B., J.A. Annema and D. Banister (eds) (2013) *The Transport System and Transport Policy: An Introduction*. Cheltenham: Edward Elgar Publishing.

World Economic Forum (2012) *New Models for Addressing Supply Chain and Transport Risk*. Geneva: World Economic Forum.

10 Methods in transport geography

Transportation is not a science, but a field of enquiry and application. As such, it tends to rely on a set of specific methodologies, since transportation is a performance-driven activity and this performance can be measured and compared. Transportation planning and analysis are interdisciplinary by nature, involving among others: civil engineers, economists, urban planners and geographers. Each discipline has developed methodologies dealing with their respective array of problems. Still, transportation is an infrastructure-intensive activity, implying that engineering has been the dominant methodological paradigm for transportation studies.

Method 1 – Methods in transport geography

Transportation and methodologies

Transportation is not a science, but a field of enquiry and application. Two common traits of transportation studies, regardless of disciplinary affiliation, are a heavy reliance on empirical data and the intensive use of data analytic techniques, ranging from simple descriptive measures to more complex modeling structures. In some respects, transport geography stands out from many other fields of human geography by the nature and function of its quantitative analysis (Figure 10.1).

There is a growing complexity and data requirements for the four common models in transport geography. Each is building upon the other, implying, for instance, that the estimation of accessibility cannot be assessed without information about distance and that spatial interactions are derived from accessibility assessments:

- **Distance**. The most fundamental element of geography in general and transport geography in particular. Distance can be represented in different manners, from a simple Euclidean distance calculation to a complex estimation of a logistical distance that considers all the tasks necessary for the realization of a movement.
- **Accessibility**. Defined as the measure of the capacity of a location to be reached by, or to reach different locations. Therefore, the capacity and the arrangement of transport infrastructure are key elements in the determination of accessibility. It is thus based upon the concept of location and distance.
- **Spatial interaction**. A realized movement of people, freight or information between an origin and a destination. It is a transport demand/supply relationship expressed over a geographical space. Routing is a specific category of spatial interaction that considers a given set of origins and destination for which specific (often optimal) routes are found.

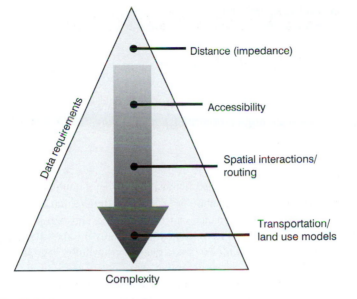

Figure 10.1 Models in transport geography

- **Transportation/land use models**. A complex framework trying to assess the numerous relations and feedback effects between transportation and the spatial structure.

In fact, transport geography was one of the main forces in the **quantitative revolution** that helped to redefine geography in the 1960s with the use of inferential statistics, abstract models and new theories. Although this perspective provided much-needed rigor, it also favored a disconnection between empirical and theoretical approaches. Like in economics, the quantitative revolution led to a mechanistic perspective where concordance to reality became somewhat secondary; realities were made to fit into models. Even if contemporary transport geography has a more diversified approach, the quantitative dimension still plays an important part in the discipline.

Thus, in addition to providing a conceptual background to the analysis of movements of freight, people and information, transport geography is much an applied science. The main goal of methods aims to **improve the efficiency of movements** by identifying their spatial constraints. These constraints can be capacity, cost, time, environmental impacts, but more often in combination. It is consequently possible to identify relevant strategies and policies and provide some scenarios about their possible consequences. There are various ways of classifying the methods that are used by transport geographers:

- Whether they are qualitative or quantitative.
- Whether they deal with infrastructures (e.g. terminals) or flows.
- Whether they provide interpolation or extrapolation.
- Whether the technique provides description, explanation or optimization.
- According to the level of data aggregation, the nature of the assumptions or the complexity of the calculations.

Like in geography, spatial and temporal process cannot be considered separately. A basic taxonomy can divide them into transport-related methods and multidisciplinary methods.

Transport-related methods

A first group of methods concern those directly related to the study of transportation since most draw their origins from transport planning. The methods mainly used in transport geography include:

- **Network analysis** (also referred to as graph theory), which is used to study transport network forms and structures, particularly how they change in time. For example, one could use network analysis to study the evolution of the hub-and-spoke configuration of airline services.
- Transport geographers also play a key role in studying **land use–transport interactions**. Numerical models have been developed which, over time, have become increasingly complex.
- Transport geographers are also interested in **flow and location allocation models** that can be used to define such things as school district boundaries or the location for a new retail outlet. These techniques are optimization procedures rather than methods for describing or understanding current transport systems.

In addition, there are various methods of general use in transportation studies that are readily applicable in transport geography:

- First, a diverse set of techniques is used in **urban transportation modeling** exercises, the purpose of which is to understand and predict urban spatial patterns.
- Second, **traffic surveys** that are used to gather empirical information about movements such as their routing and frequency.

Multidisciplinary methods

Include the whole range of methods that were not specifically developed for transportation studies, but are readily applicable to its analysis. They are labeled as multidisciplinary since they can be applied to a wide range of issues irrespective of the discipline. First, there are methods that are central to geography, but are not restricted to the study of transportation systems:

- **Cartography** is the most obvious example of a geographic technique. Indeed, various types of maps are used in the analysis of transport systems, including land use maps, depictions of transport infrastructure, isoline maps of transportation costs or schematics of transportation activity patterns.
- **Geographic information systems (GIS)**, which are an outgrowth of digital cartography, provide a set of tools for storing, retrieving, analyzing and displaying spatial data from the real world. GIS technology has been applied to some large-scale transportation planning and engineering applications. More often, however, GIS are applied in a prescriptive way to small-scale problems, for example, to plot optimal routes for buses, delivery trucks or emergency vehicles.

- There are also various **statistics** that have been developed or modified by geographers to describe urban-economic systems. Examples include the Gini coefficient and indexes of concentration and specialization.

Second, there are various methods that are used in many different applications, including transportation analysis. They underline that transportation analysts are not restricted to those methods that have been developed with transportation in mind, but to whatever is relevant to a specific problem. In fact, many methods that were initially developed for other problems have widespread use in transportation studies:

- Some methods are used to **collect primary data**, e.g. questionnaires and interviews, while others are used to analyze data. Some of the analytic techniques are straightforward to implement and interpret; graphs (e.g. scattergrams, distance–decay curves) and tables (e.g. origin–destination matrices) are two examples. Others are more complex, such as inferential statistics like the t-test, analysis of variance, regression and chi-square.
- Increasingly, transportation studies are concerned with **impacts and public policy issues**. They rely more on qualitative information such as policy statements, rules and regulations. Various types of impacts are considered, including economic (e.g. community development), social (e.g. access to services), environmental (e.g. air or water pollution) and health (e.g. road accidents). The broad fields of environmental impact assessment, risk assessment and policy analysis are relevant to these issues.

The development and application of methods to transport studies in general and transport geography in particular has been increasingly complex, particularly as improvements in **information technologies** made more powerful analytical tools available. For instance, a commercial geographic information system package has analytical and modeling capabilities well beyond what is undertaken by most researchers, analysts or policy makers. Future developments are therefore more likely to focus on **empirical data analysis** using known methods but with more extensive datasets. This will lead to more detailed and consequential analysis of real-world transport phenomena and help better connect theoretical knowledge and real-world applications.

Method 2 – Graph theory: definition and properties

Authors : Dr Jean-Paul Rodrigue and Dr César Ducruet

Basic graph definition

A graph is a **symbolic representation** of a network and of its connectivity. It implies an abstraction of the reality so it can be simplified as a set of linked nodes. **Graph theory** is a branch of mathematics concerned with how networks can be encoded and their properties measured. It has been enriched in the last decades by growing influences from studies of social and complex networks.

The goal of a graph is to represent the structure, not the appearance, of a network. The conversion of a real network into a planar graph is a straightforward process which follows some basic rules:

- The most important rule is that **every terminal and intersection point becomes a node**.
- Each connected node is then linked by a **straight segment**.

The outcome of this abstraction is the actual structure of the network (Figure 10.2). The real network, depending on its complexity, may be confusing in terms of revealing its connectivity (what is linked with what). A graph representation reveals the connectivity of a network in the best possible way. Other rules can also be applied, depending on the circumstances:

- A node that is not a terminal or an intersection point can be added to the graph if, along that segment, **an attribute is changing**. For instance, it would be recommended to represent the shift from 2 lanes to 4 lanes along a continuous road segment as a node, even if that shift does not occur at an intersection or terminal point.
- A "**dummy node**" can be added for aesthetical purposes, especially when it is required that the graph representation remains comparable to the real network.
- Although the relative location of each node can remain similar to their real-world counterpart, this is not required.

In transport geography most networks have an obvious spatial foundation, namely road, transit and rail networks, which tend to be defined more by their links than by their nodes. This is not necessarily the case for all transportation networks. For instance, maritime and air networks tend to be more defined by their nodes than by their links, since links are often not clearly defined. A telecommunications system can also be represented as a network, while its spatial expression can have limited importance and would actually be difficult to represent. Mobile telephone networks or the Internet, possibly the most complex graphs to be considered, are relevant cases of networks having a structure that can be difficult to symbolize. However, cellular phones and antennas can be represented as nodes while the links could be individual phone calls. Servers, the core of the Internet, can also be represented as nodes within a graph, while the physical infrastructure between them, namely fiber optic cables, can act as links.

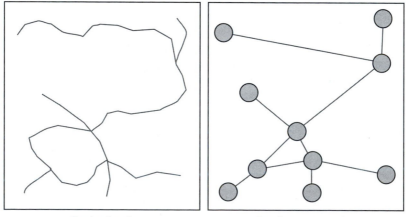

Real network   Graph representation

Figure 10.2 Graph representation of a real network

Consequently, all transport networks can be represented by graph theory in one way or the other.

The following elements are fundamental to understanding graph theory:

- **Graph**. A graph G is a set of vertex (nodes) v connected by edges (links) e. Thus $G = (v, e)$.
- **Vertex** (Node). A node v is a terminal point or an intersection point of a graph. It is the abstraction of a location such as a city, an administrative division, a road intersection or a transport terminal (stations, terminuses, harbors and airports).
- **Edge** (Link). An edge e is a link between two nodes. The link (i, j) is of initial extremity i and of terminal extremity j. A link is the abstraction of a transport infrastructure supporting movements between nodes. It has a direction that is commonly represented as an arrow. When an arrow is not used, it is assumed the link is bidirectional.
- **Sub-graph**. A sub-graph is a subset of a graph **G** where **p** is the number of sub-graphs. For instance, **G'** = (**v'**, **e'**) can be a distinct sub-graph of **G**. Unless the global transport system is considered in its whole, every transport network is in theory a sub-graph of another. For instance, the road transportation network of a city is a sub-graph of a regional transportation network, which is itself a sub-graph of a national transportation network.
- **Buckle** (loop). A link that makes a node correspond to itself is a buckle.
- **Planar graph**. A graph where all the intersections of two edges are a vertex. Since this graph is located within a plane, its topology is two-dimensional. This is typically the case for power grids, road and railway networks, although great care must be inferred to the definition of nodes (terminals, warehouses, cities).
- **Non-planar graph**. A graph where there are no vertices at the intersection of at least two edges. This implies a third dimension in the topology of the graph, since there is the possibility of having a movement "passing over" another movement such as for air and maritime transport. A non-planar graph has potentially much more links than a planar graph.
- **Simple graph**. A graph that includes only one type of link between its nodes. A road or rail network is a simple graph.
- **Multigraph**. A graph that includes several types of links between its nodes. Some nodes can be connected to one link type, while others can be connected to more than

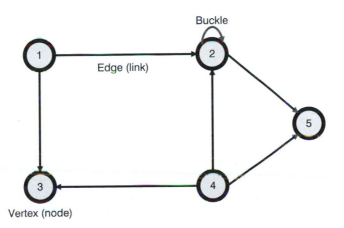

Figure 10.3 Basic graph representation of a transport network

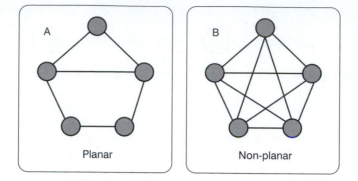

Figure 10.4 Planar and non-planar graphs

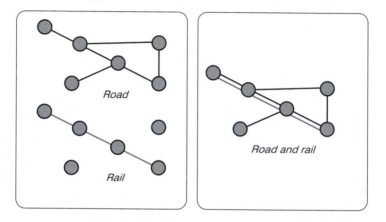

Figure 10.5 Simple and multigraph

one that are running in parallel. A graph depicting a road and a rail network with different links between nodes serviced by either or both modes is a multigraph.

Links and their structures

A transportation network enables flows of people, freight or information, which are occurring along its links. Graph theory must thus offer the possibility of representing movements as linkages, which can be considered over several aspects:

- **Connection**. A set of two nodes as every node is linked to the other. Considers if a movement between two nodes is possible, whatever its direction. Knowing connections makes it possible to find if it is possible to reach a node from another node within a graph.
- **Path**. A sequence of links that are traveled in the same direction. For a path to exist between two nodes, it must be possible to travel an uninterrupted sequence of links. Finding all the possible paths in a graph is a fundamental attribute in measuring accessibility and traffic flows.
- **Chain**. A sequence of links having a connection in common with the other. Direction does not matter.

Figure 10.6 Connections and paths

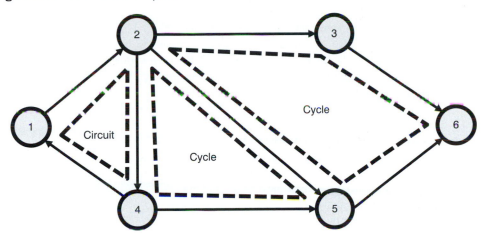

Figure 10.7 Cycles and circuits

- **Length of a link, connection or path**. Refers to the label associated with a link, a connection or a path. This label can be distance, the amount of traffic, the capacity or any attribute of that link. The length of a path is the number of links (or connections) in this path.
- **Cycle**. Refers to a chain where the initial and terminal node is the same and that does not use the same link more than once in a cycle.
- **Circuit**. A path where the initial and terminal node corresponds. It is a cycle where all the links are traveled in the same direction. Circuits are very important in transportation because several distribution systems use circuits to cover as much territory as possible in one direction (delivery route).
- **Clique**. A clique is a maximal complete sub-graph where all vertices are connected.
- **Cluster**. Also called community, it refers to a group of nodes having denser relations with each other than with the rest of the network. A wide range of methods are used to reveal clusters in a network; notably, they are based on modularity measures (intra- versus inter-cluster variance).
- **Ego network**. For a given node, the ego network corresponds to a sub-graph where only its adjacent neighbors and their mutual links are included.

- **Nodal region**. A nodal region refers to a subgroup (tree) of nodes polarized by an independent node (whose largest flow link connects a smaller node) and a number of subordinate nodes (whose largest flow link connects a larger node). Single or multiple linkage analysis methods are used to reveal such regions by removing secondary links between nodes while keeping only the heaviest links.
- **Dual graph**. A method in space syntax that considers edges as nodes and nodes as edges. In urban street networks, large avenues made of several segments become single nodes, while intersections with other avenues or streets become links (edges). This method is particularly useful to reveal hierarchical structures in a planar network.

Basic structural properties

The organization of nodes and links in a graph conveys a structure that can be described and labeled. The basic structural properties of a graph are:

- **Symmetry and asymmetry**. A graph is symmetrical if each pair of nodes linked in one direction is also linked in the other. By convention, a line without an arrow represents a link where it is possible to move in both directions. However, both directions have to be defined in the graph. Most transport systems are symmetrical, but asymmetry can often occur, as is the case for maritime (pendulum) and air services. Asymmetry is rare on road transportation networks, unless one-way streets are considered.
- **Assortativity and disassortativity**. Assortative networks are those characterized by relations among similar nodes, while disassortative networks are found when structurally different nodes are often connected. Transport (or technological) networks are often disassortative when they are non-planar, due to the higher probability for the network to be centralized into a few large hubs.
- **Completeness**. A graph is complete if two nodes are linked in at least one direction. A complete graph has no sub-graph and all its nodes are interconnected.
- **Connectivity**. A complete graph is described as connected if, for all its distinct pairs of nodes, there is a linking chain. Direction does not have importance for a graph to be connected, but may be a factor for the level of connectivity. If $p > 1$, the graph is not connected because it has more than one sub-graph (or component). There are various levels of connectivity, depending on the degree at which each pair of nodes is connected.
- **Complementarity**. Two sub-graphs are complementary if their union results in a complete graph. Multimodal transportation networks are complementary, as each sub-graph (modal network) benefits from the connectivity of other sub-graphs.
- **Root**. A node r where every other node is the extremity of a path coming from r is a root. Direction has an importance. A root is generally the starting point of a distribution system, such as a factory or a warehouse.
- **Trees**. A connected graph without a cycle is a tree. A tree has the same number of links as nodes plus one ($e = v - 1$). If a link is removed, the graph ceases to be connected. If a new link between two nodes is provided, a cycle is created. A branch of root r is a tree where no links are connecting any node more than once. River basins are typical examples of treelike networks based on multiple sources connecting towards a single estuary. This structure strongly influences river transport systems.

Figure 10.8 Complementary graph

Figure 10.9 Tree graph

Figure 10.10 Articulation node

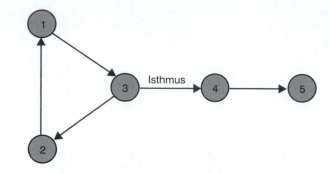

Figure 10.11 Isthmus connection

- **Articulation node**. In a connected graph, a node is an articulation node if the sub-graph obtained by removing this node is no longer connected. It therefore contains more than one sub-graph (p > 1). An articulation node is generally a port or an airport, or an important hub of a transportation network, which serves as a bottleneck. It is also called a bridge node.
- **Isthmus**. In a connected graph, an isthmus is a link that is creating, when removed, two sub-graphs having at least one connection. Most central links in a complex network are often isthmuses, the removal of which by reiteration helps to reveal dense communities (clusters).

Method 3 – Graph theory: measures and indices

Authors : Dr César Ducruet and Dr Jean-Paul Rodrigue

Measures at the network level

Transportation networks can be composed of many nodes and links, which makes their comparison challenging. For instance, it may not be evident visually to assess which of two transportation networks is the most accessible or the most efficient. Several measures and indices can be used to analyze network efficiency. Many of them were initially developed by Kansky in the 1960s and can be used for:

- Expressing the relationship between values and the network structures they represent.
- Comparing different transportation networks at a specific point in time.
- Comparing the evolution of a transport network at different points in time.

Outside the description of the network size by the **number of nodes and edges**, and its total length and traffic, several measures are used to define the structural attributes of a graph; the diameter, the number of cycles and the order of a node.

- **Diameter** (*d*). The length of the shortest path between the most distanced nodes of a graph is the diameter. *d* measures the extent of a graph and the topological length between two nodes.

The diameter enables the development of a network in time to be measured. The higher the diameter, the less linked a network tends to be. In the case of a complex

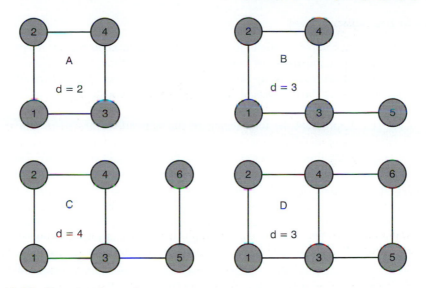

Figure 10.12   Diameter of a graph

graph, the diameter can be found with a **topological distance matrix** (Shimbel distance), which computes for each node pair its minimal topological distance. Graphs whose extent remains constant, but with a higher connectivity, have lower diameter values. Planar networks often have a large diameter due to the presence of many intermediate stops between two distant nodes.

- **Number of cycles** (u). The maximum number of independent cycles in a graph. This number (u) is estimated through the number of nodes (v), links (e) and of sub-graphs (p). Trees and simple networks have a value of 0 since they have no cycles. The more complex a network is, the higher the value of u, so it can be used as an indicator of the level of development and complexity of a transport system.

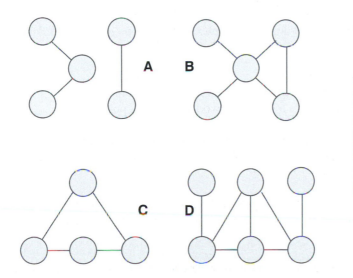

$$u = e - v + p$$

	e	v	p	u
A	3	5	2	0
B	5	5	1	1
C	5	4	1	2
D	7	6	1	2

Figure 10.13   Number of cycles in a graph

Indices at the network level

Indices are more complex methods to represent the structural properties of a graph since they involve the comparison of one measure over another. Some indices take into account spatial features (distance, surface) as well as the level of activity (traffic), while others solely rest on the topological dimension of the network.

- **Cost** (*C*). Represents the total length of the network measured in real transport distances where *aij* is the presence (1) or absence (0) of a link between *i* and *j* and *lij* the length of the link. This measure can also be calculated based on two other dimensions of the network: the Minimum Spanning Tree (*MST*) and the Greedy Triangulation (*GT*). The *MST* represents the shortest and/or lowest cost subtree of the network; it can be obtained by applying, among other shortest path algorithms, the Kruskal algorithm, which allows finding the lowest cost route connecting all nodes in the network. The *GT* refers to the maximal connected planar graph keeping the same number of nodes as in the original network but adding all possible links without breaking its planarity. Such operations take into account both the topology and the geography of the network, while comparing the latter with its optimal configurations. More efficient networks have relative costs near to 1, while less efficient networks are closer to 0.

$$Cost = \sum_{i,j} a_{ij} l_{ij}$$

$$Cost_{rel} = \frac{Cost - Cost^{MST}}{Cost^{GT} - Cost^{MST}}$$

- **Detour Index**. A measure of the efficiency of a transport network in terms of how well it overcomes distance or the friction of distance. The closer the detour index gets to 1, the more the network is spatially efficient. Networks having a detour index of 1 are rarely, if ever, seen and most networks would fit on an asymptotic curve getting close to 1, but never reaching it. For instance, the straight distance, *D(S)*, between two nodes may be 40 km but the transport distance, *D(*T*)*; real distance, is 50 km. The detour index is thus 0.8 (40/50). The complexity of the topography is often a good indicator of the level of detour.

$$DI = \frac{D(S)}{D(T)}$$

In order to derive a measure of relative efficiency, the **Detour Index Relative Efficiency** (*Erel*) is thus the ratio between the Detour Index calculated from the original network and the Detour Index calculated either from the *MST* (Minimum Spanning Tree) or the *GT* (Greedy Triangulation).

$$E_{rel} = \frac{DI - DI^{MST}}{DI^{GT} - DI^{MST}}$$

- **Network density**. Measures the territorial occupation of a transport network in terms of km of links (*L*) per square kilometers of surface (*S*). The higher it is, the more a network is developed.

$$ND = \frac{L}{S}$$

- **Pi index**. The relationship between the total length of the graph $L(G)$ and the distance along its diameter $D(d)$. It is labeled as pi because of its similarity with the real pi value (3.14), which expresses the ratio between the circumference and the diameter of a circle. A high index shows a developed network. It is a measure of distance per units of diameter and an indicator of the shape of a network.
- **Eta index**. Average length per link. Adding new nodes will cause a decrease of eta as the average length per link declines.

$$\eta = \frac{L(G)}{e}$$

- **Theta index**. Measures the function of a node, which is the average amount of traffic per intersection. The higher theta is, the greater the load of the network. The measure can also be applied to the number of links (edges).

$$\Theta = \frac{Q(G)}{v}$$

- **Beta index**. Measures the level of connectivity in a graph and is expressed by the relationship between the number of links (e) over the number of nodes (v). Trees and simple networks have beta value of less than one. A connected network with one

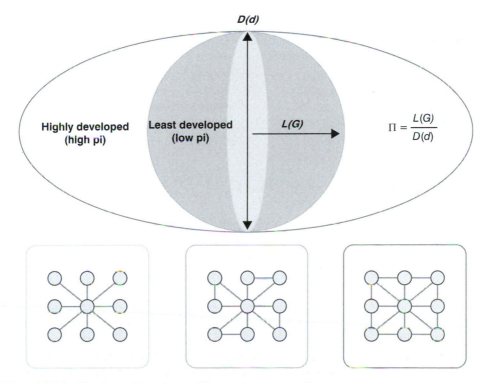

Figure 10.14 Pi index and the shape of transportation networks

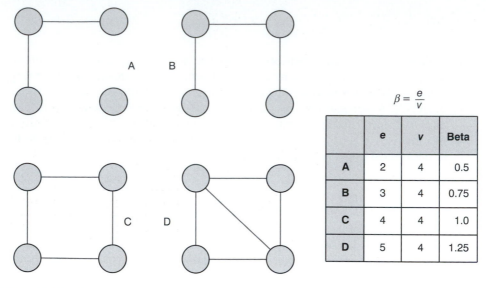

$$\beta = \frac{e}{v}$$

	e	v	Beta
A	2	4	0.5
B	3	4	0.75
C	4	4	1.0
D	5	4	1.25

Figure 10.15   Beta index

cycle has a value of 1. More complex networks have a value greater than 1. In a network with a fixed number of nodes, the higher the number of links, the higher the number of paths possible in the network. Complex networks have a high value of beta. The rich-club coefficient is the beta index applied to relations among larger order (degree) nodes; it verifies whether the connectivity is higher among larger degree nodes than for the whole network.

On Figure 10.15 four graphs are of growing connectivity. Graph A and B are not fully connected and their beta value is lower than 1. Graph C is connected and has a beta value of 1. Graph D is even more connected with a Beta value of 1.25.

● **Alpha index**. A measure of connectivity which evaluates the number of cycles in a graph in comparison with the maximum number of cycles. The higher the alpha index, the more a network is connected. Trees and simple networks will have a value of 0. A value of 1 indicates a completely connected network. Measures the level of connectivity independently of the number of nodes. It is very rare that a network will have an alpha value of 1, because this would imply very serious redundancies. This index is also called Meshedness Coefficient in the literature on planar networks.

The graphs on Figure 10.16 have a growing level of connectivity. While graph A has no cycles, graph D has the maximum possible number of cycles for a planar graph.

● **Gamma Index** (*g*). A measure of connectivity that considers the relationship between the number of observed links and the number of possible links. The value of gamma is between 0 and 1, where a value of 1 indicates a completely connected network and would be extremely unlikely in reality. Gamma is an efficient value to measure the progression of a network in time.

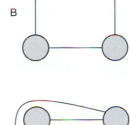

$$\alpha = \frac{u}{2v - 5}$$

	$\frac{u}{(e-v+p)}$	$2v-5$	Alpha
A	0	3	0.0
B	1	3	0.33
C	2	3	0.66
D	3	3	1.0

Figure 10.16   Alpha index

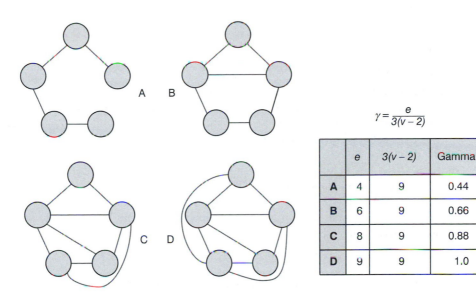

$$\gamma = \frac{e}{3(v - 2)}$$

	e	$3(v-2)$	Gamma
A	4	9	0.44
B	6	9	0.66
C	8	9	0.88
D	9	9	1.0

Figure 10.17   Gamma index

Being solely based on the number of nodes and links, alpha, beta and gamma indices remain limited in revealing structural differences between two networks of equal size. More robust measures have thus been proposed by physics, which take into account the internal complexity of the graph.

Measures and indices at the node level

Numerous measures exist for highlighting the situation of a node in a network. Some of them are made at the "local level" based on links with adjacent nodes, while others on the "global level" consider the node's situation in the whole network.

- **Order (degree) of a node** (*o*). The number of its attached links and is a simple, but effective measure of nodal importance. The higher its value, the more a node is important in a graph, as many links converge to it. Hub nodes have a high order, while terminal points have an order that can be as low as 1. A perfect hub would have its order equal to the summation of all the orders of the other nodes in the graph and a perfect spoke would have an order of 1. The percentage of nodes directly connected in the entire graph is thus a measure of reachability. An isolate is a node without connections (degree equals to 0). The difference between in-degree and out-degree in a directed graph (digraph) may underline interesting functions of some nodes as attractors or senders. The order may be calculated at different depths: adjacent nodes (depth 1), adjacent nodes of adjacent nodes (depth 2), etc. The weighted degree is simply the total of values associated with links.

$$k_i = C_D(i) = \sum_{j}^{N} x_{ij}$$

- **Koenig number** (or associated number, eccentricity). A measure of farness based on the number of links needed to reach the most distant node in the graph.

$$e(x) = \max_{y \in X} d(x, y)$$

- **Shimbel index** (or Shimbel distance, nodal accessibility, nodality). A measure of accessibility representing the sum of the length of all shortest paths connecting all other nodes in the graph. The inverse measure is also called closeness centrality or distance centrality.

$$A_i = \sum_{j=1}^{N} d_{ij}$$

- **Hub dependence** (*hd*). A measure of node vulnerability that is the share of the highest traffic link in total traffic (weighted degree). Weak nodes depending on few links will have a high hub dependence, especially if they locate in the neighborhood of a large node, while hubs will have a more even traffic distribution among their connections. It indicates to what extent removing the largest traffic link would affect the node's overall activity. The measure can be extended to more links (2, 3 . . . 10 largest flow links).

Several critiques have been made addressed to such indices, as they do not always take into account the real length, quality and weight of the links; networks of equal size may exhibit contrasted topological forms. However, they remain useful for describing the changing structure of a given network.

Method 4 – Geographic Information Systems for Transportation (GIS-T)

Authors: Dr Shih-Lung Shaw and Dr Jean-Paul Rodrigue

GIS in transportation

In a broad sense a Geographic Information System (GIS) is an information system specializing in the input, management, analysis and reporting of geographical (spatially related) information. Among the wide range of potential applications GIS can be used for, transportation issues have received a lot of attention. A specific branch of GIS applied to transportation issues, commonly labeled as GIS-T, is one of the pioneer GIS application areas. **Geographic Information Systems for Transportation** (GIS-T) refers to the principles and applications of applying geographic information technologies to transportation problems.

The four major components of a GIS – encoding, management, analysis and reporting – have specific considerations for transportation (Figure 10.18):

- **Encoding**. Deals with issues concerning the representation of a transport system and its spatial components. To be of use in a GIS, a transport network must be correctly encoded, implying a functional topology composed of nodes and links. Other elements relevant to transportation, namely qualitative and quantitative data, must also be encoded and associated with their respective spatial elements. For instance, an encoded road segment can have data related to its width, number of lanes, direction, peak hour traffic, etc.
- **Management**. The encoded information is often stored in a database and can be organized along spatial (by region, country, census units, etc.), thematic (for highway, transit, railway, terminals, etc.) or temporal (by year, month, week, etc.) considerations. It is important to design a GIS database that organizes a large amount of heterogeneous data in an integrated and seamless environment such that the data can be easily accessed to support various transportation application needs.
- **Analysis**. Considers the wide array of methodologies and tools available for transport issues. They can range from a simple query over an element of a transport system (e.g., what is the peak hour traffic of a road segment?) to a complex model investigating the relationships between its elements (e.g., if a new road segment was added, what would be the impacts on traffic and future land use developments?).

Figure 10.18   Geographic information systems and transportation

- **Reporting**. A GIS would not be complete without its visualization and data reporting capabilities for both spatial and non-spatial data. This component is particularly important, as it offers interactive tools to convey complex information in a visual format (displayed or printed). A GIS-T thus becomes a useful tool to inform people who otherwise may not be able to visualize the hidden patterns and relationships embedded in the datasets (e.g. potential relationships among traffic accidents, highway geometry, pavement condition and terrain).

Information in a GIS is often stored and represented as layers, which are a set of geographical features linked with their attributes. On Figure 10.18 a transport system is represented as three layers related to land use, flows (spatial interactions) and the network. Each has its own features, related data and can be used independently or in combination with other layers.

GIS-T research can be approached from two different, but complementary, directions. While some GIS-T research focuses on issues of how GIS can be further developed and enhanced in order to meet the needs of transportation applications, other GIS-T research investigates the questions of how GIS can be used to facilitate and improve transportation studies. In general, topics related to GIS-T studies can be grouped into three categories:

- **Data representations**. How can various components of transport systems be represented in a GIS-T?
- **Analysis and modeling**. How can transport methodologies be used in a GIS-T?
- **Applications**. What types of applications are particularly suitable for GIS-T?

GIS-T data pepresentations

Data representation is a core research topic of GIS. Before a GIS can be used to tackle real-world problems, data must be properly represented in a digital computing environment. One unique characteristic of GIS is the capability to integrate spatial and non-spatial data in order to support both display and analysis needs. There have been various data models developed for GIS. The two basic approaches are object-based data models and field-based data models:

- An **object-based data model** treats geographic space as populated by discrete and identifiable objects. Features are often represented as points, lines and/or polygons.
- On the other hand, a **field-based data model** treats geographic space as populated by real-world features that vary continuously over space. Features can be represented as regular tessellations (e.g. a raster grid) or irregular tessellations (e.g. triangulated irregular network, or TIN).

GIS-T studies have employed both object-based and field-based data models to represent the relevant geographic data. Some transportation problems tend to fit better with one type of GIS data model than the other. For example, **network analysis** based on the graph theory typically represents a network as a set of nodes interconnected with a set of links. The object-based GIS data model therefore is a better candidate for such transportation applications. Other types of transportation data exist which require extensions to the general GIS data models. One well-known example is **linear referencing data** (e.g. highway mileposts). Transportation agencies often measure locations of features or events along transportation network links (e.g. a traffic accident occurred at the 52.3 milepost on a specific highway). Such a one-dimensional linear referencing system (i.e. linear measurements along a highway segment with respect to a pre-specified starting point of the highway segment) cannot be properly handled by the two-dimensional Cartesian coordinate system used in most GIS data models. Consequently, the dynamic segmentation data model was developed to address the specific need of the GIS-T community.

Origin–destination (O–D) flow data are another type of data that are frequently used in transportation studies. Such data have been traditionally represented in matrix forms, a two-dimensional array, for analysis. Unfortunately, the relational data model widely adopted in most commercial GIS software does not provide adequate support for handling matrix data. Some GIS-T software has developed additional file formats and functions for users to work with matrix data in a GIS environment. Conventional GIS approaches can thus be further extended and enhanced to meet the needs of transportation applications. The creation and expansion of add-ons for GIS software represents a way in which specific methods and models can be implemented in existing packages.

Developments of enterprise and multidimensional GIS-T data models also have received significant attention. Successful GIS deployments at the enterprise level (e.g., within a state department of transportation) demand additional considerations to embrace the diversity of application and data requirements. An enterprise GIS-T data model is designed to allow "each application group to meet the established needs while enabling the enterprise to integrate and share data." The needs of integrating 1-D, 2-D, 3-D and temporal data in support of various transportation applications also have called for the implementation of multidimensional (including spatio-temporal) data representations.

Modern **information and communication technologies** (ICT) such as the Internet and cellular phones have changed the ways that people and businesses conduct their activities. These changing activity and interaction patterns in turn lead to changing spatio-temporal traffic patterns. The world has become more mobile and dynamic due to modern ICT. With the advancements of location-aware technologies (e.g. the Global Positioning System, cellular phone tracking system and Wi-Fi positioning system), it is now feasible and affordable to collect large volumes of tracking data at the individual or vehicle level. Consequently, how to best represent and manage dynamic data of moving objects (people, vehicles, or shipments) in a GIS environment presents new research challenges to GIS-T, especially when we have to deal with the **Big Data issues**.

In short, one critical component of GIS-T is how transportation-related data in a GIS environment can be best represented in order to **facilitate and integrate the needs of various transportation applications**. Existing GIS data models provide a good foundation of supporting many GIS-T applications. However, due to some unique characteristics of transportation data and application needs, many challenges still exist to develop better GIS data models that will improve rather than limit what we can do with different types of transportation studies.

GIS-T analysis and modeling

GIS-T applications have benefited from many of the standard GIS functions (query, geocoding, buffer, overlay, etc.) to support data management, analysis and visualization needs. Like many other fields, transportation has developed its own **unique analysis methods and models**. Examples include shortest path and routing algorithms (e.g.

traveling salesman problems, vehicle routing problem), spatial interaction models (e.g. gravity model), network flow problems (e.g. minimum cost flow problem, maximum flow problem, network flow equilibrium models), facility location problems (e.g. p-median problem, set covering problem, maximal covering problem, p-centers problem), travel demand models (e.g. the four-step trip generation, trip distribution, modal split, traffic assignment models, and, more recently, activity-based travel demand models) and land use–transportation interaction models.

While the basic transportation analysis procedures (e.g. shortest path finding) can be found in most commercial GIS software, other transportation analysis procedures and models (e.g. travel demand models) are available only selectively in some commercial software packages. Fortunately, the component GIS design approach adopted by GIS software companies provides a better environment for experienced GIS-T users to develop their own custom analysis procedures and models.

It is essential for both GIS-T practitioners and researchers to have a thorough understanding of transportation analysis methods and models. For GIS-T practitioners, such knowledge can help them evaluate different GIS software products and choose the one that best meets their needs. It also can help them select appropriate analysis functions available in a GIS package and properly interpret the analysis results. GIS-T researchers, on the other hand, can apply their knowledge to help improve the design and analysis capabilities of GIS-T. Due to the increasing availability of tracking data that include both spatial and temporal elements, development of spatio-temporal GIS analysis functions to help to better understand the dynamic movement patterns has attracted significant research attention in recent years.

GIS-T applications

GIS-T is one of the leading GIS application fields. Many GIS-T applications have been implemented at various transportation agencies and private firms. They cover much of the **broad scope of transportation and logistics**, such as infrastructure planning and management, transportation safety analysis, travel demand analysis, traffic monitoring and control, public transit planning and operations, environmental impacts assessment, intelligent transportation systems (ITS), routing and scheduling, vehicle tracking and dispatching, fleet management, site selection and service area analysis, and supply chain management. Each of these applications tends to have its specific data and analysis requirements. For example, representing a street network as centerlines may be sufficient for transportation planning and vehicle routing applications. A traffic engineering application, on the other hand, may require a detailed representation of individual traffic lanes. Turn movements at intersections also could be critical to a traffic engineering study, but not to a regional travel demand study.

These different application needs are directly relevant to the GIS-T data representation and the GIS-T analysis and modeling issues. When a need arises to represent transportation networks of a study area at different scales, what would be an appropriate GIS-T design that could support the analysis and modeling needs of various applications? In this case, it is desirable to have a GIS-T data model that allows multiple geometric representations of the same transportation network. Research on enterprise and multidimensional GIS-T data models aims to address these important issues of better data representations in support of various transportation applications.

With the rapid growth of the Internet and wireless communications in recent years, a growing number of Internet-based and wireless GIS-T applications can be found, particularly for driving directions, which is the most common commercial use. Global Positioning System (GPS) navigation systems are available as built-in devices in vehicles, as portable devices and predominantly as built-in applications in smartphones. Coupled with wireless communications, these devices can offer real-time traffic information and provide helpful **location-based services** (LBS). Another trend observed in recent years is the growing number of GIS-T applications in the private sector, particularly for logistics applications. Since many businesses involve operations at geographically dispersed locations (e.g. supplier sites, distribution centers, retail stores and customer location), GIS-T can be a useful tool for a variety of logistics applications. Many of these logistics applications are based on the GIS-T analysis and modeling procedures, such as the routing and facility location problems.

GIS-T is interdisciplinary in nature and has many possible applications. Transportation geographers, who have appropriate backgrounds in both geography and transportation, are well positioned to pursue GIS-T studies and assist in GIS-T implementations addressing real-world problems.

Method 5 – Transportation and accessibility

Defining accessibility

Accessibility is a key element to transport geography, and to geography in general, since it is a direct expression of mobility either in terms of people, freight or information. This mobility is a choice made by users and is therefore a means to evaluate the impacts of infrastructure investment and related transport policies on regional development. Well-developed and efficient transportation systems offer high levels of accessibility (if the impacts of congestion are excluded), while less-developed ones have lower levels of accessibility. Thus accessibility is linked with an array of economic and social opportunities. It is defined as the measure of the capacity of a location to be reached by, or to reach, different locations. Therefore, the capacity and the arrangement of transport infrastructure are key elements in the determination of accessibility.

All locations are not equal because some are more accessible than others, which implies inequalities. Thus, accessibility is a proxy for inequalities. The notion of accessibility consequently relies on two core concepts:

- The first is **location** where the relativity of space is estimated in relation to transport infrastructures, since they offer the mean to support movements. Each location has a set of referential attributes, such as its population or level of economic activity.
- The second is **distance**, which derived from the physical separation between locations. Distance can only exist when there is a possibility to link two locations through transportation. It expresses the friction of distance, and the location which has the least friction relative to others is likely to be the most accessible. Commonly, the friction of distance is expressed in units, such as kilometers or time, but variables such as cost or energy spent can also be used.

There are two spatial categories applicable to accessibility problems, which are interdependent:

- The first type is known as **topological accessibility** and is related to measuring accessibility in a system of nodes and paths (a transportation network). It is assumed that accessibility is a measurable attribute significant only to specific elements of a transportation system, such as terminals (airports, ports or subway stations).

- The second type is known as **contiguous accessibility** and involves measuring accessibility over a surface. Under such conditions, accessibility is a cumulative measure of the attributes of every location over a predefined distance, as space is considered in a contiguous manner. It is also referred to as isochrone accessibility (Figure 10.19).

Space/time convergence is far from being a uniform process, as differences in transport infrastructures and basic landscape constraints have a discriminatory effect on accessibility. Figure 10.19 represents travel time, from less than 1 hour to 10 days, to the nearest city of more than 50,000 people. It is the outcome of an overlay of several friction of distance factors, including the road and rail networks, navigable rivers, shipping lanes and land cover. It can be considered as a proxy for global accessibility with only 10 percent of the world's population being more than 48 hours away from a large city. While it depicts the general ease of accessing urban markets, it does not depict well the effectiveness of global freight flows. For instance, South Asia appears highly accessible because of the density of large cities, the quality and capacity of inland transport infrastructures is generally poor.

Accessibility is a good indicator of the underlying spatial structure, since it takes into consideration location as well as the inequality conferred by distance to other locations.

Due to different spatial structures, two locations of the same importance will have different accessibilities (Figure 10.20). For a spatial structure where locations are uniformly distributed (A), locations 1 and 2 have different accessibilities, with location 1 being the most accessible. As distance (Euclidean) increases, location 1 has access to a larger number of locations than location 2. To access all locations, location 2 would require about double the traveled distance than location 1. This is particularly the case, as the spatial structure changes to one having a concentration of activities around location 1 (B). In this case, the number of locations that can be reached by location 1 increases rapidly and then eventually peaks. The third example (C) has a spatial structure having roughly two foci. Although the number of locations that can be reached from location 2 initially increases faster than for location 1, it catches up and is actually the most accessible, but by a lesser margin.

Connectivity and total accessibility

The most basic measure of accessibility involves **network connectivity** where a network is represented as a connectivity matrix (C1), which expresses the connectivity of each node with its adjacent nodes. The number of columns and rows in this matrix is equal to the number of nodes in the network, and a value of 1 is given for each cell where this is a connected pair and a value of 0 for each cell where there is an unconnected pair. The summation of this matrix provides a very basic measure of accessibility, also known as the **degree of a node**:

$$C1 = \sum_{j}^{n} C_{ij}$$

- $C1$ = degree of a node.
- cij = connectivity between node i and node j (either 1 or 0).
- n = number of nodes.

Figure 10.19 Global accessibility: time to the nearest large city

Source: A. Nelson (2008) *Estimated travel time to the nearest city of 50,000 or more people in year 2000*. Global Environment Monitoring Unit – Joint Research Centre of the European Commission, Ispra, Italy.

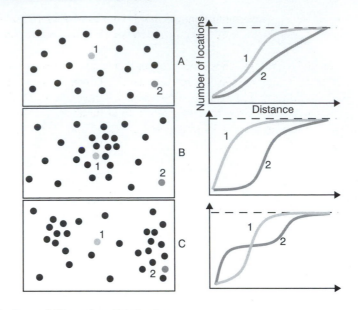

Figure 10.20 Accessibility and spatial structure

The network on Figure 10.21 can be represented as a connectivity matrix, which is rather simple to construct:

- **Size of the connectivity matrix**. Involves a number of rows and cells equivalent to the number of nodes in the network. A connectivity matrix is always a square matrix. Since the above network has five nodes, its connectivity matrix is a five-by-five grid.
- **Connection**: Each cell representing a connection between two nodes receives a value of 1 (e.g. Cell B–A).
- **Non-connection**: Each cell that does not represent a direct connection gets a value of 0 (e.g. Cell D–E).
- If all connections in the network are bidirectional (a movement is possible from node C to node D and vice versa), the connectivity matrix is **transposable**.

Adding up a row or a column gives the degree of a node. Node C is obviously the most connected, since it has the highest summation of connectivity comparatively to all

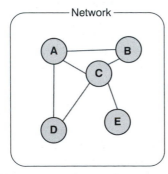

Connectivity matrix

	A	B	C	D	E
A	0	1	1	1	0
B	1	0	1	0	0
C	1	1	0	1	1
D	1	0	1	0	0
E	0	0	1	0	0

Figure 10.21 Connectivity matrix

other nodes. However, this assumption may not hold true on a more complex network because of a larger number of indirect paths which are not considered in the connectivity matrix.

The connectivity matrix does not take into account all the possible indirect paths between nodes. Under such circumstances, two nodes could have the same degree, but may have different accessibilities. To consider this attribute, the total accessibility matrix (T) is used to calculate the total number of paths in a network, which includes direct as well as indirect paths. Its calculation involves the following procedure:

$$T = \sum_{k=1}^{D} Ck$$

$$C1 = \sum_{j}^{n} C_{ij}$$

$$Ck = \sum_{i}^{n} \sum_{j}^{n} c_{ij}^{1} \times c_{ji}^{k-1} (\forall k \neq 1)$$

- D = the diameter of the network.

Thus, total accessibility would be a more comprehensive accessibility measure than network connectivity.

Geographic and potential accessibility

From the accessibility measure developed so far, it is possible to derive two simple and highly practical measures, defined as geographic and potential accessibility. Geographic accessibility considers that the accessibility of a location is the **summation of all distances** between other locations divided by the number of locations. The lower its value, the more a location is accessible.

$$A(G) = \sum_{i}^{n} \sum_{j}^{n} d_{ij} \bigg/ n$$

Although geographic accessibility can be solved using a spreadsheet (or manually for simpler problems), Geographic Information Systems have proven to be a very useful and flexible tool to measure accessibility, notably over a surface simplified as a matrix (raster representation). This can be done by generating a distance grid for each place and then summing all the grids to form the total summation of distances (Shimbel) grid. The cell having the lowest value is thus the most accessible place.

The construction of a geographic accessibility matrix, A(G), is a rather simple undertaking:

- Build the **valued graph matrix** (L). The L-matrix in Figure 10.22 shows the shortest distance in kilometers between five nodes (Node A to Node E).
- Build the **geographic accessibility matrix** A(G). The A(G) matrix is similar to the L-matrix, except that the summation of rows and columns is divided by the number of locations in the network. The summation values are the same for columns and

L

	A	B	C	D	E
A	0	8	4	9	15
B	8	0	7	12	18
C	4	7	0	5	11
D	9	12	5	0	6
E	15	18	11	6	0

A(G)

	A	B	C	D	E	Σ/n
A	0	8	4	9	15	7.2
B	8	0	7	12	18	9.0
C	4	7	0	5	11	5.4
D	9	12	5	0	6	6.4
E	15	18	11	6	0	10.0
Σ/n	7.2	9.0	5.4	6.4	10.0	38.0

Figure 10.22 Geographic accessibility

rows, since this is a transposable matrix. The most accessible place is Node C, since it has the **lowest summation of distances**.

$$A(P) = \sum_{i}^{n} P_i + \sum_{j}^{n} P_j/d_{ij}$$

- $A(P)$ = potential accessibility matrix.
- d_{ij} = distance between place i and j (derived from valued graph matrix).
- P_j = attributes of place j, such as its population, retailing surface, parking space, etc.
- n = number of locations.

The potential accessibility matrix is not transposable since locations do not have the same attributes, which brings the underlying notions of emissiveness and attractiveness:

- **Emissiveness** is the capacity to leave a location, the sum of the values of a row in the $A(P)$ matrix.
- **Attractiveness** is the capacity to reach a location, the sum of the values of a column in the $A(P)$ matrix.

By considering the same valued graph matrix (L) than the previous example and the population matrix P, the potential accessibility matrix, P(G), can be calculated:

- The value of all corresponding cells (A–A, B–B, etc.) equals the value of their respective attributes (P).
- The value of all non-corresponding cells equals their attribute divided by the corresponding cell in the L-matrix.

The higher the value, the more a location is accessible, node C being the most accessible. The matrix being non-transposable, the summation of rows is different from the summation of columns, bringing forward the issue of attractiveness and emissiveness.

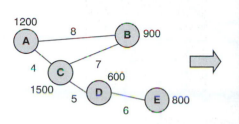

L

	A	B	C	D	E
A	0	8	4	9	15
B	8	0	7	12	18
C	4	7	0	5	11
D	9	12	5	0	6
E	15	18	11	6	0

P

A	1200
B	900
C	1500
D	600
E	800

P(G)

i\j	A	B	C	D	E	Σi
A	1200.0	150.0	300.0	133.3	80.0	1863.3
B	112.5	900.0	128.6	75.0	50.0	1266.1
C	375.0	214.3	1500.0	300.0	136.4	2525.7
D	66.6	50.0	120.0	600.0	100.0	936.6
E	53.3	44.4	72.7	133.3	800.0	1103.7
Σj	1807.4	1358.7	2121.3	1241.6	1166.4	7695.4

Figure 10.23   Potential accessibility

Node C has more emissiveness than attractiveness (2525.7 versus 2121.3), while Node B has more attractiveness than emissiveness (1358.7 versus 1266.1).

Method 6 – Network data models

Nature and utility

Graph theory developed a topological and mathematical representation of the nature and structure of transportation networks. However, graph theory can be expanded for the analysis of real-world transport networks by encoding them in an information system. In the process, a digital representation of the network is created, which can then be used for a variety of purposes such as managing deliveries or planning the construction of transport infrastructure. This digital representation is highly complex, since transportation data is often multimodal, can span several local, national and international jurisdictions and has different logical views depending on the particular user. In addition, while transport infrastructures are relatively stable components, vehicles are very dynamic elements.

It is thus becoming increasingly relevant to use a data model where a transportation network can be encoded, stored, retrieved, modified, analyzed and displayed. Obviously, Geographic Information Systems (GIS) have received a lot of attention over this issue since they are among the best tools to store and use network data models. Network data models are an implicit part of many GIS, if not an entire GIS package of its own.

The core purpose of a network data model is to provide an accurate representation of a network as a set of links and nodes. **Topology** is the arrangement of nodes and

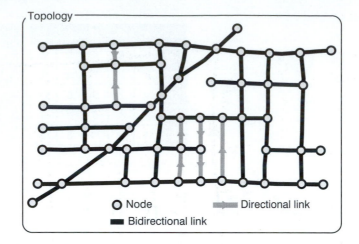

Figure 10.24   Topology of a network data model

links in a network. Of particular relevance are the representations of location, direction and connectivity. Even if graph theory aims at the abstraction of transportation networks, the topology of a network data model should be as close as possible to the real-world structure it represents. This is especially true for the usage of network data models in a GIS.

Figure 10.24 represents the basic topology of an urban transport network composed of linked nodes. It has been encoded into a network data model to represent the reality as close as possible, both topologically and geographically. Topologically, each node has been encoded with the connectivity it permits, such as whether a left turn is possible or not (although this attribute is not displayed here). Further, a direction has been encoded in each link (directional or bidirectional) to represent one-ways. Geographically, each node is located at a coordinate which matches to the actual intersection it represents. In addition, the links between each node have been decomposed into several segments (not implicitly shown) to respect the positional accuracy of the road they represent.

Cartography allows the visualization of a transport network for the purpose of reckoning and simple navigation and serves to indicate the existence of a network. Different elements of the network can have a symbolism defined by some of their attributes. For instance, a highway link may be symbolized as a thick line with a label such as its number, while a street may be symbolized as an unlabeled simple line. The symbolized network can also be combined with other features, such as landmarks, to provide a better level of orientation to the user. This is commonly the case for road maps used by the general public.

By using attributes encoded in the network data model, such as road type, each segment can be displayed to reflect its importance. For instance, Figure 10.25 displays three road classes (highway, main street and street) differently. Descriptive labels for the most important elements and directional signs for one-ways have also been added. To enrich the cartographic message, additional layers of information have been added, namely landmarks. Nodal attributes can also have a cartographic utility, such as displaying if an intersection has traffic lights.

Figure 10.25 Cartography of a network data model

Transportation network models can be used to derive a precise location, notably through a linear referencing system. For instance, the great majority of addresses are defined according to a number and a street. If address information is embedded in the attributes of a network data model, it becomes possible to use this network for **geocoding** and pinpoint the location of an address, or any location along the network, with reasonable accuracy.

Geocoding is possible if a linear referencing system is embedded in a network data model. One of the most common linear referencing systems is the address system, where each link has a corresponding street name and address range. The address range on Figure 10.26 illustrates even (right side) and odd (left side) addresses, very common attributes in most network data models such as Topologically Integrated Geographic Encoding and Referencing (TIGER) (developed by the US Census Bureau). For instance, finding the approximate location of the address "197 East Ave" would first imply querying the network data model to find all the links that have "East Ave" as a name attribute. Then, the appropriate address range is found and the location interpolated. "197" corresponds to the 191–209 address range, located on the left side of East Ave. Its approximate location would be at one-third [1 − (209–197)/(209–191)] of the length of the link that has the 191–209 address range. The same procedure can be applied to the "188 East Ave" address, which in this case would be located at one quarter of the length of the link that has the 172–210 address range.

Network data models may be used to find optimal paths and assign flows with capacity constraints in a network. While **routing** is concerned with the specific behavior of a limited number of vehicles, **traffic assignment** is mainly concerned with the system-wide behavior of traffic in a transport network. This requires a topology in which the relationship of each link with other intersecting segments is explicitly specified.

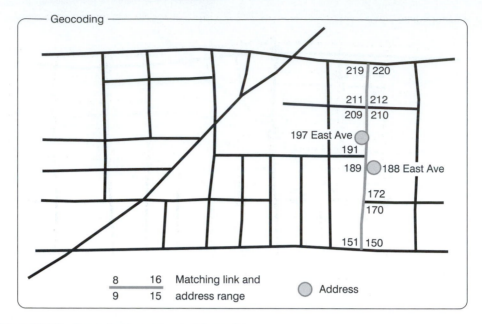

Figure 10.26 Geocoding in a network data model

Impedance measures (e.g. distance) are also attributed to each link and will have an impact on the chosen path or on how flows are assigned in the network. Routing and traffic assignment at the continental level is generally simple, since small variations in impedance are of limited consequences. Routing and traffic assignment in an urban area is much more complex, as it must consider stop signs, traffic lights and congestion in determining the impedance of a route.

Routing in a network data model can be simulated if impedance is available to links and nodes. For links, impedance if often characterized by travel time, while turn penalties are often used to characterize impedance at nodes, which is how difficult (if possible) it is to turn in one direction, as opposed to another. Figure 10.27 represents a typical routing "traveling salesperson" type of problem. Starting and ending at a warehouse, a delivery truck has a set of deliveries and pickups to perform. The locations of those pickup and delivery points could have been derived from address matching (geocoding). Considering link and node (turn penalties) impedance attributes that are encoded in the network data model, it is possible to plot an optimal route minimizing travel time that would satisfy basic constraints related to the start and end points, pickup and delivery points, as well as link and turn penalty impedances.

Layer-based approach

Most conventional GIS data models separate information in **layers**, each representing a different class of geographical elements symbolized as points, lines and polygons in the majority of cases. As such, a network data model must be constructed with the limitation of having points and lines in two separate layers; thus the layer-based approach. Further, an important requirement is that the geometry of the network matches the reality as closely as possible, since these networks are often part of a geographic information

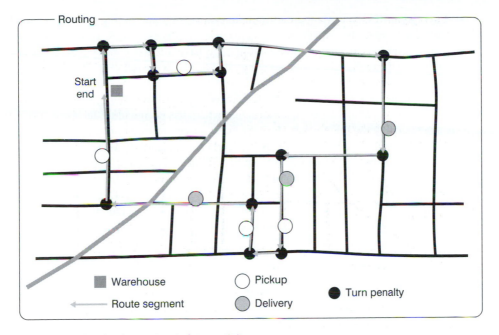

Figure 10.27 Routing in a network data model

system where an accurate **location and visualization** is a requisite. This has commonly resulted in the fragmentation of each logical link into a multitude of segments, with most of the nodes of these segments mere intermediate cosmetic elements. The topology of such network data models is not well defined, and has to be inferred. However, these network data models benefit from the attribute-linking capabilities of the spatial database models they are derived from. Among the most significant attributes that can be attached to network layers are:

- **Classification and labeling**. Each segment can be classified into categories such as its function (street, highway, railway, etc.), importance (number of lanes) and type (paved, non-paved). Also, a complex labeling structure can be established with prefixes, proper names and suffixes.
- **Linear referencing system**. Several systems to locate elements along a segment have been established. One of the most common is the address system where each segment is provided with an address range. Through linear interpolation, a specific location can be derived (geocoding).
- **Segment travel costs**. Can consider a vast array of impedance measures. Among the most common is the length of the segment, a typical travel time or a speed limit. Congestion can also be assessed, either as a specific value of impedance or as a mathematical function.
- **Direction**. To avoid unnecessary and often unrealistic duplication of links, especially at the street level, a directional attribute can be included in the attribute table.
- **Overcrossing and undercrossing**. Since the great majority of layer-based network models are planar, they are ill designed to deal with non-planar representations. A provision must be made in the attribute table to identify segments that are overcrossing or undercrossing a segment they are intersecting with.

- **Turn penalties**. An important attribute to ensure accurate routing within a network. Each intersection has different turn constraints and possibilities. Conventionally in road transportation, a right turn is assumed to have a lesser penalty than a left turn. The opposite applies for countries where driving is on the left (e.g. the UK).

The Topologically Integrated Geographic Encoding and Referencing (TIGER) model is a notable example of a layer-based structure which has been widely accepted. TIGER was developed by the US Census Bureau to store street information constructed for the 1990 Census and has been continuously updated since then. It contains complete geographic coordinates and in a line-based structure. The most important attributes include street name and address information, offering an efficient linear referencing system for geocoding. The layer-based approach is consequently good to solve the cartography and geocoding issues. However, it is ill suited to comprehensively address routing and assignment transport problems.

Object-oriented approach

The object-oriented approach represents the latest development in spatial data models. It assumes that each geographical feature is an object having a set of properties and a set of relationships with other objects. As such, a transportation network is an object composed of other objects, namely nodes and links. Since topology is one of the core concepts defining transportation networks, relationships expressing it are imbedded in object-oriented representations. The basic elements of an object-oriented transportation network data model are:

- **Classes**. They categorize objects in a specific taxonomy, which has a proper set of properties and relationships. The two basic classes of a network are obviously nodes and links, but each of these classes can be subdivided into subclasses. For instance, a link can be subdivided as a road link, a rail link, a walkway, etc.
- **Properties**. These refer to a set of measurable characteristics that are associated with a specific class. For instance, the properties of a road class could be its length, number of lanes, name, surface, speed limit, etc.
- **Relationships**. The type of logical relations objects have with one another. Instance (is-a) and membership (is-in) are among the most common relations. For example, a street is an instance of the road class, which itself is an instance of a transport infrastructure. A specific road segment can be considered part of a specific transport system through a membership relation. From these relations inheritance can be derived, where the characteristics of one object can be passed to another. Using the previous example, it is logical to derive that a street is a transport infra-structure, thus the object street inherits the properties of the object transport infrastructure.

By their structure, especially with their embedded topology, an object-oriented transport network data model would be effective to solve the routing issue in transport. Object-oriented data models. such as UNETRANS (Unified NEtwork-TRANSportation data model), have gradually become implemented standards. The potential of the object-oriented approach for GIS remains to be seen, as well as the amount of effort required to convert or adapt existing transport network databases, which are mainly layer-based, into the new representational structure.

Method 7 – Transport technical and economic performance indicators

Authors : Dr Jean-Paul Rodrigue and Dr Claude Comtois

Network and operational indicators

Multimodal transportation networks rest upon the combinatory costs and performance of transport modes, or what is referred to as economies of scope. For instance, a single container shipped overseas at the lowest cost from its origin can go from road, to maritime, to railway and to road again before reaching its destination. For passengers, a commuter may also undertake a journey involving a sequence of modes such as walking, riding a bus and then a subway. Freight shippers and carriers therefore require quantitative tools for decision making in order to compare performances of various transport modes and transport networks. Time efficiency becomes a set imperative for both freight and passenger transit, in private as well as in public sector activities.

Performance indicators are widely used by geographers and economists to empirically assess the technical performance of differing transport modes, in other words their capacity to move goods or passengers around. They are ratios, since a value such as traffic or capacity does not express a performance, but the ratio of traffic over capacity is a performance indicator. Technical performance should not be confused with economic performance, which mostly relates to how much transport output (e.g. traffic) can be supported with specific inputs (e.g. capital or labor). Performance measures are relative, implying that they mean little by themselves and must be interpreted within a comparative framework, which can be across space (e.g. systems or jurisdictions) or across time (e.g. monthly variations). Basic technical performance calculations can be particularly useful for the analysis of global network performance as well as for modal comparison, analysis and evaluation by bridging both physical attributes (length, distance, configuration, etc.) and time-based attributes (punctuality, reliability, etc.) of networks. Some indicators are currently used to measure the technical performance of freight and passenger transport:

- **Passenger or freight density**. A standard measure of transport efficiency.
- **Mean distance traveled**. A measure of the ground-covering capacity of networks and different transport modes. Used to measure the relative performance of transport modes.
- **Mean per capita ton output** (freight) or **mean number of trips per capita** (passenger).
- **Mean utilization coefficient**. Especially useful with increasing complexity of logistics associated with containerization of freight (i.e. the problem of empty returns). Can also be used to measure transit ridership.

More specifically, such indicators are of great utility by allowing **cross-temporal analysis** of a transport nexus or given transport modes. Another fundamental dimension of technical performance concerns operations and relates to specific parts of the transport network such as a segment or a terminal. The most salient indicators include:

- **Transport time/speed/turnover**. An expression of the velocity of passengers or freight along segments (speed) and at terminals or distribution centers (turnover).
- **Reliability**. The consistence of operations within defined parameters such as capacity, safety, duration and punctuality.

- **Punctuality**. The on-time performance of transport services. Particularly important for scheduled services such as flights, public transit, railways and containerized maritime shipping.
- **Load factor**. The level of transport asset utilization of modes and terminals in relation to their capacity. High load factors may be indicative of congestion.

On-time arrivals are a commonly used performance measure in air transportation, since passengers plan their trips according to the arrival schedule. The main sources of delays as reported by airlines are:

- **Air carrier delay** (5 percent). The cause of the cancellation or delay was due to circumstances within the airline's control (e.g. maintenance or crew problems, aircraft cleaning, baggage loading, fueling).
- **Extreme weather** (0.5 percent). Significant meteorological conditions (actual or forecasted) that, in the judgment of the carrier, delays or prevents the operation of a flight such as a tornado, thunderstorm, blizzard or hurricane.
- **National Aviation System** (6 percent). Delays and cancellations attributable to the national aviation system that refer to a broad set of conditions, such as non-extreme weather conditions, airport operations, heavy traffic volume and air traffic control.
- **Late-arriving aircraft** (7 percent). A previous flight with same aircraft arrived late, causing the present flight to depart late. This is the outcome of propagation effects on schedule integrity.
- **Security** (0.04 percent). Delays or cancellations caused by evacuation of a terminal or concourse, reboarding of aircraft because of security breach, inoperative screening equipment and/or long lines in excess of 29 minutes at screening areas.

Fluctuations in the flight delay pattern are mainly attributed to the growth and decline in air traffic. If air transport grows rapidly, the outcome tends to be a decreasing performance of on-time arrivals, as the system is trying to cope with additional demands with a

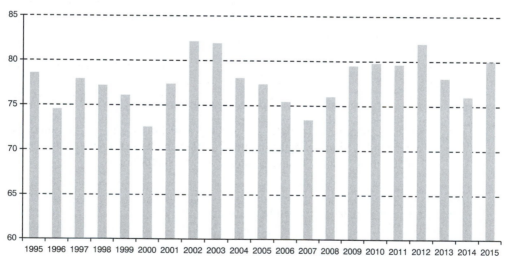

Figure 10.28 On-time arrivals of domestic flights in the United States, 1995–2015 (%)

Source: Research and Innovative Technology Administration (RITA), US Department of Transportation (US DOT).

similar level of capacity (e.g. 1995–2000, 2003–7, 2012–14). On the other hand, if air transportation stops growing or even declines, the performance improves, since some flights are removed (e.g. 2000–2 or 2007–10).

Road traffic performance

Technical performance indicators have predominantly been applied to road transportation, although other modes such as air and maritime transport are also increasingly monitored. There are two major operational types of traffic influencing the capacity of modern roads: continuous and discontinuous traffic. The **capacity of a road** is the maximal hourly flow of people or vehicles that can be supported by any link. This value is influenced by three major concepts:

- **Road conditions**. Physical attributes of the road, such as its type (paved, non-paved), number of lanes, width of lanes, design speed and the vertical and horizontal alignment.
- **Traffic conditions**. Attributes of the traffic using the road, such as its temporal distribution and its direction.
- **Control conditions**. Attributes of the control structures and existing traffic laws, such as speed limit, one-ways and priority.

Considering the above conditions, the capacity of a road is about 1,000 vehicles per lane per hour for continuous traffic roads and about 500 vehicles per lane per hour for discontinuous traffic roads. The operational goal of traffic planning is thus to make it so that road, traffic and control conditions ensure an adequate, if not optimal, service. Several guidelines will favor such a goal, such as wide enough lanes for a safe maximum speed in both directions and limited grades to limit speed differentials. The capacity of a road is also linked to the level of service, which is a qualitative measure of operational conditions of roads and its perception by users. The spatial distribution of bottlenecks, notably within urban areas, also has a strong impact on capacity, as they are the chokepoints of the whole road transport system. Traffic can be valued according to three primary measures: speed, volume or density:

- **Speed** is a rate of distance covered per unit of time. The average speed is the most commonly used measure to characterize traffic on a road.
- **Volume** is the number of vehicles observed at a point or a section over a period of time.
- **Density** is the number of vehicles that occupy a section at any point in time. For example, a road section having a volume of 1,000 vehicles per hour with an average speed of 50 km per hour will have a density of 20 vehicles/km.

The critical density is the density at which the volume is maximal and the critical speed is the speed at which the volume is maximal.

Economic performance indicators

Undoubtedly, transportation plays a considerable role in the economy with its omnipresence throughout the production chain, at all geographic scales. It is an integral constituent of the production–consumption cycle. Economic impact indicators help to show the relationship between transport systems and the economy, as well as information on the economic weight of this type of activity. Geographers should be familiar with basic econometric impact indexes. Maritime transport is still the most cost-efficient way to transport bulk merchandise over long distances. On the other hand, while air transport is recognized for its unsurpassed time efficiency versus other modes over long distances, it remains an expensive option. Thus, **vertical integration**, or the absorption of transportation activities by producers, illustrates the search for these two efficiency attributes by gaining direct control over inputs.

The relationship between transport systems and their larger economic frame becomes clear when looking at restructuring patterns which carriers and firms are currently undergoing. Structural mutations, best illustrated by the popularity of **just-in-time practices**, are fueled by two opposing yet effective forces: transporters seek to achieve economies of scale while having to conform to an increasingly "customized" demand.

Factor substitution is a commonly adopted path in order to reduce costs of production and attain greater efficiency. Containerization of freight by substituting labor for capital and technology is a good illustration of the phenomenon. Measures of capital productivity for such capital-intensive transport means are of central importance; an output/capital ratio is then commonly used. While the output/labor ratio performs the same productivity measurement but for the labor input (this form of indicator can be used for each factor of production in the system), a capital/labor ratio aims to measure which factor predominates within the relationship between capital and labor productivity. The above set of indicators therefore provides insights on the relative weight of factors within the production process.

More scale-specific indicators can also be used to appreciate the role of transport within the economy. Knowing freight transport both contributes to and is fueled by a larger economic context, freight output can be confronted against macroeconomic indicators: an output/GDP ratio measures the relationship between economic activity and traffic freight – in other words, the traffic intensity. At the local level, the status of the transport industry within the local economy is given by a transport sector income/local income ratio. Still at a micro-scale, finally, a measure of the relative production value of freight output is provided by an output/local income ratio.

Underlying objectives of the application of such indicators are as varied as they are numerous. Efficiency indicators constitute valuable tools to tackle project viability questions as well as to measure investment returns and cost/subsidy recovery of transport systems. Input–output analyses making use of some of the above indicators are also instrumental to the development of global economic impact indexes and productivity assessment concepts such as the **Total Factor Productivity** (TFP) and to identify sources of productivity gains.

Method 8 – The Gini coefficient

The Lorenz curve

The Gini coefficient was developed to measure the degree of concentration (inequality) of a variable in a distribution of its elements. It compares the Lorenz curve of a ranked empirical distribution with the **line of perfect equality** (Figure 10.29). This line assumes that each element has the same contribution to the total summation of the values of a variable. The Gini coefficient ranges between 0, where there is no concentration (**perfect equality**), and 1, where there is total concentration (**perfect inequality**).

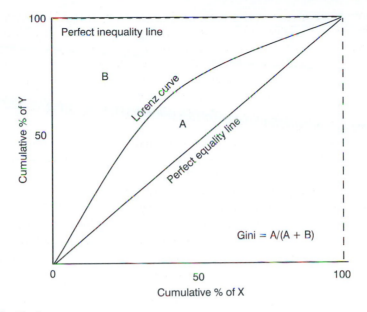

Figure 10.29 The Lorenz curve

The **Lorenz curve** is a graphical representation of the proportionality of a distribution (the cumulative percentage of the values). To build the Lorenz curve, all the elements of a distribution must be ordered from the most important to the least important. Then, each element is plotted according to their cumulative percentage of X and Y, X being the cumulative percentage of elements and Y being their cumulative importance. For instance, out of a distribution of 10 elements (N), the first element would represent 10 percent of X and whatever percentage of Y it represents (this percentage must be the highest in the distribution). The second element would cumulatively represent 20 percent of X (its 10 percent plus the 10 percent of the first element) and its percentage of Y plus the percentage of Y of the first element.

The Lorenz curve is compared with the perfect equality line, which is a linear relationship that plots a distribution where each element has an equal value in its shares of X and Y. For instance, in a distribution of 10 elements, if there is perfect equality, the fifth element would have a cumulative percentage of 50 percent for X and Y. The perfect inequality line represents a distribution where one element has the total cumulative percentage of Y, while the others have none. The Gini coefficient is defined graphically as a ratio of two surfaces involving the summation of all vertical deviations between the Lorenz curve and the perfect equality line (A) divided by the difference between the perfect equality and perfect inequality lines (A + B).

Figure 10.30 represents a simple system of five ports along a coast. In case A, the traffic for each port is the same, so there is no concentration and thus no inequality. The Lorenz curve of this distribution is the same as the perfect equality line – they overlap. In case B, there is some concentration of the traffic in two ports and this concentration is reflected in the Lorenz curve, as it is different from the perfect equality line. Case C represents a high level of concentration in two ports and the Lorenz curve is significantly different from the perfect equality line.

Figure 10.30   Traffic concentration and Lorenz curves

Figure 10.31   World's 50 largest container ports, passenger airports and freight airports, 2010

Source: Airport Council International and Containerization International.

The world's 50 largest container ports and airport terminals shows a level of concentration in their distribution, with container ports having the highest level as depicted on its Lorenz curve (Figure 10.31). The 10 largest terminals accounting for about 49.7 percent of the traffic handled by world's largest 50 container ports. Air passenger traffic has a much lower concentration level (the 10 largest airports handling

30.8 percent of the traffic of the 50 largest airports), which is reflective of its widespread use as a mode of long distance transportation. Geographical concentration is also significant with most of the activity taking place around East Asia, Western Europe and North America.

Calculating the Gini coefficient (G)

The Gini coefficient represents the area of concentration between the Lorenz curve and the line of perfect equality, as it expresses a proportion of the area enclosed by the triangle defined by the line of perfect equality and the line of perfect inequality. The closer the coefficient is to 1, the more unequal the distribution. Figure 10.32 shows a hypothetical set of terminals with varying amounts of traffic. X refers to the traffic proportion if the traffic was distributed evenly throughout all the terminals. Y refers to the actual proportion of traffic of each terminal. sX and sY are cumulative percentages of Xs and Ys (in fractions) and N is the number of elements (observations).

Geographers and many others have used the Gini coefficient in numerous instances, such as assessing income distribution among a set of contiguous regions (or countries) or to measure other spatial phenomena, such as industrial location. Its major purpose as a method in transport geography has been related to measuring the concentration of traffic, mainly at terminals, such as assessing changes in port system concentration. Economies of scale in transportation can favor the concentration of traffic at transport terminals, while other considerations, such as accessibility to regional markets, can be perceived as a countervailing force to concentration. So, the temporal variations of the Gini coefficient reflect changes in the comparative advantages of a location within the transport system.

$$G = 1 - \sum_{i=1}^{N} (\sigma Y_{y-1})(\sigma X_{i-1} - \sigma X_i) = 0.392$$

Y	σX (Cumulative)	σY (Cumulative)	$\sigma Y_{i-1} + \sigma Y_i$ (A)	$\sigma X_{i-1} - \sigma X_i$ (B)	A*B
0.25	0.10	0.25	0.25	0.10	0.025
0.20	0.20	0.45	0.70	0.10	0.070
0.15	0.30	0.60	1.05	0.10	0.105
0.10	0.40	0.70	1.30	0.10	0.130
0.08	0.50	0.78	1.48	0.10	0.148
0.07	0.60	0.85	1.63	0.10	0.163
0.05	0.70	0.90	1.75	0.10	0.175
0.05	0.80	0.95	1.85	0.10	0.185
0.03	0.90	0.98	1.93	0.10	0.193
0.02	1.00	1.00	1.98	0.10	0.198
1.00					1.392

Figure 10.32 Calculation of the Gini coefficient

Method 9 – Spatial interactions and the gravity model

Overview

One methodology of particular importance to transport geography relates to how to estimate flows between locations, since these flows, known as spatial interactions, enable the evaluation of demand (existing or potential) for transport services. A **spatial interaction** is a realized movement of people, freight or information between an origin and a destination. It is a transport demand/supply relationship expressed over a geographical space.

Spatial interactions cover a wide variety of movements, such as journeys to work, migrations, tourism, the usage of public facilities, the transmission of information or capital, the market areas of retailing activities, international trade and freight distribution. Economic activities are generating (supply) and attracting (demand) flows. The simple fact that a movement occurs between an origin and a destination underlines that the costs incurred by a spatial interaction are lower than the benefits derived from such an interaction. As such, a commuter is willing to drive one hour because this interaction is linked to an income, while international trade concepts, such as comparative advantages, underline the benefits of specialization and the ensuing generation of trade flows between distant locations. Three interdependent conditions are necessary for a spatial interaction to occur (Figure 10.33):

- **Complementarity**. There must be a supply and a demand between the interacting locations. A residential zone is complementary to an industrial zone because the first is supplying workers while the second is supplying jobs. The same can be said concerning the complementarity between a store and its customers and between an industry and its suppliers (movements of freight). If location B produces/generates something that location A requires, then an interaction is possible because a supply/demand relationship has been established between those two locations; they have become complementary to one another. The same applies in the other direction

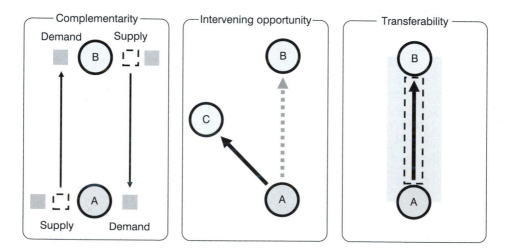

Figure 10.33   Conditions for the realization of a spatial interaction

(A to B), which creates a situation of reciprocity common in commuting or international trade.

- **Intervening opportunity**. There must not be another location that may offer a better alternative as a point of origin or as a point of destination. For instance, in order to have an interaction of a customer to a store, there must not be a closer store that offers a similar array of goods. If location C offers the same characteristics (namely complementarity) as location A and is also closer to location B, an interaction between B and A will not occur and will be replaced by an interaction between B and C.
- **Transferability**. Freight, persons or information being transferred must be supported by transport infrastructures, implying that the origin and the destination must be linked. Costs to overcome distance must not be higher than the benefits of related interaction, even if there is complementarity and no alternative opportunity. Transport infrastructures (modes and terminals) must be present to support an interaction between B and A. Also, these infrastructures must have a capacity and availability which are compatible with the requirements of such an interaction.

Spatial interaction models seek to explain spatial flows. As such it is possible to measure flows and predict the consequences of changes in the conditions generating them. When such attributes are known, it is possible, for example, to better allocate transport resources such as highways, buses, airplanes or ships, since they would reflect the transport demand more closely.

Origin/destination matrices

Each spatial interaction, as an analogy for a set of movements, is composed of an origin/destination pair. Each pair can itself be represented as a cell in a matrix where rows are related to the locations (centroids) of origin, while columns are related to locations (centroids) of destination. Such a matrix is commonly known as an origin/destination matrix, or a spatial interaction matrix.

Figure 10.34 represents movements (O/D pairs) between five locations (A, B, C, D and E). From this graph, an O/D matrix can be built where each O/D pair becomes a cell. A value of 0 is assigned for each O/D pair that does not have an observed flow. In the

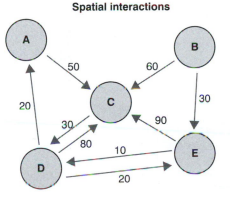

Spatial interactions

O/D matrix

	A	B	C	D	E	Ti
A	0	0	50	0	0	50
B	0	0	60	0	30	90
C	0	0	0	30	0	30
D	20	0	80	0	20	120
E	0	0	90	10	0	100
Tj	20	0	280	40	50	390

Figure 10.34   Constructing an O/D matrix

O/D matrix the sum of a row (Ti) represents the total outputs of a location (flows originating from), while the sum of a column (Tj) represents the total inputs of a location (flows bound to). The summation of inputs is always equal to the summation of outputs. Otherwise, there are movements that are coming from, or going to, outside the considered system. The sum of inputs or outputs gives the total flows taking place within the system (T). It is also possible to have O/D matrices according to the age group, income, gender, etc. Under such circumstances they are labeled sub-matrices, since they account for only a share of the total flows.

In many cases where spatial interactions information is relied on for planning and allocation purposes, origin/destination matrices are **not available** or are **incomplete**. Palliating this lack of data commonly requires surveys. With economic development, the addition of new activities and transport infrastructures, spatial interactions have a tendency to change very rapidly as flows adapt to a new spatial structure. The problem is that an origin/destination survey is very expensive in terms of efforts, time and costs. In a complex spatial system such as a region, O/D matrices tend to be quite large. For instance, the consideration of 100 origins and 100 destinations would entail 10,000 separate O/D pairs for which information has to be provided. In addition, the data gathered by spatial interaction surveys are likely to rapidly become obsolete as economic and spatial conditions change. It is therefore important to find a way to estimate as precisely as possible spatial interactions, particularly when empirical data is lacking or is incomplete. A possible solution relies on using a spatial interaction model to complement and even replace empirical observations.

Spatial interaction models

The basic assumption concerning many spatial interaction models is that flows are a function of the attributes of the locations of origin, the attributes of the locations of destination and the friction of distance between the concerned origins and the destinations. Figure 10.35 resumes the general formulation of the spatial interaction model.

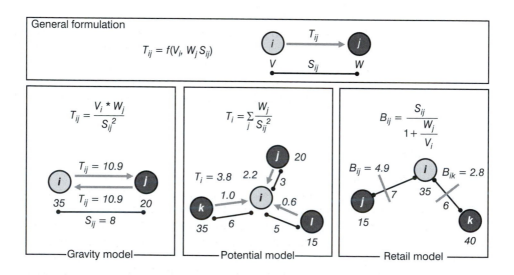

Figure 10.35 Three basic interaction models

- Tij : Interaction between location i (origin) and location j (destination). Its units of measurement are varied and can involve people, tons of freight, traffic volume, etc. It also relates to a time period such as interactions by the hour, day, month or year.
- Vi : Attributes of the location of origin i. Variables often used to express these attributes are socioeconomic in nature, such as population, number of jobs available, industrial output or gross domestic product.
- Wj : Attributes of the location of destination j. It uses similar socioeconomic variables to the previous attribute.
- Sij : Attributes of separation between the location of origin i and the location of destination j. Also known as transport friction. Variables often used to express these attributes are distance, transport costs or travel time.

The attributes of V and W tend to be paired to express complementarity in the best possible way. For instance, measuring commuting flows (work-related movements) between different locations would likely consider a variable such as working age population as V and total employment as W. From this general formulation, three basic types of interaction models can be constructed:

- **Gravity model**. Measures interactions between all the possible location pairs by multiplying their attributes, which is then pondered by their level of separation. Separation is often squared to reflect the growing friction of distance. In Figure 10.35, two locations (i and j) have a respective "weight" (importance) of 35 and 20 and are at a distance (degree of separation) of 8. The resulting interaction is 10.9, which is reciprocal.
- **Potential model**. Measures interactions between one location and every other location by the summation of the attributes of each other location pondered by their level of separation (again squared to reflect the friction of distance). In Figure 10.35, the potential interaction of location i (Ti) is measured by adding the ratio "weight"/ squared distance for each other location (j, k and l). The potential interaction is 3.8, which is not reciprocal.
- **Retail model**. Measure the boundary of the market areas between two locations competing over the same market. It assumes that the market boundary between two locations is a function of their separation pondered by the ratio of their respective weights. If two locations have the same importance, their market boundary would be halfway between. In Figure 10.35, the market boundary between locations i and j (Bij) is at a distance of 4.9 from i (and consequently at a distance of 2.1 from j).

The gravity model

The gravity model is the most common formulation of the spatial interaction method. It is named as such because it uses a similar formulation to Newton's law of gravity. Gravity-like representations have been applied in a wide variety of contexts, such as migration, commodity flows, traffic flows, commuting and evaluating boundaries between market areas. Accordingly, the attraction between two objects is proportional to their mass and inversely proportional to their respective distance. Consequently, the general formulation of spatial interactions can be adapted to reflect this basic assumption to form the elementary formulation of the gravity model:

$$T_{ij} = k \frac{P_i P_j}{D_{ij}}$$

- P_i and P_j : Importance of the location of origin and the location of destination.
- d_{ij} : Distance between the location of origin and then location of destination.
- k is a proportionality constant related to the rate of the event. For instance, if the same system of spatial interactions is considered, the value of k will be higher if interactions were considered for a year comparative to the value of k for one week.

Thus, spatial interactions between locations i and j are proportional to their respective importance divided by their distance. The gravity model can be extended to include several calibration parameters:

$$T_{ij} = k \frac{P_i^{\alpha} P_j^{\lambda}}{D_{ij}^{\beta}}$$

P, d and k refer to the variables previously discussed.

- β (beta). A parameter of transport friction related to the efficiency of the transport system between two locations. This friction is rarely linear, as the further the movement, the greater the friction of distance. For instance, two locations serviced by a highway will have a lower beta index than if they were serviced by a road.
- λ (lambda). Potential to generate movements (emissiveness). For movements of people, lambda is often related to an overall level of welfare. For instance, it is logical to infer that, for retailing flows, a location having higher income levels will generate more movements.
- α (alpha). Potential to attract movements (attractiveness). Related to the nature of economic activities at the destination. For instance, a center having important commercial activities will attract more movements.

A significant challenge related to the usage of spatial interaction models, notably the gravity model, is related to their calibration. Calibration consists in finding the value of each parameter of the model (constant and exponents) to ensure that the estimated results are similar to the observed flows. If it is not the case, the model is almost useless, as it predicts or explains little. It is impossible to know if the process of calibration is accurate without comparing estimated results with empirical evidence.

In the two formulations of the gravity model that have been introduced, the simple formulation offers a good flexibility for calibration, since four parameters can be modified. Altering the value of beta, alpha and lambda will influence the estimated spatial interactions (Figure 10.36). Furthermore, the value of the parameters can change in time due to factors such as technological innovations, new transport infrastructure and economic development. For instance, improvements in transport efficiency generally have the consequence of reducing the value of the beta exponent (friction of distance). Economic development is likely to influence the values of alpha and lambda, reflecting a growth in the mobility.

Variations of the beta, alpha and lambda exponents have different impacts on the level of spatial interactions. For instance, the relationship between distance and spatial interactions will change according to the beta exponent. If the value of beta is high

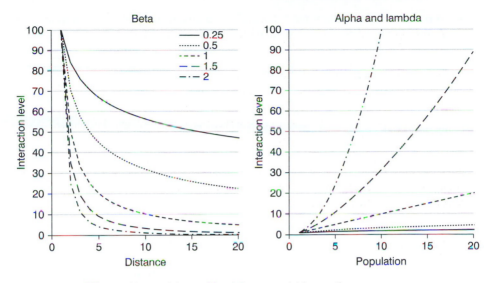

Figure 10.36 Effects of beta, alpha and lambda on spatial interactions

(higher than 0.5), the friction of distance will be much more important (steep decline of spatial interactions) than with a low value of beta (e.g. 0.25). A beta of 0 means that distance has no effect and that interactions remain the same whatever the concerned distance. Alpha and lambda exponents have the same effect on the interaction level. For a value of 1, there is a linear relationship between population (or any attribute of weight) and the level of interactions. Any value higher than 1 implies an exponential growth of the interaction level as population grows.

Calibration can also be considered for different O/D matrices according to age, income, gender, type of merchandise and modal choice. A part of the scientific research in transport and regional planning aims at finding accurate parameters for spatial inter-action models. This is generally a costly and time-consuming process, but a very useful one. Once a spatial interaction model has been validated for a city or a region, it can then be used for simulation and prediction purposes, such as how many additional flows would be generated if the population increased or if better transport infrastructures (lower friction of distance) were provided.

Method 10 – Market area analysis

Market size and shape

Each economic activity has a location, but the various demands (raw materials, labor, parts, services, etc.) and flows each location generates also have a spatial dimension called a **market area**. It is the surface over which a demand or supply offered at a specific location is expressed. For a factory, it includes the areas to where its products are shipped; for a retail store, it is the tributary area from which it draws its customers.

Transportation is particularly important in market area analysis because it impacts on the location of the activities as well as their accessibility. The size of a market area is a function of its threshold and range:

- **Market threshold**. Minimum demand necessary to support an economic activity such as a service. Since each demand has a distinct location, a threshold has a direct spatial dimension. The size of a market has a direct relationship with its threshold.
- **Market range**. The maximum distance each unit of demand is willing to travel to reach a service or the maximum distance a product can be shipped to a customer. The range is a function of transport costs, time or convenience in view of intervening opportunities. To be profitable, a market must have a range higher than its threshold.

Figure 10.37 considers a fairly uniform distribution of customers on an isotropic plain and a single market where goods and services may be purchased. If each customer is willing to purchase one unit per day and the market needs to sell 11 units per day to cover its costs (production or acquisition), then the threshold of the market would be the yellow circle of distance $D(T)$ from the market. However, 29 customers per day, including customers 1 and 2, patronize the market, of which an extra 18 are beyond the threshold distance $D(T)$. They contribute directly to the profitability of the market. The market range of all these customers is below distance $D(R)$. Beyond this range, customers are unwilling to go to the market, such as customer 3. There are different thresholds according to the variety of products or services that can be offered on a market. A threshold may be as low as 250 people for a convenience store or as high as 150,000 people for a theater. If the demand falls below the threshold level, the activity will run at a loss and will eventually fail. If the demand increases above the minimum, the activity will increase its profits, which may also lead to the entry of competitors. The frequency of use of goods or services is important in assessing the extent of the market threshold, which is often linked to the level of income. A movie theater needing 500 visitors per night will require a threshold population of around 150,000 if the average number of visits is one per year. But, if the average number of visits is three per year,

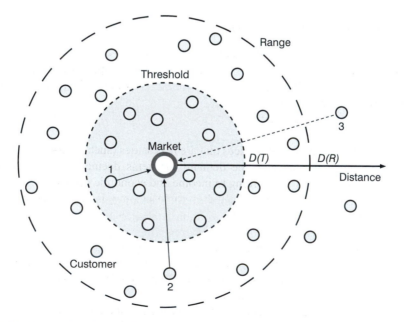

Figure 10.37 Market threshold and range

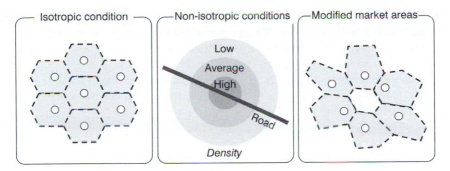

Figure 10.38 Non-isotropic conditions and the shape of market areas

the population threshold drops to 50,000. Three movie theaters instead of one can be supported by the same population.

In the case of a single market area, its shape in an isotropic plain is a simple concentric circle, having the market range as radius. Since the purpose of commercial activities is to service all the available demand, when possible, and that the range of many activities is limited, more than one location is required to service an area. For such a purpose, a hexagonal-shaped structure of market areas represents the optimal market shape under a condition of isotropy. This shape can be modified by non-isotropic conditions mainly related to variations in density and accessibility.

Under **isotropic conditions** each market has the same polygonal evenly spaced area (Figure 10.38). This theoretical condition is obviously rarely found in reality. The two most important **non-isotropic conditions** impacting on the shape market areas are differences in density (depicted here as concentric circles) and accessibility (depicted here as the presence of a road). The modified market areas are the possible outcome of non-isotropic conditions.

Economic definition of a market area

A market depends on the relationships between supply and demand. It acts as a price-fixing mechanism for goods and services. Demand is the quantity of a good or service that consumers are willing to buy at a given price. It is high if the price of a commodity is low, while in the opposite situation – a high price – demand would be low. Outside market price, demand can generally be influenced by the following factors:

- **Utility**. While goods and services that are necessities (such as food) do not see much fluctuation in the demand, the demand for items deemed of lesser utility (even frivolous) would vary according to income and economic cycles.
- **Income level**. Income, especially disposable income, is directly proportional with consumption. A population with a high income level has much more purchasing power than a population with a low income.
- **Inflation**. Involves an increase in the money supply in relation to the availability of assets, commodities, goods and services. Although it directly influences prices, inflation is outside the supply–demand relationship and decreases the purchasing power, if wages are not increased accordingly.
- **Taxation**. Sale and value-added taxes can have an inhibiting effect on sales of goods and services, as they add to the production costs and claim a share of consumer income.

- **Savings**. The quantity of capital available in savings can provide a potential to acquire consumption goods. Also, people may restrain from consuming if saving is a priority, namely in periods of economic hardship.

Supply is the amount of goods or services that firms or individuals are able to produce, taking account of a selling price. Outside price, supply can generally be influenced by the following factors:

- **Profits**. Even if the sales of a product are limited, if profits are high an activity providing goods or services may be satisfied with this situation. This is particularly the case for luxury goods. If profits are low, an activity can cease, thus lowering the supply.
- **Competition**. Competition is one of the most important mechanisms for establishing prices. Where competition is absent (an oligopoly), or where there is too much (over-competition), prices artificially influence supply and demand.

According to the market principle, supply and demand are determined by the price, which is an equilibrium between both. It is often called equilibrium price or market price. This price is a **compromise** between the desire of firms to sell their goods and services at the highest price possible and the desire of consumers to buy goods and services at the lowest possible price.

For many economists, the market is a point where goods and services are exchanged and does not have a specific location, since it is simply an abstraction of the relationships between supply and demand. It is important to underline that, most of the time, **consumers must move** in order to acquire a good or service. The producer must also **ship a commodity** to a location where the consumer can buy it – a store or a residence (in the case of online shopping). The concept of distance thus must be considered concomitantly with the concept of market. In those conditions, the real price includes the **market price plus the transport price** from the market to the location of final consumption.

Competition over market areas

Competition involves similar activities trying to attract customers. Although the core foundation of competition for a comparable good or service is price, there are several **spatial strategies** that impact the price element. The two most common are:

- **Market coverage**. Activities offering the same service will occupy locations in order to offer goods or services to the whole area. This aspect is well explained by the central place theory and applies well for sectors where spatial market saturation is a growth strategy (fast food, coffee shops, etc.). The range of each location will be a function of customer density, transport costs and the location of other competitors.
- **Range expansion**. Existing locations try to expand their ranges in order to attract more customers. Economies of scale resulting in larger retail activities are a trend in that direction, namely the emergence of shopping malls. Taken individually, each store would have a limited range. However, as a group they tend to attract additional customers from wider ranges for many reasons. First, a complementarity of goods or services is offered. A customer would thus find it convenient to be able to buy clothes, shoes and personal care products at the same location. Second, a diversity of the same goods or services is offered (more choice) even if they compete between one

other. Third, other related amenities are provided, such as safety, food, indoor walking space, entertainment and also parking space.

Making market area competition models operational has been the object of numerous approaches. Initial work undertaken in the first half of the twentieth century focused on simple market competition (Hotelling's law), which was the foundation of market area analysis by considering factors such as retail location and distance–decay. It is assumed that the product was uniform so customers would buy from the most convenient location (nearest seller) and that the friction of distance was linear and isotropic (Figure 10.39). The total price for the customer is thus the market price plus the transport price (time or effort spent to go to the market). Under such circumstances, two competitors will select locations A and B for optimal market coverage. With P1 being the market price, the market boundary would be F1 (point of cost indifference), since right of F1 customers would get a lower price at location B instead of at location A and, left of F1, customers would get a lower price at location A. If, for any reason, location A is able to lower the market price from P1 to P2, then its market area would expand at the expense of location B, from F1 to F2.

Later, factors such as market size were taken into consideration (Reilly's law), enabling complex market area areas to be built. Since market areas are often non-monopolistic, this factor was included with market areas becoming ranges of probabilities that customers will attend specific locations (Huff's law). The purpose of Reilly's law of retail gravitation (1931) is to find a point of indifference between two locations, so the trading area of each can be determined. This point is assumed to be a function of the distance between two locations pondered by their respective size (population often used for this purpose). One location can thus be more attractive than the other. For instance, in Figure 10.40 two locations are 75 km apart. According to Hotelling's principle, the point of indifference should be halfway in between (35 km). However, since location a has a larger population (more weight), it is assumed that it will draw more customers. Under such circumstances, the point of indifference is 45.9 km away from location a.

Huff's retail model (1963) assumes that customers have a choice to patronize a location in view of other alternatives. Thus, a market area is expressed as a continuous line of probabilities, unless there are no other alternative locations. The point of indifference

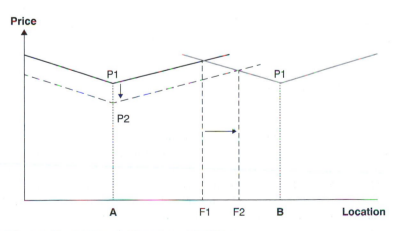

Figure 10.39 Hotelling's principle of market competition

Figure 10.40 Reilly's and Huff's laws

becomes the point of equal probability that a customer will patronize one location or another. In Figure 10.40, a customer has a greater chance (0.71) to patronize location a at the midpoint than to patronize location b (0.29). The advantage of Huff's retail model is that it leaves room for customer choice. Although market areas are particularly relevant for retail analysis, the methodology also applies to time-dependent activities, such as freight distribution, since distribution centers are located to service specific national or regional markets.

Geographic Information Systems and market areas analysis

Geographic Information Systems (GIS) have become fundamental tools to evaluate market areas, especially in retailing. With basic data, such as a list of customers and their addresses (or ZIP codes), it is relatively simple to evaluate market areas with a reasonable level of accuracy, a task that would have been much more complex beforehand. With GIS, market area analysis left the realm of abstraction to become a practical tool used by retailers and service providers in complex real-world situations. In the spatial representation of a GIS, the market area is a polygon which can be measured and used to perform operations such as intersection (zones of spatial competition) or union (area serviced). Among the major methods a GIS can be used to evaluate market areas are (Figure 10.41):

- **Buffer creation**, a common GIS procedure, associates each concentric circle with a distance or a time value. They can include the threshold and the range of a store. Another dimension of this method concerns Thiessen polygons, where the market area is calculated as halfway distances from the location of other competitors.
- **Share by polygon** can be estimated as an aggregation of individual customers within a geographical unit of reference (ZIP code, census bloc, etc.) or a statistical

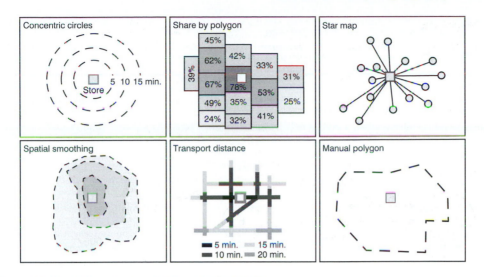

Figure 10.41 GIS methods to estimate market areas

calculation based on a set of representative variables, such as distance, population, income and age.

- A **star map** is a vector creation where segments have different origins (one for each customer) but the destination is the same (the store). It depicts a market area as a set of customers connected to a store. Qualitative and quantitative attributes can be attached to each vector, such as frequency or sales.

- **Spatial smoothing** is the outcome of statistical modeling that interpolates data from a known set of points (customers) to a continuous surface. The density of customers thus becomes a statistical surface expressing the market area.

- **Transport distance** measures the accessibility, expressed in distance or time, of road segments to the store. It takes into consideration the different capacities of road segments (number of lanes, driving speed, turn penalties, etc.), which may be quite different from Euclidean distances, such as those calculated by buffer creation. A new layer is created where each former road vector is segmented according to distance/time decay through a routing procedure that originates from the store.

- **Manual polygons** are created with tracing where the analyst evaluates a market area from a set of assumptions, often based on specific expertise and empirical knowledge about that market. For instance, the analyst may empirically know that for various reasons few customers may be coming from a nearby neighborhood, excluding it from the market area. It could also be assumed that few customers are coming from further away than a specific street, making that street a boundary for the market area.

Bibliography

Arlinghaus, S. L., W.C. Arlinghaus and F. Harary (2001) *Graph Theory and Geography: An Interactive View.* New York: John Wiley.

BTS (2001) Special Issue of *Methodological Issues in Accessibility, Journal of Transportation and Statistics* 4(2/3, September/December). Bureau of Transportation Statistics.

Butler, J.A. (2008) *Designing Geodatabases for Transportation.* Redlands, CA: ESRI Press.

Colwell, P. F. (1982) "Central place theory and the simple economic foundations of the gravity model." *Journal of Regional Science* 22(4): 541–546.

FHWA (2001) *Transportation Performance Measures Toolbox.* Operations, Federal Highway Administration. Washington, DC: US DOT.

Fotheringham, A.S. and M.E. O'Kelly (1989) *Spatial Interaction Models: Formulations and Applications.* London: Kluwer Academic.

Guimerà, R. and L.A.N. Amaral (2005) "Cartography of complex networks: modules and universal roles." *Journal of Statistical Mechanics* 2: 1–13.

International Transportation Forum (2015) *Big Data and Transport: Understanding and Assessing Options.* Paris: OECD.

Isard, W. (1956) *Location and Space-Economy: A General Theory Relating to Industrial Location, Market Areas, Land Use, Trade, and Urban Structure.* Cambridge: MIT Press.

Miller, H.J. and S.L. Shaw (2001) *Geographic Information Systems for Transportation: Principles and Applications.* New York: Oxford University Press.

Miller, H. J. and S.L. Shaw (2015) "Geographic information systems for transportation in the 21st century." *Geography Compass* 9: 180–189.

Oum, T.H. et al. (1992), "Concepts, methods and purposes of productivity measurement in transportation." *Transportation Research* A, 26A(6): 493–505.

O'Kelly, M.E. (1998) "A geographer's analysis of hub-and-spoke networks." *Journal of Transport Geography* 6(3): 171–186.

Taaffe, E., H.L. Gauthier and M.E. O'Kelly (1998) *Geography of Transportation*, 2nd edition. Upper Saddle River, NJ: Prentice Hall.

Ullman, E.L. (1956) "The role of transportation and the bases for interaction," in W.L. Thomas jr et al. (eds), *Man's Role in Changing the Face of the Earth.* Chicago: University of Chicago Press, pp. 862–880.

Victoria Transport Policy Institute, "Defining, evaluating and improving accessibility." Transport Demand Management Encyclopedia, available at www.vtpi.org/tdm/tdm84.htm Accessed: 01 July 2016.

Conclusion

Issues and challenges in transport geography

Authors: Dr Jean-Paul Rodrigue, Dr Claude Comtois and Dr Brian Slack

Transport geography seeks to understand the spatial organization of mobility. It has emerged as a full-fledged field within geography with a strong propensity to include concepts and methods from other disciplines such as economics, engineering, environmental sciences and sociology. Because transportation systems are involved in a wide variety of scales and modes, from local public transit to global maritime shipping, the approach has a tendency to be partitioned. It is indeed difficult to reconcile perspectives such as pedestrian mobility issues related to land use or the selection of air cargo hubs. Multidisciplinary approaches remain at the core of transport geography simply because its modes are at the same time independent but interconnected at different scales. Irrespective of the scale and the mode, transport geography shares several common issues and challenges.

Congestion

The issue of congestion is likely to remain as one of the ongoing issues in transport geography because there are **unprecedented demands for transportation** being generated by a global economy that is ever more dependent upon the transport industry. The causes of congestion are well understood, even if the solutions are not. Congestion occurs across modes and locations and arises from two causes. Most important is when demand for mobility **exceeds the capacity to support it**. It can also occur when random events bring about a temporary disruption to service, such as an accident or a natural hazard such as flooding. In the case of the second set of causes, it is possible to mitigate their effects if the occurrence is frequent, such as accidents, or if the risks are great, as for example flooding in a flood plain. A common and attractive solution is to increase capacity. However, increasing capacity engenders a hidden demand, so that adding lanes to an expressway tends to attract even more circulation. Furthermore, demand is increasing consistently, so that the practicality of this solution may be questioned.

The expected growth of the demand is likely to have major impacts on the nature and form of the future transport industry. In the short term at least, road transport is likely to continue its dominance of the transport industry. There are two basic reasons for this assertion. In the developed world automobiles and trucks already dominate the market, and the spatial patterns of people, industries and services have adjusted themselves somewhat to the demands of these modes. Such low density, space extensive patterns are pushing the traffic congestion ever further out, and make it very difficult for other higher-capacity modes to compete. At the same time the demand for mobility is growing as a result of the rapid industrialization in developing countries such as China and India. There, a modal shift is occurring in favor of road transport. Increasing prosperity represents a great potential for growth in road transport.

Congestion is not limited to internal urban-generated traffic. International trade is likely to continue to be dominated by maritime transport (in terms of weight) and air transport (in terms of value). This has already led to a **concentration of traffic** in a relatively small number of gateways and hubs, which are capable of extracting scale economies. For example, the 20 largest container ports handled more than 49 percent of global traffic in 2012. The traffic concentration, however, is already producing capacity problems in many of these gateways, particularly in terms of accessing their hinterlands. International trade has grown at a rate faster than economic growth as measured by the GDP in recent decades and there are expectations that congestion related to trade flows (or long-distance freight transportation) will remain an issue in the future.

For geographers there are a whole range of issues arising out of the growth of demand and congestion. First are a series of questions surrounding **how to provide solutions**. Second are the **effects on future spatial patterns**. Conventionally, the solution to congestion was to provide more capacity by building more infrastructure. Such a response depended heavily on engineering solutions. It is now recognized that a multidisciplinary approach is required. Engineering capabilities to design and construct infrastructure and systems, and to develop further technological innovations, remain fundamental. However, **transport policy and planning requires a broader perspective**, one that considers different goals and alternatives, responds to different needs for mobility, and that seeks ways to manage demand.

Congestion is **spatially bound**. It takes place in specific locations with impacts at a multitude of scales, from a particular highway intersection that may delay traffic over a few hundred meters, to blockage in a port that may disrupt the flow of goods over half a continent. Each event produces a spatial response, from the car driver who searches out an alternative route to the shipper who selects a different mode or point of entry for succeeding shipments. Increased demand and the rising likelihoods of congestion will intensify new spatial responses and thus it appears very likely that new spatial flows and structures will come into being. They involve:

- **Demand management**. Concerns the conditions and in what types of locations travel demand can be modified. In a market context, when supply is fixed and demand increases, an upward price adjustment inevitably takes place. This is common in maritime and air transport with yield management strategies. However, many transport infrastructures, such as roads, are provided free of access, implying no cost changes as congestion levels increase. There is thus a growing need to provide incentives (or disincentives) and reassess the priority in the use of infrastructure, particularly in urban areas.

- **Concentration versus deconcentration**. Accessibility and infrastructure improvements usually lead to a concentration of activities, while congestion acts as a counteracting force to concentration since it creates various diseconomies. Already there is evidence of deconcentration in air transport for growth in passengers and freight in some smaller airports. The density of economic and social activities and the related intensity of transport use imply a balance between the forces of concentration and deconcentration.

- **Economic and social impacts**. In a context where transport networks are increasingly synchronized, congestion can create multiplying effects not just impacting costs, but also the reliability of transport systems. The economic and social impacts of congestion remain a salient issue, particularly in developing countries where it can impede economic growth.

- **Passengers versus freight**. Congestion also raises the issue of the prioritization of passengers versus freight when they share transport infrastructure or when freight activities such as terminals or distribution centers are in proximity to locations where large numbers of passengers transit. This will require a careful assessment of the respective costs of congestion on specific passenger and freight transport systems and in which circumstances congestion exerts the most externalities. A salient issue concerns how freight distribution could be better integrated in the urban environment, where passenger movements tend to dominate: the realm of city logistics.

Infrastructure

Regardless of the specific solutions to congestion that are considered, increasing demand is placing unprecedented requests for investment in transport infrastructures. A major question confronting all countries around the world is **how to finance** the construction and maintenance of transport infrastructures. As economies of scale are applied to transport systems, such as larger container ships or double-stacked rail corridors, capital requirements increase in proportion. Governments have traditionally been the primary source of funding in the transport sector, but the costs of keeping pace with the growth in demand are making it difficult for even the richest countries to provide public funding on the scale required to meet expectations about the mobility of passengers and freight.

Capital requirements are particularly prevalent on both sides of the infrastructure life-cycle spectrum. The highways in China and North America represent two salient cases. For China, the last decade has seen an impressive level of highway construction with the setting of a national highway network, the longest in the world. Comparatively, the American Interstate highway system is nearing a phase in its life cycle where a substantial amount of capital investment will be required to upgrade the system and maintain its operability, including thousands of aging highway bridges. While most of the Interstate is publicly funded, almost all Chinese highways were funded by private interests that are using tolls to recover their investments. Irrespective of the context, the issue of the role of private and public actors in transport infrastructure, as well as pricing mechanisms, will remain salient:

- **Public–private partnerships** and completely private solutions are one set of solutions. For many developing countries this is the only solution, since public finances are inadequate for the task. Thus, in the future, a greater private involvement in the provision of transport infrastructure is to be expected. Several models are already well tested: BOT (Build–Operate–Transfer), where the private sector builds and operates a facility or system for a period of time, but then transfers it back to the government after an agreed period; BLT (Build–Lease–Transfer), where, after building the facilities, it is leased for a fixed period for operation, and finally transferred back; ROT (Rehabilitate–Operate–Transfer), where the private party refurbishes an existing facility to be operated for a term prior to being turned back to the state.
- **Pricing**. Another approach that is gaining momentum is charging for use of transport infrastructure. Several segments of the transport system are privately owned and operated, such as maritime shipping and air transportation, implying that pricing is generally set by market forces. Still, many transport infrastructures such as roads and airports are wholly or partially owned by the public sector. Pricing is becoming an important

feature of transport planning in urban areas where common use transport infrastructures are under stress. Whether it is cordon pricing, congestion pricing or tolling, drivers are being forced to pay for their use of roads and limited price elasticity has been observed so far. With growing concerns over the environment, charging for the externalities of transport modes is becoming a reality in many jurisdictions. It remains to be seen how effective these alternatives are and their effects on travel behavior.

The difficulties are not to be underestimated, however. Most transport infrastructure projects are **long term**, but are typified by the heaviest capital investment requirements being incurred over a short initial phase. Even if transport infrastructure can be built in phases, most private enterprises cannot take a long-term perspective, because they need to cover their expenses and recover their capital investments over short periods of time. With the growing unwillingness or inability of the public sector to fund and provide transport infrastructure, new forms of infrastructure provision, maintenance and operation need to be achieved. This is where the financial sector, particularly long term investment funds (such as pension funds) can be involved with a better synchronism between capital and time horizons of transport infrastructure projects.

Management of transport systems

The transportation industry is changing so significantly in form and function that the very important changes in the way it is **organized** and **managed** tend to be overlooked. Yet, it is through different management practices that the spatial manifestations of the industry are expressed. It is perhaps easiest to see the changes in management through the lens of governance, where an industry that used to be largely managed and controlled by the public sector has become increasingly controlled by the private sector. The privatization of transport companies and infrastructures has been an important feature of the last decades, and is likely to continue further into the present century. However, many issues about the role of the public sector in transportation and deregulation that have prevailed could be reversed.

The growing role of the private sector over an industry that has become global and multifunctional has necessitated a shift in management and ownership relationships that are still evolving. They include:

- The emergence of **horizontally linked global corporations** that through a series of acquisitions and mergers have bought up similar operating companies in different markets. A good example is the global port terminal operators.
- The development of **vertically integrated corporations** that have grown by merger and acquisition to control several segments of the transport chain, namely modes and terminals.
- **Intermediaries** that provide transport services on a global scale, without direct ownership of infrastructure. 3PL (third-party logistics) companies operate in many markets and are major actors in the transport chain.
- **Alliances**, informal groupings of transport providers that pool resources and offer joint services between major global markets as the partners combine their respective regional networks.

At the same time transport is being increasingly **integrated in global production systems**, it is becoming an integral part of production and distribution chains. These management and business structures give rise to distinct patterns of spatial organization, with different operating practices. The operational interests of a vertically integrated enterprise are different than one that is horizontally linked. This highlights the need to understand the nature of the organization of the businesses involved in transport as a means of explaining existing patterns and predicting their future forms. The concentration of traffic (and resultant congestion) is as much explained by the organization of transport firms as it is by traditional explanations involving demand and capacity. In turn, the organization of the global firms themselves is shaped by conditions of local markets. A distinct geography of transport firms exists, a geography that is still ill understood.

Another change in the management of transport systems concerns information technologies and **vehicle automation**, which open new venues in operations and the management of vehicle assets. Although self-driving vehicles are still in the design phase, their potential implementation may lead to a much higher level of use of existing vehicle assets. The same number of vehicles could carry more people or freight while putting less pressures on existing roads, highways, terminal or rail lines. Congestion, which has been a recurring challenge for transportation, could be more effectively mitigated.

Transportation and society

The role of transportation in society has been increasingly acknowledged, a role that goes beyond its economic contribution. Concerns over **energy efficiency**, **safety** and **security** are becoming more salient. While energy prices have been subject to significant volatility in recent years, the long-term trend is indicative of higher energy prices with adjustments in transport modes to be expected. While technologies may make alternative fuel vehicles a commercial option to the internal combustion engine, the main question is the effect of higher prices on automobiles and trucks. Energy, particularly the availability of oil, has been a salient factor in the development of transport systems. It is expected that an ongoing shift in the energy price structure, as well as the commercial availability of alternate energy sources, will encourage a transition to more energy-efficient modes such as rail or maritime shipping. It remains to be seen which forms of transport and mobility will take shape as the energy transition away from fossil fuels takes place.

Transportation safety issues are somewhat paradoxical. On one hand transportation modes and terminals are incrementally becoming safer as accident rates are declining. This is particularly the case for air transportation, which safety performance has steadily improved in spite of a substantial growth of passengers being carried. Similar trends are observed for road transportation, particularly in developed countries, as fatality rates have declined. However, road transport safety remains a salient issue in developing countries where vehicle ridership is increasing and where enforcement of safety regulation is lacking. Therefore, an enduring issue, in light of growing mobility levels, is to ensure that transportation safety continues to improve through better modal and infrastructure design, operational practices and the enforcement of existing regulations.

Another prevalent matter concerns security practices that are now part of the business environment in which passenger and freight transport systems are evolving. Most of these measures are imposed by regulatory agencies and their consequences are often difficult to assess, but always involve additional costs and delays for transport operators. A balance between security measures and the efficient flow of passengers and freight will need to be achieved through a variety of regulatory, operational and technological innovations. The years since 11 September 2001 have clearly underlined that security issues in transportation have played a more prevalent role.

New patterns of consumption, social interactions and usage of transportation are also emerging. The rapid growth of e-commerce, including in developing economies such as China, has transformed retailing and the use of commercial space. With growing home deliveries, a switch is taking place from retail space to warehousing space, involving different location patterns and forms of distribution. Vehicle sharing services, including bicycle pools, are changing how people are using transportation in a manner that breaks the conventional dichotomy between full vehicle ownership or the reliance on public transit.

Sustainability challenges

The issue of sustainability has become an increasing important consideration for the transport industry. It is now broadly recognized that there needs to be a balance between economic efficiency, social factors and the environment. Of these three, the issue of economic efficiency has always been to the forefront, and governments have been important in regulating social conditions (safety, security and working conditions). Despite the strong historic relationships between transport and the environment, the latter has tended to be overlooked by the industry. This is changing, and environmental issues are likely to play an ever more **important role in the transport industry**, particularly over four core dimensions:

- **Transport and climate change**. Transportation both influences and is impacted by climate change. Transport activities, particularly vehicles, account for 24 percent of CO_2 emissions worldwide. They are thus subject to regulatory pressures to improve their environmental performance with regard to the greenhouse gases they emit. Concomitantly, transportation activities can be negatively impacted by climate change. Severe weather occurrences have a disruptive effect on transport systems, particularly for air transportation, which has become a crucial element of global and regional mobility. Potential impacts on infrastructure need to be assessed, since infrastructures are built with an expected life cycle and climate change may reduce it or increase maintenance costs. The prospects of sea level rises are particularly problematic for coastal transport systems. The extent to which climate change is influenced by and will impact global transport systems, modes and terminals needs to be seriously considered.
- **Transport and atmospheric pollution**. Air quality standards are being implemented with increasing rigor in more and more countries around the world. There are still striking differences between regions and between the modes. For example, most of the countries of the developing world still have to go a long way to fixing and enforcing standards. However, the trend is towards greater control over emissions, which will have effects on modes and their respective competitiveness, particularly if a mode is subject to a greater degree of legislation than another.
- **Transport and water quality**. The contribution of transport to the pollution of rivers and oceans is considerable, and is only recently being addressed by international legislation. Considerable progress has been made in a number of areas, such as ballast water, waste and oil spills. As legislation increases in its comprehensiveness, the more the transport industry is impacted. This is particularly evident in matters

relating to dredging, where environmental constraints are placing a growing financial burden on ports that seek to deepen channels in order to keep pace with the growth of vessel size. It can be expected that these constraints may impact port competitiveness, particularly in light of the pressures to dredge to keep up with the growth in vessel size.

- **Transport and land take**. Increased demand for transport is already placing enormous pressures on the need for new infrastructures. Many of these transport facilities, such as airports and ports, require very large amounts of land for their own internal operations and for the external transport links that have to be provided. Rapid motorization in developing countries has resulted in the conversion of land to provide road infrastructure. This expanded scale of transport infrastructure questions the capacity of environmental systems to mitigate the disruptions and will likely have an impact on how transport infrastructure is designed.

Prospects for transport geography

Transport geography played a relatively small role in the field of transport studies, a field that has been dominated by engineers and economists. This was due in part to the needs of the industry being focused on providing infrastructures and technologies, at what cost and benefits and at what level of pricing. The contemporary industry is much more complex, with issues as varied as safety, aesthetics, working conditions, equity, the environment and governance being necessary considerations. A much broader set of skills are required, therefore, and **transport studies have become a multidisciplinary field of application**. Transport geography thus has opportunities to contribute to transport studies, transport planning and transport operations, in part because of the breadth of the approach and training. Still, transport geography, like the field of transportation in general, does not receive a level of attention in academia proportional to its economic and social importance.

It is also a fundamental fact that transport is a **spatial activity**. It has always been a space-adjusting service, but over the last few decades it has become increasingly global in scope. Contemporary transport operates at a wider range of scales than ever before. There are complex interactions between the local and the global. For example, the issues surrounding the expansion of an airport are usually decided at the local level, and the impacts are likely to be felt locally, namely its externalities such as noise and congestion. However, the effects on passenger and freight flows may have a global impact. The spatiality of transport and the many scale levels at which it operates are elements of particular concern to transport geography. No other discipline has as its core interest the role of space in shaping human activities. The globalization of transport activities thus has represented unique opportunities in the development of transport geography.

One reason for the success of engineers and economists in transport studies and applications is that their training has been rigorous in the application of mathematics and multivariate statistics. They have demonstrated the ability to provide precise answers to the questions that decision makers have required – what to build, at what cost, with what cost effects. There has evolved a culture in the transport industry that, unless it can be quantified, is of little value. Transport geography provides the **quantitative skills** in modeling, graph theory and multivariate statistics. However, there are newer techniques that provide geographers with opportunities to contribute to transport studies. GIS-T in particular should be an essential element in transport geography training. The multiscalar, multivariate nature of the transport industry makes GIS-T an invaluable tool, and one that will raise the profile of transport geography in the transportation industry.

One of the key challenges in transport studies is **data availability**. Many times census and survey data are inadequate or unavailable in the form required. However, online availability of large datasets increasingly offer a richer array of information to analyze transport issues. New opportunities also arise from what came to be known as "big data," where a large amount of digital information is made available at a low cost through mobile devices, sensors, remote sensing and RFID (radio-frequency indentification devices). Mobility can now be observed at an unprecedented scale and level of detail, where people, vehicles and cargo can be tracked. Knowledge of survey techniques and their limitations are also an important part of the transport geography toolkit. In spite of the appeal of ICT, many of the traditional tools and approaches are still relevant. They address problems that are frequently overlooked by other disciplines because of the lack of data or the inability to spatially represent these data. Questionnaires and interviews represent a vital source of information in many situations. Content analysis is extremely useful in providing quantified data from non-quantified sources. At the same time, fieldwork provides the opportunity to obtain detailed understanding of the particularities of the local conditions that cannot be obtained otherwise. Data methods and models are no palliative to common sense, which remains a constant challenge when the approach is more focused on the tools than the reality in which transportation is evolving.

A look back at the subject matter and topics covered in this book indicates an industry that is growing in significance and changing in the face of challenges and drivers of change. The issues that are achieving greater importance – sustainability, congestion, governance and management – are ones to which transport geography has the **opportunity to contribute**. As the transport industry becomes more complex, conventional approaches, focusing on a narrow range of factors, have to be replaced by more **nuanced analysis and solutions**. Further, issues related to the mobility of freight are assuming a greater importance within the discipline, in part driven by the setting of global supply chains and the complexities of urban freight distribution. In the transport industry itself, in public planning, and in research institutions, the scope for transport geography remains diverse.

Glossary

Many of the glossary terms are adapted from the Bureau of Transportation Statistics, the European Conference of Ministers of Transport, the Economic Commission for Europe, the Intermodal Association of North America and the Mineta Transportation Institute.

Absolute advantage

A trade theory underlining the ability of an actor (an individual, or firm, or country) to produce a greater quantity of a good, product, or service than competitors, using the same number of resources.

Access

The capacity to enter and exit a transport system. It is an absolute term implying that a location has access or does not.

Accessibility

The measure of the capacity of a location to be reached by, or to reach, different locations. The capacity and the structure of transport infrastructure are key elements in the determination of accessibility.

Aframax

A tanker of standard size between 75,000 and 115,000 dwt usually carrying half a million barrels of oil. The largest tanker size in the AFRA (Average Freight Rate Assessment) tanker rate system.

Agglomeration economies

See *economies of agglomeration*.

Air cargo

Total volume of freight, mail and express traffic transported by air. Includes the following: freight and express commodities of all kinds. Includes small package counter services, express services and priority reserved freight.

Air carrier

Commercial system of air transportation, consisting of domestic and international scheduled and charter service.

Air transportation

Includes companies that provide domestic and international passenger and freight services, and companies that operate airports and provide terminal facilities.

Airport

(1) An area of land or water that is used or intended to be used for the landing and take-off of aircraft, and includes its buildings and facilities (if any); (2) A facility

used primarily by conventional, fixed-wing aircraft; (3) A facility, either on land or water, where aircraft can take off and land. Usually consists of hard-surfaced landing strips, a control tower, hangars and accommodations for passengers and cargo; (4) A landing area regularly used by aircraft for receiving discharging passengers or cargo.

Airspace

The segment of the atmosphere that is under the jurisdiction of a nation or under an international agreement for its use. They include two major components, one being land-based (take-offs and landings) and the other air-based, mainly composed of air corridors. These corridors can cover altitudes up to 22,500 m. Most commercial air transport services are limited to the use of predetermined corridors.

Alternative fuels

Low-polluting fuels which are used to propel a vehicle instead of high-sulfur diesel or gasoline. Examples include methanol, ethanol, propane or compressed natural gas, liquid natural gas, low-sulfur or "clean" diesel and electricity.

Arterial street

A major thoroughfare, used primarily for through-traffic rather than for access to adjacent land, that is characterized by high vehicular capacity and continuity of movement.

Association of Southeast Asian Nations (ASEAN)

Free trade area established on 8 August 1967 in Bangkok, Thailand, with the signing of the Bangkok Declaration. The members of ASEAN are Brunei Darussalam, Indonesia, Laos, Malaysia, Myanmar, Philippines, Singapore, Thailand and Vietnam. The Secretariat of the Association is located in Jakarta, Indonesia.

Backhaul

Traffic for the return movement of a car or container towards the point where the initial load originated or to handle a shipment in the direction of the light flow of traffic.

Balance of payments

A record of receipts from and payments to the rest of the world by a country's government and its residents. The balance of payments includes the international financial transactions of a country for commodities, services and capital transactions.

Baltic Dry Index (BDI)

Assessment of the average price to ship raw materials (such as coal, iron ore, cement and grains) on a number of shipping routes and by ship size. It is an indicator of the cost paid to ship raw materials on global markets and an important component of input costs. The index is considered as a leading indicator (forward-looking) of economic activity, since it involves events taking place at the earlier stages of global commodity chains.

Barge

A non-motorized water vessel, usually flat-bottomed and towed or pushed by other craft, used for transporting freight. Predominantly used on river systems.

Barrel

A unit of volume equal to 42 US gallons (or 159 liters) at 60 degrees Fahrenheit, often used to measure volume in oil production, price, transportation and trade.

Base period

The period between the morning and evening peak periods when transit service is generally scheduled on a constant interval. Also known as "off-peak period." The time of day during which vehicle requirements and schedules are not influenced by peak-period passenger volume demands (e.g. between morning and afternoon peak periods). At this time, transit riding is fairly constant and usually low to moderate in volume when compared with peak-period travel.

Base fare

The price charged to one adult for one transit ride; excludes transfer charges, zone charges, express service charges, peak period surcharges and reduced fares.

Berth

A specific segment of wharfage where a ship ties up alongside at a pier, quay, wharf or other structure that provides a breasting surface for the vessel. Typically, this structure is a stationary extension of an improved shore and intended to facilitate the transfer of cargo or passengers.

"Big data."

Datasets that are so large or complex that traditional data processing applications are inadequate. They offer new opportunities for the analysis, capture, search, sharing, storage, transfer, visualization and querying of information related to transportation, such as the tracking of individuals, vehicles, items or loads.

Bill of lading

A document that establishes the terms of a contract between a shipper and a transportation company. It serves as a document of title, a contract of carriage and a receipt for goods.

Block

A group of rail cars destined to the same location.

Break-bulk cargo

Refers to general cargo that has been packaged in some way with the use of bags, boxes or drums. This cargo tends to have numerous origins, destinations and clients. Before containerization, economies of scale were difficult to achieve with break-bulk cargo, as the loading and unloading process was very labor- and time-consuming.

Bridge

A structure including supports erected over a depression or an obstruction, such as water, highway or railway, which has a track or passageway for carrying traffic or other moving loads. Its opening is measured along the center of the roadway of more than 20 ft between undercopings of abutments or spring lines of arches, or extreme ends of openings for multiple boxes. It may also include multiple pipes, where the clear distance between openings is less than half of the smaller contiguous opening.

British Thermal Unit (BTU)

The amount of energy required to raise the temperature of 1 pound of water 1 degree Fahrenheit (F) at or near 39.2 degrees Fahrenheit and 1 atmosphere of pressure.

Bulk cargo

Freight, both dry or liquid, that is not packaged, such as minerals (oil, coal, iron ore) and grains. It often requires the use of specialized ships such as oil tankers, as well as specialized transshipment and storage facilities. Conventionally, this cargo has a single origin, destination and client. It is also prone to economies of scale.

Bulk carriers

All vessels designed to carry bulk cargo such as grain, fertilizers, ore and oil.

Bulk terminal

A purpose-designed berth or mooring for handling liquid or dry commodities, in unpackaged bulk form, such as oil, grain, ore and coal. Bulk terminals typically are installed with specialized cargo handling equipment such as pipelines, conveyors, pneumatic evacuators, cranes with clamshell grabs and rail lines to accommodate cargo handling operations with ships or barges. Commodity-specific storage facilities such as grain silos, petroleum storage tanks and coal stock yards are also located at these terminals.

Bus (motorbus)

Any of several types of self-propelled vehicles, generally rubber-tired, intended for use on city streets, highways and busways, including but not limited to minibuses, 40- and 30-ft buses, articulated buses, double-deck buses and electrically powered trolleybuses. They are used by public entities to provide designated public transportation service and by private entities to provide transportation service including, but not limited to, specified public transportation services. Self-propelled, rubber-tired vehicles designed to look like antique or vintage trolleys are considered buses.

Bus, trolley

An electric, rubber-tired transit vehicle, manually steered, propelled by a motor, which draws current through overhead wires from a central power source not onboard the vehicle. Also known as "trolley coach" or "trackless trolley."

Cabotage

Transport between two terminals (a terminal of loading and a terminal of unloading) located in the same country irrespective of the country in which the mode providing the service is registered. Cabotage is often subject to restrictions and regulations. Under such circumstances, each nation reserves for its national carriers the right to move domestic freight or passenger traffic.

Canal

An artificial open waterway constructed to transport water, to irrigate or drain land, to connect two or more bodies of water, or to serve as a waterway for watercraft.

"Capesize."

Refers to a rather ill-defined standard which has the common characteristic of being incapable of using the Panama or Suez canals, not necessarily because of their tonnage but because of their size. These ships serve deep-water terminals handling raw materials, such as iron ore and coal. As a result, "Capesize" vessels transit via Cape Horn (South America) or the Cape of Good Hope (South Africa). Their size ranges between 80,000 and 175,000 dwt.

Carbon dioxide (CO_2)

A colorless, odorless, non-poisonous gas that is a normal part of the ambient air. Carbon dioxide is a product of fossil fuel combustion.

Carbon monoxide (CO)

A colorless, odorless, highly toxic gas that is a normal by-product of incomplete fossil fuel combustion. Carbon monoxide, one of the major air pollutants, can be harmful in small amounts if breathed over a certain period of time.

Carpool (or car sharing)

An arrangement where two or more people share the use and cost of privately owned automobiles in traveling to and from prearranged destinations together.

Carrier

The company moving passengers or freight.

Catchment area

Area or region whose economic, political, cultural, social, etc. influence is felt over a larger area, it is the radius of action of a given point. In transportation, it consists in the area under influence of a focal point towards which centripetal fluxes converge – an interception zone of several carriers. Also called "area of influence" or "hinterland."

Centrality

Focus on the terminal as a point of origin and destination of traffic. Thus, centrality is linked with the generation and attraction of movements, which are related to the nature and the level of economic activities within the vicinity of the concerned terminal. The function of centrality also involves a significant number of intermodal activities.

Charter

Originally meant a flight where a shipper contracted hire of an aircraft from an air carrier, but has usually come to mean any non-scheduled commercial service.

City logistics

The means over which freight distribution can take place in urban areas as well as the strategies that can improve its overall efficiency, such as mitigating congestion and environmental externalities.

Clean Air Act (CAA)

Federal legislation that sets national air quality standards.

Coach service

Transport service established for the carriage of passengers at special reduced passenger fares that are predicated on both the operation of specifically designed aircraft space and a reduction in the quality of service regularly and ordinarily provided.

Coal

A black or brownish-black solid, combustible substance formed by the partial decomposition of vegetable matter without access to air. The rank of coal, which includes anthracite, bituminous coal, subbituminous coal, and lignite, is based on fixed carbon, volatile matter and heating value. Coal rank indicates the progressive alteration, or coalification, from lignite to anthracite. Lignite contains approximately 9 to 17 million British Thermal Units (BTU) per ton. The heat contents of sub-bituminous and bituminous coal range from 16 to 24 million BTU per ton, and from 19 to 30 million BTU per ton, respectively. Anthracite contains approximately 22–28 million BTU per ton.

Cold chain

A temperature-controlled supply chain linked to the material, equipment and procedures used to maintain specific shipments within the appropriate temperature range. Often relates to the distribution of food and pharmaceutical products.

Commercial geography

Investigates the spatial characteristics of trade and transactions in terms of their cause, nature, origin and destination. It leans on the analysis of contracts and transactions.

Commodity

Resources that can be consumed and having no qualitative differentiation. They can be accumulated for a period of time (some are perishable, while others can be virtually stored for centuries), exchanged as part of transactions or purchased on specific markets (such as futures market). Some commodities are fixed, implying that they cannot be transferred, except for the title. This includes land, mining, logging and fishing rights. In this context, the value of a fixed commodity is derived from the utility and the potential rate of extraction. Bulk commodities are commodities that can be transferred, which includes for instance grains, metals, livestock, oil, cotton, coffee, sugar and cocoa. Their value is derived from utility, supply and demand (market price).

Comparative advantages

The relative efficiencies with which countries (or any economic unit) can produce a product or service.

Compressed Natural Gas (CNG)

Natural gas which is comprised primarily of methane, compressed to a pressure at or above 2,400 lb per square inch and stored in special high-pressure containers. It is used as a fuel for natural gas-powered vehicles, mainly by buses.

Commuter

A person who travels regularly between home and work or school.

Commuter bus service

Fixed-route bus service, characterized by service predominantly in one direction during peak periods, limited stops, use of multi-ride tickets and routes of extended length, usually between the central business district and outlying suburbs. Commuter bus service may also include other services, characterized by a limited route structure, limited stops and a coordinated relationship to another mode of transportation.

Commuter rail

Railroad local and regional passenger train operations between a central city, its suburbs and/or another central city. It may be either locomotive-hauled or self-propelled, and is characterized by multi-trip tickets, specific station-to-station fares, railroad employment practices, and usually only one or two stations in the central business district. Also known as "suburban rail."

Conference (liner).

An association of shipowners operating in the same trade route who operate under collective conditions such as tariff rates and shared capacity. They provide international liner services for the carriage of cargo on a particular route (or routes) within specified geographical limits and which has an agreement or arrangement within the framework of which they operate under uniform or common freight rates and any other agreed conditions with respect to the provision of liner services.

Congestion

Occurs when transport demand exceeds transport supply in a specific section of the transport system. Under such circumstances, each vehicle impairs the mobility of others. Urban congestion mainly concerns two domains of circulation, private and public, often sharing the same infrastructures.

Consignee

A person or company to whom commodities are shipped. Officially, the legal owner of the cargo.

Constant dollars

Figures where the effect of change in the purchasing power of the dollar has been removed. Usually the data are expressed in terms of dollars of a selected year or the average of a set of years.

Container

A large standard-size metal box into which cargo is packed for shipment aboard specially configured ocean-going container ships and designed to be moved with common handling equipment enabling high-speed intermodal transfers in economically large units between ships, rail cars, truck chassis, and barges using a minimum of labor. The container, therefore, serves as the transfer unit rather than the cargo contained therein.

Container On Flat Car (COFC)

The movement of a container on a railroad flat car. This movement is made without the container being mounted on a chassis.

Container ship

A cargo vessel designed and constructed to transport, within specifically designed cells, portable tanks and freight containers which are lifted on and off with their contents intact. There are two types of container ships: full and partial. Full container ships are equipped with permanent container cells with little or no space for other types of cargo. Partial container ships are considered multipurpose container vessels, where one or more but not all compartments are fitted with permanent container cells, and the remaining compartments are used for other types of cargo. This category also includes container/car carriers, container/rail car carriers and container/roll-on/roll-off (RORO) vessels.

Container terminal

A set of facilities supporting the handling (loading and unloading) of containers. The intermodal relation defines the nature of the container terminal, such as a container port, an intermodal terminal (rail) or a barge terminal.

Containerization

Refers to the increasing and generalized use of the container as a support for freight transportation. It involves a process whereby the intermodal container is increasingly used because it substitutes cargo from other conveyances, and is adopted as a mode supporting freight distribution and its spatial diffusion in terms of the transport systems able to handle containers.

Corridor

A linear orientation of transport routes and flows connecting important locations that act as origins, destinations or points of transshipment. Corridors are multiscalar entities depending on what types of flows is being investigated. Thus, they can be composed of streets, highways, transit routes, rail lines, maritime lines or air paths.

Costs (transport)

Monetary measure of what the transport provider must pay to produce transportation services and comes as fixed (infrastructure) and variable (operating). They depend on a variety of conditions related to geography, infrastructure, administrative barriers, energy, and on how passengers and freight are carried. Three major components, related to transactions, shipments and the friction of distance, impact on transport costs.

Costs–Insurance–Freight (CIF)

Price of a good is a uniform delivered price for all customers everywhere, with no spatially variable shipping price, which implies that the average shipping price is built into the price of a good. The CIF cost structure can be expanded to include several rate zones.

Crossborder transportation

The activities, infrastructures and flows that ensure the passage of passengers and freight across an international border. Cross-border transportation can be facilitated, monitored, controlled and even prevented.

Cross-docking

A form of inventory management where goods are received at one door of the distribution center/sorting facility and shipped out through the other door in a very short amount of time without putting them in storage. It consequently contributes in the reduction of operating costs with an increase in the throughput and with a reduction of inventory levels.

Current dollars

The dollar value of a good or service in terms of prices current at the time the good or service is sold. This contrasts with the value of the good or service measured in constant dollars.

Cycle time

The amount of time required from the receipt of an order to when this order is completed (assembled) and ready for delivery. Often labeled as the completion rate, it is mostly linked with the function of production in the manufacturing sector – its level of responsiveness.

Deadweight tons (dwt)

The lifting capacity of a ship, including cargo, fuel, ballast and crew. Reflects the weight difference between a fully loaded and an unloaded ship.

Demand (transport)

The expression of the transport needs, even if those needs are satisfied, fully, partially or not at all. Similar to transport supply, it is expressed in terms of number of people, volume or tons per unit of time and space.

Demand responsive

Non-fixed-route service utilizing vans or buses with passengers boarding and alighting at prearranged times at any location within the system's service area. Also called "Dial-a-Ride."

Deregulation

Consists in a shift to a competitive economic climate by reorienting and/or suppressing regulatory mechanisms. Deregulation, however, does not necessarily refer to complete absence of free market regulation measures but rather to the promotion of competition-inducing ones (which can seek elimination of monopolies, for example). Particularly observed in the transport and telecommunications sectors.

Design capacity

A theoretical capacity of a transport infrastructure such as a road or terminal based on specific operating conditions.

Distribution center (freight)

Facility or a group of facilities that perform consolidation, warehousing, packaging, decomposition and other functions linked with handling freight. Their main purpose is to provide value-added services to freight and are a fundamental component of freight distribution. DCs are often in proximity to major transport routes or terminals. They can also perform light manufacturing activities such as assembly and labeling.

Dock

A feature built to handle ships. Can also refer to an enclosed port area used for maritime operations.

Double-stack

The movement of containers on articulated rail cars which enables one container to be stacked on another for better ride quality and car utilization.

Downstream

Refers to the relative location of a given activity along a supply chain. downstream refers to the customers, whereas upstream generally refers to the suppliers.

Drayage

The movement of a container or trailer to or from the railroad intermodal terminal to or from the customer's facility for loading or unloading.

Dunnage

Packaging materials used to keep cargo in place inside a container or transportation vehicle.

Dwell time

The time a vehicle (bus, truck, train or ship) is allowed to load or unload passengers or freight at a terminal. For freight operations, it refers to the amount of time cargo stays in a terminal yard or storage area while waiting to be loaded. Dwell time can be operational, which reflects the performance of terminal infrastructures and management, including the scheduling and availability of transport services. It can also be transactional, which is usually linked with the performance of clearance procedures (such as customs). Finally, dwell time can be storage-related, implying that the owner or the carrier of the cargo deliberately leaves the cargo at the terminal as part of a transport or supply chain management strategy.

Economies of agglomeration

The benefits of having activities locate (cluster) next to another, such as the use of common infrastructures and services.

Economies of density

The benefits derived from the increasing density of features on the costs of accessing them. This could involve markets (e.g. consumption, labor) or resources (e.g. mining, agriculture).

Economies of scale

Cost reductions or productivity efficiencies achieved through size increase. The outcome is a decrease in the unit cost of production associated with increasing output.

Economies of scope

Cost savings resulting from increasing the number of different goods or services produced.

Electronic data interchange (EDI).

Communication mode for inter- and intra-firm data exchange in the freight forwarding and logistics business.

Energy

The capacity for doing work as measured by the capability of doing work (potential energy) or the conversion of this capability to motion (kinetic energy). Energy has several forms, some of which are easily convertible and can be changed to another form useful for work. Electrical energy is usually measured in kilowatt hours, while heat energy is usually measured in British Thermal Units (BTU).

Environmental impact assessment

A process for carrying out an appraisal of the full potential effects of a development project on the physical environment.

Ethanol

An alternative fuel – a liquid alcohol fuel with vapor heavier than air, and produced from agricultural products such as corn, grain and sugarcane.

European Union (EU)

Formerly the European Community (EC), became the European Union since the signing of the Maastricht Treaty in November 1993. A regional trade block composed of 28 European states (as of 2016). Its core institutions are known as the "institutional triangle," comprising the European Parliament (Strasbourg), the Commission (Brussels) and the EU Council (Brussels). The European Bank manages the common currency (euro), used by several EU countries.

Exclusive right-of-way

A highway or other facility that can only be used by buses or other transit vehicles.

Externality (external cost)

Economic cost not normally taken into account in markets or in decisions by market players.

Fare

The price paid by the user of a transport service at the moment of use.

Fare structure

The system set up to determine how much is to be paid by various passengers using a transit system at any given time.

Feeder

Short sea shipping service which connects at least two ports in order for the freight (generally containers) to be consolidated or redistributed to or from a deep-sea service in one of these ports. By extension, this concept may be used for inland transport services and air transportation.

Ferry

A boat providing fixed-route service across a body of water, which can be short or long distance.

Fixed cost

Costs that do not vary with the quantity shipped in the short run, i.e. costs that must be paid upfront to begin producing transportation services.

Fixed route

Service provided on a repetitive, fixed-schedule basis along a specific route with vehicles stopping to pick up and deliver passengers or freight to specific locations; each fixed-route trip serves the same origins and destinations, unlike demand responsive. The terms apply to many modes of transportation, including public transit, air services and maritime services.

Flag of convenience

A means by which shipowners can obtain lower registration fees, lower operating costs and fewer restrictions by registering their ships to a third country.

Flat car

A freight car having a floor without any housing or body above. Frequently used to carry containers and/or trailers or oversized/odd-shaped commodities. The three types of flat cars used in intermodal are conventional, spine and stack cars.

Fleet

The vehicles in a transport system. Usually, "fleet" refers to highway vehicles, rail vehicles as well as ships.

Foreland

A maritime space with which a port performs commercial relationships. It includes overseas customers with which the port undertakes commercial exchanges. Forwarding agent/Freight forwarder. Intermediary who arranges for the carriage of goods and/or associated services on behalf of a shipper.

Fourth-party logistics provider (4PL)

Integrates the resources of producers, retailers and third-party logistics providers with a view to build a system-wide improvement in supply chain management. They are non-asset-based, meaning that they mainly provide organizational expertise.

Free trade zone

A port or an area designated for duty-free entry of any non-prohibited goods. Merchandise may be stored, displayed, transformed, used for manufacturing, discarded, etc., within the zone and re-exported without duties. The area is thus a form of extraterritoriality since it is outside the customs regime of a country.

Freight forwarder

An individual or company that accepts less-than-truckload (TLT) or less-than-carload (LCL) shipments from shippers and combines them into carload or truckload lots. Carriers collecting small shipments to be cumulatively consolidated and transported relying upon a single or several modes of transportation to a given destination. Functions performed by a freight forwarder may include receiving small shipments (e.g. less than a containerload) from consigners, consolidating them into larger lots, contracts with carriers for transport between ports of embarkation and debarkation, conducts documentation transactions and arranges delivery of shipments to the consignees.

Freight village

A concentration (or a cluster) of freight-related activities within a specific area, commonly built for such a purpose, masterplanned and managed. These activities include distribution centers, warehouses and storage areas, transport terminals, offices and other facilities supporting those activities, such as public utilities, parking space and even hotels and restaurants. Although a freight village can be serviced by a single mode, intermodal facilities can offer direct access to global and regional markets.

Fuel cell

A device that produces electrical energy directly from the controlled electrochemical oxidation of the fuel, commonly hydrogen. It does not contain an intermediate heat cycle, as do most other electrical generation techniques.

Gasohol

A blend of motor gasoline (leaded or unleaded) and alcohol (generally ethanol but sometimes methanol) limited to 10 percent by volume of alcohol. Gasohol is included in finished leaded and unleaded motor gasoline.

Gasoline

A complex mixture of relatively volatile hydrocarbons, with or without small quantities of additives, obtained by blending appropriate refinery streams to form a fuel suitable for use in spark ignition engines. Motor gasoline includes both leaded or unleaded grades of finished motor gasoline, blending components and gasohol.

Gateway

A location offering accessibility to a large system of circulation of freight, passengers and/or information. Gateways reap the advantage of a favorable physical location such as highway junctions, confluence of rivers, seaboards, and have been the object of a significant accumulation of transport infrastructures such as terminals and their links. A gateway generally commands the entrance to and the exit from its catchment area. In other words, it is a pivotal point for the entrance and the exit of merchandise in a region, a country, or a continent. Gateways tend to be locations where intermodal transfers are performed.

General cargo

General cargo consists of those products or commodities such as timber, structural steel, rolled newsprint, concrete forms, agricultural equipment that are not conducive to packaging or unitization. Break-bulk cargo (e.g. packaged products such as lubricants and cereal) are often regarded as a subdivision of general cargo.

Geographic information system (GIS)

A special-purpose system composed of hardware and software in which a common spatial coordinate system is the primary means of reference. GIS contains subsystems for: data input; data storage, retrieval, and representation; data management, transformation, and analysis; and data reporting and product generation.

GIS-T

Acronym for "Geographic Information System for Transportation."

Graph theory

A branch of mathematics concerned with how networks can be encoded and their properties measured.

Great circle distance

The shortest path between two points on a sphere. The circumference inferred out of these two points divides the earth in two equal parts, thus the great circle. The great circle distance is useful to establish the shortest path to use when traveling at the intercontinental air and maritime level. The great circle route follows the sphericity of the globe; any shortest route is the one following the curve of the planet, along the parallels.

Green logistics

Supply chain management practices and strategies that reduce the environmental and energy footprint of freight distribution. They focus on material handling, waste management, packaging and transport.

Gross Domestic Product (GDP)

A measure of the total value of goods and services produced by a domestic economy during a given period, usually one year. Obtained by adding the value contributed by each sector of the economy in the form of profits, compensation to employees and depreciation (consumption of capital). Only domestic production is included, not income arising from investments and possessions owned abroad, hence the use of the word "domestic."

Haulage, carrier/merchant

Carrier haulage is an inland container movement (to or from a port terminal) done by the ocean shipping company, often through a parent company. The carrier is liable if the merchandise is lost or damaged during transport, or if there is a delay. Merchant haulage is when the importer or the exporter assumes the transport of the container to or from a port terminal. The merchant is liable if the cargo is lost or damaged. One of the main advantages of merchant haulage is that it gives importers and exporters more flexibility in the timing of inland distribution, However, the merchant must pick and bring back the container at a predesigned location and time.

Heavy rail

An electric railway of high capacity and characterized by exclusive rights-of-way, multi-car trains, high-speed and rapid acceleration, sophisticated signaling and high platform loading.

Hinterland

Land space over which a transport terminal, such as a port, sells its services and interacts with its clients. It accounts for the regional market share that a terminal has relative to a set of other terminals servicing this region. It regroups all the customers directly bounded to the terminal. The terminal, depending on its nature, serves as a place of convergence for the traffic coming by roads, railways or by sea/fluvial feeders.

Hub

Central point for the collection, sorting, transshipment and distribution of goods and passengers for a particular area. This concept comes from a term used in air transport for passengers as well as freight. It describes collection and distribution through a single point such as the "hub-and-spoke" concept. Hubs tend to be transmodal (transfers within the same mode) locations.

Inflation

Increase in the amount of currency in relation to the availability of assets, commodities, goods and services. Commonly the outcome of an indirect confiscation of wealth through an over-issuance of currency by central banks and governments. Although it directly influences prices, inflation is outside the supply–demand relationship and decreases the purchasing power, if wages are not increased accordingly. Almost all Central Banks have inflationary policies which enable governments to run deficits for decades by slowly devaluating the debt they contracted in the past.

Infrastructure

Capital goods that are not directly consumed and serve as support to the functions of a society (individuals and corporations). 1) In transport systems, all the fixed components, such as rights-of-way, tracks, signal equipment, terminals, parking lots, but stops, maintenance facilities, etc. 2) In transportation planning, all the relevant elements of the environment in which a transportation system operates.

Inland port

A rail or a barge terminal that is linked to a maritime terminal with regular inland transport services. An inland port has a level of integration with the maritime terminal and supports a more efficient access to the inland market both for inbound and outbound traffic. This implies an array of related logistical activities linked with the terminal, such as distribution centers, depots for containers and chassis, warehouses and logistical service providers.

Intermediacy

Focus on the terminal as an intermediate point in the flows of passengers or freight. This term is applied to the frequent occurrence of places gaining advantage because they are between other places. The ability to exploit transshipment has been an important feature of many terminals.

Intermodal terminal

A terminal which can accommodate several modes of transportation. They increasingly tend to specialize in handling specific types of passengers or freight traffic, while they may share the same infrastructures.

Intermodal transport

The movements of passengers or freight from one mode of transport to another, commonly taking place at a terminal specifically designed for such a purpose.

Intermodalism

A system of transport whereby two or more modes of transport are used to transport the same loading unit or truck in an integrated manner, without loading or unloading, in a transport chain. Typically used in three contexts: (1) most narrowly, it refers to containerization, piggyback service, or other technologies that provide the seamless movement of goods and people by more than one mode of transport; (2) more broadly, intermodalism refers to the provision of connections between different modes, such as adequate highways to ports or bus feeder services to rail transit; and (3) in its broadest interpretation, intermodalism refers to a holistic view of transportation in which individual modes work together or within their own niches to provide the user with the best choices of service, and in which the consequences on all modes of policies for a single mode are considered. This view has been called balanced, integrated or comprehensive transportation in the past.

International Air Transportation Association (IATA)

Established in 1945, a trade association serving airlines, passengers, shippers, travel agents and governments. The Association promotes safety, standardization in forms (baggage checks, tickets, weight bills) and aids in establishing international airfares. IATA's headquarters are in Geneva, Switzerland.

International Civil Aviation Organization (ICAO)

A specialized agency of the United Nations whose objective is to develop the principles and techniques of international air navigation and to foster planning and development of international civil air transport. ICAO regions include: (AFI) African Indian Ocean Region, (CAR) Caribbean Region, (EUR) European Region, (MID/ASIA) Middle

East/Asia Region, (NAM) North American Region, (NAT) North Atlantic Region, (PAC) Pacific Region and (SAM) South American Region.

International Commercial Terms (Incoterms.)
Predefined commercial contract terms which stipulate exactly which party owns cargo over the course of a shipment, as well as who bears responsibility for transporting the cargo.

International Maritime Organization (IMO)
Established as a specialized agency of the United Nations in 1948, the IMO facilitates cooperation on technical matters affecting merchant shipping and traffic, including improved maritime safety and prevention of marine pollution. Its headquarters are in London, England.

International Organization for Standardization (ISO)
Worldwide federation of national standards bodies, the ISO is a non-governmental organization established in 1947. The mission of ISO is to promote the development of standardization and related activities in the world with a view to facilitating the international exchange of goods and services and to developing cooperation in the spheres of intellectual, scientific, technological and economic activity. ISO's work results in international agreements which are published as International Standards.

International trade
An exchange of goods or services across national jurisdictions. Inbound trade is defined as imports and outbound trade is defined as exports. Subject to the regulatory oversight and taxation of the involved nations, namely through customs.

Jet stream
A migrating stream of high-speed winds present at high altitudes.

Jitney
Privately owned, small or medium-sized vehicle usually operated on a fixed route but not on a fixed schedule.

Just-in-time
The principle of production and inventory management in which goods arrive when needed for production or consumption. Warehousing tends to be minimal or nonexistent, but in all cases much more efficient and more limited in duration.

Knot, nautical
The unit of speed equivalent to one nautical mile: 6,080.2 ft per hour or 1.85 km per hour.

Lading
Refers to the freight shipped; the contents of a shipment.

Landbridge
An intermodal connection between two ocean carriers separated by a landmass, linked together in a seamless transaction by a land carrier.

Lead time
The time it takes for an order to be fulfilled, which includes preparation, packing and delivery to a designed location. Often labeled as the arrival rate and is mostly linked with the function of distribution, mainly its efficiency and reliability; its level of responsiveness.

Less than Truckload (LTL)

A shipment that would not by itself fill the truck to capacity by weight or volume.

Letter of credit

A document issued by a financial institution that provides a promise of payment for a trade transaction, implying that it can be redeemed if certain conditions are satisfied. They are mainly used in international trade for transactions between actors, such as a buyer and a seller, in different countries.

Level of service

(1) A set of characteristics that indicate the quality and quantity of transportation service provided, including characteristics that are quantifiable and those that are difficult to quantify; (2) for highway systems, a qualitative rating of the effectiveness of a highway or highway facility in serving traffic, in terms of operating conditions, the rating of traffic flow ranging from A (excellent) through F (heavily congested), and comparing actual or projected traffic volume with the maximum capacity of the intersection or road in question; (3) for paratransit, a variety of measures meant to denote the quality of service provided, generally in terms of total travel time or a specific component of total travel time; (4) for pedestrians, sets of area occupancy classifications to connect the design of pedestrian facilities with levels of service.

Light-rail transit (LRT)

Fixed guideway transportation mode that typically operates on city streets and draws its electric power from overhead wires; includes streetcars, trolley cars and tramways. Differs from heavy rail – which has a separated right of way, and includes commuter and intercity rail – in that it has lighter passenger capacity per hour and more closely spaced stops.

Lighter-aboard-ship (LASH)

A type of barge-carrying vessel equipped with an overhead crane capable of lifting barges of a common size and stowing them into cellular slots in athwartship position. LASH is an all-water technology analogous to containerization.

Liner

Derived from the term "line traffic," which denotes operation along definite routes on the basis of definite, fixed schedules. A liner thus is a vessel that engages in this kind of transportation, which usually involves the haulage of general cargo as distinct from bulk cargo.

Liquefied natural gas (LNG)

An alternative fuel – a natural gas cooled to below its boiling point of –260 degrees Fahrenheit so that it becomes a liquid. It is stored in a vacuum type container at very low temperatures and under moderate pressure. LNG vapor is lighter than air.

Load factor

The ratio of passengers or freight actually carried versus the total passenger or freight capacity of a vehicle or a route.

Location-allocation models

A family of models used to optimize the location of a series of facilities such as manufacturing facilities, distribution centers or any other market-servicing activities. The goal is to optimally service a set of locations expressing demand, often with the purpose of minimizing transport costs.

Logistics

A wide set of activities dedicated to the transformation and distribution of goods, from raw material sourcing to final market distribution as well as the related information flows. Derived from Greek *logistikos* (responsible for counting), the word is polysemic. In the nineteenth century the military referred to it as the art of combining all means of transport, revictualling and sheltering of troops. In a contemporary setting, it refers to the set of operations required for goods to be made available on markets or to specific locations.

Logistic zone

Grouping of activities dealing with freight distribution such as distribution centers (warehousing, storage, light transformations), transportation (freight forwarders, shippers, transport operators, customs brokers) and supporting services (human resources, maintenance and repair) within a defined and often planned area.

Long ton

2,240 pounds (100 kg).

Lowry model

One of the first transportation/land use models to be designed, in 1964. The core assumption is that regional and urban growth (or decline) is a function of the expansion (or contraction) of the basic sector. This employment in turn has impacts on the employment of the retail and residential sectors.

Maglev

Short for "magnetic levitation." Technology enabling trains to move at high speed above a guideway on a cushion generated by magnetic force.

Manifest

A list of the goods being transported by a carrier.

Maritime route

Corridor a few kilometers in width that tries to avoid the discontinuities of land transport by linking ports, the main elements of the maritime/land interface. Maritime routes are a function of obligatory points of passage, which are strategic places, of physical constraints (coasts, winds, marine currents, depth, reefs, ice) and of political borders. As a result, maritime routes draw arcs on the earth water surface as intercontinental maritime transportation tries to follow the great circle distance.

Maritime terminal

A designated area of a port, which includes, but is not limited to, wharves, warehouses, covered and open storage spaces, cold-storage plants, grain elevators and bulk cargo loading and unloading structures, landings and receiving stations. Used for the transmission, care and convenience of cargo and/or passengers in the interchange of the same between land and water carriers or between two water carriers.

Market area

The surface over which a demand offered at a specific location is expressed. Commonly, a customer is assumed to go to a location where a product or service can be acquired, or a part or a finished good has to be shipped from the place of production to the place of consumption.

Materials management

Considers all the activities related in the manufacturing of commodities in all their stages of production along a supply chain. It includes production and marketing activities such as production planning, demand forecasting, purchasing and inventory management. It must ensure that the requirements of supply chains are met by dealing with a wide array of parts for assembly and raw materials, including packaging (for transport and retailing) and, ultimately, recycling discarded commodities. All these activities are assumed to be inducing physical distribution demands.

Mercosur

A trade alliance between Argentina, Brazil, Paraguay and Uruguay, with Chile and Bolivia as associate members.

Methanol

An alternative fuel – a liquid alcohol fuel with vapor heavier than air, which is primarily produced from natural gas.

Mobility

Refers to a movement of people or freight. It can have different levels linked to the speed, capacity and efficiency of movements.

Modal share

The percentage of total passengers or freight moved by a particular type of transportation.

Modal split (share)

(1) The proportion of total person trips that uses each of various specified modes of transportation; (2) the process of separating total person trips into the modes of travel used; (3) a term that describes how many people use alternative forms of transportation, and is frequently used to describe the percentage of people who use private automobiles, as opposed to the percentage who use public transportation.

Mode, transport

The physical way a movement is performed.

Model

An analytical tool (often mathematical) used by transportation planners to assist in making forecasts of land use, economic activity, travel activity and their effects on the quality of resources such as land, air and water.

North American Free Trade Agreement (NAFTA)

Came into force on 1 January 1994. NAFTA binds Canada, the United States and Mexico in respect of a series of common economics rules. Besides the liberalization of exchange of goods and services, NAFTA regulates investments, intellectual property, publics markets and the non-tariff barrier. NAFTA is a result of a tradition of trade negotiations between Canada and the USA that became explicit with the 1989 Free Trade Agreement (FTA) and the 1991 Canada–US Trade Agreement (CUSTA).

Net tonnage

The net or register tonnage of a vessel is the remainder after deducting from the gross tonnage of the vessel the tonnage of crew spaces, master's accommodations, navigation spaces, allowance for propelling power, etc. It is expressed in tons of 100 cubic ft.

Network

Framework of routes within a system of locations, identified as nodes. A route is a single link between two nodes that are part of a larger network that can refer to tangible routes such as roads and rails, or less tangible routes such as air and sea corridors.

Network analysis

The pattern of transportation systems, the location of routes or rails, the location of inter-sections, nodes and terminals can be considered as a network. Networks analysis aims at identifying flows, shortest distances between two given points or the least expensive road to take for transporting goods between those points. To facilitate the task, networks have been approximated by the use of the graph theory relying on topology.

New Panamax

The ship class able to fit into the locks of the expanded Panama Canal. It is defined by the new lock dimensions of 427 m (length), 55 m (width) and 18.3 m (depth). This represents a capacity of about 12,500 TEU or 120,000 dwt.

Nitrogen oxides

A product of combustion of fossil fuels whose production increases with the temperature of the process. It can become an air pollutant if concentrations are excessive.

Off-peak period

Non-rush periods of the day when travel activity is generally lower and less transit service is scheduled. Also called "base period."

Offshore hub

A port terminal that dominantly serves transmodal operations, implying limited connections in relation to its total traffic with its hinterland. They are mainly used to feedering, relay and interlining between maritime shipping routes. The term "offshore" can be misleading, as many ports performing this function are located at standard port locations.

Offshoring

The transfer of an organizational of production function to another country, whether the work is outsourced or stays within the same corporation.

Operating cost

Costs that vary with the quantity shipped in the short run: (1) fixed operating cost refers to expenditures that are independent of the amount of use, which for a car would involve costs such as insurance costs, fees for license and registration, depreciation and finance charges; and (2) variable operating cost is the expenditure dependent on the amount of use, which for a car would involve costs such as the cost of gasoline, oil, tires and other maintenance.

Organization of Economic Cooperation and Development (OECD)

In 1961, this replaced the Organization for European Economic Cooperation (OEEC), which was created in 1948 to facilitate postwar reconstruction of Europe via American aid. It acts as a policy-leveling forum where government representatives of member states seek to harmonize economic policies, touching such sectors as commerce, industry, cooperation, foreign aid and agriculture.

Outsourcing

The practice of having some activities that used to be performed within a corporation by another corporation. It often enables costs to be reduced and the business to focus on core competencies by outsourcing low productivity tasks to a subcontractor.

Pallet

A raised platform, normally made of wood, facilitating the handling of goods. Pallets are of standard dimensions.

Pandemic

An epidemic of infectious disease that spreads through human populations across a large area, even worldwide.

Panamax

A maritime standard corresponding to about 65,000 dwt or 4,200 TEU. Refers to a ship with dimensions that allow it to pass through the Panama Canal: maximum length 295 m, maximum beam overall 32.25 m, maximum draft 13.50 m.

Particulates

Carbon particles formed by partial oxidation and reduction of the hydrocarbon fuel. Also included are trace quantities of metal oxides and nitrides, originating from engine wear, component degradation and inorganic fuel additives. In the transportation sector, particulates are emitted mainly from diesel engines.

Passenger-km (or Passenger-mile)

The total number of miles (km) traveled by passengers on vehicles; determined by multiplying the number of unlinked passenger trips by the average length of their trips.

Peak oil

A theory concerning oil production initially published by geophysicist King Hubbert in 1956, that assumes, due to the finite nature of oil reserves, that production will at some point reach maximum output. Once peak production has been reached, production declines and prices go up until oil resources are depleted or become too costly to have a widespread use.

Peak period (hour)

Represents a time period of high usage of a transport system. For transit, it refers to morning and afternoon time periods when ridership is at its highest.

Physical distribution

The collective term for the range of activities involved in the movement of goods from points of production to final points of sale and consumption. It must ensure that the mobility requirements of supply chains are entirely met. Physical distribution comprises all the functions of movement and handling of goods, particularly transportation services (trucking, freight rail, air freight, inland waterways, marine shipping and pipelines), transshipment and warehousing services (e.g. consignment, storage, inventory management), trade, wholesale and, in principle, retail. Conventionally, all these activities are assumed to be derived from materials management demands.

Piggyback trailers

Trailers which are designed for quick loading on rail cars.

Pipeline

A continuous pipe conduit, complete with such equipment as valves, compressor stations, communications systems and meters for transporting natural and/or supplemental gas from one point to another, usually from a point in or beyond the producing field or processing plant to another pipeline or to points of utilization. Also refers to a company operating such facilities.

Planning

Refers to a process that allows people's needs, preferences and values to be reflected in decisions. Planning occurs at many different levels, from day-to-day decisions made by individuals and families, to major decisions made by governments and businesses that have comprehensive, long-term impacts on society. Management can be considered a short-term form of planning, while planning can be considered a longer-term form of management.

Platform/modular manufacturing

Strategy in which a multinational corporation retains its core competencies, namely its research and development, retailing, marketing and distribution, while subcontracting (outsourcing) much of the manufacturing to the lowest bidders.

Policy, transport

The development of a set of constructs and propositions that are established to achieve particular objectives relating to social, economic and environmental development, and the functioning and performance of the transport system.

Port

A harbor area in which are located marine terminal facilities for transferring cargo between ships and land transportation.

Port authority

An entity of state or local government that owns, operates or otherwise provides wharf, dock and other marine terminal investments at ports.

Port holding

An entity, commonly private, that owns or lease port terminals in a variety of locations. It is also known as a port terminal operator.

Port of entry

A port at which foreign goods are admitted into the receiving country. Also refers to an air terminal or land access point (customs) where foreign passengers and freight can enter a country.

Port regionalization

A strategy aiming at improving the regional accessibility and connectivity of a port by better linking it to its hinterland. This includes the development of intermodal services, particularly by rail and barges, and the setting of intermodal facilities such as inland terminals.

Post-Panamax

Refers to ship classes that are higher than the standard size of the Panama Canal locks (Panamax) before its expansion.

Product life cycle

Defined as the period that starts with the initial product design (research and development) and ends with the withdrawal of the product from the marketplace. A product life cycle is characterized by specific stages, including research, development, introduction, maturity, decline and obsolescence.

Propane

An alternative fuel – a liquid petroleum gas (LPG) which is stored under moderate pressure and with vapor heavier than air. It is produced as a by-product of natural gas and oil production.

Public transportation

Passenger transportation services, usually local in scope, that are available to any person who pays a prescribed fare. It operates on established schedules along designated routes or lines with specific stops and is designed to move relatively large numbers of people at one time.

Radio-frequency identification device (RFID)

Technology that uses small devices attached to objects that transmit data to a receiver. An alternative to bar coding used for identification and tracking purposes, notably for items shipped in units (boxes, containers, etc.), but can also be attached to an individual item. Main technical advantages include data storage capacity, read/write capability, and no line-of-sight requirements during scanning.

Rail, commuter

Railroad local and regional passenger train operations between a central city, its suburbs and/or another central city. It may be either locomotive-hauled or self-propelled, and is characterized by multi-trip tickets, specific station-to-station fares, railroad employment practices and usually only one or two stations in the central business district. Also known as "suburban rail."

Rail, heavy

A high-capacity electric railway characterized by exclusive rights-of-way, multi-car trains, high-speed and rapid acceleration, sophisticated signaling and high platform loading. Also known as "rapid rail," "subway," "elevated railway" or "metropolitan railway (metro)."

Rail, high-speed

A rail transportation system with exclusive right-of-way which serves densely traveled corridors at speeds of 124 miles per hour (200 km per hour) and greater.

Rail, light

An electric railway with a light-volume traffic capacity compared to heavy rail. Light rail may use shared or exclusive rights-of-way, high or low platform loading and multi-car trains or single cars. Also known as "streetcar," "trolley car" and "tramway."

Railroad

All forms of non-highway ground transportation that run on rails or electro-magnetic guideways, including: (1) commuter or other short-haul rail passenger service in a metropolitan or suburban area; and (2) high-speed ground transportation systems that connect metropolitan areas, without regard to whether they use new technologies not associated with traditional railroads. Such a term does not include rapid transit operations within an urban area that are not connected to the general railroad system of transportation.

Rapid transit

Rail or motorbus transit service operating completely separate from all modes of transportation on an exclusive right-of-way.

Rate

The price of transportation services paid by the consumer. They are the negotiated monetary cost of moving a passenger or a unit of freight between a specific origin and destination. Rates are often visible to the consumers, since transport providers must provide this information to secure transactions.

Reefer ship

General cargo ship with 80 percent or more insulated cargo space.

Ridesharing

A form of transportation, other than public transit, in which more than one person shares the use of the vehicle, such as a van or car, to make a trip. Also known as "carpooling" or "vanpooling."

Ridership

The number of rides taken by people using a public transportation system in a given time period.

Roll-on/roll-off (RORO) vessel

Ship which is especially designed to carry wheeled container trailers, or other wheeled cargo, and uses the roll-on/roll-off method for loading and unloading. Main method to transport automobiles on international markets.

Rolling stock

The vehicles used in a transit system, including buses and rail cars.

Semi-trailer

A non-powered vehicle for the carriage of goods, intended to be coupled to a motor vehicle in such a way that a substantial part of its weight and its load is borne by the motor vehicle.

Shelf life

A term used to describe the length of time a commodity (e.g. food, drugs, chemicals) is suitable to be used or consumed. It mostly applies to temperature-sensitive goods.

Shimbel index

Measures the minimum number of links necessary to connect one node with all other nodes in a defined graph.

Shipper

The company sending goods.

Short-sea shipping

Commercial waterborne transportation that does not transit an ocean. It is an alternative form of commercial transportation that utilizes inland and coastal waterways to move commercial freight from major domestic ports to its destination.

Shunting

Operation related to moving a rail vehicle or set of rail vehicles within a railway installation (station, depot, workshop, marshalling yard, etc.). It mainly concerns the assembly and disassembly of unit trains.

Shuttle

A public or private vehicle that travels back and forth over a particular route, especially a short route or one that provides connections between transportation systems, employment centers, etc.

Silk Road

Historical trade route linking the Eastern Mediterranean basin to Central and East Asia. Named as such because of many prized commodities, namely silk, tea and jade, that were carried from China. Was operational between the first century BCE and the sixteenth century.

Site

The geographical characteristics of a specific location.

Situation

The relationships a location has in regard to other locations.

Spatial interaction

A realized movement of people, freight or information between an origin and a destination. It is a transport demand/supply relationship expressed over a geographical space. Spatial interactions cover a wide variety of movements such as journeys to work, migrations, tourism, the usage of public facilities, the transmission of information or capital, the market areas of retailing activities, international trade and freight distribution.

Spatial structure

The manner in which space is organized by the cumulative locations of infrastructure, economic activities and their relations.

Suezmax

Standard which represents the limitations of the Suez Canal. Before 1967, the Suez Canal could only accommodate tanker ships with a maximum of 80,000 dwt. The canal was closed between 1967 and 1975 because of the Israel–Arab conflict. Once it reopened in 1975, the Suezmax capacity went to 150,000 dwt. An enlargement to enable the canal to accommodate 200,000 dwt tankers is being considered.

Supply chain

A functionally integrated network of production, trade and service activities that covers all the stages in a supply chain, from the transformation of raw materials, through intermediate manufacturing stages, to the delivery of a finished good to a market. The chain is conceptualized as a series of nodes, linked by various types of transactions, such as sales and intrafirm transfers. Each successive node within a commodity chain involves the acquisition or organization of inputs for the purpose of added value.

Supply Chain Management (SCM)

The management of the whole commodity/supply chain, from suppliers, manufacturers, retailers and the final customers. To achieve higher productivity and better returns, SCM mainly tries to reduce inventory, increase transaction speeds and satisfy the needs of the customers in terms of cost, quantity, quality and delivery as much as possible.

Supply (transport)

The capacity of transportation infrastructures and modes, generally over a geographically defined transport system and for a specific period of time. Therefore, supply is expressed in terms of infrastructures (capacity), services (frequency) and networks. The number of passengers, volume (for liquids or containerized traffic) or mass (for freight) that can be transported per unit of time and space is commonly used to quantify transport supply.

Sustainable development

Development which meets the needs of the present without compromising the ability of future generations to meet their own needs.

Tanker

An oceangoing ship specially designed to haul liquid bulk cargo, particularly oil.

Tariff

A general term for any listing of rates or charges. The tariffs most frequently encountered in foreign trade are: (1) tariffs of international transportation companies operating on sea, land and in the air; (2) tariffs of international cable, radio and telephone companies; and (3) the customs tariffs of the various countries that list goods that are duty free and those subject to import duty, giving the rate of duty in each case.

Telecommuting

Using information and telecommunication technologies to perform work at a location away from the traditional office location and environment.

Terminal

Any location where freight and passengers either originates, terminates or is handled in the transportation process. Terminals are central and intermediate locations in the movements of passengers and freight. They often require specific facilities to accommodate the traffic they handle.

Terminal costs

Costs of loading and unloading. They do not vary with distance shipped.

Third-party logistics provider (3PL)

An asset-based company that offers logistics and supply chain management services to its customers (manufacturers and retailers). It commonly owns distribution centers and transport modes.

Threshold

The minimum and vital market size required to support a given type of economic activity. A mean number of passengers per trip can be identified to sustain profitability of a coach line, for example. A threshold thus rests on a level of demand and can play a determining role in organizing both freight and passenger transport structures on the basis of demographic dynamics, geographic relations to markets and intensity of economic activities.

Ton

A unit measurement of weight, frequently used in freight transport statistics. A metric ton is equivalent to 1,000 kg or 2,205 lb. A short ton is equivalent to 2,000 pounds or 0.908 metric tons (in the United States, the term "ton" is commonly used but implies short ton). A long ton, a term not as frequently used, is equivalent to 2,240 lb or 1.06 metric tons.

Ton-km (or ton-mile)

Measure expressing the realized freight transport demand. Although both the passenger-km and ton-km are most commonly used to measure realized demand, the measure can equally apply for transport supply.

Track gauge

The distance between the internal sides of rails on a railway line. The standard gauge is generally 1.435 m. Other gauges are used – for instance, in Spain and Portugal (1.676 m) or in the Russian Federation (1.524 m).

Trailer on flat car (TOFC)

A rail trailer or container mounted on a chassis that is transported on a rail car. Also known as "piggyback."

Tramp

An oceangoing vessel that does not operate along a definite route or on a fixed schedule, but rather calls at any port where cargo is available.

Transaction costs

Costs required for gathering information, negotiating and enforcing contracts, letters of credit and transactions. Often referred to as the cost of doing business.

Transactions

In the business domain, a transaction is synonymous with exchange and refers to a commercial operation. Generally, before a transaction, there are some negotiations. Transactions generate varying costs, depending on the stakes, the competition, the context of the economic market, etc.

Transit system

An organization (public or private) providing local or regional multi-occupancy-vehicle passenger service. Organizations that provide service under contract to another agency are generally not counted as separate systems.

Transloading

The transshipment of loads from truck to rail and vice versa. It is done to exploit the respective advantages of trucking and rail, namely avoid long-distance trucking. Also refers to the moving of the contents of a container such as a 40 ft maritime container, into another container, such as a 53 ft domestic container, or a regular truckload.

Transmodal transportation

The movements of passengers or freight within the same mode of transport. Although "pure" transmodal transportation rarely exists and an intermodal operation is often required (e.g. ship to dockside to ship), the purpose is to ensure continuity within the network.

Transport geography

Subdiscipline of geography concerned with movements of freight, people and information. It seeks to link spatial constraints and attributes with the origin, the destination, the extent, the nature and the purpose of movements.

Transportability

The ease of movement of passengers, freight or information. It is related to transport costs as well as to the attributes of what is being transported (fragility, perishable, price). Political factors can also influence transportability, such as laws, regulations, borders and tariffs. When transportability is high, activities are less constrained by distance.

Transshipment

The transfer of goods from one carrier to another and/or from one mode to the other.

Trip assignment

In planning, a process by which trips, described by mode, purpose, origin, destination and time of day, are allocated among the paths or routes in a network by one of a number of models.

Trip generation

In planning, the determination or prediction of the number of trips produced by and attracted to each zone.

Twenty-foot equivalent unit (TEU)

A standard unit based on an ISO container of 20 ft length (6.10 m), used as a statistical measure of traffic flows or capacities. One standard 40 ft ISO Series 1 container equals 2 TEUs.

Ultra-large crude carriers (ULCC)

Tanker ships from 300,000 to 550,000 dwt in size. Used for carrying crude oil on long-haul routes from the Persian Gulf to Europe, America and East Asia, via the Cape of Good Hope or the Strait of Malacca. The enormous size of these vessels requires custom-built terminals.

Unit load

Packages loaded on a pallet, in a crate or any other way that enables them to be handled as a unit.

Unit load device

A container that has been specifically designed to fit the cargo storage area of an airplane.

Unlinked passenger trips

The number of passengers who board public transportation vehicles. Individual passengers are counted each time they board a vehicle even though they may be on the same journey from origin to destination.

Upstream/downstream

Refers to the relative location of a given activity along a supply chain. Upstream generally refers to the suppliers, while downstream refers to the customers.

Urban form

The spatial imprint of an urban transport system as well as the adjacent physical infrastructures and socioeconomic activities. Jointly, they confer a level of spatial arrangement to cities.

Variable cost

A cost that varies in relation to the level of operational activity.

Very-large crude carrier (VLCC)

A crude oil carrying ship of between 150,000 and 320,000 dwt. They offer a good flexibility for using terminals, since many can accommodate their draft. They are used in ports that have depth limitations, mainly around the Mediterranean, West Africa and the North Sea. They can be ballasted through the Suez Canal.

Vessel

Every description of watercraft, used or capable of being used as a means of transportation on the water.

Warehouse

A place for the reception, delivery, consolidation, distribution and storage of freight. Designed to store goods for longer periods of time.

Waterway

River, canal, lake or other stretch of water that by natural or man-made features is suitable for navigation.

Weight, gross

The weight of the goods including packing, wrappers or containers, both internal and external. The total weight as shipped.

Weight, net

The weight of the goods themselves without the inclusion of any wrapper.

Weight, ton

Metric measure equals 1,000 kg. A short ton is 2,000 lb and a long ton is 2,240lb.

Wharf

A landing place where vessels may tie up for loading and unloading of cargo.

World Bank

A financial body part of the United Nations system. The World Bank was created in 1944 at the Bretton Woods financial and monetary conference. First loans helped finance reconstruction of Western Europe and Japan following World War II, but today the World Bank has considerably broadened its presence throughout the globe, lending to countries of Africa, Asia, Central Europe, Latin America, the Middle East and the former Soviet Union. Its priority is to lend capital to governments of developing countries to promote economic growth through financing of large infrastructure projects, economic reform packages and technical assistance. It thus has vested interests in a number of developing countries worldwide. Loans are also aimed to encourage private sector development. Presently, the World Bank comprises four main branches: the International Bank for Reconstruction and Development (IBRD), the Multilateral Investment Guarantee Agency (MIGA), the International Development Agency (IDA) and the International Financial Society (IFS). Its headquarters are in Washington, DC.

World Trade Organization (WTO)

The WTO was established on1 January 1995 as a result of the Uruguay Round negotiations (1986–94). The seat of the WTO is located in Geneva, Switzerland. It performs various functions, including: administering WTO trade agreement, organizing forums for trade negotiations, handling trade disputes, monitoring national trade policies, providing technical assistance and training for developing countries, and cooperating with other international organizations.

Yard

A system of auxiliary tracks used exclusively for the classification of passenger or freight cars according to commodity or destination, assembling of cars for train movement, storage of cars or repair of equipment.

Yield management (transportation)

The process of managing the usage price of a transport asset, such as the fare paid by users, in view of changes in the demand. The goal of such an approach is to maximize profit in the context where the transport supply is fixed. Commonly used in air transportation.

Index